The Mind and Society

[*Trattato di Sociologia generale*]

BY VILFREDO PARETO

EDITED BY ARTHUR LIVINGSTON

TRANSLATED BY ANDREW BONGIORNO AND ARTHUR LIVINGSTON
WITH THE ADVICE AND ACTIVE COOPERATION OF
JAMES HARVEY ROGERS

VOLUME TWO
Theory of Residues

HARCOURT, BRACE AND COMPANY
NEW YORK

The Mind and Society

VOLUME I

NON-LOGICAL CONDUCT

VOLUME II

ANALYSIS OF SENTIMENT
(THEORY OF RESIDUES)

VOLUME III

SENTIMENT IN THINKING
(THEORY OF DERIVATIONS)

VOLUME IV

THE GENERAL FORM
OF SOCIETY

PRINTED IN THE UNITED STATES OF AMERICA
BY QUINN & BODEN COMPANY, INC., RAHWAY, N. J.
Typography by Robert Josephy

CONTENTS

VOLUME II

Had we been following a deductive procedure this chapter would have stood first in this work. Resemblances and differences, as regards the elements *a* and *b,* between logico-experimental and non-logico-experimental sciences. The element *a* corresponds to certain instincts but is far from covering them all. Furthermore, interests too have to be considered among the forces determining social forms. Objective and subjective aspects of theories. Examples of a technique for distinguishing *a* from *b.* We finally assign names (they are quite arbitrary) to the things *a, b* and *c,* for mere convenience in talking about them: we call the things *a* "residues," the things *b* "derivations," the things *c* "derivatives." Residues as corresponding to instincts are devoid of any exactness. An analogy between the investigations we have been making in social phenomena and investigations in philology. That analogy arises in the fact that language is just one among the many social phenomena. Classification of residues. Study of Classes I and II.

Study of Classes III and IV.

Study of Classes V and VI.

THE MIND AND SOCIETY

Volume II: Analysis of Sentiment
(Theory of Residues)

CHAPTER VI

Residues: Combinations and Group Persistence

842. Since social phenomena appear in complex form in the concrete, we saw at once that it would be helpful to divide them into at least two elements, distinguishing logical from non-logical conduct; and that gave us a first conception of the nature of non-logical conduct and of its importance in human society. But at that point a question arose: If non-logical conduct plays such an important rôle in human life, why has it been so generally neglected (§ 252)? We found in reply that almost all writers on social or political subjects have indeed observed such conduct, or at least caught glimpses of it. Many elements, therefore, of the theory we are framing in these volumes are to be found scattered about here and there in the works of various writers, though often under hardly recognizable forms.

843. But we saw that all such writers had ideas of their own to which they very expressly attached capital importance—ideas on religion, morality, law, and the like, which have been battle-grounds for centuries. So, if they did recognize non-logical conduct implicitly, explicitly they glorified logical conduct, and most of them regarded it as the only conduct worth considering in social phenomena. We were therefore called upon to see what truth there was in theories of that type, and to decide whether we were to abandon the course on which we had set out or take heart and push on.

We then proceeded to examine those various manners of considering social phenomena, and we saw that from the logico-experimental standpoint they were devoid of all exactness and of any strict accord with the facts; though from another standpoint, we could not deny the great importance that they had had in history

[1] Had we been following the deductive method, this chapter would have been placed at the beginning of Vol. I. I may find it desirable to follow that method in treatises to come. Here I have preferred the inductive approach, that my reader might follow the road i have myself traversed in arriving at the theories with which we shall hereafter be dealing.

and in determining the social equilibrium. That discovery lent force to a suspicion which had already occurred to us, and which will acquire greater and greater prominence in the course of these volumes: that the experimental "truth" of certain theories is one thing and their social "utility" quite another, and that the two things are not only not one and the same but may, and often do, stand in flat contradiction (§§ 1682 f., 1897 f.).

844. We found that it was as important to separate those two things as it had been to distinguish logical from non-logical conduct, and our inductive survey showed that the failure to make such a distinction had been the main cause of error, from the scientific standpoint, in most social theories.

845. So we looked at them a little more closely and saw how and why they went astray, and how and why, though fallacious, they enjoyed and still enjoy such great prestige. In the course of that investigation we came upon things which we had not thought of at the outset. But we went on analyzing, distinguishing, and soon we observed another possible distinction that struck us as being quite as important as the others we had made—on the one hand an instinctive, non-logical element that was constant, on the other, a deductive element that was designed to explain, justify, demonstrate, the constant element. Arriving at that point, we found that induction had given us the elements of a theory.

846. Here, now, we are called upon to frame it, that is to say, we must now drop the inductive for the deductive method, and see what consequences result from the principles that we have found, or think we have found. After that we shall have to compare our inferences with the facts. If they fit, we shall keep our theory. If they fail to fit, we shall discard it.

847. In this chapter (and since the subject is a vast one, in the next two) we are to study the constant element a (§ 798), going on, after that, to the deductive element b. But we are dealing with a very difficult matter, and a few more remarks in general on the elements a and b, and their resultant c, will not come amiss.

848. We saw in § 803 that in the theories of the logico-experi-

mental sciences one may discern a basic element A, and a deductive element B, which in some respects are analogous to, in some respects different from, the elements a and b in theories that are not strictly logico-experimental.

The social sciences as hitherto cultivated show elements that bear a closer resemblance to a than to A, through their failure to avoid intrusions of sentiments, prejudices, creeds, or other predilections, tendencies, postulates, principles, that carry the thinker outside the logico-experimental domain.

849. The deductive element in the social sciences as hitherto cultivated sometimes comes very close to B, and there are cases where the logic is so adequate that the coincidence with B would be exact were it not for a lack of definiteness in the premises a, which deprives the reasoning of strict validity. But oftentimes in the social sciences the deductive element stands very close to b, as containing many non-logical and non-experimental principles and showing great susceptibility to inclinations, bias, and the like.

850. So let us make the elements a and b our main concern. The element a corresponds, we may guess, to certain instincts of man, or more exactly, men, because a has no objective existence and differs in different individuals; and it is probably because of its correspondence to instincts that it is virtually constant in social phenomena. The element b represents the work of the mind in accounting for a. That is why b is much more variable, as reflecting the play of the imagination.[1]

851. But if the element a corresponds to certain instincts, it is far from reflecting them all; and that is evident from the very manner in which we found it. We analyzed specimens of thinking on the look-out for a constant element. We may therefore have found only the instincts that underlay those reasonings. There was no chance of our meeting along that road instincts which were not so logicalized. Unaccounted for still would be simple appetites, tastes, in-

850 [1] As we have already seen (§ 802), the part b has in its turn to be subdivided, since it varies all the way from one extreme, where it is pure logic, to another extreme where it is pure instinct and fancy. We shall deal with that situation at length in Chapters IX and X.

clinations, and in social relationships that very important class called "interests."

852. We may also have found only a part of one of the things *a*, the other part being a mere appetite. If the sex instinct tended only to unite the sexes it would not figure in our investigations. But that instinct is often enough logicalized and dissembled under guise of asceticism; there are people who preach virtue as a way of lingering, in their thoughts, on sex matters. Examining their thinking, we accordingly find an element *a* corresponding to the sex instinct, and an element *b* that is the reasoning under which it hides. Diligent search might reveal similar elements corresponding to the appetites for food and drink. But in those cases the rôle played by simple instinct is far more considerable, at any rate, than in the case of sex.

853. The fact of being provident or improvident depends upon certain instincts, certain tastes, and from that point of view it would not figure in *a*. But in the United States the improvident instinct has fathered a theory that people ought to spend all they can earn; and so analysis of that theory yields a quantum *a*, which will be improvidence.

854. A politician is inspired to champion the theory of "solidarity" by an ambition to obtain money, power, distinctions. Analysis of that theory would reveal but scant trace of his motives, which are, after all, the motives of virtually all politicians, whether they preach white or black. First prominence would be held by principles *a* that are effective in influencing others. If the politician were to say, "Believe in 'solidarity' because if you do it means money for me," he would get many laughs and few votes. He therefore has to take his stand on principles that are acceptable to his prospective constituents.

If we stopped at that, it might seem that in the case before us the *a*'s were located not in the principles that suggested championing the theory to the politician, but in the principles that inspired acceptance of it by his hearers. But going a little deeper, such a distinction is seen not to hold. Oftentimes the person who would persuade others begins by persuading himself; and even if he is moved in the beginning by thoughts of personal advantage, he comes eventually to believe that his real interest is the welfare of others. Unbelieving apostles are rare and ineffective, but ubiquitous and ubiquitously effective is the apostle who believes, and he is the more effective, the more sincere his belief. The element a in a theory c is present both in the persons who accept and in the persons who propound it, but not to be overlooked in either case are the advantages accruing from the theory c, to the ones and the others.

855. In analyzing a theory c, we must keep the objective standpoint sharply distinguished from the subjective (§ 13). The two researches are very very often confused, and so two errors, in chief, arise. In the first place, as we have so often cautioned, the logico-experimental value of a theory is not kept distinct from its persuasive force or its social utility. Then again—and this is a peculiarly modern error—the objective study of a theory is replaced by a subjective research as to how and why it was evolved or adopted by its author. This second research certainly has its importance, but it ought to supplement the other, not replace it. Whether a theorem of Euclid is true or false, and how and why he came to discover it, are two separate questions, and the one does not preclude the other. If the *Principia* of Newton had been written by an unknown writer, would that in any way affect the value of the book? So two of the aspects under which a writer's theory may be considered (§ 541) become confused: (1) his manner of thinking, his psychic state, and how he came by it; (2) what he meant in a given passage. The first aspect, which is personal, subjective to him, is mixed in with the second, which is impersonal, objective. A factor in the confusion oftentimes is regard for the writer's authority. In deference to that sentiment it is assumed *a priori* that everything he thinks and believes must necessarily be "true," and that to determine his thought is tantamount to testing the "truth" (or when the logico-experimental sciences are concerned, the accord with experience) of what he thought.

856. Long prevalent was an inclination to consider theories exclusively from the standpoint of their intrinsic merit (sometimes their

logico-experimental soundness), which, much more often, was determined with reference to the sentiments of the critic or to certain metaphysical or theological principles. Nowadays the tendency is to consider them exclusively from the extrinsic standpoint (aspects 1 and 3, § 541), as to the manner of their genesis, that is, and the reasons for their acceptance. Both methods, if used exclusively, are equally incomplete and to that extent erroneous.

857. The second error (§ 855) is the opposite of the first. The first considered only the intrinsic merit of the theory (aspect 2, § 541); the second only its extrinsic merit (aspects 1 and 3, § 541). It appears in the abuse of the historical method, which is frequent enough nowadays, especially in the social and economic sciences. In the beginning, in their eagerness to free their science of contingencies of time and place, the fathers of political economy made the mistake of viewing their findings as absolutes. It was a salutary reaction, therefore, when just such contingencies came to be taken into account, and from that point of view the historical method was a notable contribution to the progress of science. And a forward step no less important was taken when the effort to derive the forms of social institutions from dogmatic absolutes was abandoned in favour of historical studies that made it possible to learn how institutions had developed, and their bearing on other social phenomena. We are altogether within the domain of logico-experimental science when we ask not what the family ought to be, but what it has actually been. But the historical study is to be thought of as supplementing, not as replacing, our inquiry into the relations between the constitution of the family and other social phenomena. It is useful to know how, historically, theories of income have been evolved; but it is also useful to know the relations of such theories to the facts—their logico-experimental value.

858. However, this latter type of research is much more difficult than the mere writing of history; and there are plenty of people who are utterly incapable even of understanding, let alone of creating, a logico-experimental theory in political economy, yet who blithely presume to write histories of that science.

859. In the literary field historical studies often degenerate into mere collections of anecdotes that are easy to write and agreeable to read. To find out what a writer ate and drank, how he slept, the clothes he wore, is intellectually and scientifically easier than to deal with the relations between his theories and experimental realities. And if a critic can find something to say about a writer's love-affairs, he is certain to make a very entertaining book indeed (§ 541).

860. To study the element b is to study the subjective element in a theory. But the subjective element may be further subdivided into two: the general causes and the special causes that account for the genesis and success of a theory. General causes would be causes operative over fairly extensive periods of time and affecting considerable numbers of individuals. Special causes operate in an essentially contingent manner. If a theory comes into vogue because it serves the interests of a social class it has, in that fact, a general cause. If a writer invents a theory because he is paid to do so or because he wants to spite a rival, the cause is special.[1]

861. Things that exert powerful effects upon the social order give rise to theories, and we shall find them, therefore, in the course of our quest for a's. In addition to such a's there are, as we have just seen, appetites and interests. Taking them all together we have the sum of the things that operate to any appreciable extent towards determining the social order (§ 851), bearing in mind of course that the social order reacts upon them, so that we are all along dealing not with a relationship of cause and effect, but with an interrelation or a relationship of interdependence. If we assume, as in fact seems probable, that animals have no theories, they cannot have an element a of any kind and perhaps not even interests—all that is left in their case is instincts. Uncivilized peoples, however close to animals they may seem to stand, do have theories of one sort or another, and an element a has to be considered in dealing with them. And beyond

860 [1] In our study of b theories that is to follow (Volume III) we are to deal strictly with general causes. The study of special causes is of minor importance and can come later.

a doubt they have instincts and interests. Civilized peoples have theories for very very many of their instincts and interests. An element *a* figures through virtually the whole range of their social life.

862. In this volume we are to go looking for the element *a*. In many cases already (*e.g.*, §§ 186 f., 514, 740) we have distinguished *a* elements and *b* elements that we found combined and confused in some single phenomenon, *c*. That was in itself a start towards finding a norm for making such analyses. Suppose we get a still clearer view of the method from an example or two and then proceed with our systematic study.

863. *Example I.* Christians have the custom of baptism. If one knew the Christian procedure only one would not know whether and how it could be analyzed (§§ 186, 740). Moreover, we have an explanation of it: We are told that the rite of baptism is celebrated in order to remove original sin. That still is not enough. If we had no other facts of the same class to go by, we should find it difficult to isolate the elements in the complex phenomenon of baptism. But we do have other facts of that type. The pagans too had lustral water, and they used it for purposes of purification. If we stopped at that, we might associate the use of water with the fact of purification. But other cases of baptism show that the use of water is not a constant element. Blood may be used for purification, and other substances as well. Nor is that all; there are numbers of rites that effect the same result. In cases where taboos have been violated (§ 1252), certain rites remove the pollution that a person has incurred in one set of circumstances or another. So the circle of similar facts widens, and in the great variety of devices and in the many explanations that are given for their use the thing which remains constant is the feeling, the sentiment, that the integrity of an individual which has been altered by certain causes, real or imaginary, can be restored by certain rites. The given case, therefore, is made up of that constant element, *a*, and a variable element, *b*, the latter comprising the means that are used for restoring the individual's integrity and the reasonings by which the efficacy of the means is presumably explained. The human being has a vague feeling that

water somehow cleanses moral as well as material pollutions. However, he does not, as a rule, justify his conduct in that manner. The explanation would be far too simple. So he goes looking for something more complicated, more pretentious, and readily finds what he is looking for.

864. The nucleus *a,* now that we have found it, is seen to be made up of a number of elements: first of all an instinct for combinations; people want "to do something about it"—they want to combine certain things with certain acts. It is a curious fact, also, that the ties so imagined persist in time. It would be easy enough to try some new combination every day. Instead there is one combination, fantastic though it be, that tends to prevail and sometimes does prevail over all competitors. Discernible, finally, is an instinct which inclines people to believe that certain combinations are suited to attaining certain objectives.[1]

865. *Example II.* We have seen many cases (§§ 186 f.) where people believed that they could raise or avert tempests. If we knew only one such case, we could make little or nothing of it. However, we know many cases and can identify a constant nucleus in them. Ignoring, for the moment, the element in the nucleus that relates, as in the case of baptism, to the persistence of certain combinations and the faith in their efficacy, we find a constant element, *a,* corresponding to the feeling, the sentiment, that a divinity exists and that, by a variable means, *b,* he (or "it") may be made to interfere and influence the weather. And then, right away, there is another sort of belief, the belief that it is possible to produce the desired effect by certain rites or practices, which mean nothing in themselves —the practice, for instance, of tearing a white cock asunder and carrying the two halves around a field to protect it from drought (§ 189). So the circle widens, and another constant *a* appears: an

---

864 [1] As for "causes" or "origins," we might guess that actually effective combinations, such as striking a flint to get a fire, may have led people to believe in the efficiency of imaginary combinations. But we need not, for the present, concern ourselves with that explanation or any other. We can rest content with establishing the fact, and stop at that. In some other connexion we might try to go further and explain the fact by other facts, then the latter by others still, and so on.

instinct for combinations, whereby things and acts designed for producing given effects are brought together haphazard.

866. *Example III.* Catholics believe that Friday is a day of evil omen as—so it is averred—the day of the Passion. If we knew just that, and nothing else of the kind, it would be difficult to determine which of the two facts, the evil omen or the Passion, was the main, and which the secondary, fact. But we do have other facts of the kind, many of them. The Romans had their "black" or "vicious" days (*dies atri* or *vitiosi*), which were days of evil omen—for instance, the eighteenth of July, the anniversary of their defeat by the Gauls at Allia, A.U.C. 365. That is one kind of *a*—the feeling that the day which is associated with some catastrophe is a day of evil omen. But there are other facts. Both the Romans and the Greeks had days of evil omen and days of good omen without there being any special causes in the nature of public successes or disasters. Hence there has to be a more comprehensive class of *a*'s, which includes the *a* just mentioned and expresses an impulse to combine days (and other things too) with good or evil omens (§§ 908 f.).

867. These examples give us an inkling as to how a composite situation, *c*, may be broken up into *a* elements and *b* elements.[1]

868. Before going any farther it might perhaps be advisable to give word-names to the things we have been calling *a, b,* and *c*. To designate them by mere letters of the alphabet in a measure embarrasses our discussion and makes it harder to follow. For that reason, and for no other (§ 119), suppose we call the things *a, residues*, the things *b, derivations*, and the things *c, derivatives*. But we must always and at all times remember that nothing, absolutely nothing, is to be inferred from the proper meanings of those words or their etymologies, that they mean respectively the things *a, b,* and *c* and nothing else.[1]

867 [1] We shall perform many other similar analyses in the course of this chapter.

868 [1] [Pareto makes no very extensive use of the term "derivative," probably because its functions are filled just as well by the term "theory," or better, "non-logico-experimental theory." Etymologically, a "residue" would be "what is left" (the constant element) when the variable elements have been eliminated from an action or a reasoning by a comparative analysis. It is always reducible to the synonymous phrase: "principle underlying a non-logical action or reasoning."—A. L.]

869. As we have already seen, the residues *a* constitute a multifarious mass of facts, which have to be classified according to the mutual analogies they present. In that way we get "classes," "genera," and "species." And so for the derivations *B*.[1]

870. Residues correspond to certain instincts in human beings, and for that reason they are usually wanting in definiteness, in exact delimitation. That trait, indeed, nearly always serves to distinguish them from scientific facts or principles *A,* which otherwise bear some resemblance to them. Many times *A*'s have come out of *a*'s as a result of making the *a*'s more exact. The term "warm" is indefinite. Using it, it has been possible to say that well-water is "warm" in winter and "cold" in summer. But as used by physicists the term "warm" corresponds to certain degrees of heat as registered by a thermometer; it is definite. That made it evident that the water in wells is not in that sense warmer in winter than in summer, for a thermometer lowered into a well registers about the same temperature in winter as in summer, or if anything a lower one.

871. Curious the number of different meanings the term "warm" has in Macrobius, *Saturnalia,* VII, 6-8, all of them showing as their residue the sentiments that the term "warm" awakens in the minds now of this, now of that, individual (§ 506). The doctors say that wine is warm; but a character in the *Saturnalia* disagrees, finding wine by nature cold. A woman's body, says another, contains a large amount of cold. No, answers a companion, the female body is naturally warmer than the male—it is so warm, in fact, that when it was the custom to dispose of dead bodies by cremation, a female corpse was commonly burned with each ten males so that the latter might more quickly be consumed. Women have so much heat in their bodies that they are able to wear light clothing in winter. Heat, moreover, is the principle of conception. All that is disputed by another, except as regards conception, the cause of which seems really to be heat. Why is it that in a very hot country wine has the property of cold instead of heat? The reason is that when the air

---

869 [1] [The classification of "derivatives" having already been given under "theories" in Volume I, §§ 523, 525, 526 f., 574 f.—A. L.]

is hot it drives the cold into the ground. The air is always hot in Egypt, so the cold permeates the soil and reaches the vine-roots, imparting its own properties to the wine. And we are told why a fan cools.[1]

872. That is the type of the metaphysical reasoning, whether ancient or modern. The premises contain terms altogether devoid of

871 [1] Says Macrobius, *loc. cit.*: "I have heard doctors say all the same thing, that wine should be reckoned among the warm substances; and only just the other day, in a discussion on the causes of drunkenness, Eustathius was preaching the warmth of wine. [The reasoning is clear: a drunken man feels hot, therefore wine is hot.] But pondering frequently on the matter myself, I have come to the conclusion that wine by nature stands closer to cold than to warmth." Heat, however, is not substantial to ("inborn in") wine but an incidental attribute (*accidens*): "*Dabo aliud indicium accidentis magis vino quam ingeniti caloris.*" The proof alluded to is that all warm things stimulate sensuousness: ". . . *omnia calida Venerem provocant*": but not wine, for "after abundant drinking of undiluted wine *fiunt viri ad coitum pigriores.*" Here then warmth would be associated with degrees of amorousness. "Is anything colder than vinegar, which is only soured wine (*quod culpatum vinum est*)?" Not only vinegar: "The fruits of trees are coldest when their juices taste most like wine, such as the ordinary apple, the pomegranate, or the quince (*cydonia, cotonia*) described by Cato." In that case, warmth would have something to do with tastes. How explain the fact [which is not a fact] that women are harder to intoxicate than men? One suggestion is the abundance of damp in the female body (so that the wine is diluted?): "*Mulier humectissimo est corpore.*" Another of the disputants points out that the wine the woman drinks gets chilled inside her by her natural cold. That statement brings a sharp retort: "It is no use, Symmachus, for you to go on saying that the female is cold by nature. I can show you easily, if you will allow me, that she is hotter than the male. . . . How can you say women are cold when it is undeniable that they are full of heat, being full of blood [*i.e.*, in menstruation]? Then there is another thing. In our day, of course, it is no longer the custom to cremate the dead. But the books tell us that in the days when it was considered an honour to the dead that they should be given to the flames, if occasion arose to burn a large number of bodies all at one time, the ministers of the rites used to add one female corpse to every ten of males. With the help of that one, which was as it were inflammable by nature and therefore burned rapidly, all the others caught fire. So you see, female heat was not unknown even to the ancients." Furthermore, don't we see women going around lightly clad in cold weather, and not at all bundled up as men are, so offsetting the cold in the air by their natural warmth? The argument seems weak to another in the party: "If they stand the cold better than men, it is because of their own cold: *similibus enim similia gaudent.* They are used to cold from the fact that they have a colder nature. That is why their bodies do not mind it." Macrobius, of course, does not fail to mention the usual story about well-water: "You know yourself, Albinus, from your own experience, that water drawn from deep wells or springs steams in winter and is cold in summer."

exactness, and from the premises, as from mathematical axioms presumably trustworthy, conclusions are drawn by strict logic. They serve, after all, to probe not things but the notions that given individuals have of things.[1]

873. The Macrobius example again shows how inexact terms may readily be used to prove both the pro and the contra. Women can wear lighter clothing than men because of the heat in their bodies. No, someone objects, it is because of the cold in their bodies.

874. In general terms, it is the indefiniteness of the residues *a*, chiefly, that unsuits them to serve as premises in strict reasonings, whereas *A* propositions can be and are constantly being so used in the sciences.

875. The residues *a* must not be confused with the sentiments or instincts to which they correspond (§§ 1690 f.). The residues are the manifestations of sentiments and instincts just as the rising of the mercury in a thermometer is a manifestation of the rise in temperature. Only elliptically and for the sake of brevity do we say that residues, along with appetites, interests, etc. (§§ 851 f.) are the main factors in determining the social equilibrium, just as we say that water boils at 100° Centigrade. The completed statements would be: "The sentiments or instincts that correspond to residues, along with those corresponding to appetites, interests, etc., are the main factors in determining the social equilibrium." "Water boils when its calorific state attains the temperature of 100° as registered by a Centigrade thermometer."

876. It is only by way of analysis and for the sole purposes of study that we distinguish various residues $a_1, a_2, a_3. \ldots$ What is at work in the individual is sentiments corresponding to the groups (a_1, a_2, a_3); (a_1, a_3, a_4); (a_3, a_5); and so on. These are composites, as compared with the residues $a_1, a_2 \ldots$ which are simpler. We might go on and break up $a_1, a_2 \ldots$ as well into simpler elements; but we must know how to stop in time, because if made too general

872 [1] Some people are willing as an extreme concession to bar that type of reasoning from the physical sciences, but insist on retaining it for the social sciences. If we keep within experimental limits, however, there is nothing to justify any such distinction.

propositions end by meaning nothing. So the multifarious circumstances conditioning life on our globe may, in general, be reduced to solar light, the presence of an atmosphere, and so on; but the biologist needs conditions that are much less general than that as a basis for a greater number of biological laws.

877. It sometimes happens that a derivative, *c*, reached from a residue, *a*, by way of a derivation, *b*, becomes in its turn the residue of other phenomena and itself subject to derivations. The bad omen, for instance, that is associated with the presence of thirteen persons at a table may be a derivative from a sentiment of horror at Judas's betrayal followed by his suicide; but that derivative has become a residue by this time, and people feel ill at ease at a table of thirteen without the least thought of Judas.

878. All the pointers just given must be kept in mind at all times in the investigations following. Anyone forgetting them will get everything askew (§ 88).

879. This research as so far outlined has certain points of analogy with the ordinary researches of philology that deal with the roots and derivatives in which the words of a language originate. The analogy is not altogether artificial. It arises in the fact that products of the mental activity of the human being are involved in both cases, that their processes are the same. Take, for instance, Greek. The words in that language may be grouped in families, each family having its own root. There are the nouns meaning "anchor" (ἄγκυρα), "fish-hook" (ἄγκιστρον), "curved object" (ἀγκάλη), "bent arm" (ἀγκαλίς), "bend of the arm" (ἀγκύλη), "elbow" (ἀγκών); the adjectives "curved" (ἀγκύλος) and "hook-shaped" (ἀγκιστρωτός,-ή-όν); the verbs "to fish with a hook" (ἀγκιστρεύω) and "to bend" (ἀγκυλῶ). They all have the same root (residue) ἀγκ, which originates in, and expresses, the rather vague notion of something curved, hooked, crooked. By processes of derivation, which have their rules, words are derived from these roots, just as the derivatives, *c*, are derived from the residues, *a*. We find combinations of roots just as we find combinations of residues. The adjective "biting a hook" (ἀγκιστροφάγος)

has ἀγχ and φαγ for its roots, the first referring to something vaguely hook-shaped, the second to eating. There are some very common derivations in Greek. The suffix ματ, for instance, combining with various roots, gives large numbers of words designating the effects of the actions indicated by the roots. So in social phenomena, certain derivations are very very common. The Will of the Divinity, for instance, serves to justify no end of prescriptions. Combined with the residue of filial love, it yields the precept: "Honour thy father and thy mother, for God so ordains."

880. Actually observable in society are certain derivatives, *c*, that derive from residues, *a*, by way of derivations, *b*. Other derivatives (γ) may be as regularly deducible from the residues as the *c*'s but are not observable in the concrete.

881. That situation has its philological counterpart in regular and irregular verbs. In point of fact such terms must not be taken literally. A so-called irregular verb is as regular as any other. The difference lies in the differing methods of derivation. A process of derivation used for certain roots gives a class of verbs that actually occur in the language. Used for other roots, it gives verbs that do not occur in the language. Conversely, the process of derivation used for these second roots yields verbs that occur in the language, but non-existent verbs when used for the other roots.

882. Derivatives treated as residues have their counterparts in language. The word ἀγχιστροφάγος ("biting a hook") was not derived directly from the roots ἀγχ and φαγ, but from ἀγχιστρον and φαγεῖν. Inflections, conjugations, comparatives, superlatives, locatives, to mention only a few, are all examples of derivations based on other derivations.

883. That is not all. The philologists of our time know that language is an organism which has developed according to its own laws and is not an artificial invention. Only a relatively few technical terms, such as "oxygen," "meter," "thermometer," and the like, are products of logical activity on the part of scholars. Such terms would correspond to "logical actions" in society. The majority of

the words in ordinary usage correspond in their formation to "non-logical" actions.[1]

884. We have noted these analogies merely to facilitate a clear comprehension of the theories that we are expounding. They of course are not and could not be offered as proofs. Proof must come from direct examination of the facts and in no other way. The method that relies on analogies is a very bad method.

885. Investigations into the "origins" of social phenomena, which have so far concerned sociology in the main, have oftentimes been, though their authors were not aware of the fact, searches for residues. It was taken for granted, more or less vaguely, that the simple must have preceded the complex—that the residue must have been anterior to the derivative (§ 693). When Herbert Spencer locates the chronological origin of religion in the deification of human beings, he thinks he has found the residue of all religious phenomena, the simple phenomenon from which the complex religions observable in our day derive.

886. Two criticisms are to be made of that view. 1. No proof is offered of the hypothesis that knowledge of the residue is chronolog-

883 [1] It is high time that sociology were making some progress and trying to get to the level that philology has already reached. Many other analogies between the two sciences might be noted—to mention just one, the analogy between the abuse of the historical method in sociology and of hypercriticism of texts in philology. Reinach, *Manuel de philologie,* Vol. I, § 3, p. 48: "Boeckh has very properly called attention to a vicious circle to which philological criticism is not immune. In order to explain a text it has to be read under a certain form, and to read it under that form *without change* one has to be able to understand it and explain it. Hence a tendency in many scholars to correct or suppress all passages they do not understand. [That is a way also with writers interested in the "origins" of (social or historical) phenomena.] Says Nauck, in Schneidewin's edition of Sophocles: 'The conjecture that can claim plausibility is the conjecture that best realizes from every point of view what the most exacting mind would like to find in a Greek tragic author.' Boeckh seems almost to have been writing for Nauck's benefit when he said: 'The Athenians, at the suggestion of Lycurgus, had forbidden any alteration in the texts of the tragic authors. One could almost wish the ancient classics were protected by a similar law today.'" Nowadays, in the quest for "origins" everybody takes account of the facts that agree with his notions, and nothing else. Show me if you can the humanitarian who will accept an account of facts that runs counter to his beliefs, or the Marxian who does not test all facts by his doctrine of capitalism!

ically anterior to knowledge of the derivative. That has been the case in some instances, but certainly not in others. So in chemistry certain chemical compounds have been discovered later in time than the elements of which they are compounded, but many other compounds have been known earlier in time. In sociology the "latent" principles of law (§ 802 [1]) are an excellent example of derivatives that were known before their residues. An illiterate peasant woman in the mountains around Pistoia knows the conjugations of many Italian verbs by practice perfectly well and much better than any number of educated people; but she has not the remotest idea of the rules that govern the derivation of those conjugations from their roots.[1] 2. Even if knowledge of the residue is anterior in time to knowledge of the derivative, it is better to follow a course directly opposite to the one that has so far been followed. A chronological quest for the residue *a* is difficult, often impossible, because there are no documents for times so remote from ours; and it is illegitimate to take the imagination and the "common sense" of the modern man as substitutes for them. Imagination and common sense may, to be sure, yield fascinating theories, but they have little or nothing to do with the facts. To try to discover in primitive periods the residue, *a,* from which the phenomena, *c,* observable today, are derived is to try to explain the known by the unknown (§§ 548, 571). To the precise contrary, the less well known must be inferred from the better known; one must try to discover the residues, *a,* in the phenomena, *c,* that are observable today and then see whether there are traces of *a* in documents of the past. If in so doing we find that *a* existed before *c* was known, we might conclude that *a* is anterior in time to *c,* and that, in the particular case, the *origin* is one and the same with the *residue.* Where such proof is lacking no such identity can legitimately be assumed.

887. So far in these volumes we have tried, and we shall continue

886 [1] [In Pareto's 1916 edition in place of the Pistoian peasant woman one finds: "The good Athenian housewife who recognized Theophrastus for a foreigner the moment she heard him speak (Cicero, *Brutus,* 46 . . .) knew the conjugation of a certain number of Greek verbs perfectly well by practice and much better than many modern scholars."—A. L.]

at all times trying, to explain facts of the past by other facts that we are able to observe in the present (§ 547); and in any event, we shall always be at the greatest pains to work from the better known to the less known. We are not dealing with "origins" here, not because origins are not important historically, but because the question of origins has little or no bearing on the inquiry into the conditions determining the social equilibrium with which we are at present engaged. Of great moment, instead, are the instincts and sentiments that correspond to residues.

888. Suppose we begin by classifying residues.[1] Present also, of course, in social phenomena, in addition to the sentiments manifested by residues, are appetites, inclinations, and so on (§ 851). Here we are dealing strictly with the element that corresponds to residues. In that element many, sometimes indeed a great many, simple residues figure, just as rocks contain many simple elements that can be isolated by chemical analysis. In the concrete, one residue may prevail over others in given phenomena, so that they may be taken roughly as representing that residue. The present classification is made from the objective standpoint (§ 855); but we shall be called upon, here and there, to add some few subjective considerations.

CLASS I

INSTINCT FOR COMBINATIONS (§§ 889-990)

I-α. Generic combinations (§§ 892-909)

I-β. Combinations of similars or opposites (§§ 910-43)

I-β1. Generic likeness or oppositeness (§§ 913-21)

I-β2. Unusual things and exceptional occurrences (§§ 922-28)

I-β3. Objects and occurrences inspiring awe or terror (§§ 929-31)

I-β4. Felicitous state associated with good things; infelicitous state, with bad (§§ 932-36)

I-β5. Assimilation: physical consumption of substances to get effects of associable, and more rarely of opposite, character (§§ 937-43)

888 [1] For our classification of derivations, see § 1419.

I-γ. Mysterious workings of certain things; mysterious effects of certain acts (§§ 944-65)

    I-γ1. Mysterious operations in general (§§ 947-57)

    I-γ2. Mysterious linkings of names and things (§§ 958-65)

I-δ. Need for combining residues (§§ 966-71)

I-ε. Need for logical developments (§§ 972-75)

I-ζ. Faith in the efficacy of combinations (§§ 976-90)

CLASS II
GROUP-PERSISTENCES (PERSISTENCE OF AGGREGATES) (§§ 991-1088)

II-α. Persistence of relations between a person and other persons and places (§§ 1015-51)

    II-α1. Relationships of family and kindred groups (§§ 1016-40)

    II-α2. Relations with places (§§ 1041-42)

    II-α3. Relationships of social class (§§ 1043-51)

II-β. Persistence of relations between the living and the dead (§§ 1052-55)

II-γ. Persistence of relations between a dead person and the things that belonged to him in life (§§ 1056-64)

II-δ. Persistence of abstractions (§§ 1065-67)

II-ε. Persistence of uniformities (§ 1068)

II-ζ. Sentiments transformed into objective realities (§ 1069)

II-η. Personifications (§§ 1070-85)

II-θ. Need of new abstractions (§§ 1086-88)

CLASS III
NEED OF EXPRESSING SENTIMENTS BY EXTERNAL ACTS (ACTIVITY, SELF-EXPRESSION) (§§ 1089-1112)

III-α. Need of "doing something" expressing itself in combinations (§§ 1092-93)

III-β. Religious ecstasies (§§ 1094-1112)

CLASS IV

RESIDUES CONNECTED WITH SOCIALITY (§§ 1113-1206)

IV-α. Particular societies (§ 1114)

IV-β. Need of uniformity (§§ 1115-32)

    IV-β1. Voluntary conformity on the part of the individual (§§ 1117-25)

    IV-β2. Uniformity enforced upon others (§§ 1126-29)

    IV-β3. Neophobia (§§ 1130-32)

IV-γ. Pity and cruelty (§§ 1133-44)

    IV-γ1. Self-pity extended to others (§§ 1138-41)

    IV-γ2. Instinctive repugnance to suffering (§§ 1142-43)

    IV-γ3. Reasoned repugnance to useless sufferings (§ 1144)

IV-δ. Self-sacrifice for the good of others (§§ 1145-52)

    IV-δ1. Risking one's life (§ 1148)

    IV-δ2. Sharing one's property with others (§§ 1149-52)

IV-ε. Sentiments of social ranking; hierarchy (§§ 1153-62)

    IV-ε1. Sentiments of superiors (§ 1155)

    IV-ε2. Sentiments of inferiors (§§ 1156-59)

    IV-ε3. Need of group approbation (§§ 1160-62)

IV-ζ. Asceticism (§§ 1163-1206)

CLASS V

INTEGRITY OF THE INDIVIDUAL AND HIS APPURTENANCES (§§ 1207-1323)

V-α. Sentiments of resistance to alterations in the social equilibrium (§§ 1208-19)

V-β. Sentiments of equality in inferiors (§§ 1220-28)

V-γ. Restoration of integrity by acts pertaining to the individual whose integrity has been impaired (§§ 1229-1311)

    V-γ1. Real subjects (§§ 1240-95)

    V-γ2. Imaginary or abstract subjects (§§ 1296-1311)

V-δ. Restoration of integrity by acts pertaining to the offender (vengeance, "getting even") (§ 1312)

V-δ1. Real offender (§§ 1313-19)
V-δ2. Imaginary or abstract offender (§§ 1320-23)

CLASS VI
THE SEX RESIDUE (§§ 1324-96)

889. Class I. *Instinct for combinations.*[a] This class embraces the residues corresponding to the instinct for combinations, which is intensely powerful in the human species and has probably been, as it still remains, one of the important factors in civilization. Figuring as a residue in vast numbers of phenomena is an inclination to combine certain things with certain other things. The scientist in his laboratory makes combinations according to certain norms, certain purposes, certain hypotheses, for the most part rational (at times he combines at random). His activity is primarily logical. The ignorant person makes combinations in view of analogies that are mostly fantastic, absurd, childish (and often also by chance [1]). In any event they are in large part non-logical acts. There is an instinct that prompts to combinations in general, for reasons which are fleeting, momentary, undetectable. It deserves a separate classification as our genus I-α. Similar things often, less often opposites, are combined. That gives us a genus I-β. If the similarities or contrasts are generic, we get a species I-β1. Unusual things are often combined with important occurrences (I-β2); or things and happenings alike impressive are brought together (I-β3). A felicitous state attracts good or

889 [a] [Pareto seems to have adopted the term "combination" (*combinazione*) from the use made of it in Frazer's *Golden Bough*. However, the term is much more comprehensive in Italian than in English. In English, and especially in slang, we use many particular terms to cover the ground for which *combinazione* suffices for the Italian: for example, "deal," "happy inspiration," "idea," "big idea," "scheme." The term "combination" itself has a certain use in American slang in this sense. Unsatisfactory as it is, I have followed Mr. Bongiorno in transferring the Italian term as "combination," but Pareto's explanations must be borne in mind at all times. Synonyms of "the instinct for combinations" in one connexion or another might be "the inventive faculty," "ingeniousness," "originality," "imagination," and so on. The "instinct for combinations" is the progressive element in human society, as contrasted with the "myth-making instinct," or "instinct of group-persistence," which is the conservative force (see Chapter XII).—A. L.]

889 [1] The term "by chance" means simply that the causes underlying such acts are unknown.

praiseworthy things, and *vice versa* (I-β4), whereas an infelicitous contingency attracts bad, unpleasant, horrible things, and *vice versa*. In a genus I-γ we place combinations of things and acts that have something mysterious about them, and that genus falls into two species: mysterious operations in general (I-γ1), and mysterious linkings of names with things (I-γ2). The human beings feels a need for combining various residues (I-δ). Then again, we note a need that is the more keenly felt the higher the degree of civilization in a people: a need for cloaking acts that are in themselves non-logical with a logical veneer, for devising theories that may be altogether imaginary so only they be logical. We make a special genus for that: I-ε. Finally we have to provide for the belief in the efficacy of combinations (I-ζ). Taking Class I as a whole, one notes: (1) a propensity for combinations; (2) a search for the combinations that are deemed best; (3) a propensity to believe that they actually do what is expected of them.

890. There are, moreover, passive and active aspects to combinations. On the passive side the human being is subject to them; on the active side he interprets, controls, or produces them. The propensity, too, is a vague generic sentiment that operates passively and actively. It may be seen in vigorous action in games of chance among all peoples. There the quest for the best possible combinations is conspicuous and eager. As for the propensity to believe in the efficacy of combinations, it also has a passive and an active aspect. On the passive side, a person may believe that A is necessarily conjoined with B so that if A occurs, B must ensue. On the active side, the idea is that if one can manage to produce A, one can get B as a consequence (§§ 976 f.).

891. In the concrete case residues from other classes also figure, notably residues from Class II. Were it not for the persistence of certain relations, the combinations in Class I would be ephemeral insubstantial things. One might compare the situation to a building. The instinct for combinations, the quest for the best possible one, the faith in its efficacy, provide the materials. Persistence of associations gives stability to the structure; it is the cement that holds it

together. Then faith in the efficacy of combinations again interposes to incline people to use the building. In many phenomena, especially among civilized peoples, one notes mixtures: logical actions, scientific inferences, non-logical actions, effects of sentiment. Here we are segregating by analysis things that occur in a compound form in concrete reality.

892. I-α: *Generic combinations.* There are reasons for generic combinations, just as there are reasons for specific combinations such as I-β; and if there were any point in doing so, one might subdivide our α variety into a number of subvarieties corresponding to the various reasons. Thousands and thousands of persons play the lottery assigning numbers to things they have seen in their dreams or to happenings that have impressed them.[1] One can imagine why the number 1 has been assigned to the Sun. It is a case of a β1 residue (similarities); there being only one Sun, it goes very well with the number 1. But why does the Moon get the number 6, a pair of scissors, the number 7, a white cat, 31, a black cat, 36? We hope no one will try to tell us that experience has led to the belief in such correspondences. That may have happened in some few cases; but one need only glance at a "dream-book" to see that it would never have been possible to record enough experiments to justify all the assignments of numbers there made. It would take a maniac for logic to believe that the meaningless rigmaroles used in magic were chosen by experience—that Cato, for example, or someone acting in his behalf, put first one word and then another to the test before fixing on the ones he recommends in his magical recipe for sprains (§ 184 [2]).

893. It is all the other way round. One begins by believing in this

892 [1] See, for example, *The Book of Dreams, or Echo of Fortune* (*Il libro dei sogni* . . . Florence, A. Salani, n.d.). It contains 672 pages. In France, in the days when the lottery still flourished, publications of that type were abundant: for instance, *La Liste générale des rêves* . . . Paris, 1787—*General Catalogue of Dreams . . . With the Names of Things That Are Dreamed and the Numbers That Correspond to Them in the Drawings of the Royal Lottery of France,* translated from the Italian of Fortunato Indovino ("The Lucky Guesser"), illustrated with numerous cuts similar to said lottery. New edition, revised, corrected, and enlarged, with tables of drawings in the same lottery."

or that combination. Not till later on does someone come along who tries to justify the belief by logic and experience. The Greeks believed in dreams long before any Artemidorus volunteered to show by experience that dreams came true.[1]

894. No reader of Pliny's *Natural History* can fail to be struck by the vast numbers of combinations that have been tried for curing one disease or another. It would really seem as though every combination conceivable had been thought of! Take epilepsy, for instance. First we get laser-juice (distilled from the root of *laserpitium chironium*) with sea-calf's rennet, taken in doses of three parts juice and one part rennet, then plantain, betony, or agaric, mixed with oxymel (XXVI, 70, Bostock-Riley, Vol. V, pp. 196-97). Pliny mentions twelve plants in this one paragraph, in addition to rennet from the milk of the seal and the beaver. Then come remedies for epilepsy derived from the animal kingdom, XXVIII, 63 (Bostock-Riley, Vol. V, p. 353): bears' testicles, wild boars' testicles, wild bores' urine (which is more effective when allowed to evaporate in the animal's bladder); hog's testicles dried, triturated, and beaten in sow's milk; hares' lungs taken with frankincense and white wine. In all, nineteen combinations in the paragraph—not counting gladiator's blood (XXVIII, 2)! Another paragraph, XXXII, 37 (Bostock-Riley, Vol. VI, p. 46) mentions eight more combinations from the animal kingdom; another, XXX, 27, twenty-nine. Adding, we get sixty-nine combinations for epilepsy, and there must certainly have been others that Pliny failed to mention. For jaundice, Pliny recommends wine in which chicken's feet, previously cleansed in water, have been washed. He adds that the chicken's feet must be yellow (XXX, 28). That seems to indicate a residue of our I-β variety (similarities). But when one is told, XXX, 30, that to cure the ague one must wear the longest tooth of a black dog as a charm, no reason, however fantastic, is discernible for the treatment. Similar

---

893 [1] One of my critics has contended that non-logical actions arise from "excogitation" (which means logic all the same, no more, no less) and that only when the logical reasons have been forgotten do people invent explanations that make their conduct seem non-logical!

prescriptions are to be found not by the hundreds but by the thousands all over the face of the globe, and in our Western countries they have held their own down to very recent times. Cardinal Richelieu was once treated with horse-dung steeped in white wine. One treatment for fever was to wear around one's neck a live spider shut up in a nutshell.[2] Snakes and toads long played an important part in pharmacy. Absurdities all, one may say; yet if those absurdities had never been, experimental science would never have been either.[3]

895. Du Chaillu relates an incident that is characteristic.[1] On his killing a leopard, the natives asked him for the tip of the tail to use as an erotic amulet. They also wanted the brain; it promoted courage and good luck in hunting. Finally they begged him carefully to destroy the gall-bladder, since it was poisonous. The first of the combinations was of our I-α variety (generic); the second may have been of the I-β1 species (generic similarity), the leopard being a good hunter. Both were certainly ineffective. The third may conceivably have been effective in view of the ptomaines originating in putrefaction.[2]

896. When one is trying to discover the ways in which great events have come to pass in human society it may seem ridiculous to waste a paragraph on the tip of a leopard's tail. But if one is to argue in that fashion one ought not to worry either over the spittle of a patient in diagnosing tuberculosis, or bother with a rat in trying to fight the bubonic plague. So at one time philology disdained mere dialects and confined itself to the language of "recognized authors." That time is long since past in philology. So it should be in sociology (§ 80). The instinct for combinations is among the major forces determining the social equilibrium; and if it sometimes manifests itself in ridiculous and absurd ways, that fact detracts no whit from its importance.

894 [2] For no end of particulars, see Gallier, *Les mœurs et la vie privée d'autrefois*.

894 [3] It has been suggested that civilization originated in games of chance. There is an element of truth in the notion, in the sense that games of chance figure among the many manifestations of the instinct of combinations, which has been and remains a most significant factor in progress.

895 [1] *Explorations and Adventures in Equatorial Africa*, pp. 202-04.

895 [2] [Pareto is here following the outline in § 151.—A. L.]

897. Scientists interested in the origins of things have exerted themselves to discover how animals could ever have come to be domesticated; and they have met with very serious difficulties, especially when they were overeager to regard all human conduct as logical. We need not go into all the various hypotheses that have been advanced. Let us consider one, a theory of Reinach. It happens to suggest reflections pertinent to the matter here in hand.

898. Reinach begins by eliminating simple combinations:[1] "There may be domesticable animals about, but of that man knows nothing. Experience alone, long experience, could have enlightened him in that regard. But how and why would he even venture on such an experiment when he has no conception of domestication? Chance may reveal a flake of gold to primitive man, a mineral such as copper or iron, but chance could never show him a domestic animal! There can be no domestic animal except as a result of training received from man."

899. The reasoning would be excellent if all human conduct were logical, if—except in the case specified by Reinach, where pure chance throws in the savage's way the one completed object that he needs and can use—the only road to discovery were first to know what one wants, and then to look around for the best means of obtaining it. That in fact is the route which is followed in making scientific discoveries by rational processes. There is a demand for a source of power, light in weight and of high productive capacity. People hunt and they eventually find the gasoline engine. But most discoveries, especially in times past, were not made in that way. There is another way, and it lies precisely in the instinct for combinations, which impels the human being to put things and acts together without pre-established design, without knowing exactly what he is driving at—much as a person rambles about in a forest for the mere pleasure of rambling about. Even when design exists, it oftentimes has nothing to do with the result actually achieved. Very frequently the thing that was sought was not the thing that was discovered. What the alchemists wanted, for a decisive example,

898 [1] *Cultes, mythes et religions*, Vol. I, p. 88.

was a way for making gold. What they found was a variety of chemical compounds. It occurred to someone to allow a quantity of human urine to putrefy, then to mix the product with fine sand, and then to distill the mixture. The outcome of that weird and complicated process was the discovery of phosphorus. In many other cases the combination did not result in anything useful. One gropes blindly forward. Sometimes one finds. More often one does not.

900. In the case of domesticating animals human beings may have had some vague notion of the purposes of certain things they did. It happens every day about us that children will pick up a young bird that has fallen from its nest, and raise it. If the bird happened to be of any particular use, it would surely end by being domesticated. Children are not dreaming of any such purpose. They are just trying to amuse themselves by humouring their instinct for combinations, just as they do when on a romp they make the strangest combinations of the things at their disposal. In rural districts people will often raise young rabbits they happen to catch alive in the fields. They rarely become tame rabbits. The only purpose in raising them is the fun of raising them. Why in the world might such a thing not have been done with a rabbit in some earlier period of history? Why may not the rabbit have first been domesticated in some such way?

901. But there is better yet. Cowper Rose reports an incident in which the simple instinct for combinations may be seen at work in domesticating animals:[1]

"In Hinza's territory, a Kaffer, whose possessions excited envy and dislike, was accused of keeping a wolf, which, though confined during the day, roamed about the country at night, and destroyed the cattle. On this plea he was seized and deprived of everything, half of the cattle being taken by Hinza, while the other half was distributed among the councillors. The man was banished the country; and on leaving it, seized on the cattle of another, and carried them with him to Voosani, a neighbouring chief of Tambooki's. Hinza

901 [1] *Four Years in Southern Africa*, pp. 142-43.

sent to complain of the robbery, to demand the cattle, and to inform the chief of the crime of the man, whom he had protected. The cattle were returned, and great horror expressed at the crime. The missionary, who told me the story, in speaking to Hinza on the subject, said: 'You have plenty of cattle, why did you ruin the poor man?' when the chief turned to him with a peculiar smile which marked that he was not deceived, and, with a tone of mock seriousness, said: 'Yes, but it is a shocking thing, you know, to keep a witch-wolf.' "

902. Prominent here are two residues: the residue of combinations, in the man raising the wolf; and then the residue of neophobia (IV-β3) in the people who drove him out of town. Two residues can both work side by side in the same person; the man who raised the wolf might himself have been horrified at other novelties, just as those who considered raising a wolf a crime may have had practices of their own that involved strange combinations.

903. According to Reinach the animals that have been domesticated were ancient totems; and he goes on from there, heaping hypothesis on hypothesis and telling all about things of which he knows nothing as though he had seen them with his own eyes. That is the procedure of Spencer and many other sociologists. An ingenious, intelligent, well-read author advances a hypothesis, infers things from it in the light of his logic, his learning, his sentiments, and then imagines he is reconstructing the past of lethargic, uneducated savages who were endowed with little native intelligence, and who into the bargain lived under conditions entirely different from the ones surrounding the scientist-creator of the hypothesis and its implications.

904. "Imagine," says Reinach, *Op. cit.*, p. 93, "a race of savage huntsmen living in ancient France, a country where bulls, horses, deer, bears, wolves, not to mention other animals, were indigenous. The hunters are split up into clans or little tribes, each of them claiming a different animal for its ancestor. The wolf-clan thinks it is descended from the wolf, that it has made a pact of alliance with the wolves, and that, save in cases of legitimate self-defence,

it must not kill wolves. . . . Each of the clans will refrain from hunting and killing this or that species of animal, but it will not stop at that. Since the animal is the protector of the clan, guides it in its wanderings, raises alarms in times of danger by crying and signs of uneasiness, there must always be two or more of its species living with the clan to act as its sentinels." The facts do not stand just that way. We know of many clans that have totems but do not use the totem animals as sentinels. However, suppose we let that pass; other clans may have used them that way. But why "two or more" such animals? Would one not be sufficient? One would be enough to act as watch-dog for the clan. But not enough to reproduce the species! That is the point Reinach has to get to! "These animals, captured young, get used to human beings, grow tame. Their young, born in contact with members of the clan, become their friends." So, you see, that is why there had to be two or more totem animals. But that is not all: one had to be male, the other female! If a clan's totem is a rooster (a rooster crows in time of danger) the rooster has to have a hen—one or more hens! But in the realm of hypotheses everything can readily be accounted for. We may guess that since those ancient Frenchmen worshipped Chantecleer they must surely have been French enough to provide him with the ordinary comforts of home.

905. The discovery of certain plants that are specific remedies for certain diseases is as difficult to explain as the domestication of animals. How could mere chance ever have led the Peruvians to discover that cinchona bark is a specific for malaria? Are we to say that the cinchona was the totem of a clan, and that out of reverence for its totem the clan elected to use its bark in cases of sickness? But in that event the same explanation would have to serve for other cases of the kind, and we would need as many totems as there have been folk-remedies for diseases. But there are infinite numbers of such remedies, so that we should have to assume, contrary to fact, the same infinite number of totems.

906. One may doubt whether there is a plant that has not been considered suitable for curing not just one but any number of dis-

eases. How many ills the radish can cure, according to Pliny! Which all goes to show what scant resemblance such combinations bear to the experiments that are nowadays made in our laboratories. The idea would be that a plant was tried first for one disease, then for another, and that its use was eventually retained just for diseases for which it had shown itself effective. But the fact is, Pliny's prescriptions were kept even though ineffective, and many of them have been handed down to our day. What really underlay them was the instinct for combinations, and the same instinct is asserting itself even in our civilized day when in case of illness people say that "something has to be done" (residues, Class III) and medicines are administered catch as catch can (residues, Class I).

907. It may well be that at the time when animals were first domesticated cases such as Reinach imagines occurred—indeed more probably than not they did occur. The fact that an animal was a totem may have been one of any number of reasons that inspired combinations from which the domestication of animals resulted. Reinach's error lies chiefly in his giving as the only reason a reason that may have existed simultaneously with others. We know nothing of those early times. We cannot therefore deny a thing that is in itself possible. But neither can we affirm it; and it is to reason fallaciously to assert that because it was possible for a thing to be thus and so, thus and so it must have been. We may go even further. Even if we, now in our time, could see only one way in which a thing can have occurred, that might warrant the presumption that the thing took place in that way. But it may still have happened in some other way, of which we, *now* in our time, cannot conceive.

908. In the instinct to regard certain days as of good or of evil omen many residues may figure. Sometimes there is the residue of mere combination (I-α); it is difficult to see any others in certain of the correspondences noted by Hesiod. Sometimes present may be a residue of the I-β variety (similarities and opposites). But even in such a case, one can, as we have already seen (§ 894), get back in the long run, to our I-α variety. So the plain man in Rome ended, as Aulus Gellius notes, *Noctes Atticae,* IV, 9, 9-11, by confusing *religiosi dies,* which originally commemorated baleful events, with mere *dies nefasti,* on which the praetor was forbidden to sit in judgment or convoke the *comitia.*[1] In addition to the public holidays there were private holidays and certain families had special holidays of their own. Individuals, then as now, celebrated birthdays and kept other personal holidays on one account or another.[2] The Greeks also deemed it unlucky to work on certain days. In a diatribe against one Timarchus, Lucian says that the Athenians applied the term ἀποφράδες to baleful, abominable, unpropitious, unlucky days when "neither do magistrates sit in judgment, nor are cases brought before the courts, nor are religious ceremonies performed, nor anything of good omen. . . . That is the custom for a variety of reasons: whether because of great battles that have been lost, their an-

908 [1] *Loc. cit.,* 5: " 'Religious days' ('*dies religiosi*') are days of mourning, of accursed memory (*infames*) or of inhibiting omens. Limitations are placed on celebrating divine services and beginning new enterprises on such days. The ignorant masses mistakenly and reprehensibly call them *dies nefastos*" [as it were, "court holidays," or just "holidays"]. Says Varro, *De lingua latina,* VI, 29 (Goetz-Scholl pp. 68-69): "On 'court days' [*i.e.,* days of good omen, *dies fasti*] praetors can utter any words at all without pollution. Their opposites are called 'court-holidays' [*i.e.,* days of bad omen, *nefasti*] and a praetor must not pronounce the words *do, dico, addico* ["I give, award, adjudge," in which he registers his judgments]. Court actions cannot therefore be prosecuted, for it would be necessary to pronounce one of those words." It may have been the other way round, in the beginning. Roman writers of the historical period did not know why certain days were of good omen, others of bad. A praetor who inadvertently uttered the words *do, dico, addico* on a court holiday had to atone for the slip by expiatory sacrifices. Quintus Mucius held that no atonement was possible for a praetor who had uttered them in deliberate violation of the interdict [and therefore that he had to resign]: Varro, *loc. cit.,* 30: ". . . *si imprudens fecit, piaculari hostia facta piatur; si prudens . . . eum expiari ut impium non posse.*"

908 [2] Macrobius, *Saturnalia,* I, 16: "There are, in addition, holidays peculiar to families, such as the Claudian, the Aemilian, the Julian, the Cornelian, clans, and each family observes such holidays as it has by domestic gatherings and processions (*domesticae celebritatis*). And there are individual holidays, such as birthdays and the days when [personal] auspices are taken, the death anniversaries [of relatives] and days of [personal] expiations. Among the ancients anyone naming the goddesses Salus [of public safety], Semonia [of crops in general], Seia [of sowing], Segetia [of reaping], or Tutilina [of protection of wheat] had to keep holiday. Every time a member of the Flaminian gens heard thunder, he kept holiday until he had made a propitiatory offering to the gods."

niversaries being decreed holidays inappropriate to any legal action; or indeed in honour of Zeus. . . ." [8]

909. Such combinations—such superstitions, as Christian writers call them—survived for long periods of time. Muratori notes that "Egyptian days" were observed and even registered in public calendars from a remote antiquity down to the sixteenth century of the Christian era.[1] This is one of the most tenacious of residues; we find it in every age of history, in every country, and no more among the ignorant than among the educated, even the highly educated, and whether they are temperamentally superstitious or the reverse.[2]

908 [8] *Pseudologista, De die nefasto, contra Timarchum,* 12-13 (*Opera,* Vol. VIII, pp. 66-67). The sentence was broken off by Lucian himself, as though he thought it hardly worth while to list things so well known.

909 [1] *Dissertazioni sopra le antichità italiane,* LIX (Vol. III, pp. 227-29): "Also to be counted among superstitions is the 'observance of times,' or 'of days' (*observatio temporum, dierum*). This one was very general in former times, the pastors and Fathers of the Church preaching against it in vain. . . . How tenacious this impious observance was even among Christians is apparent from the fact that 'Egyptian days' were scrupulously observed by many people from a remote antiquity down to the sixteenth century of our era, and even registered in public calendars. . . . Two days were so marked (*suis sedibus indicati*) in each month, and they were supposed to be so unlucky and of such bad omen that anyone doing anything on them could only look forward to an unpleasant outcome. Not only the plain people but gentlefolk of politer education stood scrupulously on guard against such days, judging that a tradition so ancient must rest on very trustworthy foundations. All the same it was fabricated nowhere save in the clouds, or else in the ingenious imaginations of impostors. [The usual mistake of regarding non-logical conduct as logical.] Of course, we have no great right to be surprised at such customs in our forefathers, nor at their unintelligent credulity and superstition, since not a few people in our time, and people more pretentious about their learning than minds of the darker ages ever dared to be, will not start out on a journey on Friday in fear of becoming the examples that prove the truth of a certain Spanish adage: 'Never start a wedding or a journey on a Tuesday or a Friday.' There are also people who shiver if they discover that they are sitting at table with twelve other guests, in the firm conviction that a whole year will not pass without one of the thirteen dying in some unexpected manner. And there are those . . . who think some misfortune is impending if they see salt accidentally spilled on the table." These latter superstitions, or rather combinations, have held on down to our time.

909 [2] Of the Emperor Augustus Suetonius remarks, *Divus Augustus,* 92, 2: "He observed certain signs and omens, trusting them implicitly. . . . He also observed certain days. He would never start out for any destination on the day after a *nundina* (market-day) nor begin any important business on the nones [fifth or seventh of the month], for no other reason, as he wrote to Tiberius, than the δυσφημία, the unfavourable omen, of the name." [Apparently a number 9 superstition—residues

912. I-β: *Combinations of similars or opposites*. Similarity or contrast in things, no matter whether real or imaginary, is a potent cause of combinations. The reason is at once apparent if one but consider the associations of ideas that such things provoke. Nonlogical reasonings are often reasonings by association of ideas.

911. It is important to note that if *A* and *B* are similar things, and *C* and *D* their opposites, the phenomenon opposite to the combination *A* + *B* is not the combination *C* + *D*, but the absence of any combination. The opposite of belief in God is not belief in the Devil, but absence of belief in either. The state of mind of the person who is continually dwelling on matters of sex has its opposite in the state of mind, not of the person who is continually alluding to sex with horror, but of the person no more concerned with it than with any other bodily function. The novelists have long been telling us that the opposite of love is not hate, but indifference (§ 957 [1]).

912. The homoeopathic principle, *similia similibus curantur,* combines similars. The opposite principle, *contraria contrariis,* combines opposites. Antithetical to both is experimental science, which entertains no *a priori* principles but allows experience to pass judgment in every case.[1]

I-*a*; and *cf.* § 892. Rolfe explains the feeling as due to the resemblance of *nonis* (on the nones) to *non is*: "You do not go."—A. L.] Busch, *Tagebuchblätter,* Vol. II, p. 239 (English, Vol. I, p. 473), May 1, 1871: "As I saw later, Jules Favre telegraphed that he would be in Frankfort on Friday, and the Chief [Bismarck] replied that he would arrive there on Saturday, perhaps because he considers Friday unlucky." That may have been a diplomatic pretext; but the fact that Bismarck used it shows that there were people to take him seriously. [In the case of Busch's diary, the English translation from Busch's first manuscript takes precedence both over the published German text and over the French translation. The latter shows considerable adaptation to French sentiments. As for the German, it was not published for many years after it was written and suffered much reworking at Busch's senile hands and at the hands of others.—A. L.]

912 [1] Heim, *Incantamenta magica Graeca Latina,* pp. 484-85, *Similia similibus:* "Belief in the potency of similars, which may be briefly stated in the adage *similia similibus,* had a great and universal vogue in magic and medicine. Superstitious writers of ancient times wrote and raved extensively on the subject, as, for instance, the physicists Democritus and Nepualius, whose works *On Sympathies and Antipathies* have survived to our time. It was believed that actual evils could be banished by certain fancied similitudes, people choosing deliberately to be so deceived. [A logical explanation of the instinct for combining similars or opposites.] Kopp

913. I-β1: *Generic likeness or oppositeness*. Residues of this variety are of very frequent occurrence. They oftentimes figure in magic —similar things and similar operations are combined, a human being, an animal, a thing, are influenced by working on some small particle that has been removed from their bodies; and in that there is the twin similarity of things and procedures.[1] Contraries are also associated, and active in many cases apparently are sentiments that prompt a deliberate search for contrasts (§§ 738 f.).[2]

mentions many examples, *Paleographia critica*, Pt. III, §§ 511-16 f.; Wuttke, § 477. Amazing the comments that superstition and fatuous thinking have provoked in this regard (*hic*), as, for instance, *Geoponicon*, II, 42, 2. . . . I have already dealt with the portrayals of Hercules strangling the lion that are frequently to be found on medallions and jewellery." [The Wuttke reference I fail to solve.—A. L.]

913 [1] Réville, *Les religions des peuples non-civilisés*, Vol. I, pp. 152-53: "The Kaffir is not as addicted to fetishes . . . is, therefore, not so much of an idolator, as the Negro, but he has, if such a thing be possible, even more charms and amulets of all varieties and names. . . . The idea is that the qualities or defects of a given object are transmitted by simple contact, and that the similarity between two facts, the one already accomplished, the other desired, is tantamount to a relationship of cause and effect. [The usual error of assuming rational processes of thinking where none such exist. Imagine a Kaffir indulging in metaphysical reflections on cause and effect! What really is there is a non-logical sentiment inspiring a belief that things and acts go in pairs with other things and acts of the same sort.] A Kaffir's string of beads contains a sheep-bone, an iron ring, a lion's claw, a shrike's claw. Why? That the wearer may fly with the speed of the shrike, have the strength of a lion, the hardness of a bone, the resistance of iron. Under threat of death the Kaffir will fasten to his chest an insect that lives a long time after being pierced with a pin: he wants to borrow its endurance. If he would soften the heart of a man of whom he is to buy some cattle or a daughter, he chews at a piece of wood till he has reduced it to pulp."

913 [2] It is interesting just here to note that the inductive and the deductive methods get us to the same point. Some distance back (§§ 733 f.) we made a direct study of cases involving similar facts, and we wondered whether the resemblances were due to imitation. Our answer was in the negative. We saw that there were cases where imitation was out of the question, and we were therefore led by induction to consider some other cause for the resemblances, namely, sentiments inclining human beings to put certain things together. Following the deductive method, we would have begun by recognizing, as we do here, the existence of the sentiments. From that we would have inferred that human beings entertaining the same sentiments would be likely in certain cases to act in similar ways without any reciprocal imitation whatever. In that case the facts we presented back there, instead of serving for purposes of induction, would have served for purposes of verifying conclusions already reached. Whether we proceed in the one way or the other, the method is strictly logico-experimental, since the facts remain at all times sovereign over the whole discussion.

914. Says the witch in Theocritus, *Idyllia,* II, vv. 24-31: "Delphis [her lover] has tormented me. A laurel-branch I burn upon Delphis. Even as this crackles aloud when it is kindled, and burns in a flash so that not even its ashes do we see, so may the flesh of Delphis be consumed by the fire. . . . Even as I melt this wax with the help of a god, so may Delphis the Myndian be likewise melted by love; and as I turn this rhomb of bronze, so may he [Delphis] be turned by Aphrodite towards my threshold." She works moreover on an object that has belonged to her lover, *Ibid.,* vv. 53-54: "This fringe from his mantle has Delphis lost, and, lo, I rend it and cast it into the unrelenting flame."[1] It was once and still is believed that a person can

914 [1] The scholiast notes (Dübner, pp. 20, 125-26): "As the laurel vanishes straightway when thrown into the fire, so may Delphis be consumed in body in the fire of love." Farther along, v. 58, the witch speaks of crushing a lizard for Delphis, and says that she will carry him a curse in a potion. There is no trace of any similitude in all that. It is just a residue of generic combination (I-*a*). Virgil imitates Theocritus in *Eglogae,* VIII, vv. 79-81, and adds a few items derived from popular superstitions:

> "*Ducite ab urbe domum, mea carmina, ducite Daphnim.*
> *Limus ut hic durescit et haec ut cera liquescit*
> *uno eodemque igni, sic nostro Daphnis amore.*"

("Bring Daphnis home from town, bring him, songs of mine! Even as this clay hardens and this wax melts in the same fire, so may Daphnis in love of me.") Servius explains (Thilo-Hagen, Vol. III, p. 105, note): "She had made two images, one of clay which hardens in the fire, the other of wax which melts in the fire: in other words, that the heart of her lover might harden towards the woman he was at the time loving and all other women, the way clay hardens in the fire, but might soften and melt toward her as wax melts in the fire." In short, she would have her lover hardened to other women as clay in fire, and like wax melted by her love. Virgil continues, *loc. cit.,* vv. 82-83:

> "*Sparge molam et fragilis incende bitumine laurus.*
> *Daphnis me malus urit: ego hanc in Daphnide laurum.*"

("Sprinkle sacred meal [on the fire] and burn these frail laurels in tar. The cruel Daphnis consumes me in fire; I burn this laurel for [on] Daphnis.") Servius notes, *loc. cit.: "In Daphnide laurum:* Either it is a case of an archaism for *in Daphnidem,* or we must understand that she is burning the laurel upon an image of Daphnis, in view of the similarity of the names." It is better to understand: "*in hac lauro uro Daphnidem.*" The similarity becomes more exact in Virgil because the incantation is performed on relics of Daphnis. The witch buries them under her threshold, that they may bring Daphnis to her door, v. 92:

> "*Pignora cara sui, quae nunc ego limine in ipso,*
> *terra, tibi mando! Debent haec pignora Daphnim.*"

("These mementoes [of the traitor] on my threshold, O Earth, I commit to thee. These pledges make Daphnis my due."—Fairclough).

be harmed if one tortures a wax figurine made in his image.[2] Tartarotti writes:[3] "Jean Bodin, one of the greatest writers ever for magnifying the powers of witches, sorcerers, and the Devil, alluding to people who make wax figurines and burn them or pierce them with needles in hopes so of wreaking vengeance on their enemies, cannot but confess, *De la démonomanie,* II, 8, that 'the incantation rarely works, since out of a hundred people perhaps not more than two are ever harmed, as has been learned from confessions by sorcerers.'" The judges who sat at the trial of La Môle, who was accused of making a wax image of Charles IX and piercing it with pins, believed, or feigned to believe, in such practices, as did the judges who tried the wife of the Maréchal d'Ancre.[4]

915. Here, as usual, we get a nucleus with a number of amplifications concentrated about it—one residue with a variety of deriva-

---

914 [2] Ovid, *Epistulae, Hypsipyle Iasoni,* VI, v. 91 (Ehwald, Vol. I, p. 92):

"*Devovet absentis simulacraque cerea figit*
et miserum tenues in iecur urget acus."

("She makes waxen images of the absent one, and lays a curse upon him, driving sharp needles into the quivering liver.")

914 [3] *Del congresso notturno delle lammie,* II, 17, 2 (p. 192).

914 [4] Hayem, *La maréchale d'Ancre: Léonora Galigai,* p. 280. The Maréchale (Eleonora Dori Galigai) testifying: "She [*i.e.,* the witness] does not know what wax images they are talking about, that that is the business of witches, she having never been aught but a Christian, and that they will never find out any such thing about her. *Q.* What did you use the images for? Answers that God might strike her dead if she knew anything about any wax images. *Q.* In the house, when it was broken into, pillaged, and torn down, there was a high room, like a garret, and in said room (*maison*) a coffin on a table and on the table a wax image covered with a shroud of black velvet, with four candlesticks with white candles at the corners. Answers that she would rather die than see a thing like that." *Registre criminel du Châtelet de Paris,* Vol. II, p. 287: "Prosecution of Jeanne de Brigue, *anno* 1390: And then witness asked said Jehennete whether she knew who the woman was who was causing him to suffer such torment; and she replied that it was the said Gilete . . . that she [Gilete] had made a wax face and put on it hair belonging to witness, and that every time he was sick in that way it was because she was putting the said face on the fire in a copper pan and turning it with a copper spoon, which spoon and pan he had himself given her. And then witness asked her [Jehennete] how she knew that, and she answered that she knew it because she had talked of his case (*à ses choses?*) and that never had anyone been so cruelly 'faced' (*envoulté,* bewitched, in the manner described) and that she had had a great deal of trouble in trying to cure him, more trouble than she had ever had in her life before."

tions. In Theocritus and Virgil there is an ungarnished resemblance between a wax image that is melting and a man burning with love. That seed sprouts, grows, and blossoms into an ample legend that is told [in Hector Boece's *Croniclis,* XI, 4] about one Duffus, King of Scotland. Said king was suffering from a disease unfamiliar to his physicians. He perspired every night and was unable to rest during the day. After numerous vicissitudes, it came to light that at Fores, in the nearby township of Murray, certain witches were in possession of a wax figure of the King. Whenever they set the image in front of the fire, the King began to sweat; and it was the incantations they recited before it that kept him from sleeping. All that, of course, was the work of the Devil, a derivation not available for Theocritus and Virgil, but which is never missing in Christian times. Theocritus, it is true, had a derivation of the same sort: thanks to Aphrodite the whirling of a rhomb is to bring the straying lover back. John Weier was a doctor and had a smattering of that experimental art which was so distasteful to metaphysicists and theologians, as it still is.[1] Weier takes no stock whatever in the story of the Scottish king. But it was swallowed whole by the Boutroux's and William Jameses of those days, seeming doubtless to them to possess a "truth" far superior to experimental truth and far more majestic.[2]

915 [1] In his *De operatione daemonum,* 14 (*Opera,* p. 851), Michael Psellus censures physicians who refuse to recognize works of the Devil and resort to experimental explanations of facts. Says he: "Small wonder that doctors think as they do, for they refuse to see anything that does not fall under the senses, and attend only to the body." Metaphysicists who adore Hegel and Kant, or the sublimities of a law of nations, are still finding the same fault today with scholars who insist on keeping within the limits of experimental realities.

915 [2] Weier, *Histoires, disputes et discours,* III, 14 (Vol. I, pp. 339-43): "*Ie proposerai en cest endroit une esmerueiable histoire . . . laquelle a esté escrite par Hector Boece. Le Roy Dussus* [sic] *tomba en vne maladie, laquelle de soy mesme n'étoit si dangereuse que dificile à conoistre par les plus doctes medecins. . . . Car il suoit toute nuit et ne pouuoit dormir, et de jour il se reposoit, à peine soulagé de la douleur qu'il auoit enduree toute la nuit.*" Finally people in Scotland get an inkling, we are not told how, "*que le Roy estoit detenu par vne si longue espace de temps en langueur . . . non par maladie naturelle mais au moyen de l'art diabolique des sorcieres, lesquelles exerçoient contre luy l'art de Magie et sorcellerie en vne ville de Morauie* [sic] *nommee Forres.*" The King investigates in that town, and discovers that soldiers there already had their suspicions, due to the talk of a mistress of one

916. It was, and still is, a trick of magicians for swindling simpletons to persuade them to bury gold or jewels in a certain place, with the idea that more gold and jewels will be attracted by them, the enchanter, in due course, appropriating the "bait." The newspapers report some instance of the use of this trick every so often.

917. If some incompatibility, real or imaginary, exists between certain things, the one can be used for getting rid of the other. The *Geoponicon* of Cassianus Bassus, II, 42, explains how a garden may be saved from the ravages of a parasitic weed called *orobanche,* "broom-rape," which destroys vegetables. The plant was also called "lion-grass," and that was enough to justify the assumption that anything believed to be at outs with the lion would be at war with that weed: "If you would have this grass appear not at all, take five shells [*variant:* or pieces of broken crockery] and thereon with chalk or some other white substance draw Hercules strangling the lion. Place one shell in each of the four corners of the field and one in the centre. Another cure has been found, physical and by antipathy, and it is vouched for by Democritus. He says that since the lion is stricken with terror at sight of a cock and runs away, if one takes a cock in one's hands and resolutely walks the round of the field, the lion-grass straightway departs and vegetables grow the better, the lion-grass fearing the cock." Present here are residues of two varieties: 1. A residue of the I-γ2 type links the name with the thing.

of them who happened to be the daughter of a witch. The soldiers go to her house by night: "*Lesquels entrans de force en la maison fermee trouerent vne sorciere qui tenoit vne image de cire representant la figure de Dussus, laquelle estoit faicte, comme il est vraysemblable, par art Diabolique et attachee à vn pau de bois deuant le feu, là où elle se fondoit, ce pendant que vne autre sorciere en recitant quelques charmes distilloit peu à peu vne liqueur par dessus l'effigie. Ces sorcieres doncques estant prises . . . et interroguees . . . elles respondirent que le Roy Dussus fondoit en sueur pendant que son effigie estoit devant le feu; et que tandis que l'on prononçoit les charmes il ne pouuoit dormir, tellement qu'à mesure que la cire fondoit il tomboit en langueur, et qu'il mourroit incontinent qu'elle seroit du tout fondue. Elles dirent aussi que les Diables les auoyent ainsi apprises.*" The witches are burned, and "*ce pendant que ces choses se faisoyent . . . le Roy commença à se reuenir, et passa la nuict sans suer, si bien que le iour suyuant il reprit ses forces.*" Weier concedes that the Devil may have done all that, but later qualifies: "I say that, on the assumption that the story is true, which I do not believe." [Pareto follows Weier.—A. L.]

Since the weed is called lion-grass, it has the characteristics of the lion. 2. A residue of the variety here in hand (I-β1) sets up an oppositeness between the cock and the lion.[1] Cleisthenes, tyrant of Sicyon, desired to abolish the cult of Adrastus in his city as constituting a bond between his people and the Argives with whom he was at war. Accordingly, says Herodotus, *Historiae,* V, 67, he began by asking the Pythia if he might not simply throw Adrastus out. On receiving a scornful negative, he devised a plan for being rid of the god indirectly. He asked the Thebans for Melanippus and having obtained him, dedicated a chapel in the Prytaneum to him. That he did because Melanippus had been a mortal enemy of Adrastus, and he assumed that if he paid honour to Melanippus and held in his name the feasts that had formerly been dedicated to Adrastus, the latter would withdraw of his own accord.

918. The act of parodying the rites of a religious cult shows a residue of this same variety, I-β1. The purpose of such travesties, which were frequently practised in ages past among the Catholic peoples, was to obtain things contrary to religion and morality. The "black masses" were of this type.

919. Sacrifices in Graeco-Roman antiquity are often determined by arbitrary, strange, absurd resemblances, being obtained from religious residues by derivations in which a residue of our I-β1 variety plays the principal part. In Greece the victim's head was turned towards the sky when the sacrifice was to the Olympian gods, towards the ground when it was to the nether gods. As a general rule, with many exceptions for that matter, male animals were sacrificed to male divinities, female to female. Likeness was the determining

917 [1] A variant shows how legends arising from the same residue grow more and more complicated. Instead of saying "one" or "someone," one of the manuscripts of the *Geoponicon* reads: "A virgin of marriageable age, barefoot, nude, wearing nothing about her loins, her hair hanging loose, holding a cock in her hands," *etc.* That gives another residue of our I-β2 variety (unusual things): one unusual thing, a virgin circling a field naked, is associated with an exceptional occurrence, the vanishing of the broom-rape. Note that she has to be of marriageable age—ὥραν ἔχουσα γάμου. If she were a child there would be nothing unusual in her going about naked.

factor in many cases; but in many others the reasons are either unknown or seem childish and extravagant.[1]

920. Resemblances appear in interesting ways in many other connexions. In Rome "the bride was girdled with a sash, which was loosed by the groom in the nuptial bed. The sash was made of sheep's wool, to the end that just as the wool when sheared in tufts is tangled and intertwined, so the husband might be bound and attached to the wife. The husband unties the Herculean knot in the sash as an act of good omen, that he may be as lucky in begetting offspring as was Hercules, who left seventy children."[1]

919 [1] Arnobius, *Disputationes adversus gentes,* VII, 19 (Orelli, p. 240; Bryce-Campbell, p. 326): " 'You are in error and apostasy (*erras et laberis*),' he said, 'for the reasons why female animals are sacrificed to female divinities and male to male are abstruse and recondite, lying beyond common knowledge.' " For the sacrifices of Aeneas, and the comment of Servius, *In Vergilii Aeneidem,* III, vv. 118-20, see above, § 192 [1]. Schoemann, *Griechische Alterthümer,* Vol. II, p. 208: "Goats were offered to Hera nowhere save in Sparta. Athena also disapproved of them and it was thought that her animosity came from the damage they did to olive-trees. [Derivation to explain a I-α residue.] For the same reason goats could not be taken to the Acropolis for purposes of sacrifice to any of the divinities who were neighbours of the tutelary goddess of the city. Dionysus must have reasoned the other way round [A common thing with derivations, one argument serving two opposite purposes.]; for he was supposed to take peculiar delight in offerings of he-goats in view of their ravages in the vineyards." Constant in all this the residue of combinations (I-α); variable, the reasonings that serve to logicalize the residue—the derivations. Daremberg-Saglio, *Dictionnaire, s.v. Sacrificium:* "As for the reasons given by the ancients for the preference or repugnance of this or that divinity for this or that victim, they are at times quite fatuous [residue I-α]. In any event they by no means derive from a single principle. At times it is a question of a mere play on words [residue I-γ]. Perch were offered to Hecate, says Apollodorus [*De diis,* XX, *Fragmenta,* 16 (p. 431)], and after him, Athenaeus, *Deipnosophistae,* VII, 92, *s.v. Mainides,* because the word for perch (τρίγλη) was associated with current epithets of the goddess: τρίμορφος, τριοδῖτις, τρίγληνος. The pig, suggests the Megarian of Aristophanes [*Archanenses,* v. 739], was a suitable victim for Aphrodite because its name, χοῖρος, was also the word for the female organ of sex. At other times the reason was sought in some resemblance more or less real between the temperaments of the god and the victim. . . . Now the alleged hostility of a god or goddess towards a certain species of animal is taken as a reason for sacrificing that species to them. Then again the same antipathy serves to prohibit such victims. . . . In sacrifices to the dead, the victim (when a victim was offered) seems ordinarily to have been a sheep; and the sheep was also the sacrifice for heroes, save in the case of warriors killed in battle. They were accorded heroic honours, with sacrifices of bulls (residue I-β1).

920 [1] Festus, *De verborum significatione,* III, *s.v. Cingulum* (London, Vol. I, pp. 156-57): "*Cingulo nova nupta praecingebatur quod vir in lecto solvebat, factum ex lana ovis, ut sicut illa in glomos sublata coniuncta inter se sit sic vir suus secum*

921. The I-β1 residue, combined with others from Class V (personal integrity), figures in a custom observed by Augustus in going begging once a year (opposites, contrast), and more generally in the various devices that were used for evading the "envy of the gods" (§ 1986).[1] It is present also in the complex of sentiments that leads people to treat inanimate objects as animate, and animals and things as if they were rational beings. In general it figures to a greater or lesser extent in the human inclination to reason by analogy (similars); and we shall therefore meet with it again when we come to derivations (§§ 1614 f.).

922. I-β2: *Unusual things and exceptional occurrences.* The instinctive feeling that rareties and exceptional happenings are connected with other rareties and exceptional happenings, or merely with things eagerly desired, serves also to sustain faith in the efficacy of such combinations. For the very reason that the things (occurrences) are unusual, the many proofs and counter-proofs that might show the fatuity of the belief are not provided. That fact, however, is not the cause of the belief, for observation proves that experiences to the contrary, even if exceedingly frequent, fail to shake faith in the combinations to any great extent, if at all. In Southern Italy many people wear horns on their watch-chains as infallible preventives against the evil eye, and experience has nothing whatever to do with the case.

923. The rarity of the object (occurrence) may be intrinsic or extrinsic, that is to say, it may belong to a class of objects (acts) that are rare in themselves, or the interest may derive from some accidental circumstance, even imaginary. Talismans and relics often belong to this latter category.[1]

cinctus vinctusque esset. Hunc Herculeaneo nodo vinctum vir solvit ominis gratia, ut sic ipse felix sit in suscipiendis liberis ut fuit Hercules qui septuaginta liberos reliquit."

921 [1] Suetonius, *Divus Augustus,* 91, 2: "He saw an apparition one night, and after that he went begging alms in public on a certain day every year, holding out cupped hands to those who offered coins." And *cf.* Dio Cassius, *Historia Romana,* LIV, 35, 3.

923 [1] Suetonius, *Nero,* 56: "Nero was seized by another superstition and clung to it most stubbornly. From a man of the people whom he did not know he had received an ordinary doll, such as a girl might use (*imagunculam puellarem*). He

924. Omens very often yield residues of the I-$\beta 2$ variety. They are often invented after the fact. Sometimes they are announced beforehand, and then some sort of verification is recognized. Expectation of an occurrence may even contribute to its happening. Omens derive their main appeal from belief in the efficacy of combinations (§§ 926 f.).

925. Suetonius never neglects to report the prodigies that presaged future ascents of Emperors to the throne and strange happenings that foretold their deaths. He always finds them in plenty. There is, for instance, the pretty story of the white hen that an eagle dropped into Livia's lap, Livia being Augustus's wife. The hen was holding a laurel-branch in its beak. There is no doubt about the unusualness of such a happening, and it naturally had to be associated with something equally extraordinary (§ 988). And that, in fact, was the case, at least in the fancy of the person who invented the story. Livia kept the hen and reared its chickens, and planted the sprig of laurel. The shoot grew into a tree and from the tree the Caesars cut the branches of which they made the crowns for their triumphs. Then it became customary to plant such branches all in the same place, and it was observed—such the value of experience [1] —that after the death of a Caesar, the laurel that he had planted withered away. During the last years of Nero the whole grove of laurels withered up to the very roots, and likewise all the descendants of the hen perished. All that, evidently, presaged the end of the

regarded it as a charm against plots on his life. Straightway a conspiracy chanced to be discovered, and he insisted on worshipping the image as a supreme divinity by triple sacrifices each day, trying to give the impression that he knew the future from warnings the doll gave him." The rarity in this case was the exceptional coincidence. In the following the object is rare in itself: Ollivier, *L'Empire libéral*, Vol. II, p. 55: "Among the effects left by his mother, Louis Napoleon [the future Napoleon III] found a variety of precious mementoes, one especially from which he could never be separated—'the talisman.' It was a jewel set with a piece of the True Cross, which had been found in Charlemagne's tomb about his neck and sent to Napoleon I at the time of the coronation. Great importance was attached to the possession of it in the family as a guarantee of divine protection. Josephine coaxed it from her husband with some difficulty and after the divorce she was not deprived of it. Eventually it went to Hortense."

925 [1] It is the experience of our theologians and metaphysicists nowadays; it yields exactly what has been put into it.

line of Caesars, which in fact became extinct in Nero.[2] Why should the birth of a colt from a mule necessarily presage some great event? One can find no other reason save that one rare event has to go with some other rare event. That particular omen among the Romans was adjudged baneful.[3] Just before the consul Lucius Cornelius Scipio set sail for Asia, the high-priests kept their eyes peeled for prodigies, and notable among them was the fact that a mule had had a colt.[4] Once upon a time a thunderbolt fell on the walls of Velitrae (Vellitri), and that incident was taken as a presage that a citizen of that city was to hold supreme power. Strong in that faith the Velitrians made war on the Romans, but with little success. "Not till years later did it become manifest that the presage had foretold the advent of Augustus," who came of a family of Velitrae.[5] That is one of the many prophecies—when they are not outright invention—that are not comprehended till after the fact (§ 1579).

Though Christians attribute everything to God, they often have their omens without reference, explicit at least, to divine interposition, so natural does it seem that rare things and exceptional occurrences should go together. The legend of Charlemagne records the "signs" that presaged his death. The Sun and the Moon were darkened, and the name of Charlemagne vanished of its own accord from the wall of a church that he had founded. No less than five such signs in all![6]

925 [2] Suetonius, *Galba*, 1; Pliny, *Historia naturalis*, XV, 40 (Bostock-Riley, Vol. III, p. 336); Dio Cassius, *Historia Romana*, XLVIII, 52. Pliny and Dio do not mention any withering of the laurels. Pliny in fact says that some of them were still flourishing in his day.

925 [3] Pliny, *Ibid.*, VIII, 69: "Our annals record many instances of mules having colts, but it was taken to be a prodigy"—*i.e.*, in the bad sense. (Bostock-Riley, Vol. II, p. 325: "But such cases must be looked upon only as prodigies.")

925 [4] Livy, *Ab urbe condita*, XXXVII, 3.

925 [5] Suetonius, *Divus Augustus*, 94, 2.

925 [6] Pseudo-Turpin, *Les fais et les gestes le fort roy Charlemaine*, pp. 285-86: "*Plusieurs signes avindrent par trois ans devant qui apertement signifioient sa mort et son deffinement. Le premier fu que le soleil et la lune perdirent leur couleur naturelle par trois jours, et furent ainsi comme tous noirs, un pou avant ce qu'il mourust.*" The fifth was that "one day while he was riding from one place to another on his horse, the sky suddenly darkened and a great sword of fire (*brandon*) waved across the heavens in front of him moving from right to left."

Taken as manifestations of divine activity presages and divination are derivations from I-β residues and more especially from those of the I-β2 species. Anything exceptional might correspond to the residue. Divine intervention was then introduced to explain the correspondence.

926. Constant over many centuries is the ascription of divine origins to heroes and great men. Every individual, be he real or imaginary, whose name appears at all prominently in history or legend owes his birth to some divine act, or it is at least attended by prodigies.[1] We must not confuse legends of divine origins with the fre-

926 [1] The conception of Buddha was attended by so many that it would be a long and not very profitable task to recount them even in brief proportion. Kern, *Histoire du bouddhisme*, Vol. I, pp. 23-24: The virtuous queen Maya dreamed that "the four divine sovereigns, the Cardinal Points, gathered her up with her bed and transported her to the Himalayas, where they set her down in the shade of a wide-spreading tree. . . . The Bodhisatva assumed the form of a white elephant, departed from the Golden Mount on which he dwelt, ascended the Mount of Silver, entered the Golden Grotto with a terrible thunder and, bearing a white water-lily in his trunk, marched thrice about the bed where Maya was resting, moving to the right as a sign of courtesy, opened the right side of the queen, and so entered her body. . . . At the moment of the Bodhisatva's conception in his mother's womb all nature was set in motion, and thirty-two presages were observed: an incomparable radiance encompassed the Universe. . . ." Latins do not indulge in these Oriental extravagances. Suetonius, on the authority of Asclepias Mendes, recounts the conception of Augustus by Atia as follows, *Divus Augustus*, 94, 4: "She had entered the temple of Apollo in the middle of the night to perform a sacrifice. Her litter was set on the floor and the other matrons went home (*domi irent:* also *dormirent:* went to sleep). She fell asleep. A serpent suddenly made its way to her side, and soon after departed. Awaking, she purified herself as was her custom after her husband's embrace. And at once on her body appeared a spot of the shape and colour of a serpent, and she could never remove it, and in view of it abstained from the public baths." Serpents, be it said in no disrespect to the reptile that tempted our Mother Eve, seem to have had a peculiar predilection for relations with women. One of them, whether on its own account or in behalf of Zeus, was responsible for Olympia's becoming the mother of Alexander the Great. Justin, *Historiae Philippicae*, XII, 16 (Clarke, p. 126): "The night in which his mother, Olympia, conceived him, she dreamed in her sleep that she lay with a huge serpent. Nor was the dream a mere illusion, for assuredly she was not fertilized by any mortal man." [So Pareto; literally: "She bore in her womb a work too great for human mortality."—A. L.] In XI, 11 (Clarke, p. 105), Justin tells how Alexander "hastened to the oracle of Jupiter Amon for light on his future and on his origin; for his mother had confessed to her husband Philip that 'she had conceived Alexander not of him but of a serpent of gigantic size.' Thereafter, being come almost to the end of his days, Philip proclaimed openly that 'her son was not his' and therefore divorced

quent cases where the appellative "divine" is bestowed on individuals merely to indicate their eminence in admirable, venerable, or excellent qualities—so Homer, *Odyssey,* XIV, v. 413, calls a swineherd divine (δῖος ὑφορβός).

Olympia as proven guilty of adultery." The legend grows and grows. Plutarch, *Alexander,* 2, 3-4 (Perrin, Vol. VII, pp. 227-29), relates that Philip saw a serpent near his sleeping wife (adding, 6, that according to one story Olympia kept tame serpents). Philip, he goes on, lost an eye, the eye "which he had applied to the chink in the door in order to see the god in the form of a serpent in embrace with his wife." [In reality Philip lost the eye at the siege of Methone.] [In reality, Plutarch (Clough, Vol. IV, pp. 3-4) merely records a prophecy that Philip *would* lose the eye.—A. L.] New embellishments finally evolve the story of Alexander's birth that is given by the Pseudo-Callisthenes, *Historia fabulosa Alexandri Magni,* I, 1-13 (Budge, pp. 1-13). It matters little for our purposes just what share in it is to be ascribed to naïve credulousness and what to sheer artifice, or whether there may have been some real basis for the legends, such as the fact that is vouched for by Lucian, *Pseudomantis,* 7 (Harmon, Vol. IV, p. 185), that Macedonian women often kept pet snakes. The mere fact that the legends existed, and more especially the fact that they met with a favourable reception, show that they corresponded to certain sentiments; and that is the one point we are concerned to establish. Here too and as usual, we get a nucleus with a fog of derivations extending around it. Publius Scipio, the first Africanus, also had a serpent for a father, an unusually big one, of course, and, of course also, divine: Livy, *Ab urbe condita,* XXVI, 19: Scipio's manner of living led to the belief that "he was a man of divine lineage, and so revived the story that was earlier told of Alexander the Great and was equally fatuous and fictional, that he was conceived of intercourse with a huge snake, and that the semblance of that prodigy [*i.e.,* something shaped like a snake] was time and again seen in his mother's bed, suddenly crawling away at the approach of human beings and vanishing from sight." And *cf.* Aulus Gellius, *Noctes Atticae,* VI, 1, 1-3. Servius Tullius could not be allowed to remain the son of a slave. Livy, *Ibid.,* I, 39, 5, assigns a less marvellous origin to that legendary character, suggesting that his mother was already with child by her husband, headman at Corniculum, at the time when she was made a prisoner. That is also the story told by Dionysius of Halicarnassus, *Antiquitates Romanae,* IV, 1 (Spelman, Vol. II, pp. 144-45). But for so great a man our present residue could be relied upon to provide something more and better. And in fact, Dionysius himself relates, IV, 2, that in the annals of Corniculum and in many Roman histories he has found another family-tree that smacks more of the legendary; and he tells a long story, which is later repeated by Ovid and Pliny, according to which Vulcan is to be held responsible for Servius Tullius and in a somewhat fantastic manner. Pliny, *Historia naturalis,* XXXVI, 70 (Bostock-Riley, Vol. VI, p. 384), tells the story as though he believed it, but robs Vulcan of the fatherhood and bestows it on the god of the hearth: "I must not omit one episide (*exemplum*) involving the hearth-fire that is famous in Roman letters. The story goes that while Tarquinius Priscus was on the throne, genitals of the male sex arose from the ashes in the flame of his hearth [*i.e.,* the sacred home-fire] and that the woman who was tending it, a slave, Ocresia, maid to queen Tanaquil, arose from her work with child. So was born Servius Tullius, who succeeded the Tarquin as king." Ovid,

In concrete cases of divine generations a number of residues figure. The central nucleus is made up of: (1) residues of group-persistence (Class II) whereby gods and spirits become projections of the human personality;[2] (2) sex residues (Class VI), that satisfy the

Fasti, VI, vv. 627-34, hands the paternity back to Vulcan, the latter functioning as in the miracle recounted by Pliny:

> *"Namque pater Tulli Vulcanus, Ocresia mater,*
> *praesignis facie Corniculana, fuit.*
> *Hanc secum Tanaquil sacris de more paratis*
> *jussit in ornatum fundere vina focum.*
> *Hic inter cineres obscaeni forma virilis*
> *aut fuit aut visa est—sed fuit illa magis.*
> *Iussa loco captiva fovet: conceptus ab illa*
> *Servius a coelo semina gentis habet."*

("Tully's father was Vulcan and his mother, Ocresia, a beautiful girl from Corniculum. Having prepared for the rites according to custom, Tanaquil bade her assist in pouring the wine upon the hearth, which had been adorned for the ceremonies. There among the ashes an unsightly shape of male form was visible—or they thought it was (and my belief is that it was). At the command of her mistress, the slave Ocresia leaned upon the hearth, and since she there became his mother, Servius has his lineage of heaven.") Whatever Ovid's inner thought, he leaves the impression (*sed fuit illa magis*) of believing that it was not an illusion on the part of Ocresia. Arnobius, *Disputationes adversus gentes,* V, 18 (Bryce-Campbell, pp. 241-42), is impressed only with the obscenity of the story and charges it to the account of the pagans. Divine origins may be found even for philosophers when they are very very great. Origen says, *Contra Celsum,* I (Augsburg, p. 30): "Some writers—not in ancient or heroic histories, but in books dealing with matters of very recent date—have seen fit to assert as a fact altogether possible that Plato was born of his mother Amphiction [Perictione], . . . Ariston [her husband] having been forbidden to have knowledge of her until she should have borne fruit of Apollo. But such are mere tales born of a belief that men esteemed superior to others in wisdom must have sprung of some divine seed, as would befit natures greater than human." And so it is, but without going such a long way round. It is simply because in the human mind sublime things are associated with sublime things and bad things with bad.

926 [2] Grote, *History of Greece,* Vol. I, pp. 80-81: "And thus the genealogy was made to satisfy at once the appetite of the Greeks for romantic adventure, and their demand for an unbroken line of filiation between themselves and the gods. The eponymous personage, from whom the community derive their name, is sometimes the begotten son of the local god, sometimes an indigenous man sprung from the earth, which is indeed itself divinized. It will be seen from the mere description of these genealogies that they included elements human and historical, as well as elements divine and extra-historical. . . . In the point of view of the Greeks . . . not only all the members were alike real, but the gods and heroes at the commencement were in a certain sense the most real; at least, they were the most esteemed and indispensable of all."

human hankering to dwell on procreative acts; (3) residues of the variety here in hand (I-β2) whereby a thing in itself remarkable must have a remarkable origin—and that is achieved in two ways: either by going back from a real thing to an imaginary origin, or by coming down from an imaginary origin to a thing equally imaginary.

927. Divine generations fall into two groups: 1. Divine beings unite with other divine beings and produce a divine progeny. Such the source of the many theogonies current among different peoples. This class, further, has a number of appendages. Instead of being strictly divine the entities may be merely spiritual; or they may so far depart from personification as to become mere metaphysical abstractions (§§ 1070 f.). In another direction, another residue of our present variety (I-β2) also comes into play. If divine procreation is the rule, the unborn one becomes the exceptional being, the eternal, "increate" being, and so too the person with one parent only, such as Minerva, engendered of Jupiter without female cooperation, or Vulcan born agamogenetically of Juno.[1] 2. Divinities unite with human beings or, very rarely, with animals. Unions of gods and women are more frequent among our Western races than unions of female divinities with men; and that because the myths were

927 [1] Ovid, *Fasti*, V, vv. 231-32:

> "*Sancta Iovem Iuno, nata sine matre Minerva,*
> *officio doluit non eguisse suo.*"

("On the birth of Minerva motherless, holy Juno complained of Jove that he had not done his duty by her.") Flora instructs her as to how she may become a mother independently of a male, and tells of a flower someone had given her, *Ibid.*, vv. 253-56:

> "*Qui dabat, 'Hoc,' dixit, 'sterilem quoque tange iuvencam—*
> *mater erit. Tetigi. Nec mora mater erat.'*
> *Protinus haerentem decerpsi pollice florem:*
> *Tangitur—et tacto concipit illa sinu!*"

("He who gave it to me said: 'Touch a fallow heifer with this flower and she will bear a calf. I touched her, and in a trice she was a mother.' I plucked the clinging flower in my fingers forthwith and touched her [Juno], and at the touch on her body she conceived.") The myth of Hephaestus (Vulcan) goes back as far as Hesiod, *Theogonia*, v. 927; but Homer, *Iliad*, I, vv. 572, 578, makes him a son of Zeus and Hera. Apollodorus, *Bibliotheca*, I, 3, 5 (Frazer, Vol. I, p. 21), follows Hesiod: "Hera bore Hephaestus without embrace."

composed chiefly by men among peoples where the patriarchal family prevailed. So only can we account for the fact that in the Bible male angels fall enamoured of the daughters of men, never female angels of the sons of men.[2] This group like the preceding has its variations and postscripts, till step by step one gets to the point where the wind is fertilizing mares and, for that matter, women.[3] Here again I-β2 residues pile up one on the other. Procreations by divine commerce with human beings becoming common-

927 [2] Gen. 6:1-4: "And it came to pass, when men began to multiply on the face of the earth, and daughters were born unto them, that the sons of God saw the daughters of men that they were fair; and they took them wives of all which they chose. . . . There were giants in the earth in those days; and also after that, when the sons of God came in unto the daughters of men, and they bare children to them, the same became mighty men which were of old, men of renown." Kahn, *La Bible . . . traduite par les membres du rabbinat français,* Vol. I, p. 6: "Now when men had begun to multiply upon the earth and daughters were born to them, the sons of divine lineage found that the daughters of men were beautiful and chose as their wives such as were pleasing in their sight." In his *Quaestiones sive traditiones hebraicae in Genesim* (*Opera,* Vol. III, pp. 947-48) St. Jerome remarks (Gen. 6:2) ("saw the daughters of men that they were fair"): "The Hebrew word *eloim* is both singular and plural (*communis est numeri*) and God and gods may of course be rendered by the same word. That is why Aquila [a reviewer of the Septuagint] made bold to say 'sons of gods' in the plural, meaning divine holy creatures, in other words, angels."

927 [3] In his edition of Ovid, Vol. VIII, pp. 327-28, Panckoucke quotes a note of Saintange on *Fasti,* V, vv. 231-56 (see above, § 927 [1]): "If one feels any temptation to ridicule the mythical tale that Ovid has handed down to us, one should remember that in the eighteenth century a strait-laced English physician published a pamphlet called *Lucina sine concubitu* or *Lucina Freed from the Laws of Competition,* which was designed to show that a woman may conceive and bear offspring apart from any male commerce, like the mares in Virgil's *Georgics,* III, vv. 265-283, which were fertilized by no other stallion than the west wind—Zephyr. . . . There are women in fact who have found the charm of the west wind more delectable than any vulgar pleasure; as witness a formal decision of the superior court (Parlement) of Grenoble, Feb. 13, 1637, declaring legitimate a son born to a certain Mme. d'Aiguemère in the absence of her husband. . . . [The woman testified that] she had been sleeping on a summer's night with the windows of her room open to the west, and her coverlets in some disarray. She had dreamed that her husband had returned from Germany and been with her. She had been exposed to the west wind and had breathed deeply of it." Burette adds, and he seems not to be jesting: "Certainly there are occult mysterious forces in nature of which science has not yet mastered the secret. There are powers in the human imagination to which the wonders of magnetism have strikingly called attention." The decree of Grenoble was of 1637; but Panckoucke's edition of Ovid appeared in the year of grace 1835.

Pliny, *Historia naturalis,* VIII, 67 (Bostock-Riley, Vol. VI, p. 322): "It is well

place, other exceptional circumstances supervene. It is not enough that a man have a god for a father: he must also have a virgin mother, and bearing the child she still remains a virgin. It is not enough that Zeus engender Hercules: he must devote three nights to the task. Three is generally, though not exclusively, specified as the number of nights. In that a sacred-number residue, the three superstition, figures (§ 960 [8]). This whole process is just a particular case of a fact that is general: the re-enforcement of the principal residues in a legend by a cumulation of secondary residues.[4]

known that in Lusitania, near the city of Olysipo [Lisbon] on the Tagus, mares standing against the west wind (Favonius) conceive thereof and become gravid. The colts so born are very swift of foot but live not longer than three years." Aristotle, *Historia animalium*, VI, 18 (Thompson, p. 572a), records the belief that mares may be fertilized by a wind, but refuses to go bond for the fact. Varro, *De re rustica*, II, 2, 19 (Leipzig, p. 211; Harrison, pp. 191-92), notes the same thing as true of hens and says that the fact is well known: "In this matter of conception there is something incredible in Spain, though it is true enough. On the sea-coast in Lusitania, in the neighbourhood of the town of Olysippo and Mount Tagrus, mares at certain times are fertilized by the wind, just as hens are in our part of the world, their eggs being known as ὑπηνέμια ("wind-eggs"). However, the colts born of such mares never live longer than three years." Pausanias, *Periegesis*, VII, *Achaia*, 17, 9-14, gives a detailed account of the birth of the god Attis. To begin with, and making a long story very short, Agdistis was born of Zeus in an unusual manner, springing from seed that Zeus had dropped on the ground. Eventually from a part of the body of Agdistis that had been cut off and thrown away an almond-tree sprouted. Finally, a daughter of the river Sangarius placed some almonds from the tree in her corsage. They mysteriously vanished, and she gave birth to Attis. Here we get a series of strange procreations and strange details leading up to a single birth. There are many other such examples. The literature of divine procreation could be quoted to indefinite lengths. All of the stories involve a nucleus of residues with a nebula of poetic, or merely fantastic, embellishments gathering about it.

927 [4] As a descendant of Perseus, too, Alcmene was of Jovian lineage. According to Apollodorus, *Bibliotheca*, II, 4, 6 (Frazer, Vol. I, pp. 171-73), Electryon, Alcmene's father, gave her to Amphitryon along with his kingdom, but stipulating that Amphitryon should keep her virgin until Electryon's return from an expedition on which he was about to set out against the Teleboans. Electryon dying, Amphitryon himself, after various adventures, undertook the expedition against the Teleboans. Zeus outstripped him on his way home, assumed the guise of Amphitryon to make his way into his house and enjoyed Alcmene for a night, tripling it [in length] (καὶ τὴν μίαν τριπλασιάσας νύκτα). That was why Lycophron, *Cassandra*, v. 33 (Mair, pp. 496-97), calls Heracles the "lion of the three nights." Apollodorus, *Epitome*, 23 (Frazer, Vol. I, p. 172, note): ". . . τὴν μίαν νύκτα πενταπλασιάσας ἢ κατά τινας τριπλασιάσας (quintupling or, according to others, tripling the one night)." Palladas, *Greek Anthology*, IX, 441 (Paton, Vol. III, pp. 246-47), applies

As regards early classical antiquity, it would be easier to give the list of famous persons of human origin than those of divine. The divine seems actually to be the normal rule. Proof of the enduring permanence of the residue over long periods of time is the fact that in deference to it the Christians also made extensive use of legends about unions of spiritual beings with women in the genealogies of exceptional persons, merely substituting Christian demons for the pagan gods. To tell the full truth, the service of devils for purposes of generation has been abused rather than used by the Christian peoples. Merlin the magician was a child of the Devil, and there

the epithet τρισέληνος ("three-mooned," *i.e.,* "three-nighted") to Heracles. Statius, *Thebaid,* XII, v. 299 (Juno addressing the Moon):

> *"Da mihi poscenti munus breve, Cynthia, si quis*
> *est Iunonis honos: certe Iovis improba iussu*
> *ternoctem Herculeam: veteres sed mitto querelas."*

("Give me a brief favour, O Cynthia, I beg you, if you have any regard for Juno! Surely that matter of the Herculean thri-night at the bidding of Jupiter was not to your credit, but we can let bygones be bygones.") Commenting on the lines, Luctatius Placidus explains (Leyden, p. 781): "That oncoming day might not cut his pleasure short, Jupiter ordained that the night be lengthened thrice, the Moon traversing her course three times. It is said that Hercules was born of that union with Alcmene. Very aptly he [Statius] says 'Herculean thri-night' for the night on which Hercules was conceived." Diodorus Siculus brings out the residue very clearly, *Bibliotheca historica,* IV, 9, 2-3 (Booth, Vol. I, p. 225): "When Zeus deceived Alcmene he made a night of triple length, foreshowing by the labour spent in the procreation how great the might of the progeny was to be." Diodorus further notes that Zeus sought Alcmene not of lecherous desire, but for the purpose of begetting a son. Servius, *In Vergilii Aeneidem,* VIII, v. 103 (Thilo-Hagen, Vol. II, p. 213): "Amphitryon was king of Thebes. Jupiter fell enamoured of his wife Alcmene, and while he was absent at the siege of the town of Oechalia, possessed her for a night which he tripled in length. Alcmene thereupon gave birth to two sons, the one by Jove, Hercules, the other, Iphiclus, by her husband." For Iphiclus less effort was required than for Hercules. The scholiast of the *Iliad,* XIV, v. 323 (Dindorf, Vol. II, pp. 50-51), remarks that Amphitryon also begat a son by Alcmene on the same night as Zeus, and Apollodorus makes Iphiclus the junior of Hercules by one night. Latin writers more especially limit the conception of Hercules to two nights instead of three: *e.g.,* Ovid, *Amores,* I, 13, vv. 45-46; Propertius, *Elegiae,* II, 22, vv. 25-26; Martianus Capella, *De Nuptiis inter Mercurium et Philologiam,* II, 157 (Berne, p. 64); Seneca, *Agamemnon,* vv. 814-15. St. Jerome also mentions two nights: *Adversus Vigilantium,* X (*Opera,* Vol. II, p. 348; Schaff-Wace, p. 421): "Jupiter spent two nights in adultery with Alcmene that Hercules might be born a man of great strength." And see Hyginus, *Fabulae,* XXIX, *Alcumena.* But on the whole the Church Fathers are much more generous, allowing Zeus nine nights for his escapade: *e.g.,* Clement

have been those to ascribe a similar parentage to Luther. Nowadays regard for great men has fallen off considerably and such genealogies are things of the past.[5][6] (For footnote 6 see page 551.)

928. Legends are first built up by residues and then explained by derivations. So long as the divine or merely spiritual entity which is brought into being by group-persistence (Class II) remains not far removed from its human origin, no difficulty is experienced in conceiving its copulation with other beings of its own kind or with human beings. From that trunk a branch shoots off which also occasions no great difficulties: divine beings are more or less transformed

of Alexandria, *Protrepticus* (*Exhortation to the Greeks*), II, 28 (Butterworth, pp. 67-69). Says Arnobius, *Disputationes adversus gentes*, IV, 26 (Bryce-Campbell, pp. 208-09): "Are you not uncomplimentary to your Jupiter, king of the world? . . . It is you who aver that he spent nine continuous nights with Alcmene. . . . And I must say you gained a precious deal if you have been blessed with a god, Hercules, who at such lubricious business outstrips a father who took nine nights to compile, compress, compound, an infant and then hardly had enough!" And *cf.* St. Cyril, *Contra impium Julianum*, VI (*Opera*, Vol. IX, p. 799).

927 [5] As for the theoretical question, see Del Rio, *Disquisitiones magicae*, II, 15 (Louvain, Vol. I, p. 180; Cologne, pp. 160-61): "We assert therefore that at times it is quite possible for offspring to result from commerce of a devil (*incubi*) with a woman, though in such cases the real father of the child would not be the demon but the man of whose seed the demon has made wicked abuse. This has been denied by Plutarch in his *Numa* [4] . . . but it is affirmed by the Egyptians, according to Plutarch, and by the Scholastics as a whole—and they were excellent philosophers. . . . And then we have instances in great numbers reported now by one writer, now by another, and if they are true they are doubtless to be accounted for on the hypothesis above. Antiquity offers its demigods, its Herculeses, its Sarpedons, its Aeneases, its Servius Tulliuses; England her Merlin, Pannonia her Huns, born of Arluns [*Arlunis*], Gothic witches, and fauns . . . nor is there any lack of people to place Luther in this same class. [See our note next following.] Six years ago, in the leading city of Brabant [Brussels] a woman was punished for having had a child by the Devil. Coming down to the present time, Louis Molina, one of the theologians of our Society, has stated that the thing has occurred, and many other writers of different nationalities have corroborated him, citing examples." For the "Huns" of Pannonia, *cf.* Jornandes, *De rebus Gothorum*, 24, 8 (p. 67): "Filimer, King of the Goths . . . who also invaded Scythia with his hordes, found among his people certain females, witches, whom he himself designated in his own tongue as 'Aliorumnas.' Suspecting them, he drove them in a body from his midst (*de medio sui*), and forced them to live in out-of-the-way parts of the land, keeping far from his soldiers. Unclean spirits wandering through the desert places laid eyes on them and mingled with them freely in carnal commerce, whence they brought forth that very fierce race of people." A people so savage and so hated had to have had some such origin. St. Augustine, good soul, knows quite as much about demoniacal gen-

into metaphysical abstractions that copulate with one another. Group-persistence facilitates the transition from cases where, for instance, heat and damp combine to produce grain, to other cases in which metaphysical principles procreate real or imaginary beings. But along another branch the difficulties seem rather to increase, in the case, namely, where the spiritual creatures remain personifica-

eration as he does about the antipodes and other such matters (§ 1438). Says he, *De civitate Dei*, XV, 23: "It is a matter of general knowledge, and many people claim to know of experience or to have heard from trustworthy persons who have had the experience, that sylvans and fauns, which are commonly called *incubi*, have often appeared in their wickedness to women and sought and consummated intercourse with them. Many persons, also, and of such merits that it would be the part of impudence [Just so: nothing less than impudence!] to dispute them, assert that certain demons which the Gauls call 'Dusii' attempt such impurity assiduously [Healy: "tempt others to impurity"] and succeed in it." Bodin inquires, *De la démonomanie*, II, 7, "Whether witches have carnal commerce with devils." "I have read," he says, "extracts from the examinations of the witches at Longny-en-Potez, who, I may add, were burned alive, with which Lawyer Adrian de Fer, Lieutenant-General at Laon, has supplied me. I will introduce some of their confessions here in regard to this matter. . . . [A number of confessions of women to carnal knowledge of the Devil follow.] Similarly we read in Meyer's book, XVI . . . that in the year 1459 large numbers of men and women were burned in the city of Arras, on mutual accusations, and on their own confessions, that they had been transported at night to 'dances' and had there had commerce with the devils. . . . Jacob Sprenger and his four colleagues on the Inquisition on witchcraft write that they have prosecuted no end of witches and executed very large numbers of them in Germany and that all of them in general and without exception confessed that the Devil had had criminal intercourse with them. . . . Henry de Coulongne . . . says that nothing is more commonly known in Germany, and not only in Germany, it being notorious all through Greece and Italy [*i.e.,* ancient Greece and Rome]; for fauns, satyrs, sylvans, are nothing but demons and evil spirits. Proverbially the word 'satyrize' means 'to act the [licentious] rogue.' . . . We read, further, in the history of St. Bernard, that there was once a witch who was regularly attended by the Devil at her husband's side without his perceiving it. The question as to whether such copulation be possible, and notably as to whether anything can come of it, was debated before the Emperor Sigismund; and it was decided, against the brief of Cassianus, that such copulation was possible, and conception likewise. . . . We also read in the *Histories of the West Indies*, Bk. I, Chap. XXVII, that those peoples took it as a fact that their god, Cocoto, cohabited with women, the gods of those countries being nothing but devils." For the remainder of the passage see § 928 [1]. A modern writer, in a book published in the year of grace 1864, refers to and believes in the endless amount of trash that has been concocted on the subject of generation by demons and concludes that the objective fact of intercourse between demons and human females cannot be denied: Des Mousseaux, *Les hauts phénomènes de la magie*, p. 297: " 'To deny these strange facts,' says a distinguished

tions and the gap between them and human beings widens. The Greeks did not feel in the least called upon to decide just how the seed of Zeus managed to fertilize the many women of whom he had carnal knowledge; whereas the Christians felt an irresistible compulsion to solve that problem in the case of relations between devils and women.[1]

jurist of unquestioned integrity [In a note: "A. de Gasparin, *Surnaturel*, Vol. II, p. 154." Another fine specimen!], the learned and widely experienced De Lancre [who caused the deaths of hundreds of men and women on charges of witchcraft] 'would mean to undo what all antiquity and *our own* court *procedures* [italics Mousseaux's] have shown.' And I repeat that it would also mean undoing what flesh and blood have shown of old and *in our own day*, what medical examination and theological science have established, each by its own peculiar methods." A fine example of the experimental value of that universal consensus which has of late been transfigured into universal suffrage. It may be, of course, that this latter-day divinity is immune to the blunders into which its predecessor was forever stumbling!

927 [6] For the genealogy of Luther, see Del Rio, *Op. cit.*, II, 15 (Louvain, Vol. I, p. 180; Cologne, p. 161) and *cf.* § 927 [5] above. Del Rio quotes Simon Fontaine, *Historia ecclesiastica nostri temporis* [For Pareto's strange title see Index.—A. L.]. It was not enough that the Devil should have figured in the birth of Luther; he also had to have a hand in his death. Del Rio himself writes, *Ibid.*, III, 1, 7 (Louvain, Vol. II, p. 76; Cologne, p. 429): "It was indubitably observed [at the age-old refuge for the insane] at Gheel [Geila] in the Brabant that the demons left the victims they obsessed and flew to Luther's funeral." Luther many times averred during his lifetime that he had seen devils. There is nothing strange therefore in the attendance of those estimable creatures at his funeral. In his *Histoires disputes et discours*, III, 25 (Vol. I, pp. 418-20), Weier tells a long story about the diabolical conception of Luther and then remarks: "The Catholic history of the state of religion in our time, written in French by a certain S. Fontaines, doctor in theology, says that an opinion which appears in print in many books is well founded, and to wit, that Marguerite, Luther's mother, conceived him of the Devil, who had had her company before that at a time when she was not married to John Luther." Maimbourg feels called upon to refute these fabrications, *Histoire du Luthéranisme*, Vol. I, pp. 22-24: "Luther was born at Islebe [Eisleben], a town in the county of Mansfeld, in the year 1483, and not of a devil (*incube*) as some have written without shadow of truth in order to whet the hatred against him, but the way other men are born; and that fact was never questioned until after he turned heretic."

928 [1] The question as to whether and how demons could fertilize women was answered in various senses by the Fathers of the Church. St. Thomas disserts learnedly on the point in the *Summa theologiae*, I[a], *qu.* 51, *art.* 3 (*Opera*, Vol. V, p. 19): "If, however, offspring sometimes results from intercourse with demons, the fact is due not to any seed deriving from them or from the bodies they assume but through the seed of some man, which has been assumed for that purpose (*ad hoc acceptum*), the same demon first becoming a woman to a man and then a man to a woman (*utpote quod idem daemon qui est succubus ad virum fiat incubus ad mulierem*), just as they take up the seed of other things for purposes of propagating those

Anti-clericals condemn the Christian religion on the basis of these absurd stories. But Christianity did not invent them, it inherited them from antiquity; and after all they are not more extravagant than others that are still enjoying wide currency. Judged by strictly logico-experimental standards, a person believing in the dogmas of universal suffrage may just as well believe in the divine origins of heroes, there being no great difference in the intellectual effort required for adopting either position. From the standpoint of social utility both those ancient absurdities and their modern counterparts may have had or may have a utility great, small, zero, zero minus. Nothing can be said on that point *a priori*. It all depends on times, places, circumstances.

929. I-β3: *Objects and occurrences inspiring awe or terror.* This residue appears almost always by itself in certain situations of which the following is typical. Speaking of the Cataline affair, Sallust relates, *Bellum Catilinae,* XXII: "There were those at the time who said that after Catiline had finished his address he pressed his comrades in crime to an oath, and passed around bowls of human blood mixed with wine, whereof after they all had tasted, with imprecations upon traitors, as is the custom in solemn sacrifices, he made known his design to them, saying that he had done as he had to

things, as Augustine says; with the result that the child that is born is not the child of the demon but of the man whose seed has been utilized." The passage of St. Augustine alluded to, *De Trinitate,* III, 8-9 (*Opera,* Vol. VIII, pp. 875-79; *Works,* Vol. VII, pp. 90-96), is full of interesting information—among other things: "Bees certainly do not conceive the seed of their offspring through copulation, but seem to find it scattered about on the ground and collect it in their mouths." Continuing the Bodin quotation in our § 927 [5], *De la démonomanie,* II, 7: "The Doctors are not in agreement on the point, some of them holding that the devils called 'hyphialtes' or 'succubi' [first] receive seed from men and [then] utilize it with women as 'ephialtes' or 'incubi,' as Thomas Aquinas says—a thing very hard to believe. In any event, Sprenger writes that the Germans, who have had the most experience with witchcraft, having had sorcerers from most ancient times and in greater numbers than people in other countries, hold that such copulation at times results in children who are called *Vechselkind* [*sic*], or 'changelings.' They are heavier than other children and are always lean, and they will suckle three nurses dry without growing any fatter. The others are devils in the guise of children; and they copulate with nurses that are witches and oftentimes [vanish] without one's ever knowing what becomes of them."

the end that each having such a great crime to the charge of the other, they would be the less likely to betray one another. Some hold that these and many other stories were invented by certain individuals who thought to mitigate the unpopularity that later arose against Cicero by stressing the enormity of the crime of the men who had been punished."[1] Whether this story be true or a fabrication, the fact of the association of two terrible things remains: a drinking of human blood and a conspiracy to destroy the Roman Republic. This residue also appears in certain cases where human sacrifices are substituted for animal sacrifices. Animals will do under ordinary circumstances. Human sacrifices come to the rescue in extraordinary, terrifying situations.

The oath of Catiline and his accomplices is not reported in the same way by all historians; but whatever the form, the same residue transpires. Of Catiline and his accomplices both Plutarch says, *Cicero,* X, 3 (Perrin, Vol. VII, p. 107): "To bind themselves mutually by oath, they killed a man and tasted of his flesh." Says Dio Cassius of Catiline alone, *Historia Romana,* XXXVII, 30: "He killed a boy and took an oath on his entrails; then both he and the other conspirators confirmed the oath, their hands on the entrails."[2] We saw the working of this same residue in the human sacrifices that were offered in Rome after the defeat at Cannae (§ 758). Dio Cassius, *Historia Romana,* XLIII, 24, tells how Caesar's soldiers mu-

929 [1] Simpler the account of Florus, *Epitoma de Tito Livio,* II, 12, 3-5 (IV, 1, 3-5; Forster, p. 263): "A pledge of comradeship in conspiracy was also taken: human blood was passed around in cups and drunk. The greatest of crimes, had not the crime for which they drank been greater!" The last sentence formulates the ungarnished residue.

929 [2] The exact meaning of Dio's text has been disputed. It reads: Παῖδα γάρ τινα καταθύσας καὶ ἐπὶ τῶν σπλάγχνων αὐτοῦ τὰ ὅρκια ποιήσας, ἔπειτα ἐσπλάγχνευσεν αὐτὰ μετὰ τῶν ἄλλων. Gros, in the notes to his French translation of Dio, Vol. III, p. 219, remarks very soundly on the words ἔπειτα ἐσπλάγχνευσεν: "Xylander's rendering, 'he then tasted of them in company with the others,' has been repeated by Reimar and Sturz, by Wagner and Tafel. But that is not the meaning of ἐσπλάγχνευσεν, as Mérimée well points out in a note to his *Histoire de la conjuration de Catiline,* p. 113. The true meaning was indicated by Henri Étienne: Σπλαγχνεύω: 'I take these entrails in hand and touch them,' that is, as an oath binding conspirators in a plot." *Cf.* Duncan, *Novum lexicon Graecum, s.v.;* Eustathius, *Commentarii ad Homeri Iliadem,* Vol. I, p. 111 (*Iliad,* I, v. 464).

tinied because they had not received their wages, Caesar having spent all his money on certain games. Caesar seized one of the mutineers and had him put to death. "So he," says Dio, "was punished for the reason stated [as a mutineer]. But two other men were slain in guise of a sacrifice. The reason for that I could not imagine." The reason is to be sought, in part at least, in the residue here in question. The crime of the mutineers seemed an unheard-of thing, and could be expiated only in some terrible manner. Doubtless logical pretexts for justifying the sacrifice were afterward evolved in plenty.[8]

930. And just so the *ver sacrum* of the Romans. In ordinary times it was sufficient to promise the gods animal sacrifices, games, temples, a tithe of the war-booty, and so on. But when some extraordinary, some very critical, situation arose, the gods were promised all the living creatures that should be born during a specified spring season. It would seem that in remote ages the Italic peoples included human beings among the creatures in question, but in historical times the Romans made exceptions of children.[1] A *ver sacrum* was

929 [8] Marquardt, *Römische Staatsverwaltung: Sacralwesen*, p. 254, develops one such pretext: "Caesar had one of the mutineers put to death. Two others were sacrificed in the Campus Martius by the pontiffs, assisted by the *flamen* of Mars, and their heads were exposed at the Regia [headquarters of the state religion]. If the facts were really as reported, the sacrifice celebrated on that occasion was a *piaculum*, or atonement, necessitated by the selfish opposition of the soldiers to the offering to the gods of the sacrifices and thanksgivings due them. But why should the *piaculum* take the form of a human sacrifice? That is the surprising thing, in Caesar's time, whatever one may otherwise think of human sacrifices in Rome." The answer to Marquardt's question is simple. Whether the sacrifice was or was not a *piaculum*, whether the story be true or a fabrication, those who ordered the men slain or those who invented the story felt the appropriateness of matching with some terrifying act a case of insubordination on the part of·Caesar's soldiers, who owed him such great gratitude.

930 [1] Festus, *De verborum significatione*, XIX-XX, *s.v. Ver sacrum* (London, Vol. III, p. 1002): "The Italians had the custom of vowing the 'sacred spring.' Under pressure of great perils they took a vow to sacrifice such living creatures as should be born among them during the spring season next ensuing. But since it seemed a cruel thing to slaughter innocent boys and girls, they waited till they grew up (*perductos in adultam aetatem*), then veiled them, and banished them across the borders." And *cf. Ibid.*, XI, *s.v. Mamertini* (London, Vol. I, pp. 378-79, and again with variants in a *Fragmentum*, Vol. III, pp. 1031-32); Strabo, *Geographica*, V, 4, 12 (Jones, Vol. II, p. 465); Dionysius of Halicarnassus, *Antiquitates Romanae*, I,

pledged, for instance, in the days when Rome was being hard pressed by Hannibal.[2] The contract with the gods was drawn up with the minute formalistic definiteness characteristic of the Roman People (§§ 220 f.).[3] The gods kept their compact loyally, but the Romans renegued. Not till twenty-one years later did they make up their minds to fulfil their vow,[4] and even then they did not comply with it very strictly, so that the sacrifices had to be repeated again.[5]

931. The same residue recurs in the sacrifices of children that are connected with certain rites of magic. Well known the allusions that Horace, *Epoda*, 5 (Canidia's incantation), and Juvenal make to such sacrifices.[1] In Europe accusations, true or false, in the premises, are frequent down into the seventeenth century. A child sac-

16 (Spelman, Vol. I, p. 38); Servius, *In Vergilii Aeneidem*, VII, v. 796 (Thilo-Hagen, Vol. II, p. 196); Nonius Marcellus, *De compendiosa doctrina*, 12 (Mercier, p. 522).

930 [2] Livy, *Ab urbe condita*, XXII, 9, 10; 10, 1.

930 [3] With what ingenious circumspection the compact was drawn is evident from some of the terms as given by Livy. It is a question of the animals that are being kept for sacrifice: "If an animal being kept for sacrifice (*quod fieri oportebit*) shall die, it shall be profane [not available for sacrifice] but no defilement shall result. If one shall be accidentally maimed or killed, no evasion shall stand. If one shall be stolen, no defilement shall result to the Roman People or to the individual robbed. If a sacrifice shall unknowingly be offered on a 'black day,' it shall stand as valid."

930 [4] [Pareto seems not to notice that according to the passage in Festus, which he read in Latin, the twenty-one years' delay would be the time required for the children born during the *ver sacrum* to grow up.—A. L.]

930 [5] Livy, *Op. cit.*, XXXIII, 44; XXXIV, 44.

931 [1] Juvenal, *Saturae*, VI, vv. 551-52:

> "*Pectora pullorum rimabitur, exta catelli*
> *interdum et pueri—faciet quod deferat ipse.*"

("He will probe the breasts of a chicken, the entrails of a pup or even of a child—he will do things of which only he could tell.") Another allusion can be found in Cicero, *In Publium Vatinium*, 6, 14: "What depravity was ever so great in you, what madness so extravagant, that you should ever have undertaken such unheard-of, such criminal rites, as to evoke souls from the other world, and sacrifice to the dead with the entrails of boys?" And *cf.* Quintilian, *Declamationes*, 8 (*Gemini languentes*) (Leyden, pp. 103-19); Lucan, *Pharsalia*, VI, v. 558; Lampridius, *Antoninus Heliogabalus*, 8 (Magie, Vol. II, pp. 121-23); Eusebius, *Historia ecclesiastica*, VIII, 14, 5 (Lake, Vol. II, pp. 304-05); IX, 9, 3 (Lake, Vol. II, pp. 358-59); *Idem, De vita Imperatoris Constantini*, I, 36 (English, p. 492); Ammianus Marcellinus, *Res gestae*, XXIX, 2, 17; Theodoret, *Ecclesiastica historia*, III, 21 (*Opera*, Vol. III, p. 1119; Jackson, p. 106).

rifice seems to have been performed in behalf of Madame de Montespan in her efforts to retain the affections of Louis XIV.[2]

932. I-β4: *Felicitous state associated with good things; infelicitous state, with bad.* When a given state A is considered a happy one, there is an inclination to associate anything that is deemed good with it. When a state B is considered bad, the tendency is to associate all bad things with it. This residue often goes in company with another residue from Class II (group-persistences). So we get a nucleus, with many notions of good or evil things clustering about it, and so, by a process of abstraction, the way is opened for a personification of the whole nebulous complex whereby it becomes an entity by itself, first existing subjectively in the minds of people, but eventually by the usual procedure (§§ 94 f.) acquiring an objective existence.[1][2]

933. For a long time in Europe everything good was placed under the aegis of the "wisdom of the forefathers." Nowadays everything

931 [2] Funck-Brentano, *Le drame des poisons,* pp. 171-72: "On the day fixed, they met at Villebousin: Mme. de Montespan, the Abbé Guibourg, Leroy, a 'lady of high rank,' who was certainly Mlle. Descœillets, and an unidentified person said to have been a representative of the Archbishop of Sens. In the chapel of the château the priest said a mass over the body of the favourite, who lay naked on the altar. At consecration, he chanted the formula of conjuration, the text of which he later surrendered to the Commissioners of the Chamber: 'Astaroth, Asmodea, princes of friendship, I conjure you to accept the sacrifice I here offer of this child [in exchange] for the things which I ask of you, namely, that the favour of the King and the Dauphin, my lord, be continued unto me and honoured [recognized] by the princes and princesses of the Court, so that nothing shall be denied me of what I shall ask of the King in behalf of my relatives and servitors.' According to Reynie, Guibourg bought the child who was sacrificed at the mass for £1—15 francs in our money. . . . The details of the mass were divulged by Guibourg, and for that matter corroborated by the testimony of Madame de Chanfrain, his mistress. The second mass celebrated over the body of Madame de Montespan took place two or three weeks after the first. . . . The . . . third was held in a house in Paris."

932 [1] For instance, "Progress": Georges Gaulis, *"La révolte des Albanais":* "There are steps towards progress that can be forced only at the point of the bayonet upon ignorant masses for whom the word 'progress' does not have the almost mystical significance that we attach to it." That is true of the Albanians. In France, Italy, England, Germany, "the ignorant masses" have a profound and mystical sense of progress!

932 [2] Just here we are interested in the nucleus, the residues, only; but it should not be forgotten that the process is extended by imperceptible degrees to the whole sum of residues and derivations.

good is credited to "progress." To have a "modern sense" of this or that is to have sound and solid sense. In the old days a man was praised for his "time-honoured virtues." Now he is praised for being a "modern man," or—to use, as some do, a neologism—for having an "up-to-date" outlook on things. It was once to one's credit to act "like a Christian"; today it is praiseworthy to act "like a human being," or better, "in a spirit of broad humanity"—when, for instance, one is defending a thief or a murderer. To succour one's neighbour was formerly a "charitable act"; today it is an "act of humanity." To suggest that a man was dangerous or prone to wrongdoing, he was once called a "heretic" or "godless man"; today it is enough to label him a "reactionary." Everything good is nowadays "democratic"; everything evil, "aristocratic." The high-priests of the god Progress and their communicants in Europe seethed with indignation when Abdul Hamid suppressed the Armenian rebellion, and they named him "the red-handed Sultan." But after such an outgiving of holy horror, they of course had none left when, in 1910, the Young Turks suppressed the Albanian rebellion in the holy name of Progress. The criterion of such people would seem to be something like this: A government has a right to suppress an insurrection if it stands in better favour with the god Progress than its rebels; otherwise it has no such right.

934. The adversaries of an institution hold it responsible for all the bad that happens. Its friends credit it with all the good. "It is raining—what a crooked administration!" So says the Opposition. "The weather is fine—what a blessed government!" So the Majority. What denunciations were hurled at the governments of the past in Italy on the matter of taxes, though they were light indeed as compared with taxes that are cheerfully tolerated today! The old Tuscan "liberals" inveighed against the Grand Duke for permitting "the immoral lottery"—see what the poet Giusti wrote on the subject in his ironical "Defence of the Lottery." But stepping into power themselves, they found it altogether natural and moral that an Italian government should run lotteries too. In France, in the days of the Empire, the Republicans raged against "official candidacies." When

they came into power, they used "official candidacies" on a wider scale and in a more thorough-going fashion than the Empire had ever dreamed of doing.[1] The same Englishmen who assert that political crimes in Russia are due exclusively to bad government are convinced that identical crimes in India are due to outbursts of criminal brutality in their Hindu subjects.

935. The ancient Romans credited the gods with the successes of their Republic. Modern peoples attribute their economic betterment to corrupt, ignorant, altogether contemptible parliaments.[1] Under the old monarchy in France the king partook of the divine. When something bad occurred, people said: "If the King only knew." Now the republic and universal suffrage are the divinities.[2] "Universal suffrage, the master of us all." Such the slogan of our Deputies and Senators who are elected by the votes of people who believe in the dogma, *"Ni Dieu, ni maître!"* When an evil cannot be denied, the blame is laid on some circumstance or other that is not seldom quite incidental. There are people who really believe that all the evils observable in countries enjoying parliamentary government are due to the Australian ballot, or the list ballot, or the majority vote, and they recommend proportional representation as the cure-all. Such people are cherishing the illusion that they can remedy evils of substance by tinkering with forms. Their eyes are blind to the funda-

934 [1] Their predecessors in 1848 had followed the same policy, which for that matter had been the policy of the monarchical governments that they had succeeded. See in evidence Dugué de la Fauconnerie, *Souvenirs d'un vieil homme*, pp. 299-330.

935 [1] And to these add considerations with which we shall deal in §§ 1070 f.

935 [2] Failing of re-election in the general elections of May, 1910, M. Paul Doumer wrote to his constituents: "In taking my leave of the Parliament after devoting all my strength and such knowledge of public affairs as I may have exclusively to the service of the country, I prefer to utter no word of bitterness or recrimination. Universal suffrage is sovereign and its will is to be respected, whatever the sentiments that dictate it, and even when it is expressed through a balloting system which deforms and debases everything and tends to make of the winning candidate not the representative of the general interest, but the prisoner of private interests often of the least defensible kind." And those are the people who ridicule Catholics because they submit to the will of the Pope! And yet a Catholic does not say that "the will of the Pope must be respected whatever the sentiments by which it is motivated." He simply believes that the Pope's will is inspired of God; and that is why he defers to it.

mentals because they will not, or cannot, think counter to a sentiment that allows them to see nothing but good in universal suffrage and democracy.[8]

936. In France a justice of the peace had ruled that a man who was an idiot in the medical sense of the term could not be a voter. The High Court of Appeals (*Cours de Cassation*), in an opinion handed down on April 8, 1910, reversed the decision and ruled that "feeble-mindedness, when it has not been itself the cause of the interdiction, is not incompatible with enjoyment of the right to vote, as regulated by the decree of February 2, 1852." Mme. Marguerite Durand forthwith presented an idiot as a candidate at a public meeting and remarked, "Women cannot vote, but idiots can, and are even eligible for office"—so putting her finger on the absurdity not only of electoral inequality between men and women, but of the very principle of universal suffrage. For that matter, an idiot is not out of place as a voter among panderers, criminals, and other such people, who on election day vote early and often. By that, remember, we are in no way showing that on the whole and at a given historical moment universal suffrage is detrimental to society. We are merely showing that the halo of sanctity which is thrown about it is, from any experimental standpoint, ridiculous; and bringing to the surface the sentiments that find their expression in worship of that divinity. Nor have we shown either that such suffrage worship is not promotive of social welfare. That may or may not be one of the

---

935 [8] In March, 1910, a number of French scientists and university professors published a manifesto containing the following: "We demand an electoral reform as a means of strengthening the Republic and ameliorating our parliamentary system. . . . The count by districts has resulted in electoral and political immoralities that are intolerable: official candidacies, arbitrary acts in administration, arbitrary decisions in the courts, displacements of justice by favouritism, disorders in the public services, deficits in budgets in which private and clique interests prevail over the general interest. Deputies to the parliament must be freed of a slavery that obliges them to satisfy appetites in order to retain mandates. More dignity, more morality, must be introduced into the exercise of the right of suffrage." It never once occurs to those gentlemen that universal suffrage and democracy may have something to do with the political evils they are complaining of. Those divinities are essentially good, in fact, they are "the good" itself and can therefore never in any way do wrong.

many instances in which a belief intrinsically false is socially advantageous. In an objective study such as ours, we have to adhere strictly to the terms of a proposition and never overstep them (§§ 41, 73-74, 1678 f.).

937. I-β5: *Assimilation: physical consumption of substances to get effects of associable, and more rarely of opposite, character.* Human beings have often believed that by eating certain substances one may come to partake of the properties of those substances. On rare occasion such phenomena may imply belief in some form of mysterious communion between a man and his totem or divinity; but more often those are different things.

938. Zeus had received a prediction that Metis would one day bear him a child who would become Lord of Heaven. He swallows Metis, the latter being pregnant with Athena. A line of Hesiod, *Theogonia,* v. 899, adds: "to the end that the goddess might impart to him a knowledge of good and evil."[1] Pindar, *Olympia,* I, 62 (Turner, p. 10), says that Tantalus made bold to steal from Zeus the nectar and ambrosia with which he had himself been made immortal and to give them to his own comrades. Elsewhere, *Pythia,* IX, 63 (Turner, pp. 88-89), he says that the Hours bestowed immortality on Aristeus by pouring nectar and ambrosia between his lips. Familiar the important part played by the "soma" in the Vedic religion.[2]

938 [1]　　　'Αλλ' ἄρα μιν Ζεὺς πρόσθεν ἐὴν ἐγκάτθετο νηδύν,
　　　　　　　ὡς οἱ συμφράσσαιτο θεὰ ἀγαθόν τε κακόν τε.

The verse may be an interpolation, but that has no bearing on the matter in hand. Thereafter, as is well known, Athena emerged from the head of Zeus. And *cf.* Apollodorus, *Bibliotheca,* I, 3, 6 (Frazer, Vol. I, p. 25).

938 [2] Oldenberg, *Religion des Veda,* pp. 175-76, 181, *Soma, der Göttertrank:* "The drink that gives Indra the strength to execute his mighty feats is a juice pressed from the soma plant. The notion of an intoxicating beverage belonging to the gods seems to go back to Indo-European days. A liquor that instils a mysterious vigour, an ecstatic exhilaration, in the human being must be divine by nature and an exclusive perquisite of the gods. So among the American Indians tobacco was called a 'sacred plant' as a source of supernatural inspiration, and they believed that the gods smoked it in order to taste the same ecstasy. So the Indo-Europeans in their time located the home of the sacred drink in heaven. . . . But the liquor was carried off by a bird from the celestial repository where it lay under the eye of a vigilant demon. . . . Poets laud the wisdom, splendour, sub-

939. In view of and considering the strength, courage, and fleetness of foot of Achilles, some were pleased to assume that in his childhood he had been fed on marrow from the bones of lions and stags, and others specified bear's marrow and the viscera of lions and of wild boars.[1] The residue in that case is apparent enough, unless the fanatics of totemism are to insist that the lion, the bear, the wild boar, the stag, were all and at one time totems of Achilles. New Zealanders eat their enemies to become possessed of their strength. As usual, there is no lack of wide-roaming logical explanations (derivations), but the residue remains easily recognizable. Dumont d'Urville explains that the New Zealanders devour the "souls," the *waiduas*, of enemies whom they have slain.[2] The diet of Achilles

limity, of the soma, but rarely ascribe human form and conduct to it. . . . It is praised, Rig-Veda, VIII, 48, v. 3 (Griffith, Vol. III, p. 265), for the joy it brings to men: 'We have drunk of the soma, and, lo, we are immortals: we have ascended to the light and found the gods! What have we now to fear, O deathless ones, from the hatred or malice of men?' "

939 [1] Apollodorus, *Bibliotheca*, III, 13, 6 (Frazer, Vol. II, p. 71). For further dietary particulars, see Bayle, *Dictionnaire historique, s.v. Achille*.

939 [2] *Voyage de la corvette l' "Astrolabe,"* Vol. II, pp. 524-27 (royal edition): "The New Zealanders think that the soul, or spirit, which they call *waidua*, is an inner breath or puff of air, entirely distinct from the bodily substance. Upon death the two substances hitherto united separate. The *waidua* lingers hovering for three days about the body and then departs for the famous rock of Reinga (the word means 'departure'), which we have mentioned as the Cape Tenares of those savages. Thence an *atua* carries the *waidua* off to an abode of glory or shame, while the body, the impure part, vanishes into the dark. [The account so far is offered as an explanation of what follows. It is not a very good one, for "devouring" an "inner breath" or "puff of air" is at best a very strange procedure. It is evidently all an invention to get some sort of logic into the custom.] With such superstitious ideas it is only natural that they should think of eating the bodies of their enemies. In so doing, they believe, they will be absorbing the souls of their foes, adding them to their own and growing that much stronger. The more enemies of distinguished rank a chieftain has devoured in this world, the happier and more enviable will his triumphant *waidua* be in the next. This future bliss, moreover, is just one round of fish-and-potato banquets and of stubborn combats in which the chosen *waiduas* always come off victorious. The New Zealanders think the *waidua* is located in the left eye. On overwhelming a rival, therefore, a warrior never fails to dig out that eye and swallow it. . . . He also drinks the blood of his enemy to avoid the wrath of the swallowed *waidua*; for the blood being so imbibed, the *waidua* gets back some of the food that formerly sustained it and is so dissuaded from doing any harm thereafter." As usual the residue (the eating of a portion of the enemy's body) remains constant. The derivations are variable (inner breath, food).

as a child might be described in exactly the same terms. The idea, we may say, was to have him eat the *waidua* of lions, bears, stags, boars; and since the *waidua* resides in the marrow or viscera, those portions of the animals were given him to eat. Many customs of savage peoples analyze into the residue we are here considering, and which, for that matter, appears in somewhat disguised forms among civilized peoples.[8]

940. The eating of totems by savages is just a particular instance of the general custom of eating things held to be beneficial; but as a result of the now fashionable abuse of totemism, this totem "communion" has been represented as the "primitive fact" from which other "communions" have been derived. That in no wise results from our present knowledge. What we have is simply a series of communions showing one common residue—the residue of assimila-

939 [8] Frazer, *The Golden Bough*, Vol. II, pp. 353-55: " 'The savage commonly believes that by eating the flesh of an animal or man he acquires not only the physical but even the moral and intellectual qualities which were characteristic of that animal or man. . . . Thus, for example, the Creeks, the Cherokees, and kindred tribes of North American Indians, believe that nature is possest of such a property as to transfuse into men and animals the qualities either of the food they use or of those objects that are presented to their senses. He who feeds on venison is, according to their physical system, swifter and more sagacious than the man who lives on the flesh of the clumsy bear or helpless dunghill fowls, the slow-footed tame cattle, or the heavy wallowing swine' (James Adair, *History of the American Indians*, p. 133). . . . The Namaquas abstain from eating the flesh of hares, because they think it would make them faint-hearted as a hare. But they eat the flesh of the lion, or drink the blood of the leopard or lion, to get the courage and strength of these beasts (Theophilus Hahn, *Tsumi-Goam, the Supreme Being of the Khoi-Khoi*, p. 106). . . . The flesh of the lion and also that of the spotted leopard are sometimes cooked and eaten by native warriors of South-eastern Africa, who hope thereby to become as brave as lions (Macdonald, *Light in Africa*, p. 174; and *Idem, Superstitions and Religions of South African Tribes*, p. 282). . . . Sometimes if a Zulu has killed a wild beast, for instance a leopard, he will give his children the blood to drink, and will roast the heart for them to eat, expecting that they will thus grow up brave and daring men. . . . When a serious disease has attacked a Zulu Kraal, the medicine-man takes the bone of a very old dog, or the bone of an old cow, bull, or other very old animal, and administers it to the healthy as well as to the sick people, in order that they may live to be as old as the animal of whose bone they have partaken." Chardin, *Voyage en Perse*, Vol. VII, p. 115: "The Persians rate the sheep higher than all butcher animals, claiming that it has no bad habits and that none, therefore, can be contracted by eating its flesh; for their doctors hold unanimously that a man comes to resemble the animals on which he feeds."

tion. The residue also transpires in what Justin Martyr says of the Eucharist, *Apologia*, I, 65-66 (Migne, p. 427a; Davie, pp. 50-51): "Then bread and a cup of watered wine is brought to the presiding elder. He takes these things, praises and glorifies the Father of the Universe in the name of the Son and the Holy Spirit, and then makes a long thanksgiving [Eucharist] for all the favours we have received from Him. . . . After the presiding elder has offered thanks and all the people have responded, those whom we call deacons give of the consecrated bread, and of wine and water, to each of those present, and carry of it to absent ones. . . . We call this 'Eucharist food.'[1] . . . For we do not partake of it as of common bread or common beverage; but even as, through the word of God, Jesus Christ our Saviour became incarnate and assumed flesh and blood for our salvation, so through the words of His prayer are we taught that the consecrated food, whereof our blood and flesh by transmutation are nourished, is flesh and blood of the incarnate Jesus."[2]

941. As is well known, derivations without end have been appended to that simple fact, and theologians—and detractors of Christianity as well—have quarrelled copiously and fiercely on the subject. That is no concern of ours here. Let us note simply that to have identified the sentiment that figures as the residue in all communions does not in the least impair Catholic doctrine or the teaching of any other theology. If it did, to recognize the sentiment of love for a powerful and beneficent Being as the residue underlying the Christian's love of God would impair every religion inspired by that love. Whatever the faith may be, it can be expressed only in the language spoken by human beings and through the sentiments pres-

---

940 [1] Εὐχαριστηθεῖσα τροφή is, properly, the consecrated food that bears the grace of the Lord within it.

940 [2] A freer rendering would be: ". . . through the words of His prayer do we know that the consecrated food is the flesh and blood of the incarnate Jesus and that our flesh and blood are fed on that food by transmutation." Justin continues: "Evil daemons have imitated this institution in the mysteries of Mithras, wherein initiates are offered bread and a cup of water and are addressed with certain words that you know, or can know [if you choose]." The usual error of assuming that two similar derivations from one residue must be imitations one of the other. They are really parallel expressions of one same residue.

ent in them. To study such modes of expression in no way affects the things that are expressed (§ 74).

942. Disputes such as have raged about the Eucharist might have arisen in connexion with other cases of the kind. Had Graeco-Roman paganism survived down to our own day and the Eleusinian mysteries enjoyed continued popularity, people might have quarrelled just as vociferously over the cyceon, and sent just as many heretics to the stake. Initiates in the Eleusinian mysteries repeated the formula: "I have fasted; I have drunk the cyceon (κυκεών); I have drawn from the box; I have seen; I have put into the basket, and then from the basket into the box."[1] The cyceon that the initiates drank was evidently no ordinary cyceon, such as was commonly drunk; it acquired mystical properties from the ceremony in which it was used. Demeter had drunk the cyceon when, in sorrow, she was hunting for her daughter (Homer, *Hymnus in Cererem,* vv. 208-09; White, p. 303). According to her recipe it was made of water, flour, and grated mint-leaves. The recipe for the potion seems subsequently to have changed, wine being added, though Demeter herself had refused to drink wine. In the *Argonautica,* one of the Orphic compositions, vv. 323-30 (Leipzig, pp. 53, 525), the Argonauts seal their oath by drinking a still different cyceon made of flour, bull's blood, sea-water, with a touch of olive-oil.[2]

943. Of little interest to sociology is the rich harvest of derivations that is eventually garnered from these facts. Its concern rather is

---

942 [1] Clement of Alexandria, *Protrepticus (Exhortation to the Greeks),* II, 18. (Butterworth, p. 43): Ἐνήστευσα ἔπιον τὸν κυκεῶνα ἔλαβον ἐκ κίστης· ἐργασάμενος ἀπεθέμην εἰς κάλαθον, καὶ ἐκ καλάθου εἰς κίστην. The word ἐργασάμενος, "having done" does not yield a satisfactory meaning. Migne proposes θεασάμενος, that is, "I have then inspected the sacred ῥῶπον, and the secret wares." That would be satisfactory. Arnobius renders in Latin, *Disputationes adversus gentes,* V, 26 (Bryce-Campbell, p. 251): *"Ieiunavi atque ebibi cyceonem: ex cista sumpsi et in calathum misi: accepi rursus, in cistulam transtuli."* (Butterworth: "I fasted; I drank the draught; I took from the chest; having done my task, I placed in the basket, and from the basket into the chest.")

942 [2] And *cf.* Hesychius, *Lexicon, s.v.* Κυκεῶ: "A beverage made of a mixture of wine, honey, water, and flour." The scholiast of the *Odyssey,* X, v. 290, adds cheese.

with the residue, which is at work in many social phenomena and helps to explain them. In the incident described in the *Argonautica* we have passed, as frequently happens, from a special to a general— from a I-$\beta 5$ to a I-α—residue. Observable among many peoples is a custom of having the sick swallow pieces of paper inscribed with certain symbols, certain letters, or else the ashes from such bits of paper, or water in which the ashes have been mixed.[1]

944. I-γ: *Mysterious workings of certain things; mysterious effects of certain acts.* This residue figures in many rites of magic, in amulets, in oaths taken on certain objects, in ordeals, judgments of God, and the like. It is also the principal element in taboos, with or without sanction. It corresponds to a sentiment whereby things and acts are invested with an occult power that is often vague and not clearly explained.

945. If we had nothing but the mediaeval "judgment of God" to go by we might be left in doubt as to whether the principal element in it were the alleged interposition of the Divinity. But ordeals appear more or less everywhere, often with judgments by a divinity, and often without. In the Middle Ages the "judgment of God" itself was forced upon a reluctant Church by popular superstition. It is evident, therefore, that the main element is the instinct for combinations, and that the introduction of a supposedly divine judgment is a derivation designed to explain and justify that instinct.[1]

946. We shall find it helpful to distinguish from our general case,

943 [1] Davis, *The Chinese*, Vol. II, p. 135 (1836, pp. 142-43): "The written spells which the Chinese sometimes use consist of mystical compounds of various characters or words, in which astrology is generally introduced, with the eight diagrams of Fo-by, the twenty-eight lunar mansions, the five planets, and so on. Some of these spells are kept about the person, others are pasted on the walls of rooms. 'Occasionally,' observes Mr. Morrison, 'they are used as cures for sick persons, by being either written on leaves which are then infused in some liquid, or inscribed on paper, burned, and the ashes thrown into drink which the patient has to swallow.' " [A favourite Italian story of a day gone by was that "Of the simple-minded rustic who gets a prescription from a doctor, thinks it the medicine, eats it, and gets well." Sagredo, *L'Arcadia in Brenta*, Venice, 1667, p. 60. But the jest is as old as Poggio and Domenichi (1574).—A. L.]

945 [1] The ordeal would be a subject for a "special"—as opposed to a "general"—sociology. Here we need go no farther than to note it as a case in which the instinct for combinations figures.

I-γ1, a special case, I-γ2, in which the names of things are supposed to have occult powers over them.

947. I-γ1: *Mysterious operations in general.* Cases are exceedingly numerous. Here we shall mention just a few. The residue often comes out strikingly in little incidents in themselves of scant moment. On May 2, 1910, a certain Muff was beheaded at Lucerne for arson and murder. One newspaper carried the following details:[1] "The last sacraments were administered. On the march to execution Muff carried on his person a genuine piece of the True Cross which Mme. Erica von Handel-Mazzetti had sent him, with a consoling message." Logically, a place for that relic in any judgment which God may pass on the man's crimes or on his repentance would be hard to find. We have to conclude that a sort of mysterious power was ascribed to it, something like the emanations from a bit of radium sealed in a glass tube.

948. The residue is more commonly observable under the disguise of one of its derivations. Feeling better if their attitudes are logical (residue I-ε) people wonder: "How do these things, these acts, come to have the effects they have?" And the answer is: "Through the interposition of a spirit, a god, the Devil." That is like explaining that opium induces sleep because it contains a sleep-inducing property.

949. An anecdote related by St. Gregory of Tours, *Historia ecclesiastica Francorum*, VIII, 16 (*Opera*, p. 460; Dalton, Vol. II, p. 342), lays bare both the residue and the derivation. A man had been accused of setting fire to a neighbour's house. Said he: "I shall go to St. Martin's Church, and taking oath upon my faith I shall return innocent of this crime." St. Gregory's informant declares: "Now it was certain that the man had set fire to the house. As he was on his way to take the oath, I turned to him and said: 'According to what our neighbours are saying you are not innocent of this crime. Now God is everywhere, and His power is the same outside [the church] as inside.[1] If therefore you are nursing the illusion that God or His

947 [1] *Gazette de Lausanne*, May 3, 1910.

949 [1] ". . . *sed tamen Deus ubique est, et virtus eius ipsa est forinsecus quae habetur intrinsecus.*"

saints will take perjury lightly, here is the church—swear, if you wish, but outside! For you will not be allowed to step foot across the threshold.'" He swears, and straightway falls dead, blasted by celestial fire! It is clear that the narrator wavers between two notions that are not easily reconcilable: a feeling that an oath is just as effective in one place as another, and then a feeling that it is more effective in some places than in others.[2] It was for daring to take oath in very front of the Church of St. Martin that the perjurer was struck dead; for the witness adds: "That was an object lesson to many [rascals] that they had better not take any false oaths *in that place* again!"[3]

950. Marsden[1] explains how oaths are administered in Sumatra and upon what strange objects: an old sword (kris), a broken gun-barrel, a rifle, sometimes the earth, the witness stooping to lay a hand upon it. As usual thinking in terms of logical conduct primarily, Marsden observes, p. 243: "It is a striking circumstance that practices which boast so little of reason in their foundation, which are in fact so whimsical and childish, should yet be common to nations the most remote in situation, climate, language, complexion, character, and everything that can distinguish one race of people from another."[2]

949 [2] Pertile, *Storia del diritto italiano,* Vol. VI, Pt. I, p. 372: "Such solemnities and precautions notwithstanding, perjuries were still very frequent. With the idea of protecting sacred objects from such misuses, King Robert ordered that oaths be administered upon reliquaries that were either empty or filled with counterfeit relics."

949 [3] *"Multis haec causa documentum fuit ne in hoc loco auderent ulterius periurare (misprint: peierare)."*

950 [1] *History of Sumatra,* pp. 240-43.

950 [2] Says Marsden: "The place of greatest solemnity for administering an oath is the *krammat,* or burying ground, of their ancestors, and several superstitious ceremonies are observed on the occasion. The people near the seacoast, in general, by long intercourse with the Malays, have an idea of the *Koran* and usually employ this in swearing, which the priests do not fail to make them pay for. But the island people keep laid up in their houses certain old reliques . . . which they produce when an oath is to be taken. The person who has lost his cause, and with whom it commonly rests to bind his adversary by an oath, often desires two or three days' time, to get ready his swearing apparatus, called on such occasions *sumpalian,* of which some are looked upon as more sacred and of greater efficacy than others. They consist of an old rusty *kris,* a broken gun barrel, or any ancient

951. Ordinarily, in fact, human beings try to fortify their faith in the occult powers of things in just such ways. In the *Iliad,* III, vv. 271-91, Agamemnon sacrifices victims to make his oath with Priam valid and formal. He cuts tufts of hair from the lambs' heads, and the hair is distributed among the Trojan and Achaian optimates. He then cuts the lambs' throats and utters an oath, to which Priam responds with a similar oath. Years, hundreds of years, after that legendary episode, acts of the same sort are being daily repeated. Forms alone change. It matters little whether the oath be taken upon sacrificial victims, upon the relics of saints, or upon other objects; whether the power invoked be Zeus, Helius, the Rivers, the Earth, the God of the Christians and His saints, a devil, or some other being. The essential point is that people believe that they can mutually and effectively bind each other by virtue of certain acts in part mysterious. The residue is that belief, and it is observable among all peoples from the earliest periods of history. Even today there are countries where oaths must be taken by laying a hand on the Bible or the New Testament; and the hand must be bare. One cannot imagine any logical reason why an oath should be less binding for the presence of a layer of leather between the hand and the Book. What evidently is working is a vague, indefinite feeling that the layer of leather may somehow impair the mysterious action of the Book, much as a non-conductor impedes the transmission of an electric current. However, the feeling is not expressed in any such definite form. It remains just an instinct whereby certain things are accepted and others rejected, and which can well be described in terms of this residue.

trumpery, to which chance or caprice has annexed an idea of extraordinary virtue. These they generally dip in water, which the person who swears drinks of, after having pronounced the form of words before-mentioned. The most ordinary *sumpalian* is a *kris,* and on the blade of this they sometimes drop lime-juice, which occasions a stain on the lips of the person performing the ceremony—a circumstance that may not improbably be supposed to make an impression on a weak and guilty mind. Such would fancy that the external stain conveyed to the beholders an image of the internal." The formula for the oath: "If what I now declare, namely . . . [Here the testimony is recited.] is truly and really so, may I be freed and clear from my oath: if what I assert is wittingly false, may my oath be the cause of my destruction."

952. A similar sentiment underlies conceptions as to the virtues of relics. As for objects deemed beneficent, it is important to distinguish between the mysterious powers they have intrinsically and the feeling of veneration for them, for the powers may exist independently of the veneration and *vice versa,* and things may be venerated that are not deemed beneficent. Both elements, however, may be present simultaneously. That is the situation with relics. Numberless the cases where an object belonging to a saint operates apparently in and of itself. In general terms, people may believe in the efficacy of certain rites of a religion without believing in the religion, a fact that emphasizes the non-logical character of the conduct (§§ 157, 184 [2]). Logically, one ought first to believe in a given religion and then in the efficacy of its rites, the efficacy, logically, being the consequence of the belief. Logically, it is absurd to offer a prayer unless there is someone to hearken to it. But non-logical conduct is derived by a precisely reverse process. There is first an instinctive belief in the efficacy of a rite, then an "explanation" of the belief is desired, then it is found in religion. This is one of the many cases where the residue figures as the principal element and the derivation as the secondary. In the particular, there are numberless instances where objects connected with saints function of and by themselves upon anybody who comes into contact with them.[1]

We read in Acts 19: 11-12 that "God wrought special miracles by the hands of Paul: So that from his body were brought unto the

952 [1] Chardin, *Voyage en Perse* (*Nouvelle bibliothèque,* Vol. VII, p. 11; Vol. VIII, p. 149): "The Persians believe that the prayers of all men are good and have their effects, and in cases of sickness and other troubles they accept and even court the devotions of the faithful of different religions, as I have seen them do on numberless occasions. . . . They make lavish use of magical and other such remedies when they are sick, and seek help not only of all their own saints but of the saints of all religions—pagan, Jewish, Christian, anything. Christians read the Gospel according to St. John over the sick—the Gospel that is used in the mass. Missionaries of the Roman, to an even greater extent than those of the Eastern, Church make a practice of such readings and for the benefit of men, women, and children alike. That can only be regarded as magic, for, as you can well imagine, the Persians understand Latin about as much as Europeans understand Persian. But, in addition, it must be accounted downright sacrilege, for those Mohammedans do not believe in the Word proclaimed in the Gospel, but believe ours the falsest and most damnable of all religions." Chardin argues throughout from the logical

sick handkerchiefs or aprons, and the diseases departed from them, and the evil spirits went out of them." [2]

953. Magic furnishes mysterious acts in countless numbers. If we were acquainted with Christian magic only, where "powers" invariably are ascribed to the Devil, or only with magics where "powers" are ascribed to some supernatural being, we could never determine whether the belief in the magic were a I-γI residue or a derivation— a consequence, that is, of beliefs in the Devil or other supernatural beings.

954. But the doubt is dispelled the moment we find cases of magic where no interference on the part of supernatural beings is presupposed. That shows that the constant element in magic is not the divine intervention, but the belief in mysterious operations, and that the introduction of the supernatural entity is a derivation designed to explain and justify the combinations showing the residue. There are many cases, moreover, where magic or quasi-magic is mixed in with religion inadvertently, unconsciously, without trace of evil intent. The Catholic Church has found itself obliged to con-

standpoint. In his *Travels and Adventures in the Persian Provinces,* J. Baillie Fraser tells a story of an old man who wore a copper box hanging about his neck (translation from the French translation in the *Bibliothèque universelle des voyages,* Vol. XXXV, p. 469): "It contained two small figures, the one a copper Lama, the idol usual in worship of the Grand Lama, and which is presented to pilgrims visiting His temple; the other a small Chinese image, painted on porcelain or terra cotta. The two relics were wrapped in a piece of yellow silk. He said he had received them from the Grand Lama at the Hassa, whither he had gone on a pilgrimage some years before. The man was a Hindu by religion, and worshipped idols in the Hindu manner. Nevertheless the relics came to him from the high-priest of another faith whom he had doubtless visited with a religious purpose. The man offered an interesting example of tolerance and ignorance at the same time."

952 [2] And *cf. Dictionnaire encyclopédique de la théologie catholique, s.v. Reliques* (Wetzer, *s.v. Reliquien*): "If the handkerchiefs and linen of St. Paul, which were things external to his person, cured diseases, that virtue should with all the more reason be ascribed to the very bodies of the saints that housed the souls from which such powers emanated. In his homily on St. Julitta [of Tarsus] St. Basil says: 'Her body now rests in the sumptuous vestibule of a church in that city and sanctifies the place where it lies and those who visit it.' 'Under the old dispensation,' he says elsewhere, *Homilia in Psalmum* CXV, § 4 (*Opera,* Vol. II, p. 111), 'the bodies of the dead were deemed unclean things. That is not the case under the new dispensation. Whosoever touches the bones of saints obtains by that contact somewhat of the sanctifying grace which dwells in saintly bodies.' "

demn misuses of holy water, of the Host, of this or that rite—any number of superstitions, in short.[1] St. Thomas does his best to save both the goat and the cabbages and justify the residue by the derivation. Speaking of the practice of carrying relics (scapularies) about

954 [1] *Decretum Gratiani, pars 2, causa 26, quaestio 5, canon 3* (Friedberg, Vol. I, pp. 1027-28): "It shall not be lawful for Christians to keep to the traditions of the heathen. . . . 1. Nor shall they use rites (*observantia*) or incantations in collecting medicinal herbs, save only with the divine [*i.e.*, the Apostles'] Creed (*cum symbolo divino*), or the Lord's Prayer, that so honour be paid only to God the creator and lord of all men. . . . 3. Nor shall Christian women, either, perform false rites (*vanitatem observare*) in their spinning and weaving (*lanificiis*) but rather pray for the help of God who has given them the skill they have in that art (*texendi*)." Ferraris, *Bibliotheca canonica juridica moralis theologica, s.v. Superstitio*: "49. The 'health-rite' (literally 'observances of healths': *observantia sanitatum*) is a superstition whereby fatuous and ineffective agencies are applied to the preservation or recovery of health for human beings and animals. They become guilty of this superstition who use meaningless names (*ignota nomina*), certain prescribed words, certain characters, certain scripts, wrappings, signs, certain numbers of prayers and signs of the cross (*certum numerum crucium*), and other ineffective things of the sort for curing illnesses, healing wounds, stopping pains, staunching blood, or for making themselves or others invulnerable to spears, swords, cannon-balls, so that they may be immune to injury from the enemy and exempt from any misfortune or sickness; since all the said things and their like have never been appointed, whether by God, by Nature, or by the Church, to such purposes. . . . 54. Guilty of superstition are they who change seats or packs of cards while at play in order to avoid bad luck; who touch some particular wood in order to win at play; who refuse to sit down at table when their doing so would bring the number to thirteen . . . women who pray on St. John's Night [June 24] that they may see in their dreams the men they are going to marry; men who believe that if a fire has been covered with ashes in their presence they will not marry within the year; persons who stand brooms upside down so that if the woman whom they suspect of being a witch (*saga*) is one, she may be able to walk in no wise save backward, like a crab; persons who paste certain notes on door-posts that thieves may be forced to come thither; who think that when a hen crows like a cock some misfortune impends; who think that somebody's death or bad luck is foretold when a bird sings mournfully, when a crow caws, or a rabbit crosses their path; who fear some grave disaster if they see two priests raising the Host at the same time at mass; who think hens become safe from hawks if their first eggs are given to the poor; who keep eggs laid by hens on Saturday (*die Parasceves*: 'day of preparation for the Sabbath') for putting out fires; and so on for countless other superstitions almost infinite in number." All that is but an infinitesimal proportion of the countless ways in which the residues of combination assert themselves in such connexions. I will add just one more example—a discussion of the uses of holy water, from Thiers, *Traité des superstitions* (Avignon, Vol. II, pp. 20-21; Amsterdam, *Superstitions anciennes et modernes*, Vol. II, Pt. II, Bk. I, 2, 6, pp. 5-6): "Remarking that there is an element of superstition in using holy objects for purposes other than those to which they were appointed, Cardinal Cusa mentions the instance

one's person he says:[2] "If they are worn as evidence of faith in God and the saints whose relics they are, it is not illicit; but if some fatuous thing be held in view, for instance the triangular shape of the container (*quod vas esset triangulare*), or some other thing of the sort not pertaining to veneration of God and the saints, it would be superstitious and illicit."[3] As for scripts that may be worn on the person, one must be careful "that they contain no unknown words, lest some illicit thing be concealed therein."[4] In such a case evidently the sin would be involuntary.[5] Superstitions abide, while religions change: in other words, the residue endures and the derivations vary. The Christians did not invent the magic "spell"—the *fascinum*. They did not derive it from the fact that there was a Devil. They merely explained it, finding it ready-made in pagan society.

955. Tertullian says that "among the heathen there is a dreadful thing called the *fascinum,* 'the spell,' which comes as the unfortunate result of excessive praise and glory. This we sometimes believe

of holy water, which is drunk in order to recover lost health, sprinkled on lands and fields to make them more fertile, and given to animals to drink to cure them of this or that malady. . . . But in calling those three practices superstitions the learned Cardinal did not pay due attention to the words that the Church uses in blessing the water. It is stated very definitely that holy water is very good for casting out devils, driving away diseases, dissipating unhealthy air and bad winds, purifying houses and all other places where it is sprinkled and freeing them of anything disturbing to the peace and tranquillity of the faithful dwelling in them. . . . There is nothing superstitious, therefore, in giving human beings and animals holy water to drink, nor in sprinkling it about the houses and on the lands of Christians, provided such things be done in a pure faith and in perfect trustfulness in the goodness and omnipotence of God."

954 [2] *Summa theologiae,* II^a II^ae, qu. 96, art. 3-4 (*Opera,* Vol. IX, pp. 334-35: *Utrum suspendere verba divina ad collum sit illicitum*).

954 [3] The Saint draws the general conclusion, *loc. cit., art.* 4: "The wearing of divine words about the neck, unless they contain something false or doubtful, is in no wise illicit, though it would be the more praiseworthy part to abstain from such things."

954 [4] *"Similiter etiam videtur esse cavendum si contineat ignota nomina, ne sub illis aliquid illicitum lateat."*

954 [5] [I wonder whether Pareto states the Saint's position quite adequately. St. Thomas seems to mean that scapularies may be worn as acts, signs, of faith (*per*), but not for purposes of magic. The presence of meaningless rigmaroles (*verba ignota*) would be *prima facie* evidence of magical intent and therefore sinful.— A. L.]

to be the work of the Devil, because he hates whatever is good, sometimes the work of God, for of Him comes judgment on pride in an exalting of the lowly and a humbling of the haughty."[1] Two things in the passage are noteworthy: first, the variability of the derivations, which go from one extreme to the other, from the Devil to God; and, second, God's humbling of the vainglorious, which is something similar to the "envy of the gods" of the pagans. St. Basil observes[2] a belief that envious people could harm others by a mere glance—"as it were by a maleficent emanation gushing from their eyes, harming and blasting."[3] That notion he rejects as ignorant folk-lore and an old wives' tale (*fabulam . . . popularem*): the truth is that the devils hate the righteous, and use the eyes of the envious to harm them. Del Rio bows to such holy authority, and, rejecting all other causes, holds the spell to be the work of the Devil. As usual the derivation sprouts, branches out, thrives luxuriant. Del Rio—lo, what wisdom!—knows just how the Devil goes about it:[4] "The spell is a pernicious capacity acquired by contrivance of demons in pursuance of a compact, tacit or explicit, between a man and the Devil. The pernicious property is spread generally about by the Devil in the ambient air. The man breathes in this polluted air in his immediate neighbourhood and it is drawn to the heart through the arteries thereof, so that shortly disease and corruption are distributed to every part of the body."[5] Ingenious explanations of the

955 [1] *De virginibus velandis*, XV (*Opera*, Vol. III, p. 24; English, Vol. III, p. 177): "*Nam est aliquid etiam apud ethnicos metuendum quod fascinum vocant, infeliciorem laudis et gloriae enormioris eventum. Hoc nos interdum diabolo interpretamur, ipsius est enim boni odium; interdum deo deputamus, illius est enim superbiae iudicium, extollentis humiles et deprimentis elatos.*"

955 [2] *Homilia de invidia*, 4 (*Opera*, Vol. II, p. 132).

955 [3] . . . οἷον ῥεύματός τινος ὀλεθρίου ἐκ τῶν φθονερῶν ὀφθαλμῶν ἀπορρέοντος, καὶ λυμαινομένου καὶ διαφθείροντος. [Garnier: *exitioso quodam quasi fluento . . . tabefaciente atque corrumpente.*]

955 [4] *Disquisitiones magicae*, III, 1, 4, 1 (Louvain, Vol. II, pp. 25-26; Cologne, pp. 379, 388), *De fascinatione*.

955 [5] Del Rio's definition is really more prolix. It began: "The spell, as properly so called in common parlance, is something not natural but of an imaginary superstitious character, as has been excellently shown by Léonard Vair, Lorenzo Annania, Francisco Valles, and Julius Scaliger. . . . It [this thesis] is further proved by the authority of the great Basil, who alludes to the belief contemptuously,

same sort had long been familiar. Plutarch, *Symposiaca*, V, 7 (Goodwin, Vol. III, pp. 327-33), discusses the spell at length. That there is such a thing is, he says, certain; but it is so hard to account for it that many people do not believe in it. And he goes on to show how the spell can arise in natural course. Another naturalistic explanation is given by Heliodorus, *Aethiopica*, III, 7.[6] It would be idle to go into such nonsense in detail. For our purposes we need simply remark this interesting example of derivations varying about a constant residue. Of course, once the disease is diagnosed, there is a scamper for the remedy; and there will naturally be remedies of various kinds according to the temperament of the doctor, naturalistic, magical, religious.

956. While such branches are growing out from the central trunk, the trunk itself endures through the ages; and the simple notion of a mysterious influence due to the evil eye holds its own down to our very day. Says Hesiod, *Opera et dies*, v. 348: "You would not lose your ox if you did not have a wicked neighbour." [1] Columella, *De re rustica*, I, 3, strengthens the dose. He quotes Hesiod's proverb and adds: "And it applies not only to our ox but to all our possessions," so seeming to combine the evil-eye with the malicious-neighbour superstition (§ 185). Catullus, kissing his mistress, fears the evil eye of the envious,[2] and in the *Eclogues* Virgil too dreads the

Homilia de invidia, loc. cit., as female chatter (Garnier: *fabulam . . . introductam in muliereum coetum*). . . . The spell results from a pact when the Devil, in ways known to himself, harms the victim of the spell by the gaze or praise of the spellbinder (*aspiciente malefico vel laudante*)." Then follows the definition given in the text.

955 [6] Underdowne version, Boston, p. 83: "The ayre which is about us on every side, enteringe into us by our eyes, nosthrilles, mouth and other poares, carrying with it suche outwarde qualities as it is indued withal, doth ingrafte a like infection in them who have received it."

956 [1] Οὐδ' ἀν βοῦς ἀπόλοιτ', εἰ μὴ γείτων κακὸς εἴη. And *cf.* § 185.

956 [2] *Carmina*, V, vv. 12-13:

> "aut ne quis malus invidere possit
> cum tantum sciat esse basiorum."

(". . . or that no evil person may cast the spell of envy, knowing of so many kisses") [L. Beebe in F. P. A.'s "Conning Tower," New York *World*, Sept. 21, 1916, renders: "Lest we should know, or evil eye discover How many kisses Lesbia gave her lover."] Muret, *In Catullum commentarius* (*Opera*, Vol. II, p. 727), notes: "The

spell.[3] Pliny, *Historia naturalis,* VII, 2 (Bostock-Riley, Vol. II, pp. 126-27), relates that "in Africa according to Isigonus and Nymphodorus, there are families of spellbinders, a word of praise from whom kills the flocks, withers the trees, and brings death to children. Isigonus adds that among the Triballi and the Illyrii there are individuals of the same sort who cast spells with their eyes and kill those upon whom they fix their gaze for any length of time, especially if it be in wrath. Grown people, in particular, fall ready victims. Such spellbinders have two pupils in each eye. There are women of the same sort in Scythia, called 'Bythiae,' according to Apollonides. Philarchus places the Thibii and many other such people in the Pontus. They are recognizable, he says, from having a double pupil in one eye and the image of a horse in the other. They do not sink in water even if weighted down by clothes.[4] Damon mentions people not unlike these, the Pharnaces of Ethiopia. Their sweat induces consumption in any human body touched by them. Even among the Romans Cicero says that when women have double

spell was thought to be unable to injure things of which the names or the number were unknown. [As usual the instinct for combinations working.] Even rustics of our day and country make it a matter of religion [not] to count the apples on young trees."

956 [3] *Eglogae,* III, v. 103:

"*Nescio quis teneros oculus mihi fascinat agnos.*"

("I know not what evil eye has its spell on my young lambs.") And VII, vv. 27-28:

"*Aut si ultra placitum laudarit, baccare frontem*
cingite ne vati noceat mala lingua futuro."

("Or if he praise beyond the due, wreathe my brow with nard that his evil tongue harm not the future of your bard.") As for the "evil tongue," Servius interprets (Thilo-Hagen, Vol. III, p. 86): "the tongue that casts a spell in intent of harm." Horace, *Epistulae,* I, 14, vv. 37-78:

"*Non istic obliquo oculo mea commoda quisquam*
limat, non odio obscuro morsuque venenat."

("There where you live no one disturbs my peace of mind with leering eye nor poisons with bite of slinking hate.")

956 [4] In the Middle Ages, and for that matter later, the same peculiarity was ascribed to persons guilty of some crime, especially heresy, and most of all, witchcraft. Hence the belief that they could be detected by the "cold-water test." Father Le Brun, *Op. cit.,* Vol. II, pp. 240-41, 253, 271, 284: "The 'cold-water test' was conducted as follows: The suspect was stripped naked, his left hand tied to his right

pupils in their eyes their gaze is always baneful." [4a] People still believe in the evil eye in our day, without crediting the Devil with any share in it. One need only reflect that many very good Catholics were convinced that Pius IX was a *jettatore*. It is interesting that spellbinders are more often women than men, and almost invariably old and ugly women, or at the very least ugly. Young women, pretty girls, never have the evil eye. In that the determining factor is a residue of the I-β4 variety. [5]

957. Mysterious the disease, mysterious also the working of the remedies, though on occasion some sort of an explanation is sup-

foot, his right hand to his left foot, so that he could not move. He was then thrown into the water at the end of a rope. If he sank, as a man so bound and unable to make any movement naturally would, he was deemed innocent; if he floated and could not be made to sink, he was adjudged guilty." Then again a person who floated was assumed to do so because of divine protection (§ 587 [5]). Clearly apparent in such cases is the mysterious efficacy of certain acts. Floating is adjudged an unnatural circumstance. It must therefore be associated with ethical traits in the individual. It may, however, go equally well with innocence and with guilt. Whichever it is, "explanations" will be available in plenty. For innocence, God's help will serve: "Good Christians have always believed, and rightly, that a miracle is required to keep persons so thrown into the water afloat; and innocent and devout individuals, on appealing to God for help, have many a time been saved when thrown into the water to drown." For guilt, more ingenuity will be required. According to Hincmar [*De divortio Lotharii regis*, VI (*Opera*, Vol. I, p. 669)], "since the coming of Jesus Christ a number of things have been changed. Water, for instance, which has been hallowed by contact with the body of Jesus in the Jordan and appointed to sanctify men by baptism, must no longer receive the guilty in its embrace when information is sought as to their crimes." Adolphus Scribonius, a philosopher of repute, studied cold-water tests at first hand in the year 1583 [*De examine et purgatione sogarum per aquam frigidam*] and concluded "that sorcerers are necessarily lighter than other people, because the Devil, a being of spiritual volatile substance, permeates all parts of their bodies and communicates his lightness to them, so that they become less heavy than water and accordingly cannot sink."

956 [4a] [This text of Cicero is not otherwise known: Lemaire ed. of Cicero's *Opera*, Vol. XXV, p. 263 (*Fragmenta incerta*).—A. L.]

956 [5] Carefully examining how a given person, man or woman, comes to get a reputation for possessing the evil eye, one gets the impression that it is very much the case of seed scattered on the ground, some of it sprouting, some of it dying. A report goes abroad that the individuals *A, B, C* . . . have the evil eye. As for *A* and *B*, that is the end of the matter; but the charge sticks in the case of *C*, often on most idiotic grounds. I may mention a personal experience. A lady, old, of course, and of unprepossessing physique, was alleged to have the evil eye. At a ball where she was a guest a chandelier chanced to fall. And everybody, at once,

plied by other residues.[1] Taboos would be a good illustration, but we can deal more advantageously with them when we come to derivations (§§ 1481 f.).

958. I-γ2: *Mysterious linkings of names and things.* Names may be linked to things in two ways: either mysteriously, for no experimental reason; or else because they suggest certain experimental, or even imaginary, properties of things. We distinguish the first case under this category. The second case yields residues of group-persistence (Class II). From the scientific point of view a name is a mere label serving to designate a thing. The label may be changed at will whenever some advantage is to be gained by doing so. It is from this standpoint that definitions are chiefly to be judged (§§ 119 f.).

959. But matters are different when viewed from the two standpoints mentioned. The name is joined to the thing by certain mysterious ties, now abstract, now experimental, now pseudo-experimental, sentimental, imaginary, fantastic. In such linkings of names and things there is nothing arbitrary. In experimental science names are quite arbitrary.

"There, now, tell me she hasn't the evil eye!"—quite disregarding the fact that the same proof might have served just as well against every other individual present. In accord with the proprieties, all the guests, including the *jettatrice,* soon after paid their calls on the hostess. A few days later her children came down with the measles! That was a final proof that the woman was what she was said to be; and she was subjected to such general and such cruel mistreatment that she left town.

957 [1] As for other devices see Daremberg-Saglio, *Dictionnaire, s.v. Fascinum.* Most of those mentioned were used in ancient times, but not a few have continued popular down to our own day. Notable, in the same article, the following: "The Romans placed their children under the protection of a special divinity, Cunina, whose function was to stand guard over the cradle (*cuna*), and shield little ones from the influence of the evil eye. Finally it was imagined that wild animals too might suffer from the spell and that instinct prompted them to ward it off by placing plants and pebbles of secret properties known to them in their lairs. . . . The insect known as the praying mantis (μάντις σέριφος) passed for having the evil eye and casting the spell not only on human beings but on animals. On the other hand, by an association of ideas constant in all superstitions of this variety, images of the praying mantis were supposed to be very effective for warding off spells. Pisistratus had one carved on the Acropolis at Athens as a preservative." However, such inconsistency is by no means peculiar to "superstitions of that variety." It is the general case, a residue being equally valid pro and contra, and the opposite of the pro being not the contra but absence of action (§ 911).

960. An excellent illustration of the sort of residue involved in mysterious linkings of names and things is the so-called perfect number, and it emphasizes with peculiar clearness the contrast between the logico-experimental reasoning and the reasoning by accord of sentiments. For mathematicians the term "perfect" is just a label (§§ 119, 963), serving to designate a number equal to the sum of its aliquots. For the number 6, for instance, the aliquots are 1, 2, 3, and their sum, in fact, is 6. The "perfect" numbers so far discovered are 6, 28, 496, 8128, and others. They are all even numbers. "Perfect" odd numbers are unknown. We might designate such numbers by some other name than "perfect." We might, for example, call them "imperfect," and nothing, absolutely nothing, would be changed. Euler's formula for discovering "perfect" numbers would yield imperfect numbers, but they would still be numbers equal to the sum of their aliquots.[a] It is quite a different matter when we are reasoning on sentiments. Then the name is of great importance: "perfect" is the opposite of "imperfect" and traits that make a number "perfect" prevent it from being "imperfect." What, exactly, the word "perfect" means in such cases no one knows, any more than one knows the meaning of the kindred terms, "just," "good," "true," "beautiful," and so on. All that is clear is that all such terms are symbols for certain sentiments which this or that individual experiences as pleasurable. It would be a waste of time to go over all the nonsense of which the Pythagoreans have delivered themselves on the subject of numbers. Aristotle clearly perceived the fantastic and arbitrary nature of such chatter. Of their numerical theories he writes: "And if their theories were defective in some respect, they made heroic efforts to have results tally. For example: They say that since the decade is perfect, comprising the whole nature of numbers, the planets have to be ten in number. But since only nine

960 [a] [The allusion seems to be to Euler's *Tractatus de numerorum doctrina*, III, §§ 106-09 (*Commentationes,* Vol. II, pp. 514-15). Euler's formula for perfect numbers was $2^n - 1 (2^n - 1)$, where $n = 1, 2, 3, 5, 7, 13, 17, 19$, Euler remaining doubtful about 31, 41 and 47. Strictly, a perfect number would be a number equal to the sum of its aliquots (divisors without remainder) including 1 but excluding the number itself. The aliquots of 28 are 1, 2, 4, 7, 14, 28.—A. L.]

are visible, they add an 'anti-Earth.' " [1] It may even be that 10 *is* a
"perfect" number! How are we to say yes or no unless we are told
what, exactly, the word "perfect" means? Philolaus does not enlighten us any more than the rest of them, but lets go with a hymn
to the decade: [2] "Marvellous to contemplate the efficiency and nature
of numbers according to the power residing in the decade. Supreme
is the decade, perfect. It is the creatrix of all things, the principle,
the guide, the regulatrix of divine, celestial, and human existence.
Without the decade all is purposeless, uncertain, obscure." His Serene
High-and-Mightiness, Number 4, is also divine, and in the "Golden
Verses" of the Pythagoreans, vv. 45-48, he is used to swear by. [2a] Commenting thereon, Hierocles asks: [3] "How does the Number Four
come to be a god?" And he answers: "The decade is the interval
which separates numbers. For if one counts beyond [10], one returns
once more to the numbers 1 and 2 and 3, and counts the second
decade as far as 20, doing the same for the third decade as far as 30,
and so on until one has counted the tenth decade and comes to 100;
and then again 110 is counted in the same fashion; and so one may
go on forever by decades. [In humble prose, without so much
palaver, 10 is the basis of Greek numeration.] The number 4 is the
virtue [the hidden principle] of the decade, the reason being that
the sum of the numbers 1, 2, 3, 4 is 10. Moreover the number 4 ex-
ceeds the number 3 by unity, and is itself exceeded by 3 by the number 7." Verily, as Hierocles assures us, "unity and the number 7 have
most beautiful and excellent properties!" That blessed number 7 has
had hosts of admirers, the illustrious Auguste Comte, almost of our
day, among them. It may therefore be worth while to see what
Hierocles thinks of it: "The number 7 being motherless and a virgin,

---

960 [1] *Metaphysica*, I, 5, 3 (Ross, p. 986a): τέλειον ἡ δεκὰς εἶναι δοκεῖ: "The decade
seems to be perfect." Clement of Alexandria, *Stromata*, VI, 11 (*Opera*, Vol. II, p.
306A; Wilson, Vol. II, p. 352) says: ἡ δεκὰς δὲ ὁμολογεῖται παντέλειος εἶναι: "By unan-
imous consent the decade is perfect."

960 [2] *Fragmenta*, 18 (Chaignet, Vol. I, pp. 239-42; Newbold, pp. 177-78).

960 [2a] [Strictly the *Carmen* reads, v. 47: *Per eum certe qui nobis tradidit quarter-
narium*. Lowe: "This by his name I swear, whose sacred lore First to mankind explained the mystic four."—A. L.]

960 [3] *Commentarius in Aureum carmen*, vv. 45-48 (Lowe, pp. 223-24).

stands next after unity in dignity."[4] The expression "motherless" means that 7 has no factors, that it is a prime number. The epithet "virgin" means that no multiple of 7 is to be found between 1 and 10. Why those two properties should give one number greater dignity than any other remains a mystery. In any event plenty of other properties are mentioned that enhance nobility in the number 7.

We need not dwell on the marvellous properties the Pythagoreans found in other numbers; but it would be a shame not to pay our respects to that most celebrated of numbers, the number 3, which has played and is still playing so important a rôle in the worship of human beings. Know ye, therefore, that "as the Pythagoreans also say, the universe and all things are based on the number 3; for the end, the middle, and the beginning make up the number of the universe, that is, the triad. We use that number as a thing received of Nature according to her laws in celebrating sacrifices to the gods."[5] Other vagaries follow. Then: "In as much as the all, the universe, the perfect, differ from one another not in concept, but only in substance, in the attributes after which they are named, mass would seem to be the only perfect magnitude. For it alone is defined by 3, and 3 is the all." People talk like that when they are dreaming.

The term τριττύς, "perfect sacrifice," was applied by the Greeks to the sacrifice of three animals: a pig, a ram, and a goat.[6] It was the *suovetaurilia* of the Latins, where the victims were a pig, a goat,

960 [4] ἡ δὲ ἑβδομάς ὡς ἀμήτωρ καὶ παρθένος τὴν τῆς μονάδος ἀξίαν δευτέρως ἔχει. (Lowe: "A septenary being motherless and a virgin has secondarily the dignity of an unite.") In his *Commentarius in Timaeum Platonis,* 36 (Mullach, pp. 188-89), Chalcidius dwells at length on the marvellous properties of the number 7: "Noteworthy another property of the number 7 that other numbers do not have. Of all the numbers comprised within the limits of the number 10, some engender other numbers, some are engendered by others, some both engender and are engendered. Only the number 7 neither engenders any other number lower than 10 nor is engendered by any other. . . . That was why it was called 'Minerva' by the ancients, as having no mother and being itself forever virgin."

960 [5] Aristotle, *De coelo,* I, 1, 2-3 (Hardie-Gaye, Vol. II, p. 268a).

960 [6] Suidas, *Lexicon, s.v.* Τριττύς: ἡ ἐντελὴς θυσία, ἐκ συὸς, κριοῦ καὶ τράγου, ἐκ τριῶν. —"The perfect sacrifice: [a sacrifice] of three victims: a pig, a ram, a goat."

and a bull.[7] "Uneven numbers are pleasing to the gods," says Virgil;[8] and in his commentary Servius explains how the number 3, or any other odd number, is to be interpreted.[9] The fact that the number 3 was sacred must have had something to do with the divising of the number 333,333 1/3, for use in votive offerings in Rome.[10]

961. Auguste Comte[1] plagiarizes the Pythagoreans and makes their number nonsense his own. He credits the deification of numbers to fetishism, and talks of "certain numerical speculations which, though sound enough at first in days of fetishistic spontaneity, came eventually to be vitiated by metaphysical mysteries. They concern what may properly be called the philosophical or religious properties

960 [7] According to Festus, *De verborum significatione*, XVII, *s.v.* (London, Vol. III, p. 880), the term was *solitaurilia*, because the three animals had to be uncastrated. He derives the latter word from an Oscan *sollum*, "whole," "intact."

960 [8] *Eglogae*, VIII, v. 75: "*Numero deus impare gaudet.*"

960 [9] Virgil's word "*deus*" Servius interprets (Thilo-Hagen, Vol. III, pp. 104-05) as "any one of the gods, following the Pythagoreans, who assign the perfect number 3 to the supreme Deity of whom are the beginning, the middle, and the end; or in particular, Hecate, who is said to wield a threefold power. For that matter, the powers of virtually all the gods are represented by threefold symbols, as the three-forked lightning of Jupiter, Neptune's trident, Pluto's three-headed dog; and so for Apollo, the Sun, and Liber." Of "*impare*" he says: "Odd, because everything goes by 3's, the Fates, the Furies. Hercules was conceived in a triple night. Muses go by 3's. Or else, any odd number at all, there being 7 strings [to a lute?], 7 planets, 7 days named after gods, 7 stars in the North, and so on. Furthermore the odd number is immortal, being indivisible [What a pretty reason!], whereas the even number is mortal, being divisible. To be sure, the Pythagoreans, according to Varro, considered the odd number as having an end, and the even number as infinite, and therefore used odd numbers for healing and many other purposes, the gods of heaven liking the odd numbers, the nether gods the even."

960 [10] Marquardt, *Römische Staatsverwaltung: Sacralwesen*, p. 255: "Public prayers were drawn up with the help of the pontiffs, and the offerings, games, and sacrifices that were vowed could be evaluated at certain sums while they were being written. . . . Livy, XXII, 10, 7: 'on account of the same things, great games were vowed, to cost to the amount of 333,333 1/3 in brass asses (*aeris*).' That was a sacred number. It is still current under the Empire, as witness an inscription from Ephesus, *Corpus inscriptionum Latinarum*, Vol. III-2, no. 6065 (p. 979), in which a Roman dedicates that amount, substituting one-half a sestertium [in silver] for the 'heavy copper' (*triens*) that was no longer in circulation."

It would take us too far afield to review the many divine trinities that have held and still hold sway over the minds of men. To just one, as of modern coinage, we will advert farther along (§ 1659)—the trinity of the Saint-Simonians.

961 [1] *Système de politique positive*, Vol. III, pp. 129-30.

of numbers, which are altogether unappreciated by our academic doctors. Their true evaluation, which has been left for sociology to make, rests on the logical aptness of the first three numbers. . . . Ingenious experiments have shown that in animals distinct numeration ceases after 3. But one would try in vain to claim a more extensive privilege for our species. . . . In both cases, however, one can consider only abstract coexistence, which is always confused after 3, whereas concrete coexistence may, with human beings and animals alike, be exactly measured beyond 3, objects there taking the place of words. It is upon such abstraction, strictly, that the philosophical character of each number, considered with respect to its logical functions, depends. Going more deeply into this intellectual process, one perceives the source of the mental properties that I above assigned to sacred numbers, 1 representing any kind of systematization, 2 always distinguishing combinations, 3 everywhere defining progression."

This "positivistic" metaphysics is identical with metaphysics stripped of that epithet. Why must a combination always be of two elements, and not of three, or more? It is all quite childish! And as usual Comte gets out of his predicament by reasoning in a circle, declaring, *loc. cit.*, p. 130, any non-binary combination "vicious." [2]

961 [2] Says he, *loc. cit.*: "Dynamically considered any given entity (*existence*) presents three successive stages, a beginning, a middle, and an end. [Comte might at least have mentioned a writer or two who had said as much before him (§ 960 [5]).] Considered statically, its constitution results from the permanent concurrence of two opposite but comparable elements. [A prize for anybody who can explain what that means.] Considered as a whole it always appears as a unit. [Tautology.] So any structure where unity of principle does not prevail, any more than binary combination (*composition*) and any succession going beyond three degrees, are necessarily vicious, the operation being badly conducted or being left unfinished. [So saith the high-priest of Positivism, and that is that!] Their fully subjective synthesizing enables people who think in fetishistic terms to feel these fundamental properties of the three numbers that alone can be conceived without symbols [The learned philosopher is in error: the number 4 is very readily conceived without symbols, and so are other numbers, according to the individual.], especially when a developing number-system is concentrating [general] attention on the rudiments of arithmetic. All philosophical speculations on numbers arise from the subordination of other numbers to those three. Such speculations must therefore especially concern numbers that, not being susceptible of division [It would have been nice of Comte to mention some predecessor here—Hierocles, say (§ 960 [4]).], are appropriately

If any combinations containing more than two elements is not a combination, one can say, of course, that all combinations are of two elements. Comte apparently bars the number 4 from the sacred numbers, though the Pythagoreans regarded it as divine. When all is said and done, the feeling of a modern Positivist is as good as the feeling of a philosopher of old. No one can say who is right and who wrong, since there is no judge to decide the quarrel. Having exalted the number 7 to such great dignity, Comte forthwith sets out, *Synthèse subjective,* pp. 127-28, to force it upon the world as the basis for a numerical system: "Formed by two progressions followed by a synthesis,[8] or by a progression between two couples,[4] the number 7, coming next after the sum of the three sacred numbers,[5] determines the largest group that we can distinctly imagine. Reciprocally, it fixes the limits of the divisions that we can directly conceive in any given magnitude. [Arbitrary assertions on Comte's part. Like all metaphysicists he does not derive his theories from the facts, but moulds the facts to his theories.] Such a privilege should lead systematically to its adoption as the basis of final numeration, concrete as well as abstract." What connexion is there between the number 7's being equal to $3 + 3 + 1$ or to $2 + 2 + 2 + 1$ and its being chosen as the basis of a number-system? But the word "systematically" saves the situation! So "true" liberty stands in contrast to the liberty that has no adjective (§§ 1554 f.)! But there are other good reasons still: "Such a base must be a prime number [So saith the high-priest of Positivism. Mathematicians say that the number with the largest number of factors is the best, 12 therefore being preferable to 10], especially in view of the general need of irre-

called primes (*premiers*) as universal roots. That explains the spontaneous fondness they everywhere inspire. [Everywhere? Did Comte investigate to see?] Here we need merely think of the popularity of the number 7, which derives in two ways from the three radicals by taking now a couple of progressions, now a progression of couples, according as the purpose be static or dynamic, and adding a synthesis [*i.e.,* unity?] either before or after them." This gibberish seems to mean first that $7 = 3 + 3 + 1$, and second that $7 = 2 + 2 + 2 + 1$. A most striking example of a reasoning by accord of sentiments!

961 [8] [*I.e.,* $7 = 3 + 3 + 1$.—A. L.]
961 [4] [*I.e.,* $7 = 2 + 3 + 2$.—A. L.]
961 [5] *I.e.,* 1, 2, 3.

ducibility [It cannot be so general, for quite a few peoples have chosen the number 10], but also because of the special advantage deriving from a full periodicity in fractional transformations."

962. Hebrew and Christian writers might be expected to feel great reverence for the numbers 6 and 7, because of the number of days God spent on the Creation. Philo the Jew, who repeats not a few Pythagorean fancies about numbers, remarks:[1] "Since the whole world was completed according to the perfect nature of the number 6, the Father honoured the seventh day, praising it and calling it holy. For a holy day it is, not of one people nor of one country but of the universe, and it alone is really worthy to be called popular and the birthday of the world. I know not who could adequately celebrate the nature of the number 7, since it is more excellent than words could say."[2] All the same, Philo tries to find words for at least some of the many beautiful properties of that holy number. He returns more than once to a subject so important. In his *Allegories of the Holy Laws* he begins by glorifying the number 6.[3] It would be absurd to imagine that the world was created in six days, for time could not have existed before the creation of the world. The expression "six days" must therefore be taken not as a period of time but as a "perfect" number. The number 6 is "perfect" because it is the first that is equal to the sum of its factors. Furthermore it is the product of two unequal factors (2×3). Then comes an explanation that must be surpassingly inspiring to anyone able to understand what on earth it means: "The 2 and the 3 have overcome 1, which is incorporeal nature. Two is the symbol of matter, and, like matter, divisible and sunderable. Three is the symbol of mass, for mass has three dimensions." Other beautiful properties of the number 6 appear in animate bodies, which move in six directions, backwards, forwards, upwards, downwards, to right and to left.

962 [1] *De mundi opificio*, 30 (Cohn, Vol. I, p. 31; Yonge, Vol. I, p. 26).

962 [2] Τὴν δὲ ἑρδομάδος φύσιν οὐκ' οἶδ'εἰ τις ἱκανῶς ἀνυμνῆσαι δύναιτο, παντὸς οὖσαν λόγου κρείττονα.

962 [3] *Sacrarum legum allegoriae*, I, 2 (Cohn, Vol. I, pp. 61-62; Yonge, Vol. I, pp. 52-53). Strickly speaking, Philo deals with the "diad," the "triad," the "hebdomad," and so on, rather than with the numbers 2, 3, 7 in themselves.

It is also important to know that Moses "sets mortal things in correspondence with the number 6, immortal and divine things with 7." [4] Our old and estimable acquaintance, Dame Nature, loves the number 7 and rejoices in it. [5]

963. St. Augustine is in doubt as to whether the six days of Genesis are to be taken literally, but he has no doubt whatever as to the perfection of the number 6: "We have called the number 6 perfect because it is equal to the sum of its parts, and the parts are such that if they alone are multiplied together they give the number of which they are parts." [1] In other words, the parts are the factors of 6. Six is equal to the sum of its factors, namely, of 1, 2, and 3. That is an experimental fact. Mathematicians put a label (§ 119) on the numbers having that property. On the label they write "perfect number"; but they might just as well write "imperfect number," or any other name. People reasoning by accord of sentiments make a thesis of the definition. The feeling they have of the "perfect" accords, for reasons unknown, with the feeling awakened in them by the reflection that a number is equal to the sum of its factors. Hence such a number is "perfect"; and since 6 is a number of that kind, it is a "perfect" number. But as a matter of fact, reasonings by accord of sentiments are not as strict as that. There is a confused sum of sentiments originating in contemplation of the number 6; and that, roughly, accords with another indeterminate sum of sentiments originating in contemplation of the word "perfect." This latter sum of

---

962 [4] Τὰ μὲν θνητὰ ὡς ἔφην καταμετρῶν ἐξάδι, τὰ δὲ μακάρια καὶ εὐδαίμονα ἐβδομάδι.

962 [5] Χαίρει δὲ ἡ φύσις ἑβδομάδι. In his treatise, *De decalogo*, 5-7 (Cohn, Vol. IV, pp. 272-74; Yonge, Vol. III, p. 140), Philo discourses on the "most perfect number 10," as also in *De congressu quaerendae eruditionis gratia*, 16-22 (Cohn, Vol. III, pp. 89-97; Yonge, Vol. II, pp. 175-82). For the number 7 see his *De septenario et festis*, 23 (*De legibus specialibus*, II; Cohn, Vol. V, pp. 95-141; Yonge, Vol. III, pp. 264-91). St. Epiphanius, *De numerorum mysteriis*, II, IV, V, treats first of the mysteries of the number 3 (*Opera*, Vol. III, p. 510); then of the excellences of the double of 3, in plain English, 6 (p. 514); and finally demonstrates overwhelmingly that the number 7 is perfect (*quod et septenarius perfectus sit numerus*) by listing at great length the sacred or important things that are 7 in number (pp. 514-18).

963 [1] *De Genesi ad litteram* (*Opera*, Vol. III, p. 245 f.), IV, 2, 2: "*Proinde istum senarium ea ratione perfectum diximus quod suis partibus compleatur, talibus dumtaxat partibus quae multiplicatae possint consummare numerum cuius partes sunt.*" Briefly, $6 = 1 + 2 + 3$, and $1 \times 2 \times 3 = 6$.

sentiments accords just as readily, depending on the individual case, with the sums of sentiments originating in other numbers, such as 4, 10, and so on. According to the definition mathematicians use, 10 is not a perfect number; but from the standpoint of sentiment it may very well be, since the word "perfect" stands for something altogether indefinite (§ 509).

From the logico-experimental standpoint it would be absurd to say: "Six is equal to the sum of its factors; therefore God had to create the world in six days." There would be no connexion between the premise and the conclusion. On the other hand, a reasoning by accord of sentiments establishes just such a connexion by virtue of the term "perfect," which, following a procedure that is general (§ 480), it goes on to eliminate. "The number 6 is perfect; the creation is perfect; therefore it had to be completed in six days." St. Augustine states unequivocally: "In a perfect number of days, to wit, in six, did God finish his handiwork" (§ 1546).[2]

964. It might seem to someone that we have been going into such fatuities too seriously, and that would surely be the case were we considering them strictly from the objective, logico-experimental standpoint. But if from the subjective standpoint we consider that

963 [2] *Op. cit.*, IV, 2, 6: "*Perfecto ergo numero dierum, hoc est senario, perfecit Deus opera sua quae fecit*"; and even more explicitly in *Ibid.*, 7, 14: "Wherefore we cannot say that the number 6 is perfect because God completed all his work in six days, but that God completed his work in six days because the number 6 is perfect. So even if God's work had not been done, the number 6 would still be perfect; but if the number 6 were not perfect, God's work would not have been perfect in respect of that number." Speaking of the Trinity in his treatise on the mysteries of numbers, *De numerorum mysteriis*, III (*Opera*, Vol. III, p. 510), St. Epiphanius advances the thesis "that even the very number of the Trinity as written in Scripture is of a marvellous and mysterious nature"; and facts without end he adduces to prove as much. Suffice the following specimens: three things are in us; mind, spirit, and reason; three the things that cannot be sated; hell, lust, fallow soil. Three the virtues, Faith, Hope, Charity. Jonah dwelt in the belly of the whale three days and three nights. The Saint then goes on to laud the number 6 and finds it perfect also. To show that we have no bias or favouritism against any number, we had better mention a *Theological Arithmetic* (*Theologoumena arithmeticae*) by Nicomachus of Gerasa, wherein tribute of just praise is paid to all the numbers from 1 to 10. Photius, *Myriobiblon*, 187 (Geneva, p. 459) dares aver that Nicomachus talks nothing but nonsense, quite arbitrarily taking numbers as gods and goddesses.

such nonsense has been taken seriously by huge numbers of people in all periods of history, it becomes apparent that it must correspond to wide-spread and very cogent sentiments and that it cannot be ignored in a study of the forms of society.

965. Our study of sacred and perfect numbers has achieved the following purposes:

1. It has given another example of a constant element (residues) and a variable element (derivations) in complex phenomena.[1] The constant element in this case is a sentiment that links "perfection" to numbers in some mysterious way. The number to which the attribute of perfection is ascribed varies according to individual inclinations, and more variable still are the fanciful reasons suggested to account for the perfection.

2. It has given a striking example of the reasoning by accord of sentiments—an example, in other words, of derivation.[2] To base an argument on the perfection of numbers is altogether parallel to basing an argument on "natural law," "solidarity," and the like. Men like St. Augustine held such arguments no less sound, in fact rather more sound, than other arguments by accord of sentiments. In our time, however, it is easier to find people who would not take "perfect" numbers seriously but who hold "natural law," and such things, in high esteem. Such people will grasp the general bearing of our criticism of "perfect" numbers more readily than they would any criticism of "natural law" or "solidarity." That is the chief reason why we have lingered on the subject.

3. It has given an excellent example of the difference we have so often stressed between the definition of logico-experimental science and the metaphysical, theological, sentimental assertion. People who continue asking whether a thing be "just," "good," and so on, (§ 1551) are not aware that to ask such a question differs little if at

965 [1] It is true that we had already given so many examples that another was hardly necessary to prove the point.

965 [2] The study of numbers therefore would belong, strictly, to our chapter on derivations—Chapter IX. However, it saves us some repetition to consider them here.

all from asking whether a given number be "perfect" (§§ 119, 387, 506, 963).

4. It has served to contrast the exactness of the logico-experimental sciences with the vagueness of metaphysical, theological, and sentimental speculations. One need only compare the mathematical concept of "perfect" numbers with the sentimental concepts of individuals who apply the term "perfect" to any number they happen to like.[8]

5. It has given an example of the non-logical action that has no apparent social utility. The non-logical actions corresponding to disquisitions on natural law often seem to have, and sometimes actually do have, their social usefulness. That makes it not so easy to see their absolute fatuousness from the logico-experimental point of view.

966. I-δ: *Hunger for combining residues.* The human being often feels prompted to combine certain residues that are present in his mind. That is a manifestation of a synthetic tendency which is indispensable to practical life. Disjoining residues by analysis is a scientific process of which few people are capable (§ 30). Ask some individual who is not familiar with scientific method (or even, at a venture, someone who is, or ought to be) to solve the problem as to whether $A = B$. It will be found that almost irresistibly he will be inclined to consider at the same time, and without the slightest effort to keep them separate, other questions, such as: "Is it a good idea that A should be equal to B? Is it better to believe that $A = B$? Does the identification of A and B meet with the approval of certain people? Or do they disapprove?" And so on and on. Take the question, "Will the man who follows the precepts of morality achieve material prosperity?" (§§ 1898 f.). It is, virtually, impossible for many people to consider such a question by itself.

967. The human being is loath to dissever faith from experience; he wants a completed whole free from discordant notes. For long

965 [8] We shall be meeting other examples arising under captions 2, 3, 4, above. Our present lengthy discussion of perfect numbers will enable us to be more brief in dealing with them.

centuries Christians believed that their Scriptures contained nothing at variance with historical or scientific experience. Some of them have now abandoned that opinion as regards the natural sciences, but cling to it as regards history. Others are willing to drop the Bible as science and history, but insist on keeping at least its morality. Still others will have a much-desired accord, if not literally, at least allegorically, by dint of ingenious interpretations. The Moslems are convinced that all mankind can know is contained in the Koran. The authority of Homer was sovereign for the ancient Greeks. For certain Socialists the authority of Marx is, or at least was, just as supreme. No end of felicitous sentiments are harmonized in a melodious whole in the Holy Progress and the Holy Democracy of modern peoples.

968. The ancient Epicureans absolutely divorced the residues associated with their gods from other sorts of residues. But that case stands by itself, or is at least very rare. In general, many varieties of residues are blended in concepts of divinity. A similar process of concentration also takes place among the various divinities. That is one of the main forces at work in the development from polytheism to monotheism.

969. The impulse to combine residues plays a not inconsiderable rôle in the use people make of certain words of vague indeterminate meanings but which are supposed to correspond to real things (§ 963). The term "good," and the kindred term "well-being," are quite generally taken as standing for real things. "Good," at bottom, is something pleasing to the sense of taste. Then the sense circle widens and "good" is anything pleasing to the taste and promotive of physical health, and from that, anything promotive of physical health alone. Then the sense-circle widens again to embrace moral sensations, and they come to dominate in what is considered "good," and in "well-being." In the end, among philosophers and moralists especially, moral sensations are the only ones considered at all. In other words, the terms gradually come to designate a sum of residues towards which the person who uses them chances to feel sentiments of attraction and not of revulsion.

970. In "intellectuals" the impulse to combine residues goes farther still. They make one general blend of "well-being," "the true," "the beautiful," "the good," and some of them add "altruism," "solidarity," "the human," or better yet, the "broadly human," thus forming a simple complex gratifying as a whole to their sentimentality. Then that complex (or any other like it) which rests merely on the need for combinations may, eventually, acquire in virtue of residues of group-persistence (Class II) an independent existence, and in certain cases even be personified [for example, Progress, Democracy, Reason].

971. Far from negligible among the differences obtaining between a scientific research and a piece of literature is the fact that the former separates residues while the latter combines them. Literature satisfies the human hunger for combining residues and that need is left unsatisfied by science. As for the demand for logic, to which we shall soon be coming (§ 972), one might guess that it should be better satisfied by science than by literature; and so it may be with some few individuals. But not so for the majority of men. Most people are entirely satisfied with the pseudo-logic of literary compositions. Literature is much better suited to their understanding and their tastes than the exact, rigorous thinking of the experimental method. A scientific work may therefore convince the few specialists who understand the subject with which it deals; but literature is always better able to influence mankind in the mass. That is one of the reasons why political economy has remained so largely literary; and it might just as well be left such for people who are inclined to preach—but not for anyone interested in discovering the uniformities prevailing in economic or social phenomena (§ 77).

972. I-ε: *Hunger for logical developments.*[1] The demand for logic is satisfied by pseudo-logic as well as by rigorous logic. At bottom what people want is to think—it matters little whether the thinking be sound or fallacious. We need only reflect on the tangle-wood of

972 [1] This variety might be considered a species of the preceding, since it involves a combination of the logical residue with other residues. In view of its great importance, however, we find it advisable to make a separate classification for it.

fantastic discussion that has flourished and still flourishes around such incomprehensible subjects as come up in the various systems of theology and metaphysics—wild speculations as to the Creation, the purposes for which human life was ordained, and such things—to gain some conception of the imperiousness of the need that is satisfied by such lucubrations.

973. Those who proclaim "the bankruptcy of Science"[1] are right in the sense that science cannot satisfy the insatiable need of pseudo-logical developments that the human being feels. Science can merely relate one fact to another. There is always, therefore, a fact at which it comes to a halt. The human imagination refuses to stop there. It insists on going on, insists on drawing inferences even from the ultimate fact, on knowing its "cause," and if it cannot find a real cause it invents an imaginary one.

974. We should not forget that if this insistence on having causes at all costs, be they real or imaginary, has been responsible for many imaginary causes, it has also led to the discovery of real ones. As regards residues, experimental science, theology, metaphysics, fatuous speculations as to the origins and the purposes of things, have a common point of departure: a resolve, namely, *not* to stop with the last known cause of the known fact, but to go beyond it, argue from it, find or imagine something beyond that limit. Savage peoples have no use for the metaphysical speculations of civilized countries, but they are also strangers to civilized scientific activity; and if one were to assert that but for theology and metaphysics experimental science would not even exist, one could not be easily confuted. Those three kinds of activity are probably manifestations of one same psychic state, on the extinction of which they would vanish simultaneously.

975. This residue explains the need people feel for covering their non-logical conduct with a varnish of logic—a point we have already stressed time and again and at length. It also accounts for that element in social phenomena which we have designated as *b* (§ 798)

973 [1] See Pareto, *Manuale,* Chap. I, § 48.

and which constitutes the whole subject of derivations.[1] The usual purpose of a derivation, in fact, is to satisfy with pseudo-logic the need of logic, of thinking, that the human being feels.[2]

976. I-ζ: *Faith in the efficacy of combinations.* As we have already noted (§ 890), one may believe that *A* is necessarily conjoined with *B*. That belief may be based on experience, on the fact, that is, that *A* has always been observed in conjunction with *B*. From such a fact, however, logico-experimental science infers merely that it is more or less probable that *A* will always appear in conjunction with *B* (§ 97). To ascribe an attribute of "necessity" to the proposition, one has to add to it a something that is non-experimental—an act of faith (§ 1531).

977. That much being granted, if imagination were equivalent to demonstration,[1] the scientist working in his laboratory would note the combinations *AB* without preconception. But that is not the case. In prosecuting his researches, imagining, inventing, he allows himself to be guided by guesses, assumptions, preconceptions—perhaps even prejudices. That does no harm in the case of the scientist. Experience will be there to rectify any error that may develop from the sentiments he feels.

978. For the person who is not grounded in the logico-experimental method, rôles are inverted. Sentiments now play the leading part. Such a person is chiefly moved by faith in the efficacy of combinations. Oftentimes he is indifferent to experimental verifications. Often again, if he does give them a thought he rests content with utterly insufficient, sometimes even ridiculous, proofs.

979. Such conceptions reign sovereign in the minds of the majority of men, and that is why the mind of the scientist sometimes succumbs to them. That will happen the more readily, the more closely, in the pursuit of his calling, the scientist keeps in touch with the population at large and to the same extent the less aware will he be that his sentimental results are in conflict with experience.

975 [1] See Volume III.

975 [2] We need dwell no further here on residues of this type because they are virtually the subject of this work as a whole.

977 [1] Pareto, *Manuale,* Chap. I, § 51.

That is why the student of the social sciences finds it more difficult to adhere to the logico-experimental method than, for instance, the chemist or the physicist.

980. But let us ignore the logico-experimental sciences for the present, and look at things from the standpoint of sentiments and residues. If the combination *AB* is a fact not of the laboratory, but of ordinary life, it will in the long run engender in the minds of people a sentiment linking *A* indissolubly with *B*, and such a sentiment is virtually indistinguishable from a sentiment originating outside experience or pseudo-experimentally.

981. If there is a cock in the hen-coop, the eggs will produce chicks. When a cock crows at midnight, someone dies in the house. For the person reasoning on sentiment, those two propositions are equally certain and, for that matter, equally experimental; and the sentiment that dictates them derives in the one case as in the other from direct experience and from indirect experiences reported by other persons. If one objects that a rooster has been known to crow at midnight without anybody's dying, there is the answer that an egg from a hen living with a rooster often fails to produce a chick. The scientist distinguishes the two phenomena not only by direct experience, but also by the check of likeness—(assimilation) (§ 556). The plain man is not equal to that; and even when he declares the belief about the cock crowing at midnight an absurd superstition, he can offer no better reasons than he could when he held it to be an undebatable truth.

982. Speaking in general, the ignorant man is guided by faith in the efficacy of combinations (§ 78), a faith which is kept alive by the fact that many combinations are really effective, but which none the less arises spontaneously within him, as may be seen in the child that amuses itself by trying the strangest combinations. The ignorant person distinguishes little if at all between effective and ineffective combinations. He bets on lottery numbers according to his dreams just as confidently as he goes to the railroad station at the time designated in the time-table. He thinks it quite as natural to consult the faith-curer or the quack as to consult the most expert

physician. Cato the Elder hands out magical remedies and directions for farming with the same assurance.

983. As experimental science progresses, people try to give an experimental gloss to the products of their sentiments and assert that their faith in combinations derives from experience. But one need only examine the facts a little closely to see the fatuousness of such explanations.

984. If superstition has on the whole fallen off in the masses in our day, the fact is due not so much directly to the influence of the logico-experimental sciences as indirectly to the prestige of scientists —they meantime having introduced quite a number of new superstitions of their own. And it is partly due to the enormous development of industrial life, which is to a large extent an experimental life and has had the effect of disputing—in no very explicit way, to be sure—the dominion of sentiment.

985. The belief that A must necessarily be linked with B is strengthened and becomes stable in virtue of residues of group-persistence. For the very reason that it is rooted in sentiments it takes over from them the vagueness which is their distinguishing trait; and A and B are oftentimes not definite things, definite acts, but classes of things or acts, usually corresponding to our I-β and I-γ varieties (similars or opposites, mysteries). Hence a thing A is linked to anything B provided it be a similar or an opposite, or exceptional, terrible, propitious, and so on. A comet presages the death of some important person, but who the person is nobody very definitely knows.[1]

985 [1] Examples are available for the asking—the old chronicles are literally crammed with them: *e.g.*, Foulcher de Chartres, *Histoire des Croisades*, pp. 33, 155, 217, 233: "When we reached the city of Heraclea, we saw a prodigy in the sky. A great light suddenly appeared, brilliant, and of dazzling brightness. It was shaped like a sword with the point turned toward the east. What the sign portended for the future we did not know, but committed present and future alike into the hands of God. . . . In the year 1106 a comet appeared in the sky. That sign began to glow during the month of February, on the very day of the new Moon. It evidently foretold some future happening, but not presuming to draw any prognostic from such a prodigy, we committed ourselves for all that it might portend into the hands of God. . . . At that time Balak had revealed to him through a dream a misfortune that was to come upon him; for he thought he saw Josselyn tearing out his

986. Whatever the origin of the belief that A is linked to B, whether it be experimental, pseudo-experimental, sentimental, fantastic, or of some other character, once it exists and has been consolidated, stabilized, by the residues of group-persistence, it exerts a powerful influence upon sentiments and conduct, and that in two directions, the one passive, the other active (§§ 890 f.).

987. On the passive side, given one element of the combination AB, the individual is uneasy if the whole combination does not materialize. So, B being posterior to A, on observing A he looks for B (comets, and events announced by them—presages in general). B being given, there is the conviction that it must have been preceded by A, and the past is ransacked until a corresponding A is found (events that were supposed to have foretold the rise of Roman Emperors to the throne). If A and B both lie in the past, they are brought together even if they have nothing whatever to do with each other (presages recorded by historians, when they are not inventions pure and simple).

988. Oftentimes B is left undefined or is defined only to the extent of belonging to a certain class. Something has to happen—exactly what no one really knows (§ 925). Under pressure of group-persistences the combination AB has acquired a personality of its own, independent, within certain limits, of B.

989. On the active side there is a feeling that if one can get A, one can get B. In that way the passive science of divination (§ 924) becomes the active science of sorcery. The Romans already had introduced an active element into divination through their rules for accepting or rejecting presages. Not all

[Balak's] eyes, as he thereafter made known to his men. His priests [He was an infidel.], to whom he reported his vision at once, asking for an interpretation thereof, told him that that misfortune, or some other equivalent, would surely happen to him if ever chance should will that he fall into Josselyn's hands. . . . [Balak is eventually slain in battle with Josselyn and decapitated.] Josselyn ordered it [the head] to be carried forthwith to Antioch as evidence of the victory he had won. . . . So was the aforesaid dream fulfilled, which Balak, gloomy prophet of his own fate, had recounted at the time of Josselyn's miraculous escape from prison. At that time, in fact, he had seen Josselyn tearing out his eyes; and tear them out he did, and well, taking with them his head and the use of his bodily members."

combinations lend themselves to such transformation. In the first place, combinations in which *A* does not lie within human powers —thunder, for instance, or the appearance of a comet—are of course barred. But there are cases even when *A* does lie within human powers where there is no belief that *B* can be obtained by use of *A*. A superhuman being is born of a virgin, but no one believes that a virgin will always yield such a child. It took thirty-six hours or more to engender Hercules, but no one imagines that by exerting oneself to that same extent one will as a matter of course beget a son of Herculean stature. There are cases, then, where there is a mixture of the active and the passive—words of good omen, for instance. If they are heard accidentally, they presage good fortune. It is also a good idea to utter them deliberately, to facilitate the advent of good fortune. Similarly, but *vice versa,* for words of evil omen.

990. In general terms, the concept of the capacity of *A* to produce *B* adds something to the simple concept of the combination *AB*.[1]

991. Class II: *Group-persistences*[1] (Persistence of aggregates).

990 [1] This would be the place for a study of magic and kindred arts, which, however, being a special investigation must be referred to Special Sociology.

991 [1] [The Italian phrase is *"persistenza degli aggregati."* The aggregate is an aggregate (combination, association, group) of *sensations.* The tendency to consolidate such groups of sensations and make them permanent in time Pareto regards as one of the great and fundamental forces in society. Pareto likes to clarify some of his conceptions by showing that they are merely scientific definitions of the hazy concepts of ordinary parlance, such as one notes in the comparison of the ordinary concept of "heat and cold" with the scientific concept of "temperature." In this sense the concept of "group-persistence" would be a definition of the ordinary concept of "habit" or "custom." The concept of "group-persistence" is basic in Pareto's theories of the social equilibrium and class-circulation, and in general in his whole conception of history. It is therefore one of the most important technical phrases in this work. All the difficulties, syntactical, rhetorical, expositional, that we met in the expression "non-logical actions" recur with "the persistence of aggregates." I fix on the phrases "group-persistence," "residues of group-persistence," "group-persistences" (for the eleven shown in his table, § 888), after careful and painful experimentation with all possible other translations. The obscurity that arises (when it arises) in connexion with the concept is due to the fact that in ordinary language the "group-persistences" are widely different in appearances: "Uncle Sam," "the Devil," "Russia," "goodness," "honour," "Santa Claus," "the individual," "Vilfredo Pareto" (to include the word "God" among such examples would be to tear the veil from a studious reticence on Pareto's part). These, analytically and experimentally con-

Certain combinations constitute a group of elements closely united as in one body, so that the compound ends by acquiring a personality such as other real entities have. Such combinations may often be recognized by the fact of their having names of their own, distinct from the mere enumeration of their component elements. The presence of such a name in its turn gives greater consistency to the concept of the group as a personality (§ 1013), by virtue of a residue which assumes that a name always has a thing corresponding to it.[2] The sentiments associated with the group may remain virtually constant, but they may also vary in intensity and in diffusion. Such variation must be kept distinct from that other and much greater variability which affects the forms in which the sentiments express themselves—from variability in derivations, in other words. There is, briefly, first, a nucleus, which has a personality of its own but which may vary, much as a chick varies in becoming a hen, or a

sidered, are groups (aggregates, combinations, associations) of sensations that the mind consolidates into units abiding (persisting) in time, denotes with a name and then more or less personifies. Different as they seem, they are alike from Pareto's point of view, as groups of sensations abiding (persisting) in time. The tendency of the mind (the instinct, sentiment, impulse) that creates such units is the force now of first, now of second, importance in determining the social equilibrium. The intensity of the impulse or sentiment in individuals determines what we ordinarily call "character." In society at large it determines the type of civilization or "culture." Anyone who chances to dislike the phrase "group-persistences" can restore the original Italian by reading "persistences of aggregates" or, "persistences of associations of ideas and acts," or if one is a real Paretan enthusiast, by reading "persistences of associations of the sensations P, Q, R. . . ." As for some of the possible translations that I discard. To use the term "persisting aggregates" would involve a far-reaching misunderstanding of Pareto's thought. Not the aggregate or group of associations does the work, but the fact that it persists in time. The same associations by and large are shared by all members of a community. They endure however only in some of them, and the people in whom they endure are different sorts of people from the ones who take up new associations each day. "Persistence of combinations": I am conscious of one defect in Pareto's exposition of his "group-persistences." He seems to hesitate as to whether he should establish some organic connexion between Class I and Class II residues, whereby the function of the latter would be to make the combinations of Class I habitual and permanent in time. If that was his idea, he should have made it far more explicit. If it was not his idea, then it would seem that persistence of specific combinations should appear as a special genus among Class II residues. "Persistence of combinations" has at any rate to be discarded in the light of this ambiguity.—A. L.]

991 [2] See Chapter X (Verbal Proofs), and especially § 1544.

caterpillar in becoming a butterfly; and then, second, there are the manifestations under forms of derivations of that nucleus, and they would correspond to the capriciously varying conduct of the chick or the caterpillar.

992. After the group has been constituted, an instinct very often comes into play that tends with varying energy to prevent the things so combined from being disjoined, and which, if disintegration cannot be avoided, strives to dissemble it by preserving the outer physiognomy of the aggregate. This instinct may be compared roughly to mechanical inertia: it tends to resist the movement imparted by other instincts. To that fact the tremendous social importance of Class II residues is to be ascribed.

993. Combinations that disintegrate as soon as they are formed do not constitute groups of subsisting individuality. But if they do persist, they end by acquiring that trait. Not by abstraction only do they take on a sort of individuality, any more than by abstraction only do we recognize groups of sensations by such names as "hunger," "wrath," or "love," or a number of sheep by the name of "flock." The point must be clearly grasped. There is nothing corresponding to the noun "flock," in the sense that the flock may be separated from the sheep which constitute it. At the same time the flock is not a mere equivalent to the sum of the sheep. The sheep, by the very fact that they are members of the flock, acquire characteristics which they would not have apart from it. A male and a female thrown together at an age for reproduction are something different from the same male and female taken by themselves. Yet that does not mean that there is an entity X distinct from male and female which represents the male and the female coupled.[1]

994. To these considerations must be added another, to which frequent reference has already been made in these pages, namely, that though the abstraction corresponding to the group may not have an objective existence, it may have a subjective existence, and that fact is most important in its bearing on the social equilibrium.

993 [1] [The Spanish have a word for it: *un matrimonio*, "a married couple."— A. L.]

An example will make that clear. Let us imagine that certain people have taken a river for their god. The fact may be explained in a great variety of ways: *a.* It may be said that by a process of abstraction the people in question have distinguished from the concrete river an ideal river that they regard as "a force of nature" and worship as such. *b.* It may be said that they have ascribed human attributes to the river, assuming that it has a soul, just as a man is assumed to have a soul, and that that soul has been deified. *c.* It may be said that the river has given rise within the people in question to a variety of sensations to an extent at least not clearly defined, but very potent. These sensations persist, and their sum, their combination, their aggregate, constitutes, *for the subject* and *for those people,* a thing to which they have given a name, just as people give names to all other subjective things deemed worthy of their notice. This entity together with its name is attracted by other similar entities and may take its place in the pantheon of the people, just as it may take its place near the flag in the patriotic aggregate (the German Rhine), or a more modest place in the baggage-train of the poets. No one of these three manners of approach is to be barred; but the third explains a number of facts that are not accounted for by the other two, and which sometimes even stand in conflict with them. The residue underlying the third hypothesis is therefore much more generally used than the other two residues.

995. We came upon cases of this kind on a previous occasion in our discussion of the gods of ancient Rome (§§ 176 f.); and we saw that they corresponded to certain associations of acts and ideas. We now carry the analysis a step further, and see in those cases residues of Class I which have become permanent under pressure of residues of Class II. A cult of that type is a sort of fetishism where the fetish is not a thing, but an act. If we tried to explain it by hypotheses *a* or *b,* we should never succeed in understanding how the Roman, whose mind was undoubtedly more practical, less subtle, less ingenious than the Greek mind, could have come out with so many abstractions, seen everywhere about him so many "forces of nature" (probably not even having the remotest notion corresponding to

that term!), and so shown himself more idealistic than the Greek. It would seem, indeed, that the opposite should be the case. On the hypothesis *c,* the facts are very readily explainable. Class II residues were much stronger among the Romans than among the Greeks.[1] Hence it ought to follow—and it actually has followed—that a larger number of aggregates would acquire independent individuality, and it is such aggregates, precisely, that have been passed off as "personifications of forces of nature" by rationalizing historians far surpassing in subtlety of mind the rough and rude people among whom the associations in question originated.

996. We find inscriptions to the goddess Annona (the year's crop).[1] It seems hard to believe that by a process of abstraction the Romans should have personified the victualling of Rome, and then have proceeded to exalt the personification to divine rank. One readily sees, however, how strong and deep-seated the sensations associated with the maintenance of a food-supply at once so important and so difficult must have been. They came to constitute a group, which by the fact of permanency acquired an individuality of its own—became a *thing.* That thing, eventually, under its name, Annona, took its place with many other things of the same kind in the Roman pantheon.

997. The *annona,* the food-supply, existed not objectively but

995 [1] That we showed by proofs in Chapter II *passim,* but especially §§ 226 f. [And Pareto will show it again in Chapters XII and XIII (Vol. IV).—A. L.]

996 [1] De Ruggiero, *Dizionario epigrafico, s.v. Annona (dea):* "From the Capital itself (*Corpus,* Vol. VI, no. 22; Orelli, *Inscriptionum . . . collectio,* no. 1810): *Annonae sanctae Aëlius Vitalio mensor perpetuus dignissimo corporis pistorum siliginiariorum d(ono) d(edit).* ("To Holy Annona, Aëlius Vitalio, surveyor in perpetuity, by most reverent gift of the guild of millers and bakers (this tablet) inscribes.") From Russicade [in Numidia] (*Corpus,* Vol. VIII, no. 7960; Orelli-Henzen, *Inscriptionum . . . collectio,* no. 5320): *M. Aemilius Ballator praeter (sestertium) X m(illia) n(ummum), quae in opus cultumve theatri postulante populo dedit, statuas duas, Genium patriae n(ostrae) et Annonae sacrae urbis sua pecunia posuit,* etc. ("Marcus Aemilius Ballator, in addition to 10,000 sestertia in cash that he gave at the request of the people for the building and operation of a theatre, has erected at his own expense two statues [the one to the] Genius of our country and [the other] to Holy Annona of this city.") Her cult developed most notably in Rome and its vicinity under the Empire, at a time when Rome had come to be liberally and cheaply provided with victuals, as a result of a reorganization in storage and marketing (*curae annonae*)."

subjectively. If anyone had thought in the old Roman days of having such religious pseudo-experiences as are had in ours, he would have found the goddess Annona in the minds of the Romans, along with other gods like her, male and female. That would have proved that certain associations of sentiments and notions were present under certain names in the minds of the Romans; but it would not in the least have proved the objective existence of such groups. In a certain sense, if we chose to use poetic language, we might say that such groups were "alive" in the consciousness of the Romans; but we could not say that they had any "life" outside that consciousness.[1]

998. Phenomena of this kind differ the more widely the farther they stand removed from their residues. The Romans stuck close to residues, for the very reason that they were but slightly inclined to theological and philosophical speculation. Owing to their aptitude for such speculations, the Greeks were carried far afield from residues by derivations, and one such derivation results in the anthropomorphism of the Greek gods—which explains why the Greek gods are so much more "alive" than the gods of the Romans (§ 178).

999. Viewed from any logical standpoint, the apotheosis of the Roman emperors was an absurd and ridiculous thing; but considered as a manifestation of abiding residues, it seems natural and reasonable enough. The Emperor, no matter who he was, personified the Empire, orderly administration, justice, the *pax Romana;* and such sentiments did not in the least languish because one man died and another succeeded him. The permanence of that aggregate was

997 [1] Sorel, *Le système historique de Renan,* Vol. IV, p. 341; Pt. III, Chap. I, entitled: *"La vie posthume de Jésus et les traces qu'elle a laissées"*—in question, the Apostles, after the death of Jesus: "During this period they thought they had before them a Jesus as real as the Jesus they had known in Galilee and that they were going on with their former life with him. And there is no doubt that that was the situation for a long time, for the claim was that the rules for fasting and for the Christian Passover went back to the revelation made by the risen Jesus (*Didascalia,* XXI [Gibson, Vol. I, pp. 92-101]). That presupposes that, according to very ancient traditions, the posthumous life of Jesus lasted long enough for ecclesiastical laws to have had time to form. I believe it has to be considered as lasting down to the martyrdom of St. James the Apostle. The surmise rests on a number of details that are intelligible on no other basis."

the fact, the apotheosis one of the forms under which it found expression.

1000. Similar considerations hold for many other instances of the deification of human beings. The thing did not take place, as Spencer imagines, as a result of a logical analysis (§§ 682 f.). It is just one of the many manifestations of the permanence of groups of sensations. We shall see farther along (§ 1074 [1]) that in the first place, Rome is made a goddess; and not till afterwards does someone imagine that there was a woman who had that name and so came to be deified. Similar examples occur in great abundance. Sometimes the development is from a god to an imaginary person, and sometimes from a real person to a god. All such are derivations and essentially variable, whereas the sentiments which find expression in that manner are constant.

1001. It has been observed that customs sometimes endure after the circumstances in which they originated have disappeared, and the phenomenon has—not generally, to be sure, but in one particular case—been called a "survival." Says Tylor, *Primitive Culture* (1871, Vol. I, p. 62; 1873, Vol. I, p. 70): "When a custom, an art, or an opinion is fairly started in the world, disturbing influences may long affect it so slightly that it may keep its course from generation to generation." That is what Tylor calls a "survival," but it is just a particular case of a thing much more general. The persistence of a custom may be due to its meeting weak resistance, but it may also be due to its having found support in a force superior to any opposing force, considerable though this latter may have been. So the Christian Church certainly fought might and main against pagan "superstitions," but with varying success. Some of them were demolished and disappeared. Others could not be conquered, and held their ground. When the Church realized that the resistance was too great, it ended by compromising, and contented itself with giving a new garb—often a very transparent one—to an old superstition.

1002. In such phenomena one clearly detects the working of residues constituted by group-persistences. But we get something more and better than that simple observation: They enable us to explain many other phenomena. Says Monsignor Duchesne:[1] "The litanies were solemn supplications instituted to invoke heavenly protection upon earthly possessions. They were sung in the springtime, in the season of the late frosts so dreaded by farmers. It is not surprising that on a point of that kind Christianity should have found itself in agreement with religious customs of an earlier period. [Christianity did not "find itself in any agreement"; Christianity simply had to resign itself to accepting certain customs—an entirely different matter.] . . . The same needs, the same sense of this or that danger, the same confidence in divine aid, inspired very similar rites." It would seem, from that, that paganism and Christianity, each operating independently, happened by chance, or as the result of identical causes, to institute the same festival. Such a thing might at a hazard be granted as a rule; but it is devoid of any probability in the present case, the moment we consider that the two religions were in no wise independent, that the newer was superimposed upon the older, and that the details of the ceremonies are identical—as Monsignor Duchesne himself notes: "In Rome the holiday selected was the twenty-fifth of April, a traditional date on which the ancient Romans celebrated the festival of the Robigalia. The principal rite in that festival was a procession, which, issuing from the city through the Porta Flaminia, made its way toward the Pons Milvius. . . . The Christian procession that replaced it followed the same route to the same bridge."

1003. In other cases the Church offered a greater and more effective resistance to the continuance of ancient customs. It arranged matters so that the Christian Easter did not fall on the same date as the Hebrew Passover. It tried to put an end to the celebration of the pagan festival of the first of January, and partially won its point by replacing it with Christmas. We may guess, therefore, that had it been able, it would also have changed the date of the Rogations.

1004. Monsignor Duchesne (whom we quote because he cannot be suspected of hostility to the Catholic Church) gives other examples,

1002 [1] *Origines du culte chrétien*, Vol. I, pp. 293 f.

Vol I, pp. 283-84: "The [Philocalian] calendar of the year 336 contains, for the twenty-second of February, a feast called the *Natale Petri de cathedra*. Its purpose was to commemorate the inauguration of the episcopate, or apostolate, of St. Peter. . . . The choice of the day had not been dictated by any Christian tradition. We need only glance at the ancient calendars of the Roman religion (*Corpus Inscriptionum Latinarum*, Vol. I, p. 386) to see that the twenty-second of February was devoted to the most popular of all festivals, the festival of the family dead. The observance of that festival and the rites which accompanied it was considered incompatible with the Christian profession of faith. But it was very difficult to uproot habits so particularly dear and deep-rooted. That, doubtless, was the reason why the feast of the twenty-second of February was established."

In that Monsignor Duchesne is entirely in the right. The explanation he gives is the one that best harmonizes with the facts. The Catholic Church had no end of difficulty in putting an end to pagan banquets in honour of the dead, and often enough it had to be prudent and rest content with transforming what it could not abolish.[1]

1004 [1] In his *Epistolae*, XXIX, 8 (*Ad Alypium*) (*Opera*, Vol. II, p. 118; *Works*, Vol. VI, p. 89), St. Augustine tells how he tried to abolish the custom of holding banquets in the churches in honour of the dead. His hearers were not convinced. Said they: *"Quare modo? Enim antea qui haec non prohibuerunt Christiani non erant?"* ("How is that? Bishops heretofore have not prohibited such things. They were not Christians?"). The Saint had a moment of perplexity and was about to withdraw, when those who had disputed him came and called on him; and he therefore explained just why the Church had had to tolerate such banquets in the past: "When peace was at last made after such long and cruel persecutions, throngs of heathen were disposed to adopt the Christian faith, but they were restrained by the fact that along with their idol-worshipping they had been accustomed to spending their holidays in riots of drinking and feasting, and it was not easy for them to give up enjoyments that were as ancient as they were wicked. Our elders, therefore, in order to condone such weakness in part and for a time, thought that in exchange for (*post*) the festivals they were giving up there should be others which could be celebrated in honour of the Holy Martyrs with the same splendour, though not with the same sacrilege." And he exhorts his flock to imitate the churches overseas, which were doing away with such wrongful things. When he was met with the rejoinder that "banquets were held every day in the basilica of the blessed Apostle Peter," he replied that "it was well known that they had often been pro-

1005. Examples without number show the saints taking over cults of the pagan gods, and so make clear that, at bottom, it is a case of one identical thing assuming different forms.

1006. Says Maury: [1] "This substitution of Christian ceremonies for pagan rites occurred whenever the latter were of such nature as to be susceptible of sanctification. It was especially the case in countries like Gaul, Great Britain, Germany, and the northern lands, where the Gospel was not preached until a fairly late date and where pagan beliefs showed themselves vigorous and less docile. The Church herself enjoined this compromise with popular superstition on her apostles, and so we still find numerous traces of it today in our rural districts. In certain places [in France] Charon's penny is still placed in the mouth of the dead. The statue of the saint is plunged, as was the statue of Cybele, in a sacred bath. The fountain continues to receive in the name of a saint libations that were poured of yore to a divinity. Oracles are obtained in practically the same manner as our ancestors obtained them [And just as naturalistic paganism had obtained them before the advent of anthropomorphic paganism.], and there is nothing, down even to the cult of the phallus, which has not been sanctified under evasive forms."

hibited. However, they did occur in places far removed from the bishop's influence (*conversatione* [Pareto renders: *abitazione*]). In a metropolis such as Rome there were always many licentious people about, especially foreigners, who arrived in town every day and observed heathen customs with a fidelity proportionate to their ignorance. It had therefore so far been impossible to eradicate the evil altogether." In the *Confessions*, VI, 2, St. Augustine voices commendation of St. Ambrose for prohibiting offerings of victuals in honour of the saints in the churches in Milan, "so avoiding giving the intemperate occasion for indulging in strong drink, and because such things smacked of the superstitions of the heathen *parentalia*." In his *De moribus ecclesiae catholicae et de moribus Manichaeorum*, I, 34, 75 (*Opera*, Vol. I, p. 1342; *Works*, Vol. V, p. 47), the Saint says anent bad Christians: "I know that many worship tombs and paintings. I have heard that many drink most excessively at the graves of the dead, offering banquets to the corpses, burying themselves [in wine] over those who lie buried [in earth], and setting such gluttony and tippling to the account of piety." The persistence of ancient customs is manifest in another of his letters, *Epistolae*, XXII (*Opera*, Vol. II, p. 92; *Works*, Vol. VI, pp. 53-54): "The drunken and licentious banquets that are held in the cemeteries are believed by the ignorant and carnally-minded masses to be not only

---

1006 [1] *La magie et l'astrologie dans l'antiquité et au moyen âge*, pp. 157-59. *Cf.* Saintyves, *Les saints successeurs des dieux*.

1007. A residue built up of certain associations of ideas and acts in ancient Rome comes down to our time under successive guises (§ 178). It does not change with the invasion of Greek anthropomorphism, whereby the fountain becomes a personified divinity, nor with the rise of Christianity—the god or goddess merely becoming a saint. On a parallel line, a metaphysical transformation gives the residue abstract form as a "natural force" or as a "manifestation of divine power"; but such transformations are kept for the use of writers and philosophers, and are not very warmly welcomed by the masses at large. The power inherent in the residue becomes evident enough in the fact of its persistence in the face of so many and such varying vicissitudes; and so it is clear that as regards deter-

an honour to the martyrs but a great comfort to the dead," and he advises Aurelius to suppress them. It is clear enough that the Church was doing everything in its power to extirpate customs such as these and tolerated them only when it could do no better. On that point it would be well to read the whole of a letter by Gregory the Great to Mellitus, *Epistolae*, XI, 4, 76 (*Opera*, Vol. III, pp. 1215-16; Barmby, Vol. I, p. 85). Just an excerpt here: Gregory is giving directions as to the manner of dealing with the English. First of all, he observes, heathen temples may be retained: "Take holy water (*aqua benedicta fiat*) and sprinkle it about in such temples; then let altars be built and relics be deposited in them. If such temples are well constructed (*i.e.*, worth the trouble), they should be made over from the cult of devils to the worship of the true God; for when those people see that their shrines are not being destroyed, they will dismiss error from their hearts, and acknowledging and worshipping the true God, feel more at home in gathering (*familiarius concurrat*) at their accustomed places. [Here the Church is evidently trying to make capital out of the popularity of certain heathen shrines.] And in cases where it is the custom to slaughter many cattle in sacrifices to devils, that too must be turned into a certain solemnity for them. For instance, on days of dedication or on the birthdays of the Holy Martyrs whose relics are being deposited there, let them make shrines to them out of the branches of trees about those same churches that have been made over from temples, and let them celebrate such occasions with religious banquets. . . . For evidently not everything can be eradicated from such untutored minds all at once." Muratori, *Dissertazioni sopra le antichità italiane*, LXXV (Vol. III, p. 464): "And since sometimes in these reunions [of the confraternities] it is thought that feasts are more solemnly celebrated with some sort of banquet and good wine, the which not seldom gives rise to quarrels and enmities, it behooves us once more to hearken to Hincmar, who attests that the same thing was going on in his day, nay, his words seem to be describing the customs of our own: 'For,' says he, 'there are banquets and feasts which the Divine authority forbids, and of them come expense and undue levy, and wicked and silly pleasures are the rule, and quarrels, hatreds, and dissensions, and often, as we have observed, even murders. Wherefore we forbid them.'"

mining the social equilibrium, it is far more important to consider the residue than to consider the various ephemeral vestments that it assumes in course of time.

1008. And it is also clear that forms change more readily than substance, derivations more readily than residues. Banquets in honour of the dead become banquets in honour of the gods, and then again banquets in honour of saints; and then finally they go back and become merely commemorative banquets again. Forms can be changed, but it is much more difficult to suppress the banquets. Briefly (and therefore not very exactly) one might say that a religious custom or a custom of that general character offers the less resistance to change, the farther removed it stands from its residues in simple associations of ideas and acts, and the larger the proportion it contains of theological, metaphysical, or logical concepts.[1]

1009. That is why the Catholic Church won an easy victory over the major gods of paganism, but found it much more difficult to deal with the little secondary divinities. And that again is why it could gain the acceptance of Graeco-Latin civilization for the theological concept of a single God—or Trinity—but at the price of permitting the abiding residues of the old religion to continue expressing themselves in the worship of saints and in many customs that at bottom were not greatly at variance with those which had prevailed in the past. That, finally, is the reason why it is easier to change a people's form of government than its religion, manners and customs, and language. Even in changes of government under

---

1008 [1] In his *Narrative of a Voyage to the Pacific and Behring's Strait*, pp. 309 f., Beechey writes of the Indians who were being taught in the missions at San Francisco: "The neophytes being thus arranged, the speaker began, 'Santíssima Trinidad, Diós, Jesú Cristo, Espíritu Santo,' pausing between each name to listen if the simple Indians, who had never spoken a Spanish word before, pronounced it correctly or anything near the mark. . . . They did not appear to me to pay much attention to what was going forward, and I observed to the *padre* that I thought their teachers had an arduous task; but he said they had never found any difficulty, that the Indians were accustomed to change their own gods, and that conversion was in a measure habitual to them. I could not help smiling at this reason of the *padre* but have no doubt it was very true; and that the party I saw would feel as little compunction at apostatizing again, whenever they should have an opportunity of returning to their own tribe."

its varying forms the substance remains but little changed. The prefect under the Third Republic in France is the twin brother of the prefect under the Second Empire, and the "official candidacy" under the two governments differs little if at all.

1010. The fanaticism and idiocy that inspired the old prosecutions for witchcraft are present point for point in modern prosecutions for offences against the sex religion. Offenders are no longer burned at the stake, to be sure; but that is because criminal penalties have been mitigated all along the line. When severity was the rule witches were burned and thieves were hanged. Today sex heretics and thieves alike get off with mere terms in prison. But the forms of the phenomenon and the principles that it betrays are the same. Procedure under the Inquisition deprived the defendant of guarantees he enjoyed in the episcopal and civil courts. Says Lea:[1] "The procedure of the episcopal courts . . . was based on the principles of the Roman law, and whatever may have been its abuses in practice, it was equitable in theory, and its processes were limited by strictly defined rules. In the Inquisition all this was changed."

1011. And lo! the same thing is now being done for crimes of sex heresy, for the crime, for instance, of printing stories that are, or are reputed to be, obscene or even merely "immoral," the crime of photographing women scantily clad, the crime of mentioning the embrace of Daphnis and Chloe—things that have always been done and will always be done so long as the human race endures. Civilized governments give asylum to political exiles even if guilty of homicide, but they hand over sex heretics to their prosecutors, sex heresy being a more serious crime than murder, as was the crime of heresy in Catholic countries in days of yore. In England, the land of the habeas corpus, and in the year of grace 1912 (June), the House of Commons approved on second reading a bill permitting the police to arrest without warrant any person suspected of being about to commit a crime connected with the "white-slave trade." If the term designated nothing more than the fraudulent and deceitful alluring of a woman to a house of prostitution, there would be no question

1010 [1] *History of the Inquisition*, Vol. I, p. 399.

of any sex religion; it would be a crime like any other crime involving fraud or deception, aggravated in some instances by the greater damage inflicted on the victim. But such is not the case. In many many instances seaport authorities have halted prostitutes who deliberately and in full awareness of what they were doing expressed intentions of sailing overseas for the simple reason that they hoped to make more money in some foreign country. Not the remotest suggestion of fraud or deception! The crime could only be viewed as a transgression of a special taboo. So at Basel in Switzerland the police on one occasion raided all lodging-houses in the middle of the night, roused the guests, and whenever they found a man and a woman in the same room, demanded that they give proof of legal marriage. In this case it was evident that whatever the name of the law applied in such fashion, there was no question of fraud, deception, or any other such crime, but only of a violation of a sex taboo, much like the sin of the Catholic in eating meat on Friday or the sin of the Moslem in eating, drinking, or having commerce with his wife between sunrise and sunset on a day of Ramadan.[1]

1011 [1] A correspondent writing in the *Journal de Genève*, July 11, 1913, declares himself in favour of "suppressing the white-slave trade," but is nevertheless forced to admit on the strength of the facts that there is an element of farce in the whole business. Reporting the Convention on the White-Slave Trade held in London, June 30-July 5, 1913, he comments: "This convention will certainly equal in importance the Madrid convention of 1910, which marked an epoch in the battle against this new scourge [The good soul finds "new" a thing that has gone on from the days when Greek hetairai were inspiring Greek poets and dramatists down to our own.], which was brought to world-wide attention less than fifty years ago by the sagacity of a few philanthropists and specialists in sex morality [Some such specialists are closer students than they need be.]. Those gentlemen had some trouble in convincing their contemporaries that there was any such thing as the abominable traffic which they had set out to combat. But when the genuineness of certain allegations was placed beyond dispute, there was a shift from excessive scepticism to excessive credulousness, the public being inclined to accept without investigation and with evidence of real appetite yarns that were as dramatic as they were without basis in fact. The 'movies' came to corroborate this sensation-mongering with the fabricated testimony of their films, with the result that educated people, in the habit of using their minds, are no longer so easily taken in and are beginning to move the previous question. That is why, in this domain as in any other, it is important to have trustworthy organs of information and investigation. Those organs now exist and they are gradually coming to cooperate through the central international

1012. Exceptional procedures are usually justified by the seriousness of a crime, which is deemed so great as to warrant the risk of punishing some few innocent persons provided no guilty person escape. Such, in fact, is the experimental justification of exceptional procedures, like the French *loi des suspects,* in times of war or revolution. The justification is sentimental in the case of procedures against religious heretics; and with these must in our day be classed dissenters from that sex religion which our Inquisitors on Purity are trying to force upon civilized societies.[1]

1013. In many cases where the permanence of groups of sensations is involved, a development of great importance arises. The residue originates in the permanence of certain facts, but then contributes to maintaining that permanence until there is a clash with some obstacle that disintegrates or modifies the group. It is a question of a series of actions and reactions (§ 991).

1014. Erroneous the idealistic theory that regards the residue as the cause of the facts. Likewise erroneous, but at times less so, is the materialistic theory that regards the facts as the cause of the residue.

bureau in London and national Committees on the White-Slave Trade, so called. The reports presented by the delegates make it clear beyond shadow of doubt that if the 'trade' is not flourishing to any such fantastic proportions as certain writers have claimed, there is in fact such a 'trade' and that it is operating everywhere. There is not a large city in the world that does not have its 'traders,' its secret organization, its 'girl-market.' Only—and that is what explains the negative or sceptical attitude of certain court authorities towards the presentments of the vice societies—the 'white-slave trade' is no longer, as a rule, carried on by brutal methods that fall directly under the penal code, but by a sequence of shrewdly manipulated and progressive influences, contacts, temptations, degradations, whereby the young girl, but yesterday unsullied and self-respecting, embraces her ruin ostensibly of her own choice." *Habemus confitentem reum!*

1012 [1] Taking due account of the general mitigation of punishments, which applies to thieves and murderers quite as well, very much the same things may be seen going on today as in the days of the Inquisition. To avoid scandal the Inquisitors recognized secret accusations and kept the names of witnesses confidential. *Cf.* Bernard Guidon, *Practica inquisitionis heretice pravitatis,* p. 189: "If the Inquisitors find that any danger to witnesses is involved in the publication of their names, they may mention the names of such witnesses in the presence of a certain number of persons, not publicly but confidentially. There is a ruling on this point in a letter of Pope Innocent IV to the Friars Inquisitors of the Order of Preachers, *Cum negotium fidei catholicae.* . . . 'We urgently order that the names of accusers of heresy and witnesses thereto be strictly withheld from publication in view of the scandal

In reality the facts re-enforce the residue, and the residue the facts. Changes occur because new forces come into play to affect either the facts or the residue or both facts and residues—new circumstances occasion changes in modes of life (§ 976).

1015. II-α: *Persistence of relations between a person and other persons and places.* This variety falls into three subvarieties presenting similar and closely related characteristics, so that the residues readily blend and they also compensate one for the other.[a] These residues are common to men and animals. It is said that certain animals have a sense of "property," which is just a way of saying that they have a permanent sentiment attaching them to places and things. Also persistent in them is a sentiment attaching them to people and to other animals. The dog knows not only his master, but other individuals and animals about the house. A dog kennelled in a garden will not harm the cats and the poultry that belong there. Once outside the gate he chases all the cats and hens he sees; and he will attack a strange cat that enters his garden. In a case I have in mind, a number of cocks hatched in the same brood and kept together did

or danger possibly resulting from such publication.' " In our day, actually if not legally, procedure against "immoral literature" and other crimes of the modern heresy is the same. Many individuals are eager enough to be informers, but they also desire to remain anonymous, and their charges are lodged at second hand through the chairman, or executive secretary, of some "society for the suppression of vice." Such societies induce complaisant newspapers not to print news of prosecutions of "immoral literature" or of trials relating to the white-slave traffic, and for the very reasons alleged by Pope Innocent IV: "in view of the scandal or danger possibly resulting from such publication." The consequence now as then of such secret procedures is that their crookedness is never brought to public notice. Says Lea, *Op. cit.*, Vol. I, p. 406: "Had the proceedings been public, there might have been some check upon this hideous system, but the Inquisition shrouded itself in the awful mystery of secrecy [As our high-priests of purity do today.] until after the sentence had been awarded." In our day not even verdicts are published by newspapers that are politically controlled; to find out about them one must hunt them up in special publications, so that they remain unknown to the public at large. The interesting thing is that many of these modern inquisitors and their admirers hate the mediaeval Inquisitors and regard them as very wicked men; thinking they have cleared their traces when they have said that the faith of the old Inquisitors was "false," while theirs is "true."

1015 [a] ["Compensate" is a technical term with Pareto. For his theory of compensation among residues, a subdivision of his theory of varying intensities, see §§ 1701 f., and Index.—A.L.]

not fight. One of them was taken away and kept apart for six days. It was taken for granted that he could be put back with the others as a matter of course, but he was immediately attacked and killed. The same thing happened with two male cats that were born together and lived together peacefully. They were separated for a short time. When they were again brought together they went at each other furiously. The human sentiments of family, so called, of property, patriotism, love for the mother-tongue, for the ancestral religion, for friends, and so on, are of just that character, except that the human being dresses his sentiments up with derivations and logical explanations that sometimes conceal the residue.[1]

1016. II-α1: *Relationships of family and kindred groups.* Among animals that rear their offspring there is necessarily a temporary union between one or both parents and the young, but no notable residues seem, as a rule, to develop from such association. As soon as the young are able to take care of themselves, they separate from their parents and cease to recognize them. Among human beings, probably because the young need their parents or foster-parents for a much longer time, interesting and sometimes very powerful residues develop.

1017. These correspond to the forms of family association prevalent in the given country, and they also serve to strengthen or modify such forms. The best known, or rather the only, literature we have comes from peoples who have had a patriarchal family system—and they, after all, are the civilized peoples; so the only residues with which we are at all familiar are residues corresponding to the patriar-

---

1015 [1] Davis, *The Chinese,* 1806, Vol. I, p. 248 (1836, pp. 260-61): "To the system of clubbing together in families—we might almost say in clans—is to be attributed that sacred regard to kindred which operates better than a public provision for the relief of the poor and serves as one of the best means for the *distribution of wealth.* . . . Hence, too, that regard for the place of his birth, which always clings to a Chinese through life, often making him apply for leave to quit the honours and emoluments of office and retire to his native village. The same feeling makes the colonists who venture abroad in search of gain return home as soon as they have acquired something like a competency, though at the risk of being oppressed under the forms of law for having left China. They have a popular saying, 'If he who attains to honours or wealth never returns to his native place, he is like a finely-dressed person walking in the dark'—it is all thrown away."

chal type. We find them all through Graeco-Roman antiquity, in the Bible, and in the literatures of China, India, and Persia. That fact gives grounds for the notion that the patriarchal type of family was the only one concretely existing, and that deviations from it, which had been noted even in ancient times, were of little or no account. Those good souls who dreamed of a "natural law" did not fail to conclude that the patriarchal family was part of that law. But the day came when it was discovered, to the extreme astonishment of the learned world, that not only were other types of family extant among uncivilized or barbarous peoples, but that these may have played a part in the family organization of our own prehistoric ancestors, leaving traces that were still discernible in historic times.

1018. As usual there came a leap from one extreme to the other. It was a day when the concept of unitary evolution reigned supreme. So the manufacture of theories began at once. Starting with a primitive stage of the family—according to some writers, sex promiscuity or community in women—and going on through various intermediate stages (they are duly described in all details, as though anyone had ever been able to observe them with his own eyes!) it was shown how all peoples had modified their family organizations in a uniform direction and how civilized peoples had come by the type of family that prevails at present among them.

1019. The very few and very faint vestiges of families differing from the patriarchal type that are to be found in classical literature were put under high-powered magnifying glasses and became the foundations of rounded theories which do honour to the mental ingenuity and lively imaginations of their authors, but fail to testify as eloquently in favour of their historical and especially their scientific sense. Engels, for his part, killed two birds with one stone (§ 822): He reconstructed a history unknown to anybody except to himself, and brought the infamy and hypocrisy of the *bourgeoisie* to clearer light along with the ideal beauty of that evolutionary limit which we are to reach through Socialism.

1020. Though scientifically erroneous, these new theories of the family were didactically useful in that they served to break the circle

within which every study of the family had formerly been confined
by the prevalence of a single concept of family type: the patriarchal.
Even the story by Engels may have had its use as showing to many
people who had no aptitude for scientific investigation the immense
amount of fatuity, stupidity, and hypocrisy that lurked in certain
forms of bourgeois idealism.

1021. Whatever the causes, groups came to be formed among
many peoples. Presumably they were bound to the soil and endured
in time, the dead being one by one replaced by successors. It also happened that the nucleus of such groups was constituted by individuals
bound to one another by ties of kinship. The existence of such groups
stands in a relationship of interdependence with the existence of
sentiments tending to make the groups permanent and which manifest themselves in various ways, but chiefly through what is called
religion. We do not know the "origins" of such groups. The historical documents at our command present them in an advanced
stage of evolution, often indeed in decadence. That much certain,
three principal explanations of the historical phenomenon have been
suggested: 1. Considering the nucleus primarily, it was explained
that the groups in question originated in the family and that if in
historic times they were no longer mere families, the fact was due
to deviations from the type or from the "origin," because of abuses
that had altered the "primitive" institution. 2. Stressing primarily
the sentiments that prevail in the group and strengthen it, it was
explained that the origin of the groups lay in religious beliefs (§ 254),
and the family nucleus was accounted for by the religious prescription that certain religious rites should be performed by persons bound
by ties of kinship (§ 254). In this case, deviations are much less
marked than in the first, and in historic times in the countries
considered the religious tie coincides exactly with the tie binding
the group. That does not in the least prove that the groups originated in religion. Only the mania for logical interpretations and the
gravely mistaken notion that sentiments have to precede acts can
lead to the conclusion that the religious tie is the "origin" of the tie
binding the group. 3. It was once possible to imagine that the groups

were altogether artificial things, devised by legislators, but that interpretation now enjoys very little consideration, and properly so.

1022. But there is a fourth hypothesis that explains the known facts much better. It considers the groups as natural formations growing up about a nucleus which is generally the family, with appendages of one sort or another, and the permanence of such groups in time engenders or strengthens certain sentiments that, in their turn, render the groups more compact, more stable, better able to endure.

1023. These general considerations apply in the particular to the Roman gens, the Greek γένος, and the Hindu caste. The difficulties encountered in early efforts to determine what the gens and the γένος exactly were arose partly from the fact that definiteness was sought where, at least in very ancient times, nothing of the kind existed. It was the usual error of imagining that crude people with little or no propensity for abstraction and scientific thinking reason with the strictness and exactitude of jurists living in far more civilized and better-educated communities. The jurists of a later day had to solve very complicated problems and solve them in clear, precise, and logical terms, in order to determine who belonged to gens or γένος, and who did not. But in primitive times the problems were much simpler and came down to questions of fact; which in no wise means that the fact was arbitrary, but merely that it was determined by any number of considerations that later on, when it became important to define and classify them, were reduced in numbers and even changed in their relative importance.

1024. It is certain that in historical times the family was the nucleus of the Roman gens; but it is just as certain that the tie of kinship was not the only thing that figured in making up the gens. We must not become involved here in the intricate question as to whether the gens was made up of one, or of more than one, family. In the historical period girls of one gens were given in marriage to men of another gens. To be rid of one difficulty we might assume that that did not occur in times more ancient, but there would still be the question of adoption and "adrogation," which admitted outsiders to the gens. We might ignore that too. But still insuperable difficulties would remain. Legitimate birth was not alone enough to make a male child a member of the gens. He was presented to the father soon after birth, and the father might accept or repudiate him (*liberum repudiare, negare*). That arrangement was common to Greece and Rome. It has not the slightest appearance of being a custom of late date. Indeed it has all the ear-marks of coming down from a remote antiquity, and it is sufficient all by itself to show that there is something more to the gens and the γένος than descent from a common ancestor.

1025. Then come the appendages to the family, and consequently to the gens and the γένος—they are considered "appendages" because it had been decided *a priori* that blood-descent had to be the sole origin of the family group. But can we be sure that such "appendages" were not really organic survivals of the more primitive group? So in India now the practice of admitting outsiders into a caste is regarded as an abuse, and an abuse it may well be today; but who can be sure that in ancient times that was not one of the ways in which a caste was formed?[1]

1025 [1] Sénart, *Les castes dans l'Inde,* pp. 94 f.: "There has always been a rank growth of sects in India, and that sort of vegetation is far from dying out today. New sects turn up from year to year—only to be absorbed very soon, to be sure, in the rising tide of orthodox Hinduism, so called in spite of its composite character. As a rule such religious movements are very circumscribed, coming down to mere handfuls of ascetics who decide to consecrate themselves to penitence and celibacy and therefore reject the basic premise of caste—heredity. They recruit their forces from voluntary applicants or from children borrowed from other castes. All the same a number of such brotherhoods have members from both sexes and themselves develop into castes that are more or less hereditary. The movements so arising in the castes and continually modifying their inner structure are either individual or collective. Now by favour of influential patrons, now by trickery, now by fraud, now by corruption, certain people find ways of getting into this caste or that as individuals. That is the frequent case in the frontier districts, where observances are less strict. There have been instances where individuals from all the different castes have been made Brahmans by caprice of some ruler. A caste, moreover, may not be very strict and may open its ranks quite readily under certain conditions. There are clans of nomads and criminals that make a practice of admitting new members on money-terms." Such things have always happened. It is the grossest of errors to imagine that reality always tallies exactly with the abstractions of law-makers and men of letters.

1026. The Graeco-Roman clientage is the most interesting example of such appendages to the family. It throws a vivid light on the character of the vital cell in those ancient societies, as constituted not merely by the nucleus of individuals of common descent, but by individuals living together in close association and bound together by ties of common rights and duties. In Athens the new slave was made a part of the family by a religious initiation. Under the law of Gortyna, when a family became completely extinct, its lands went to such of its serfs as were bound to the soil.

1027. All that being undeniable, the tie of common descent had to be supplemented with the tie of religion in order to account for family, gens, and γένος. And in that we do get a little closer to reality, since religion is indeed one of the forms in which the ties of fact that supplement the tie of blood find expression. But it is a dangerous procedure to substitute the sign for the thing, the manifestation of a thing for the thing itself. It might lead one to imagining that religion was the "origin" of family, gens, and γένος, and that would be to go wide of the mark.

1028. Fustel de Coulanges assigns that very office to religion. The only hypotheses he considers are the first (the family unit) and the third (legal artifice) (§ 1021). He has no difficulty in showing that the blood-tie is not sufficient to account for the gens and the γένος, and to that extent his demonstration serves to call attention to other ties too. He also shows that the gens and the γένος cannot have originated as devices of law-makers. But he gives no evidence to show that his argument, which designates religion as the "origin" of those groups, is anything more than the usual *post hoc, propter hoc*. And just that is the weak point in his theory.

1029. On the theory that the gens was an artificial creation, he says, *La cité antique*, p. 119 (Small, p. 141): "Another defect in that system is that it assumes that human societies can have been instituted by agreement, by artifice. Historical science can grant no such assumption."

1030. Quite so. But it is just as impossible to assume that beliefs can have preceded the facts to which they relate. At the most, it is conceivable that believers in a revealed religion may admit as much in the case of *their own* religion. A Christian may well believe that the dogmas of his faith antedate the facts to which they relate; but that same Christian will not grant as much for pagan rites. And even if one adopt the theory of the decadence and perversion of a revealed religion, it must further be admitted that that decadence and perversion must have been determined by the facts, and did not arise independently of them.

1031. The religion of Graeco-Roman antiquity stands in close relation to the constitution of the groups comprising the social cellules. It grew out of residues originating in the permanence of those organisms and in turn guaranteeing their existence and permanence (§ 1013).

1032. The residues were very much alike in Greece and Rome. They developed differing derivations owing to the different temperaments of the two peoples. The residues that built up the family religions became, with a few modifications and additions, the residues that built up the city-state religions. Small wonder that those religions should show the trait noted by Reinach (§ 383)—"a sum of scruples interfering with the free exercise of human faculties"; since those residues corresponded exactly to the sum of ties—of obstacles to the free exercise of the faculties—that gave being and strength to the social cellule. Every theory is inclined to overstress the importance of its own principles; hence religion, which was a manifestation of existing ties, created in its turn new ties, and sometimes absurd ones. It has been many times said and well said that religion embraced every act of ancient life; but it would be even better to say that religion was the manifestation of ties, whether spontaneous or artificial, that figured in every act of ancient life. The separation of religion and state may have some meaning for modern peoples; but it could have had none for Graeco-Roman antiquity, where it would have meant the separation of the ties of civic life from the ties of the state. The tolerance of the ancient Roman city for various religions provided they wrought no offence to the national worship corresponds exactly to the tolerance the modern civil state has for various systems of morality and certain personal individual codes, provided these involve no infringement on positive legislation.

1033. The city cults were largely patterned on the family cults, and the imitation was direct. The worship of the domestic hearth-fire became the worship of the sacred fire of the city, in the Greek Prytaneum and in the Roman Temple of Vesta. But there are cases where a public cult originates not in the domestic cult but in the same residues that engendered the latter, there being no direct imitation, or at least apparently none.

1034. The Roman Penates correspond, in part at least, to the notion of domestic food-supply. The importance attached to provisioning by ancient families, the precautions that had to be taken to avoid famine, the agreeable sentiments connected with abundance, all corresponded to a powerful residue that expressed itself in the religious status of the Penates, divinities which were also associated with other residues of the same sort.

1035. Similar, at a much later day, the origin of the deification of the harvest—Annona (§§ 996 f.). Yet in that, so far as we know, no direct imitation was involved; the deification of Annona was not a copy either of the household worship or of the public worship of the Penates. It originated in the very same sentiments that found expression earlier in the ascription of a religious status to domestic provisioning.

1036. The Greek tribes had eponymic heroes and Greek and Latin cities had founders more or less deified. Those facts have been regarded as copies of real facts of descent, family, gens, and γένος coming from a single ancestor. That may well be. It may also well not be, the original ancestor being as much of a fiction as the eponymic hero and the divine founder. We can come to no decision so long as direct proofs are lacking.

1037. The Middle Ages saw a recurrence in the Latin countries of Europe of circumstances in part similar to the conditions under which the ancient families of the Latin races came into being; and just as a confederation of independent families produced the ancient city, so the feudal hierarchy produced the monarchies of centuries past. The feudal group had a family nucleus with appendages of extraneous elements. Says Flach:[1] "A family grouped around its chief forms the kernel of a far more extensive comradeship, the importance of which seems not to have received sufficient stress from historians—the *maisnie*, the lord's house, his chosen body-guard, the centre of resistance in his army, his best counsel, his daily *entourage*. The *maisnie* fills out, apart from the natural family, with the children and relatives of the vassals or the more trusted allies, and even with foreigners."[2] As was the case in more ancient times, religion interposes to give expression to the ties binding the group and to re-enforce them. But the circumstances were in part different. Ancient families built up their own religions and therefore deified the things that promoted the ties. Feudal families had a religion ready-made outside their circle, and the process of deification was already complete. They therefore created no new divinities, but applied those already existing to their own needs. After describing the rites of *commendation* and *homage*, Flach adds, *Op. cit.*, p. 522: "But the authority thus established over the person was so established only with a view to his becoming a member of the household, which was

1037 [1] *Les origines de l'ancienne France*, Vol. II, pp. 455-56.

1037 [2] Fustel de Coulanges, *Op. cit.*, pp. 96, 126-27 (Small, p. 116): "Thanks to the domestic religion, the family was a small organized body, a diminutive society with its leader and its government. [Drop the allusion to the domestic religion and the description serves just as well for the feudal *maisnie*. Amend the wording to read that religion strengthened the association and gave it new power, and the parallel becomes complete.] . . . But the family of those distant ages was nothing like as small as the modern family. In great societies the family is broken up and reduced in numbers. But in the absence of any other society, it spreads out, develops, ramifies, without dividing. A number of junior branches remain grouped about the elder branch [So far the description applies exactly to the feudal family, a difference appearing only in the following:] before a single hearth around a common tomb. Another element also entered into the composition of this ancient family [and of the feudal clan]. The reciprocal need that the poor man has of the rich man and the rich man of the poor man created servants. But in that sort of patriarchal régime servant is synonymous with slave. One can readily see, in fact, that the principle of free voluntary service to be ended at the will of the subordinate can hardly be consonant with a social situation where the family lives in isolation all to itself. [The remark applies to the feudal family also.] The servant must in some way become a member of the family, and an integral part of the family." And both the ancient family and the feudal *maisnie* made provision for that very thing.

embodied in the lord [As it was of yore, in the *paterfamilias*.⁸], to his affiliation with the family unit, along with the rights and duties which such association entailed. Now that initiation took place with the most earnest, the most solemn, ceremony known to human beings in primitive societies—the swearing of a religious vow. In pagan times the person so affiliated became a participant in the domestic worship: he delivered himself, 'devoted' himself, body and soul, to a new family, and if he failed to keep faith he drew upon his head the vengeance of the gods. [Those are derivations: in more ancient times, religion was itself the manifestation of those ties.] In the Christian era the vow by which the vassal engaged his person was a most formidable one. It made martyrs of individuals who sacrificed their lives to remain faithful to it, outcasts of those who violated it."

1038. Pertile rejects the theory that fiefs originated in the clientage of ancient Roman law or in the military benefices of the Empire: [1] "Just as there is no continuity in time," he says, "between those institutions and the fiefs, so there can have been no connexion between them." Pertile is right in the sense that there was no direct imitation, just as we saw above that the goddess Annona was not directly derived from the Penates. But it would be erroneous not to recognize their common origin. The same sentiments (residues), acting under circumstances of fact in large part similar, and in part also different, resulted in institutions in large part similar, and in part also different—ancient clientage on the one hand, and on the other "commendation," benefices, fiefs.

1039. Pertile says, *Op. cit.*, p. 203, that "in clientage . . . the real element is entirely missing." That is the common error of jurists, who are more inclined to consider forms than substance. In ancient clientage the real element was lacking in law, but not in the fact.

1037 ⁸ *Ulpian, Digesta, Lib. L., tit.* 16, sec. 195, § 2 (*Corpus iuris civilis*, Vol. I, p. 970; Scott, Vol. XI, p. 286): *"Pater autem familias appellatur qui in domo dominium habet, recteque hoc nomine appellatur quamvis filium non habeat."* ("The term 'paterfamilias' is applied to the man who has authority over the household, and he is properly so called even though he have no child.")
1038 ¹ *Storia del diritto italiano*, Vol. I, p. 204.

Nor was the military element lacking in the fact, in the sense that the client stood by his patron even in quarrels involving violence.

1040. Consider, for example, the story of Eumaeus in the *Odyssey,* XIV, vv. 55-71. Eumaeus, a servant of Ulysses, says that his lord, were he to return, would give to him, Eumaeus, "the things that an affectionate patron giveth to a servant who hath laboured well," that is, a house, a piece of land, and a wife. In the house and the land we have, *in the fact,* the real element. Ulysses reveals his identity to Eumaeus, and the latter fights at his patron's side to defeat the suitors. From all of which it is evident that *in the fact* he stands towards Ulysses in the same relation as a vassal towards the feudal lord.

1041. II-α2: *Relations with places.* These residues often blend with residues of the preceding variety (family and group relations) and with II-β residues (living and dead). Even moderns speak of their "native land," their "old home," which is not necessarily the birthplace but the place where the family lives, or has lived, and where they have spent their childhood. Among the ancients of the Graeco-Roman world relations to places combined with relations of family and groups (*gens, γένος*) and with relations to the dead to form a unit sum of residues.

1042. Something similar takes place among modern peoples. Looking at things superficially, one might imagine that patriotism of the modern type is a matter of territory, since the modern nations take their names from the territories they occupy. But looking a little more closely, one perceives that in awakening sentiments of patriotism the territorial name suggests a sum of sentiments, language, religion, traditions, history, and so on. In reality patriotism cannot be exactly defined, any more than "religion," "morality," "justice," "the good," "the beautiful," can be exactly defined. All such terms merely call to mind certain cumulations of sentiments of no sharply defined forms and with very vague limits (§§ 380 f.), the various units being held together by the residues of group-persistence.

1043. II-α3: *Relationships of social class.* Living in a given group impresses the mind with certain concepts, certain ways of thinking and doing, certain prejudices, certain beliefs, which, as is the case with so many other entities of the kind, endure in time and acquire a pseudo-objective individuality. The residues corresponding to them have in the past often assumed the forms of residues of family relationships. It has been imagined that social classes and even nations were so many lineages each with some common ancestor, real or mythical, and each indeed with its own gods, who were enemies of the gods of other groups. But the latter is a mere derivation, and among modern peoples it has fallen into desuetude.

1044. The form of the caste in India is unique, but the underlying substance is very very general. Something similar is observable in all countries, and oftentimes with greatest intensity in countries that make a show of some principle of equality. The distance between an American millionaire and a plain American is greater than the distance between a German nobleman and a German factory-hand. It is something like the distances between the castes in India, which is nothing like the distance between whites and blacks in the United States.

1045. In Europe the propaganda of the Marxian "class struggle," or rather, the conditions that found their expression in that manner, served to awaken or intensify corresponding residues in the "proletariat," or to be more exact, in a part of the population; whereas the concern felt by business men (*entrepreneurs*) not to run counter to democratic sentiments, in fact to exploit them for purposes of money-making, weakened or destroyed certain residues of collectivity in the higher social classes.

1046. A number of traits observable in the Jews of our time, and which are ordinarily ascribed to race, are mere manifestations of residues produced by long centuries of oppression. And the proof is easy; one need only compare a Russian Jew with an English Jew. The Russian Jew is readily distinguished from his Christian neighbours; not at all so the English Jew. And then there are the intermediary types, corresponding to the longer or shorter duration of the oppression. It is a well-known fact that the various professions often develop distinct types of individuality—in other words, present different residues corresponding to the respective type of activity.

1047. The associations known as sects, when held together by strong and exclusive sentiments, have well-known traits that have been observed in all periods of history. The persistence of relations within the sect strengthens such traits and weakens the effect that conflict with other sentiments operating outside the sect would otherwise have upon them. Hence one of the outstanding characteristics of sectarians: They lose the perception other people generally have of the relative values of things. What others may regard as a very mild sin, the sectarian may deem a serious crime;[1] and *vice versa,* what the former consider shameful or criminal the sectarian may regard as honourable and above-board.[2] The spy, the informer, is generally considered a dishonourable person; but in the days of the Inquisition many people thought spying a duty, as contributing to the extermi-

1047 [1] Countess Lydia Rostoptchine, *Les Rostoptchine,* pp. 222-26: "I remarked above how my grandmother detested drunkenness, a very natural vice that is intensified in the Russian by the severity of our climate. She made no distinction between the inveterate drunkard and the man who had overtasted by mere chance—a matter of a good time or of forgetting. Both in her eyes were equally deserving of the knout and Siberia. . . . On another occasion painfully graven in my memory, we were again walking on the drive when a woman, her clothing torn and stained with blood, came running towards us as fast as she could, pursued by the hostlers. She had escaped from the stable where she had been receiving a flogging. The poor woman threw herself at my grandmother's feet sobbing. I shall never forget the horror of the scene . . . the prostrate victim, and the impalcable suzerain sternly inquiring as to the cause of the punishment that Timothy had ordered. At mention of the hated name of vodka, and deaf to the vehement prayers of my mother and my father's more timid protests, my grandmother, whom I was enraged at that moment to call by that name, turned her back without a word and resumed her walk. The hostlers approached, seized the woman by the wrists, and dragged her off to receive the remainder of her punishment. And the poor thing was with child!"

1047 [2] Cunningham, *Two Years in New South Wales,* Vol. II, pp. 257-58 (anent convicts deported to Australia): "Designations of individual character have among them a very different meaning to what is attached thereto in honest society. A *good fellow* is one who divides fairly with his companions whatever he thieves in partnership, and who never confesses a theft or gives evidence against an associate. A *clever fellow* is a bang-up, bold, thorough-going knave, an able 'actor of all work'; while a *great scoundrel* is one who will be *base* enough to acknowledge his crime, or inform upon his partner." So now in our countries, in the eyes of certain people, a "good judge" is a judge who rules against the law, a "bad judge," one who conscientiously upholds it.

nation of heretics of Catholicism. Today it is also considered honourable and obligatory by many persons, as contributing to the extermination of heretics of the sex religion of our high-priests of purity. Notorious, in Italy, the Camorra and the Maffia; but the basic principles of Camorra and Maffia are applied in various cases in other quarters, as when members of the parliament refuse to permit prosecutions of their colleagues for crimes or misdemeanours that are in no sense political, for private slanders, and even for violations of the traffic regulations: that certainly is a legislators' Camorra, no more and no less. To satisfy a humanitarian caprice a jury at Interlaken allowed Tatiana Leontieff to get off with a very light penalty for murdering an aged and harmless unfortunate. To humour another whim, whether humanitarian or merely half-witted would be hard to say, a French jury acquitted a young man who had killed his father. Such people really consider themselves superior to criminals and far, far superior to the "despots who rule unhappy peoples."

1048. Sentiments may become so cogent in sectarians as to impel them to any extreme of crime—the very term "assassin" is derived from the feats of a certain historic association of criminals. All that is very well known; but not so commonly realized is the fact that the difference between certain acts, from the abject delations of our paladins of purity down to a murder committed by a gangster, is a difference only in intensity of sentiments, and sometimes only a difference in the courage of the persons involved—the difference, let us say, between the murderer who poisons an enemy and the murderer who faces his enemy revolver in hand.

1049. The notion, widely prevalent among uncivilized peoples, that anything is permissible against a foreigner or an enemy, that the moral laws in force in relations between citizens of the same country cease to apply in dealings with outsiders and enemies, is another expression of the residues of class. Such notions have been entertained even by civilized peoples—the Romans, for instance—and have not entirely disappeared among our contemporaries (§ 1050 [2]). Modern civilized peoples, as was the case in ancient Greece, have mutual relations with one another not greatly at variance with the moral laws prevailing at home; but they feel no obligation to consider them in dealing with uncivilized peoples, or peoples whom they consider such.

1050. Aristotle's theory of natural slavery, *Politica,* I, 2, 3-23 (Rackham, pp. 15-31), is the theory put forward by modern civilized peoples to justify their conquests of peoples whom they call "inferior" and their dominion over them. Aristotle said that some men are naturally slaves and others masters, and that it is proper for the ones to obey and the others to command, the which is just and of benefit to all concerned. So say the modern peoples who decorate themselves with the title "civilized." They assert that there are peoples—themselves, of course—who were intended by Nature to rule, and other peoples—those whom they wish to exploit—who were no less intended by Nature to obey, and that it is just, proper, and to the advantage of everyone concerned that they do the ruling and the others the obeying. Whence it follows that if an Englishman, a German, a Frenchman, a Belgian, an Italian, fights and dies for his country, he is a hero; but if an African dares defend his homeland against any one of those nations, he is a contemptible rebel and traitor. So the Europeans are performing a sacrosanct duty in exterminating Africans in an effort to teach them to be civilized. And there are always plenty of people to admire such work "of peace, progress, and civilization," with mouths agape! With a hypocrisy truly admirable, these blessed civilized peoples claim to be acting for the good of their subject races in oppressing and exterminating them; indeed so dearly do they love them that they would have them "free" by force. So the English freed the Hindus from the "tyranny" of the rajahs. So the Germans freed the Africans from the tyranny of their black kings. So the Italians freed the Arabs from the oppression of the Turks. So the French freed the Madagascans and—to make them freer still—killed not a few of them and reduced the rest to a condition that is slavery in all but the name. Such talk is uttered in all seriousness, and there are even people who believe it. The cat catches the mouse and eats it; but it does not pretend to be doing so for the good of the mouse. It does not proclaim any dogma that all animals are equal, nor lift its eyes hypocritically to heaven in worship of the Father of us all.[1]

1051. The theory of the superiority of the civilized peoples is for the most part used only against non-Europeans. But Prussians use it

1050 [1] For example, the Belgian Congo. Besides the minutes and documents of official investigations see Conan Doyle, *The Crime of the Congo.* As for the Portuguese, I quote from *Liberté,* Aug. 9, 1912: "In answer to charges of cruelty made against Portuguese planters in Angola, one of them has published a large volume vaunting the good treatment that Negroes 'bonded under contract' have been receiving from his fellow-residents in the colony. In [? an article in] *France d'outre mer,* M. René Claparède, general secretary of the International Committee on the Congo Leagues, refutes such assertions. He claims that the Negroes bonded under alleged contracts are actual slaves, the contracts being automatically renewable. That transforms the contract into servitude for life. As for the good treatment boasted by the Portuguese, it is so effective that the mortality-rate among the blacks is more than 10 per cent on the Portuguese islands, whereas it is lower than 2.6 per cent in Jamaica and Trinidad. The unhappy Negroes therefore do their best to escape from the plantations and get into the woods. Then comes the man-hunt that M. Claparède describes, following an account given him by a planter who had taken part in one. "The hunters," says M. Claparède, "had been taken by guides to a place for which it was known the fugitives had started. They came to some huts that had just been deserted. An old Negro was found near by hiding in the grass. 'We took him,' said the planter, 'and forced him to tell where the other slaves were. At first we could get nothing out of him, but after a time, without uttering a word, he pointed with his hand towards the tallest trees. There they were, men and women, clinging to the branches like so many bats! It was not long, I can assure you, before we had brought them all down through the foliage. What a bag we made that day!' " Such criticisms were published against Portugal and Belgium because they were not very powerful countries; but nothing was said about things equally bad or even worse that the English, Germans, and French were doing. The Belgian Government made reparation to a large extent for the oppression practised in the Congo by King Leopold's "Administration"; and the Portuguese Republic made full reparation for the oppression tolerated by the monarchy; whereas the larger "civilized" countries continue conquering the lands of so called barbarous peoples or maintaining their former rule over them, spreading death, affliction, and ruin in all such territories. Even the ultra-civilized Americans are acting no differently in their treatment of the wretched natives of the Philippines and the remnants of the Redskins, whom they have robbed of their ancestral lands. I will quote in point a document published in *Liberté,* July 21, 1913: *"Le Sort des Peaux-Rouges"* ("The Lot of the Redskins"): "A recent investigation by the New York *Herald* specifies the misdeeds of the Yankee administration, and here is the opinion of a specialist, Robert G. Valentine, formerly Commissioner of Indian Affairs: 'It is astounding to note that the whites follow quite different moral codes according as they are dealing with other white men or with Indians. People who would never think of stealing from their white neighbours find it quite natural to swindle an

also against the Poles; and there are Germans who would use it against the Latin peoples, regarding them as barbarians in comparison with the surpassingly excellent, moral, virtuous, intelligent, civilized, and so on, Germanic stock. In England and North America there are those who arrogate the same outstanding superiorities to the divine breed of the Anglo-Saxon. Such people always consider themselves rigidly "scientific" and ridicule those who differ with them as victims of outworn prejudices.[1]

1052. II-β: *Persistence of relations between the living and the dead.* The sum of relations between an individual and other individuals persists, by abstraction, in the absence of that individual or after his death. That explains residues which figure in vast numbers

Indian. They know, furthermore, that in doing so they run no risks. The swindlers themselves are not so much to blame as the American public which encourages their crimes by its indifference. I have plenty of proof available, and the facts in my possession are so abominable that a jury could not fail to punish them as they deserve. . . . A device often resorted to to deprive Indians of their money is to induce them to deposit their funds in banks which shortly afterwards go into fraudulent bankruptcy, the dishonest bankers then dividing the spoils with government agents. They have nine chances out of ten of going unpunished. Worse yet, Indians resisting the demands of white intruders have been murdered. A case of that kind occurred last year in Johnston County, Oklahoma, where two Cherokees who were not willing to "come across" were mercilessly "executed." In this case the courts had to interfere, and it developed that the county judge was in league with a gang of criminals engaged in fleecing the Indians of the county. The judge was impeached, and three or four convictions were obtained. However, the courts are in general very lax, and prosecutions involving the tribes very long protracted. . . . Then there is the case of the Pimas. That tribe had shown itself very industrious and was making a comfortable living off its lands. The activities of white men have reduced the Pimas to idleness, pauperism, and ruin. Land speculators have so manoeuvred as to get possession of the timber, pastures, and mines of the Pimas for insignificant sums. Arizona had hardly been admitted to the Union before white speculators were at work on the Navajos, a peaceful self-respecting people, because their lands had risen in value. It was again a story of intimidation and seizure.' " Such things are nothing as compared with the lynchings of Negroes and other such trifles. American missionaries are at sedulous pains to note the motes in other countries. They would do well to attend to some of the beams lying about in their own.

1051 [1] Napoleone Colajanni has well shown the fatuity of all such race chatter in his *Latini e anglo-sassoni: razze inferiori e razze superiori.* Arcangelo Ghisleri has also deflated various balloons of racial hypocrisy in a number of publications: [*e.g., Le razze umane ed il diritto nella questione coloniale; Metafisica tedesca e mentalità italiana.*]

of phenomena.[1] They are in some respects similar to II-α residues, and that explains why they are found combined with them in many many cases, such as family, caste, patriotism, religion, and so on. In combination with IV-δ2 residues (§§ 1149 f.), which prompt sharing of possessions with the objects of one's love or goodwill, they appear in such complex phenomena as honouring or worshipping the dead, or banquets and sacrifices connected with funerals or commemorations.

1053. Those who will have logical explanations for all human beliefs imagine that such phenomena presuppose belief in the immortality of the soul, for without such a postulate they would not be logical. To refute that notion, one need merely observe, ignoring countless other proofs, that among the people right about us, materialists are not less punctilious than others in honouring their dead, in spite of their philosophy; and that in London and Paris, to say nothing of other cities, there are cemeteries for dogs where such pets are buried by people who certainly do not credit the dog with an immortal soul.

1054. Ghosts, apparitions of the dead, which have at all times been taken seriously more or less everywhere, are nothing but tangible forms given to residues of persisting relations between the living and the dead, which by analogy also figure to some extent in ap-

---

1052 [1] Describing the Tahitians in his *Account of a Voyage to the Pacific Ocean*, Vol. II, pp. 164-65, Captain Cook speaks largely in terms of derivations, but that does not altogether conceal the residue: "The only great privilege they seem to think they shall acquire by death is immortality; for they speak of spirits being in some measure not totally divested of those passions which actuated them when combined with material vehicles. Thus if souls who were formerly enemies should meet, they have many conflicts; though it should seem, to no purpose, as they are accounted invulnerable in this invisible state. There is a similar reasoning with regard to the meeting of man and wife. If the husband dies first, the soul of his wife is known to him on its arrival in the land of the spirits. They resume their former acquaintance in a spacious house called *Tourova*, where the souls of the deceased assemble to recreate themselves with the Gods. She then retires with him to his separate habitation, where they remain forever, and have an offspring which, however, is entirely spiritual, as they are neither married, nor are their embraces supposed to be the same as with corporeal beings." The derivations are illogical and absurd simply because they are so irrelevant, the residues being the important thing.

paritions of divinities, angels, devils, fairies, and other personified entities of the kind. In our day they are satisfied by "double personalities," telepathy, and other such trumpery.

1055. It is apparent, on close scrutiny, that the concept of the survival of the dead is at bottom merely the extension of another notion which is very powerful in the human being, the notion that the individuality of a person is a unit over the course of the years. In reality both the physical and the psychic elements in the human being change. Neither materially nor morally is an aged man identical with the child he was. And yet we feel that in him there is something which endures the same. Overstepping the experimental field, people call it a "soul," without being able to explain very clearly what becomes of such a soul in lunacy, for example, or in "second childhood," or just when, between the time when the human egg is fertilized and the first cry of the new-born babe, such a soul finds its way into the body. Such matters need not concern us here, since they transcend the confines of the experimental field within which we have chosen to remain. Our point is merely to show that one same residue is present in the belief in the unity of the living individuality and in the belief in survival after death.

1056. II-γ : *Persistence of relations between a dead person and the things that belonged to him in life*. The relations of a man to the things once belonging to him endure in the minds of the living after his death. Hence the widely prevalent custom of burying or burning such objects with a corpse, or otherwise destroying them, and that of killing his wives, his slaves, his animals.

1057. As usual a logical explanation of such customs puts in an appearance; and again as usual, they are regarded as corollaries of a belief in another life for the person who has died. If a man's weapons are laid in his tomb, it is in order that he may use them in a life to come. Libations are poured on his grave, and food left, that his soul may eat and drink. Living beings are sacrificed that he may find company and service over there.

1058. Such beliefs there certainly were; but they are derivations —that is to say, they are essentially variable; whereas the constant element in all that is the persistence of the relations between the dead person and the things that were once his.

1059. Read, for example, the account of the funeral of Patroclus in the *Iliad,* XXIII, vv. 65-98. The ghost of Patroclus appears in a dream to Achilles. He in no wise asks him for utensils or living beings for his service in another life. All he asks of his friend (vv. 83-84) is that their ashes may rest together in the same urn. There we have our residue, virtually without any derivation whatever; and it is a residue so powerful that it has stood intact over these many centuries and over so many changes in peoples and beliefs. It is usual enough in our day for people to provide in their wills that their bodies shall rest near the bodies of loved ones. Be they Christians or free-thinkers, there is nothing in their beliefs that logically can prompt them to do any such thing; they are merely inspired by the sentiments manifested in this residue. The Myrmidons of Achilles each consecrate their shocks of hair to Patroclus (vv. 135-36). What use could he have for such a gift in another life? Nor could the twelve Trojan prisoners who were slaughtered on his pyre have made very agreeable companions for him. Why should we think differently of the four horses and the two dogs that were likewise slaughtered? In any event there is nothing whatever in the poem to justify the assumption that they were to be of service to the soul of Patroclus. Champions of the logical explanation may object that, "originally," living creatures were sacrificed to attend on the soul of the dead, and that later on, the meaning of the tradition being lost, human beings and animals were slain more or less at random. But that would be a mere hypothesis not supported by any facts, nor even by any analogy with other facts; for in general, the non-logical act precedes the logical act, and the assumption there would be that the opposite was the case.

1060. The pyre on which the body of Patroclus has been burned is extinguished with wine (*Ibid.,* v. 250). The intention was to honour the hero with the use of that precious liquid (I-β2). Not the slightest hint in the poem suggests that Patroclus was to drink the wine. In the *Odyssey,* Ulysses pours libations of water, honey, and wine in honour of the dead, and sprinkles flour. The dead do not taste of any such offerings. They do come running to drink the blood of the victims! Elpenor requests Ulysses to burn his panoply with his body, but there is no indication that he is to use the weapons in another life. They are burned for the same reason that an oar is planted on the mound covering the body of Elpenor. What we have there is simply a persistence of the relations between a man and the things that belonged to him. The mother of Ulysses says: ". . . as soon as life has left the white bones, the soul flits hither and thither abroad like a dream." She makes no mention whatever of having with her the objects that were placed on her tomb or burned on her pyre.

1061. So cogent is the preconception in favour of logical explanations that a writer will often add one quite unconsciously to a description. In the more ancient tombs in Egypt objects that were once used by the living are found with their bones. We have no documents whatever to indicate just what relations obtained between such things in the eyes of the Egyptians of those days. Yet a very distinguished Egyptologist, Erman, no less, describes what he sees as follows (gratuitous logical explanations in italics): "In those ancient times, some object was placed in the hands of the deceased, *in the belief that it would be of service to him in death.* So one of the ancient cadavers in our collection still holds the large stone on which in his lifetime he was wont to grind the green pigment that he used for colouring his body. Another has a leathern purse in his hand. But a great many other things are placed near the corpse: pots, above all, and ladles, with food and drink, *in order that the deceased may not suffer from hunger;* harpoons and stone knives, *that he may hunt his food and defend himself against his enemies;* a chequer-board, *for his entertainment during leisure hours.* . . . There are other things too which can have had no use save in a supernatural sense. The little clay bark is to aid him in crossing the lakes that . . . surround the celestial fields of the blest. The clay bull will be slaughtered for him, and the hippopotamus, of the same material, will be his game. The clay maidservant in the large vat will knead barley-meal with her feet in preparing his beer for him. . . . To the other female figure, coy, composed, *the duty evidently falls of supplying her lord with the consolations of love;* and so she is painted in beautiful colours of varied hue, as though she were about to be decked and crowned with flowers; and her thighs and legs have that sinewy development which the African of our day still regards as the supreme ideal of feminine beauty." [1]

1062. It is certain that in later ages such logical explanations corresponded exactly with popular beliefs; but that in no way proves that there was the same correspondence in a much earlier period for which we have no documents. Yet these logical explanations assume just that.

1063. Finally, the fact of chronological evolution is one thing and the fact of residues and derivations quite another. There is no occasion for speculating as to how the first fact arose in ages about which we know nothing, when we are studying the second in times that we know very well, as witness the following example.

1064. In December, 1911, a band of thieves desecrated the tomb of

---

1061 [1] *Aegyptische Religion,* p. 116 (Johns, pp. 115-16). Naville, *La religion des anciens égyptiens,* pp. 45-47: "In historical times one notes in the Egyptians very positive ideas that inclined them to make mummies of their dead. They attached great importance to that rite, and it was so solidly grounded in their consciousness that the custom lasted down into the Christian era and even called forth severe reproof from certain of the Church Fathers. (*Cf.* § 1004 [1].) The mummy has become almost symbolic of the dead of the Land of Egypt, and that seems always to have been the case. Great, therefore, was the astonishment of the early excavators who found that in a very ancient period, prehistoric or primitive as one may choose to call it, things were not the same. Modes of burial at that time seem to have corresponded to quite a different conception than came to prevail later on. [Better: burial customs changed with changes in the concepts correlated with such customs.] In the necropolès of the native population that was eventually subjugated by conquerors from abroad, one finds little rectangular or oval graves. The corpses are buried in them intact without any trace of a mummification process. The knees are drawn up against the chest. . . . That has been called the embryonic position and has been interpreted as a posture preparatory to second birth, it being the one best adapted to a body about to be reborn to a new life. [The usual abuse of logical interpretation.] I find that explanation a little abstruse for such a crude people. Another much simpler one is suggested by the Father of History, Herodotus." The suggestion was, in brief (*Historiae,* IV, 190), that the custom came from such peoples as the Nasamones, who kept the dying in a sitting posture after the Oriental manner.

Mme. Lantelme for the purpose of stealing the very rare and very valuable jewels that had been buried with the actress some days previous. Their venture was not successful. The envelope that contained the jewels was found in the grave. Now in this case two things are as certain as certain can be: 1. That the jewels were buried with the dead actress. 2. That the persons responsible for that act did not in the least imagine that the jewels would be of actual use to the lady in some other life. Now supposing two or three thousand years hence that tomb were to be discovered with its jewels, just as we are nowadays finding other tombs of past ages containing weapons and jewels; and supposing the discoverers, reasoning as we do now, were to conclude that people of this age of ours believed that a dead person was to use the things that were buried with him in an after-life. Such a conclusion would be manifestly erroneous. Now we are drawing similar conclusions about peoples of the past in the same way from identical facts. Why are ours not just as far wrong? We are merely stressing the possibility of the error. We are not saying that it is necessarily so. But the mere possibility is enough to discredit a reasoning that may be summarized in the following terms: "To our way of thinking, certain facts have only one logical explanation. Those facts, therefore, necessarily arose in the manner indicated by our explanation." No, they may have taken place in some other way; and the choice between the various ways must be made in the light of direct proofs and not indirectly on the basis of inferences that facts have often proved to be fallacious. We must work from the known to the unknown, explaining facts with other facts, not with the impressions our minds have of them (§ 547).

1065. II-δ: *Persistence of abstractions.* After an agglomerate of relations has grown up, either in the manner described in § 991 or in some other, a corresponding abstraction appears that may persist in time; and then a new subjective entity comes into being.

1066. Such residues underlie theologies and systems of metaphysics, which might properly be defined as cumuli of derivations from such residues. Hence the great importance of theologies and metaphysical systems—not the importance they are supposed to have when considered as logical sciences, but as expressing residues that correspond to powerful social forces.

1067. From that standpoint past and present alike show remarkable uniformity. There is, however, a difference in the matter of personification of abstractions, which among our Western people was far more characteristic of the past than it is of more recent times. Let us glance at one or two abstractions that are so important as to deserve classification by themselves.[1]

1068. II-ε: *Persistence of uniformities.* An important instance of the persistence of abstractions is the common procedure of generalizing a particular uniformity or even a single, isolated fact. A fact is observed. It is stated in abstract language. The abstraction persists and becomes a general rule. The thing is a matter of everyday occurrence. We may even go so far as to say that that is the characteristic manner of reasoning of people not trained to scientific thinking and even of many who are. Very few people indeed state particular facts under particular forms, and are able to distinguish that form of expression from the other which states a general rule, and furthermore to distinguish the rule that is an instrument of research and subject to experimental verification from the rule that is assumed to be above such verification (§ 63). Going to extremes in the direction of abstractions superior to experience, we get metaphysical principles, "natural" principles, "necessary" relationships, and the like (§ 531).[1]

1069. II-ζ: *Sentiments transformed into objective realities.* Such residues are exceedingly numerous, so much so that they are rarely absent from any discussion that is not conducted with strictest scientific exactitude. They underlie all subjective proofs derived from sentiments, and they exert a powerful influence upon the considerations that inspire the production and acceptance of theories (§ 13). The introspection of the metaphysician, the "inner experience" of the

---

1067 [1] To avoid repetitions we shall postpone our discussion of certain other abstractions till later on (§§ 1070 f.), when we come to the matter of personifications.

1068 [1] Of these as well as of the following residues (II-ζ) we need give no examples here, since we deal with them in great numbers in the whole course of these volumes.

Christian, and other similar manners of thinking, all involve transformations of sentiments into objective realities.

1070. II-η: *Personifications.* The lowest degree of personification lies in the naming of an abstraction, a uniformity, or a sentiment, and so transforming them into objective individualities. Thence, step by step, we mount to the highest degree, where the personification is complete and we get anthropomorphism.[1] Bringing in the sex residue we get male and female principles, or divinities in every respect similar to men and women. Places and things may also be personified, without there being on that account any deification. Such personifications arise spontaneously in the mind independently of any process of reasoning.[2]

1071. Language is a very effective instrument for lending continuity to such groups and for personifying them; and the mere bestowal of a name on a sum of abstractions is often sufficient to transform it into an objective individuality. Conversely, every name is supposed to have some such reality corresponding to it (§§ 1543-1686). Language also may play a part in endowing the abstractions with sex, but the sex residue is itself sufficient to account for that development. Language thereupon comes in to determine what the sex shall be.

1072. Anthropomorphism works in different ways among different peoples and in different periods of history. There was a great dif-

1070 [1] In his *Cultes, mythes et religions,* Vol. III, pp. 186-96, Reinach calls attention to a small figure published by Mommsen, bearing the inscription ΓΕΡΜΑΝΙΑ and then to a figure in mosaic with the inscription ΓΑΛΛΙΑ. In that mosaic, says he, "we are privileged to pay our respects to the first certain portrayal of [a personified] Gallia [Gaul] that Graeco-Roman art has handed down to us. The medallion that ornaments the bust is part of a very extensive mosaic dating from the reigns of the Antonines. . . . Already known were some few specimens of [personified] provinces or towns in mosaics of the second century. The tradition of topical personification of this kind was not lost during the high Middle Ages." Many examples of such personification of Rome are to be found on Roman coins and medallions.

1070 [2] Robiou, *L'état religieux de la Grèce et de l'Orient,* p. 22: "In Pindar [*Olympia,* VIII, 86; *Pythia,* X, 44 (Turner, pp. 81, 93)], and a little later in the *Electra* of Sophocles [v. 792], Nemesis is personified, but neither Aeschylus, nor even Herodotus in a work in which she plays an important part, make her an anthropomorphic creature properly so called. In other words, the conception seems to

ference between Greek anthropomorphism and the more archaic religion in Rome. There is also a very great difference between the anthropomorphism of Graeco-Roman antiquity and the religious notions of our own time. Yet we moderns have abstractions in plenty, and except for the one point of personification, they are very like the abstractions of old.

1073. It has often been said that Socialism is a religion. In the field of anthropomorphic derivations such a proposition is absurd; for surely nobody in our day has ever conceived of Socialism in a male form, the way the ancient Romans conceived of the goddess Roma in female form. But in the domain of residues the proposition corresponds quite to the facts, in the sense that the sentiments which in times past found their expression in worship of the goddess Roma, or the goddess Annona, and the sentiments which now find their expression in such faiths as Socialism, Progress, Democracy, and the like, are exactly similar.

1074. In the case of Rome sentiments begin by suggesting a mere image. They then develop in intensity to the point of a deification. They end by degenerating into objects of poetic or literary admiration, which endures down to our own very day. The Romans began by picturing Rome as a woman, and then made the woman a goddess. The vivid sentiment that found expression in the deification of the city persisted, in another form, even after the fall of paganism,

have been wavering at the time between the abstract and the mythological senses." According to the editor of *La sagesse de Jésus fils de Sirach*, pp. 390-91, the author of Ecclesiasticus "at times personified Wisdom, as the writers of his people had done before him; but he gradually slips back towards a more concrete representation, and one cannot be sure in many cases where he mentions Wisdom whether he is thinking of the metaphysical entity or of the practical virtue. His various statements are quite inconsistent. She is the first of creatures, eternal, omnipresent. Every man partakes of her. . . . God has bidden her to abide with Jacob and she has made Jerusalem her capital. She is more or less completely identified at times with the fear of the Lord and even with the Law." Toutain, *Les cultes païens dans l'Empire romain*, Vol. 1 (*Les cultes officiels*), pp. 415-16: "If we except the two goddesses Fortuna and Victoria, who deserve a special examination in view of their importance, the abstract divinities whose names we have remarked in [Roman] inscriptions are: Aequitas, Bonus Eventus, Concordia, Copia, Disciplina, Fama (?), Felicitas, Fides Publica, Gloria, Honos, Iuventus, Libertas, Mens or Bona Mens, Pax, Pietas, Prosperitas Deorum, Providentia, Salus Generis Humani, Sanctitas, Virtus."

eventually losing vigour and becoming a mere rhetorical expression. So we get a nucleus of sentiments persisting in varying intensity in time and expressing themselves under a variety of forms. The peoples who enjoyed the blessings of the *pax Romana* cherished, with regard to Rome, a sum of sentiments and concepts corresponding to the power of Rome and the benefits vouchsafed by Roman rule. In terms of the language then common among men the expression of such sentiments and concepts took the form of calling Roma a goddess and rearing temples to her. The same sentiments were expressed in worship of Rome and the ruling Emperor in common— *Romae et Augusto,* say the inscriptions; and a similar worship we find of Rome-and-Venus.[1][2]

1074 [1] Daremberg-Saglio, *Dictionnaire, s.v. Roma: Rome personnifiée ou déifiée* (E. Maynial): "The most ancient portrayal of Roma as a symbolic personification of the state appears on the recto of the first denarii of the Republic beginning with the year 269 B.C. . . . In engraving that head on their coins the Romans had no idea whatever of representing Roma as a divinity, but intended merely to create an emblem for their city under guise of an armed woman, following in that the example of many Greek cities. The foreign peoples, in a spirit of flattery or gratitude, were the ones who endowed the personification of Roma with the status and attributes of a divinity. . . . While they were deifying Rome, the Greeks gave the new goddess a definite history and personality. The most ancient tradition relative to Roma is reported by Dionysius of Halicarnassus after the historian Callias [*Antiquitates Romanae,* I, 72 (Spelman, Vol. I, p. 165)]. It represents her as a Trojan. Under the Empire the cult of Roma became elaborate and fixed rites were established. . . . The Emperor Hadrian formally recognized the worship of the deified State and gave it official status in the capital." Toutain, *Les cultes païens dans l'Empire romain,* Vol. I, pp. 41, 74, 376: "Worship of the goddess Roma survived at one point or another of the Roman world during virtually the whole period of the high Empire. As distinguished from the worship of the Emperor it seems not to have been very wide-spread in the Latin provinces. . . . The worship of Roman power, under one or another of its various forms, was general in the Latin provinces. If the goddess Roma had fewer worshippers than she had in Greece and Asia during the last two centuries of the Republic, the imperial divinity at least received boundless homage. To say nothing of the Augustus himself, living or dead, a veritable worship was paid to his associates, his house, his qualities, his exploits." Toutain goes on to show that such worship was quite spontaneous and was never forced upon the masses. In the large, people worshipped Rome and the Emperor; in the detail—and sometimes a very petty detail—individuals and groups of individuals paid worship to anybody or anything that they thought might be in a position to help them: "The miller's guild at Guntia worshipped the god of that river because the river drove their millstones."

1074 [2] On being rescued by Titus Quintus Flaminius, the Chalcedonians consecrated the most beautiful buildings in their city to him. Plutarch, *Flaminius,* XVI,

1075. From the logical standpoint an engrossing admiration for Rome and a fact of deification of that city are different things; but from the standpoint of sentiment they are altogether similar, the second oftentimes being a mere translation of the first into the language current. Martial is expressing only popular sentiments when he exclaims: "Rome, goddess of the world and the peoples, without a peer and without a second!" [1]

1076. Such sentiments endure in time by mere force of inertia, even after the circumstances in which they originate have passed away. The abstraction becomes detached from the facts and lives a life of its own. St. Jerome will still be saying of Rome: "City powerful, city queen among cities, city praised of the Apostle, thy name,

3-4 (Perrin, Vol. X, p. 369), gives the text of two of the inscriptions on the edifices, one: "This gymnasium to Titus [Flaminius], and to Heracles the people [consecrates]"; the second, "To Titus and Apollo this Delphineon, the people." In Plutarch's time a "priest of Titus" was still being appointed, and still in use was a paean ending with the words: "We venerate the faith of the Romans, a faith we vow to cherish, and which we pledge ourselves to serve. Sing, O Virgins, to Zeus the great, and to Rome and to Titus, and therewith to the Faith of the Romans. *Io! Paian! Oh! Titus, Saviour!*" At about that time at Locris an altar was consecrated "To Jupiter Optimus Maximus, the immortal gods and goddesses, and eternal Rome": (Orelli, *Inscriptionum . . . collectio,* no. 1799): "*Iovi optimo maximo diis deabusque immortalibus et Romae aeternae Locrenses.*" At Melos a statue and a bronze wreath were offered to Rome by the people. And *cf.* Livy, *Ab urbe condita,* XLIII, 6, 2: "The people of Alabanda [Asia Minor] urged the point that they had built a temple to the City of Rome and held annual games in honour of that goddess." Tacitus, *Annales,* IV, 56, 1, relates that in a competition of eleven cities for the privilege of building a temple to Tiberius, the people of Smyrna urged their long-standing fidelity to the Roman people and added that "they had been the first to rear a temple to the City of Rome, during the consulship of M. Porcius, at a time when the Roman People had done great things, to be sure, but had not yet attained its present supremacy, Carthage still flourishing and there being powerful kings in Asia." Dio Cassius, *Historia Romana,* LI, 20, 6: "Among other things which he set in order, Caesar [Augustus] permitted Ephesus and Nicaea to rear a temple to Roma, and to Caesar his father, whom he designated as the Hero Julius." Orelli mentions a number of individual priests of the cult of Roma and other gods: *Ibid.,* no. 155: "*sacerdoti Romae et Aug. P.H.C.* [*i.e., Provinciae Hispaniae citerioris*]"; nos. 488, 606: "*Romae et Augusto Caesari divi F. Patri patriae.*" ("To Rome

1075 [1] *Epigrammata,* XII, 8, vv. 1-2:

"*Terrarum Dea gentiumque Roma,*
   cui par est nihil et nihil secundum!"

[Pareto read: ". . . who is second to nothing."—A. L.]

O Rome, among the Greeks signifieth power and among the Hebrews sublimity."[1] And so on and on till nothing but the mere poetic reminiscence is left among the poets of our day.[2] But if today it is mere reminiscence, at one time it was a vital and influential sentiment.

1077. From the middle of the nineteenth century on the peoples of Western Europe witnessed a progressive improvement in their living conditions, the progress becoming more remarkably rapid towards the end of that century, and during the first years of the twentieth. Great prosperity engendered a group of agreeable sentiments and ideas that eventually came to cluster about nuclei known as Progress and Democracy. These powerful and beneficent entities are contemplated by people of our time with sentiments very like the emotions our ancestors felt for the power of Rome.

1078. Countless examples of this process might be mentioned, because, in general, any sentiment that is keenly felt tends to assume the form of faith in some abstraction or other. I will halt at the

and Augustus Caesar, son of the Divine [Julius] and father of his country"); nos. 732, 1800, 3675: ". . . *mun. L. restitutae in maiorum libert. Roma*" ("Roma [*i.e.*, a statue of the goddess Roma], by gift of the Lycians [Asia Minor] restored to their ancient liberties"); "*Iovei Capitolino et populo romano* [*virtutis*] M[*aximae*] *benivolentiae beneficiq. caussa.*" ("In recognition of its great valour, benevolence and generosity"); no. 5211: ". . . *sacerdos Romae et Aug.*; no. 7172: *in aede Romae et Augusti.*" From a later period, Rutilius, *Itinerarium*, I, vv. 47-50 (Paris, pp. 88-89):

> "*Exaudi, Regina tui pulcherrima mundi,*
> *inter sidereos Roma recepta polos:*
> *exaudi, genetrix hominum genetrixque Deorum,*
> *non procul a caelo per tua templa sumus.*"

("Hearken, O Queen, fairest of thy world, Rome now welcomed among the stars of heaven; hearken, O mother of men and gods: thy temples have brought us nigh unto heaven.")

1976 [1] *Adversus Jovinianum*, II, 38 (*Opera*, Vol. II, p. 337; Schaff-Wace, p. 415): "*Urbs potens, urbs orbis domina, urbs Apostoli voce laudata, interpretare vocabulum tuum, Roma, aut fortitudinis nomen est apud Graecos, aut sublimitatis iuxta Hebraeos.*"

1076 [2] Carducci, "Before the Baths of Caracalla" (*Poesie*, pp. 795-97):

> "*Religioso è quest' orror: la dea*
> *Roma qui dorme.*"

("A holy thing this awe: here sleeps the goddess Rome!")

single case of "pacifism." Says George Kemeny:[1] "It is of a doctrine, therefore, that I intend to speak, not of a religion, much less of a creed. The meanings of those two last terms have been so altered in the course of the ages, they have undergone so many reincarnations, that they have become quite disfigured and often serve today to express ideas that stand in direct conflict with the pacifist ideal. [So the religious idea is being thrown out through the door, but we will soon find it coming back through the window.] I trust that I am not falling into any sin of blasphemy when I declare that pacifism in the highest sense of the term is neither a means nor an end, but a belief based on a sort of revelation. [The salient feature in many doctrines called religions.] The moral substance of pacifism being of a higher order [There is no definition to enable us to distinguish a "higher" from a "lower" order.] and present in every universal conception of life [What can that wonderful thing be?], pacifism must be placed on a footing with Buddhism, Judaism, Islamism, Christianity [Why then did he begin by saying that it was not a religion?], though it is safe to say that it surpasses all these conceptions in that it is common to them all, is present in them all, unites them all."[2]

1079. The example is of special interest in that it is one of many in which the residues clearly transpire through the derivations. Stress of sentiment puts logic to flight. Kemeny began by banishing pacifism from the "religions." A few lines further on he puts it

1078 [1] *Le mouvement pacifiste, Correspondence bimensuelle du Bureau International de la Paix à Berne*, Apr. 15, 1912, no. 7, pp. 99-101.

1078 [2] The whole article is a sermon such as we find in other religions; in fact it seems to be a reminiscence of some sermon he may have heard in a church, p. 101: "There are no miracles without faith. Pacifism as a world-doctrine will work miracles only if it reigns in your hearts." The flexibility of derivations is well illustrated in the case of certain Italian pacifists who preached war in the name of peace (§§ 1705 f.)! There is an apparent contradiction, and the contradiction is real enough from the standpoint of logic; but not so from the standpoint of sentiment. The pacifists in question were attaching the term "pacifism" to a sum of sentiments of benevolence and brotherly love, and that same group of sentiments is one of the elements in patriotism. "Pacifism" and "patriotism" therefore become two names for one same thing, and one is conscious of no contradiction in following the various impulses of the group of sentiments. In just the same way, how many wars have been fought in the name of Christianity, which preaches peace!

"on a footing" with doctrines that beyond any doubt everybody calls religions. The contradiction is not apparent to him, since he is writing under the influence of a powerful sentiment, whereby pacifism "like an eagle soareth" over other religions—that must be why it is not one of them, though it is in other respects like them! He shows that pacifism does not conflict with any religion—the eagle is flying like a humble sparrow—but then he adds, pp. 100-01: "There is another analogy between religion and pacifism, an analogy expressed in words that are often uttered in jest: 'It is faith that saves!' Pacifism, too, encompasses salvation. All those who have worked in the pacifist movement consistently, sincerely, without selfish ulterior purposes, have certainly been conscious of being better men therefor. Pacifism destroys the germs of evil one by one. It purifies our thoughts, ennobles our instincts; and by that very fact exercises a regenerating influence on individuals and races." If one had a weakness for personification along with such notions, one would get an image of Pacifism, just as we got images of the pagan deities—something like the statues of the goddess Roma, or like the picture some people have of the God of the Christians, a rather handsome old gentleman with a long beard, sitting on a cloud.

1080. There have been—to be sure by way of exception—no end of modern derivations fashioned on the ancient pattern. Auguste Comte personified the Earth, rebaptizing it as "the Great Fetish"; and Humanity, too, for which he ordained a ritual of worship. Our present-day "humanitarians" are expressing not a few of Comte's ideas in a language of their own.

1081. The word "Socialism" has stood, and still stands, for something great, powerful, beneficent; and about that nucleus, again, no end of hopes, dreams, agreeable sensations, have come to cluster. Just as the ancient divinities multiplied, subdivided, competed, so in our day, alongside the godhead of Socialism, we have the godheads of Social Reform and Social Legislation—not to mention lesser gods such as Social Art, Social Hygiene, Social Medicine, and countless other things, which in grace of the affix "social" become partakers of the divine essence.

1082. Lyall classifies the various styles of deification among the Hindus, and they hold, with some slight modification, for many other peoples:[1] "1. The worship of mere stocks and stones and of local configurations, which are unusual or grotesque in size, shape, or position. [Cf. Class I residues.] 2. The worship of things inanimate, which are gifted with mysterious motion. 3. The worship of animals which are feared. 4. The worship of visible things, animate or inanimate, which are directly or indirectly useful and profitable, or which possess any incomprehensible function or property. [These, so far, have been groups of sensations of the simpler forms. The following involves a process of abstraction more remote from simple sensation:] 5. The worship of a *Deo,* or spirit, a thing without form and void—the vague impersonation of the uncanny sensation that comes over one at certain places. [Then come categories involving the persistence of certain sensations in time:] 6. The worship of dead relatives and other deceased persons known in their lifetime to the worshipper. 7. The worship of persons who had a great reputation during life, or who died in some strange or notorious way—at shrines. [From there we go on to abstractions of greater and greater complexity:] 8. The worship in temples of the persons belonging to the foregoing class as demigods or subordinate deities. 9. The worship of manifold local incarnations of the older deities, and of their symbols. 10. The worship of departmental deities. 11. The worship of the supreme gods of Hinduism and of their ancient incarnations and personifications, handed down by the Brahmanic scriptures."[2]

1083. So far Lyall's description is perfect; but thereafter he succumbs to the general weakness for logical explanations, assuming that the worship of certain inanimate objects is to be attributed to

1082 [1] *Asiatic Studies,* pp. 7-9.

1082 [2] Hovelacque, *Les nègres de l'Afrique suséquatoriale,* p. 397: "The religion of the superequatorial blacks is a fetishism of a most rudimentary character. Let the sight of some creature, object, or spectacle stir the individual to some unusual degree and he will attribute to that creature, object, spectacle, some special power. It is not spiritualism, or spiritism, that we get: there is so far no notion of immaterial being. It is something in the direction of animism."

the "intelligence, which argues that a stock or stone embodies divinity only because it has a queer, unusual form." He inadvertently refutes himself when he says: "Now the Brahmanic explanation of this reverence for curious-looking things, especially for things conical and concave, is always at hand and producible to the earnest inquirer after divine emblems and manifestations; but these interpretations appear to belong to a later symbolism, which is habitually invented by the more ingenious to account upon orthodox principles for what is really nothing but primitive fetishism rising into a higher atmosphere." [1]

1084. Examining the facts directly, Lyall was able to get at the underlying residues. If the residues are not always apparent, it is because we do not get the facts directly, but know them only under the gloss laid over them by poets, philosophers, theologians, and

1083 [1] The passage continues, pp. 9-10: "For the feeling which actuates the uninitiated Indian worshipper of stocks and stones, or what are called freaks of nature, is in its essence that simple awe of the unusual which belongs to no particular religion. It survives in England to this day in the habit of ascribing grotesque and striking landmarks or puzzling antiquities to the Devil, who is, or has been, the residuary legatee of all obsolete Pagan superstitions in Christian countries. In any district of India such objects or local configurations as the Devil's Quoits . . . would be worshipped. Similar things are actually worshipped all over Berar, and in every case some signification, either mythical or symbolical, has been continued or sanctioned by some expert Brahman to justify and authorize the custom. [The derivation, and admirably described!] Yet it seems certain that among the vulgar there is at first no *arrière pensée* in their adoration. [A good description of the residue.] The worshipper requires no such motive, he asks for no sign, offers no prayer, expects no reward. He pays reverent attention to the Unaccountable Thing, the startling expression of an unknown power, and goes his way. [Next come derivations.] It is not difficult to perceive how this original downright adoration [Residues.] of queer-looking objects is modified by passing into the higher order of imaginative superstition. [In other words, how derivations originate.] First, the stone is the abode of some spirit; its curious shape or situation betraying *possession*. Next, this strange form or aspect argues some *design*, or handiwork, of supernatural beings, or is the vestige of their presence on earth. One step further lands us in the world-wide regions of mythology and heroic legend, where the naturally remarkable features of a hill, a cleft rock . . . commemorate the miracles and feats of some saint, demigod, or full-blown deity. Berar is abundantly furnished with such fables, and beyond them we get, as I think, to the regarding of stones as emblems of mysterious attributes . . . and to all that class of notions which entirely separate the outward image from the power really worshipped. So that at last we emerge into pure symbolism, as when anything appears to be selected arbitrarily to serve as a visible point for spiritual adoration." The passage is continued in § 1090.

men of letters. Of the ancient religion of the Vedas, for instance, we know nothing but a literary-theological product passed on to us in religious hymns of a prolix vacuity that is truly remarkable, and which are quite as devoid of sense as of definiteness. And we have no other documents for determining the character of parallel forms of popular belief that in all probability existed then, as they exist now, expressing themselves in the facts studied by Lyall.[1]

1085. So the mythology of the Greek tragic poets, superior as their poems are to the Vedic hymns in meaning, definiteness, and clarity, is probably—one might say certainly—different from the popular mythology that we at least descry through the few documents known to us on the subject—the writings of Pausanias, for instance.

1086. II-θ: *Need of new abstractions.* Abstractions become outworn or untenable for one reason or another; they disappear or lose their appeal. But the need for them endures and new abstractions are required to take the places of those which disappear or weaken. So popular mythologies are superseded, among the educated, by scholarly, subtle, abstruse mythologies; ingenious theogonies become the order of the day—speculations as to the creation of the world, the primitive state of humanity, and so on. Then another onward step is taken: supernatural abstractions give ground to metaphysical abstractions; there are speculations as to the "essences" of things, and people expatiate in incomprehensible language on even more incomprehensible subjects. Finally these metaphysical abstractions are topped off with pseudo-scientific abstractions. Laplace's nebular theory was holding a prominent place in Socialist sermons a few years

1084 [1] There are many other cases like that—for instance, Pallas, *Reise durch verschiedene Provinzen des Russischen Reichs,* Vol. III, pp. 60-61: "The Ostiaks also manifest a sort of worship for certain mountains and trees that have struck their imagination or have been declared sacred by their priests. They never go by one such without discharging an arrow—a testimony of respect that they pay. What I have been saying applies to individual worship. Public worship is addressed to first-class idols, which their priests have blessed. . . . In days gone by the Ostiaks used to worship many trees in that particular forest, where they hung up the furs and hides of animals they had sacrificed. But the Cossacks began to steal the furs, so they resolved to cut down the trees. They cut them up into logs or large wheel-like blocks (*Klötze*), which they decorated with ribbons and signs and set up in safe places. It is to such places that they go with their offerings today."

back and supplying conclusive proof that Evolution, Holiest of Holies, was to lead the world to a Socialist golden age. People who have ceased worshipping the relics of saints turn to worshipping "solidarity." Those who cannot accept the theology of Rome turn to the theology of the Modernists as something more "scientific." Numberless the cases of this kind where forms change and the need of persisting abstractions endures.[1]

1087. To judge by the little we know of it, the primitive religion of the Roman people was deficient, to some extent at least, in this element of theological and metaphysical abstraction. That must have been one among the many causes that opened the doors to the invasion of Hellenism; nor could it have been altogether stranger to the vogue, later on, of the Oriental cults of Mithras and Christ, though in that the succession of new races to the ancient Roman stock was the most decisive factor. The meagreness of theological and metaphysical abstraction in present-day humanitarianism is impeding its progress as a religious creed; and the same is true of the closely kindred doctrine of Liberal Protestanism.

1088. Not only does the human being need abstractions: he also needs to develop them—he wants them alive in his mind, not dead. So it comes about that the more flourishing a religion is, the more vigorous and vital are the heresies arising within it. There is a static demand, and a dynamic demand, for abstractions.

1086 [1] A single individual can run this whole gamut in one lifetime. In July, 1913, a monument was unveiled in Paris to Father Hyacinthe. The inscription on it reads: "Father Hyacinthe, a priest of Saint-Sulpice, then a barefoot Carmelite, preached from the pulpit of Nôtre-Dame (1864-1869), then left the Church and married, September 3, 1872. For twenty years thereafter he preached the reform of Catholicism and the brotherhood of the churches (1873-1890). During the twenty years thereafter he rose above all churches and died as a monotheistic free-thinker." By no means an isolated case. It is a general rule that people begin by severing connexions with the Catholic Church on the claim that all they want is a better, more liberal form of Catholicism. But they very seldom stop there. They go on evolving. Their Catholicism becomes theism. Sometimes their theism becomes materialism. Sometimes, again, the evolution halts at a certain point, and there comes a retrogression, the individual dying in the Catholic faith of his childhood. [The American example might be the spiritual Odyssey of Henry James the Elder, who travelled leagues and miles in quest of truth and finally pounced on Swedenborgianism. That would be something like the monk's pursuit of Angelica in the *Orlando Furioso*.—A. L.]

CHAPTER VII

Residues: Activity and Sociability

1089. Class III: *Need of expressing sentiments by external acts.* Powerful sentiments are for the most part accompanied by certain acts that may have no direct relation to the sentiments but do satisfy a need for action. Something similar is observable in animals. A cat moves its jaws at sight of a bird; the dog twists and turns and wags its tail at sight of its master; the parrot flaps its wings.

1090. Says Lyall further:[1] "The present writer knew a Hindu officer of great shrewdness and very fair education who devoted several hours daily to the elaborate worship of five round pebbles which he had appointed to be his symbol of Omnipotence. Although his general belief was in one all-pervading Divinity, he must have something symbolic to handle and address." Notable in that is not merely the need for the symbol, but the need for "doing something," acting, moving the limbs, fixing the attention on something concrete—escaping, in a word, from a state of passive abstraction. In our day, Flammarion and other scientists hold a meeting at the spring equinox and watch a sunrise.

1091. The acts in which sentiments express themselves reinforce such sentiments and may even arouse them in individuals who were without them. It is a well known psychological fact that if an emotion finds expression in a certain physical attitude, an individual putting himself in that attitude may come to feel the corresponding emotion. The residues of this class, accordingly, stand conjoined with emotions, sentiments, and passions in a complex concatenation of actions and reactions.

1092. III-α: *Need of "doing something" expressing itself in combinations.* As regards combinations we come across residues of Class I again. It is a question really of a variety of compound residues. Few the cases in which, as in the Lyall example, combinations are

---

1090 [1] *Asiatic Studies*, p. 10 (concluding quotation in §§ 1082-83 [1]).

due to pure chance, or better, to vague or very complicated motives. In general some more or less fantastic rule determines the choice of the combination. The impulse to "do something" is overwhelming; the fancy sets to work, and finds a way to satisfy it. In such cases the III-α residue—in other words, the demand for action—is the chief factor; Class I residues, in other words, the combinations, are secondary. The norms governing the combinations—in other words, the derivations from the Class I residues—are incidental and generally of little importance.

1093. For that reason it is difficult, and not seldom impossible, to distinguish operations in magic from religious rites, with the result that the common mania for substituting the search for "origins" for the search for residues has led people to conclude that magic was the "origin" of religion. The demand for action, which corresponds to the III-α residue, gives rise to occult, magical, and religious rites. There is a transition by imperceptible degrees from the first variety to the last. Numberless the examples in procedures devised for healing the sick.[1]

1094. III-β: *Religious ecstasies*. One may feel a calm and thoughtful need for "doing something." But that sentiment may rise in intensity to the point of exaltation, exhilaration, delirium. There is a merely quantitative difference, therefore, between the III-α and the III-β types. Religious chants, contortions, dances, mutilations performed in states of delirium, belong to the III-β variety. However, mutilations and, more generally, voluntary sufferings often involve another kind of residues—the ascetic type of which we shall speak hereafter (§§ 1163 f.).

1095. Shamanism is an interesting case where our "action" residues come to light with relatively few complications. Says Sir John Lubbock:[1] "Wrangel, however, regarding Shamanism as religion in the ordinary sense, was astonished at this: 'It is remarkable,' he says (*Siberia and Polar Sea*, p. 123), 'that Shamanism has no dogmas

---

1093 [1] The great variety in the rites inspired by the need human beings have felt for averting or producing storms was noted in Chapter II (§§ 186 f.).

1095 [1] *Origin of Civilization*, pp. 222-23.

of any kind. It is not a system taught or handed down from one to another; though it is widely spread, it seems to originate with each individual separately, as the fruit of a highly excited imagination, acted upon by external impressions, which closely resemble each other throughout the deserts of Northern Siberia.' [Lubbock, like everyone else who has dealt with such matters, has the fixed idea of logical derivations, so he explains:] It is far from easy in practice always to distinguish Shamanism from Totemism on the one hand, and Idolatry on the other. The main difference lies in the conception of the Deity. In Totemism the Deities inhabit our earth. In Shamanism they live generally in a world of their own, and trouble themselves little about what is passing here. The Shaman is occasionally honoured by the presence of the Deity or is allowed to visit the heavenly regions."

1096. In that we get the usual mistake of assuming a development from the abstract to the concrete. In reality the route is the precise opposite. The idea would be that before there were any concrete cases of the kind, human beings began by evolving an abstract, logical conception of the Deity; thence inferring the rules that were to guide their conduct; and finally acting concretely in the light of that conception and those rules! In general the very opposite is the case. Theories that divinities inhabit the Earth or some other world are altogether accessory to the concrete facts of totemism and Shamanism. They did not produce the observed facts. They have been devised to explain them.

1097. Religious frenzy is not peculiar to any one religion or people. It appears in most religions and among most peoples, now in mild, now in very exaggerated, forms. It is not therefore a logical derivative of any one of the religions in which it is observable. To the contrary, the religious theory is devised to explain it. We are in a position to study it in cases that are taking place before our eyes, and so are enabled to proceed from the known to the unknown in dealing with phenomena more remote in place or more ancient in time. There is, for example, the Salvation Army, whose chief instrument of conversion is religious exhilaration. It considers itself a branch of Christianity, yet its procedures would be no whit different if it belonged to some other religion, the Mohammedan, let us say.

1098. The Welsh "revival" differs but slightly from the Salvation Army. The theological element is negligible: religious frenzy is the main thing. A Frenchman, M. Henri Bois, attended the Welsh revival of the year 1904-05. He was impressed by the fact that individuals in the throes of religious fervour shrank from arguments with unbelievers.[1] The Torrey Mission was to some small extent theological, the revival, not at all.[2] The meeting of April 11 was (p. 269) "a strange meeting! Fervid, passionate prayers, men and women boxing with their clenched fists! Several lapse into the *hwyl!*[3] . . . In a *hwyl* one loses all self-control—one is almost unconscious—the subconscious in fact comes to the fore. A little girl is sitting two seats to my right. She begins to pray along with others. They begin to sing, but that makes no difference to her. She continues praying. She catches their attention for a moment; they listen with cries of *Amen! Yes! Very good!* Then, apparently, the meeting has had enough of her. It breaks forth into a great hymn. The little girl continues praying. She has been praying now for a long time. She is in a *hwyl,* completely oblivious to everything about her. She sits with

1098 [1] *Le réveil au pays de Galles,* p. 147: "There were unbelievers in the galleries. Sidney Evans [the evangelist] advises 'Christian workers' not to argue with them but to 'bear witness,' exemplify, 'show forth,' the 'life that is in them'—to pray. In the front row at the meeting is a woman who would like to be converted but cannot make up her mind. A Christian sitting at her side begins praying for her in a loud voice. Still she cannot make up her mind. The meeting draws to a close. She does not stir. And the Christian also keeps his seat beside her, talking to her, exhorting her."

1098 [2] *Ibid.,* p. 129: "While the Torrey Mission is more dogmatic, more concerned with doctrines, the revival is all emotion, all excitement—it is stirring, vital. At the Torrey Mission the address is a long affair and a very important feature. Torrey is so much the schoolmaster that some of his hearers may be seen taking notes. The address is nothing at the revival. There everything comes down to singing and praying."

1098 [3] *Ibid.,* pp. 268-69: "If at times the Welsh 'pray singing' they also 'sing praying.' They call that the *hwyl* in Welsh." And *cf.* Rogues de Foursac, *Un mouvement mystique contemporain,* p. 140: "The word *hwyl* designates not a mere exercise in oratory, but a peculiar state of the soul of which the plaintive melopoeia in question is, or is supposed to be, a translation. Psychologically it is made up of an intense emotion that leads to unconsciousness of the outer world and a consequent amnesia." Shamanism could not be described in terms at all different.

her eyes closed as though possessed by an outer power which controls her utterly."

1099. This state of unconsciousness through emotional stress is identical with the exaltation trance of the Shaman, though the derivations with which the respective states are explained are so widely different. The Welsh fanatic, during a "revival" as described by Bois, offers the counterpart of well-known phenomena observable in all peoples in all periods of history.[1]

1100. One may claim that the cries of the Angekok are inspired of the Devil, while cries of the revivalists are inspired of God. That is a problem which experimental science cannot consider and which it could in no wise solve. What is certain, experimentally, is that the two cases are identical and manifest the same residues.

1101. Prophets of all eras seem to have had at least something in common with such enthusiasts. Modern democracy has chosen to seek its ancestors among the Hebrew prophets. That is one of those fantastic genealogies which pleasantly tickle the vanity of the *parvenus*. In attributing the inspiration of their prophets to God and the inspiration of pagan prophets to the Devil, the early Christians were coming pretty close to the truth, in the sense that they were to an extent aware that the two things were manifestations of the same residue. The old view that the prophets of both schools were

1099 [1] *Ibid.*, p. 227: "I saw a young man lying full-length on the steps leading to the platform. His face was distorted, his fists clenched. He delivered a vehement prayer in that posture, and did not rise even when he had finished praying. As the meeting was protracted and 'warmed up' I could see emotions gradually rise. Men would clench their fists and start boxing, as it were, in rhythm, keeping their seats and uttering not a word; or else they would begin beating their heads, or burying their faces in their two hands, or waving their arms wildly about, all in silence. I saw women and girls gradually succumb to the contagious nervous excitement and grow more and more unconscious of the outer world. They would sit there with flushed cheeks and vacant eyes or sometimes with their eyes closed. If the inner excitement became too strong, they would burst forth, men and women, and apparently quite unconsciously, into prayers or hymns." *Ibid.*, p. 241: "In addition to 'thanksgivings' there are prayers that amount to mere shouting: 'crying unto the Lord,' 'wrestling with God,' 'agonizing in prayer'—such in exact literalness are the expressions they use. One hears piercing shrieks from sinners who believe themselves lost and are appealing to God to have mercy on them: 'Lord, be merciful to *me, me, me!*' "

charlatans and rogues went farther astray, mistaking the exception for the rule.[1]

1102. In the same way the view that the Hebrew prophets were just degenerates and half-wits also goes wide of the mark. To be sure mental pathology must have played some part in such phenomena, but it does not account for them entirely; and to be persuaded of that one need only observe phenomena going on before our eyes (§ 547). In the United States there have been prophets, like the so-called Elias, who enjoyed perfect mental health and had the sole purpose—which they sometimes realized—of making money. Similar occurrences have been common in all countries at all times. Not long ago the Marconi investigation in England showed that certain politicians who stand high in the esteem of the Welsh fanatics and affect the language of the prophets of Israel in their public utterances do not forget their own interests nor scruple to speculate in the stock-markets. Such facts have no bearing on the phenomena we are here examining. But then again, in the ranks of the Salvation Army, among the enthusiasts of the Welsh revival, the fanatics of prohibitionism and purity campaigns, among humanitarians and prophets of the god Progress, and so on and on, there are undeniably individuals who vary little if at all from the normal type of the sane man; and if others do, that merely proves that exaltation may readily go hand in hand with a pathological state, but not that sane people are necessarily immune to it.[1]

1101 [1] Sorel, *"Quelques prétentions juives,"* pp. 230 f.: "The fact that leaders of popular insurrection have at one time or another, in the Middle Ages, or in earlier modern periods, pretended to base their revolt on words uttered by the prophets of Israel does not justify the inference that those prophets were revolutionaries. It is in point to recall a sage remark of Renan: 'In religious history a text means not what the author meant, but what the needs of the moment made him mean.'" (For the remainder of the quotation see § 541 [4].) That is all very true. The case is general and arises in the fact that the derivation is secondary and that as many derivations are always available as are required to justify residues, inclinations, interests. Renan used one of the usual phraseologies: the "needs of the moment." What can that new entity be? In order to keep within experimental limits, it has to be rectified to read: "what people get out of it in order to justify their sentiments, inclinations, interests, at a given moment."

1102 [1] Binet-Sanglé, *Les prophètes juifs,* pp. 76-77 (the ancient prophets of Israel in question): "The Jahvist *nabi* is a degenerate with an incompletely developed cere-

1103. Furthermore, the social significance of prophecy lies not so much in the prophets as in the people who believe in them; and when we find a genius like Newton among such people, we have to admit that our action residue plays no small part in social phenomena.

bral cortex that contains a limited number of mnesic neurones, in other words of frames for images and ideas. For that reason the field of his thinking is also limited. Furthermore, as a consequence of this arrested development of the neurones and the hypercontractibility that results from it, the *nabi* has a special disposition towards cerebral dissociation, to the formation of those independent groupings of neurones which constitute the theatre for those mnesic short-circuits which supply the conditions for hallucinations and obsessions." Not a few Protestant writers concede that there may have been something pathological about the ancient seers: *e.g.*, Piepenbring, *Théologie de l'Ancien Testament*, pp. 16-17: "The prophets have sometimes been regarded as lunatics or abnormals because all sorts of eccentricities crept into ancient prophecy. A thing that further contributed to their earning that reputation was their resort to in fact strange symbolic acts to give plastic expression to their thoughts. [But siding with the incendiaries as regards ancient prophecy, they turn fireman to save the prophecy of a later day, nor can they do otherwise, if they would keep the Gospels: *Ibid.*, p. 73 (the "new prophecy" in question):] It appears in its full purity, purged of the traditional usages that one meets in the other peoples of antiquity and which exerted a powerful influence upon the ancient prophets of Israel. The latter still practised the art of divination and their work was not immune to a more or less unhealthy exhilaration. The prophets of our period, instead, are preachers, speaking under divine inspiration but without losing consciousness of themselves, and following the trend of political events of which they are attentive observers. [So saving both the goat and the cabbages; believers will be satisfied with the divine inspiration, pseudo-experimentalists with the political outlook.] All that proves beyond dispute that the prophets of Israel manifested something similar to 'glossolalia'—that lower degree of Christian inspiration [Piepenbring, notice, does not reject inspiration outright, but merely demotes it to a lower grade.], and other similar phenomena that have been witnessed since that time in the Church, especially under the influence of American Methodism. But it does not prove that all [Some were, but not all!] of them were in that condition when they received the Divine Word. The two kinds of Christian inspiration described by St. Paul (I Cor., Chapter 14) are evidently something very similar to the two types of prophecy in ancient Israel. And just as the Apostle ranks plain evangelical preaching higher than 'glossolalia,' so we must give simple prophetic preaching under the inspiration of the Spirit of God a higher plane than ancient ecstatic prophecy." Piepenbring does not define what a "higher plane" of prophecy would be, so we can neither accept nor refute his thesis. He does not, and cannot, give a single experimental proof that such prophets were "inspired by the spirit of God." Such a thing can be believed only as an act of faith. Nor can one imagine why the act of faith should stop at the general proposition and not go on to accept as true all the particulars of prophecy, both old and new, no criterion being given for determining where faith is to halt and experimental research to begin.

1104. Only the mania for judging things by the incidental element in them, by derivations, can obscure the exact similarity of all phenomena of religious exaltation, or frenzies of kindred type.

1105. "Ecstasy," for example, the *mania* of the Pythia, had the same residue as other phenomena of religious ecstasy; and as far as good sense is concerned, the Pythia gave more signs of it than many a Hebrew prophet. Says Bouché-Leclerq:[1] "Intoxicated, it was said, by the vapours of the cave and utterly possessed by the god, the Pythia lapsed forthwith into an ecstasy that the poets have been pleased to depict in the loudest colours and which we shall not describe after them. Such nervous excitement was not always simulated, for in Plutarch's time one Pythia died of it" (*De defectu oraculorum*, 51; Goodwin, Vol. IV, pp. 62-63).[2]

1105 [1] *Histoire de la divination dans l'antiquité*, Vol. III, p. 101.

1105 [2] The prudish reticence of the author who cannot muster the courage to describe the ecstasy of the Pythia (in a scientific work in four volumes!) is characteristic of the fatuous sexophobia prevalent in our day. Van Dale lived at a time when scientists were not affected by that malady. He does not mince words when it comes to describing what took place. The idea, in two words, was that an evil spirit entered the body of the Pythia through her sexual organs and gave answer through her mouth. Such the great mystery that cannot be revealed without offence to our bigots of prudery! Sorry as I am for their discomfort, I am going to quote what Van Dale has to say, *De oraculis veterum ethnicorum*, pp. 153-54: "It is said not only that the 'Cacodaemon,' or Devil, was taken into the body of the Pythia while she was sitting on the Tripod, but that he entered thither through her female or private parts and gave out through her mouth answers which the heathen (*Ethnici*) called divine and the Christians diabolical. The pagan writers themselves make no mention of any such thing, and the numerous early Christians who assert it do so without giving any proof (*non nisi nuda assertatione*), many modern theologians carelessly following them. The first of Christian writers, to my knowledge, to make that assertion was Origen, *Contra Celsum*, VII (Augsburg, p. 343, Latin, p. 338), who writes: 'The Pythia was assuredly the most celebrated of soothsayers. It is said that that prophetess of Apollo squatted over a hole in the cave at Castalia and took in the spirit issuing from it through her private organs, until, entirely filled by said spirit, she gave forth those celebrated and divine utterances which the Oracles were supposed to be.' Chrysostom, *Homilia in 1 Cor.*, 22 [read, 29] (Gaume, Vol. X, p. 304; Chambers, p. 170) follows Origen, and just as hesitantly using *dicunt* (λέγουσι) where Origen has *narrant*: 'It is said that the Pythia, a certain woman, at times squatted on the Tripod of Apollo, her legs apart, and that an evil spirit entering her body from below (*inferne*) filled her with its frenzy (*furore*).' The scholiast of Aristophanes seems to have borrowed what he says (*sua*) from this latter, Chrysostom, since he uses virtually the same words." The scholium mentioned by Van Dale relates to the *Plutus*, v. 39 (Dübner, pp. 327, 545-46, 688).

1106. The phenomena of the Welsh revival enable us to understand phenomena observable in the days of the Crusades (§ 547). It is a mistake to see in the latter mere effects of "mediaeval superstition." They were products of many circumstances, some of which are still observable in our time, in the "revival trance" for example, and other such things. The important part played by children in revivals serves to show how crusades by children may have come about.[1]

1107. The English are a more level-headed people than the Welsh, and not a few were shocked at doings in the revival. One of them said to M. Bois, *Op. cit.*, p. 261: "Those hymns of praise are paeans! Why, they remind me of the Corybantes!" A remark not so far from the truth, after all, since the two phenomena have the same residue.[1]

1106 [1] Michaud, *Histoire des croisades*, 1877, Vol. I, pp. 28-29 (Robson, Vol. I, pp. 56-57): "In those days the pilgrim spirit, which became more violent as it passed from person to person and might be called, in line with a phrase of St. Paul, 'Cross-madness,' was a flaming, obsessing passion that overwhelmed all other feelings. . . . Women, children, clerics, branded crosses on their foreheads or other parts of their bodies as evidence of God's will. . . . A thing hardly believable, thieves, brigands, left their hidden retreats, came forward to confess their crimes, and on receiving the Cross promised to go to Palestine to expiate them." Exactly what happens nowadays at revivals and in Salvation Army missions. Then as now such conversions were ephemeral things. Lea, *History of the Inquisition*, Vol. I, pp. 147-48: "It was during the preaching of this crusade [against the Albigenses] that villages and towns in Germany were filled with women who, unable to expend their religious ardour in taking the cross, stripped themselves naked and ran silently through the roads and streets. Still more symptomatic of the diseased spirituality of the time [Lea might have observed a spirituality just as diseased in his own country. That harpy who went about dismantling barrooms with a hatchet [Mrs. Carrie Nation] was a modern sufferer from the crusader malady.] was the Crusade of the Children, which desolated thousands of homes. From vast districts of territory . . . crowds of children set forth, without leaders or guides, in search of the Holy Land . . . and the few who eventually found their way home again could give no reason for the overmastering longing which had carried them away."

1107 [1] Horace, *Odes*, I, 16, vv. 5-9:

> "*Non Dindymene, non adytis quatit*
> *mentem sacerdotum incola Pythius;*
> *non Liber aeque, non acuta*
> *sic geminant Corybantes aera,*
> *tristes ut irae.*"

("Not so doth Dindymene (Cybele), not so doth the Pythian (Apollo) who dwelleth in the shrine, shake the minds of their priests, not so doth Liber (Bacchus), not so

M. Bois also records the opinion of a lady of Anglican affiliation to whom he was enthusiastically describing a revival meeting. Says he, *Op. cit.,* p. 137: "My admiration and enthusiasm found scant echo. My hostess belonged to the Anglican Church. She had attended a Welsh meeting and had been quite scandalized at the absence of orderliness, regularity, decorum. Think of it! She had taken her Anglican hymn-book with her, as one always does in attending a respectable service. She had not been able to use it once!"

1108. Such more or less must have been the sentiments of many Roman Senators when they voted the *senatus consultus* against the Bacchanals; and not greatly different the sentiments that Euripides puts upon the lips of Pentheus.[1]

1109. Livy's account, *Ab urbe condita,* XXXIX, 8-16, is obviously exaggerated. The rebukes for obscenity levelled at the Bacchanals are the usual insults that religious sects hurl at each other—so regularly, indeed, that there is no way of knowing how much truth there is in them. We cannot accept Livy's testimony as altogether trustworthy nor decide just to what extent the indictments laid

do the Corybantes, beat their ringing bronze, as black wrath doth [the human heart].")

1108 [1] *Bacchae,* vv. 215-28 (Coleridge, Vol. II, p. 94): "Sometime absent from this city, I now hear of new misfortunes that have befallen it. Our women have left their homes for a feigned inspiration, and are wandering the shady hills, hailing this new god, Bacchus, whoever he may be, with dances. Each revel-troop has its brimming wine-cups, and each and all depart to the solitudes to enjoy the embraces of men, pretending to be 'Maenads' performing sacrifices—but with more thought, I hear, to Aphrodite than to Bacchus. Such as my guards have been able to seize, they hold manacled in the public prisons. Those who have escaped will I capture on the hills and bring hither." Cicero, *De legibus,* II, 14, 35-36, expressed himself in terms no different. What he is condemning evidently is unruly chaotic ceremonies. Anything governed by public authority he is ready to allow:

"*Marcus.* We can hardly agree as to what comes next!

"*Atticus.* What would that be?

"*Marcus.* The matter of religious ceremonies conducted at night for women.

"*Atticus.* But I do agree [to the requirement that private worship should be performed with priests appointed by the state], especially since orderly (*solenni*) sacrifice in public you expressly except."

But Cicero sees fit to expatiate:

"*Marcus.* But if we prohibit night-time services, what about our Iacchus [the Bacchus of Eleusis], our Eumolpidae [his priests] and their rites—most majestic

against the Bacchanals were justified. Let us assume for the moment that they were true: the fact still stands that the Senate also prohibited mysteries celebrated in Magna Graecia that were not in the least held to be obscene. It is therefore clear that the Senate had quite other purposes in view than the mere safe-guarding of morals; and one has only to read a speech of the consul Postumius, which Livy quotes, 15-16, to see that political considerations were the chief ones. "No one would care, particularly," says Postumius, 16, 1-2, "if they had become mere perverts through these filthy acts which are a great disgrace to them, provided they had kept their hands clean of crimes and their minds of treason to the State. Never has there been so great an evil in the Republic involving either more individuals or more things. I assure you that all the roistering, all the cheating, all the corruption, that has gone on during these past years has originated in that sanctuary of crime. This conspiracy has itself not revealed the full measure of the wrongdoing: it has stopped at private crime merely because it has never yet been strong enough to destroy the state." [1]

ones? We are not legislating for the Roman People, remember, but for the [average] law-abiding, well-governed country.

"*Atticus*. Well, I suppose you would except the rites to which we were initiated ourselves.

"*Marcus*. Yes, I would."

All the same Cicero does not care to have such things going on in Rome. He concedes at the most that women may be initiated into the rites of Ceres but in clear light of day and according to Roman ritual, *Ibid.*, 15, 37: "*Marcus* . . . The sternness of our forefathers in such matters is evident from the ancient decree of the Senate against the Bacchanals, and the investigation and suppression [of those practices] by the consuls, with an army raised for that special purpose. If you find that rather severe of us Romans, you should remember that in the very heart of Greece Diagondas of Thebes prohibited all nocturnal rites by a permanent law." In a word every legitimate requirement of religion can be met by a cult that has been well organized by the state: "The public priest should absolve from fear [of prosecution] minor oversights [of a religious character: *imprudentiam*] that have been sanely (*consilio*) expiated [by sacrifices]; but any effrontery in the practice of obscene (*foedis*) rites he should condemn and brand as sacrilegious." [The text of Cicero is corrupt and his exact meaning obscure. For various reconstitutions and renderings see Keyes, ed. of *De legibus*, Loeb Classical Library, p. 417. Pareto read: *audaciam in admittendis religionibus foedis damnet.*—A. L.]

1109 [1] Reinach does not believe the accusations made against the Bacchanals. He well remarks, *Cultes, mythes et religions*, Vol. III, p. 269: "The charges spread

1110. The legends about enemies whom Dionysus meets and vanquishes betray the working in Greek sentiment of a certain resistance to religious frenzies. It was less effective among the Greeks than among the Romans, for Greek life was less earnest, less restrained, less decorous than Roman life.

1111. Before opening his biography of Epaminondas, Cornelius Nepos cautions the Roman reader that he must not judge foreign manners by the standards of his home country: "We know, of course, that according to our notions music does not become a person of distinction, while dancing we class frankly among the vices. Those things are enjoyed and held in high honour among the Greeks." [1] All the same, singing and dancing figure in the Roman cults of the Salii (cult of Mars) and the Arvales (cult of the Lares). In the Lupercalia the Luperci, perfumed, almost naked, raced around the Pomerium of the old Palatine City and lashed with goat-hide whips such women as they encountered, so stimulating fertility in them. That festival, curious to note, was one of the last to succumb to the pressure of Christianity. Residues of that sort, as we have already seen (§§ 1004, 1008), are much more stubborn than derivations.

1112. Religious exaltation frequently eventuates in the belief that certain persons are in communication with the Deity. Not infrequently excursions into the supernatural world also occur. Williams describes a case of that kind, which he witnessed in the Fiji Islands.[1]

abroad as to the immorality of the mysteries are all crude or ridiculous fabrications such as were circulated in that same Rome against the early Christians, then in the Christian world against Manicheans, Jews, Templars, and many others. Human malice is not very imaginative. Murder, sodomy, and rape always stand at the head of the list of complaints against sectarians whom hatred would destroy." But from then on Reinach gives free rein to his fancy, and describes the Bacchanalia in terms far overreaching the documents at our disposal. That is guessing, not writing, history.

1111 [1] *De excellentibus ducibus*, XV, 1-2.

1112 [1] Lubbock, *Origin of Civilization*, pp. 339-40 (quoting Williams, *Fiji and the Fijians*, Vol. I, p. 224): "Unbroken silence follows. The priest becomes absorbed in thought, and all eyes watch him with unblinking steadiness. In a few minutes he trembles; slight distortions are seen in his face, and twitching movements in his limbs. These increase to a violent muscular action, which spreads until the whole frame is strongly convulsed, and the man shivers as with a strong ague fit. In some

If that description be compared with what Bois says of certain occurrences at the Welsh revival it will be evident beyond shadow of doubt that the derivations are different in the two cases, but that the residue is the same.[2]

1113. Class IV: *Residues connected with sociality.* This class is made up of residues connected with life in society. Disciplinary residues might also be grouped here, if one agrees that the sentiments corresponding to them are strengthened by living in society. In that direction, it has been observed that with the exception of the cat all domestic animals when at liberty live in groups. On the other hand society is impossible without some sort of discipline, and therefore the social structure and the disciplinary structure necessarily have certain points of contact.

1114. IV-α: *Particular societies.* A need for particular associations is observable among the majority of peoples. They are of many different kinds. Some are for purposes of mere amusement, others for

instances this is accompanied with murmurs and sobs, the veins are greatly enlarged, and the circulation of the blood quickened. The priest is now possessed by his god, and all his words and actions are considered as no longer his own, but those of the deity who has entered into him."

1112 [2] Bois, *Le réveil au pays de Galles*, pp. 493 f.: "On reaching the platform, Evan Roberts rises at once, halts the singing and asks: 'Is there light in this place? I fear not! Have we come here just to see with our eyes, or to worship the living God? Have we come here for amusement's sake or to be sanctified?' A pause. 'No, there is no light in this place! And,' he asks savagely, 'what is the meaning of it, my friends?' He leans forward over the pulpit, his face flushed, red, congested, the veins bulging. 'There is something unusual here, something that will not do!' He shouts the words. Someone starts a prayer: 'If there is something here that is hurting . . .' 'Do not say yes,' cries Roberts, interrupting. 'Do not say yes!' And he falls into his chair, weeping and moaning: 'Restrain them, O Lord!' His heavy sobs are a terrible thing to hear. Dr. McAfee rushes to his side. 'O Lord,' cries Roberts desperately, 'it is greater than I can bear!' Then he turns to the audience: 'It is a greater burden than I have ever been called upon to bear!' He falls silent. The whole hall is now in prayer. Sobbing violently, Roberts cries: 'It is hard always to be obedient to God!' . . . He pauses, then: 'It is the same trouble as last evening! I have to give a message . . . !' And again he succumbs to his emotion. Finally, summoning all his strength, mastering himself, he says: 'God entrusted this message to me some days ago, but I was not to reveal it until this evening. This is the message. Do with it as you see fit. It comes directly from God. The foundations of this Church do not rest on the rock! . . .' A profound sensation in the hall!"

purposes of individual advantage. Still others have religious, political, literary, or other purposes.[1]

Alluding to the wide-spread prevalence of burial colleges in Rome, Renan observes that the members of such associations became closely united, almost as closely as blood-relatives.[2] The fact emphasizes the power that sentiments engendered by associations of the kind may acquire. Renan himself found similar sentiments among the Oriental Christians of his time, and they are little different from the sentiments readily observable in many religious, political, and social sets and sects today. The gilds of the Middle Ages were very like the colleges of ancient times. The fact that their patron was a Christian saint and not a pagan god certainly did not change their character. Also interesting is the fact that the activities of the gilds and the ancient colleges were very much the same—the banquets included. That is just another of the many instances in which forms are seen to change, substances remaining the same: derivations vary, the residue endures. The sentiments that prompt human beings to organize in particular societies are to be kept distinct from the sentiments which develop inside such societies: the latter correspond to all sorts of residues, notable among them the residues of the II-α3 variety (relations of class, §§ 1043 f.).

1115. IV-β: *Need of uniformity*. That need is felt also by animals that live in society. If a hen is painted red and returned to its flock, the other hens at once attack it. The need of uniformity is much more strongly felt among uncivilized than among civilized peoples.

1116. In human societies the uniformity desired may be general throughout a people, but it may also differ according to the various groupings of individuals within the people. We get a picture of the situation in the crystallization of salt solutions. Around a central nucleus successive stratifications cluster to form a thick crystal. But there is not one crystal only in the solution; there are a number of

1114 [1] This is not the place to give even a summary account of such societies. We are interested merely in noting the residues that, in general, are observable in them.

1114 [2] [Pareto seems to be referring to Renan, *Histoire des origines du Christianisme*, Vol. II, pp. 354-58. However, Renan deals repeatedly and *passim* with the Roman burial colleges, or gilds, in that work and in *Marc-Aurèle*.—A. L.]

crystals. In the same way there is not one centre of similarity in a given society, but a number of centres. Sometimes there is conflict between the different "sets," the one trying to extend its own particular uniformity to others. Then again there is no such conflict, each individual resting content with the uniformity of the group to which he belongs and respecting others.

1117. IV-β1: *Voluntary conformity on the part of the individual.* Imitation is of that variety. Imitation plays an important rôle in social phenomena: one individual imitates other individuals; one group, one nation, imitates other groups, other nations. We have of course seen (§§ 733 f.) how mistaken it is to regard similar institutions as necessarily imitations. The similarities may have evolved from similar circumstances. It may also happen that imitation serves to strengthen similarities. Laws against theft, for instance, grow up among various peoples out of similar circumstances; but when such peoples come to have mutual relations, they may to some extent copy each other's laws. So for political institutions and other branches of social activity.

1118. The imitation may have a purpose: to attain some result that is beneficial, or is deemed beneficial, by means which have been seen to yield those results when used by others. Such an imitation would be a logical action. But oftentimes no such purpose exists, at least no conscious purpose; and we then get non-logical actions, which, as usual, come to be tinted with logical colourings.

1119. The residue finds expression in virtually pure form in the temporary uniformities imposed by fashion. It is often impossible to find any imaginable utility in a style. For people to say, "We follow the fashion in order to do as others do," amounts to saying that they imitate because they imitate. It is true that the person refusing to fall in line would become a victim of public censure, but the censure would be merely the sanction of the general sentiment and with it we would be moving from our present residue (IV-β1) to the variety next following (enforced uniformities).[1]

1119 [1] On fashion in general, see Squillace, *La moda,* p. 24. Squillace rightly observes that "these collective currents or tendencies peculiar to periods of time

1120. The origins of things that come to be imitated are often obscure. How and why they are imitated frequently depends upon combinations of circumstances that are for the most part unknown and which we roughly designate by the term "chance." It is therefore altogether erroneous to insist on finding logical causes for the facts observable at a given moment, and the inferences drawn in that direction are oftentimes quite fanciful.

1121. In the year 1909 women in Europe were wearing huge broad-brimmed hats in the so called Merry Widow style. Suppose some traveller who knew nothing of European life had chanced to arrive in Europe just then. He might have sought a logical explanation for the customs just as European travellers seek logical explanations for the similar things they see among uncivilized peoples. In writing an account of his travels, he might have said that women in Europe believed they could make sure of a merry widowhood by wearing broad-brimmed hats of a peculiar shape. Another traveller might have held, instead, that such hats were preservatives against widowhood. Still another might have seen in the fad remnants of the customs of some other social state.

1122. What here is an arbitrary hypothesis on our part is reality itself in no end of studies on the customs of antiquity and uncivilized or barbarian societies. Anyone observing a taboo sets out forthwith to find a logical reason for it. It is not beyond the range of possibility that such a reason may have existed, but that case would be rare indeed. It may also happen that a reason may be discovered or at least divined, but that case would be rarer still. In the most frequent case, the logical reason never existed; or if it did, we have no way of knowing what it was; and we therefore guess at some other.

more or less brief may be grouped under the generic and comprehensive term of 'styles,' that is to say, modes of thinking and feeling, under certain circumstances, and at certain moments, in full uniformity with other individuals of the same society at the same historical moment." At times such "styles" have general causes operating on large numbers of individuals, many others adopting them by mere imitation. Then again, the whim of a single individual may give rise to a style and be imitated by others. Edward VII long set styles of dress for men in England.

1123. The Wahabis prohibit the use of tobacco. Tobacco is taboo for them. There is no question of running down any archaeological reason in this case, for the prohibition is of recent date. Palgrave went looking for a logical explanation for the taboo. He found one in the passion of sectarians for distinguishing marks—"the passion for sectarian discrepancy"; and there was some truth in that, in the sense that members of sects imitate customs that are peculiar to their "set." But then Palgrave strays farther from the facts, by ascribing the prohibition to a logical design on the part of leaders of the sect. If he had documents or direct testimony to substantiate his explanation, we could do nothing but accept it. But his theory is just an inference from an implicit premise that a taboo must have a logical cause, which one may find by considering the intentions of law-givers who established it.[1]

1124. That method is quite generally fallacious. Founders of religions are not shrewd hypocrites endeavouring surreptitiously to attain certain ends. The apostle, as a rule, is a man convinced of his own message—that, in fact, is an almost indispensable requisite if he is to win any following. So in cases where documents are lacking, to ascribe astute and knavish intentions to him carries one, in all probability, far from the truth. It may well enough be that after tobacco had been prohibited for any number of reasons unknown to us, the prohibition may have been retained because, as Palgrave observes, it was a convenient means for distinguishing Wahabis from other Mohammedans. The logical explanations which the Wahabis

---

1123 [1] *Journey through Central and Eastern Arabia*, Vol. II, pp. 14-15: "The early history of the Wahhabee sect, narrated in my first volume, may have, I think, sufficiently shown my readers that the idea of aggression and conquest was no less present to Mohammed-ebn-'Abd-el-Wahhâb and his disciple, the chief Sa'ood, than that of dogma or proselytism; both of these men, and the latter perhaps even more than the former, had in view not only to found a sect, but an empire; not only to convert their neighbours, but to subdue them. . . . Now, to embark on such a career, some decent pretext was wanted, while a visible and unequivocal badge was equally required to counterdistinguish their party from all others. The profession of the Unity of God, the regular performance of prayers almost identical with those of all other Mahometans . . . would not suffice for either one or the other end, would neither warrant the sword, nor sufficiently distinguish those who unsheathed it from those against whom it was unsheathed. . . . Something additional was requisite, and tobacco stepped in conveniently for the Wahhabee."

themselves give for the prohibition of tobacco are in the nature of derivations.

1125. Some customs connected with taboos are so strange that they defy any possible logical explanation. Consider, for example, what Frazer has to say, and anyone desirous of further instances may find them at will in the literature of travel.[1] But, without roaming afield from our own countries, there are the strange customs of many of our own sects such as the Masons or the Good Templars. In French-speaking countries the Good Templars are an anti-alcoholic society. In a secret convention recently held at Lausanne nothing could be seen except their usher, an individual dressed in a flaming red uniform. Discover if you can any possible relation between a flaming red uniform and total abstinence!

1126. IV-β2: *Uniformity enforced upon others.* The human being not only imitates to become like others; he wants others to do likewise. If a person departs from the uniform rule, his conduct seems to jar, and produces, quite apart from any reasoning, a sense of discomfort in the persons associated with him. An effort is made to eliminate the jar, now by persuasion, more often by censure, more often still by force. As usual, there is no lack of logical chatter to explain such procedures; but they originate not in the causes so alleged, but in great part at least in a sentiment of hostility to violations of uniformity, re-enforced by sentiments of asceticism and other sentiments of that type.

1127. The requirement of uniformity is particularly assertive in matters of logic. From the logical standpoint the maximum of absurdity would seem to be reached in condemning a man to the stake

---

1125 [1] *Golden Bough,* Vol. I, p. 327: "Thus, among the Creek Indians a lad at initiation had to abstain for twelve moons from picking his ears or scratching his head with his fingers: he had to use a small stick for these purposes. For four moons he must have a fire of his own to cook his food at; and a little girl, a virgin, must cook for him. During the fifth moon any person might cook for him, but he must serve himself first, and use one spoon and pan. On the fifth day of the twelfth moon he gathered corn cobs, burned them to ashes, and with his ashes rubbed his body all over. . . . While the ceremony lasted, he might touch no one but lads who were undergoing a like course of initiation. Caffre boys at circumcision live excluded in a special hut." Frazer gives no end of similar examples.

because he does not think as others think on some theological question that is incomprehensible to any rational human being. But that criticism is valid only for the derivation, for the logical reason devised to explain what has been done. The act itself is just the manifestation of a sentiment of hostility to a violation, regarded as particularly flagrant, of a uniformity. Today transgressors of that kind are no longer burned at the stake, because the whole scale of penalties has been lowered; but people who preach birth-control are sent to prison. One is allowed to deny the actual presence of Christ in the Host, but not to believe that if a man is not well enough off to support children, he would do better to keep them from coming into the world and use measures calculated to prevent conception.[1] But marvellous to relate, people who condemn and persecute the birth-controllers, who are heretics of the sex religion, speak with bleeding hearts of the heretics of the Church, loathing those who

1127 [1] On July 22, 1913, a police detective in Paris tried to kill a certain Mme. Roudier, with robbery in view. He was arrested and on being questioned confessed the crime. *Liberté*, July 23, 1913: " 'I am a wretch,' he cried, after stating his name and position. 'I had to get money somehow. Poverty drove me to it. I have a little boy a year old. My wife is expecting another. I was at the end of my resources, with just 13 cents in my pocket. I have been living on the rue Nationale for only a week. Moving expenses and then the rent took everything I had.' 'Why didn't you ask assistance of your superiors? They would certainly have helped you out.' 'I didn't dare. I was too young in the service. Besides, I was afraid such a step would get me a bad mark. . . . I met Mme. Roudier a year ago. In my predicament I at once thought of that woman, with the idea of going and asking a loan of 50 francs. Once in her presence I could not find the courage to make my request. I was just leaving when I suddenly thought of my little family, which would soon be without anything to eat. . . . A hellish idea came into my mind. . . . I saw red. . . . I rushed upon the woman. She screamed. I began to choke her to rid my ears of her piercing shrieks. Then I realized that I was lost and I took to my heels. . . . Oh, I'm guilty all right! But I swear to you it was just a moment's madness.' " Now the question arises: Was that man right or wrong in having two children whom he could not support? We are not here concerned with deciding the question either one way or the other; but evidently if the question is to be considered, people must be free to speak of birth-control, anti-birth-control, and even of contraceptive measures; for, after all, if one would have an end, one must accept the means. If that is forbidden, if such problems are not to be discussed, we go back to the times when it was forbidden to discuss the dogmas of the Catholic Church. Those who admire those times may, consistently, be willing to go back to them; but those who condemn them are ridiculously illogical when they try to imitate their procedures.

persecuted them, calling them ignorant fanatics, and saying and believing in all good faith that they themselves are wiser than they, know more than they, and are freer from superstition—that, no more and no less! There are people who think that in order to condemn Catholicism they have only to mention the Inquisition and the tortures it inflicted upon heretics, but at the same time admire English judges who condemn to the whipping-post a man guilty of no greater crime than selling pictures deemed obscene.[2]

Joinville relates how St. Louis, King of France, punished blasphemers against the Faith—and that is grievously shocking to our free-thinkers, who, for their part, deem it altogether proper that blasphemers against any one of their dogmas should be just as severely punished.[3] The fanatics of the goddess Science say that it is their veriest intention never to stray outside the field of logic and experience, nay, that is why they consider themselves so superior to believers in other religions. But really if one would keep strictly to that field, one could not prove that showing a picture of a naked woman is a greater crime than blaspheming the god of any religion,

1127 [2] Of the countless examples available suffice the following: *Liberté*, June 13, 1912: "Yesterday forenoon H. J. B., 22, appeared in court at Newington on a charge of persistent loafing on the sidewalks of Piccadilly, despite orders from the police to move on, and of offering obscene pictures for sale to passers-by. Magistrate Lowrie embellished his sentence with a few remarks: 'I am sorry I cannot give you the punishment you deserve. I shall however do the best I can. You will receive twenty-nine lashes from the cat-o'-nine-tails and serve nine months at hard labour in prison.'" We may expect from this exalted magistrate some day a *Malleus maleficarum* of his own, granted of course that he has the brains to write a book. Believers in metempsychosis might imagine that the soul of that Meletus who accused Socrates of corrupting Athenian youth, after making a short sojourn in the body of that Pierre de Lancre who had so many witches burned in the *"pays de Labourd"* (Gascony), finally ended up in the person of this estimable English magistrate.

1127 [3] *Histoire de Saint Louis,* CXXXVIII, 685: "The King had such affection for God and His Gentle Mother that all whom he could convict of uttering improprieties anent God and His Mother or vulgar oaths he caused to be severely punished. So at Cesarea one day he ordered a goldsmith to the stocks in his underdrawers and shirt-tail with the bowels and lights (*fressure*) of a pig about his neck, and so many of them that they came up to his nose. Since my return from overseas I have heard that he had a Parisian merchant branded on the nose and lips with a red-hot iron, for the same reason, though I did not see it myself. And the holy King said [on that occasion]: 'I would willingly be branded with a hot iron myself so only my realm were cleansed of all dirty oaths.'"

or that crimes of the one species do greater harm to society than crimes of the other. In fact, precisely because they cannot enlist the support of reason, fanatics of all times and countries are inclined to resort to force to impose on others the uniformities that they hold so dear. The same Joinville tells a story in which the resort to violence is candidly espoused without any dressing of hypocrisy. The Catholic clergy invite some Jews to a debate at Cluny. A knight on the Catholic side uses no other arguments than his fists, and the good King approves and blesses him.[4] "There you have Catholic superstition," many a contemporary of ours will say. But, after all, that knight had the high honour of being a predecessor of Senator Bérenger, who meets those who disagree with him not with arguments, but with complaints to the State Prosecutor, and who also finds himself in the precise situation in which King Louis held that force

1127 [4] *Ibid.*, X, 51-53: "The King told me that there had been a great conference of clerics and Jews at the monastery at Cluny. A knight was there and he asked that the leading cleric and the chief scholar of the Jews be called before him and so that was done. And he asked a question of the Jew as follows: 'Master,' said the knight, 'I ask you whether you believe that the Virgin Mary who bore God in her womb and in her arms had that child as a Virgin and whether she was Mother of God.' and the Jew replied that of all that he believed not a word. And the knight answered that truly he had acted the lunatic in entering her church and her house not believing in her, nor loving her; 'And forsooth,' said the knight, 'you shall pay for it.' Whereupon he picked up his staff (*béquille*) and struck the Jew a blow behind the ear and knocked him to the floor. And the Jews took flight carrying their master with them in a sorry state, and so the conference came to an end. Then the Abbot came to the knight and told him he had done a very crazy thing. And the knight replied that the Abbot had done a still crazier thing in getting such a conference together; for before it closed, any quantity of good Christians in there would have gone away unbelievers from not having understood what the Jews were talking about. 'So,' said the King, 'I tell you that nobody, unless he is a very good clerk, ought to argue with them; but when a layman hears someone speaking badly of the Christian law, he should defend the Christian law only with his sword, giving it to him in the belly and up to the hilt.'" Such disputes were frequent in the old days, and continued down to the Reformation. St. Gregory of Tours, *Historia ecclesiastica Francorum*, VI, 5 (*Opera*, p. 375c; Dalton, Vol. II, pp. 237-38), tells of a debate with a Jew that took place before King Chilperic. The Saint said some very beautiful things to the unbeliever, but was unable to persuade him; whereupon the King allowed him to go in peace, without receiving harm from anyone: "*Haec et alia nobis dicentibus, numquam compunctus est miser ad credendum. Tunc rex silente illo cum videret eum his sermonibus non compungi ad me conversus postulat ut accepta benedictione discederet.*"

should be used; since a defective education, an obtuse mind, and an appalling lack of good sense prevent the Senator from effectively showing the faith that is in him in any other way.

1128. The requirement of conformity does not apply in the same way in all directions. The Romans were not at all theologically-minded, and required uniformity only as regarded external ceremonies of worship. The Chinese government tolerates all sorts of religions provided they remain subject to the state. Our modern governments confiscate newspapers printing pictures of naked women, and do not interfere with the sales of papers that preach pillage, arson, and slaughter of the *bourgeoisie*.[1]

1129. Such manifestations of the instinct of uniformity are, moreover, spasmodic and irrational, as are almost all manifestations of such instincts. There were few prosecutions for impiety in Athens but the impious were many. Roman persecutions of Christians were carried out by fits and starts without system or method. Persecutions by the Catholic Church were better systematized and logically more coherent because they were not manifestations of the instinct of uniformity pure and simple; the Church organized the business and

1128 [1] Many instances might be mentioned to point this contrast. We have already noted several. Add to them the following: *Corriere della sera*, Jan. 12, 1913: "At Boston the women who crowded the opera-house for the first production of Puccini's *Tosca* were scandalized at the so called sofa scene between Scarpia and the heroine in the second act. Suffice it to say that the chief of police interfered and gave orders that on moral grounds the scene should be either deleted or radically altered on following nights." The actors rebelled. "A telegram was sent to Puccini, who replied that the scene must be presented in its entirety, and that if that could not be done, the show should be suppressed without further ado." A compromise was arrived at: Tosca remained standing, "and the Bostonians, the chief of police included, were satisfied." That for the recto; here now is the verso: *Gazette de Lausanne*, Jan. 21, 1913: "*Sabotage and Digestion:* Mr. Ettor, one of the leaders of the I.W.W., who was recently acquitted of criminal complicity in strike violence at the textile factories in Lawrence, Massachusetts, advises hotel and restaurant waiters in New York to poison capitalists or at least to sabotage the meals they eat. 'If you are forced to return to work under bad conditions,' said Ettor, 'do so with the firm resolve to make it uncomfortable for the capitalists to eat meals prepared by your union.' Large hotels and restaurants in New York are engaging private detectives to supervise their kitchens and dining-rooms." According to the worthy legislators of Massachusetts less harm is done to a man by poisoning him than by allowing him to see two opera-singers, the one male, the other female, sitting on

added a pinch of logic. Logic vanishes again in the persecutions by modern governments of heretics of the sex religion, now become the official religion. The sale of most obscene books is permitted without trace of hindrance, while newspapers much less obscene are confiscated. Certain writers are prosecuted, others enjoy immunity, and one can discover not the slightest reason to justify such discriminations. Indictments are brought at crudest random, and one is reminded for all the world of one of those big flies that are caught in a room and go buzzing round and round because they cannot find a way out.

No less capricious the attitude of certain governments towards anti-militarism. In Germany that doctrine has always been suppressed; but in Italy and France it is now tolerated, now prosecuted. In France Hervé is put in prison, but school-teachers are allowed to preach anti-militarism in the class-room—what is more, the lay school is protected by threats of fine and imprisonment against anyone's criticizing it. In Italy a few years ago it was permissible to preach anti-militarism and insult the army. In 1912 a newspaper in Naples, the *Propaganda,* was brought to trial for publishing anti-

the same sofa on a stage. If we leave Massachusetts, we find things even better. In New York an association has been discovered that has burned more than a thousand houses in order to collect the insurance. While these praiseworthy things are going on, the police are busy keeping obscene or merely sensuous books from getting into the city from Europe. In Indianapolis, just south of Chicago, the trial of a number of criminals who had been dynamiting industrial plants and private homes and killing people gave Federal Judge Anderson occasion for declaring that if local authorities had done their duty, such crimes might have been avoided. It would seem, in fact, that there would have been a greater social advantage in doing that than in hunting down young men who are spooning with young women in the parks. The corruption of American Congressmen may well be called a "trade" if that name is to be applied to the corruption of willing women; with this difference, that Congressmen are selling other people's goods, such women their own. American virtuists are so deeply concerned with the "white-slave trade" that they have no time to think of the first, and it is well known that the "white Congressman trade" is prospering, blossoming, and bearing fruit in the United States. Even very recently a certain Mulhall publicly accused a great many legislators of corruption, and declared himself ready to prove his accusations with no end of documents referring to over twenty thousand letters and telegrams. The Congressional Labor Commission seems to have been the principal "victim" of this trade in white Congressman, victims, of course, in the sense in which most of the women involved in the so called white-slave trade are victims.

militaristic articles, one of which had been written by a high army officer and published in the *Riforma sociale* in 1887. The apparent contradiction disappears once one reflects that governmental policies follow and favour variations in derivations that partisan sentiment in the public will have uniform, the requirement of uniformity persisting through all such changes.

1130. IV-β3: *Neophobia*. This is a sentiment of hostility to innovations that are calculated to disturb uniformities. It is very very powerful among uncivilized or barbarous peoples, and shows a very considerable strength among civilized peoples, being surpassed only by the instinct for combinations (Class I residues).

1131. In Paris in February, 1911, women who appeared on the streets in *jupe-culottes* ("bloomers") were attacked and beaten by mobs. Similar incidents took place in Italy and Spain, and more or less everywhere. Much the same things had happened previously when "picture hats" first came into vogue, and on occasions of other innovations in fashion.

1132. It is interesting that many individuals who suffer from neophobias in some departments of life may look with favour upon anything new in some other direction, say in politics or religion, and for the simple reason that it is new. They are shocked at innovations in tailoring and dressmaking, but fume at the mouth because the Pope does not take kindly to the innovations of the Modernists, and heap abuse on governments that make haste slowly in adopting "social reforms." Fresh proof that contradictory residues can function simultaneously in the mind of one same person! In the case just mentioned the conflict is between the residues of neophobia and the residues of the religion of Progress.

One might also consider the opposite of neophobia—eagerness for innovations; but one may doubt whether that be a sentiment by itself and not rather a product merely of the instincts for combinations and, in our time, also of sentiments of adoration for the god Progress.

1133. IV-γ: *Pity and cruelty*. These contrary sentiments are better taken together. As we observed some distance back (§ 911), the opposite of the two would be indifference. It is not easy to distinguish the sentiment of pity from many others that ape its forms. Undeniable the fact that for a century or more past the punishment of crime has grown progressively milder. Hardly a year goes by but new laws are passed in favour of criminals, while existing laws are applied by courts and juries with greater and greater leniency. It would therefore seem as though pity for criminals were increasing, and pity for their victims decreasing.

1134. On the other hand there are cases from which it would seem that pity in general is increasing, the difference just noted depending on the fact that the criminal brought to bar is present, while his victim is absent. Sentiments of pity at all intense are felt, chiefly, for people who stand before one's eyes. They are much weaker for the absent. The jury sees the murderer and pities him, and that is true of judges too. The victim is not visible—he has vanished. To think of him is just a painful duty. The juryman who acquits a murderer today will as likely as not join a mob to lynch a murderer tomorrow if the crime is committed before his eyes.

1135. Characteristic in this connexion is an anecdote related by Meng-Tseu, a Chinese writer. A king sees an ox that is being led to sacrifice. He is stirred to pity for it, and orders that a sheep be used its stead. He confesses that he did that because he could see the ox, but not the sheep.[1]

1136. Typical of a long list of examples is the case of Liabeuf, thief, panderer, and murderer, who was glorified by revolutionaries because he had slain a policeman, and mourned by society women and wealthy members of the French *bourgeoisie* who dally as a

1135 [1] Pauthier, *Confucius et Mencius*, p. 209. Meng-Tseu says to the King: "A tender heart inspired you to do that. The ox was there before your eyes. The sheep you had not yet seen. When a superior man has seen animals alive he cannot endure the thought of their dying. When he has heard their death-cries he cannot eat of their flesh. That is why the superior man locates his slaughter-house and his kitchen in out-of-the-way places."
There may be other cases where the murderer is absent and the victim remains. In that situation evidently what we have just said no longer applies.

sport with Tolstoian or some similar brand of pity.[1] With the revolutionaries such conduct may have been logical; they were enemies of the state, and it is quite natural therefore that they should applaud anyone fighting its police. It may also have been logical with certain members of the *bourgeoisie* who thought they might win votes or the favour of certain politicians by standing by Liabeuf. But still left would be persons for whom those considerations, or others of the sort, would not apply, who were acting sentimentally, non-logically. Such behaviour is very complex. It is motivated not only by the generic sentiment of pity, but also by a special sentiment of pity for the particular wrongdoer, a sentiment that is the more

1136 [1] The story is told in the *Journal de Genève,* July 3, 1910: "On Febuary 26, 1907, in the lower criminal court at Saint-Etienne, Liabeuf was sentenced to four months in prison for theft. On June 7, 1907, he received three months for the same offence in the same court. On August 14, 1909, in the lower criminal court of the Seine, he received three months in prison and was fined 100 francs for 'special vagrancy.' [A phrase from the jargon of a hypocritical age. Dante would have called a spade a spade and Liabeuf a pimp.] On May 14, 1910, he was sentenced to death in Criminal Assizes. . . . After sharing in the exploits of a gang of thieves and becoming entangled with professional criminals, Liabeuf left Saint-Etienne and went to Paris. There, far from mending his ways, he again began frequenting the haunts of vice and prostitution. On his conviction for 'special vagrancy,' he had sworn mortal hate against Detectives Vors and Maugras, whose sworn testimony had proved his undoing. With his vengeance in view he made himself a pair of arm protectors (*brassards*) and another pair of leather mittens bristling with nails. He set out from his favourite bar one evening with that formidable armament to hunt up the two detectives. But they were not the ones to fall under his fury. His victims were policemen whom the bandit had never seen before. The frightful butchery is still fresh in the public memory: Patrolman Deray mortally wounded from a bullet and stabs from a butcher's knife. His comrades Fournès, Février, and others literally cut to shreds. . . . Liabeuf to be sure protested all along against his conviction for 'special vagrancy.' But in the course of the debate before the jury, no new fact, no new circumstance came to light to cast any real doubt on the man's guilt on that charge." With the women who are fascinated by such criminals the poet Carducci dealt in his satire "On the Fadda Case" (*Poesie,* pp. 492-94). They turned up again at the trials of Musolino and other bandits. They may usually be seen at trials of exploiters of female vice. The verses of Juvenal still hold fresh, *Saturae,* VI, vv. 110-12:

> *"Sed gladiator erat—facit hoc illos Hyacinthos.*
> *Hoc pueris patriaeque, hoc praetulit illa sorori*
> *atque viro: ferrum est quod amant . . ."*

("But he was a gladiator! That fact makes them all so many Hyacinths! That she prefers to her children, her sister, her husband, her country! What such females

intense, the worse he is as a criminal. There were members of the *bourgeoisie* who at the urge of sentiment sought the acquittal of Liabeuf, sympathized with him, sided with him. Had their conduct been altogether determined by the generic sentiment of pity, that sentiment should have spoken as vehemently for the victim, or at least for his widow, as for the murderer. But not one of the individuals in question gave a thought to the wretched plight of Policeman Deray's widow.[2] Vigorous opposition was expressed, moreover, in many quarters to granting policemen the right to use arms in self-defence. It took the exploits of the ruffians Garnier, Bonnot, and Co. to strike a balance between humanitarian pity and fear of future mischief in the hearts of the French *bourgeoisie,* good souls, and induce the Government to allow the police to use their weapons against criminals bent on killing them.[3]

1137. In individuals sentiments are always more or less complex, sometimes very much so. In making a scientific analysis, therefore, we have to fix our main attention on sentiments, not on individuals. Examining the complex of sentiments involved in pity for

love is the bleeding steel!") The scholiast notes very soundly: *"Sed gladiator:* Cruelty lent charm to such beastliness and revealed him to her as something beautiful and fair."

1136 [2] Of her *Liberté* spoke as follows: "The innocent victim of the tragedy in rue Aubry-le-Boucher has led a cruel life since her husband met his death. Already smitten in her tenderest affections, Mme. Deray has been subject to daily insults from the underworld. Public discussion as to the fate of the murderer served to keep her grief and sufferings alive. What the poor woman has undergone since Liabeuf's execution is indescribable. She has been obliged to leave the home to which so many memories bound her. The police themselves advised her to leave. Fortunately she has found a modest situation in house-work, which will enable her to earn her living and support her little boy, who was heart-broken at his father's failure to come home, fell sick, and is hardly well even now." One writer went so far as to say that Liabeuf's victim deserved no sympathy, because it was part of the policeman's trade to get killed. That same writer, however, is agitating for a law to place the occupational risk of the employee on the shoulders of the employer. Another case of two contradictory residues working side by side in the same individual!

1136 [3] *Liberté,* May 6, 1912: "All the papers are commending the exploit of the patrolman at Bougival who shot a burglar as the latter made a motion to draw his revolver—all the papers except *Humanité.* The Socialist organ says: 'We consider that "courageous exploit" both execrable and dangerous.' Dangerous it undoubtedly is—for our crooks. But execrable? Hardly execrable!"

criminals, one is led to breaking it up along the following lines: 1. The sex residue. It figures in nearly all judgments on crimes of passion, so called. 2. Residues of sectarian, patriotic, and other group sentiments. We are inclined to great indulgence towards persons belonging to our "set." We are indifferent, when not actually hostile, to persons not of our "set." 3. Residues of Class II (group-persistences). Religious and political convictions tend to make us indulgent towards those who share them with us, ill-disposed towards those who do not.

Not to be overlooked, further, is the question of interest in cases where individuals give evidence of pity as a means to some personal end. Such would be logical conduct. The residues that are left over pertain strictly to pity; they fall into three varieties. In one, a sentiment of personal pain prevails, and it is extended to embrace pain in others (IV-γ1). In the other two, the sentiment is less personal or not at all so. It leads to an instinctive repugnance to pain in others (IV-γ2), or to a reasoned repugnance (IV-γ3).

1138. IV-γ1: *Self-pity extended to others.* If people are unhappy and are inclined to lay the blame for their woes on the environment in which they live, on "society," they are apt to view all who suffer with a benevolent eye. That is not a logical reasoning; it is a sequence of sensations. If we try to state them in rational form we deprive them of the very thing that gave them force and efficacy— their indefiniteness. Bearing that in mind, one may, roughly, state the reasoning corresponding to such sensations as follows: "I am unhappy, and 'society' is to blame. So-and-so is unhappy, and so 'society' must also be to blame. We are comrades in misfortune, and for my comrade I have the indulgence that I should have for myself; he has my pity."

1139. Something more or less of the kind figures in the humanitarianism of our time. People in poor economic circumstances are convinced that "society" is to blame. By analogy, the crimes of thieves and murderers are also felt to be chargeable to "society." So thieves and murderers come to look like comrades in misfortune worthy of benevolence and pity. "Intellectuals" are convinced that

they are not playing a sufficiently important rôle in the social hierarchy; they envy people of wealth, army officers, prelates, in short
all others in the higher social rankings. They imagine that criminals
and the poor are also victims of the same classes. They feel that in
that respect they are like them, and therefore feel benevolence and
pity for them. While Mme. Tarnowska was on trial in Venice, she
received a poem by a schoolmistress voicing a hope for her speedy
liberation. The teacher in question may well have been an upright
but unhappy woman. Unhappiness drew her close to the murderer,
and filled her with pity for her. The novels of George Sand, Victor
Hugo's *Les misérables,* sold widely to people harbouring just such
sentiments. Certain women are vaguely conscious of how nice it
would be if they had a husband to provide them with the necessaries
and luxuries of life, and a number of paramours to satisfy their
amorous yearnings. Certain men are likewise aware of the advantage of having other men support the women they enjoy. All such
sentiments find expression in a theory that is called "the right to
happiness." In plainer language, it might be called the right to adultery. Hence sentiments of benevolence for adulterers and to some
extent even for panderers.

1140. Such sentiments may drive individuals to rebellion and murder. Just after the bandits Bonnot and Garnier met their death in a
clash with the French police, many persons who thought they had
been wronged by the authorities, even in respect of some minor
traffic summons, raised one shout—"Good for Bonnot!" Attempts
upon the lives of kings, presidents, or other eminent men are largely
the work of unhappy individuals, more or less out of their heads,
who vent their feelings by striking out haphazard at the first person
of note who crosses their path.[1]

1140 [1] In its issues of July 5-6, 1912, the *Matin* published Garnier's diary. There
the criminal may be seen voicing his various sentiments under the derivations
brought into fashion by the literature of the day. Says Garnier: "Every being born
into this world has a right to life. That is undeniable, since it is a law of nature.
[Garnier must have got that from some newspaper, which must have got it from
some hack writer, who, in turn, must have got it from some first-liner such as
Victor Hugo, Anatole France, or Léon Bourgeois.] In my earliest childhood I came
to know authority in the persons of my father and mother; and before reaching the

1141. The existence of such residues makes it probable that many who are seeking their own advantage, but claim to be working for the good of "society," do so in all good faith. It may therefore be that many people who are doing practical Socialism with profit to themselves really believe they are doing theoretical Socialism for the good of all, or at least of the greater number.

1142. IV-γ2: *Instinctive repugnance to suffering.* This is a sentiment of disgust at the sight of all suffering, regardless of whether it

age of understanding, I rebelled against that authority as well as against authority in school. [Mere expressions of sentiment.] I was thirteen at the time, and just beginning to work. Awakening to reason, I began to understand what life and the social machine were like. I saw that individuals were bad. I said to myself: 'I must find some way to get out of this rot of bosses, workers, *bourgeois,* magistrates, police, and all the rest. [Another derivation taken from some Socialist newspaper.] All such people disgusted me, the ones because they did the bossing, the others because they were spineless enough to go through all those motions. Refusing either to exploit or be exploited, I began shop-lifting, but could not make very much at that. [All derivations, just to say that he wanted to enjoy life without working. At bottom he was neither better nor worse than other individuals, such as the Tarnowska woman, for whom our estimable humanitarians feel such exceptional pity.] I got caught, for the first time. For the first time—I was seventeen then—I got three months in jail. On being released I went home to my parents, and they gave me terrible scoldings. But my term in prison, my having had my taste of what is called justice, had made me more of a rebel than ever. It was then that I became an Anarchist. I was about eighteen. I did not want to go back to work again [The real reason for all the patter. People of that kind cannot live in a civilized society, but our kind-hearted humanitarians object to eliminating them.], so I returned to individual reprisal. [A derivation copied from some third-rate paper, which got it from some "thinker."] But no better luck than the first time! Within three or four months I was caught again. I got two months. . . . [He then goes on to tell how he came to hob-nob with Anarchists and to believe in their theories:] My mind was soon made up. I became what they were. [That is to say, he adopted that particular expression for sentiments he had all along held.] I resolved never again to work for other people. I also resolved to work for myself. But how go about it? I didn't have very much, but I had acquired a little more experience; and I was full of energy. I was determined to defend myself from that pack of wolves, so full of stupidity and iniquity, that present-day society is. [A derivation not unlike the derivation of the "thinkers" when they say they are trying to work towards "a better humanity with a little more justice." That is why they want the votes of the Garniers, to send them to parliament. The Garniers of course find it more expeditious and more rational to get the little more justice directly for themselves.] I left Paris when I was about nineteen and a half, for I looked forward to my term of military service with loathing. [People of that sort dislike civil discipline, but military discipline they loathe.] Will that sly, irresponsible mass change some day? It may! I hope so! Meantime, for my part, I am not going to

be beneficial or otherwise. It has provoked the proverb, "The merciful doctor aggravates the sore." The sentiment is often observable in weak, submissive, spineless individuals. If they chance to succeed in overcoming it, they are likely to show themselves exceedingly cruel. That explains a remark one sometimes hears to the effect that women are more tender-hearted and at the same time more cruel than men.[1]

sacrifice myself for it. Now is the time I am living on this earth. Now is the time I have a right to live, and live I am going to with all the means that science [The god of his religion.] puts at my disposal. I will meet trickery with trickery, force with force. . . . [He recounts various adventures in crime in Belgium. "Wanted" by the police in Brussels, he slips back to Paris,] where I took a job on *L'anarchie* and set to work with a will. I worked almost every day, and since the pay was rather small I joined some of my comrades in a number of burglaries, though the intake did not amount to very much. So I turned to counterfeiting, but that was not a success either. The risks were greater than in night-work and I made more at that. . . . [These estimable humanitarians may say what they will; but it is evident enough that if such people were eliminated from society, their exploits would come to an end. Mild punishments allow them to continue. Garnier joins a gang of criminals and tells about a large number of burglaries he carries out with them:] During the two months of September and October our chief job was the post office at Chelles, where we got 4,000 francs. There were others of less account. Finally, early in November we did another at Compiègne, which netted 3,500 francs. . . . [Garnier teams up with Bonnot and learns how to drive a car. He describes his "first big haul"—the murder of a bank messenger carrying funds:] I go up to about three yards from the boy. I pull my gun and coolly give him a first bullet, then a second. He falls, his companion taking to his heels, scared out of his wits. I pick up one bag. My pal gets the other, which that fool of a boy will not let go of, for he is not dead. But he ends by dropping it, for he loses consciousness. [Humanitarians pity poor wretches like Garnier but give not a thought to their victims. The second instalment of Garnier's "Memoirs" in the *Matin* recounts many other crimes. I will transcribe just one story—the murder of a chauffeur!] I picked up a big piece of wood . . . and gave it to him with all my might just over the left temple. The chauffeur dropped without a cry. He was dead or what amounted to that. To be sure he wouldn't come to, one of my pals went and got a jack weighing some hundred and fifty pounds and set it on his chest. Within a few moments he stopped moving. He was dead." Anatole France sells no end of books showing that such ghouls are unfortunates (§ 1638 [1]). It is instructive to set side by side the sentiments voiced by Garnier and the sentiments of people who buy such books and dote on them.

1142 [1] *Liberté*, May 8, 1912: "At Sceaux, 8 rue de Bagneux, stands a garden-lodge that goes with the mansion there. It is the home of Mme. Herbuté de Bute, 51, a gentlewoman. She is deaf and nearly blind. She lives there alone. She has always passed for a woman of some property and one of her former maids said as much to Gabriel Gaugnon, 18, a mechanic, living at Fontenay-aux-Roses. Gaugnon made up his mind to rob the lady, and suggested to friends of his that they join

1143. The fact that among the Greeks and the Romans heads of families were called upon to make animal sacrifices may have served to arrest the development of the sort of pity here in question. Such pity is often the mainstay of those who condemn wars of whatever description. They dwell chiefly on the sufferings of the killed and the wounded, never stopping to consider the advantages a war may have won. But not a few such sentimentalists of this type readily forget their declamations when other sentiments gain the upper hand. The sufferings of the killed and the wounded are important only so long as it suits the convenience of the pacifist (§ 1559). This variety of pity is widely prevalent in decadent ruling classes. In fact it may serve as an adequate diagnosis of such decadence.

1144. IV-γ3: *Reasoned repugnance to useless sufferings.* This sentiment is characteristic in strong, energetic people, who know what they want and are able to stop at the exact point that they consider it desirable to attain. In judging its government, a people instinctively understands the difference between this sort of pity and pity

him in the venture. They accepted. They are Fernand Le Bas, 17, from Bourg-la-Reine, and Fernand Léard, 21, of Sceaux. On January 10 last Léard presented himself at Mme. Herbuté's cottage under guise of a delivery man sent by a grocer in Paris to deliver an order. Léard made sure that the lady was deaf and so informed his accomplices. The three went back there the following evening, January 11, at six o'clock. Léard broke open the garden-gate, which was locked with a key. With the help of Gaugnon he then broke open the door of the cottage. Le Bas stayed outside on watch and the other two made their way into the house. Mme. Herbuté was reading the evening paper in her bedroom. She heard no sounds. Léard suddenly seized her by the throat with the idea of holding her and keeping her from making any outcry, while Gaugnon was going through the things in the room. But Mme. Herbuté tried to free herself. Falling to her knees, she managed to extract a knife she carried from her pocket and made a pass at Léard, who leapt back instinctively. The lady was so enabled to rush from the room and snatch up her revolver. She dashed out into the garden, where Le Bas fell upon her, threw her to the ground, and held her down. Mme. Herbuté did not lose her presence of mind. She fired one shot from her revolver in Le Bas's direction, calling meantime for help. The three rogues were arrested shortly after. This afternoon they appeared before Criminal Sessions, Department of the Seine. All three made a full confession, and Mme. Herbuté de Bute on giving her testimony begged for the jury's leniency in their favour. To the astonishment of everybody, the jury brought in a verdict of not guilty and the three toughs were dismissed from the bar. . . . The verdict is baffling only in appearance. It is explainable on the one hand in view of the terror that the Bonnot-Garnier gang and

of the preceding type. They respect, they esteem, they love the pity of a strong government; they ridicule and scorn the pity of a weak government. The latter they regard as cowardice, the former, as generosity. The term "useless" above is subjective; it reflects a feeling of the person who uses it. In certain cases it is possible to determine that a thing is objectively "useless" to society; but in many many others there is doubt, and sociology is far from being sufficiently advanced to dispel it. However, it would be a mistake to conclude, in the light of an eventual and remote chance of some advantage, that the infliction of suffering will prove beneficial. Decisions have to be based on the greater or lesser probabilities. It would be manifestly absurd, for instance, to say that it might be a good thing to kill a hundred or so people at random on the chance that a future murderer might so be disposed of. There was more room for doubt in the argument often advanced to justify prosecutions of witches, that many common criminals were to be counted among them. And the doubt would probably be insuperable were

its avengers are spreading on every hand; for it is only too certain, alas, that so far the people who ought to be executed are doing most of the executing. Then again, jurymen who are cowardly enough to be afraid find a further excuse in the fact that criminal legislation during these past years has been inspired exclusively by the increasing sympathy with which gunmen and Anarchists have been viewed by those in power; whence the conclusion, for that matter logical enough, that the maxim 'Be kind to animals' is a humanitarian watchword that altogether conforms with signs 'from on High.' Finally there is a third prime factor. The policy of 'No enemies to the Left' has also affected the jury system in the direction of increased incompetence. Criminal Sessions have been blessed with a new set of jurors and among these 'self-conscious proletarians' not a few, we may guess, have a real esteem for Bonnot, whom the 'unified' [Socialist] Hervé has described as a 'professor of energy.' " *Liberté*, May 9, 1912: "A Seine jury yesterday acquitted a trio of unusually distinguished rascals who broke into a little cottage one evening last January and did their best to kill, in the thought of robbing her, an elderly gentlewoman, deaf and half-blind, who was living alone there. They did not succeed in their twin and very laudable intent, but assuredly through no fault of their own. It was because their victim was ill-mannered enough not to let herself be plucked without raising an outcry. The jury however concluded that it was only fair to give these youths of such tender age a chance to return to their favourite studies in murder and theft. The astonishment is general. The lawyers [of the defence] have hardly got their breath back yet, and their clients much less. They in fact will not understand till some day in the near future they appear in court again between three other pairs of gendarmes. By that time they will have grown up and learned how to do a better job."

there no means of distinguishing between a poisoner and a hysterical female who thinks that she is having commerce with the Devil. There are such means, however, so the doubt vanishes, and the sufferings so inflicted may be judged objectively useless.[1]

1145. IV-δ: *Self-sacrifice for the good of others*. Life in society necessarily rests on a certain reciprocal goodwill between individual and individual. The sentiment may be weak or strong, but it cannot be entirely wanting. It is manifested in both animals and human beings in acts of mutual assistance and common defence—in other words, by the sufferings an individual takes upon himself for the good of others. Such phenomena are observable even among non-social animals in their relations to their young, which are fed and protected by one or both of the parents. The lioness shares her prey with her cubs, the hawk and its mate share their prey with their chicks. In our own homes male canaries may be seen feeding their mates and their little ones.

1146. All known facts incline one to the belief that the sentiment which prompts a man to help and protect his family and the group to which he belongs is, in part at least, similar to the sentiment observable in animals. The difference lies in the fact that the human being cloaks such conduct with a logical varnish. Very beautiful theories have been evolved to show that a man *ought* to love his country. However, the effect of such theories is virtually nil. It is insignificant at any rate as compared with the influence of the non-logical sentiment that inspires patriotism. One would really have to have the sickly brains of the day-dreamers of the "social contract," or of the "debt to society" of the "solidarists," to imagine that people fight for their countries the way a partner in a business concern pays in an assessment.

1147. Not only do the sentiments that inspire a man to self-sacrifice for the benefit of others influence the members of a society directly to perform certain acts and to approve of those who do them and admire them. They exert an indirect influence upon the

1144 [1] Such considerations are not strictly in point here, since they overstep the domain of residues and bring up questions of logical conduct.

individual who is encouraged to this or that behaviour, not only by a sentiment of his own favourable to such conduct, but also and often even more forcibly, by a desire to win the admiration of others or to avoid their censure. Conversely, as we shall see for the general case in § 1161, if we find that certain things are done to satisfy this desire for public approval, we may safely conclude that functioning in the group in question are sentiments corresponding to these IV-δ residues.

1148. IV-δ1: *Risking one's life.* People risk or even sacrifice their lives out of deep feelings of sociality, or from the importance they attach to the esteem of others. It would seem that in animals only the first sentiment figures. Polygamous males are wont to defend their females; it is a matter of everyday observation that the cock defends his hens, the bull his cows. Even domestic animals of different species defend one another when they are members of the same household. House-dogs have been known to defend the house-cat, and the house-cat a puppy. In human beings, in most cases, it is impossible to distinguish a sentiment of that variety from the desire to win the approbation of one's fellows. Tacitus records that among the Germans the chiefs were surrounded by liegemen who fought strenuously to defend them and who were forever disgraced if they returned alive from a battle in which their chief had fallen.[1] General

---

1148 [1] *Germania,* 14: *"Iam vero infame in omnem vitam ac probrosum superstitem principi suo* (surviving his prince) *ex acie recessisse."* Similar sentiments prevailed in Sparta among the citizens. It was a disgrace for a man to return alone after his comrades had been slain. Herodotus, *Historiae,* VII, 229-31, tells of two Spartans, Eurytus and Aristodemus, whom Leonidas sent home from Thermopylae because of serious trouble with their eyes. They stopped at Alpene. The news coming that the Spartans were surrounded by the Persians, Eurytus had himself guided to the battle-field by his helot, and died fighting. Aristodemus lingered at Alpene. (According to another story, they had both been sent on a mission, Eurytus returning promptly, Aristodemus delaying.) "When Aristodemus returned to Lacedaemon he was branded with infamy and disgrace." Plutarch, *Lacaenarum apophthegmata* (*Sayings of Spartan Women,* 22, Babbitt, Vol. III, p. 467): "A man was telling his sister how her son had fallen gloriously in battle. She replied: 'I am as glad for his sake as I am sorry for you who played false to such valiant company.'" *Ibid.,* 6 (Babbitt, Vol. III, p. 461): "A man was describing to his mother the glorious death of his brother. 'Are you not ashamed,' she said, 'to have missed such company on such a journey?'" Herodotus, *Historiae,* V, 87, also tells how one man

Nogi, victor for the Japanese at Port Arthur, killed himself with his wife on the day of the Mikado's funeral. In that case the sacrifice of life had no direct utility. It was a pure manifestation of sentiments of sociality, subordination, hierarchy, combined with certain group-persistences of the old-fashioned Samurai, and with a desire for the approbation of people sharing those sentiments.

1149. IV-δ2: *Sharing one's property with others.* There are any number of shadings between the state of mind where one gives up one's life and this milder form of sentiment where there is a mere renunciation of certain enjoyments for the benefit of other individuals. Here too examples are exceedingly numerous among both animals and human beings.

1150. The little girl who dresses up her doll and offers it food is not merely imitating her mother; she is expressing a spontaneous sentiment of her own, as is the case with the swallow that has hatched a brood for the first time and carries food to her nestlings.

1151. Combining with Class II residues (group-persistences), the present residue accounts for sacrifices offered to objects inanimate or animate, to the dead, to gods. In the more complex cases other causes may also figure.

1152. At first blush one might imagine that this residue was at work in all individuals of the ruling class who sided with the subject classes. But that is not the case. As one looks more closely it is apparent that such persons may be classified in the following manner: 1. Persons who assume leadership of the subject classes to attain some political, financial, or other advantage. History is replete with the doings of such people. Aristocracies usually owe their falls to them. In a day gone by violence was the only recourse, and that limited their number. Nowadays, when there is a pacific instrument, the ballot, their number has increased inordinately, since revolutions are no longer necessary to assure them some measure of success. Democracy, moreover, affords outlets for all ambitions, from the

alone returned from an Athenian expedition against Aegina and how he was slain upon his return to Athens by the wives of those who had fallen, "indignant that he alone of all should have saved himself." Whether such tales be history or legend matters little for our purpose, which is merely to get at certain sentiments.

ambition of the political boss (Pareto: *grande elettore*) in a township to the ambitions of aldermen, councilmen, Deputies and Senators; and outlets from the modest "job" obtained through the influence of a Congressman, to the directorship of a department or the control of a treasury. In Europe today how many people are Socialists just to obtain such a post, just as tomorrow they would be conservatives if a conservative government should come into power! 2. Persons who, with an eye to their interests, tie the donkey where the "boss" directs. Under the Restoration in France the "level-headed young man" went to mass; under Louis Philippe he read Voltaire; under the Second Empire he found it highly praiseworthy to say that he was "uninterested in politics." Today, he has to be "interested in politics"—he has to be a *blocard,* a humanitarian, a Socialist.[1] He may have to be a Nationalist tomorrow. Today financiers and captains of industry have discovered that it is to their interests to abet the Socialists. Captains of industry and financiers of a wealth to be computed in millions are to be heard calling for "social legislation"; and one might believe that they were inspired solely by love of their neighbour, with whom they are passionately bent on sharing their worldly goods. But keep your eye on what happens after said "social legislation" has been passed. You will see that their wealth has not decreased, but increased, that they have given nothing away, but have rather received. The Caillaux-Bertaux ministry in France was made up largely of millionaires. In them even with a microscope you could detect no trace of a desire to share their goods with others. Giolitti's "democratic" majority in Italy was made up of people who understood "business" (and a very good business they did indeed);

1152 [1] The term *"blocard,"* now in common use, may perhaps be unintelligible a few years hence. I will explain, therefore, that M. Clemenceau once founded in France a newspaper called the *Bloc.* In it he exhorted all "republicans" to consolidate in one mass, one "block," to fight reaction. He was aped in France and Italy by hosts of good souls who clasped hands in order to clamber the more easily into control of the public weal and fatten thereon. The traditional terms for their kind—"Camorrist" in Italy or "grafter" elsewhere—fell into desuetude, the newly coined term *"blocard"* being used instead. [In these volumes we follow the late M. Clemenceau's own caprice in the spelling of his name. The usual form of the word is *Clémenceau.*—A. L.]

nor did his ministry lack the support of the "steel men" or the "sugar men"; yet one may doubt whether those estimable people were inspired by any desire to share their goods with others. They became Nationalists and fire-eaters (*guerrafondai*—militarists) when it turned to their interest to do so; and they passed the bill extending universal suffrage to illiterates the moment "the old man" assured them that that was a first-class device for securing "good elections," and therefore for "sitting pretty." [2] In England Lloyd George is quite willing to distribute the properties of the peers among "the poor"; but he keeps an eye on his own pocket-book, and does not disdain a risk on the stock exchange. And there is his team-mate, John Burns. No one can see what he has given to others; but anyone can see what he has received and the fat salaries he has been able to earn—assiduously striving for the welfare of others. 3. Persons who are sincerely inclined to give something to others because they instinctively feel that they will receive more than they give. They give away a sparrow in the hope that he will come home a capon. Working in them is

1152 [2] Fradeletto, *Dogmi ed illusioni della democrazia:* "Today we are witnessing most unexpected changes of heart, which—such the mysterious workings of chance!—never coincide with a sacrifice or a personal risk, but always, or almost always, coincide, with a striking 'clean-up' on Exchange. People who a short time since were shouting the war-slogans of sedition that they might elbow their way into public life with the applause of the revolutionary parties are now voicing counsels of prudence that they may hold their places by the votes of the reactionaries. . . . But a spectacle even more astonishing to the naïve must be these mass-conversions that are taking place, these descents of grace from on high which suddenly enlighten a whole Chamber and convert it. The proofs are close at hand in time and in space: *domestica facta!* Before the sixth of April, 1911, how many partisans of universal suffrage were there in the Italian parliament? Luzzatti's reform bill, which would have given the vote to anyone able to read and write and so would have increased the electorate by a little more than a million, seemed to a great many people premature, unseasonable, a thing not 'wanted by the country,' a dangerous concession to extremist parties on the Left. But since the sixth of April, since the descent of tongues of fire in the shape of a few words dropped by the Head of the Government, the devotees of universal suffrage have become legion, and among the warmest are those who voted against Luzzatti's cautious measure. But that is not all. In the summer of 1910, while the Daneo-Credaro bill was up for debate, illiteracy was solemnly proclaimed our worst sore, our shame, our ruin [It is not at all proved that those who expressed that opinion were right.], our abiding title to discredit in the eyes of foreign countries. Two years later, while the new electoral bill was before the parliament, we heard at times a sort of idyllic paean lifted to illiteracy, now held to constitute a presumption of instinctive good

the present residue combined with other residues looking to the advantage desired. 4. A few "intellectuals," defective in energy, knowledge, and good sense, who take the declamations of the types named above seriously. But they are few in numbers, and some who might seem to belong among them really belong to the other types. 5. It cannot be denied that conceivably there may be individuals of energy, knowledge, and good sense who propound social and "solidarian" doctrines out of a sincere desire to share their goods with others; but it is not easy to find examples of them. Saint-Simon was rich. He died poor and friendless. It might seem as though he could be mentioned as one. But his wealth he squandered in pleasure-seeking, and he was comforted in his friendless poverty by his pride in being a Messiah, the founder of a new religion. In such things the main motives of his conduct! All these types are to be found among those subscribing to the doctrine of "solidarity," which is more often invoked for purposes of receiving than for purposes of giving; and rare as white blackbirds are those who believe in it with-

sense, unsullied by 'fragmentary education.' " [It is not at all proved that those who expressed such sentiments were wrong.]

The explanation of such things is very simple. It was stated by Sir Edward Grey in regard to an exactly identical situation in international affairs. On Aug. 1, 1913, the House of Commons heckled him with questions on the Balkans. He was asked whether there were any principle of international law whereby Turkey might be restrained from repudiating the treaty of peace and reoccupying Adrianople and Thrace. He replied that there was not. He was reminded that on the outbreak of the Balkan War the Powers had pompously declared that, whatever the outcome of the war, the territorial *status quo* had absolutely to be maintained in the Balkans; and he was asked whether the Powers had any reasons, other than the victories of the Allies, for repudiating that solemn declaration. He replied that there was, in fact, no other reason. Finally after many other questions Sir Edward Grey had a moment of genuine frankness and said: "The questions that have been put to me seem all to be framed on the assumption that the policies of the Powers have been dictated by considerations of logic and international law. In point of fact each Power has been following the course indicated by its own special interests, and by a collective desire to preserve peace in Europe." His frankness, however, did not go so far as to mention the powerful financial interests that were guiding all the Powers, severally or collectively. The point of this long note might be summarized in a few words of Beaumarchais, in *Le Barbier de Séville,* Act IV, Scene VIII. Don Bartholo is astonished that Bazile has undergone a change of heart like the ones just mentioned: "*Bartholo:* What, Bazile? You signed? *Bazile:* What do you expect! That devil of a man always has his pockets full of unanswerable arguments!"

out ulterior motives. As we have already noted (§ 1147) and will note again (§ 1162), the existence of these various categories in no wise detracts from the social importance of the sentiments registered by these IV-δ2 residues. Indeed it emphasizes their very great significance, since they are resorted to and used, be it indirectly, in so many and such different ways.

1153. IV-ε: *Sentiments of social ranking (hierarchy)*. Sentiments of ranking on the part of inferiors as well as superiors are observable in animals. They are very wide-spread in human societies. It would seem indeed that no human society at all complex could survive without them. Relationships of superiority and inferiority are changed in forms, but none the less kept, in societies that ostensibly proclaim equality for all individuals. A sort of temporary feudalism is the rule in such societies, with a progressive descent in rankings from the politicians at the top to the politicians at the bottom. Anyone doubting this need only try to obtain something, in Italy or France for instance, without the support of the local "boss," the Deputy in the parliament, the "powers that be" in art, science, or public service; or (at the bottom of the ladder) the "fixer." With sentiments of social ranking we may class the sentiment of deference the individual feels for the group of which he is a part, or for other groups, and his desire to have their approval or admiration.

1154. It is absurd to imagine that the old-style feudalism in Europe rested solely on force. It held its own in part by virtue of sentiments of reciprocal affection, which are observable in other countries also where feudalism prevailed or has prevailed—in Japan, for instance. The same may be said of Roman clientage, of the craft-gilds of the Middle Ages, of the monarchies, and in general of all social systems in which a social ladder exists. In fact, only when it is crumbling and is about to give way to another does a hierarchy cease to be spontaneous through becoming preponderantly or exclusively a matter of force. I say preponderantly, because the element of unmixed force is never missing.

1155. IV-ε1: *Sentiments of superiors*. They are sentiments of patronage and benevolence, supplemented oftentimes by domineering sentiments, or sentiments of pride. These last may coexist with sentiments of apparent humility, as one may observe in religious corporations and among ascetics. One may in good faith thrill with the pride of being humbler than another.

1156. IV-ε2: *Sentiments of inferiors.* They are sentiments of subordination, affection, reverence, fear. They are indispensable to the constitution of animal societies, to the domestication of animals, to the ordering of human societies. They are often observable *de facto* in individuals who call themselves Anarchists. Anarchists have their "leaders," even though they do not call them such, and there are plenty of Anarchists who show almost superstitious deference to the authority of physicians and medical practitioners who are not seldom quacks. Manifestations of the sense for authority are very very numerous and endlessly varied. It is common to accept the authority of a person who has, or presumes to have, some real or imaginary symbol of superiority.[1] Hence the reverence of the young for the old, of the novice for the expert; in a day gone by, of the illiterate for the learned, of the person who spoke only a modern language for one who spoke Latin; of the plebeian for the noble— in our day, of the non-union worker and many people of the *bourgeoisie* for the union man; of the weak for the strong (or reputed strong), of the man of one race for the man of another regarded as superior; of the woman for the man (when special circumstances do not make her the dominant party); of the subject for the sovereign; of the believer for the priest, the prophet, the ascetic, the man who pretends to be to a greater extent than others in the good graces of

---

1156 [1] From no end of examples the following: Landor, *In the Forbidden Land*, Vol. II, p. 167: Held prisoner in Tibet Landor was about to be slain when he was saved by a peculiar arrangement of the fingers on his hand. "The Lama . . . examined my hands and spread my fingers apart, expressing great surprise and astonishment. In a moment all the Lamas and soldiers came round and examined my manacled hands. . . . The Pombo, too, upon being informed, immediately came and inspected my fingers, and the proceedings were at once stopped. When some weeks later I was released, I was able to learn from the Tibetans the reason for their amazement. My fingers happened to be webbed rather higher than usual and this is most highly thought of in Tibet. He who possesses such fingers has, according to the Tibetans, a charmed life, and, no matter how much one tries, no harm can be done to him."

the Deity; of the voter for the politician; of the plain man for the
man of mystery, the fortune-teller, the charlatan—and in our days,
particularly, for the physician, the hygienist, the promoter of "reform measures," or the person who otherwise comes forward as a
high-priest of the god Progress; of the poor in spirit for the emancipated woman, who, he thinks, is above sex appetites; of the old-
time bigot for the first friar who came along; of the new bigot for
the pontiffs of humanitarianism.

1157. In virtue of the persistence of abstractions (§§ 1065 f.) the
sentiment of authority may to a greater or lesser extent become dis-
engaged from the person and attached to the symbol, real or presumed, of authority. Hence the importance for those in authority
of "keeping up appearances"—"prestige," the outward semblance of
superiority. The detachment may be complete, and the sentiment of
authority may attach itself to inanimate objects, as in the reverence
felt by many people for anything that is written or printed, and in
some countries for anything written or printed on paper bearing a
seal or an official stamp (§ 1430). The residue also plays a more or
less important part in other phenomena, such as fetishism, the worship of relics, and the like.

1158. A passage in Machiavelli's *Mandragola* well brings out the
plain man's reverence for anyone speaking Latin.[1] Molière too makes
sport of it, but time was when the best minds believed that historical
truth was to be sought in Latin texts, and that a text deserved
credence from the mere fact of being written in Latin. Not so long
ago it was taken for granted that the older the manuscript, the better
it was. Palaeography has shown that some ancient manuscripts are
less correct than others more recent.[2]

1158 [1] Act II, Scene II: "*Callimaco. . . . Nam causae sterilitatis sunt aut in
semine aut in matrice . . . aut in causa extrinseca. Nicia.* The most wonderful man
that ever was!" Had Callimaco spoken in Italian, Nicia, who also knew Latin,
would not have assented with the same extravagant admiration.

1158 [2] Paulin Paris, *Les grandes chroniques de France,* Vol. I, Preface, p. xv.
Noting that the spurious chronicle of the Pseudo-Turpin was the first to be translated into French, Paris remarks: "It occurred to no one to dispute its trustworthi-
ness. It is easy enough for us to do that today. How can it be authentic, we would
say, when earlier historians make no mention of it, when Charlemagne's contempo-

1159. In England there used to be a curious privilege called benefit of clergy (*privilegium clericale*), whereby certain persons escaped punishment for crime, on a first offence at least. It applied not only to persons who had taken holy orders, but to anyone who could read. Trying to find a logical reason for the privilege, Blackstone says [1] that "everyone that could read (a mark of great learning in those days of ignorance and her sister superstition)" was "accounted a clerk or *clericus,* and allowed the benefit of clerkship, though neither initiated in holy orders, nor trimmed with the clerical tonsure." But the people of those days were not such dolts, after all, as to think that a man belonged to the clergy when they very well knew that he did not. The privilege, therefore, could not have had any such origin. It arose rather from the respect in which the clergy and other such classes of citizens were held. James I, by his Statute 21, article 6, extended benefit of clergy even to illiterate women convicted of thefts under 10 shillings in value. William and Mary (Statutes 3, 4, 5) extended to women without restriction any benefit of clergy enjoyed by men. It is evident, therefore, that in days not so remote from ours benefit of clergy was simply a privilege granted to certain classes of people deemed worthy of special consideration, among them persons able to read and write.

raries give the facts in an entirely different and far more plausible manner? But at that time no one in the world knew those contemporary historians. One thing only was known: Turpin's *Chronicle* was written in Latin and that was enough to justify the trust of the most fastidious." In another essay, *Op. cit.,* Vol. II, Preface, p. x, he says: "At the time when the monument constituted by the *Great Chronicles of Saint Denis* was being erected, anything of a certain antiquity that was written in Latin could claim by that very fact the acceptance of everybody." Davis, *The Chinese,* Vol. II, pp. 370-71 (1836, p. 163): *"The god's visit to the home of Yu-Kong."* The god is rebuking Yu-Kong, who has been saying that he has dutifully obeyed all the rules laid down for him: ". . . Among them was a rule commanding you to reverence written characters; and nevertheless your pupils and your colleagues tear leaves from ancient books and paper the walls of their rooms with them and wrap parcels. Some even use them to wipe off their tables, and then excuse themselves by saying that if they do soil the paper, they burn it afterwards at once. Such things are going on every day before your eyes, and nevertheless you never utter a word to prevent them. And you yourself if you chance to pass a piece of paper with writing on it in the street—what do you do but take it home and throw it into the fire?"

1159 [1] *Commentaries,* IV, 28.

1160. IV-ε3: *Need of group approbation.* This is one of the cases in which the difference between the sentiment and the manifestation of it which constitutes the residue comes out most clearly. The need that the individual feels for being well regarded by his group, for winning its approval, is a very powerful sentiment. On it human society may be said to rest. But it works in silence, oftentimes without being expressed. Indeed the person who most desires admiration —glory—from his group pretends to be indifferent to it. Strange as it may seem, he may really be indifferent to it, and then again unwittingly allow himself to be guided by the approbation or admiration of others. That is observable in ascetics who are such in good faith.

1161. The sentiments of sociality manifested by various sorts of residues are nearly always accompanied by a desire for the approbation of others, or for avoiding their censure. But it is not very usual for this latter sentiment to express itself in the residue corresponding to it. Conversely, the residue sometimes hides other residues. A person may say that he is prompted by a desire to win the esteem of others, whereas to some extent, however slight, he is also prompted by a desire to do the thing that after all merits such esteem. When a person does a thing and says, "It is good," or refrains from doing a thing and says, "It is bad," it is hard to say whether he means, "It is approved (or disapproved) by the group," or that it accords or disaccords with his own sentiments. The two considerations function simultaneously. As a rule the approbation or censure of the group reinforces a sentiment already present in the individual (§ 163). There may, of course, be the perfect hypocrite who is loath to do a thing but does it to win public esteem. There may be the coward who lets himself be killed in war to escape the stigma of cowardice. But such cases are not, after all, very frequent. In the commoner case, a person has a faint impulse to do a thing and does it to win public esteem, or the naturally brave man is inspired to heroism and gives his life in the thought of glory.

1162. The cases just noted where the individual is not at all, or not entirely, inspired by the sentiment corresponding to the residue that happens to be involved, but entirely or in part by the desire to win the approbation or escape the censure of his group, none the less shows the social importance of the sentiments corresponding to the residues in question. For if the residue is not acting upon the individual directly, it is doing so indirectly through the approbation or censure of the group; and only because that sentiment is influential in the group does the approbation or censure have its force. Even the ascetic who is a perfect hypocrite bears witness to the strength of the ascetic residue in the group whose opinion he values. He becomes a hypocrite and his hypocrisy is approved and admired in the group. If the group were indifferent to him his hypocrisy would serve no purpose.

1163. IV-ζ: *Asceticism*. Observable in human beings is a special group of sentiments that has no counterpart in animals. They are sentiments that prompt the human being to seek sufferings or abstain from pleasures without design of personal advantage, to go counter to the instinct that impels living creatures to seek pleasurable things and avoid painful things. They constitute the controlling nucleus in the phenomena known as asceticism.

1164. If we knew only one type of asceticism—the Catholic, for instance—it would be hard to distinguish the residue from the derivation. A man does penance because he believes that in so doing he is pleasing God and making amends for his sins. The religious feeling might well be the residue, and penance the logical consequence of it. There are, in fact, cases where matters seem to stand that way. But there are other cases where the variable element is the reason given for the penance, the penance itself coming down to mere renunciation of the pleasures of life, which would be the constant element. So long as the reasons vary with varying conceptions of the deity, we get for a constant element the religious concept in general. But lo, there are ascetics, such as the ancient Greek Cynics, who had no religious conceptions whatever, so that uniformity goes by the board. And there stand the Spartans, who practised asceticism as a means of maintaining strict discipline; and the Buddhists, who turned ascetics in order to stultify all vital energies. Among our own contemporaries we find ascetics in the name of the goddess Science who abstain, or pretend to abstain, from the use of alcoholic beverages; other ascetics who dare not look at a pretty girl in the name of a sex morality of their own, which—who can guess why?—regards the sexual act as the worst of crimes; others who cannot endure light literature; still others who make war on dramatic productions that are not altogether dull and fail to "solve some social problem." It is therefore apparent that the constant element is the self-infliction of sufferings, the variable element the reasons they have—or say they have—for doing so.[1]

1164 [1] Montet, *De l'état présent et de l'avenir de l'Islam*, pp. 59-61: "It has been observed that the Mussulman who aspires to status as a marabout and seeks distinction for his asceticism is inclined, once he has been proclaimed a saint, to relax quite readily from his acts of continence, which served merely as a ladder for attaining that status. . . . Licentiousness has more than once gone hand in hand with the most extreme austerity, as examples from the most widely differing religions show. . . . So there are obscene saints, immodest saints, immoral saints. There is plenty of trustworthy testimony as to the escapades and public scandals of such people. . . . There are degrees, furthermore, in filthiness and personal neglect. One frequently encounters marabouts who go about in tatters and never wash. Others make a boast of their uncleanliness and their lice . . . and affect the greatest contempt for the comforts of this world. . . . As may readily be imagined, continent saints, ascetic saints, antinomian saints, are veritably legion in Islam." Fraser, *Travels and Adventures in the Persian Provinces*, pp. 93-95: "In the course of two hours, my friend the dervish arrived, and recommended his hints of information in a strain which I could not at all comprehend; for I endeavoured in vain to recollect his features or the place where I could have before seen him. At last I displayed so much impatience at his continued grimaces that being convinced of their further inutility he made himself known to me. He was, it appeared, a native of Shiraz, who, being a clever but a lazy fellow, had taken to a life of wandering idleness to avoid the miseries of occupation, and now lived by his wits. He had seen much of the world, had discovered that it was easy and profitable to gull it, and practised what his experience had taught him, to the extent of his ability. . . . My friend the dervish had now thrown aside the cant of his profession, and was beginning to be communicative, when Zein-ul-Abudeen, with some other persons, unfortunately entered, upon which he suddenly relapsed into grimace and jargon." The Church Fathers often complain of monks who usurped the semblance of asceticism in order to trick people. In the fourth century Joannes Cassianus, *Collationes*, XVIII (*De tribus generibus monachorum*), makes a veritable class of them as a "fourth order of monks" (*Caput 8: De quarto genere monachorum*), holding it to be of quite recent origin. Alluding to them in his *De monastica exercitatione*, VIII (*Opera*, p. 727), St. Nilus the Abbot describes them as shunning the hard life in the monasteries, which they could not endure, and besieging the wealthy like so many parasites.

1165. The main residue appears in that constant element. But it is not the only residue that figures in it. All social phenomena are complex mixtures of many elements involving many residues. In the ascetic, oftentimes, along with the residue of asceticism one notes the residue of pride (IV-ε1). He feels himself superior to the generality of mortals, and those who admire him recognize that superiority (§ 1161, IV-ε2). Active in him sometimes is a religious residue (§ 882) and then again a residue of uniformity (IV-β2), as when he sets out to force his asceticism on others, or a residue of a presumed utility, real or imaginary (§ 851). All such residues have to be put aside to get at the residue of pure asceticism.

1166. Now that we have found it, we still have to determine its affinities with other residues, in other words, its proper classification.[1] That is not an easy thing to do, and it would almost seem as though asceticism had to stand in a class by itself. But it is soon apparent that the facts of asceticism belong to a large class comprising acts of abstinence, renunciation of pleasures, voluntary self-sacrifice. Subvarieties may be distinguished in the class by considering the purposes of such sacrifices and their degrees of intensity. Two men voluntarily reduce their consumption of food, one in time of famine, that there may be a little bread for everybody, the other in time of plenty, just to inflict a pain upon himself. Those evidently are two different sorts of acts, even though the second may be regarded as a different manifestation of certain instincts that also figured in the first. Four men abstain from drinking wine: the first because he has discovered that wine is injurious to his health; the second in order to save the money he spends on wine for the benefit of his children; the third to set an example of abstinence for a drunkard who is ruining himself and his family; the fourth to inflict

---

1166 [1] We are not trying, remember, to determine "what asceticism is" (§ 118). We are merely asking whether there is a class of facts that possess such and such characteristics in common. To that group we then give the name of asceticism, but only by analogy, there being among such facts certain facts that in ordinary parlance are called ascetic. So the botanist does not ask "what Ranunculaceae are." He is looking for a genus of plants that possess certain common characteristics. He calls the group Ranunculaceae, because among them is the plant commonly called ranunculus. He might label the genus with any other name just as well.

a pain upon himself. There we get acts of four different kinds. The first involves self-interest and residues of personal integrity (Class V). The second and third arise out of regard for one's neighbour—residues of sociality (Class IV). The fourth is distinct from these last two; in the first place, because the purpose they were seen to have is missing, in part at least; then again intensities are different —in the fourth case intensities ordinarily are greater. We are therefore justified in grouping the last three sorts of actions together and in regarding the fourth type as a particular case of the instincts that give rise to the other two.

1167. So we are placed in the way of finding the proper location for acts of asceticism in a natural classification (§ 147). They appear as depending on the residues of sociality, the social purpose being attenuated, playing a slighter and slighter rôle, even disappearing, while intensities increase, assume gigantic proportions, overreach all bounds. In general terms, individual temperance, besides conceivably having some utility for the individual himself—a case that we are not considering here—may have its utility for others, for the group. In a case where there is a shortage of food, fasting becomes a public service. In conditions of general poverty, abstinence from voluptuous consumption is a benefit to the group. If every individual yielded to the sex-instinct at sight of any woman, human society would dissolve. Abstinence in this last respect is of very great utility, and that explains why sex asceticism has come to be so general; not that it was invented of design with that in view, but because as manifesting certain sentiments it encountered no obstacles in social utility. Next in order comes asceticism in food, as manifested in fasting and in taking poor and insufficient nourishment, because food-supply was one of the major problems of ancient societies, where famines were frequent. Residues of pride, admiration, and the like are also favoured by such circumstances, for abstinence in matters of sex and eating is evidence of no common will-power.

1168. From the standpoint of the group, providence, which means abstinence from a present with a view to a future advantage, has its utility, in fact is an indispensable prerequisite to progress in civilization. In the individual case economy is a useful thing. Carried to extremes it becomes miserliness. So with the group, abstinence from present enjoyments finds its hypertrophy in asceticism. Present enjoyment, furthermore, is oftentimes a matter of merely sensuous pleasure, whereas the future blessing resulting from abstinence and saving is often a matter of intellectual reflection. In that lies one of the many encouragements to the subordination of sense to intelligence. The ascetic goes farther in that direction and declares all sensuous pleasures vain. Then some go farther still in the same direction: sensuous pleasures are not only empty things; they are sins, crimes; one should spend one's life in mortifying the senses.[1] Now it is often of benefit to a group that the individual should sacrifice himself to his faith, and admiration for the martyr originates, partially at least, in an instinctive perception of that truth. The man who dedicates himself absolutely to a faith and apart from it sees nothing else in the world readily comes to look to sensible people as though he were not altogether sound of mind. Go far enough in that direction, and we get those Christian ascetics who simulated madness as an ascetic discipline.[2]

1168 [1] Many writings of prohibitionists consider nothing but the effects—all presumably bad—of wine and other alcoholic beverages on physical health and pay no attention to the pleasure a man gets from a temperate use of liquors. The idea apparently would be that a man should think of nothing but his health, that pleasure by itself is vanity. To think logically, as people never do in arguments addressed to the sentiments, that would mean giving up almost everything a human being does. One should not go out of doors because a brick might fall on one's head, or one might meet a mad dog or have some other accident. One should never go in swimming for fear of getting drowned, nor climb a mountain for fear of falling over a precipice; nor kiss a girl—and the point has been made in all earnestness—for fear of catching a germ; nor enter a theatre or any shut-in place because of the bad air. To say it in a word with the Latins, one should *propter vitam vivendi perdere causas.*

1168 [2] Besse, *Les moines d'Orient,* pp. 48-49: "There used to be a still more extraordinary form of monastic life in the East. . . . Its adepts, who were held together by sentiments of profound self-abasement, simulated madness. Father Or seems to encourage one such disciple to carry his contempt for the world to that extreme. 'Eschew the society of men by flight afar,' he said. 'Show thy contempt for the world and its ways by semblance of madness in this or that regard.' There was a recluse at Tabenna whom everyone regarded as a lunatic. Her comrades were inclined to take advantage of her, but she never dropped a word of impatience, exhibiting to them all a most inspiring example of humility and sisterly

1169. Admiration for the external evidences of asceticism to some extent rests on the utility that acts of abnegation may sometimes and within certain limits have. As a rule people do not go beneath the surface of things and they readily mistake the sign for the thing itself. Another element figuring in the admiration is envy, an inclination on the part of the individual who is kept from certain pleasures to wish that others were kept from them too. Those who are he comes to regard as his comrades, and those who voluntarily deprive themselves of things that he does without from harsh necessity he views with admiration. That partially explains the favour the mendicant orders have always enjoyed with the poorer classes, and the admiration for chastity that is very very general. With many men the favours of young and beautiful women are luxuries that they cannot afford. Male jealousy inclines them to hate anyone who can, and sentiments of common sacrifice fill them with admiration for the man who could, but voluntarily refrains. Many feminists hate men and persecute women who have lovers simply because they have been unable to find men of their own. In every period of history there have been people to disparage what they cannot have, and to hold such disparagement a praiseworthy thing in themselves and in others.

1170. There are acts that seem incapable in any respect of being directly beneficial to society. What social advantage can there be in a man's passing his life on top of a column? But it should not be overlooked that, indirectly, the sentiments which find expression in that way or others equally ridiculous may be of benefit in so far as they indicate a mastery of sensual and worldly instincts of which not everybody can boast. In such conduct and in other behaviour that

love. So she attained to a very high grade of sanctity. But that was an exceptional case. In the course of the century following there came to be quite a number of monks in Palestine who simulated madness. It was indeed the general rule for men well advanced in years and of accomplished virtue. They spent considerable periods of time in prayer and liked to attend to pilgrims and the care of the sick. Their austere living won them general esteem." These people, notice, practised their asceticism themselves. Our contemporary Paladins of Purity, who are as much lunatics as those ever were, try to force their insanity upon other people by dint of fines and sentences to jail.

may be of benefit to the group within narrow limits, but transcends them and sometimes by far, noteworthy both in human beings and animals is a tendency to continue certain acts even when their utility to the individual performing them has come to an end. When a cat has no mice to catch, it plays with a paper ball as if it were a mouse. Give a squirrel all the food it can possibly require and it will continue laying in provisions. A dog may be given all the meat it wants, but it will bury a left-over bone and later dig it up and eat it, though it has plenty of other bones at its disposal.

1171. Acts of asceticism are quite largely acts originating in residues related to life in society that continue functioning when they have ceased to have any utility and acquire an intensity which carries them beyond the point where they might be useful. The residue of asceticism must, in other words, be classified with residues of sociality, and frequently represents a hypertrophy of sentiments of sociality.

1172. This latter circumstance explains why ascetics are oftentimes exceedingly selfish people. Asceticism in expanding has absorbed all the individual's social instinct, so that he has none left for showing benevolence to others, not even to his own family oftentimes (§ 1187).[1]

1172 [1] Literature in all periods has exploited such contrasts in human nature. Dorens, who lived under Louis XIII in France, wrote in a satire:

> *"Gardez-vous bien de lui les jours qu'il communie."*

("Look out for him on the days when he takes communion.")

Famous the verses that Molière puts into the mouth of Orgon, who has been converted by Tartuffe, Act I, scene 6:

> *"Il m'enseigne à n'avoir affection pour rien;*
> *de toutes amitiés il détache mon âme;*
> *et je verrois mourrir frère, enfans, mère et femme,*
> *que je m'en soucierois autant que de cela."*

("He teaches me to feel affection for nothing; he severs my soul from all friendship. I could see mother, wife, children, brothers die, and care no more than that!")

So there are many women among our contemporary uplifters who spend day after day trying to reclaim more or less repentant prostitutes, more or less reformed thieves, while they neglect the washing at home, keep their husbands and children in rags, and serve on the family table meals that a dog would refuse to eat. Sorbière, *Sorberiana, s.v. Dévot* (p. 80): "There is nothing more to be feared than a

1173. The instinct of sociality is much more highly developed in the human race than in animals, and that is why asceticism is a peculiarly human trait. In the same way insanity is a peculiarly human disease because the human intelligence is far superior to intelligence in animals.

1174. But if asceticism in its nucleus is a hypertrophy of certain instincts relative to sociality, it follows, as is the case in general with similar phenomena, that around that nucleus other manifestations foreign to sociality cluster. Abstinence from things of benefit to others brings on, by a process of imitation, abstinence from things that are of no benefit to others or even such that abstinence from them is harmful to others. Abstinence from useful things such as clothing, food, and the like, is often attended in ascetics by ridiculously useless doings, such as spending one's whole life erect on a column as the Stylites did, or by behaviour frankly prejudicial to society, such as uncleanliness, which often attends practices of asceticism.

1175. In our present-day societies such manifestations of asceticism as flagellations and mutilations have virtually, if not altogether, ceased. Such things, too, in a day gone by may have represented hypertrophies of instincts of self-sacrifice for the general good. That may well have been the case with the ritualistic flagellation of which examples abound in many countries at one time or another, the supporting derivations varying according to times and places (§ 1190).

1176. Oftentimes observable in the phenomena of asceticism is an element of hypocrisy. Indeed the perfect type of the hypocrite would seem to be the person who poses as an ascetic. Too much has been said on the subject to require a word from us here. But besides the case of the hypocrite, there are many other cases in which it hangs on in attenuated forms to the point of virtually disappearing, other residues claiming the leading rôle in the composite phenomenon.

devout man in anger: he becomes a vengeful snapping animal, because he thinks that God owes him tit for tat, that religion is offended in his person, that his wrath is divine." The same may be said of our contemporary humanitarian. There is nothing to match the rage of that animal when he considers that Progress, Democracy, Solidarity, have been offended in his person.

1177. Taking a given number of concrete cases of asceticism, all apparently identical, it is hard, not to say frankly impossible, to classify them even approximately into types.[1] Ordinarily it is as great a mistake to pass them all off for the genuine article as it is to take them all as mere examples of hypocrisy. There are honest, sincere ascetics, and even in them there is no telling how much influence we are to ascribe to the residue of asceticism, or to the derivation that, arising in the residue, goes on to produce the corresponding conduct even when the residue has lost its force. There are ascetics who are inspired by impulses of imitation, which are stronger than any others in many human beings. Then again there are ascetics who are inspired to a greater or lesser extent by motives of self-interest, or by any number of complex sentiments that have nothing to do with asceticism. Finally come the hypocrites, and even they are hypocritical to varying degrees: some are ascetics in part and hypocrites in part; some are pure or almost pure hypocrites.[2]

1178. Among the professional prudes of our day who are for ever persecuting what they call immorality, there are likewise some few who are really persons of conviction and are altogether stranger to sexual satisfactions. Then there are another few who are consistent in their conduct and actually repress carnal impulses in deference to "moral principles." There are quite a good few who find in militant morality a mere pretext for satisfying their interest in obscene things. Read an obscene book for pleasure? Not they! They read it to see

1177 [1] Intimate familiarity with certain particular cases may enable one, so far as those cases go, to give at least a hint as to a possible classification. Romolo Murri, in *Voce*, Dec. 7, 1911: "With regard to the matter of celibacy, the clergy of today may be divided into three categories. First, individuals whom a vocation athirst with idealism, a real calling to struggle and sacrifice, spiritually unfits for family life, silencing or anaesthetizing all cries of the flesh. Such priests are few; they may be counted on the fingers for any given generation. Second, individuals who accept celibacy as a prerequisite that is necessary, or is considered necessary, to a life of "piety," to priesthood as a profession, but whose piety and religious aspiration are strong enough to suppress any regrets for all that has been given up and to hold them to chastity. Such priests represent, I believe, not less than 10 per cent and not more than 20 per cent of the clergy. In the third group are the ones who fall. For them and through them the priesthood becomes, for a certain period of life at least, a hypocrisy and a sacrilege."

1177 [2] See Pareto, *Le mythe vertuiste*.

whether there is legal ground for suppressing it as a crime! Women who have had many lovers in younger days are prone to apply themselves in maturer age to reforming wayward girls. They enjoy lingering in thought on pleasures now materially beyond them. And that far the residue of asceticism has kept pace with others. But there is no trace of it in hypocrites; in persons who hate the opposite sex because they are too much attracted by their own; in persons who find compensation for lascivious conduct in purity of speech; in those poor in spirit who repeat parrot-like the things they hear others say. In a word, concrete acts that present appearances of identity may be due to widely differing causes.[1]

1179. Among the residues that are alien to asceticism but appear in concrete phenomena in combination with the ascetic residue, notably, are the residues of personal integrity (Class V). They manifest themselves in the ascetic's pride, and through them asceticism becomes a kind of sport. The ancient Athenian Cynics unquestionably enjoyed the astonished wonder that their antics aroused in other people. The story, truth or fiction, that was told of Plato as turning the tables on Diogenes when the latter taxed him with pride, reflects the attitude of many people towards the quaintness of the Cynics;[1] and the same may be said of Lucian's satire on the death of Peregrine (§ 1183[2]).[2] When Daniel climbed up on his pillar (§ 1187[5]), not a few believed that he was doing so out of vainglory.

1180. In all times and places, the ascetic life, genuine or partly genuine, simulated or partly simulated, has helped many individuals to honours and money at the expense of the plain man.[1] It should

1178 [1] What we say here of asceticism applies just as well to many concrete cases of behaviour resting on other residues.

1179 [1] Diogenes Laertius, *Diogenes*, VI, 2, 26 (Hicks, Vol. II, pp. 27-29): "Plato being host one day to a number of friends of Dionysius, Diogenes stamped on Plato's carpets and said, 'I stamp on Plato's vanity!' Plato retorted, 'What a lot of dust [pride] you raise—in seeming not to have any!' According to another version, Diogenes said, 'I am raising Plato's dust [pride]'; and Plato, 'Rather your own dust, O Diogenes!'"

1179 [2] *De morte Peregrini* (*Opera*, Vol. VIII, pp. 263-93; Fowler, Vol. IV, pp. 79-95).

1180 [1] Heber, *Journey through the Upper Provinces of India*, Vol. I, pp. 110-11, 99-100: "A few days since I saw a tall large elderly man, nearly naked, walking

not be forgotten either that not all men are to the same degree sensitive to pain, and just as in olden days there were those who could endure prolonged tortures while others immediately succumbed, so there are people who readily endure sufferings as ascetics that no one else could possibly withstand. The history of tattooing, of various types of mutilation, of the cruelties practised on prisoners of war

with three or four others, who suddenly knelt down one after the other and catching hold of his foot kissed it repeatedly. The man stood with much gravity to allow them to do so but said nothing. He had the string (*pectu*) of a Brahmin. Another man passed us on Sunday morning last hopping on one foot. He was a devotee who had made a vow never to use the other, which was now contracted and shrunk close to his hams. Lately, too, I saw a man who held his hands always above his head, and had thus lost the power of bringing them down to his sides. . . . The crowd on the Meidân was great and very picturesque. The music consisted chiefly of large double drums ornamented with plumes of black feathers, like those of a hearse, which rose considerably higher than the heads of the persons who played on them. . . . The devotees went about with small spears through their tongues and arms, and still more with hot irons pressed against their sides. . . . From time to time as they passed us, they laboured to seem to dance, but in general their step was slow, their countenances expressive of resigned and patient suffering, and there was no appearance, that I saw, of anything like frenzy or intoxication. . . . [The ceremony ends with a voluntary torture:] The victim was led, covered with flowers and without any apparent reluctance, to the foot of the tree: hooks were then thrust through the muscles of his sides, which he endured without shrinking, and a broad bandage was fastened round his waist, to prevent the hooks from being torn through by the weight of his body. He was then raised up and whirled round. At first the motion was slow, but by degrees was increased to considerable rapidity. In a few minutes it ceased; and the by-standers were going to let him down, when he made signs that they should proceed. This resolution was received with great applause by the crowd, and after drinking some water he was again spun round." Besse, *Les moines d'Orient*, pp. 496 f.: "Among the privations voluntarily undertaken by certain monks, St. Epiphanius makes special mention of abstention from bathing [*Panarium adversus haereses, lib.* III, *tomus* II, *Expositio fidei*, 33 (*Opera*, Vol. II, p. 830)]. . . . There were those who went farther still and spurned the most elementary precautions of cleanliness. . . . St. Hilarion was one of these, and Abraham the Recluse, who never washed his feet and hands. [The recluse Abraham may have been a great saint. He certainly was a dirty one. Let us hope and pray that no emulator of Senator Bérenger will ever take it into his head to force that type of virtue upon us.] St. Pachomus allowed a general anointing of the body with oil only in case of sickness. One had to have authority to perform such a service for a brother either by virtue of one's office or by obedience. . . . St. Ephraim enjoined on those performing such a duty to look carefully to their eyes, their hands and their tongues. . . . There were monks who condemned themselves never to cast their eyes about them, even to look at the furniture in their cells; to sleep a certain number of nights on briars; to live near pools of stagnant water; and so on. They resorted to these devices to be rid of be-among the American Indians and other peoples, corroborates these inferences.[2]

1181. Extraordinary cases of asceticism have been and are still to be witnessed in the East. Orientals have the endurance of savages and brute animals for physical pain, and it is no great wonder

setting temptations. Whenever Hammon was conscious of an importunity from the flesh, he treated his body with pitiless severity. One of his favourite measures was to burn himself with a hot iron. To banish an impure thought that was tempting him, St. Macarius of Alexandria threw himself naked into a quagmire. The stagnant water attracted quantities of mosquitoes to the place, some, avers Pallas, as big as wasps and able to pierce the hide of a wild boar. The Saint endured that new sort of sackcloth for six long months. One may imagine the state his body was in. He looked like a leper. Some thought of loading themselves down with chains and pieces of wood. That was an excellent means of subduing one's body." Examples of that type of penance are frequent enough in the West: St. Gregory of Tours, *Historia ecclesiastica Francorum*, VI, 6 (*Opera*, pp. 376-77; Dalton, Vol. II, p. 238): "In the city of Nice in those days was a recluse by the name of Hospitius, a very abstemious man, who wore iron chains next to his body and over them sackcloth and lived on naught but bread and a few dates. . . . Finding him in that condition in the pit of a tower, the Lombard invaders thought him a criminal. One of them was minded to slay him, but his arm was stiffened [in mid-air], nor did it become sound again till the holy man had made the sign of the cross upon it."

1180 [2] J. L. Burckhardt, *Travels in Arabia*, p. 259 (alluding to Hindu ascetics who pursue pilgrims to Mecca (*hadji*) begging alms): "The gates of the Mosque are always beset with them. Every coffee-house and water-stand is a station for some of them, and no *hadjy* can purchase provisions in the markets without being importuned by Indians soliciting a portion of them. I saw among them one of those devotees who are so common in the north of India and in Persia: one of his arms was held up straight over his head, and so fixed by long habit that it could not be placed in any other situation." Lafitau, *Mœurs des sauvages américains*, Vol. II, pp. 274, 280, 284-86: "Among the tribes of North America that are known, slaves are punished by roasting over slow fires, but the scene takes place with so many details of incredible barbarity that one shudders at the very thought of it. [A description follows.] . . . So the bloody tragedy came to an end—and I am at a loss to say which deserved the greatest wonder, the brutish ferocity of the inhuman savages who were treating poor slaves with such cruelty . . . or the endurance of the slaves themselves, who displayed in the face of the most frightful torments a greatness of soul, a heroism, that is altogether unimaginable. [Burned and tortured in a thousand ways] the prisoners sing their own great feats of arms and those of their tribes. Hurling curses at their tormentors, they try to intimidate them by threats, calling upon their friends to rescue or avenge them. They ridicule the executioners for not knowing their business, telling them how to apply the fire to inflict a bitterer pain, describing what they themselves did to prisoners who fell into their hands. If by chance they have ever dealt with a victim from the tribe of their captors, they enter into the greatest detail of the torments they inflicted, fearless of the consequences of such talk, which can only serve to enrage their

therefore if individuals are to be found among them who submit to cruel tortures for the sake of attracting attention, or at times for a price. Sonnerat gives a good description of the multifarious forms of asceticism in India and it may serve as typical of the thing in general.[1]

tormentors. Though the sheer violence of their anguish makes them foam at the mouth or stare with the wild eyes of madness, they never utter a word of shrinking. The women are as heroic as the men. I saw one have two finger-nails torn out in my presence. Not a cry, not a groan! The most I could catch on her face was an imperceptible expression of tedium. Some of them laugh under torture, take the whole matter as a jest, and amiably thank those who have hurt them most. The savages seem to train themselves for such exhibitions from earliest childhood. Children have been seen to clasp each other with naked arms, with a burning coal between them, wagering as to who could stand it longest and with the least show of pain. I myself saw a child between five and six years old who had been seriously scalded about the body by a vessel of hot water being accidentally upset upon him. Every time his wounds were dressed, he would strike up his death-song and sing it with incredible courage, though he was suffering the keenest anguish at the time."

1181 [1] *Voyage aux Indes orientales et à la Chine*, Vol. I, pp. 256-62: "The Sanjassi (or Sanachi) is either a Brahman or a Chouta. He dedicates himself exclusively to the divinity. He takes a vow to be poor, chaste, and sober. Owning nothing, with no interest in anything, he wanders from place to place, his head shaven, almost naked with a single strip of yellow cloth to cover his back. He lives altogether on alms and eats only enough to keep himself alive. [Those traits are typical of many ascetic associations.] The Pandaroons are not less revered than the Sanjassis. They are worshippers of Siva. They smear their faces, chests, and arms with ashes of cow's dung, and go about the streets carrying peacock-plumes in their hands, begging alms, and singing hymns of praise to Siva. . . . The Karé-Patré Pandaroon is a variation on the Pandaroon proper. He takes a vow of perpetual silence. [*Cf.* the Western Trappist.] He enters a house and claps his hands in begging alms, in order not to speak. His name is significant: *Karé* means 'hand,' *Patré,* 'plate.' . . . The Tadin goes begging from door to door, dancing and singing hymns of praise, and recounting the metamorphoses of Vishnu. . . . The Hindus, finally, have religious Penitents. The Penitents correspond among the Gentiles to the fakirs among the Mongols. They are inspired by their fanaticism to abandon family, property, and so on, and lead lives of utter misery. . . . The only articles they are allowed to possess are a lingam, to which they pay continuous worship, and a tiger's skin on which they sleep. They inflict on their bodies everything that a fanatical fury can suggest. Some tear their flesh with whips [*Cf.* the discipline of our Catholics.] or have themselves chained by the feet to trees to be released only when they die. Others take a vow to remain all their lives long in some uncomfortable position, keeping their hands always closed, for instance, so that their finger-nails, which they never cut, in the end grow through their hands. Some sit with their arms folded across their chests or raised above their heads, so that they have lost the power to bend them. Not a few bury themselves in the ground, breathing only through little

1182. Monks and ascetics have been known in India from most ancient times. The student of the Vedas had to live with his master, obey him, serve him. In that, evidently, residues of rank (IV-ε) are at work in combination with the ascetic residue, as is the case with monks in the Christian monasteries. He must, furthermore, be strictly chaste, temperate, humble, and live in poverty. Buddhism has a complete code for the ascetic life, in some respects very like the rule devised by St. Francis of Assisi—and that is another of the many cases where similar institutions have grown up spontaneously without any imitation (§§ 733 f.).[1] Just such practices, with minor

openings. Others, less fanatical, bury themselves no higher than their necks. Some have taken a vow to spend their lives standing, without ever lying down. They sleep with their bodies leaning against walls or trees, and to prevent themselves from slipping into comfortable postures, they wear frames of lattice-work about their necks. Others stand for hours at a time on one foot, staring open-eyed at the sun. To acquire greater merit still others stand with one foot off the ground, their weight resting on the great toe and their arms, into the bargain, raised above their heads. They stand between four cauldrons in which fires are burning and gaze at the sun with unwinking eyes. There are those who appear in public stark-naked to show that they have become insusceptible to any passion, that on abandoning their bodies to the Divinity they have returned to a state of innocence. The people are convinced of their virtue, look upon them as saints [Generally observable among many peoples.] and think they can get from God anything they ask for. In the belief that they are doing a very pious act, people assiduously provide them with food [Also very general.], put the morsels into the mouths of such as have vowed never to use their hands, and clean them. While the Penitent is sunk in his contemplation, there are women who approach, kiss his private parts, and pay worship to them. . . . Characteristic of the Penitents is an overweening pride; they have a very great esteem for themselves and believe in their own sanctity. They refuse to be touched by members of the lower castes and by Europeans, fearing pollution. They will not even allow their personal articles to be touched, and at once move on if anyone approaches them. They evince sovereign contempt for anyone not of their calling and look upon such as profane things. Everything about them is supposed to hide some mysterious property and to be worthy of devout worship."

1182 [1] Kern, *Histoire du bouddhisme*, Vol. II, pp. 3-5, 14-16: "One of his strictest obligations is to observe absolute chastity: he must not touch a woman or look at one, if there is any danger to his purity. He must strive incessantly and earnestly to control his tongue, his appetite, and his hands. Play, menial labour, the acquisition of objects that have not been offered to him, unkindness to living creatures, unkind words, are all strictly forbidden him, and likewise the use of wines and strong drinks (at least among the Brahmans). He must abstain from salt, honey, meat, spices. He must not sleep during the daytime. He must not use perfumes or ointments, nor wear smart clothes. He must in general avoid anything tending to encourage effeminacy, such as dancing, singing and instrumental music. . . . One

variations, are to be noted among many different peoples at many different periods of history. In our day there are people who admire them. Paul Sabatier drools unctuously over the ascetic practices, at times not so very hygienic, of St. Francis of Assisi.[2] It is evident therefore that the residue plays a far from negligible rôle in the senti-

of the most characteristic duties of the student is that he should each day beg alms for his maintenance." Each Veda had to be studied twelve years; but only one Veda was required, whereupon the student was free to return to life as a layman and marry. If he chose, he could remain a student all his life.

The mendicant monk, the Bhikshu, differs from the student in that he is not subject to a master: "The rules of conduct for the Bhikshu may be summarized as follows: He has no home and no personal property. He leads a roving life, save during the rainy season, when he has to have a fixed residence. He begs alms once a day in the village for his maintenance. He must renounce all desires, master his tongue, his eyes, his conduct, and observe the strictest continence. He may have one garment to hide his nakedness, or wear cast-off rags, first washing them. He must keep his head shaven, save for one tuft on the very top of the crown. [Such a person is hardly distinguishable from the Franciscan.] . . . Not to be confused with the mendicants properly so called, the Bhikshus, . . . are the hermits, who live lives of mortification in solitude in order to accustom themselves to renunciation of worldly things and prepare themselves for the hereafter. [As Christian hermits do.] Though they are allowed to beg alms for their support, it is exceptional for them to do so. . . . The hermit lives in the jungle, getting his own living from fruits and wild vegetables and practising asceticism. . . . The Buddhists have in the Dhûtangas a complete set of rules for the ascetic life. The Dhûtangas are thirteen in number among the Buddhists of the South, twelve in the north: I. To wear a garment made of rags gathered from a dunghill or a dump. (As a rule the monks are inclined to disregard this provision.) . . . II. To own three such garments. . . . III. To take no food save such as is received in alms. . . . IV. While begging alms for one's living to go systematically from door to door, to the poor as well as to the rich, neglecting no one. . . . V. To remain seated at the same place during a meal. . . . VI. To eat only from a single ladle or almsplate. . . . VII. To take no second repast after the morning meal. . . . VIII. To live in solitude. . . . IX. To live at the foot of a tree. . . . X. To sleep out of doors. . . . XI. To live in a cemetery. . . . XII. To spend the night at the spot one happens to reach without design. . . . XIII. To sleep in a sitting posture. . . . In the Northern rule articles IV and VI are missing. It has, however, another provision . . . prohibiting the use of felt."

1182 [2] *Vie de Saint François d'Assise*, p. 165 (Houghton, p. 144): "One day Brother John . . . who had been placed in special charge over a leper, brought him on a walk to the Portiuncola, as though he had not been suffering from a contagious malady. He did not escape rebukes and hearing them the leper could not hide his distress and sorrow. . . . Francis easily perceived that and felt a sharp pang of remorse. The thought that he had pained 'one of the sick of the good Lord' he could not bear; and not only did he beg his forgiveness, but he had him stay for the repast, sat down beside him, and ate out of the same plate with him."

ments of certain people of our time. Derivations draw sharp distinctions between the dirty practices of Hindu ascetics, Athenian Cynics, the Franciscans, and similar sects; but identical residues underlie them all.

1183. People who are not victims of the sentiments corresponding to the ascetic residues either take towards ascetics of that brand the attitude voiced by Rutilius of old, in wonderment at their dislike for the good things life has to offer;[1] or else frankly ridicule them, as Lucian ridiculed Peregrine.[2] As a rule, moreover, people laud ascetics of their own faith and censure others. Christians deride Hindu ascetics and revere their own. Humanitarians cannot endure Christian asceticism, but glorify the asceticism of teetotallers and prudes. There are people who rave at the celibacy rule for the

1183 [1] *Itinerarium*, I, vv. 439-46 (Paris, pp. 138-39):

> "*Processu pelagi iam se Capraria tollit.*
> *Squalet lucifugis insula plena viris.*
> *Ipsi se monachos Graio cognomine dicunt,*
> *quod soli nullo vivere teste volunt.*
> *Munera fortunae metuunt dum damna verentur.*
> *Quisquam sponte miser ne miser esse queat?*
> *Quaenam perversi rabies tam stulta cerebri*
> *dum mala formides nec bona posse pati?*"

("And lo, as we proceed, Capraria rises from the sea, an island infested with men who shun the light. They call themselves by a Greek name, monks, because it is their will to live alone without companionship (*monachus* from μόνος). The gifts of fortune they fear in fear of damnation. What kind of person is this that makes himself wretched in order to escape wretchedness? What stupid madness of perverted minds—in fear of an evil, to spurn all blessings!")

1183 [2] "*De morte Peregrini,*" 1-2 (*Opera*, Vol. VIII, pp. 263-64; Fowler, Vol. IV, p. 79): "Poor dear Peregrine—or Proteus, as he loved to call himself—has quite come up to his namesake in Homer. We have seen him under many shapes: countless have been his transformations for glory's sake; and now—'tis his last appearance—we see him in the shape of fire. So vast was his ambition! Yes, Cronius! All that is left of the best of men is a handful of ashes. . . . I fancy I see you chuckling away at the old dotard; or rather I hear you blurting out the inevitable comment—'Mere imbecility, mere clap-trap, mere—everything else,' that we are accustomed to attribute to these gentry. But then, you are far enough off to be comparatively safe: now I made my remarks before a vast audience, at the very moment of cremation (and before it for that matter), exciting thereby the indignation of all the old fool's admirers, though there were a few who joined in the laugh against it. I tell you I was within an ace of being torn limb from limb by the Cynics, like Actaeon among the dogs." (Fowler.)

Catholic priest, yet would legislate against premarital relations between men and women, not perceiving, in their intellectual pauperism, that both attitudes are one and the same and arise from the same causes.

1184. "In the summer-time Diogenes rolled about [in his tub] on the burning sand, and in the winter went about hugging statues covered with snow, accustoming himself to all such hardships."[1] To chasten promptings of the flesh St. Francis once threw himself naked into the snow.[2] Be such stories fact or legend, the people who invented or retold them show, now through Diogenes and now through St. Francis, the working of a residue that prompts human beings to eschew the pleasures of life and seek out suffering, whatever the reason they give for their conduct. The Cynics degenerated, just as in later times the Franciscans degenerated; but the fact that they both continued to enjoy wide-spread popularity even in their day of degeneracy shows the great power the residue must have had in the masses to sustain such popularity; nor did the ridicule of sensible people serve to weaken it.[3]

1184 [1] Diogenes Laertius, *Diogenes,* VI, 23 (Hicks, Vol. I, pp. 25-27).

1184 [2] Jacopo a Voragine, *Legenda aurea,* CXLIX (*De Sancto Francisco*): "And on a tyme as this holy man was in prayer, the deuyll called him thryes by his owne name, and whanne the holy man had answered hym he said: None in this world is soo grete a synner but yf he conuerte hym our lord wold pardone hym, but who that sleeth hymself by hard penaunce shall neuer fynde mercy. And anone this hooly man knewe by the reuelacion, the fallace and deceyte of the fende, how he wold haue withdrawen hym for to doo well. And whanne the deuyll saw that he myght not preuayle ayenst him, he tempted hym by greuous temptacion of the flesshe, and whan this holy seraunt of god felte that, he despoylled of his clothes and bete hymself right hard with an hard corde saying: Thus broder Asse it behoueth the to remayne and to be beten, and whan the temptacion departed not he went out and plonged hymself in the snow al naked, and made seuen grete balles of snowe and purposed to have taken them in to his body, and sayd, This gretest is thy wyf, and of these foure, two ben thy doughters and two thy sones, and the other tweyne, that one thy chamberer and that othir thy varlet or yeman, haste the and clothe them for they al deye for cold, and yf thy besynes that thow hast aboute them greue the sore, then serue our lord parfightely. And anon the deuyll departed from them al confused, and saynt Fraunceis retournjd ageyne in to his celle glorifying god." (Caxton.)

1184 [3] The early day of Epictetus had its equivalent for the adage "The habit does not make the monk." Epictetus, *Dissertationes,* IV, 8, 4-5: "It is not easy to judge opinions from exteriors. . . . This man is a philosopher. Why? Because he

1185. Philo the Jew wrote a treatise on the contemplative life of the Therapeutae.[1] It has been a moot question whether the treatise is really Philo's, and also, on better grounds, whether the Therapeutae were men in the flesh or a mere literary invention. The point is of little importance for our purposes. The fact that a writer, be he who he may, described such things, be they real or imaginary, shows that at the time he wrote a strong current of asceticism prevailed. That is all that need concern us for the moment. Women were admitted into the sect, but they had to remain virgin. Horror for sexual relations is an obsession seldom missing in asceticism, especially in its intenser manifestations, where it approximates insanity.

1186. There is no doubt that the Essenes, on the other hand, were real people. They were like the Hindu ascetics, and the "Perfects" of the Albigenses were, in turn, like them. "To the westward of the shores [of Lake Asphaltides] and far enough away not to be harmed by its fumes, dwell the Essenes, a solitary people and marvellous beyond all others in the world. They live without any woman, for-

wears a coarse mantle and a long beard! Yet—the mountebanks, what do they wear? And so, if one of them is caught doing some shameful thing, there comes the cry forthwith, 'See what philosophers do!' Whereas, since the thing he does is shameful, one should rather say that he is not a philosopher." In *Ibid.*, III, 22, Epictetus contrasts the true with the false Cynic, accusing the latter of every vice. Cynics were still to be seen in the day of St. Augustine: *De civitate Dei*, XIV, 20: "Even now we see that there are philosophers who are Cynics, and not only go about in sheets, but also carry the Cynic's staff." Lucian is not sparing of invective against self-styled philosophers. In *Piscator*, 11 (Harmon, Vol. IV, p. 19), he says that he has found no trace of philosophy among men who go about wrapped in sheets [Harmon: "short cloaks"] and wearing unkempt beards. The scholiast remarks that the same may be said of the monks of his time. In the *Dialogi mortuorum*, X, 8 (*Opera*, Vol. II, pp. 170-71; Fowler, Vol. I, p. 121), Mercury requires a philosopher to draw aside his mantle and then, peering at him, exclaims: "O Zeus, what boastfulness he was hiding under there, what ignorance, what quarrelsomeness, what vainglory . . . ! And here? Bless us—gold, lechery, impudence, wrath, high living, effeminacy! Hide nothing, man, for I see everything!" On the exclamation "O Zeus! What a boastfulness . . ." the scholiast comments: τὶ ταῦτα τοῖς καθ᾽ἡμᾶς μονα-χοῖς ἁρμόδια ("That goes for our monks.") An epigram, XVI, 19, in the Appendix of Maximus Planudes to the *Greek Anthology* (Paton, Vol. V, pp. 168-69) plays on the word *Irene*, which means "peace" in Greek and was also the name of a bishop's concubine. "Peace (Irene) be with you all!" says the Bishop, entering. "But how can she be with us all, if you have her in the other room all to yourself?"

1185 [1] *De vita contemplativa* (Cohn, Vol. VI, pp. 46-71; Yonge, Vol. IV, pp. 6-20).

swearing love, and without money, in the company of the palms. Their numbers are replenished day by day, because many who are weary of life and the fluctuations of fortune are attracted by their manner of living."[1] Flavius Josephus says that "property is held in common among them, the rich enjoying no more wealth than the poor. Such the custom of more than four thousand men, and they have neither wives nor slaves, because slaves are a cause of injustice and wives of discord." Josephus may be suspected of describing the causes for asceticism in those terms because he had no very clear conception of the real ones.[2]

1187. Among the countless follies of the ascetics not the least silly were the practices of the Stylites, a name given to certain devout Christians who spent portions of their lives on top of columns. The earliest known individual of this type was St. Simeon, called in fact, the Stylite, who lived in the fifth century.[1] He was born in Cilicia and entered a monastery in earliest youth. Moving on to a second, he remained there ten years, leading a life so excessively austere that, to believe the account of Theodoret, he ate only once a week, whereas the other monks ate every other day. He practised self-mortification in other ways that were deemed so extravagant by his superiors that he was expelled. He thereupon withdrew to a little cell near Antioch, where he continued his self-inflicted sufferings. After three years of that he betook himself to a mountain-top and walled himself up in a cramped cell fastened by a heavy iron chain about his foot (Garnier). Pilgrims flocked to him from all parts of the world, and he rewarded them with many a pretty miracle.[2] Annoyed,

1186 [1] Pliny, *Historia naturalis*, V, 17 (Bostock-Riley, Vol. I, pp. 430-31).

1186 [2] *Antiquitates Judaicae*, XVIII, 1, 5 (*Opera*, Vol. IV, p. 139; Whitson, Vol. IV, p. 59).

1187 [1] Theodoret, *Religiosa historia*, XXVI, *Symeones* (*Opera*, Vol. III, pp. 1463-84), claims to have seen St. Simeon personally. And *cf.* Theodorus Lector, *Excerpta ex ecclesiastica historia*, I, 12 (Migne, p. 171) and I, 18 (Migne, p. 174); Valois, [? *Theodoreti et Evagrii historia ecclesiastica* (notes), Vol. II, p. 565], Evagrius, *Ecclesiastica historia*, I, 13 (*Opera*, pp. 2454-59; English, pp. 24-28); Antonius (*Symeonis discipulus*), *Vita Symeonis Stylitae*.

1187 [2] Says Theodoret, *loc. cit.* (*Opera*, pp. 1478-79): "Not only was I present at his miracles, but I heard him prophesy the future. [On one occasion] he predicted a great drought and crop-failure, followed by famine and pestilence, two full years in advance."

finally, at so much bustle about him, he took to the top of a column, standing there erect. He first ordered one made six cubits high, then successively columns twelve, twenty-two, and thirty-six cubits high. "So great his desire to be near unto Heaven and far from this Earth!" And at that point, to silence critics who were ridiculing the Stylite, the good Theodoret recalls in his favour, *loc. cit.*, the penances of Isaiah, Jeremiah, Hosea, and Ezekiel. Perched on his column, St. Simeon converted no end of people who came to look at him. Theodoret says he saw them. Women were not allowed to enter the enclosure where the pillar rose. Simeon refused to see even his mother (§ 1172). Just how long he lived on the column is a moot question.[3] He had a spiritual successor, one Daniel, who also decided to live on top of a pillar.[4] These holy and silly

1187 [3] Baronio, *Annales ecclesiastici, anno,* 460, IV (note by Antoine Pagi): "In his supplement (*Auctarius*) to the works of Theodoret (*Dissertationes, lib.* II, *cap.* V, § 3, sec. 5-11; Theodoret, *Opera,* Vol. V, pp. 239-41) Garnier examines the celebrated question as to the year in which Simeon the Stylite mounted his column and the length of time he stood on it. He notes that Baronio mentions three things that are at variance not only with all the biographers of Simeon, including Theodoret, but with Baronio himself." He concludes that the Saint must have spent some forty years on the column.

1187 [4] Baronio, *Op. cit., anno* 460, XVII-XX: "But just as Elijah designated Elisha as the heir of his spirit and the imitator of his virtues, so Simeon seems to have made the monk Daniel the legitimate successor to his spiritual legacy, and to have exhorted him to take up that angelic manner of life by divine prophecies and visions. Like Elisha in assuming the mantle of Elijah, Daniel was found worthy to receive the cowl of Simeon shortly before the latter's death, he having sent it by his disciple Sergius to Leo the Emperor, who, however, had not accepted it. The which must evidently have been by divine plan, inasmuch as Daniel became the heir of the spirit and virtue of Simeon in the giving forth of signs, for it happened [that Daniel took the cowl] on the very day on which Simeon departed this life. In taking the cowl from Sergius, he revealed to the latter the death of Simeon, which had been revealed to him, and forthwith, in the greatest confidence, as though he were entering upon a paternal inheritance, he mounted a column that he had erected at Ostia in Pontus. It was his lot to be criticized among others by St. Gennadius, Patriarch (*antistes*) of Constantinople, who was shocked by the strangeness of his conduct and was apprehensive lest he were a man of overweening conceit (*inflatus superbia*), inspired by emulation of the great Simeon with a view to winning popular favour and so acquiring notoriety (*gloriolam*). But by signs divinely manifested the Patriarch was at length persuaded that Daniel was a lover of God, that he had made that effort not of human presumptuousness but supported by the counsel of God, governed by His authority, inspired by His spirit, sustained by His help." He lived on the column many years and worked no end of first-class miracles.

men had other emulators. They are still being mentioned as late as the year 806, when Theodore of Studa advises the Emperor Nicephorus in a letter to select the patriarch of Constantinople from among the "bishops, Stylites, and recluses."[5]

1188. If we had only the Christian Stylites to go by, we might be left in doubt as to whether such practices were logical consequences of Christian beliefs (§§ 184, 734, 829). But exactly identical cases are observable in places where there is no trace whatever of Christianity. We may suspect therefore that they all have a common cause, independent of beliefs. Not that beliefs may not have cooperated with such causes, but with them, I say, not replacing them. So in ascetic acts of penance, residues of personal integrity (Class V) are working in combination with residues of asceticism—since one among the penitent's motives is to purge himself of sin. But the residues of asceticism come to the fore again when the penance is served for the sins of others.

1189. Whoever the author of the *Syrian Goddess,* he was certainly not a Christian and was not describing customs of Christians. All the same in that document we find Stylites, temporary Stylites at least, and a type of asceticism that as far as concrete results are concerned is not so very different from the asceticism of St. Simeon. No less than four explanations of the conduct of the Stylites are given in the *Syrian Goddess,* nor are they so very different, after all, from the explanations given for Christian Stylitism.[1]

1187 [5] Baronio, *Op. cit., anno* 806, V: ". . . *ex praepositis et ex stylitis et ex inclusis."*

1189 [1] Lucian, *De Syria dea,* 28-29 (Harmon translation, Vol. IV, pp. 379-80): "The place therinne the temple sytt is a hylle; and it liggeth wel in the myddes of the cytee, and two walles enviroune it. Oon of the walles is auncien, but the tother is not mocheles elder than oure tyme. The entree of the holy place maketh out toward the Septemtryon, well a 100 fadmes of largenesse; and in that entree stont tho yerdes that leet set, on heighte a 300 fadmnes. A man goth up the oon of thise yerdes twyes in the yeer and woneth at the cop of the yerde for the space of 7 dayes. And the cause of his goynge up, as men seyn, is this. Lewed folk trowen that he speketh with the goddes on highe and axeth bones for alle Surrye, and the goddes heren his preyeres fro there nyghe. [First derivation.] But othere wenen that this also is don be cause of Deucalioun in tokene and mynde of that tribulacioun, whan men wenten into montaynes and into the gret highe trees for fere of the flode. [Second derivation.] Now to me, that is not to beleven. I suppose wel that thei don this for worschipe of Bacchus, and I conclude it thus. Yerdes

1190. Ascetic flagellation is fairly wide-spread in terms of both time and space. Familiar the Spartan institution of flogging for young men at the altar of Artemis Orthia, and the flagellation of Christian penitents in the Middle Ages. Writers have collected similar cases and suggested various explanations for them. They have been taken as demonstrations of courage and indifference to pain—and there is some truth in that. Lycurgus has been credited with the intention of accustoming his fellow-citizens to courageous endurance of pain —and explanations of that kind always have scant probability. It has been suggested that flagellations were surviving remnants of older practices of human sacrifice—and that may well be, but proofs of any such thing are entirely lacking. It used to be said that flagellation served to drive out evil spirits. That is a derivation, probably with a residue lurking underneath. It has been explained that the victims acquired the strength and vitality of the instruments used in

that thei maken for worschipe of Bacchus, on tho yerdes ther setten alle wayes wodene men; but I schalle not seye whi. [Third derivation. Add now the fact that the Stylite is doing penance and we get a fourth derivation. That shows that the many derivations are the variable, secondary element in the case, the main, the constant, element being the residue that the derivations are designed to explain.] . . . The manere of his goynge up is this. He putteth a schort corde abouten himself and the yerde and thanne he climbeth on peces of wode ynaylled on the yerde, bigge ynow for to lette setten on his toon; and ther as he climbeth he throweth up the corde with bothe hondes right as he mighte schake the reynes of a charre. If ony ther be that hath not seen this thing but hath seen men that climben trees of palme in Arabye or in Egypte, or elles where, he understondeth whereof I speke. [The description apparently of an actual eyewitness.] Whan he is comen to the ende of his weye, he letteth falle an other corde that he hath, that is long, and draweth uppe what him list, wode and clothes and purveyaunce, of the whiche he frameth a sete lyk as a nest, theron he sytteth and abydeth for the space of the before seyde dayes. And manye comynge putten gold or silver or per-aunter brasse, that thei usen for here moneyes, in to a vessele that lyeth there neer, seyinge everychon his name. Than oon that stondeth there beside calleth it uppe; and whan that other resceyveth the name of eech, he preyeth for him, and in preyinge schaketh a thynge of brass that souneth gret and schrille when it is stered. [Significant the parallel: Crowds came from the world over to St. Simeon's column. The Emperor Leo had a monastery built near Daniel's pillar for that saint's disciples.] And he ne slepeth never. For if that ever he falle on slepe, a scorpioun goynge up awaketh him and doth him pitous harm; and that is the peyne that is leyde on him for slepynge. Now this tale that is told of the scorpioun is a holy tale and wel semynge, but wher it be trewe or non, I wot neer. Natheles, me seemeth that drede of fallynge avayleth moch to wakfulnesse."

the flogging; and that too is a derivation. Flogging was also interpreted as a purifying process for the victim—again a derivation. For the Christians flagellation was a way of doing penance.

1191. The totemic explanation of course could not fail to put in an appearance, since totemism nowadays has to have a finger in everything. Reinach adopts it, following Thomsen:[1] "The young men of Sparta were flogged with hazel rods, and the goddess presiding over the ceremony was the goddess of the hazel (Lygodesma, from the Greek *lygos,* 'hazel'). The Luperci lashed women in Rome with thongs of hide from a he-goat or a she-goat, and Luperca, the goddess presiding over the ceremony, partakes of both the she-wolf and the she-goat (*lupus, hircus*). The purpose of the flogging, therefore, was to transmit to the victim's body the strength and vitality of the tree or animal—undoubtedly, former totems." That "therefore" is truly splendid! At the very least, one might expect the conclusion to be tied to the premise somewhat more effectively! The explanation would not change, notice, whatever the material used in the flogging. Would it not serve just as well for the hide of any other animal? Strength and vitality were by no means confined to he-goats and she-goats! Worth a round of applause, also, the broad jump that is taken to reach the conclusion. Granting that the purpose of the flogging was to transmit to the victim the strength and the vitality of the material from which the whip was made, or which it symbolizes—must that material necessarily have been a former totem? When one is satisfied with proofs as tenuous and fragile as that, one can prove anything.

1192. As we have repeatedly suggested (§§ 23, 670), let us not go looking in this case for "origins" destined to remain obscure. Let us look for the sentiments that underlie the conduct. Let us not go guessing at possibilities in times for which we have no documents. Let us confine our attention to facts attested by documents that we can trust.

1193. First of all, cases of flagellation in the concrete are not necessarily all of the same kind. The lashes, surely not very painful, that

1191 [1] *Cultes, mythes et religions,* Vol. I, p. 180.

were inflicted on the women of Rome during the Lupercalia may have little or nothing to do with the very painful flagellation of the Spartans. So let us look about for some case of flagellation that is very simple, and calculated, therefore, to betray the residues more clearly.

1194. Casati happens to describe just such a simple case, and it is a matter of young men flogging one another to show their courage and win the admiration of young women.[1] Our totemists will of course say that since the whip was made of hippopotamus hide the purpose of the flagellation was to transmit to the young man the strength of the hippopotamus, a former totem. If a whip chanced to be made of the hide of some other animal *A,* or were a switch from some tree *B,* substitute *A* or *B* for the hippopotamus, and we still get the same explanation. Indeed it would always serve, for the whip has to be made of something! Disregarding such fanciful explanations, we find expressed in the case described by Casati sentiments that we know to be widely diffused among human beings; and probably therefore they figure in other cases of the kind.

1195. It would be surprising indeed that they should be missing in the floggings of the young men at Sparta, and that the Spartans, so eager in everything they did to show themselves contemptuous of the comforts of life, and scornfully indifferent to pain and death, were to lay them aside in the special case of flagellation, where they would seem to be most appropriate. The view of the ancients that

1194 [1] *Dieci anni in Equatoria,* p. 48 (Clay, p. 49). "The dances open the first day with a very curious and typical ceremony. The young folks, the girls on one side, the boys on the other, begin singing joyous love-songs. Then one of the girls rises, takes a whip of hippopotamus hide, and hands it to one of the boys, who accepts it with polite thanks. He looks about him crying: 'Who would be loved and admired?' 'I!' a companion answers, stepping forward with uncovered shoulders. The youth with the whip belabours his shoulders soundly—fifteen lashes in all, and applied with a will. To comply with the rules the welts must be distinctly visible. The two actors now invert rôles and repeat the game. Then they retire, proud of having displayed their physical and moral fortitude before the eyes of their fair ones." Compare with this account Plutarch's description of the flagellations at Sparta, just below. [There are substantial differences in Casati's various texts. The English version of his work seems to have been the first published.— A. L.]

flagellation was instituted by deliberate device of the legendary Lycurgus was mistaken. Very probably, however, flagellation was a manifestation of sentiments connected with training for endurance of pain and with self-sacrifice on the part of the individual to the group. Those sentiments were very powerful in Sparta. A country where people led lives of incredible hardship, and where mothers disowned sons who fled from battle or who alone escaped where their comrades perished (§ 1148 [1]), must necessarily have had boys who courted sufferings commensurate with their age. The fact that the floggings took place at the altar of Artemis Orthia is secondary, incidental. Had there been no such goddess, it would have been no great task to find another. The concrete case of Sparta and the concrete case described by Casati seem to differ in one respect. The residue, common to them both, endurance of pain (IV-ζ) is combined, in the case of Sparta, with a feeling that the pain is inflicted in behalf of the country and its gods—a sentiment of individual sacrifice (IV-δ), therefore.[1]

1196. In the Middle Ages voluntary flagellation turns up again. It would be altogether ridiculous to see any trace of totemism or of any device for acquiring physical strength in this mediaeval case. St. Dominic Loricatus first preached flagellation. His story is well known, and nothing, absolutely nothing, in it suggests either of those notions. St. Dominic Loricatus flogged himself as a penance for himself and for others—such the derivation covering the ascetic residue. It is not surprising that at a time when all imaginable austerities were being devised to satisfy the ascetic urge, flagellation should have been one of them. It would have been surprising had it not been thought of. Condemned by many people, that new mortification was defended by St. Peter Damian, who quite soundly re-

1195 [1] Plutarch, *Instituta Laconica*, 40 (Babbitt, Vol. III, pp. 443-45); and *Lycurgus*, 18 (Perrin, Vol. I, pp. 261-65); and Lucian, *Anacharsis*, 38 (Harmon, Vol. IV, pp. 63-65). Placidus, *Commentarii in Statii Thebaidem*, IV, 227 (Leipzig, 1671, pp. 425-26): "Why he mentions the Eurota he explains himself. The Laconians play a whipping-game (*vapulando contendunt*) on the banks of that river; and he is the prouder who has had the courage for more than the prescribed number of lashes; for when anyone dies under them, he is publicly crowned at his funeral."

marked that it could not be condemned unless the other mortifications of the Holy Fathers were to be condemned likewise. To the
objection that Jesus, the Apostles, and the martyrs had been flogged
by others but had not tortured themselves, Damian replies that we
are quite able to punish ourselves and that, just as we fast of our own
accord, so we may chastise ourselves with our own hands.[1]

1197. St. Dominic Loricatus (*i.e.,* of the iron armour) got that
surname, according to his *Life* by St. Peter Damian, from at all times
wearing an iron tunic. He observed scrupulous chastity to the day
of his death and practised all sorts of corporal penances, spending
his life reciting psalms, making genuflections, and flogging himself.
Some years before his death he discovered that leathern whips inflicted greater pain than willow switches and therefore adopted
them. His was a case of mental alienation. But just as megalomania
is a mental disease taking the form of excessive pride, so the follies
of St. Dominic betray an excess of the sentiment that induces the
individual to abandon all thought of personal integrity (*cf.,* Class
V residues). St. Dominic did penance for the sins of others, sacri-

1196 [1] *Epistolae,* V, 8, *Ad clericos Florentinos* (*Opera,* Vol. I, p. 75, col. 2, C-D).
The Saint argues further: ". . . He performs excellent penance who makes up in
pain, through flagellation of the flesh, for the gain he has lost through carnal pleasures, and inflicts a present healthful discomfort upon that which, through his
noxious delight in it, was the cause of his sin. It matters little to what punishments the flesh of the penitent is subjected, so only the pleasure of the earlier
allurement be exchanged for the vicarious pain of the punished body. If to those
who do not practise it (*non facientibus*) the discipline of the rods seems strange and
therefore reprehensible and is represented (*iudicatur,* misprint for *indicatur*) to the
stupidity of envious belief as a destruction of the law and an undoing of the
decretals, are we to say that the Venerable Bede is to be rebuked (*est,* misprint for
esse) for asserting in the face of (*post*) ancient laws that certain penitents should
be shackled in iron chains? And is that manner of living (*vita*) of the Holy
Fathers to be spat upon which (*quem,* misprint for *quae*) bears witness that they
did penance for their sins, some by standing for weeks and fortnights (*ogdoadas et
pentadecas*) in [piles of] thorns, some by standing from sunrise to sunrise with
their arms uplifted stiff above their heads, and some by hiding from view for
long periods (*jugiter*) in caves they dug for themselves? And is the Blessed
Macharius properly to be ridiculed because for six months at a time—not in
penance for any sins he had committed himself (*dum se minimum quid admisisse
poenituit*)—he exposed his limbs naked to the sharp beaks of mosquitoes (? *culi-
cum*), which were fit to pierce the hide of a wild boar?" And see *Opuscula,* LI, 9,
De Dominico Loricato: De ratione disciplinae (*Opera,* Vol. III, pp. 400-01).

ficing himself for the salvation of others (IV-δ). A pretty computation in arithmetic worked out by St. Peter Damian shows that a hundred years of penance could be offset by reciting twenty Psalms [*read* Psalters] accompanied by self-flagellation with switches or leathern thongs.[1] It seems that St. Dominic managed to perform that feat in six [*read* five] days' time. On one occasion at the beginning of Lent, St. Dominic begged St. Peter Damian to impose one thousand years of penance upon him, and he had paid almost the whole debt before the end of that Lent.[2]

1198. In his efforts to promote the practice of self-flagellation, St. Peter Damian reminds one, *mutatis mutandis,* of the ascetics of our time, who would deprive human life of all material pleasures and who so fiercely persecute the smile of woman and the warmth of wine. If it be objected that ours are mere pseudo-ascetics, the comparison nevertheless holds between their admirers and the admirers of the flagellations of the "Saint in Armour."[1]

1197 [1] *Idem, Opuscula,* LI, 8-9, *De Dominico Loricato* (*Opera,* Vol. III, pp. 400-01). P. 400, col. 1, D: "According to that same author [St. Dominic Loricatus] credit for a hundred years of penance could be obtained in that way. It is our regular procedure to count three thousand blows of the rod as the equivalent of one year of penance. However, as has often been tested (*probatam,* misprint for *probatum*) the recitation of ten Psalms allows opportunity for one thousand blows. Now since there is no doubt that the Psalter contains one hundred and fifty Psalms, accurate computation shows that there are five years of penance in this discipline of the Psalter. But whether you multiply 5 by 20 [Pareto rightly corrects *vices* to *vicies.*—A. L.] or 20 by 5, the result is 100. It follows therefore that anyone reciting twenty Psalters with flagellation (*disciplina*) may be sure he has won credit for a hundred years of penance." The Saint's arithmetic does not show a wrinkle. [Pareto misread "Psalteria" as "Psalms"—a difference between 20 and 3,000! St. Dominic, still according to St. Peter Damian, usually recited two Psalters every ordinary day, and at least three Psalters on days in Lent: *loc. cit.,* C.: *vix dies ulla praetereat quin duo Psalteria modulando utraque manu scopis armata nudum corpus allidat . . . quadragesimalibus circulis . . . ad minus tres Psalteria.* On the special occasion in question here he must have performed his stint not in six days, as Pareto says, but in five.—A. L.]

1197 [2] *Ibid.,* 9: "*Memini quoque quia cuiusdam Quadragesimae imminentis initio mille annos imponi sibi per nos ad poenitentiam petiit: quos certe omnes ferme antequam ieiunii tempus transigeretur explevit.*"

1198 [1] A certain Mr. Cannon, an American, turned ninety-seven preachers loose upon his countrymen during the Christmas season of the year 1911 with the idea of persuading them to abstain from women and wine. No comparison is possible between Mr. Cannon and St. Dominic. The one makes money on the stock-market

1199. Record of the penances of St. Dominic chances to have survived in the works of St. Peter Damian. We may readily imagine that there were other cases of the kind, perhaps less severe, of which no record has come down to us. Be that as it may, towards the year 1260 an epidemic of flagellations broke out in Italy and raged for several years thereafter, now in one place, now in another, now abating and dying out, now flaring up again. Muratori believes that many of the modern brotherhoods and congregations originated in the flagellations of those days: "Forasmuch as the notion was fixed in the minds of people that flogging was a most salutary act of penance and since zeal of faith was strong with them, they came together in devout societies each with its own banners, marching about thereafter in public processions singing godly hymns, and repairing on holy days to their churches, where they practised flagellations, prayed for divine forgiveness, and performed other acts of Christian devoutness." [1]

(a place of no great repute as an abode of virtue), keeps the pleasure for himself, and presents the penances to others. The Saint lived in utter poverty and hardship, and inflicted penances upon himself to compensate for the enjoyments of others. A comparison is possible, however, between their respective followings, for these are in both cases inspired by an ascetic sense for eschewing the pleasures of life and seeking its sufferings.

1199 [1] *Dissertazioni sopra le antichità italiane,* LXXV (Vol. III, p. 468). And cf. his *Annali d'Italia,* Vol. VII, pp. 290-91: "The present year [1260] was further celebrated for a novelty in religion, which had its beginnings in Perugia, as some say with a child, according to others with a hermit who asserted that he had revelation of it from God. This man preached repentance to the people, representing a heavy scourge from Heaven as imminent unless they repented and made peace with one another. Wherefore men and women of all ages organized processions, lashing themselves and invoking the protection of the Virgin, Mother of God. This popular devotion moved on from Perugia to Spoleto, attended by a wondrous spirit of compunction, and thence into Romagna. The people in one town would gather in processions, sometimes ten and even twenty thousand strong, and march to a neighbouring town, and there in the cathedral flog themselves to the point of bleeding, crying to God for His mercy and for peace among men. [In that the residue of sociality comes into view in naked form.] Catching the spirit, the people of that town would then go to the next in the same way, so that by the end of the winter, the fashion had spread across the Alps, into Provence, Germany, and as far away as Poland. [The usual course of such epidemics, as was seen in our own times in the activities of the Salvation Army.] On October 10, the people of Imola brought the revival to Bologna. Twenty thousand Bolognese then

1200. The Roman Church, which has always been inclined to moderateness, condemned the excessive asceticism of the flagellants, just as in our day the Church of England preserved an attitude of hostility to the orgies of the Welsh revival. The flagellant epidemic of the year 1260 spread as far afield as Germany and aroused great excitement there. Rinaldi, who continued the *Annals* of Cesare Baronio, describes (following Stero) the penances practised by the German flagellants,[1] and also notes that the sect eventually turned to heresy. "This piety of the penitents," he says, *loc. cit.,* "later degenerated into loathsome heresy. Though it had a good beginning in great pomp of sanctity, it was changed by the acts of the Devil into wickedness and debauchery." Flagellants are again in the public eye in Germany in the year 1349, and this time they may be seen rising to appease the divine wrath manifested in a pestilence that

marched upon Modena, and an equal number of Modenese to Reggio and Parma. So from place to place the thing was carried on to Genoa and through the whole of Piedmont. [The Welsh revival spread in much the same way, though on a far smaller scale, in our day.] However, the Marquis Oberto Pallavicino and the Torriani refused to allow the processions to enter the territories of Cremona, Milan, Brescia, and Novara; and King Manfred also forbade them the March of Ancona and Apulia, fearing lest that pretence of piety dissembled some political stratagem. This harshness the Monk of Padua deeply deplores. As a result of this devout stirring of the people, numberless reconciliations were effected among hostile factions, and exiles were allowed to return to their homes. Numberless the confessions and communions—rites much neglected in those barbarous times; and the conversions, whether lasting I could not say, of prostitutes, usurers, criminals, and other wrongdoers." (The usual momentary effects of such epidemics, as may also be seen in the Welsh revival.) In *Dissertazioni,* LXXV above quoted, Muratori specifies further: "The rite spread from one town to the next adjoining. The people of a city, dressed in sackcloth and barefooted, formed in procession two by two, and with the crucifix at their head marched to the next city, imploring peace and the forgiveness of wrongs. Towards the end of October, for example, the Bolognese came to Modena, more than twenty thousand strong, headed by their banners, lashing themselves, and singing hymns of praise and other crude songs. The Modenese went out as far as Castello Leone to receive them and welcome them to their city. They repeated their flagellations, their prayers and wailings in the cathedral and then after service of refreshments by the citizens returned to their homes."

1200 [1] *Annales ecclesiastici, anno* 1260, VIII: "Henricus Stero claims—in that agreeing with the Monk of Padua—that the rite of the flagellants started in Perugia and spread to Germany. Their manner of supplication he describes as follows: 'That form of penance was a hard thing to bear and a horrible and pitiable thing to look upon. The flagellants marched with their bodies bared down to the middle,

was at that time ravaging those unhappy lands.[2] As usual superstition went hand in hand with asceticism, and again as usual, hypocrisy supplied the cloak for criminal doings. These German flagellants read the counterpart of a letter that had been delivered at the Church of St. Peter in Jerusalem by an angel, and which said that Jesus Christ was wroth at the sins of the world but that, in deference to prayers of the Virgin and the angels that He be merci-

then with a sort of skirt (*quadam veste*) reaching to their heels. Their heads and faces were hooded to prevent recognition. They marched in double or triple file, like priests, with a banner or a cross in front. They lashed themselves twice a day for thirty-three days in memory of the time Our Lord Jesus Christ spent in the flesh on this earth [Jesus figures here very much as did the Artemis Orthia in the flagellations of the Spartans. A devout people connects its institutions with its own gods.], the flagellations lasting for the duration (*quousque . . . compleverunt*) of certain chants that they had composed concerning the Passion and death of Our Lord, and which they sang either in the churches or outside them, with two or three leaders of the singing, and now prostrating themselves on the ground, now raising their naked arms to heaven, and regardless of mud or snow, cold or heat. Their pitiable gestures and terrifying flagellations moved many people to tears and to taking up the same form of penance.' "

1200 [2] *Ibid., anno* 1349, XVIII (quoting Albert of Strasburg, *Chronicon*, pp. 149-50): "The pestilence gradually spreading in Germany, people began marching about the country lashing themselves. In mid-June of the year mentioned [1349], two hundred came to Spires from Swabia. They had one man as leader and two other teachers, whose commands they obeyed implicitly. They crossed the Rhine at day-break. A great crowd gathering, they formed a vast circle in front of the minster in the city of Spires. Going into the circle, they stripped themselves of their garments and footwear, being left in a sort of shirt, in place of breeches (*in modum braccae*), that reached from waist to heel (*a femore ad talos*). Then as they marched about the circle they would throw themselves on their faces one after the other, their arms outspread as though crucified, the ones coming behind stepping over those prostrate on the ground and touching them lightly with their flails. Those who had been the first to prostrate themselves were the first to rise; and they would resume the march about the circle, lashing themselves with whips of four thongs tipped with iron nails, singing the Sunday doxology in German (*cantu vulgari invocationis dominicae*) with many prayers. Meantime three of them stood in the centre of the circle lashing themselves and singing in loud voices, and after them others sang. After some time, at a given signal, they all knelt and threw themselves on their faces with arms outspread like persons nailed to the cross, praying in loud sobs. The two masters walked round and round the circle exhorting them to pray to the Lord for mercy upon the people of Spires, and upon all those who had done them good or ill and upon all sinners and all souls in Purgatory. And there were many other things of the kind." [The *Chronicon* ascribed to Albertus Argentinensis seems really to have been written by Matthew of Neuburg (Mattaeus Neuburgensis). See Hamcke, *De M. Alberti Argentinensis Chronico*, n. p. [1866].—A. L.]

ful, He had prescribed that each of those persons should withdraw from the world for thirty-four days and do penance in flagellation.[8] In certain respects at least, the pseudo-scientific pronouncements that people in our time use to preach abstinence from the enjoyments of wine and women are just as silly as the letter from Jerusalem, though in a different way.

1201. The writer of a life of Pope Clement VI asserts of the flagellants of 1349 that "under guise of penance and good works, they slyly committed many crimes"; and that same Pope complains in a bull addressed to the Archbishop of Magdeburg that "under semblance of piety, they cruelly turn their hands to works of impiousness. The blood of Jews (to whom Christian pity gives shelter and protection, not suffering harm to be done to them in any way), nay, the blood even of Christians, do they shed; and to the undoing of good order they lay hold on possessions of clergy and laity alike."[1] The Pope accordingly orders that they be condemned and dispersed. Sentence was also passed against them by the University of Paris, and Philip, the king, forbade them entrance to the realm of France on pain of death.

1202. Flagellants appear again at Misura in 1414, and again they are persecuted and dispersed. This time they were saying that ordinary baptism by water did no good and had to be replaced with a baptism by blood through flagellation. Three years later, in 1417, they break out in Aragon (St. Vincent Ferrer), and Gerson writes a treatise against the abuse of flagellation, which he countenances only when exercised in moderation and at the direction of superiors. In the year 1582 Henry III of France founded congregations for flagellants; but in that case a new element creeps in—eroticism,

---

1200 [8] The Albert [or Matthew] in question summarizes, *loc. cit.*, the letter that was read on that occasion: *"Cuius literae tenor similis in sententia esse dicebatur in ecclesia S. Petri in Ierusalem per angelum praesentatae, in qua narrat angelus Christum offensum contra mundi pravitates, plurima exprimens crimina violationum diei dominicae, et quod non ieiunetur feria sexta, blasphemias, usuras, adulteria, Christumque rogatum per B. Verginem et angelos pro misericordia, respondisse quemlibet per triginta quatuor dies se debere exulando flagellare ut misericordiam Dei consequantur."*

1201 [1] Baronio-Rinaldi, *Op. cit.*, anno 1349, XXI.

the ascetic current going astray.[1] Even in later times, many very devout people were opposed to flagellation, on the ground that it often concealed erotic perversions. Such cases are entirely, or in large part, foreign to asceticism.

1203. Likewise to be distinguished from it are such acts as appear in the Lupercalia in Rome, which, on quite inadequate grounds, the totemists would classify with the flagellation of young men at Sparta. In Sparta the pain inflicted on the victims was an essential element in the rite. In the Lupercalia pain had no part, or at least no apparent part. In the Lupercalia the Luperci ran about the city streets with leather whips cut from the hides of sacrificial victims, and struck the women they encountered with them, the women thus being assured of children. That is just one of the many practices that have been invented by the human fancy to cure women of sterility, and it is of the same nature as the many practices equally numerous that have been devised to cure males of impotence. It may

1202 [1] Pierre de l'Estoile, *Registre-journal de Henri III*, pp. 159-60: "In this month of March of the present year 1583, the King decreed and established a new order, which he named the Order of Penitents, himself and his two favourites (*mignons*) joining the brotherhood; and he caused to enter it also several lords-gentlemen and others of his Court, inviting likewise the prominents of his parliament in Paris, his Exchequer, and other courts and jurisdictions, along with a goodly number of the outstanding burghers of the town. . . . On which day [March 25, 1583, the Feast of the Annunciation] a solemn procession of the said brotherhood of the Penitents took place, they coming about four in the afternoon to the Convent of the Augustinians . . . two by two, and accoutred like the flagellants of Rome, Avignon, Toulouse, and the like. . . . On Holy Thursday, the seventh of April, from about nine o'clock in the evening, the procession of the Penitents, in which the King with all his favourites (*mignons*) marched all night long about the streets and to the churches, in great magnificence of torches and excellent music, and masked (*faux-bourdonnée*). And there were some, even the royal favourites (*mignons*) it is said, who lashed themselves during the processions, their poor backs being all red from the blows they gave themselves." The public ridiculed such buffoonery. After the procession the following quip went the rounds:

> "*Après avoir pillé la France,
> et tout son peuple despouillé,
> est-ce pas belle pénitence
> de se couvrir d'un sac mouillé?*"

("After pillaging France and stripping her people clean, is it not fine penance to go about in a wet sack?")

be that among the fantastic reasons underlying these products of the imagination the reason given by the totemists may also have figured. In that case they would have made a good guess, as may sometimes happen in cases where one has no certain knowledge to go by. Pausanias, *Periegesis,* VIII, *Arcadia,* 23, 1, notes that at Alea, in Arcady, a feast was celebrated in honour of Bacchus: "At that festival," he says, "in obedience to an oracle of Delphi, women are flogged, as are the young men of Sparta at the altar of the Orthia." Trying to discover the reasons for a thing when we know so little about it is like trying to guess the numbers that will be drawn in a lottery—a sheer waste of time.[1]

1204. Among the civilized peoples of our day such manifestations of asceticism as fasts and flagellations have all but disappeared. As early as 1831 an *Instruction to Confessors* reads:[1] "The true and

1203 [1] On the Lupercalia see Ovid, *Fasti,* II, vv. 425-8:

> *"Nupta, quid exspectas? non tu pollentibus herbis*
> *nec prece nec magico carmine mater eris.*
> *Excipe fecundae patienter verbera dextrae:*
> *iam socer optati nomen habebit avi."*

("Bride, why waitest thou? Thou shalt become a mother not from potent herbs nor prayers nor magic chants. Submit in patience rather to the lashes of the fertilizing whip, and straightway thy husband's father will be the grand sire he yearns to be.")

He then recounts, vv. 441-48, an oracle of Juno and what came of it:

> *" 'Italidas matres,' inquit, 'caper hirtus inito.'*
> *Obstupuit dubio territa turba sono.*
> *'Augur erat: nomen longis intercidit annis—*
> *nuper ab Etrusca venerat exsul humo.*
> *Ille caprum mactat: iussae sua terga maritae*
> *pellibus exsectis percutienda dabant.*
> *Luna resumebat decimo nova cornua motu:*
> *virque pater subito, nuptaque mater erat."*

("'A shaggy goat,' came the voice, 'will mate with Italic mothers!' The throng stood in awed silence at the ambiguous prophecy. But an augur was there (his name has been forgotten in course of the passing years, but he had lately come as an exile from Etrurian soil). He slaughtered a goat. At his bidding the women offered their backs to lashes from thongs cut from its hide. And the new Moon was again showing pointed horns in the tenth month, when the man became a father and his bride a mother.")

1204 [1] *Pratica del confessionale compilata da un provetto confessore,* Turin, 1831, Vol. III, p. 311.

direct manner of subduing the rebellious flesh is through the use
of fasting or other mortifications, such as haircloth, the scourge, and
the like; and those were the penances prescribed for the most part
by the Holy Fathers. However, it is not always possible or expedient
to require formal fasts of nothing but bread and water several times
in the week, or over periods of years, according to Church practice
or as specified in the Sacred Canons. What penitent in our day
would accept them or observe them? According, therefore, to present regulations and to the actual usage of judicious confessors, fasts
and all other mortification of the flesh should be used as moderately
as possible." Now less than ever is there any question of hair-shirts,
flagellations, and strict fasts in Italy, France, Germany, or England.
It is said that some very moderate use is still made of them in Spain.

1205. So in modern European countries the Nazaritic vow among
the Jews seems to have fallen into disuse. Nowadays Nazarites are,
one may say, unknown, having been superseded in part by the prohibitionists of all religions (or of no religion). According to the
Bible, the Nazarite was required to abstain from the use of wine
and all other alcoholic beverages, vinegar, and all beverages obtained
from the grape or raisin.[1] He could not cut his hair, and was obliged
to observe other rules, to keep himself in a state of purity. A Nazareat lasted for thirty days, or for some other specified period, or it
might even be perpetual. The Talmud dwells on it at length.[2]

1205 [1] Num. 6:4 (*Vulgate*): *"Cunctis diebus quibus ex voto Domino consecrantur,
quidquid ex vinea esse potest, ab uva passa usque ad acinum, non comedent."*

1205 [2] Talmud of Jerusalem, Tract Nazir, III, 6, 1-3 (Schwab, Vol. IX, pp. 138-48;
Danby, p. 287): "(Mishnah) Three things fundamentally are forbidden the Nazir:
impurity, cutting of the hair, and consumption of any product of the vine. All
things coming of the vine, grape-skins, for instance, grape-pits, or dried seeds, will
be taken together in determining the regulation minimum, there being no violation
of abstinence till a quantity of grape equal in bulk to an olive has been eaten."
The "Commentary" goes into some very fine discriminations. The Nazir is forbidden to eat the flesh of an animal that has been quartered. Hence a problem:
"Rabbi Yohanan and Rabbi Simon b. Lokisch debate the question of eating an ant
that has been bitten in two in the mouth and then eaten, Rabbi Yohanan concluding
in favour of a penalty, Rabbi Simon against one. Rabbi Mescha asked Rabbi Zura:
'Do Rabbi Yohanan and Rabbi Simon b. Lokisch rule on the question of a grape-
seed which a Nazir has bitten in two in his mouth and then eaten?' [Yet teetotallers of our day have been known to refuse food they suspect of being flavoured

1206. Manifestations of asceticism under forms of mortifications of the flesh are still common among Mohammedans and Hindus, and in semi-civilized countries. They are also frequent among the more advanced savages, though much more rare among peoples living virtually on the plane of the brutes. In modern civilized countries asceticism has evolved into prohibitionism, a phobia for anything suggesting sex, the pathological humility of many sincere humanitarians. Occasionally, also, some manifestation turns up, such as the long fast that is nowadays prescribed in the name of Science Sacrosanct, after having for ages been recommended or required in the name of some other divinity.[1]

When the residues of asceticism are combined with the residues of the instinct for combinations (Class I), the result is a very elaborate code, which in any given variety of asceticism seems ridiculous to those who do not share the sentiments corresponding. But such persons usually have other sentiments of their own corresponding to other varieties of asceticism, so that they observe codes altogether similar to the ones they deride.

All these varieties of asceticism, when exacerbated by their codes,

with wine.] A person eating five ants [What a titbit!] even at one mouthful and whether wittingly or not, will be penalized for each insect so eaten, since each ant, in spite of its smallness, constitutes a separate item. But if the ants are crushed before being eaten, the Nazarite will be guilty but once, and even then the total amount consumed must be equivalent to an olive. . . . (Mishnah) Unless otherwise specified the Nazareat is a period of thirty days. A voluntary shaving during that period, or a forcible shaving at the hands of brigands, upsets the period, and it has to be begun over again. If a Nazarite has clipped his hair with scissors or shaved with a razor or pulled out any hair, regardless of the amount, he is guilty. He may rub himself and even scratch himself, but he must not comb his hair for fear of pulling one out." Failure to observe the prescriptions of the Nazareat has its penalties: "He said in the presence of Rabbi Yossé: 'The moment one has cut a single hair during a Nazareat period, one is subject to a flogging.' " People are much more humane today. One merely goes to jail, in a number of states in the American Union, for making a sly wink at a lady.

1206 [1] I am personally acquainted with a teetotaller who is an atheist and who gives not a thought to the Bible. He carries his hatred of alcoholic beverages to the point of abstaining from vinegar, seasoning his salads with lemon. He will not eat fish that has been seasoned with white wine, nor will he touch jugged hare—because of the red wine that is used in the sauce. The residue remains the same—derivations change.

and when efforts are made to enforce them upon others, are the source of huge amounts of suffering that have afflicted, and continue to afflict, the human race. The fact that people tolerate such sufferings, and sometimes even accept them voluntarily instead of rejecting them and stamping on those who promote them as on poisonous snakes, shows conclusively how powerful the sentiments corresponding to them are. Really they are perversions of the instinct of sociality, and without that instinct human society could not exist.

CHAPTER VIII

Residues: Individual Integrity and Sex

1207. Class V: *Integrity of the individual and his appurtenances and possessions.* This class is in a sense the complement of Class IV (sociality). To defend one's own things and strive to increase their quantity are two operations that frequently merge. So defence of integrity and development of personality are two operations that may differ little or even be one and the same. The sum of sentiments called interests is of the same nature as the sentiments to which the residues of the present variety correspond; hence sentiments of "interest" ought strictly to be put in it. But they are of such great intrinsic importance in the social equilibrium that they are best considered apart from residues.

1208. V-α: *Sentiments of resistance to alterations in the social equilibrium.* The equilibrium may be one actually existing, or an ideal equilibrium desired by the individual. But whether real or imaginary, if it is altered, or thought of as altered, the individual suffers, even if he is not directly affected by the alteration, and sometimes, though rarely, even if he gains by it.

1209. In a people that has the institution of slavery, the ancient Greeks, for instance, a citizen may not himself be a slave-owner, but he feels the wrong that is done to the slave-owner in taking the slave away from him—a reaction against an act that disturbs the existing equilibrium. Another citizen would keep the Barbarians slaves and make all Greeks free men; he is envisaging an equilibrium which for those times would be partially ideal. Still another citizen would abolish slavery altogether. He is contemplating an equilibrium which, for those times again, is altogether ideal.

1210. If an existing state of social equilibrium is altered, forces tending to re-establish it come into play—that, no more, no less, is what equilibrium means (§§ 2068 f.). Such forces are, in chief, sentiments that find their expression in residues of the variety we are here examining. On the passive side, they make us aware of the alteration in the equilibrium. On the active side, they prompt us to remove, repel, counteract, the causes of the alteration, and so develop into sentiments of the V-δ variety (§§ 1312 f.). The forces (or sentiments) that come into play when the social equilibrium is disturbed are nearly always perceived by the individual members of that society under some special form. Needless to say, they, as individuals, know nothing about any forces, nothing about any equilibrium. Those are just names which we, as scientists, apply to what is going on. They are conscious of an unpleasant disturbance—it may sometimes be painful, and very painful indeed—of their integrity as it was when the state of equilibrium was still being maintained. Ordinarily such sensations belong to the vague categories known as the "just" or the "unjust." When a person says: "That thing is unjust," what he means is that the thing is offensive to his sentiments as his sentiments stand in the state of social equilibrium to which he is accustomed.

1211. Where a certain kind of property exists it is "unjust" to take it away from a man. Where it does not exist it is "unjust" to bestow it on him. Cicero would have those who are in power in the state refrain from that type of liberality which takes away from the ones in order to give to the others. "Many are they," he says, "who, especially if they are covetous of splendour and glory, take away from the ones what they bestow with a free hand on others."[1] That principle, on the other hand, is fundamental to the so called social legislation that is so dear to the men of our time. Soldiers who are dividing booty taken from an enemy resent as "unjust" any alteration in the rules usually followed in making such partitions. A similar feeling prevails even among thieves in dividing their loot.[2]

1212. The various elements in the social equilibrium are very imperfectly distinguished, especially when the social sciences are at all

1211 [1] *De officiis,* I, 14, 43. And he adds: "The transfers of property made by Lucius Sulla and Gaius Caesar from its rightful owners to other parties should not be accounted liberalities, for nothing is generous that is not also just."

1211 [2] Other residues also figure in the nebulous things called "justice" and "injustice"; but this is not the place to go into them.

backward. So the sentiment that inspires resistance to alterations of equilibrium places alterations in insignificant matters on a par with alterations in very important matters, and people regard as equally "just" a sentence condemning an anti-trinitarian to the stake and a sentence condemning a murderer to death. The mere wearing of clothes different from the common fashion clashes with the sentiment as violently as other far more important transgressions against the social order. Even today, among peoples who call themselves civilized, a woman is not allowed to walk the streets in male attire.

1213. The residue we are here examining prompts a remark of great importance, though it may not appear so at first blush. Take a society in which murder is becoming a frequent occurrence. That society is evidently breaking up. To check the process of dissolution, the sentiment corresponding to our residue does not have to come into play. The immediate interest of the members of the society is enough. In ordinary parlance it will be said that the individual who opposes that state of things is not inspired by any "ideal of justice," but by his instinct of self-preservation, an instinct that he shares with animals and which has nothing to do with any "ideal" of "justice." Now take a very large community where the number of murders is very small. The probability that a given individual will be the victim of a murder is very slight, equal, let us say, to the probability of his succumbing to any number of other perils—of his being bitten by a mad dog, or killed in a railroad accident, things to which the individual pays little attention. The sentiment of direct self-preservation has but slight influence in this case. But another sentiment comes into play and functions vigorously: a sentiment of revulsion against anything disturbing to the social equilibrium as it has existed and is accepted by the individual.

1214. If that sentiment did not exist, every slight incipient alteration in the social equilibrium would meet little or no resistance, and could therefore go on growing with impunity until it came to affect a sufficiently large number of individuals to provoke their resistance from a direct concern to avoid the evil. That is what happens to a certain extent in every society, however highly civilized. But the extent to which it happens is minimized by the interposition of the sentiment of resistance to any alteration in equilibrium, regardless of the number of individuals directly affected. As a consequence the social equilibrium becomes much more stable, and a much more energetic action develops as soon as any alteration sets in.[1]

1215. Examples of such phenomena are exceedingly numerous. One of the most recent was provided by France in 1912. For many years criminals had been treated with ever increasing indulgence in the country. The lay school had become a pulpit for Anarchy, and the social fabric was breaking down in many other respects. The effects became apparent in cases of "sabotage" in the ship-yards and on the railways, and finally in the exploits of a gang of Anarchists, Bonnot, Garnier, and Co. Then some slight reaction occurred. Undoubtedly fear of direct danger on the part of inhabitants of Paris and the suburbs had something to do with it; but, after all, the probability of any given citizen's being struck down by such criminals was very very slight. What interposed with greatest effect was the sentiment of opposition to disturbance of the social equilibrium as it had been. That feeling, in human society, is somewhat analogous to the instinct in animals that makes them flee at perception of danger.

1216. It is readily understandable, therefore, that through a combination of this residue of equilibrium with the residues of our Class II (group-persistences) compound residues of great social importance are built up, corresponding to vigorous and powerful sentiments of the type very vaguely designated by the term "ideal of

---

1214 [1] An example taken from mechanics will make the matter clearer. Let us assume that a material point stands in equilibrium and that when it is moved from the position of equilibrium a force proportional to the displacement comes into play, tending to carry it back to its former position. If the displacement is slight, the equilibrating force will also be slight, and the point can move quite a distance from its position of equilibrium. Now let us assume that in addition to the force just mentioned, every displacement of the point from the point of equilibrium, whatever the degree, brings into play a constant force of considerable power. In that case the slightest displacement is immediately counteracted by a very considerable force, is unable to increase, and the point is immediately restored to the position of equilibrium. This, notice, is just an analogy—by no means an identity (§ 121).

justice." From the logico-experimental standpoint to say that an "injustice," whether done to one person or to many, involves an equal offence against "justice," is to say a thing that has no meaning. There is no such person as "Justice," and one cannot imagine what "offences" could possibly be offered her. But the wording only is faulty. At bottom what is expressed is a feeling, vague and instinctive to be sure, that it is a good thing that resistance to disturbances of the social order should not stand in direct ratio to the number of individuals affected, but should have a considerable force independent of any such number.

1217. Going back to the example of Bonnot, Garnier, and Co. A number of devotees of the goddess "Science"—the science that has nothing to do with logico-experimental science—observed in great anger that the reaction which developed at the time was absurd, that it could not be said that the criminals in question were products of any *one* of the causes against which the country was aroused. They repeated that argument for every one of the causes in point, with the usual sophistry of the bald-headed man pointing to his one hair; and added that criminals there had always been in all societies at all times in history.[1]

1217 [1] So in England, in 1913, outrages by the "suffragettes" provoked sentiments of bitter resentment in the public at large, people feeling instinctively that to grant the right of disturbing the peace to anyone desirous of using force would sooner or later bring about the dissolution of society. The fanatic humanitarian mystics who were then governing the country did not see matters in that light; nor is the fact to be wondered at, for it is characteristic of fanaticisms and mysticisms that they put people out of touch with all realities. The Prime Minister read statistics in the House of Commons which tended to show that the crimes of the suffragettes were to be counted on the fingers, and that therefore repressive measures could continue mild as in the past. A few days later the newspapers reported two incidents: the one, that one of the harpies in question, who had been in prison for her misdeeds, had been set free as a result of her going on a hunger-strike; the other, that the suffragettes had used paraffin to set fire to Treytom House at Englefield Green, near London, the mansion being completely destroyed (it belonged to Lady White, widow of General Sir George White, the defender of Ladysmith). The damage was estimated at £4,000 sterling. Near the ruins handbills were found bearing the inscription: "Stop tormenting our comrades in prison, and give votes to women." One cannot imagine just why the eminent Prime Minister neglected to state how many more such crimes would be necessary to induce humanitarian arithmetic to grant protection to law-abiding citizens and withdraw

1218. In all that, in so far as reaction had been determined not at all by logic, but by instinct, there was an element of truth. One might add that had logic been the determining factor, there would have been no reaction, for the very good reason that there would have been no action in the first place. A matter of instinct was the pity that allowed criminals to go scot-free, preached anarchy to schoolchildren, and dissolved every tie of subordination to authority. Instinctive, therefore, was the fear that prompted people to react against such outrages. Instinctive is the conduct of the animal in approaching the bait that is set to trap him; and instinctive also his flight if, when near the bait, he perceives signs, real or imaginary, of danger.

1219. The only inference that can be drawn from all that is that non-logical actions play a great part in social life and that sometimes they produce an evil, and then again the remedy for it.

1220. V-β: *Sentiments of equality in inferiors.* This sentiment is often a defence of integrity on the part of an individual belonging to a lower class and a means of lifting him to a higher. That takes place without any awareness, on the part of the individual experiencing the sentiment, of the difference between his real and his apparent purposes. He talks of the interest of his social class instead of his own personal interest simply because that is a fashionable mode of expression.

1221. Striking tendencies arise from the very character of this sentiment, and at first glance they might seem to be contradictory. On the one hand there is a tendency to make the largest possible number of persons share in the advantages that the individual asks for himself. On the other, there is a tendency to restrict that number as far as possible. The contradiction disappears the moment we consider that the tendency is to admit to the advantages all whose cooperation helps one towards obtaining them, so that their intro-

licence to commit crimes at pleasure from hysterical furies who gloated over the things they did. Meantime what the Government actually did was to take steps not to put said females in prison but to station firemen at the hydrants day and night that they might be ready wherever fires started by the suffragettes broke out.

duction yields more in profits than it costs; and to exclude all who do not help, or help less effectively, so that their participation costs more than it yields. Similarly, in a war it is a good thing to have as many soldiers as possible for the fighting, and as few as possible for the division of the spoils. Demands for equality almost always conceal demands for privileges.

1222. There is another apparent contradiction. Inferiors wish to be the equals of their superiors, but they will not allow their superiors to be their equals. From the logical standpoint two contradictory propositions cannot be true at the same time. If $A = B$, it follows necessarily that $B = A$. But the contradiction disappears on reflection that the demand for equality is nothing but a disguised manner of demanding a privilege. The member of one class who demands equality for that class with some other really intends to win it a privilege as compared with the other. If the proposition $A = B$ really means that $A > B$, it is in no way contradictory—in fact, it is the perfection of logic—to go on and say that $B < A$. People agitate for equality to get equality in general, and then go on to make countless numbers of distinctions to deny it in the particular. Equality is to belong to all—but it is granted only to the few.[1]

1223. The Athenians set surpassing store on being equals before the law—ἰσόνομοι, as they said—and they sang the praises of Harmodius and Aristogiton who had made them so. But that equality did not extend to foreigners or resident aliens or even to persons of whose parents only the father was a citizen. Among the citizens themselves it was by no means considered contrary to equality that the poor should oppress the rich. Citizens of Sparta who enjoyed full rights were the Equals, the ὅμοιοι, but in reality they constituted an aristocracy of very limited numbers, which were constantly decreasing. The bare fact that a person was not rich enough to partake of the communal repast deprived him of status as an Equal. Among the peoples of our day equality of all human beings is an article of faith; but that does not preclude great differences, in

---

1222 [1] Pareto, *Manuale*, Chap. I, § 50.

Italy and France, between "union" and "non-union" working-men, between plain citizens and citizens who have "influence" with Deputies, Senators, "grand electors" (local bosses), and the like. Before handing down decisions, judges look well to see with just whom they are dealing. There are gaming-resorts that the police dare not enter, because they would be sure to find law-makers and other important persons there. How many prominent people in Italy carry knives with blades more than four inches long? That privilege is denied (by an utterly fatuous piece of legislation) to plain citizens, but not to people who belong to the political aristocracy or enjoy its protection. So in a day gone by it was legal for the nobleman to carry arms, not so for serf or villein.[1]

1224. Such things are known to everybody. That in fact is why no attention is paid to them, why if some Simple Simon ventured to complain of them, people would laugh at him as at someone complaining of the weather. Yet that does not prevent them from believing, in all good faith, that they are enjoying equality. There are hotels in certain places in the United States where a person cannot have his boots polished because it is an offence against Holy Equality for one person to polish another's boots. But the very people who cherish that lofty doctrine of equality are eager to expel the Chinese and Japanese from the United States; are disgusted at the very thought of a Japanese schoolboy sitting at a desk near child of theirs; will not allow a Negro to be accommodated at a hotel that they frequent, or ride in a railway coach which has the honour of transporting them. The thing would seem incredible if it were not true—but there are those among these fierce believers in Holy Equality who

1223 [1] In *La Ragione*, June 16, 1911, the Italian Deputy, Pio Viazzi, writes: "Is it not a matter of common knowledge that every [Italian] court has its privileged attorney, who is called the 'prince,' usually the shrewdest intriguer in the lot? He is the lawyer who monopolizes the wealthiest clients, is unfailingly resourceful in securing last-minute evidence, is friends with all the judges, gets postponements that are denied to others; whose questionable witticisms in open court meet with considerate smiles, and whose clients always receive a benevolent consideration that is never useless even when it is not altogether unfair and iniquitous." [A magnificent portrait of such a person is drawn in the character named Malaguzzi, in Guglielmo Ferrero's *La terza Roma* (The Seven Vices), Vol. I.—A. L.]

hold that Jesus died to redeem all men (and they call them "brethren in Christ"), and who give their mite to missionaries to go out and convert people in Africa and Asia, yet who refuse to worship their God in an American church to which a Negro is admitted.[1]

1225. Both European and American democracies profess to be founded on principles of thorough-going equality between human beings. But the equality is strictly for men, not for women. "One man, one vote," cry our fanatics; and they hide their faces in holy horror if someone remarks that the vote of the educated man should not be equal to the vote of the illiterate, the vote of the delinquent to the vote of the honest citizen, the vote of the ne'er-do-well to the vote of the useful citizen. There must be perfect equality, because all human beings are equal. But that fine principle is forgotten when it is a question of women. By a neat trick of sleight-of-hand, equality of human beings becomes equality of males, nay, of certain males. The very persons who regard the principle of universal suffrage as a dogma above discussion, superior to every consideration of expediency or convenience, deny suffrage to women on grounds of expediency and convenience; because, they say, votes for women would strengthen clerical or conservative parties.

1226. We are not concerned here with the social utility of such measures. It may be great even if the arguments with which people try to support them are absurd. Then again, it may be nil. Just here we are examining these reasonings merely with reference to the sentiments that inspire them. If the reasonings are patently false but are nevertheless approved and accepted, the fact cannot be due to their logical force but simply to the strength of the sentiments that they hide. That is the fact which it is so important to grasp.

1227. The sentiment that is very inappropriately named equality is fresh, strong, alert, precisely because it is not, in fact, a sentiment of equality and is not related to any abstraction, as a few naïve "in-

1224 [1] In 1911 the United States repudiated a commercial treaty with Russia because the Russian Government was denying right of entry to Jews carrying American passports. That was regarded as an offence against equality. But the United States refuses entry to many Asiatics who are Russian subjects—and that is not at all an offence against equality!

tellectuals" still believe; but because it is related to the direct interests of individuals who are bent on escaping certain inequalities not in their favour, and setting up new inequalities that will be in their favour, this latter being their chief concern.

1228. The residues we still have to consider, the V-γ and V-δ varieties, have one trait in common, the following: Integrity having been somehow altered, the effort is to restore it, if possible, or else to obtain compensations for the alteration. If the restoration is effected by acts pertaining to the individuals who have suffered alteration in integrity, we get the V-γ variety, which subdivides into two species, V-γ1, where the subject is real, and V-γ2, where the subject is imaginary. If the restoration is effected by acts pertaining to the agent of the alteration, we get our V-δ variety, which subdivides into the species V-δ1 where the agent is real, and V-δ2 where the agent is imaginary.

1229. V-γ: *Restoration of integrity by acts pertaining to the individuals whose integrity has been impaired.* This variety embraces the purifications that were so generally used in ancient societies and which are still common among uncivilized or barbarous peoples. They have virtually or completely disappeared in the civilized societies of our day; and for that reason we might content ourselves with a bare mention of them, were it not that they provide excellent illustrations of the manner in which residues act and blossom out into derivations. Knowledge of them therefore helps indirectly to an understanding of similar phenomena and we shall therefore dwell on them at some little length here.

1230. The subject is a very complicated one; and it will help if we draw a few distinctions. We must consider the various cases first of all (*a*) from the standpoint of the persons or things, real or imaginary, that figure in them—that is to say, from the objective standpoint; and second (*b*), from the standpoint of the attitudes or feelings of the persons who participate in operations of purification or restoration of integrity—that is to say, from the subjective standpoint.

1231. *a: Objective standpoint.* Here three distinctions are in order:

1. *The subjects undergoing the alteration.* Here again a number of aspects present themselves:

Character of the subjects. They may be real or imaginary, a fact that yields our subdivision of the genus into the species V-γ1 and V-γ2. Further to be considered would be subjects that are abstractions of real subjects, for example, "the family," "the nation," and the like; but to avoid complicating our outline unnecessarily we shall consider them "unreal" and include them under species V-γ2. Someone accustomed to considering conduct from the logical point of view might imagine that the concept of alterations in integrity was first applied to human beings and then extended either by analogy or through group-persistence to things, abstractions, imaginary beings. But we have no proof of any such development, which may have occurred in certain cases and not in others. The development, furthermore, may sometimes have been in the opposite direction, the concept being carried over from things to people. But leaving origins aside and attending strictly to interdependences in facts, it seems obvious enough that analogy and group-persistence serve to maintain alterations of integrity in people, things, and abstract or imaginary beings in homogeneous masses; and it may often be said that, for those reasons, the concept of alteration passes back and forth from one such subject to another. Since the human being is the principal concern with human beings, it is understandable that the usual course is from the human being to other sorts of subjects. "Real" subjects would be human beings, animals, plants, things, buildings, cities, territories, societies, and groups such as armies, families, nations, and the like. They are exceedingly numerous and variegated.

Extension in space. Even here, without meaning to imply anything as to origins, we may say that the human being frequently appears as a nucleus in the various concepts, the alteration extending from him to the various groups of which he is assumed to form a part. Notable among such groups are the family, blood-relationships more or less far-reaching, ethnical groups, such as the tribe, the city, the nation, even the whole "human race." Group-persistences are of such effect that the individuals composing the groups are not alone considered, but the groups themselves acquire independent individuality. Alterations of integrity often follow the opposite course, being carried over from the group to individuals. Among many peoples non-logical feeling makes a unit of the family, which continues to figure as a unit in logical or pseudo-logical derivations. This trait, which was general among our Graeco-Latin ancestors, is still very conspicuous in Chinese society. That fact stands in close relation with another—the fact of "family responsibility," and with strange phenomena such as the Hebrew "levirate" or the Greek "epiclerate," whereby, within the limits of the possible, the integrity of an individual without offspring is restored, and the integrity of his posterity, or rather of the group that is called "the family," is maintained.

Extensions to animals, inanimate objects, and abstract or imaginary beings. The direct course, from the human being to these entities, is the usual one; but there are cases of the opposite. All such entities may be taken as persons and undergo alterations of integrity.

Extensions in time. This cannot fail to occur when the alteration is not materially subsistent at the moment of the restoration. The two operations being successive, it is implicitly assumed that the subject is continuous (§ 1055). If a man does penance for a sin that he has himself committed, it is taken for granted that the person who has sinned and the person who does the penance are one and the same. But extension in time takes place in many other situations. Alteration and restoration are extended in the direction of ancestry and in the direction of posterity. The former direction is preferred by the Chinese, the second by Europeans. Pushed to its extreme limit, the extension to posterity gives rise to the concept of original sin (§ 1288). Another extension in time oversteps the confines of earthly life, and we get such beliefs as metempsychosis, Nirvana, punishment or recompense for the souls of the dead, redemption, and so on.

2. *Alteration*. This may also be real or imaginary. It may be a material alteration, or a purely conceptual affair. The remarks just made on extensions in space and time apply to it.

Manners of transmitting the alteration. Transmission may result from contact; from certain relationships between the subjects involved—descent, for instance; from acts having effects now real, now imaginary. Ordinarily, thanks to group-persistences, notions and concepts applying to real manners of transmission are carried over to the imaginary.

3. *Means of alteration and restoration*. These too may be real or imaginary. The residues of combination interpose to supply an immense variety of practices that are deemed capable of altering integrity, and an even greater abundance of rites deemed suitable for restoring integrity—among them, magical practices and all sorts of religious rites. Partisans of logical conduct usually give first importance to the means and believe that the purifications take place by virtue of certain reasonings. Those who are aware of the important rôle played by non-logical conduct in human life give first prominence to sentiments, consider means as subordinate, and realize that reasonings are just cloaks for the sentiments that inspire the purification rites (§ 1239). Choice of means may be of great importance from the standpoint of social utility. The ancients purified themselves in times of epidemic with frequent baths, people in the Middle Ages with religious processions and penances, remaining in the same untold filth as when they started. The two means were different cloaks for the same sentiment, but the first was beneficial to society, the second useless, and even harmful, in view of the contacts between the healthy and the sick in the processions, and the violations of sound hygiene involved in the penances![1]

1231 [1] A legendary episode that is typical of many historic cases of purification is mentioned in the *Iliad*, I, vv. 313-14. A pestilence was raging in the Greek camp. "The son of Atreus bade them purify themselves. They did so, throwing the filth into the sea." Eustathius remarks on the passage, *Commentarii*, Vol. I, p. 90: "Purification means cleansing with ablutions. And this among the ancients was

1232. There are a few considerations that apply in common to all the distinctions just made. For all of them we find real cases historically well authenticated. Not only may a man suffer material alterations of integrity, but he may suffer alteration in his reputation, and not only as an individual, but as a member of certain groups. Extension of alteration to the family becomes a fact when there are laws to impose it, but it may also take place without the interposition of any law. The man who gets rich brings prosperity to his family; the bankrupt, distress. There are hereditary diseases that visit the sins of parents upon their children. Peoples suffer from the mistakes of their rulers and gain by their wise policies. The means by which an alteration is transmitted *de facto* are not material only. The spoken word is a powerful instrument, and defamation may be worse than a bodily wound. The transition from the real to the imaginary is often imperceptible and cannot be accurately delineated even with the methods of modern science. There is still doubt, for instance, as to whether certain diseases are or are not hereditary, and doubts as to the manner of their transmission are far from being dissipated. It seems not to be true, as the Moslems think, that contact with a hog does any harm to a man. It is known,

a very appropriate expression, for the purifications were performed in connexion with sacrifices." And he continues: "Why into the sea? Because sea-water by its very nature is appropriate to washing. They threw the filth into the sea, where, it is said, there is no filth. Hence the proverb, 'The sea cleanseth men of all their ills.'" The proverb is a line in the *Iphigenia in Tauris* of Euripides, v. 1193 (Coleridge, Vol. II, p. 377). Diogenes Laertius, *Plato,* III, 6 (Hicks, Vol. I, p. 283), claims that the verse alludes to an incident in the life of Plato, who, falling ill in Egypt, whither he had gone with Euripides, was cured by some priests with sea-water. The whole scene in the *Iphigenia* is worth a reading, to see the way in which altogether fantastic notions are jumbled together with notions that might have some bearing on cleanliness or disgust at filth. Iphigenia declares, v. 1171, that the two strangers brought to her are defiled by murder of their mother and, v. 1177, she carries the image of the goddess out of doors to save it from contamination by contact with a murderer. She also says, v. 1191, that before she can sacrifice for them she must purify them. "At the fountain or in the water in the sea?" asks the King, v. 1192. It is then that Iphigenia replies that "sea-water cleanseth (washes) men of all their ills." Further along, v. 1199, she feels that she also has to "purify the image of the goddess." The King assents, v. 1200: "In truth, the stain of the matricide hath defiled it." That is not all. The two prisoners have to be veiled so as not to defile the sunlight, and to escape the same defilement no citizen must look upon them, and the King has to draw a veil over his eyes.

on the other hand, that rats are an important factor in spreading the bubonic plague. Beliefs, in the imaginary cases, might be attributed to observations presumably made in real cases; and that may sometimes have happened—but it is not to be accepted as the general rule, for it would oblige us to believe that human knowledge originated in rigorously logico-experimental science, which then proceeded to degenerate into imaginary beliefs. All known facts point to an opposite development. In the recipes that antiquity has bequeathed to us we find remedies that are really effective along with remedies that have no effect at all. It is certain that human beings did not first know the good remedies, then going on to apply the concept of efficacy to the bad ones. They devised them all hotchpotch, and in plenty of cases the bad ones came first, the good ones not being discovered till much later.

1233. Real cases contributed to engendering a general vaguely defined belief embracing the imaginary along with the real. That belief was strengthened both by observation of real cases and by supposed effects of imaginary cases, and also by certain instincts of repugnance to certain things—the origins of such instincts being as unknown as the origins of instincts in animals. Then derivations interfere on a lavish scale to enhance the complexity of the concrete phenomenon.

1234. *b: Subjective aspect.* As regards the sentiments of those who resort to restorations of integrity, we may distinguish: 1. The sense that the individual has of his own integrity and that of his dependents and possessions, with the various extensions in space and time above noted (§ 1231). 2. The feeling that if such integrity is impaired it may be restored. 3. The sentiments prompting the use of certain means to attain that end.

1235. Variability in such things increases from 1 to 3, while their importance as regards their bearing on the social equilibrium diminishes from 1 to 3. Let us look at them separately.

1. The sentiment of the alteration of integrity is at first vague, indistinct, as all such sentiments are. The different sorts of integrity, material, moral, political, and so on, are not distinguished or not

clearly distinguished. Nor are the integrities of the human being, the animal, and the thing clearly distinguished. Then gradually step by step the different kinds of integrity are recognized and give rise to various theories.

The same confusion exists as to the causes of alterations in integrity. At first little attention is paid to whether the cause lies in conduct on the part of those whose integrity has been altered or in the conduct of someone else. But those two cases are soon distinguished. Later on and with greater difficulty the voluntary cause is distinguished from the involuntary. In this latter consideration as to will or intent a trace of metaphysics figures.

1236. Other distinctions come to be made, and other forms of alteration are segregated. Important, for instance, the distinction between the permanent alteration and the temporary. The type of the permanent would be the stain on the murderer in Greece, in the days when he was required to purify himself; or the state of mortal sin in the Catholic. The type of the temporary would be the state of a person who lies under a spell, or of the Catholic tempted of the Devil.

1237. 2. The same confusions, and in due course the same distinctions, arise as to restoration of integrity. For example, taking the one extreme, restoration of integrity is exclusively a matter of external, mechanical acts (§ 1252), which may even be performed without the knowledge of the person who is to benefit by them. At the other extreme, restoration of integrity is exclusively a matter of inner voluntary acts on the part of the individual. In the intermediate cases, which are the commoner ones among civilized peoples, the restoration takes place by means of certain external, mechanical acts, supplemented by inner acts of will, with varying conceptions as to the relative importance of the respective types.

1238. 3. The sentiment that determines choice of means corresponds to the residues of combinations (Class I), which are fertile of no end of suggestions, the supply being further augmented by derivations. Sometimes there is a feeling that some means there must be, but what it is cannot be definitely determined. The purification then either is entrusted to some indeterminate act, or many different agencies are used in the hope that the good one may be among them.

1239. The forms of usage observed in purifications are of scant importance as regards the social equilibrium. Of great importance is the feeling that the violator of a rule, a taboo, suffers an alteration of integrity, and important also the feeling that the integrity can be restored. But after all, it matters very little whether the restoration be effected by touching a pewter plate (§ 1252 ^{1}), or in some other fashion. In the theory of logical conduct, that scale of importance is inverted. It is assumed that it is faith in the means that prompts people to the act of purification and inspires the sentiments involved in the rite (§ 1231).

1240. V-γI: *Real subjects.*[1] The sense of integrity is among the most powerful sentiments human beings have. It has its roots in the instinct of self-preservation, though it radiates far afield from there. Often, also, alteration of integrity is felt instinctively and gives rise to concrete actions in numbers truly vast.

1241. What is known as "remorse" is a manifestation of the concept of altered integrity. The person who violates a certain norm that it has been his habit to observe feels ill at ease from that very fact. He is conscious of being somehow less than he was before. To escape from that painful state of mind, he looks about for some means of removing the stain, of restoring his former integrity; he finds it and he uses it. The rites that are used to escape the consequences of violating a taboo illustrate the situation in fairly simple form.

1242. When one insists on reducing everything to logical conduct, a sharp distinction is drawn between the remorse that follows violation of a norm of "true" morality or "true" religion and the remorse that follows transgression of a norm of "superstition." From the standpoint of non-logical conduct the two cases are identical. Every person, of course, believes his own morality the "true" moral-

---

1240 [1] In view of the complexity of the phenomena we shall have to make some mention of the next following residues (V-γ 2) in dealing with this species.

ity, his own religion the "true" religion.[1] The Moslem laughs at the Catholic's qualms at eating meat on Friday, and the Catholic laughs at the Moslem's remorse at grazing a hog with the hem of his garment. At them both laughs the atheistic teetotaller who cannot forgive himself a spoonful of wine. A case of remorse noted among the Australian aborigines has often been cited as something extraordinary, but substantially it is altogether on a par with the many remorses of civilized peoples.[2] Remorse, in part at least, is not a consequence of reasoning. It arises spontaneously, instinctively, from the feeling that a transgression has altered personal integrity. Many instances have been cited to show that dogs also feel remorse.

1243. What has been done cannot be undone, but one can meet one force with a counter-force of equal power and opposite tendency, so that the two will balance and effects will be neutralized. One fact can be counterpoised to another fact in such a way that the impression left by the second will cancel the impression left by the first. One can dry a man if he has been in the water, warm him if he has been out in the cold, clean him if he has been befouled. Through the persistence of abstractions these material acts, or others like them, are extended to the intellectual and moral sides of the human being, and there they sprout, leaf out, blossom, and yield a bounteous harvest of most variegated conduct.

1244. Integrity may be altered profoundly or just slightly, so that the restoration may involve regeneration of the whole personality

1242 [1] Brunet, *Les propos de table de Martin Luther,* p. 261: "Master Kinnick answered [to Luther]: 'If you say that the Holy Spirit is certainty of God, then all sectarians who have an unswerving certainty about their religion have the Holy Spirit.' Doctor Luther replied: 'They have no such certainty. Mohammed, the Papists, the sacramentalists, base their faith not on the Word of God, but on their personal convictions.'" All believers reason like that.

1242 [2] Sturt, *Two Expeditions into the Interior of Southern Australia,* Vol. II, p. 54: "The old men have alone the privilege of eating the emu; and so submissive are the young men to this regulation, that if, from absolute hunger or under other pressing circumstances, one of them breaks through it, either during a hunting excursion or whilst absent from his tribe, he returns under a feeling of conscious guilt and by his manner betrays his guilt, sitting apart from the men and confessing his misdemeanour to the chief at the first interrogation, upon which he is obliged to undergo a slight punishment."

or come down to a simple act serving to counterbalance another act defiling to him. The Catholic Church makes a distinction of that kind in its classification of sins as mortal or venial. An incantation alters the integrity of its victim but is not an indelible blemish, such as a murder committed by him would be. In general, but especially in cases of profound alterations, the restoration purports to restore the person to the state in which he was prior to the acts that have defiled him.

1245. The taint presumably contracted in such a manner may be considered as a material consequence of certain acts and therefore materially removable by certain other acts. Or, by the interposition of other residues or through derivations, the taint may depend on certain circumstances, among which oftentimes the intent of the person, and in that case too, identical or analogous circumstances have to be produced to remove the taint.

1246. So also to restore integrity strictly material instrumentalities may be used, exactly as though a material stain were to be removed. Then again, exclusively moral and intellectual means may do;[1] but in general the latter have to be supplemented by material agencies. Very very often an evolution seems to have taken place whereby material means have come to be supplemented by notions of a moral and intellectual character, these latter in the end coming to prevail exclusively, the material means figuring as mere symbols—something altogether secondary.[2] That gives rise to the common error of

1246 [1] St. Augustine, *De moribus ecclesiae catholicae et de moribus Manichaeorum*, I, 34, 76 (*Opera*, Vol. I, p. 1342; *Works*, Vol. V, p. 47): "Such as amend their ways of their own goodwill and with the help of God recover through repentance (penance) what they had lost through sin."

1246 [2] Oldenberg, *Religion des Vedu*, pp. 317-18: "On the one hand . . . sin is a transgression of the will of the gods, which has provoked their wrath. The expiation, therefore, is addressed to them, it aims to satisfy and appease them. The suppliant brings them his gifts, humbles himself before them. But on the other hand, sin is a sort of fluid that sticks to the sinner like a glue. In that sense the expiatory rite involves magic practices calculated to dissolve the glue, destroy it, or remove it to a distance at which it can do no harm, so that the sinner is left free and pure again, much as a man reeking with sweat is relieved of his grime by a bath, or the way a feathered bird is freed of its egg. . . . This second point of view is not altogether inconsistent with a divine action. The elimination of the sinful matter may be conceived of not as the direct consequence of the incantation,

assuming that the material element has always been incidental, that it has never served any other purpose than to give external form to the moral and spiritual concept. Water removes material stains. It is therefore taken for granted that it can also remove moral stains.[3] Ordinarily used by human beings to remove material impurities, it becomes chief among the agencies for removing moral impurities. Water is now and again supplemented by other things, either actually or verbally, large numbers of combinations originating in Class I residues being available for the purpose.[4] Blood, sulphur, and

but as due to the power or ingenuity of the god whose succour has been invoked." The facts are well described. Some slight retouching would remove the inevitable varnish of logical processes.

1246 [3] Dubois, *Mœurs, institutions et cérémonies des peuples de l'Inde,* Vol. II, p. 257: "These hermits [the *vanaprasta*] made no distinction between soiling of soul and body. They were convinced that the soul communicated its stains to the body and *vice versa* and thought that the bath in washing the body also served to purify the soul, especially if the water came from the Ganges or from other reputedly sacred sources. Fire completed purification, and that was why the bodies of such penitents were burned when they departed this life."

1246 [4] First come the waters of springs, rivers, the sea. Philo the Jew wrote a whole book to explain just what victims could be offered according to the Jewish rite, which he regarded as an altogether rational rite but which, in point of fact, tallies in many respects with pagan rites. Says he, *De victimas offerentibus seu de sacrificantibus,* II (Cohn, Vol. V, pp. 40-41; Yonge, Vol. III, p. 212): "The victim must be whole, entirely free from blemish, of select quality approved by the unbiased judgment of the priests and by their critical scrutiny. [Pagan rules, as well.] . . . This is not a senseless rule, but accords with intelligence and reason. However, care must be exercised with regard not only to the victims but also to the sacrificial priests, to the end that they [the sacrifices] be not vitiated by any untoward circumstance. Indeed, as I have said, let him [the priest] purify his body with baths and aspersions, and once bathed and sprinkled, let him not venture beyond the precincts of the Temple even once, save he be commanded to remain without for seven days. . . . Almost all perform their ablutions with pure water, many with sea-water, some few with river-water, others still with spring-water fetched in jars." Just such aspersions were customary among the pagans. See Pollux, *Onomasticon,* I, 1, 8 (Dindorf, Vol. I, p. 5, and see note, Vol. IV, p. 18), and Hesychius, *Lexicon, s.v.* Δάλιον. The Ebionites, says St. Epiphanius, *Panarium adversus haereses, lib.* I, *tomus* II, *Haeresis* 30, § 2 (*Opera,* Vol. I, p. 407), were like the Samaritan Jews in that "every time they come into contact with some foreigner and every time they have commerce with a woman and have left her, they wash themselves with water, either sea-water or some other, according to the supply at hand. But if after they have so immersed themselves in water and washed themselves they chance to encounter any thing of evil omen, they hasten back and wash themselves over again, often in their clothes." Of the priests in Egypt, Plutarch says, *De solertia animalium,* XX, 4

other things have also been used in purifications. Interesting the extension of the idea of purification in the belief that the Flood was a purification of the Earth.⁵

1247. Among many ancient peoples material and moral taints, whether resulting from voluntary or from involuntary acts, were regarded as all on a par. Spots equally black result from uncleanness or crime, from homicide deliberate or accidental, from the impurity of childbirth in the case of a woman, or the impurity of guilt.

(Reiske, Vol. X, p. 57), that "to purify themselves they use water of which the ibis will drink, since the ibis will not touch water that has been polluted or is otherwise unwholesome." The Romans made extensive use of river (running) water: Virgil, *Aeneid* II, v. 719: *"donec me flumine vivo abluero"* ("till I shall have cleansed myself in a living (running) stream"). Servius remarks (Thilo-Hagen, Vol. I, p. 323): *"Flumine vivo:* That never dries up *(perenni).* It is a term used in augury." IV, v. 635: *"Dic corpus properet fluviali spargere lympha."* ("Tell her to make haste and sprinkle her body with river-water.") Servius annotates (Thilo-Hagen, Vol. I, p. 574): *"Spargere lympha:* In sacrificing to the nether gods, they sprinkled themselves with water," as also in VI, v. 230: *Spargens rore levi et ramo felicis olivae* ("Sprinkling light dew with a branch of the propitious olive"). So too they purified themselves in sacrificing to the gods of heaven, as in II, v. 719: *Donec me flumine vivo abluero.* However, just here he is sacrificing to the nether gods, as witness: *Sacra Iovi Stygio."* And *cf.* VI, vv. 635-36: *"Occupat Aeneas aditum corpusque recenti Spargit aqua."* ("Aeneas gains the threshold and sprinkles his body with fresh water.") Servius annotates (Thilo-Hagen, Vol. II, pp. 88-89): *"Recenti:* ever flowing. . . . *Spargit aqua:* Cleanses himself, as having been defiled either by his glimpse of Tartarus, or his hearing *(auditu)* of crimes and punishments. *Spargit:* because purifying for the nether gods." Ovid, *Fasti,* IV, v. 778: *"Et*

1246 ⁵ John Spencer, *De legibus Hebraeorum ritualibus,* Vol. II, Bk. III, § 2, pp. 783-84: "Generally current in a day gone by was the opinion that the Flood was no less than a great catharsis of the World, which God had sent that He might cleanse the land and wash away and make amends for the taint it had suffered *(haustam)* from the impure morals of earthly inhabitants. The ancient Hebrews, the philosophers, and not a few Christians clung stubbornly to that view. That the notion had its supporters among the ancient Hebrews may be legitimately inferred from the language used by Philo [? *De confusione linguarum,* 7]: 'When therefore the Supreme Creator decided to purge the earth with water . . .' That Christians were imbued with the same belief is evident from Origen, *Contra Celsum,* IV (Augsburg, p. 179; Latin, p. 177), when he says: 'I know not why Celsus thinks the overthrowing of a tower is like the Flood, with which Christians and Jews alike assert that the Earth was purged.' Origen, *Ibid.,* VI (Augsburg, p. 325; Latin, p. 320), likewise bears witness that philosophers were of that opinion: 'The destruction of the human race by the Flood was a purification of the Earth, as altogether reputable philosophers among the Greeks relate, in the words: 'When the gods bring on a flood to purge the lands with water' (Plato, *Timaeus,* 22)."

The material taint may arise from real uncleanliness, but also and just as well from imaginary. The taint contracted by an individual may extend, by contact or otherwise, to other persons, things, abstractions.[1]

in vivo perlue rore manus" ("Wash thy hands in living (fresh) dew"), and *Fasti*, V, vv. 431-35: *"Ille memor veteris ritus . . . Terque manus puras fontana perluit unda."* ("Observant of the ancient rite . . . he thrice washes his hands clean in spring-water.") Propertius, *Elegiae*, III, 10, vv. 12-13, says to his beloved: *"Surge et poscentes iusta precare deos, Ac primum pura somnum tibi discute lympha."* ("Rise and pray the gods who seek their proper due, but first banish sleep from thine eyes with pure water.") In *Ibid.*, III, 3, v. 51, Calliope sprinkles the poet with water from a spring. Tibullus, *Nemesis*, I, vv. 11-14, is speaking of the lustration of the fields, according to the ancient rite handed down from the forefathers:

> *"Vos quoque abesse procul iubeo: discedat ab aris*
> *cui tulit hesterna gaudia nocte Venus;*
> *casta placent superis: pura cum veste venite*
> *et manibus puris sumite fontis aquam."*

("You also I bid depart! Away from these altars, you who last night enjoyed the pleasures of Venus. The gods love the chaste! Come with clean garments and in clean hands gather up the water in the spring.") In the *Argonautica*, III, v. 1030, of Apollodorus, Medea advises Jason to "wash himself in the living current of a river." The Greeks used sea-water also: *cf.* Aristophanes, *Plutus*, vv. 656-57, where Carius leads Plutus to the sea to purify him. And the scholiast remarks (Dübner, pp. 361, 577): "It was the custom of the ancients to purify there [in the sea] such as needed purification." Pausanias, *Periegesis*, IX, 20, *Boeotia*, 20, 4 (Dindorf, p. 459), says that the women of Tanagra bathed in the sea in celebrating the mysteries of Dionysus. To get lustral water, salt was sometimes added to fresh water, or burning brands were extinguished in it: *cf.* the scholiast of Aristophanes, *Pax*, v. 959 (Dübner, pp. 200, 475): ". . . since fire is good for purifying all things, as Euripides says in the *Heraclidae*, v. 928" ("His body burnt by the fire's fierce flame": Coleridge, Vol. I, p. 179). Besides fire, sulphur, tar, and like substances were used: Ovid, *Metamorphoses*, VII, v. 261: *"Terque senem flamma, ter aqua, ter sulfure lustrat."* ("Thrice he sprinkles the old man with fire, thrice with water, thrice with sulphur.") Theocritus, *Idyllia*, XXIV, vv. 94-98 (Edmonds, p. 295): "But first purify the house with fire of pure sulphur. Then, as the custom is, place a crown on thine head and take a green branch and sprinkle about with pure water mingled with salt. Then sacrifice a male swine to Zeus the Most High." And *cf. Odyssey*, XXII, vv. 481-82; XXIII, v. 50. The custom of mingling ashes with water was also wide-spread (§ 1266). The well-known cult of springs and rivers may have had some connexion with the purifying properties ascribed to their waters. As late as Nero's time it was believed that the gods punished anyone failing of respect to springs. Tacitus, *Annales*, XIV, 22, 6, relates that Nero took a bath in the springs of the Aqua Marcia. That was considered a profanation "and a sickness [with which he was smitten] bore witness to the wrath of the gods."

1247 [1] Speaking in general terms, human beings show an extensive class of non-logical actions relating to cleanliness, quite similar to the instinct for cleanliness in

1248. Ordinarily concepts of alteration of integrity depend directly upon sentiments, and have only an indirect bearing on utilities of individuals and society—and that, indeed, by way of the sentiments. Those two manners of considering alterations of integrity are there-

certain animals. Pigeons, for example, wash every day, and the cat is for ever cleaning its fur. Such actions in human beings at times present fetishistic traits, as is usual with many other non-logical actions. Close kin to them are other actions that are similar in forms and appearances, or else are prompted by one derivation or another, but which have nothing to do with cleanliness. Well-bred people in civilized countries take baths in the morning, and that is a simple act of cleanliness. With the ancients the same act takes on a religious character. Virgil, *Aeneid*, VIII, vv. 67-70: On awakening Aeneas scoops water from the river in the hollow of his hands: *"Undam de flumine palmis sustulit."* Servius explains (Thilo-Hagen, Vol. II, p. 209): "Because night is said to pollute by the mere fact of sleeping. So Persius [*Saturae*, II, v. 16]: *Et noctem flumine purgat.*" ("He washes the night away in the river.") (Actually the line in Persius reads *purgas* for *purgat.*) But then we find another notion creeping in that has nothing to do with cleanliness: *Aeneid*, IV, 6: *"Postera Phoebea lustrabat lampade terras."* ("The next day was purifying the Earth with the Phoebean lamp.") Servius explains (Thilo-Hagen, Vol. I, p. 461): "Purifying, because the night had somehow polluted the world." The Jews believed that the night spoiled the water in sacred vessels: Mishnah, Tract Yoma, III, 10 (Danby, pp. 165-66); Surenhuis, *Mischna*, Vol. II, p. 224 (comment by Sheringham): "It is a tradition of the Hebrews also that water in a sacred vessel is polluted by the night: and since the laver was a sacred vessel, they resorted to a device [So Danby; ? *machinam*] so that the water would not have to stay in the laver overnight. Maimonides in *Hilcoth Beth Habbechira*: 'They used a device (? *machinam*) to hold the water that was to be kept for any length of time (*iugiter*), and it was built outside the Temple (*prophana erat*) so that the water in it should not be polluted by the night; for the laver was a sacred vessel and sanctified [its contents]; but anything sanctified in a holy vessel is polluted if it is kept overnight.' . . . It is stated in the Gemara (commentaries) (*Sevachim*, f. 19) that the hands are polluted by the night . . . and therefore the Talmudists assert that it is lawful for priests to wash their hands and feet on leaving the Temple; but all the same when they return the next day they have to wash [again] even if they have not slept during the night . . . because the hands are polluted by the night." Surenhuis believes that the Jews took this superstition over from the Gentiles—the usual mistake of regarding products of the same sentiment as imitations (§§ 733 f.). Jews and Gentiles alike had other types of impurity, some of which at least may be connected with cleanliness. Leprosy was "unclean" among the Jews. That may be taken as something similar to the control of contagious diseases among modern peoples. Contact with dead bodies was "unclean." That prescription may have served to avert dangers of poisoning by toxins, or otherwise have been thought of as a measure of hygiene; however the notion had altogether fantastic embellishments. One might be tempted to pass the ascription of impurity to women in childbirth as a measure of hygiene; but when the Bible (Lev. 12:2) ascribes seven days of impurity to a woman who has a male child, and fourteen days (*Ibid.*, 12:5) if the child is a girl, any ra-

fore radically different. When phenomena are taken synthetically and first prominence is given to considerations of ethics or social utility, not only are there great differences but there is actual antithesis between phenomena that appear similar from the standpoint of residues and derivations. Thus from the botanical standpoint, parsley (*Carum petroselinum*) and the classic "hemlock"—("fool's parsley": *Aethusa cynapium*), are closely kindred species of the Umbelliferae; whereas from the medical or hygienic standpoint they have opposite properties, the former being a condiment, the latter a poison.

1249. In the Gospel according to St. Mark, 7:3 f., the Pharisees meet Jesus with the reproach that His disciples did not wash their hands before eating, as was the custom of all Jews. But Jesus answers them, and then explains to the disciples that not material things make a man unclean, but moral things such as evil thoughts, adultery, unchasteness, murder, and the like. For many many centuries Christians have plumed themselves on their ideal religion as contrasted with the material religion of the Jews, without observing that over bypaths devious they went back to the very practices which they laid to the charge of the Pharisees; and Catholics have believed, and still believe, that eating meat on Friday brings defilement upon a man, exactly as the Pharisees believed that one incurred a taint by partaking of food without first washing one's hands. Such the power of residues that they bring opposite doctrines to the same point, and such the power of derivations that few are they who are aware of the inconsistency! Jesus said (Mark 7:15): "There is nothing from without a man that entering into him can defile him; but the things which come out of him, those are they that defile him." It would be difficult to speak more clearly, and the further explanation Jesus gives to the disciples dispels any doubt whatever. And yet Catholics believe that meat, which surely is "without a man," defiles him if it is eaten on Friday and that certain rites are required

tional consideration of hygiene fails to explain the difference. Other forms of "uncleanness" we had better mention in Latin: *"Immundities menstruatae; concubitus coniugalis; somni seminis fluxum procurantes; ex alvo aut vesica levata."*

to cleanse him of the taint. And there are no end of derivations to show that there is not the slightest contradiction between the Saviour's declaration that nothing that is without a man can defile him by entering into him and the doctrine that the meat which he eats on Friday leaves him tainted. This is one of the many cases in which it is apparent that as regards their bearing on the social equilibrium residues far surpass derivations in importance. Residues are very very hard to modify. Derivations are stretched to any length required, like rubber bands.

1250. The case just noted in the Gospel of St. Mark is a particular case of a phenomenon that is general. When the residue of restoration of integrity is functioning alone, or virtually so, exclusively material agencies for restoring integrity may be accepted. But then other residues from the class of group-persistences come into play. In deference to them it is customary to regard individuals possessing certain traits as of a higher order; and that sentiment is shocked when material agencies of purification or other agencies lift to the higher order individuals not possessing the qualities which the persisting sensation associates with that order. Diogenes well expressed the feeling when he said:[1] "It is ridiculous that Agesilaus and Epaminondas should be left in the mire, while an abject rabble of initiates get to the Isles of the Blest."[2]

1250 [1] Diogenes Laertius, *Diogenes,* VI, 39 (Hicks, Vol. II, p. 41).

1250 [2] Plutarch, *De auditu poetarum,* IV (19), 21 (Babbitt, Vol. I, p. 113), reports the same remark in a different text. In question are the lines of Sophocles [*Fragmenta,* 58, 8, Musgrave, Vol. II, p. 274]: "Thrice blessèd they to whom it hath been given to be initiate [to the Eleusinian mysteries] ere they come to Hades, for they are they that alone shall live! The rest shall suffer all manner of evil." Then Plutarch quotes the comment of Diogenes as follows: "What? Because he is an initiate the thief Pataecion shall be better off after death than Epaminondas?" Diogenes Laertius, *Diogenes,* VI, 42 (Hicks, Vol. II, p. 45), relates of Diogenes that "seeing an individual purifying himself with water, he exclaimed: 'O unhappy man! Know you not that as you could not wash away a mistake in grammar with a purification, neither can you wash away a mistake in living?'" Euripides was conscious of the conflict between the ancient formalistic religion and the newer rationalism. He makes Iphigenia say of Artemis, *Iphigenia in Tauris,* vv. 380-86 (Coleridge, Vol. II, p. 350): "I approve not the wilful prescriptions of the goddess. If some mortal be defiled by a murder or by touching a corpse or a woman in childbed, she bars him from her altar as unclean. Yet she delights in human sacrifices! Latona, consort of Zeus, can in no way be guilty of such a stupidity!" And

1251. In the examples following, to avoid cumbersome and useless repetitions we shall consider cancellations of taints and agencies of cancellation together; but the reader will have no difficulty in keeping the two things separate in his mind.

1252. The violator of a taboo experiences sensations of degradation, fear. He rids himself of them—he restores his integrity—by performing certain acts (§ 1481). Sometimes violations of taboos are counterbalanced by certain mechanical acts devoid of any moral content.[1] That is one type. Bring in other residues and especially derivations, and other types in very large numbers result. The absence of any moral element, or at least of the moral element involved in repentance, in a resolve not to do wrong again, is char-

stupid it is, in fact, from the logical standpoint. But that sentiment is posterior to the sentiment which combines non-logical actions as simple acts of fetishism without any resort to logic whatever.

1252 [1] Domeny de Rienzi, *Océanie,* Vol. III, pp. 53-54: In the Tonga Islands, "any person who lays hands on a chief of higher rank is taboo, but the interdiction has no serious consequences if the *moë-moë* is used." He must perform that rite "before he can use his hands to eat. The ceremony consists of pressing first the flat of the hand, then the back of the hand, against the sole of the foot of a ranking chief, then in washing the hands in water or rubbing them with banana or plantain leaves. Then he can eat in all security. Anyone so unfortunate as to have eaten with tabooed hands must go and sit down in front of a chief, pick up the latter's foot, and press it against his stomach. That is to prevent the food he has eaten from doing him any harm. Otherwise his body would swell up and certain death ensue. Taboo is incurred also by eating in the presence of a relative of higher rank without turning one's back, and also by eating food a chief has handled. If taboo has resulted from touching the person or garments of the *toui-tonga,* he alone can remit the penalty, for there is no chief as high as he. For that purpose he keeps near his door a pewter plate which Captain Cook gave him as a present. It is sufficient to touch the plate to be freed of the taboo." In that the influence of combination residues (Class I) is apparent enough. The pewter plate reached the Tonga Islands long after the taboo had been established. It could therefore have had nothing to do with the original taboo. But it was a remarkable and precious object and so made its way into the rites (§ 922). Interestingly, theft too was regarded as a violation of the taboo, "and since it is thought that sharks attack thieves in preference to honest people, suspects are forced to bathe in waters infested by sharks, and if they are bitten or eaten they are adjudged guilty." Those savages regard a taboo as violated by eating certain foods, and also by stealing, and certain rites are in order. Catholics think it a sin to eat certain foods on certain days, and also to steal, and certain rites are in order. The native Tongan goes to his chief, the Catholic to his priest. For the Tongan, there are cases that have to go before the highest chief. For the Catholic there are cases with which only the Pope can deal.

acteristic in anticipatory purifications that are performed in advance of the act which they are designed to counterbalance. The prayer to Mercury that Ovid ascribes to the Roman merchants, imploring the god to absolve them of past and future sins, would, if authentic, be an example of an anticipatory purification.[2] The Catholic Church does not permit absolutions of future sins,[3] but it has its difficulties with an instinct in its faithful that inclines them to ascribe effectiveness to the material acts of Catholic worship independently of any moral element.

1253. At a certain period in Greece a custom of purifying homicide, voluntary or involuntary, comes to the fore. Let us not speculate here as to whether the custom was native to Greece or came from other countries. Certainly there is no trace of it in Homer, but that is not enough to solve the problem. At a later period, in any event, the custom is general. It is a question, at that time, of certain acts which have to be performed by some person other than the murderer. The person need not, necessarily, be the priest of a god, but neither can he be chosen at random. He had to be, it would seem, a person of prominence. The taint follows on the slaying automatically, regardless of the circumstances under which it occurs,

1252 [2] *Fasti*, V, vv. 681-88:

> " 'Ablue praeteriti periuria temporis,' inquit
>   'Ablue praeteritae perfida verba die.
> Sive ego te feci testem falsove citavi
>   non audituri numina magna Iovis,
> sive Deum prudens alium Divamve fefelli,
>   abstulerint celeres improba dicta Noti,
> et pereant veniente die periuria nobis:
>   nec curent superi si qua locutus ero.' "

(" 'Purge me,' he said, 'of the pledges I have broken in the past, purge me of the deceits of a bygone day. If I falsely have called thee to witness or invoked the great divinity of Jove (who will not hear anyhow) (Frazer: "in the hope that he would not hear"), or if knowingly I have cheated any other god or goddess, let the swift winds waft my evil words away. And may the false oaths I shall tomorrow swear be not charged to my account (*pereant*). May the gods above ignore them, if I chance to utter them.' ")

1252 [3] Dante, *Inferno*, XXVII, vv. 118-20: "For not absolved can be one who repents not. Nor both at once can one repent and will, Because a contradiction there consents not" (Fletcher).

even if the provocation is deemed legitimate. In that we get the restoration residue in a pure form. Herodotus, *Historiae*, I, 35, tells of
a man who came to Croesus to be purified: "Having come to the
house of Croesus he begged him to purify him according to the rite
of the land. Croesus did so, rites of purification being similar among
Lydians and Greeks." Not till the ceremonies are over does it occur
to Croesus to ask: "Who art thou, man, and from what part of
Phrygia comest thou whom my hearth receiveth? What man or
what woman hast thou slain?" The mechanical automatic character
of the rite is strikingly apparent in this case. Whoever the man,
whatever the murder, and be it a merit or a crime, it is all the same
—the purification has to be vouchsafed, and it is performed in the
same way in any event. The Phrygian gives his name, his father's,
his grandfather's, and adds: "Unintentionally slew I my brother."
So involuntary homicide, like voluntary homicide, leaves its taint.
Herodotus, notice, makes no mention of the gods; their interference
is a subsequent adjunct along with new residues clustering about
the basic residue. In the *Bibliotheca* of Apollodorus, I, 9, 24 (Frazer,
Vol. I, p. 115), for the Argonauts to know that they are being persecuted by the wrath of Zeus for the slaying of Absyrtus, their ship
has to speak and warn them, with the further admonition that the
persecution will not end till they have been purified by Circe. Apollodorus then remarks as naturally as can be: "They went to Circe
as suppliants, and she purified them."

1254. Apollonius of Rhodes gives the particulars of the purification, *Argonautica*, IV, vv. 585-709, probably following ancient traditions, which he tries to embellish with logical explanations, bringing
in Zeus. At first the Argonauts suffer many hardships at sea, exactly
as happens to a violator of a taboo who has not been purified. Finally
their ship, the *Argos*, speaks up, to the purport that "they should
not escape long wanderings and great storms unless Circe should
purify them of the cruel slaughter of Absyrtus." They reach Circe's
isle after a difficult voyage. Jason and Medea go up to the palace of
the goddess and sit down before the hearth according to the custom
of suppliants, without uttering a word. Jason drives the weapon

with which he had slain Absyrtus into the ground, whereat Circe understands what is being asked of her. She offers a prayer to "the Justice of Zeus of the Suppliants," and then performs, with ablutions, the sacrifices whereby, along with the ablutions, unclean suppliants are purified when they come and sit at her hearth. First she places an expiatory victim on the altar, a suckling pig, cuts its throat and sprinkles their hands with its blood.[1] And then she purifies them again with other libations, calling on the name of "Zeus the Purifier, who hearkeneth to prayers in appeasement of blood that hath been shed."

1255. Apollodorus seems to think of purifications as normal procedures after homicide. The daughters of Danaus who slew the sons of Egyptus are purified by Athena and Hermes, as representatives of Zeus (II, 1, 5; Frazer, Vol. I, p. 143). Heracles slays his children in a fit of madness and is purified by Thestius (II, 4, 12; Frazer, p. 183). He also has to be purified after slaying the Centaurs (II, 5, 12; Frazer, p. 233). In a new fit of madness he kills Iphitus, son of Eurytus, and then asks Neleus to purify him. But Neleus is a friend of Eurytus and refuses. Heracles then gets the purification at the hands of Deiphobus (II, 6, 2; Frazer, p. 239). It is interesting that in spite of the purification he is smitten with a serious illness in punishment for the murder of Iphitus, and is not cured of it till he sells himself as a slave and gives the proceeds to the youth's father (II, 6, 2; Frazer, p. 241). Evidently another tradition is here being grafted upon the first, without the author's even trying to make them agree. Legend supplies many other examples of purifications after involuntary homicide. Peleus is purified of two killings of that sort.[1] But there is better yet. In exterminating bandits Theseus

1254 [1] Literally, "the male offspring of a sow, her teats still bulging from the belly that hath borne." Of that particular victim, the scholiast remarks: "Λυτήριον means . . . 'that which purifies.' It is a suckling pig. Those who are performing a sacrifice of purification bathe the hands of the recipient in the blood of such a pig."

1255 [1] Apollodorus, *Bibliotheca*, III, 13, 2 (Frazer, Vol. II, p. 63): Peleus, purified by Eurytion, shoots at what he thinks is the wild boar of Calydon. The arrow strikes Eurytion and kills him. Peleus is purified by Acastus. Diodorus Siculus, *Bibliotheca historica*, IV, 72, 6 (Booth, Vol. I, p. 283): In a game Peleus accidentally kills a half-brother on his father's side and he is purified by Actor.

is performing a public service; yet he has to be purified of their blood.[2] Apollo himself has to be purified of slaying the Python. Living at an age later than the days when the legend originated, Plutarch thinks it ridiculous that a god should have to be purified.[3] Ajax purifies himself after killing some sheep in a fit of madness.[4] Some go so far as to require purification of hunters and dogs returning from the chase.[5] The strictly mechanical character of the taint of homicide and the ensuing purification comes out clearly in a story told by Pausanias, *Periegesis*, V, *Elis* I, 27, 10. A child at play strikes his head against a bronze bull and dies. The statue is felt to be tainted by homicide. "The Eleans thought best to remove the bronze from the Alteum as guilty of murder; but the god at Delphi prescribed that the bull be left where it was and be purified with the rites usual among the Hellenes for involuntary homicides."

1256. The legend of Orestes is one of the cases in which the wholly material purification can be seen in process of transformation, partial at least, into a moral purification. Orestes is purified at Delphi by Apollo. But that is not enough—well known his ensuing trial at Athens. Pausanias, *Periegesis,* III, *Laconia,* 17, 7-9, tells how the Spartan king Pausanias accidentally killed a girl named Cleonice. He tried all sorts of purifications, but they could not avail to cleanse the defilement contracted by such a misfortune. That was why he was the only one not saved by the refuge offered by Chalcioicus.

1257. Commerce between a man and a woman, whether legiti-

1255 [2] Plutarch, *Theseus,* 12, 1-2 (Perrin, Vol. I, p. 23): "So Theseus continued punishing the wicked." Proceeding on his journey, he comes to the river Cephisus. There he meets the sons of Phytalus. They welcome him. He begs them to purify him, and they do so with the customary rites.

1255 [3] The slaying of the serpent and the subsequent purification of Apollo were commemorated at Delphi: *Quaestiones graecae,* 12. In the *De defectu oraculorum,* 15 (Goodwin, Vol. IV, p. 21), Plutarch exclaims: "It is altogether ridiculous, my friends, that after killing the beast, Apollo should have fled to the borders of Greece because he needed purification."

1255 [4] Sophocles, *Ajax,* vv. 654-55 (Storr, Vol. II, pp. 56-57).

1255 [5] Arrian, *De venatione,* 32, 3: "After a fortunate chase a sacrifice must also be performed, and the first-fruits of the chase offered to the goddess as a purification for the dogs and hunters, according to the custom of our land."

mate or not, was considered a cause of impurity among the ancient Greeks as well as among other peoples. Here too we have a transition from a purely material uncleanness to a moral impurity. Theano, a woman of the Pythagorean sect, was once asked: "How many days after commerce with a man may a woman be considered pure?" and she answered, "If with her husband, at once; if with some other man, never."[1]

1258. Among many peoples, chiefly uncivilized or savage, not only the sexual act, but also menstruation, induces impurity.[1] Countless examples might be cited in point. Noteworthy the prescriptions

1257 [1] Diogenes Laertius, *Pythagoras*, VIII, 43 (Hicks, Vol. II, p. 359); Clement of Alexandria, *Stromata*, IV, 19 (*Opera*, Vol. I, p. 1331A; Wilson, Vol. II, p. 195); Stobaeus, *Florilegium*, LXXIV, 55 (Meinecke, Vol. III, p. 61); Theodoret, *Graecarum affectionum curatio*, Sermo XII, *De virtute activa* (*Opera*, Vol. IV, pp. 1143-46).

1258 [1] Hovelacque, *Les nègres de l'Afrique suséquatoriale*, pp. 311, 475: "During their monthly periods the women, as a rule, live apart, sometimes, as in certain districts along the Gold Coast, in huts appointed to such seclusion [Quoting "Bosman, II, 371," *i.e.*, *New and Accurate Description of the Coast of Guinea*, Letter XVIII, p. 329]. 'Women in menstruation are regarded hereabouts [on the Slave Coast] as so particularly tainted that they would never during such a period dare to enter the house of the king or of any important person, and women who violate such orders are punished with death or at least servitude for life. . . . Letter XXI, p. 416, by one David Van Nyendael: They are not allowed to enter their husbands' houses or to touch the least thing whether in the preparation of meals or in house-cleaning.' " Lafitau, *Mœurs des sauvages américains*, Vol. I, pp. 262-63: "[Such seclusions during periods and purifications] are very strict in [South] America. The women are given cabins apart, much as lepers were segregated among the Jews. They are regarded as so unclean at such times that they are forbidden to touch any article of common use. On a first infraction of that rule they are separated for thirty days from the rest of the tribe, and the fire in the cabin that they have entered is put out and the ashes are dumped outside the village. Then a new fire is lighted, as though the first had been sullied by their presence. In tribes living along the Rio de la Plata, they are sewn up in their hammocks at such periods, like corpses, with just a little opening for them to breathe through. There they stay for the duration of the period, whereafter they are subjected to all the rites usually applied to girls who have reached the age of puberty. . . . Tavernier, *Voyages en Perse*, p. 85 (1630 ed., Vol. I, p. 396), says that among the Gaures 'as soon as the women or the girls feel their periods coming on, they promptly leave the house and go off by themselves to the country to little bamboo huts with cloths hanging over the entrances in place of doors. They are provided with food and drink daily throughout the period. When it is over, each of them according to her means sends a goat, a chicken, a pigeon, to the priest as an offering, thence proceeding to bathe.' "

in the Bible, which are no longer observed by Christians.[2] Parturition is regarded among many peoples as a cause of impurity. Births and deaths were alike prohibited on the island of Delos. Both in Greece and in Rome the new-born babe was purified.

1259. In Greece contact with a dead body or the mere sight of one induced impurity. A jar of water taken from another house was set in front of the house where a person lay dead that departing visitors might perform purification.[1] People who had attended funerals made purification.[2]

1260. Countless the forms of impurity, but they all corresponded to a single sentiment, real or imaginary, of alteration in personal integrity; and they were remedied by appropriate ceremonies of purification. In such a plethora of dreaded impurities the superstitious soul was afraid of everything. Theophrastus shows one such leaving the temple after washing his hands and sprinkling himself

1258 [2] Lev. 15:2 f. (Vulgate): *"Vir qui patitur fluxum seminis immundus erit. . . . Vir de quo egreditur semen coitus lavabit aqua omne corpus suum et immundus erit usque ad vesperum. . . . Mulier cum qua coierit lavabitur aqua et immunda erit usque ad vesperum. Mulier quae redeunte mense patitur fluxum sanguinis septem diebus separabitur. Omnis qui tetigerit eam immundus erit usque ad vesperum. . . . Omne vas super quo illa sederit quisquis attigerit lavabit vestimenta sua, et ipse lotus aqua pollutus erit usque ad vesperum. Si coierit cum ea vir tempore sanguinis menstrualis immundus erit septem diebus, et omne stratum in quo dormierit polluetur."* It is customary to explain these prescriptions as hygienic. If that were so, the state of uncleanness ought to end after the prescribed washing. Instead it continues (§ 1247 [1]).

1259 [1] Pollux, *Onomasticon*, VIII, 7, 65-66 (Dindorf, Vol. I, p. 131); Hesychius, *Lexicon*, s.v. Ἀρδάνια; Suidas, *Lexicon*, s.v. Ἀρδάνιον; Eustathius, *Commentarii ad Homeri Iliadem*, VIII, v. 187, Vol. II, p. 201.

1259 [2] Virgil, *Aeneid*, VI, vv. 229-30:

"Idem ter socios pura circumtulit unda,
spargens rore levi et ramo felicis olivae."

("Aeneas thrice purged his comrades with pure water, sprinkling a light dew with a branch of the auspicious olive.") Servius annotates (Thilo-Hagen, Vol. II, p. 42): *"Thrice:* either actually three times, or more often than that. For though they had incurred pollution from the burial, every purgation is addressed to the Higher Gods. That is why he uses an odd number, or else because that particular lustration required it. *Circumtulit:* 'purged.' It is an archaic word. Says Plautus, *Fragmenta*, 48 (68): *Pro larvato te circumferam:* 'I will purge thee as one bewitched,' the lustration taking its name from the fact that a torch, or [burning] sulphur, or in some cases, victims, were 'carried around.'"

with lustral waters and walking about all day long with a laurel-leaf between his lips. Every so often he purifies his house. He dares not go near a tomb or a woman in childbed. He goes down to the sea-shore for a sprinkling with sea-water. If he chance to encounter something reputed to be of evil omen, he purifies himself by pouring water on his head, and having someone carry a shrimp and a puppy in a circle around him.[1] On driving away the courtesans with whom she has surprised Propertius, Cynthia purifies the chamber.[2] Anyone stressing derivations primarily would find an abyss between purification for a crime and this love-game. But looking strictly to the constant and significant element in such phenomena, their perfect similarity is obvious. Juvenal ridicules the purifications of a superstitious woman who in early morning in midwinter goes to the Tiber, breaks the ice, plunges in three times, and shivering washes her head in the eddying current.[3]

1261. The impurity extends from the person who has incurred it to others who have been in contact with him or are otherwise re-

1260 [1] Theophrastus, *Characteres*, 16 (18), "The Superstitious Man" (Jebb, pp. 162-65). I have used the general expression, "something reputed to be of evil omen," to avoid entering on the problem of the exact meaning of this very corrupt passage. Coray thinks it is a question of the evil eye. Plutarch, *De superstitione*, III, 166 (Babbitt, Vol. II, p. 461), speaks of the superstitious individual who has had a bad dream. He goes to a quack, then turns to "the old crone who performs purifications, then takes a plunge in the sea, and finally spends one whole day seated on the ground." Apuleius, *Metamorphoses*, XI, 23, tells of a purification: "The time for it having come, as the priest said, he led me, in the press of a great crowd of the devout, to the baths near by, and first subjecting me to the usual ablution, then praying to the god for forgiveness and sprinkling [in a circle about] me in a very pure manner, he pronounced me clean (*abluit*)."

1260 [2] *Elegiae*, IV, 8, vv. 83-86: "She fumigates all the spots that the girls had touched . . . and washes the threshold with pure water. She bids me change all my garments, and thrice my head she circles (*tetigit*) with a sulphur flame." Tibullus, *Delia*, 5, v. 11, speaks of performing lustrations for his beloved, when she was ill, by circling three times with sulphur about her:

> "Ipseque ter circum lustravi sulfure puro."

His "pure sulphur," is the καθαρὸν θεῖον of the Greeks—"purifying" sulphur.

1260 [3] *Saturae*, VI, vv. 522-24:

> "Hibernum fracta glacie descendet in amnem,
> ter matutino Tiberi mergetur et ipsis
> vorticibus timidum caput abluet."

lated to him—from parents to children, from the individual to the group to which he belongs, to animals, material things, a whole country. To lend credence to the so-called *Institutes of Manu* the mere fact that a close relative has died is a cause of impurity, though the corpse has neither been seen nor touched.[1] Evidently, therefore, it is a question of a nebula extending to greater or lesser distances about a nucleus.

1262. When the family is felt to be the social unit it follows that any alteration of integrity in one of its members extends to the family as a whole, in space and in time, much as a wound inflicted on one part of the body of a living being affects the body as a whole. In the infliction of penalties upon a whole family for a crime committed by one of its members a logical action may figure: the design to influence the individual through the affection he may be assumed to have for his family: but also active is the residue underlying the conception of the family as the social unit. That is why such collective penalties disappear when the individual becomes the unit, as has been the case in Europe. They have persisted down to our own times in China, where the family remained the unit.[1]

1261 [1] Loiseleur-Deslongchamps, *Lois de Manou*, V, 74-77 (p. 382): "Such the [ten-day] rule of impurity caused by the death of a relative when one is on the spot. But in case of absence at a distance the rule laid down for *sapindas* and *samânodakas* prescribes as follows: If news of the death of a relative in a distant locality arrives within the ten days' period of impurity, the impurity holds for the remainder of the period. If the tenth day has elapsed, the impurity holds over three nights. If a year has passed, a bath is sufficient for purification. If news of the death of a relative or the birth of a male child arrives after the expiration of the ten days, one may be purified by plunging fully dressed into water." Those are not merely theoretical prescriptions. They are put into practice. Du Bois, *Mœurs, institutions et cérémonies des peuples de l'Inde*, Vol. I, p. 244: "Hindus regard themselves as sullied by mere attendance at a funeral. They take a plunge-bath immediately after the ceremonies, and no one would dare re-enter his house without having performed purification in that manner. The mere news of the death of a relative, be it a hundred leagues away, has the same effects, and makes the same purification obligatory on all members of the family who hear of it. The taint, however, does not extend to mere friends and acquaintances of the deceased."

1262 [1] Farjenel, *La morale chinoise*, pp. 243-44: "[In Chinese law] individuality is absorbed in the paternal powers of the head of the family, the magistrate, the prince, who theoretically are elder brothers and fathers of all Chinese subjects. The terrible principle of solidarity in penal law, so incomprehensible to Westerners, used to be manifest evidence of that concept of human personality. There were certain

1263. If a man has neither sons nor daughters, the family integrity is altered (daughters are not considered when the family is perpetuated through the male line) and something has to be done about it. Hence the various arrangements for permitting a man married to a barren woman to take another wife, now divorcing, now keeping, the first. If the man dies childless, that remedy no longer avails, and we get such institutions as the Athenian epiclerate, the Jewish levirate, and so on. Derivations eventually obscure such facts, but not to such an extent as to conceal their substantial traits from an attentive observer.[1]

crimes of such enormity that they could be avenged only by the decapitation of all ascendants and descendants of the guilty person, even though they had no knowledge of the crime and the crime were not actually perpetrated but merely plotted. It is the spirit of Chinese law that the family taken *in globo* is the only real individuality. That provision figured in Chinese written law down to April 25, 1905."

1263 [1] To give some idea of such phenomena certain provisions in the *Institutes of Manu* will suffice. A thorough treatment of them would be the province of a *special* sociology, which would follow this *general* sociology.

Loiseleur Deslongchamps, *Lois de Manou*, IX, 45 f. (pp. 422-56): "He alone is the perfect man who is made up of three persons combined—to wit, his wife, himself, and his son; and the Brahmans have propounded this maxim: 'The husband makes but one same person with his wife.' . . . 48. The owner of the male that has sired with cows, mares, sheep, female camels, buffalos, and goats, and slave-girls has no property-right over the offspring. The same it is with the wives of other men. . . . 58. An elder brother who cohabits with the wife of a younger brother, and a younger brother with the wife of an elder brother, are degraded even if they have been invited to do so by the husband or by relatives, unless the marriage be barren. . . . 59. When one has no children the desired progeniture may be obtained through the union of one's wife, on suitable authorization, with a brother or another relative (*sapinda*). . . . 60. Rubbed with liquid butter and observing silence, let the relative assigned that office approach at night a widow or a childless woman and beget a single son, but never a second. . . . 61. Considering the fact that the purpose of this arrangement may not be perfectly attained by the begetting of a single child, those thoroughly versed in this question are of opinion that women may lawfully have a second son in this manner. . . . 127. A man without a male child may bid his daughter rear a son for him . . . by *saying to himself*, 'Let the male child which she shall bear become mine and perform the funeral rite in my honour.' 128. So of yore the Pradjâpati Dakcha himself bade his fifty daughters give him sons for the increase of his line. [Hence the further prescription:] *Ibid.*, III, 11 (p. 353). The sensible man will not marry a girl who has no brother or whose father is not known, in fear lest, in the first case, she be given him by the father only in the intent of adopting the son that she may have; and lest, in the second case, the marriage so contracted be illicit [? as contracted with a bastard]." And cf. *Ibid.*, IX, 136 (p. 426).

1264. Biblical prescriptions, subsequently developed in the Talmud, yield a luxuriant harvest of prescriptions pertaining to impurities and purifications.[1] Impure and unclean objects are arranged in a series according to decreasing impurities on the plan of father and sons. At the top of the lists stands the "forefather" of uncleanness.[2] Next come the "fathers of uncleanness," and then, in four degrees of descent, the "sons of uncleanness." Contact with the "forefather" gives rise to certain "fathers." "Sons" in the first degree are objects made unclean through contact with "fathers"; "sons" of the second degree acquire uncleanness through contact with "sons" of the first, the third through contact with the second, the fourth through contact with the third. "Fathers" and "sons" may be according to law (*ex lege*), or according to the commentaries (*ex instituto scribarum*). The "forefather" of uncleanness is the human corpse. According to law there are thirty-two "fathers," to wit, "creeping things" (*reptilia*), the dead bodies of beasts or human beings, and so on.[3]

1264 [1] It would be a waste of time to go into them here at length; but some notion of them will prove useful, the particular case giving a bird's-eye view of the thing in general.

1264 [2] Surenhuis, *Mischna,* preface to Part VI (Tohoroth) (Vol. VI, p. C2): "The 'uncleanness of the dead' (*immundities mortui*) embraces nine fathers of uncleanness, and flesh from a corpse to the amount of an olive defiles with 'uncleanness of the dead'; so also flesh torn [by an animal, Lev. 22:8] from the corpse to the amount of an olive, and putrefied flesh to the amount of a spoonful, and that amount of bone and blood from a corpse. The corpse of a dead man taken as a whole is the 'forefather of uncleanness.' "

1264 [3] *Loc. cit.,* p. D: "The 'fathers of uncleanness' *ex lege* are thirty-two, to wit: a creeping thing (*reptile*), the corpse of an animal, a human corpse, a man polluted by a human corpse, vessels that have touched a man polluted by a human corpse, vessels polluted by a human corpse, vessels that have touched other vessels which have been polluted by a human corpse, a tent, a grave, *eiectio seminis,* expiatory water, a red heifer, bull-calves and he-goats appointed to sacrifice (*qui comburendi erant*), a scapegoat, *vir gonorrhea affectus, et foemina gonorrhea affecta, menstruosa, puerpera,* a saddle (*equitatio*) [see Lev. 15:9] and a chair (*sessio*) [Lev. 15:6] of either sex [? *i.e.,* whether used by unclean man or woman], anyone *qui cum menstruosa corpus miscuit,* the blood of an unclean woman, her saliva, urine, *profluvium seminis, eiectio seminis illius,* a leper on the days of his numeration [*i.e.,* quarantine, Lev. 13:4-5], a leper on days of undoubted leprosy [*i.e.,* positively diagnosed, Lev. 13:8], a garment contaminated by leprosy, and finally a house contaminated by leprosy [Lev. 14:34 f.]. These, I say, are called 'fathers of uncleanness *ex lege.*' "

The "creeping things" are listed in the Bible, and they are animals of one kind or another, though just which is not certainly known, the commentators giving different lists.[4] Champions of logical conduct may rustle about as much as they choose, but they will never succeed in finding just why those particular animals should be unclean and others not. According to the Scribes the "fathers of uncleanness" are twenty-nine.[5] The "sons" of uncleanness are also either by law or by institute of the Scribes. The first degree, as regards profane things, is unclean and induces uncleanness by contact. The second, however, does not. In sacred things the first three degrees are unclean and induce uncleanness, the fourth does not.

1264 [4] Lev. 11:29-32: (Vulgate) *"Haec quoque inter polluta reputabuntur de his quae moventur in terra: mustella et mus et crocodilus singula iuxta genus suum, mygale et chamaeleon et stellio et lacerta et talpa"*; (King James version:) "These also shall be unclean unto you among the creeping things that creep upon the earth: the weasel and the mouse and the tortoise [Septuagint, κοκόδειλος, Vulgate, *crocodilus*] each after his kind, and the ferret and the chameleon and the lizard and the mole." Surenhuis, *loc. cit.*, p. C2: "By *reptilia* are meant the eight kinds of 'creeping things' mentioned in the Law, such as the weasel, the mouse, the turtle, the crawling weevil (*attelabus*), the lizard, the newt, the snail, and the mole. The blood of reptiles, their flesh and fat, have the same degree of uncleanness. The hides or skins of four of the *reptilia,* the crawling weevil, the lizard, the newt, and the snail, are of the same degree of uncleanness as the flesh. However, the bones taken from creeping things do not defile. Other creeping and loathsome things, such as the frog, toad, snake, viper, and the like, do not defile." Segond's French translation, p. 78: ". . . the mole, mouse, and lizard, according to their kinds; the porcupine, the frog, turtle, snail, and chameleon." Crampon's French translation: ". . . the weasel, the mouse, and all kinds of lizards; the shrew, the chameleon, the salamander, the green lizard, and the mole."

1264 [5] Surenhuis, *loc. cit.*, p. D2: "But if we compile the 'fathers of uncleanness' from the Institutes of the Scribes, we find that they are twenty-nine, such as bone from a corpse to the amount of a grain of barley, blood from a bruise, earth belonging to Gentiles, a cemetery (a field in which bones of dead bodies lie buried: *ager in quo cadaverum ossa latent*), a swelling (scab) over a bruise that has bled, a man polluted by those things, vessels that have touched them or been otherwise polluted by them, a man who has touched a [hallowed] vessel, [hallowed] vessels that have touched a man, vessels that have touched other vessels so polluted in the ways mentioned, a Gentile woman, a woman in irregular period, *foemina quae maculam sanguinis praepostere vidit, foemina quae in accessu menstruali se non visitavit praepostere, puerpera quae aliquod foetus membrum peperit,* her couch, saddle (*equitatio*), saliva, urine, *et immunditiei sanguis;* and further a *vir qui cum foemina immunda rem habuit quae gonorrhoea laborabat,* a male Gentile, an idolater, [objects pertaining to] an idolatrous worship, anything killed by a Gentile, and finally the dead body of a bird [otherwise] clean."

"Fathers" of uncleanness defile human beings and receptacles; "sons," only foods and beverages. "If a man has touched a 'creeping thing,' he contracts an uncleanness of the first degree, and contaminates oil, if he touches it; and if again such oil comes into contact with honey, it contaminates it . . . and if the honey comes into contact with water, it contaminates it, and in that way the oil, the honey, and the water each acquires an uncleanness of the first degree." [6] The uncleanness lasts for a greater or lesser length of time, and there are many prescriptions on the subject. The Talmud devotes an entire book to leprosy, adding many regulations to the by no means few that are laid down in the Bible (Lev., Chapters 13-15).

1265. Impurities being thoroughly identified, the next thing is to get rid of them. Luckily, washing in water happened to be lavishly recommended. That served at least towards cleanliness. However, minute prescriptions usually guided the believer in his purifications. The Bible gives numbers of them and the Talmud lengthens the list.

1266. As was the case with other peoples, Jewish purifications were performed with special waters and in special ways. Notable, among the Israelites, the sacrifice of a red heifer. It had to be undefiled and without blemish. After killing it, the priest "shall take of her blood with his finger and sprinkle of her blood directly before the tabernacle . . . seven times." So the Greeks purified with the blood of a suckling pig, and satirizing the custom Aristophanes, *Ecclesiasuzae,* v. 128, has his congress of women open with a sacrifice of the lustful weasel (§ 919 [1]). The heifer was burned in a manner prescribed, and the ashes were then gathered up and mixed in water to provide the "water of separation." [1] It was a custom of the Romans to sacrifice,

1264 [6] Surenhuis, *loc. cit.,* p. E.

1266 [1] Num. 19:19-22: "And the clean person shall sprinkle upon the unclean on the third day and on the seventh day: and on the seventh day he shall purify himself and wash his clothes and bathe himself in water and shall be clean at even. But the man that shall be unclean and shall not purify himself, that soul shall be cut off from among the congregation, because he hath defiled the sanctuary of the Lord: the water of separation hath not been sprinkled upon him: he is unclean. And it shall be a perpetual statute unto them that he that sprinkleth the water of separation shall wash his clothes; and he that toucheth the water of separation shall be unclean until even. And whatsoever the unclean person toucheth shall be unclean; and the soul that toucheth it shall be unclean until even."

about the middle of April, a heifer that was, as they said, *"forda,"* "fertile and with calf." The priests took the calf from the heifer's belly, and it was burned by the Dean of the Vestals (*Virgo Vestalis Maxima*), the ashes being kept to purify the people on the feast day of Pales (the Palilia or Parilia).[2] Already the blood of a horse, regularly sacrificed in October in the Field of Mars, had been set aside for the same purpose.[3] The Palilia were celebrated on the twenty-first of April. The people went in throngs to the altar of Vesta, got possession of the horse's blood, the ashes of the calves, and masses of dried bean-stalks. The crowd was sprinkled with water with a laurel-branch, there were fumigations with sulphur, fires were made of the bean-stalks and the people leapt over them.[4] A survival of this festival is to be seen in the bonfires that are still burned in several

1266 [2] Ovid, *Fasti*, IV, vv. 639-40:

> *"Igne cremat vitulos quae natu maxima Virgo est,*
> *luce Palis populos purget ut ille cinis."*

("The eldest of the Virgins burns the calves in the fire that the ash may cleanse the people on the morn of Pales.")

1266 [3] Festus, *De verborum significatione*, XIII, *s.v. October* (London, Vol. II, pp. 519-20): "The name *October* was applied to a horse that was sacrificed in the month of October in the Campus Martius. There was a great rivalry between the inhabitants of the Subura quarter and those living on the Sacra Via for possession of the head. If the Suburites won, it was nailed up on the Mamilian Tower, if the Sacravienses, on a wall of the Regia. The tail of the horse was rushed to the Regia that the blood in it might drip into the [sacred] fire there."

1266 [4] Ovid, *Fasti*, IV, vv. 727-28, 731-34, 739, 781-82:

> *"Certe ego transilui positas ter in ordine flammas,*
> *virgaque roratas laurea misit aquas. . . .*
> *I, pete virginea populus suffimen ab ara;*
> *Vesta dabit: Vestae munere purus eris.*
> *Sanguis equi suffimen erit vitulique favilla;*
> *tertia res: durae culmen inane fabae. . . .*
> *Caerulei fiant vivo de sulphure fumi. . . .*
> *Moxque per ardentes stipulae crepitantis acervos*
> *traiicias celeri strenua membra pede."*

("I myself have leapt over the bonfires burning in triple row while the laurel-branches sprinkled us with dewlike mist. . . . Run, O ye people, to receive your fumigation from the altar of the Virgins. Vesta will vouchsafe it: pure ye shall be by gift of Vesta. The blood of the horse will be your purification, and the ash of the calf, and a third thing, the pile of empty stalks of hard beans. . . . Let the blue fumes rise from the burning sulphur. . . . And you had better be limber and quick of foot as you leap over the burning piles of crackling tinder!")

districts in Italy. Catholics burn the palms of the previous year on Ash Wednesday and use the ashes to make the sign of the cross on the foreheads of the faithful.[5]

1267. But the cleansing power of water over persons or things is evidently lost sight of in such cases, for it is unclean to touch "water of separation," the imaginary trait taking precedence over the real. The Talmud as usual expatiates on these defiling properties of purifying water. A distinction is drawn between waters available in sufficient quantities for aspersion, and waters not available in such sufficiency. The first contaminate the carrier, the second only persons who touch them. And be sure not to forget that "if a string is attached to the unclean thing, and a man lifts the unclean thing by the string, he is defiled by the uncleanness of the weight, for the weight of the unclean thing touches him; and he in turn contaminates his garments, or all the garments and vessels that he touches, save only earthen vessels"![1]

1266 [5] *Dictionnaire encyclopédique de la théologie catholique, s.v. Cendres (Mercredi des)* (Wetzer, *s.v. Aschermittwoch*): "The ash that is spread on the heads of the faithful comes from the burning of the palms of the preceding year. It is blessed just before the Ash Wednesday mass by a special ritual."

1267 [1] Mishnah, Tract Kelim (*De vasis*), I, 2 (Danby, p. 604; Surenhuis, Vol. VI, p. 16), comment by Bartenoro [read: Bertinoro]. And *cf.* also the following, *Ibid.,* I, 1 (Surenhuis, *loc. cit.,* pp. 15-16): "Fathers of uncleanness are: creeping things, seed of copulation, a man defiled by the dead, and a leper in the days of his numeration, and expiatory waters insufficient in quantity for the sprinkling. All these things defile persons and vessels by touch, and earthen vessels by air but not by weight." Bertinoro's comment: *"Semen concubitus:* only the seed of copulation of the Israelite and full-grown (*adulti viri*). The seed of copulation of the Gentile does not defile [For similar distinctions see §§ 1278 f.], not even by institute of the Scribes, for the seed of the Gentile is altogether clean. Nor does the seed of copulation of the adolescent defile. . . . Earthen vessels, foods, and beverages that have been in contact with the dead [in a house where a person has died] do not become fathers of uncleanness. Only an Israelite becomes a father of uncleanness by contact with the dead. A Gentile and an abortion delivered after eight days do not contract uncleanness from the dead. . . . *Expiatory waters insufficient for sprinkling:* they too defile by touch, and if in quantities sufficient for sprinkling, they defile by weight as regards the person and vessels, as appears from Num. 19:21. [The passage refers only to sprinklers.—A. L.] Our doctors, however, hold that the sprinkler is not defiled, the Law meaning simply to determine a measure for the carrier, and specifying (*nempe*) that there should be sufficient for aspersion. For the Law distinguishes between waters and waters, that is to say, between waters in sufficient

1268. Legislation on the material circumstances of cases is fulsome and fine-spun. A chicken swallows a reptile and eventually strays into an oven. If the chicken remains alive it does not defile the oven: if it dies, it does.[1] If milk drops from a woman's breast into an oven, the oven is unclean; and so if in sweeping an oven a woman pricks a finger and puts it into her mouth.[2] There are rulings on cases where weasels or cats go travelling about with *reptilia* in their mouths,[3] on spittles clean and unclean, semi-fluid and dry, in public places or in private.[4] As regards matters of sex there are disquisitions a-plenty that would hold their own with the obscenities with which modern anti-Clericals so bitterly taunt the Jesuits.[5] Manners of ablution are debated at length, and their effectiveness. There are, accord-

quantities for aspersion, which defile the person, he defiling his garments, and waters insufficient for aspersion, which defile the person so that he defiles foods and beverages, but not his garments. Superior to this are the dead body and expiatory waters in quantities sufficient for aspersion. They defile a man by weight, just as he defiles his garments by touch, and garments removed from the garment by touch (*et subtractas veste tactu*)." Maimonides: "*Defilement by carrying:* it means that if a man has lifted a weight of unclean substance, he is defiled, even if he himself has not touched the body that was unclean. . . . Of similar nature is [defilement by] *inclination*, a timber being laid over the top of a wall, with the uncleanness on one end of the timber. If by leaning one's weight on the other end one raises the end on which the uncleanness is located, one is defiled by the inclination of the timber." Bertinoro: "*Et subtractas veste tactu.* It means garments withdrawn from uncleanness. In this case contact results from carrying. For anyone in contact with the dead or the *menstruae aquas* but not carrying these does not defile the garments he has on."

1268 [1] Mishnah, *loc. cit.*, VIII, 5 (Danby, p. 615; Surenhuis, Vol. VI, p. 48).

1268 [2] *Ibid.*, 11 (Danby, p. 616; Surenhuis, Vol. VI, p. 51).

1268 [3] *Ibid.*, Tract Tohoroth, IV, 2, 3 (Danby, p. 720; Surenhuis, Vol. VI, p. 327).

1268 [4] *Ibid.*, *loc. cit.*, IV, 6; V, 7-8 (Danby, pp. 720, 723; Surenhuis, Vol. VI, pp. 329, 330).

1268 [5] *Ibid.*, Tract Mikwaoth (*De lavacris*), VIII, 4 (Danby, p. 742; Surenhuis, Vol. VI, p. 381): "*Si gentilis eiecerit semen ab Israëlita immissum, immunda est. Si filia Israëlitae eiecerit semen a gentili iniectum, munda est. Si uxor domi coitum passa sit et postea se laverit sed pudenda non purgaverit, perinde est ac si non lavavisset se. Si is qui semen emisit se immerserit sed non prius minxerit, tum postquam urinam reddiderit, immundus est. R. Iose dicit: Aegrotus et senex immundus est, sed infans et sanus mundus est.*" Bertinoro: "*In iuvene et sano mundus est, quia fortissime emittunt semen ita ut nihil remaneat.*" There is even worse: *Ibid.*, VIII, 3 (Surenhuis, p. 380). A whole treatise, Tract Niddah (*De fluxu menstruo*), goes into all possible cases with the greatest fulness (Danby, pp. 748-57).

ing to the case, things that separate, and other things that do not separate, the water from the body.[6]

1269. If now we look down on all this, as it were in a certain perspective, disregarding minutiae as one does in making a map, we readily grasp the general outlines of the thing. The nucleus is an instinctive repugnance to dead bodies and to filth of one kind or another. That repugnance is in certain cases beneficial to the human being, just as it is beneficial to animals to abstain from poisonous foods.[1]

1270. How animals come by such useful instincts we do not know. That they do have them is certain. Cattle, goats, and sheep do not touch poisonous plants in the pasture. It is an interesting fact, on the other hand, that they will eat them in hay. Birds seem to avoid poisonous seeds. We might say with the Darwinists that by a process of selection animals not endowed with such instincts have perished. Some other explanation might be imagined. Whatever the causes, the fact is there, and at it we halt.

1271. In the case of the human being, the nucleus shows two supplements (§§ 1273 f.): first, an interposition of residues from Class I, which inspire numberless combinations, and their logical explanations. We have quoted the Talmud as offering a remarkable instance of such material combinations and their explanations, and all within a juridical sphere, with some very few metaphysical or theological reflections, the authority of the Bible being chiefly invoked very much as a jurist might point to a written code of law.

1272. The niceties of the Jews are not at all exceptional. Their

1268 [6] *Ibid.*, Tract Mikwaoth, IX, 1 (Danby, p. 742; Surenhuis, Vol. VI, p. 382): "*Haec in homine dividunt: fila lanae et lini, et corrigiae in capitibus filiarum. R. Iehuda dicit: fila e lana et e pilis non dividunt, quia ad illa perveniunt aquae.*" Fairly dirty remarks follow, in IX, 2. IX, 3 reads: "*Haec non dividunt: capilli, pili axillae, locus occultus in viro. R. Eliezer dicit: perinde se res habet in viro et in foemina, quidquid quis curat id dividit, sin minus, non dividit.*" Bertinoro: "*Et locus secretus in viro, nam vir istius loci non tam accuratam curam gerit, imo ne quidem foemina, nisi maritata sit, uti expositum est; si ergo quis talia loca non curat, ipsa nec dividunt, si nempe ea non sint in maxima corporis parte.*" And the commentaries keep it up.

1269 [1] It is one of the many cases of non-logical conduct that we came upon in Chapter II.

counterparts are to be met with among other peoples, especially among the Hindus and the Mohammedans. Many Hindu prescriptions tally almost word for word with the Hebrew.[1]

1273. The non-logical actions connected with uncleanness and purification supply excellent illustrations of the II-2 and II-4 varieties distinguished in §§ 151 f. They have a subjective logical purpose—obedience to certain religious injunctions. Some of them are without any objective logical end—refraining from lifting an unclean object with a string, for example. Those both belong to our II-2 variety. Some have an objective logical purpose contributing to hygiene—for instance, condemning as unclean a beverage into which a particle from a dead body has fallen. That purpose would be approved by the subject if he knew it, and we would have a non-logical action of the II-4α species.

1274. That has led people to represent such actions as logical

<hr>

1272 [1] Dubois, *Mœurs, institutions et cérémonies des peuples de l'Inde,* Vol. I, pp. 245-52: "Menstruation and childbirth lend temporary uncleanness to women. The mother of a new-born babe lives a whole month apart from other people . . . and women are subjected to the same segregation for their periodic seasons of uncleanness. . . . When the days of expiation are over, the clothing such women have been wearing is given to the washerwoman. It is carefully kept from entering the house, and no one would dare let his eyes rest on it. However, to purify themselves of such uncleanness, the wives of Sivaites (*lingamistes*) merely rub their foreheads with ash of cow's dung; and that simple ceremony they hold sufficient. . . . Earthen vessels are by nature susceptible of irremediable pollution, a thing not true of metal-ware. To be purified the latter need simply be washed. The others, being no longer usable, have to be destroyed. It is the same with clothing as with dishes: some are susceptible of defilement, others are not. . . . A scrupulous Brahman must be careful where he puts his feet when he walks. He would be defiled and required to take a bath if, by oversight, he chanced to set foot on a bone, a bit of broken crockery, a rag, a paper napkin with which someone has eaten, a piece of hide or leather, a lock of hair—anything unclean. The place where he sits down also requires his careful inspection . . . nor is his manner of eating a matter of indifference. The Hindu has an insurmountable horror for saliva. It is not so much a concern with neatness that obsesses him in that regard as his everlasting dread of the unclean. Contact with one animal or another, the dog especially, defiles the person of the Brahman, and it is amusing to watch the capers they cut, the precautions they take, to avoid the intimate caresses of one of the most faithful comrades of man. If in spite of their efforts the dog manages to reach them, they have no recourse but to hurry away and plunge fully dressed into a bath 'to be free of the pollution that the touch of the unclean animal has brought upon their persons and their garments.' "

actions, and it has contributed to the extension of the label to actions not belonging to the II-4α species. But no such logic figures in them. One may insist that the rules on menstruation were rules of hygiene; but in that case, why distinguish the menstruation of a Jewess from the menstruation of a Gentile, and the corpse of a Jew from the corpse of a Gentile?

1275. The second element that appears in the human being but not in the animal (§ 1271) is a need for explaining, not the combinations as such, but the principles that give rise to them; in other words, a desire to logicalize conduct that is non-logical. Active in that are not only the residues that reflect the hunger for logic (residues I-ε), but also residues of persisting abstractions (II-δ, §§ 1065-67). This supplement falls into two aspects—pseudo-experimental explanations on the one hand, and, on the other, explanations that overstep experience.

1276. Typical of the pseudo-experimental variety is the explanation which long enjoyed wide acceptance that the prohibition of pork for Jews was a hygienic principle supported by a religious sanction.[1]

1276 [1] Maimonides, *Guide of the Perplexed*, III, 48 (Munk, Vol. III, p. 396; Friedländer, Vol. III, pp. 251-52: "So I say that all the foods which the Law forbids constitute an unhealthy diet. Of all that has been forbidden us only pork and lard are not generally regarded as deleterious; but that is a mistake, for pork is a moister and more exuberant food than is good for us. But the chief reason why it is held in abomination by the Law is that the pig is a very uncleanly animal and feeds on uncleanly things. . . . Thus the fat of the inner organs of the pig is over-nourishing and so harmful to good digestion and productive of phlegmatic blood. . . . As for the characteristic signs [of the clean animal], the cloven hoof and cud-chewing for quadrupeds, and the presence of fins and scales in fish, the fact is that the presence of those signs is not the reason why eating them is permitted, nor lack of them the reason for their prohibition. They are just signs enabling one to recognize the good species and distinguish it from the bad." Maimonides explains and justifies all the biblical prescriptions with reasons derived from experience and logic. In some very few cases he confesses his inability to find any, *Ibid.*, III, 47 (Munk, Vol. III, p. 394; Friedländer, Vol. III, pp. 249-50): "The reason why purification was performed with cedar, hyssop, crimson wool, and two birds has been indicated in the Midrashôt; but it does not serve our purposes, and so far I have not been able to account for any of those things. Nor can I see, either, why cedar, hyssop, and crimson wool are used in the red-heifer rite, nor why a bunch of hyssop is used for sprinkling the blood of the lamb at Passover. I can find nothing to justify the preference given to those species." Logical explanations of unclean-

1277. Totemism, which explains everything, of course also explains the aversion of the Semites to the pig, presumably an ancient totem and as such revered and not used as a food! That might be true, and there are facts in favour of such a theory. J. L. Burckhardt animal prescriptions come down to our own day. Mills, *History of Muhammedanism*, pp. 311-12: "The nature of the climate of the East has rendered certain meats detrimental to health. Legislators have therefore either divided beasts into the clean or the unclean, that is to say, those that are proper, and those that are not proper food, or they have specifically prohibited some, and left the people to their discretion with respect to the use of the rest. [All that is purely fantastic, and arises merely in a desire to see logical conduct in everything.] Of the former description of lawgivers was Moses; of the latter, was Muhammed. That the flesh of the *ignavum animal* (as Tacitus so decently calls the hog) engenders cutaneous disorders, more especially in warm countries, is a well-known fact; the filthiness of the quadruped [Mills would doubtless have agreed with the dictum of another Englishman that "the swine was properly so called."—A. L.] is sufficient to give a distaste of it; and accordingly we find that the Egyptians, Arabians, and other oriental nations have always abhorred it. The necessity of the case dictated the prohibition." Reinach well demonstrates the fatuity of such explanations in his *Cultes, mythes et religions*, Vol. I, pp. 11-13: "Oftentimes the prohibition to kill animals of one or more species comes in the shape of a taboo, a non-motivated interdiction, that is, or an interdiction justified after the fact by considerations of an entirely different order, hygienic, for example. That is still observable among the Mussulmans and the Jews." But Reinach goes wrong in regarding such rules as consequences of totemism. He himself shows that they may have had a different origin when he says: "Even in our day the Russian peasant will not kill a dove because the dove is the bird of the Holy Spirit, and even in France children are taught not to harm the lady-bird, which is called 'God's little animal' (*bête-du-bon-Dieu*). [There is not the slightest indication that the lady-bird was ever a totem in France. Reinach goes on to say himself, *Op. cit.*, pp. 91-92:] One of the most ancient and most widely diffused forms of religion [He ought really to say, "of non-logical conduct."] is a scruple against killing or eating some animal. Such scruples are still common enough. Mussulmans and Jews will not eat pork. Russians will not eat pigeons. Europeans, as a rule at least, will not eat dog-meat, and many still feel for horse-meat an instinctive repugnance that goes back to some ancient religion." Perhaps, but there are other things of the kind for which no religious or totemic explanation is imaginable. Ram-mutton goes very well in France and England. There are Italians in Central Italy who refuse to touch it in any form. Is there any likelihood that the ram was their totem? If one say that it is a religious prescription, on what documents could such a contention be based? Many Englishmen stand aghast at sight of a Frenchman eating frogs' legs. In all countries there are plenty of people who have an absolute repugnance to oysters. The Arabs eat grasshoppers. I challenge anyone to offer one to a European. In all such cases, there is no trace of any totemic, religious, or if you will, hygienic reason. They are just non-logical actions like the hosts of others observable in the human race.

relates: [1] "Some years ago an English ship went ashore near Djidda [Arabia] and among various spoils obtained from the wreck by Sherif Ghaleb was a large hog, an animal probably never before seen at Djidda. This hog, turned loose in the town with two ostriches, became the terror of all the sellers of bread and vegetables; for the mere touching of so unclean an animal as the hog, even with the edge of the gown, renders the Moslem impure and unable to perform his prayers without previous ablutions. The animal was kept for six months, when it was offered by the Sherif to an American captain for fifty dollars; but such a price being of course refused, it soon after died of a surfeit, to the great satisfaction of the inhabitants." [2] Here one notes characteristic traits of reverence for the totem, and if all cases were of this kind, the explanation would acquire great probability. But there are cases where it does not fit. In the Bible the hog is not the only animal that cannot be used as food. Many others are in the same fix. If there were only a few such animals one might imagine they were all totems. But can so many many all have been—all aquatic animals, for instance, and most of

1277 [1] *Travels in Arabia,* p. 208.

1277 [2] It is well known that the dog also is reputed unclean by the Moslems. Says Burckhardt, p. 386: "It is not unworthy of remark, that Medina, as far as I know, is the only town in the East from which dogs are excluded; they are never permitted to pass the gate into the interior, but must remain in the suburbs. . . . The apprehension of a dog entering a mosque, and polluting its sanctity, probably gave rise to their exclusion." Mills, *History of Muhammedanism,* pp. 467-68: "The benevolence of the Muselmans extends to the animal creation, and it is an established article in the Moslem's belief that the irrational animals will be judged on the last day and have mutual vengeance for the injuries they have done each other in this life. From feelings of compassion, hunting is held in abhorrence by the Turks, and birds are seldom deprived of their liberty. . . . According to popular tradition Muhammed was kind to the domestic animal, the cat. Its gravity of deportment and independent indifference well accord with the sullen solemnity and pride of the Turks. Though they are far too cleanly to admit them to touch their persons, yet they are received in their houses; the dog is not treated with the same benevolent attention. . . . His touch is deemed contagious and his very name is the Turk's bitterest expression of contempt." Such differences between the cat and the dog cannot be explained by totemism. Mills quotes in a footnote a remark of Labat, *Mémoires du Chevalier d'Arvieux,* Vol. III, p. 227: "Cats are not unclean animals; therefore they may eat and drink of the same things as the faithful do. But if a dog drink in the vessel of a believer, it must be washed seven times (Mishat, Vol. I, p. 108)."

them unknown to the Hebrews—that have neither fins nor scales? [8] One might answer that the prescription not to eat totems was subsequently extended to other animals. But granting that, it has still to be shown whether the pig was the totem from which the interdiction sprang or an animal to which the abomination was extended from others that were totems—and on that point we have not the slightest information. The conclusion is that the hog may well have been an ancient totem, but that such a fact requires specific proof, which for the present is not available; while the general fact of aversion to the use of its meat or to contact with it proves nothing because it would be proving too much.

1278. Speaking of certain laws on uncleanness Rabbinovicz tries to explain the prescription that a dead Gentile is to be considered clean. But the derivations to which he resorts he refutes later on himself. [1]

1277: [8] Lev. 11:12: (Vulgate) *"Cuncta quae non habent pinnulas et squamas in aquis polluta erunt"*: (King James) "Whatsoever hath no fins nor scales in the waters, that shall be an abomination unto you."

1278 [1] *Législation criminelle du Talmud*, Preface, pp. xxxiii-xxxv. "The Jews never buried their dead along public highways; and they furthermore marked graves with a sign called *tzijon*. Gentiles did not do that. The result was, at a time when the Jews were everywhere surrounded by Gentiles, that the Jews were unable to observe the laws of uncleanness as regarded the Gentiles, being unable to recognize their graves; so that in the end they came to believe that such graves did not defile." Rabbinovicz himself supplies the means for refuting this conjecture by showing that it applies to a particular case of a theory that is general; and which it certainly does not fit. Trying to refute another theory, which he rightly regards as erroneous, he says: "So they had a tradition, which had grown up . . . that the grave of a Gentile did not defile. Following a habit of the Talmud, that tradition was tied to a word in the Bible. Scripture says that an *adam,* a man, who is dead is a cause of uncleanness. The word *adam,* it was held, meant a Jew and nobody else. ([In a note]: It was not observed that the word *ysch,* 'man,' also excluded Gentiles in connexion with another case of uncleanness.) The passage [where the word *adam* so figures] was badly comprehended by several commentators and was still being attacked by enemies of Judaism as late as the past century. . . . They did not know that the passage in question had not been found till centuries after the Jews had grown accustomed to applying the law of cleanness to the graves of Gentiles. So also the passage in the Song of Songs that forbade the Jews to revolt against Gentiles . . . was not discovered till after the last revolution of Bar Khokhbah, when any rebellion had become impossible." In his *Législation civile du Talmud,* Vol. V, p. 381, again adverting to the law that a dead Gentile was clean, Rabbinovicz adds: "Rab says: 'If, as regards certain rules of uncleanness, a dead

1279. Gentiles were considered clean in certain cases chiefly because the non-logical conduct related, in its basic nucleus, to members of the group, to Jews, that is, but later on was extended by a process of reasoning to non-Jews as well. Rabbinovicz says that the Hebrews could not distinguish the graves of Gentiles. But they could not distinguish the spittles of Gentiles either; and in that case the Talmud rules in a sense directly contrary to its ruling in the other. Rabbinovicz himself notes the fact: "If there be a Gentile woman within the city, the spittles are impure (as regards the *haberim*, who have pledged themselves to observe the Mosaic laws on purity, since the Gentile woman might chance to be in a period)."[1] So we get many other problems of the kind with varying solutions, which cannot always be brought down to considerations of convenience for the Hebrews at a time when they were forced to live in contact with Gentiles.[2]

man has to be taken as a living individual, that must have been to prevent his being considered dead in cases of merely apparent death.'" As usual, derivations are the variable element in the thing, residues the constant. See further § 1279 [2] below.

1279 [1] *Législation civile du Talmud,* Vol. V, p. 411.

1279 [2] We mentioned one such problem just above in § 1278 [1]. Add the following: Mishnah, Tract Tohoroth, V, 8 (Danby, p. 723; Surenhuis, Vol. VI, p. 335): "If there be in the city a half-witted woman, either a foreigner or a Cuthaean, then all spittles found in the city are unclean." Maimonides: "We have stated . . . that Gentiles are to be regarded as *seminiflui* in all respects. Further in our fourth article of the code *De menstruis* we stated that a Cuthaean woman must always be held open to suspicion of being in a period. But it is not to be overlooked that a half-wit does not take care of herself, nor observe the times of her periods as defined in the Law." *Ibid.,* Tract Niddah (*De fluxu menstruo*), IV, 3 (Danby, p. 748; Surenhuis, Vol. VI, p. 400): "The blood of a female foreigner, and the blood of a female leper in state of cleanness, are clean according to the School of Schammai. The school of Hillel rules that it is on a par with spittle and urine." Bertinoro: "According to the School of Schammai, the blood of a female Gentile is clean, though with respect to spittle and urine the Schools of Schammai and Hillel are in agreement." Maimonides: "We have already . . . remarked that Gentiles in no wise defile, according to the Law, but the Scribes have ruled that they are to be regarded as *seminiflui* in all respects." *Ibid., loc. cit.,* VII, 3 (Danby, p. 753; Surenhuis, Vol. VI, p. 415): "All spots coming from Raca are clean, but unclean according to Rabbi Jéhudam, because they are proselytes and prone to err (*quia proselyti sunt et errant*). Such as come from Gentiles are clean. Such as come from an Israelite and from the Cuthaeans are unclean according to Rabbi Meir, clean

1280. The purpose of the trans-experimental explanation is to account for a prescription in which people believe on faith and which requires certain practices. It begins with the simple assertion of the taboo and gradually goes on to the most abstruse metaphysical and theological hair-splitting. In Leviticus one meets a simple form of explanation: the regulation as to purity and purification is bluntly stated as coming from God. Then again the assertion is re-enforced with more or less exhortation.[1] Finally comes a type of explanation usual with taboos: it is said that the transgressor runs a risk of death, and a religious explanation is further added.[2]

1281. A new stratum of explanations was added by Christianity. The Hebrews performed sacrifices and used the blood of sacrificial victims for purifications, as other peoples did.[1] The Christians wanted to abolish the custom and, not satisfied with that, they wanted to explain why they abolished it. St. Paul says that the blood of the Christ shed once and for all is the most perfect of sacrifices

according to the Scribes because they are not suspect of blemish." Bertinoro: "Those who come from Raca, and their blood, are unclean, because the inhabitants of that place are foreigners." Maimonides: "We have several times stated that Gentiles do not defile by the *fluxu seminis vel sanguinis nec fluxu menstruo:* the Scribes ruled concerning them, but gave no ruling as to their blemishes." Bertinoro: *"From Raca:* In the Targum the words *inter Cades et Sur* are rendered as 'between Raca and Chagra.' *Because they are proselytes:* their blood being unclean. . . . *Are prone to err:* it is as though he said, they are not very neat, nor do they cover over their blood-spots. Therefore we may suspect that they may perchance be *foeminae menstruae maculae. Such as come from Gentiles are clean,* because the Scribes have made no rulings as to their blemishes, and according to the Law their blood is altogether clean." *Ibid., loc. cit.,* X, 4 (Danby, pp. 756-57; Surenhuis, Vol. VI, p. 424): *"Seminifluus, seminiflua, menstrua, puerpera,* and lepers who have died, defile if they are carried, until the flesh changes. A Gentile that dies is clean of defilement if he is carried."

1280 [1] Lev. 11:43: "Ye shall not make yourselves abominable with any creeping thing that creepeth, neither shall ye make your selves unclean with them, that ye should be defiled thereby."

1280 [2] Lev. 15:31: "Thus shall ye separate the children of Israel from their uncleanness, that they die not in their uncleanness, when they defile my tabernacle that is among them."

1281 [1] So in Ex. 29:18 the sacrifice of the ram is explained with the words: "And thou shalt burn the whole ram upon the altar: it is a burnt offering unto the Lord: it is a sweet savour, an offering made by fire unto the Lord." That, roughly, was the reason given for pagan sacrifices.

and supersedes the old.[2] Interesting in that the persistence of an association, whereby the Christians dare not do away with the notion of the sacrifice altogether, but stop at transforming it in such a way that it carries on, but under a different form.[3]

1282. Residues of restoration of integrity in persons and things figure in many other cases. The Catholic Church used to "reconcile" penitents. It still "reconciles" churches and cemeteries.[1]

1283. Group-persistences result in the extension of practices devised for human beings (such as juridical acts and restorations of integrity) to animals and things. But that does not mean that there has necessarily been any direct imitation. Imitation may figure to some

1281 [2] Heb. 10:5-14 represents the single sacrifice of Christ as sufficient for all sins. And *cf.* Heb. 9:12-14: "Neither by the blood of goats and calves but by his own blood he entered in once into the holy place, having obtained eternal redemption for us. For if the blood of bulls and of goats and the ashes of an heifer sprinkling the unclean sanctifieth to the purifying of the flesh, how much more shall the blood of Christ . . . purge your conscience from dead works to serve the living God?"

1281 [3] Really this whole subject is a matter of derivations, to which we shall come in our next chapter. We made this digression here in order to show by one more example how residues may be got at in the complex concrete case.

1282 [1] *Dictionnaire encyclopédique de la théologie catholique, s.v. Réconciliation des pénitents* (Wetzer, *s.v. Reconciliatio poenitentium*): ". . . An act whereby, in days when a severe discipline prevailed in the Church, public penitents were officially reconciled with the Church and formally admitted to its circle, after completing their penance. . . . Pope Innocent I writes to Decentius, Bishop of Gubbio, that penitents of the Roman Church receive absolution and are admitted to Church communion on Holy Thursday. . . . The admission was made with a solemnity fit to stir all hearts." *Ibid., s.v. Réconciliation des églises et des cimetières* (Wetzer, *s.v. Reconciliation der Kirche und des Begräbnisplatzes*): "When a church has once been appointed to divine worship and blessed, it can never lose its status as a sacred thing . . . but it can be profaned by acts affecting its sacred character. [A good example of altered integrity in things.] Neither church nor cemetery can continue to serve their hallowed purposes so long as they remain profane. To restore them to their proper condition a religious ceremony called 'reconciliation' [Restoration of integrity.] is required. That act has deep roots in the exigencies of religious sentiment [Quite so, owing to the residues here in question.] and in the conviction it inspires [Derivation.] that God withdraws from places where He has been insulted and that expiation is required to recall the Lord to such a sanctuary. . . . If a man who has defiled his soul, the hallowed temple of the Holy Spirit, through sin can be reconciled with God through penance, a church that has been profaned may likewise become the residence of God again as the result of a solemn rite."

extent, but in other respects it may be a question of the direct effects of a single sentiment.

1284. So the notion of purification is extensible in space. Certain signs indicate that some vague peril is impending over a group of people, a country, and steps have to be taken to avert it.

1285. The type of such phenomena would be the exorcism (*procuratio*) of prodigies by the Romans. A prodigy was a threat of on-coming disasters and something had to be done, and in a hurry, to avert them. A prodigy, moreover, involved a taint, and a purification was called for. When a man has unwittingly swallowed a poison he must find an antidote to counteract its effects. In descriptions of such cases that have come down to us, clearly apparent are, first, a feeling that *something has to be done,* and then, a breathless search for that something.[1]

1285 [1] Bouché-Leclerq, *Histoire de la divination dans l'antiquité,* Vol. IV, pp. 80-82: "Any prodigy, whatever it may have been and even if its meaning could not be divined, required expiatory ceremonies. When a man is frightened by a miracle it is natural for him to interpose sacrifices and prayers between himself and the danger he apprehends. [In general terms, he interposes some sort, any sort, of action. When an animal is frightened at the sight of some unusual object, he reacts physi-cally: a dog barks, a horse rears and prances, the lion lashes his flanks with his tail.] The Greeks and Romans hardly overstepped such merely empirical ex-orcism (*procuratio*), which the most ignorant could understand. Instead of trying to discover what will had wrought the miracle and the purpose it was designed to fulfil [A lengthy derivation.], they called upon the 'gods who avert' evils [θεοὶ ἀποτρόπαιοι, *dii Averrunci*] and took courage in the thought that they had met enemies unknown with trustworthy friends. [A much shorter derivation.] Some ritual or other, a sacrifice, an offering, the recitation of a magical rigmarole, or some other external expression [The residue working unmixed.], completed the task of propitiation that had begun with the prayer. [More probably, the prayer came afterwards.] Numa had taught the Romans how to exorcise a certain num-ber of so to say ordinary prodigies, and experience had enabled them to supple-ment the old ritual with some few empirical recipes. They had learned as far back as the day of Tullius Hostilius that a rain of stones was adequately 'taken care of' (*procuratio*) by nine days of holiday. [Whereas the haruspices came closer to the notion of purification:] As a rule they regarded prodigies less as warnings for the future than as complaints for the past. The abnormal character of the sign indicated, they thought, some imperious demand ordinarily inspired by some offence committed against the gods and not atoned for. The prodigy once recog-nized as such and, as the phrase was, 'accepted' (*suscipere prodigium*), the first problem was to determine which of the gods was the complainant. The prodigy once credited to its real author, it became easier to determine the cause of the complaint and the price for which it would be forgotten. Scrupulous investigation rarely failed

1286. In certain cases it was known exactly what the alteration in integrity had been. It was called a *piaculum,* and the same term was applied to the remedial rites. In case a sacrifice had not been performed in strict accordance with ritual, integrity was restored by repeating the sacrifice. For other sorts of violation one sacrifice or another served. Aulus Gellius, *Noctes Atticae,* IV, 6, relates that on learning that the spears of Mars had stirred in the sanctuary of their own accord, the Senate ordered a sacrifice to Jupiter and Mars, and that in case other victims should prove necessary—"*si quid succidaneis opus est*"—they should be sacrificed to Robigus (the god who averted mildew). Gellius ponders the term "*succidaneae*" at length and concludes that they are victims that served to "fill out" where previous offerings had proved insufficient. "For the same reason victims offered on the eve of solemn sacrifices were called *praecidaneae.* So the term *porca praecidanea* was given to the sow that was sacrificed by ancient custom to Ceres as a *piaculum* 'in advance of' a new harvest (*ante fruges novas captas*), in case someone had died in a family and the necessary purifications had not been, or had been inadequately, performed."

1287. The *lustratio* and the *piaculum* were often confused, since they both aimed at restoration of integrity. The *Arvales fratres* necessarily had to enter the sacred forest with cutting-knives in order to perform the sacrifices. On the other hand, it was forbidden to carry such instruments into the forest. The rule, therefore, being at all times broken, needed the support of a rite designed to restore integrity. Such a rite was performed by the Magister, or the Pro-Magister, who made an expiatory sacrifice of two pigs and a heifer in the morning and awaited the Arvals in the afternoon. That was the procedure at the annual ceremony, which fell in May or June. But then, in addition, whenever any work had to be done in the

to develop some oversight that had either not been noticed or had been inadequately repaired, and that was taken as the prime cause of the prodigy. If nothing of the kind came to light, the soothsayers were at liberty to conclude either that the inquiry had not been carried far enough or that the prodigy related to the future. To play the safer, the haruspices often looked in both directions, their findings showing mixtures of complaints and prophecies."

forest special expiatory sacrifices were required. In these customs of the College of the Arvals, which go back to very ancient times, the mechanical character of the restoration of integrity is clearly apparent. It was something very like sharpening an ax that has been dulled in cutting down a tree. Something has to be done. It is regularly done, and there is nothing wrong in doing it. All the same, it has to be offset by doing something else, to restore a certain balance that has been disturbed by the doing of it.

1288. The concept of altered integrity is extensible also in time, so leading to the notion that posterity may be held responsible for the sins of the forefathers. Hence the Christian doctrine of original sin, and other notions of the kind, such as the idea of the Orphics that the integrity of humankind had been primevally altered.[1] Such notions logically led to the belief that expiations and purifications are somehow required. Plato, in his day, mentions soothsayers who managed to persuade the rich that they held the secret of purification rites that could purge the crimes of men in general, and of their ancestors in particular.[2] Ovid retells the stories that were current in his time as to an original taint of the human race.[3]

1289. The type-case of a restoration of an integrity altered by orig-

1288 [1] Daremberg-Saglio, *Dictionnaire, s.v. Orphici:* "The Orphics believed in the divine nature of the soul and in a Fall, an original sin. Created in the first place by the gods, the soul had lived in Heaven, being exiled thence in consequence of a sin, the παλαιὸν πένθος of which Pindar speaks [*Fragmenta*, Boecke, Vol. II-2, p. 623], the μεγάλα ἁμαρτήματα alluded to by Jamblichus. Just what the sin was is unknown. Following the common explanation, humanity had sprung of the blood of the Titans, murderers of Zagreus. By birthright, therefore, man was an enemy of the gods, but at the same time there was something divine in him coming from the Titans. In addition to the general defilement attaching to all human beings, there was a particular defilement hereditary in certain families."

1288 [2] *Respublica*, II, 364 B-E. They used books of Musaeus and Orpheus and imposed not only on private individuals but even on the governments of cities.

1288 [3] *Metamorphoses*, I, vv. 155-62. Jupiter strikes down the Giants with his thunderbolts; but Earth gives life to their blood and "changes it into men, a race true to its birth in blood, being contemptuous of the gods, cruel, bloodthirsty, violent." To tell the truth, all such tales, all such derivations, in which the sense of an original taint finds its expression, are intrinsically of little significance. Yet with them many professed students of religion are chiefly concerned, quite disregarding the sentiments, the residues, that they manifest, and which are the prime factors in determining the social equilibrium.

inal sin would be Christian baptism. We are not called upon here to go into the numberless derivations that the dogma of baptism has inspired, and much less into the question of its spiritual value. Such subjects altogether transcend the experimental field in which we have elected to remain. However, from the standpoint of residues, it is impossible not to connect present-day Christian baptism with the baptism practised by St. John the Baptist, and with the ablutions that have been and are still in use among peoples and peoples without end. In Christian baptism the effect of one such ablution has acquired definite form as regards restoration of integrity: baptism removes not only original sin but all other sins that may have tainted the individual down to the precise moment of baptism. Numberless the passages in the Holy Fathers relating to the matter. They may be epitomized in the following declaration, which is usually included in the works of St. Augustine but seems to be really by an author unknown: *"Remission of sins:* Holy baptism entirely removes all sins, both original and one's own: sins of word, of deed, of thought; sins known and unknown—all are remitted. He reneweth man, who made him."[1]

1289 [1] St. Augustine, *De symbolo, Ad catechumenos sermo alius* (a), X, 10 (*Opera,* Vol. VI, p. 639). A *Decretal for the Armenians* by Pope Eugene IV rules: "The effect of the sacrament of baptism is the remission of all original and present sin, and of any penance that might be owing on the account of such sin. Therefore no satisfaction is to be required of recipients of baptism for past sins. Those who die before they have committed any sin advance straightway to the Kingdom of Heaven and the vision of God." St. Cyril of Jerusalem, *Catechisis tertia: De baptismo,* XV (*Opera,* pp. 446-47; Gifford, p. 17), makes specific mention of fornication and adultery among the sins so remitted. However, this status of Christian baptism is too well known to require any extensive documentation. A few opinions will suffice. St. Augustine states the Church doctrine over and over again: *e.g., Sermones,* LVI, *In Evangelium Matthaei,* 6:7-15, *De oratione dominica,* IX, 13 (*Opera,* Vol. V, pp. 377 f.): "Be ye baptized . . . and so shall ye enter! And be certain that you are forthwith forgiven all sins that you incurred from your parents in the fact of birth according to Adam in original sin, in view of which you hasten with your children to the grace of the Saviour, and all sins that you have added thereunto in the course of your lives—sins of word, of deed, of thought —all are forgiven you." The Saint sees in the Flood a symbol of baptism: *Contra Faustum Manichaeum,* XII, 17, (*Opera,* Vol. VIII, p. 265; *Works,* Vol. V, pp. 216-17): "It rained for forty days and forty nights, because every possible sin of a sinner is comprised within the Ten Commandments of the Law covering the whole Earth, which is in four parts, ten times four making forty. Both the sins which pertain to the day—to prosperity—and those pertaining to the night—to

1290. So, reasoning logically, one could infer that it was wiser to defer baptism until the very moment of death, so that, being cleansed of every sin by the rite, one would necessarily be saved; and support for that opinion could be found in the Gospels, where it is written, Matt. 20: 1-16, that the labourers of the eleventh hour shall be paid as those of the first. But, as everybody knows, logic has no place in such thinking—one same derivation can prove both the yea and the nay. The Church vigorously combated such interpretations, which in fact would have reduced all religion to a merely mechanical act at point of death.[1] On similar grounds the Church

adversity—are washed away in the sacrament of heavenly baptism." Gousset, *Théologie dogmatique*, Vol. II, p. 415: "This grace [of baptism] obliterates the original sin that the child bears in him at birth. In adults baptism erases all present sins that they may have committed before baptism and remits all spiritual penalties due on account of any sin whatsoever." *Canones et decreta Concilii Tridentini, sessio* V: *De peccato originali*, 5 (Richter, p. 14; Schaff, Vol. II, p. 87): "If anyone shall deny that the offence of original sin is forgiven by the grace of Our Lord Jesus Christ conferred in baptism, or assert that anything that has real and proper status as sin is not taken away, but holds that it is merely erased or not imputed, let him be anathema." The concluding remark on the notion that baptism does not obliterate original sin entirely, but merely cancels it so that it cannot be charged against one, is an allusion to a heresy that the Pelagians attributed to the Catholics. St. Augustine, *Contra duas epistolas Pelagianorum*, I, 13, 26 (*Opera*, Vol. X, p. 562; *Works*, Vol. XV, p. 256): " 'According to him, they hold that baptism does not give plenary remission of sins nor obliterate crimes, but shaves them off so that the roots of all sin still abide in a flesh that is evil.' Who but an infidel would ever sustain such a position against the Pelagians?" Calvin, *Institutions*, IV, 15, 1-3 (Allen, Vol. III, pp. 327-28): "Baptism is sent to us from Him as a letter patent signed and sealed, whereby it is enjoined, confirmed, and assured unto us that all our sins are so remitted, overwritten, abolished, erased, that they will never be considered by Him, never be refreshed in His memory, never charged by Him to our account. . . . Baptism promises us no other purification than by the aspersion of the blood of Christ, which is figured in the water through the similitude it has therewith in washing and cleansing. . . . And we must not imagine that Baptism is given to us only for times past, so that we must seek some other remedy for the sins into which we fall after Baptism. I am aware that that error arises from the fact that in olden times there were those who would not take Baptism till the end of their lives and on the point of death, that they might so have plenary remission for the whole of their lives [§ 1290]—a foolish fancy that has often been rebuked by the bishops in their writings. We must know instead that at whatever time we are baptized we are forthwith washed and purged for the whole course of our lives."

1290 [1] St. Gregory of Nazianzos, *Oratio* XL, 20 (*Opera*, Vol. II, pp. 383-86; English, p. 377): "But someone may say: 'What does it avail me to be bound earlier by baptism and by such haste deprive myself of the pleasures of life, when

condemned so-called Hemerobaptists. Also reasoning by strict logic, they baptized every day to be rid of moral blemishes, much as one might wash one's hands after the day's work.[2]

1291. Integrity before birth may be envisaged as well as integrity after death; but whereas the former has a bearing on a real subject, the living person, the subject in the latter case is abstract or imaginary.

1292. Time was when purifications with the blood of a bull (the *taurobolium*) or with the blood of a ram (the *criobolium*) became very frequent in Roman worship. The *taurobolium* was used either as a public sacrifice for the health of the Emperor or for the regeneration of a private person. A man went down into a trench over which a bull or a ram was slain by cutting the throat, and the blood of the animal dripped upon him, purifying him either forever, or for a certain period of time, after which the sacrifice had to

it is possible to enjoy them and receive divine grace at the last? For those who came early to labour in the vineyard had none the better wage, but received the same hire as those who came last.' " The Saint explains that the parable must not be interpreted in that fashion. In the first place it makes no mention of baptism. Furthermore, if the last did not work as long as the first, they were in no wise inferior in goodwill. A parable can mean anything one wants it to mean.

1290 [2] St. Epiphanius, *Panarium adversus haereses, lib.* I, *tomus,* I, *Haeresis* 17 (*Opera,* Vol. I, p. 255): "*Against the Hemerobaptists, fourth of Jewish heresies, seventeenth in order.* . . . Chiefly peculiar to this heresy is the doctrine that one should be baptized (βαπτίζεσθαι) daily at all seasons of the year, spring and autumn, winter and summer, whence the name of Hemerobaptists. They declare that there is no salvation for man save he baptize himself in water every day, washing himself and cleansing himself of every sin." St. Epiphanius assails that view, on the ground, in brief, that not all the waters in the ocean, nor all the water in the seas, rivers, and springs, nor all the water in the rain could, put together, wash away the sins of men, who must purify themselves by repentance. To which the heretic might have retorted: "Why, then, do you use water in your single baptism?" As a matter of fact, baptism involves an external act and an internal act, and now the one, now the other, takes the foreground according to the strength of the sentiments corresponding. Petau (Petavius), *Appendices geminae pro vindicandis ad Epiphanium animadversionibus,* 19-20: "That persons baptized while sick in bed are to be barred from the priesthood is the doctrine laid down in the *Canon Neocaesarensis* XII, and by Pope Cornelius, in a letter to Fabius, bishop of Antioch, quoted by Eusebius, Bk. VI, Chap. XXXV [read, *Historia ecclesiastica,* VI, 43, 14 and 17; Lawler, Vol. II, p. 123], in which he says of Novatus: 'It is unlawful to admit to the clergy anyone who has been baptized in bed because of sickness, as he [Novatus] was.' "

be repeated.[1] The Christians, naturally, resented the competition of such purifications with their own rites. Firmicus Maternus exclaims: "Why does the *taurobolium,* or the *criobolium,* cover you with blood in clots accursed? To wash away the taint that is upon

1292 [1] Daremberg-Saglio, *Dictionnaire, s.v. Taurobolium:* "The first *taurobolium* we can date belongs to the year 134 [A.D.] [It was devoted] not to the Mother of the Gods, but to the Celestial Venus of Carthage. Next in order of antiquity comes a *taurobolium* held at Lyons for the health of Antoninus Pius and his children and the welfare of the colony. The latest known was of the year 390, and it was taken by a Senator in his own behalf. In the meantime frequent public *taurobolia* must have been celebrated. . . . Private *taurobolia* can be traced, by inscriptions, from the second century down to the last days of paganism, but they were especially frequent after the reign of Julian." As Marquardt says, "at the end all pagan forms of worship seemed to converge on the *taurobolium.*" Some inscriptions: Orelli, *Inscriptionum . . . collectio,* no. 2352: ". . . *Taurobolio criobolioque in aeternum renatus . . .*" ("regenerate forever through a *taurobolium* and a *criobolium . . .*"); 2355: ". . . *iterato viginti annis ex perceptis tauroboliis VI aram constituit.*" ("this altar erected on the repetition of six *taurobolia* twenty years after their first taking [*ex perceptis*]."); 6032 (Henzen): "*Pro salute imp. L. Septimi Severi . . . taurobolium fecerunt. . . .*" ("They made a *taurobolium . . .* for the health of the Emperor L. Septimius Severus."). Prudentius, *Peristephanon, Hymni,* X, vv. 1011-50 (*Opera,* Vol. II, pp. 260-61). Vv. 1016-20 read:

> "*Tabulis superne strata texunt pulpita*
> *rimosa rari pegmatis compagibus:*
> *scindunt subinde vel terebrant aream,*
> *crebroque lignum perforant acumine,*
> *pateat minutis ut frequens hiatibus.*"

("Over [the trench] they build a platform of planks. It is full of cracks from the joints of a scanty framework. . . . Then they split the planks or pierce the floor with many borings so that it is thickly dotted with holes.") A bull is led up on the platform and his throat cut with the consecrated blade. The blood falls on the sieve-like floor. "Then through the numerous holes the blood rains as a dew infect, and the priest in the trench receives it, offering his vile head, his garments, the whole of his reeking person, to every drop." *Anthologia veterum Latinorum epigrammatum,* I, 57 (Vol. I, p. 33):

> "*Quis tibi taurobolus vestem mutare suasit,*
> *inflatus dives subito mendicus ut esses,*
> *obsitus et pannis modicis tepefactus, . . .*
> *Sub terra missus, pollutus sanguine tauri?*
> *Sordidus, infectus, vestes servare cruentas,*
> *vivere cum speras viginti mundus in annos.*"

("What bull-vendor enticed you into changing your clothes that you might turn in a flash from bloated Croesus to beggar, and be locked up, shivering in light garments, underground, to be dirtied with the blood of a bull till you reek with filth and grime and your garments are soaked with blood—and all in the hope of living clean for twenty years?")

you, you need a crystal spring, pure water you need, that after many stains the blood of Christ, with the Holy Spirit, may purify you." [3] Tertullian accuses the Devil of imitating sacraments of the Christian religion in the pagan mysteries (he may be right, for we do not know who the Devil is nor what his ways and morals). [4] "He sprinkles his believers and his faithful, and promises to wash away their sins with that ablution." And elsewhere vouching for the effectiveness of Christian baptism, he says: [5] "Even the heathen, who are strangers to all knowledge of spiritual powers, attribute the same capacity to their idols. But widowed of every virtue, their waters are deceptive. They initiate to an Isis or a Mithras with an ablution. They sprinkle even their gods. For the rest, they besprinkle round about their homes, their farms, their temples, and whole cities, and everywhere they expiate. During certain games of Apollo and at Eleusis they bathe, and presume to be regenerate and to have escaped punishment for their forswearing. So among the ancients those who had been tainted by homicide betook themselves to purifying waters."

1293. It is understandable that with such a great variety of rites to choose from the choice might prove perplexing. If the urge to purification rested on belief in a purifying power, that power would determine the consequences of the sentiment. What we observe instead is that the sentiment comes first; and then a means of satisfying it with some rite is sought; and sometimes the person desiring purification does not know to whom to turn.

1294. That is what happened in the famous purification of Athens executed by Epimenides. [1] "He took white sheep and black, led them to the Areopagus, and thence allowed them to go whither they pleased, enjoining on those who followed them to sacrifice them to

1292 [3] *De errore profanarum religionum*, 28-29 (Migne, p. 1043): ". . . *Quaere fontes ingenuos, quaere puros liquores, ut illic te post multas maculas cum Spiritu Sancto Christi sanguis incandidet.*"

1292 [4] *De praescriptionibus hereticorum*, 40 (*Opera*, Vol. II, p. 40; English, Vol. II, p. 48).

1292 [5] *De baptismo, adversus Quintillam*, 5 (*Opera*, Vol. V, pp. 161-62; English, Vol. I, p. 48).

1294 [1] Diogenes Laertius, *Epimenides*, I, 110 (Hicks, Vol. I, pp. 115-17).

the god of the place where they halted. Whereupon the plague ceased. That is why even now here and there in villages of Attica there are altars without names of gods that commemorate the expiations made at that time." Juvenal, *Saturae*, VI, vv. 511-68, satirizes a Roman matron who lends willing ear to all sorts of charlatans and pays good money to Jewess and Chaldean and to the priest of the Mother of the Gods.

1295. According to Zosimus, *Historia nova*, II, 29 (Reitemeier, pp. 150-51; Davis, pp. 51-52), Constantine decided in favour of Christianity because it offered purifying expiations for his particular crimes that he could not find in the pagan religion. That may not be the whole truth. Constantine may have had other reasons and stronger, such as the large number of Christian soldiers in his legions. All the same, superstition has its influences even on criminals! Bandits have been known to carry images of the Virgin on their persons. After ordering his mother's murder Nero, according to Suetonius, *Nero*, 34, 4, "had a sacrifice celebrated by magicians in an effort to evoke and propitiate her shade. In his journey through Greece he did not dare present himself for initiation into the Eleusinian mysteries because the voice of the herald holds the impious and the wicked afar off." [1] Eusebius says that, before advancing upon Maxentius, Constantine inquired as to the god to whom he should entrust himself in order to win the battle; and that he decided upon the God of the Christians because Emperors who had worshipped pagan gods had had bad luck.[2] The fact that Constantine inquired as to the religion best suited to his purposes is vouched for, therefore, both by a friend, Eusebius, and by an enemy, Zosimus, and they differ only in their manner of accounting for his choice. The story of Zosimus shows the residue of restoration of integrity. In the story of Eusebius the residue is a sentiment of personal in-

---

1295 [1] Dio Cassius, *Historia Romana*, LXII, 14, 4 (Carey, Vol. VIII, p. 161), says that Nero avoided going to Athens "because of the tradition about the Furies" (διὰ τὸν περὶ τῶν Ἐρινύων λόγον).

1295 [2] *De vita Imperatoris Constantini*, I, 27 (*Opera*, Vol. II, pp. 941-42; English, p. 489): Ἐννοεῖ δῆτα ὁποῖον δέοι θεὸν ἐπιγράψασθαι βοηθόν: ("inquires diligently as to which god he had better call to his aid.")

terest. Supplementary in both stories are combination residues (Class I).

Closely related to residues of restoration of integrity, so much so indeed as sometimes to be confused with them, are residues whereby men, animals, and things are endowed by certain rites with qualities that they do not have and so acquire a certain imaginary integrity. There is no question of restoring an altered integrity. The integrity is created by bringing something that was imperfect to perfection.

1296. V-γ2: *Imaginary or abstract subjects.* Here we get compounds, residues of our V-γ varieties uniting with residues of group-persistence (Class II). Suppose we begin with cases where the latter predominate. The persistence of an abstraction (II-δ) endows it with a personality, the integrity of which may be impaired; and any person with a deep feeling for the abstraction also feels the offence to its integrity, not only as a thing belonging to himself, but also as something belonging to his group, so that the II-δ residues are re-enforced by residues of the IV-β variety (sociality-uniformity).

1297. That explains the penalties which so many peoples in all periods of history have inflicted on offences offered to prevailing religions, popular customs, abstractions of all sorts. To preach that the Father came before the Son, or some other theological heresy of that sort, to utter an ill-calculated hurrah or an unfortunate hiss, to picture on a postcard the pretty figure of Paolina Borghese that Canova immortalized in marble, are deemed serious crimes and profoundly shock many people, not a few of whom are as indulgent as can be towards thieves and murderers. Numberless the cases in centuries past where mobs have risen against heretics, abused them, robbed them, put them to death. The Pan-Germanists of our time will not brook the slightest contradiction of the dogma that proclaims the Germans far superior to all the peoples that have been, are, and ever will be on this Earth of ours, or perhaps even in the solar system, modestly to say nothing of planets possibly gravitating around other suns and of the peoples that may inhabit them. Every now and then a newspaper will print a furious protest on the part of some Pan-Germanist who has turned wild beast (assuming that he was not already one) because a menu in some restaurant has been written in French. Others boil in holy wrath because a railway time-table reads "Genève" instead of "Genf." But then again there are people who lose their minds, again assuming that they once had minds, at the mere thought that a boy and girl may be exchanging love-letters through "General Delivery," when they hear the cooing of two turtle-doves, remark the absence of a fig-leaf "on a marble child exposing his male innocence to light of day"; or—moved by envy or some other form of hate—chance to reflect that somebody somewhere may be feasting his eyes on feminine beauty in the nude. (The conduct of such people, to be sure, often fails to coincide with the moral fury of their preachings.) Unfailingly, of course, deriva-tions supervene to show that such ravings are logical, nay, the very essence of logic, that they hold the public welfare in view as their one and only end; and that those who "introduce new gods into the city" were justly and for the public welfare condemned of yore to drink the hemlock and in our time are justly put into prison or made to pay a fine.[1]

1298. The concrete case commonly shows the following elements:

1. Residues of group-persistence that make it possible for an ab-stract or imaginary subject to be taken as real (II-δ).

2. Some fact, real or imaginary, whereby it is believed, or assumed, that the integrity of some entity has been impaired.

3. Residues of restoration of integrity (V-γ) inspiring acts that are designed to compensate for the supposed offence.

4. Supplementary residues of hostility to alterations in the social equilibrium (V-α).

Derivations transmute imaginary subjects and acts into real sub-jects and acts, and replace the sentiments manifested by the residues with logical and pseudo-experimental inferences.

1299. In other cases the sentiments of group-persistence, though still playing an important rôle, are not altogether predominant. Among the many peoples in widely separated periods of history

1297 [1] [The literary allusion in the text is to Carducci, *A proposito del processo Fadda* (*Poesie*, p. 494).—A. L.]

who have had criminal codes of law, the factor determining the acceptance of the code has been a sentiment made up of the three kinds of residues just mentioned. In general when criminal codes do not exist and the personal vendetta is the rule, the residues of group-persistence are either absent or extremely weak; but they come into play again wherever the vendetta widens in scope and becomes a family or tribal duty. Here again there are derivations to show that the codes have strictly logical motivations—and these are sought now in the will of some deity, now in the wisdom of some semi-divine or very wise lawgiver; now in the sound sense of the forefathers; now in the will of the people; now in some metaphysical abstraction; now in purposes of social welfare, in some pretext of reform for criminals, or some other notion of the sort.

1300. It is interesting that oftentimes all these arguments, however varying and contradictory, work up to the same objective—a fact which clearly shows that the arguments are the secondary things, whereas the main thing is the objective, or rather the sentiment that determined its choice. A man kills another man under such circumstances as not to be justified by public opinion. He is made the target now of a vendetta by the family of his victim, now of the penalties decreed by a god, by a legendary lawgiver, by a sovereign, by the people, by the hair-splitting quibbles of the lawyers—but as the proverb says, all roads lead to Rome, and whatever road is chosen, it leads to the infliction of a certain penalty upon the murderer. Scholars have been trying for centuries and centuries to discover how and why such a penalty can or ought to be inflicted. They have not so far been able to agree on any single theory and continue disputing, each in favour of his own. It is obvious, therefore, that the conclusion precedes the premise not only historically but also logically; and that in turn proves that the conclusion does not follow from the premises, but that the premises are invented to give a reason for the conclusion.

1301. Illuminating in this connexion was a development in France in our day. The humanitarians had to all intents and purposes succeeded in abolishing the death-penalty; the President of France was pardoning as a matter of practice all murderers condemned to death. The parliament was regularly refusing to appropriate money for the fees of the public executioner. Under pressure of derivations, the death-penalty had gone out of existence. Then came the Soleilland affair, a case where a brute raped and cruelly murdered a little girl of humble family. He was condemned to death and then, duly, in line with the humanitarian theories prevailing, his sentence was commuted. But derivations are effective only when they are in harmony with residues, which are the real motors behind human conduct. In the Soleilland case no such harmony prevailed. Residues of personal integrity and group-persistence still functioning in the psychic state of the French people were not in accord with the humanitarian derivation. Events therefore followed a course contrary to the derivation and in accord with the residues.[1] The Presi-

1301 [1] "Scientists" spoke contemptuously of the morbid excitement that the crime aroused in the French public, representing the crime as a product of "prejudices" and of ignorance of their sublime theories. Hesse, *Les criminels peints par eux-mêmes*, pp. 146-47: "It was an impulsive, unpremeditated crime, committed by an individual who was predisposed by his antecedents and vices to just such outrages. That is the truth which the memoirs of Soleilland reveal. Debauchery, excesses, alcoholism, a natural inclination to violence, were all abetted by unfortunate circumstances. How many immoral crimes involving murder of children are committed under just such conditions by just such criminals! [An overstatement to some extent; statistics do not show any great numbers of murders of little girls after rape.] Yet somehow the Soleilland affair has made an unusual impression on public opinion. It is hard to say why. The dramatic discovery of the little girl's body in the parcel-room of a railway station; the fact that the hunt was for many days directed by the fiend himself; the fact that this is the off season for news and that the papers needed something to fill their empty columns—all that may have contributed to work up the sensation. . . . Soleilland's picture completes this gallery of abnormals, whose examinations show that they are fitter subjects for mental pathology than for the criminologist." If this writer, Hesse, really cannot understand why "the Soleilland affair made an unusual impression on public opinion," it can only be that the metaphysics in his theories has deprived him of all grasp over the realities of life. The conduct of the French public was instinctive, like the act of the hen in defending her chicks, of the bitch or the lioness in defending her young. The public did not intend to allow brutes like Soleilland to go on raping and murdering little girls under the wing of psychiatrists, with their dictionary of ten-syllabled terms, and the criminal lawyers allied with them. M. Hesse should be made to see that the reasons underlying the conduct of such fiends are of little or no importance. The important thing is to get them destroyed, the way rattlesnakes, mad dogs, and rats with the bubonic plague are destroyed. To fan Hesse's righteous indignation to white heat we must also tell him, and people like him, that

dent of France had to resign himself to signing death-warrants again. The parliament again began to vote appropriations for the public executioner; and the worst murderers again began to wend their way to the guillotine. Something very much the same occurred later on when the Bonnot and Garnier gang set out to spread destruction far and wide among law-abiding citizens. The instinct of self-preservation was again aroused in the public.[2] And something of the sort, though on a far smaller scale, took place in Switzerland. A well-meaning jury at Interlaken had inflicted an insignificant penalty upon the "heroine" Tatiana Leontiev. Logically enough the Russian Terrorists concluded that Switzerland was getting to be a favourable climate for their exploits; so before long they tried to "expropriate" a bank at Montreux, "executing," or in plain English murdering, such employees of the bank as resisted them. But the Swiss public reawakened to good sense, and the instinct of self-

the extenuating circumstances which he alleges, to wit, "debauchery, excesses, alcoholism, natural inclinations to violence," and let us add, as a special favour to him, atavisms from alcoholic and half-witted ancestors, are not extenuating but rather aggravating circumstances from the standpoint of social defence, since they increase rather than diminish the probability that the eminent individuals blessed with such traits of character will commit crimes of rape and murder. The French public understood instinctively that the one practical effect of all the chatter about "abnormals who are fitter subjects for mental pathology than for the criminologist" was to allow said "abnormals" to continue committing crimes to the damage of "normals," who, for their part, refused to tolerate any such thing, and rose in self-defence as does an animal when its life is threatened. If the metaphysics of our criminologists suffers in consequence, that is of course a great pity; but perhaps not so much of a pity as to allow little girls to go on being raped and murdered with impunity.

1301 [2] *Liberté*, May 6, 1912: "M. Herriot, mayor of Lyons, has also bidden good-bye to humanitarianism, born 1898, died 1912. He writes this morning: 'We demand that an end be put to this counterfeit sentimentality, which is just a caricature of self-respecting kind-heartedness. We demand that the presidential pardon shall cease to be what a courageous magistrate has called "a premium on murder." This business of extenuating circumstances is being carried too far. Reprieves are being carried too far, and the privilege-of-review period should be lengthened from five to eight years. Instead of heaping the graves of policemen killed in course of duty with flowers, more severity should be shown to those who shoot them.' One thing is clear. Yesterday's policy of turning the other cheek is going to lead in France to a policy of night-stick and cudgel."

preservation won out over the stupidities of the humanitarians.[3]

1302. In the matter of anti-militarism and anti-patriotism theories have not changed in France and in Italy during recent years. But for some reason or other Class IV residues (sociality), and especially δ residues of that Class (self-sacrifice), have changed in intensity; so that juries and judges have been convicting for anti-militaristic and anti-patriotic offences for which they formerly acquitted, and meantime there has not been the slightest change in the laws.[1] The Italian Government expelled Hervé, a man whom a few years before, during the period of benevolent indulgence for detractors of the army, it would at least have regarded with indifference. The wise change as times change! Here the facts are more striking than

1301 [3] Similar cases might be mentioned for all countries in all periods of history.

1302 [1] Colajanni, *Rivista popolare,* Dec. 31, 1911, p. 653: "In the preceding number of this review we called attention to the 'new spirit' that has come over the Italian courts since Nationalism has been on the rampage. . . . Optimists have been objecting that the instances mentioned in my article might very well be regarded as accidental idiosyncrasies of individual magistrates. Today that objection is left without a leg to stand on, because arrests, prosecutions, and convictions for incendiary editorials, incitements to striking and class-hatred, and other essentially political and essentially elastic crimes, are taking place everywhere. Convictions on such counts are reported from Ferrara. De Ambris and Zocchi are arrested at Parma. Giusquiano is under arrest at Pisa. A warrant is out for Lori at Florence. . . . This sudden outburst of reactionary fury has been ascribed to orders issued by the Minister of Justice and Pardons. I do not believe that. I happen to know that Signor Finocchiaro-Aprile, the minister in question, is a man entirely stranger to reactionary sentiments. The explanation is quite different. Our magistrates . . . showed special leniency to Socialists when they had reason to believe that the Socialists were all-powerful in high circles. Today they have reason to believe that the Government's outlook has changed. Now they are hoping to win promotions by siding with the Nationalists and Clericals. So there they are, arresting, prosecuting, convicting." Very well—but why did the "Government's outlook" change? Professor Colajanni himself reveals the secret: "Down to yesterday the Nationalists were satisfied with writing patriotic songs. Now they have an excited public on their side [The primary cause of the change.] and they are now resorting to violence in direct ratio to the amount of leeway accorded them by the police. . . . They spat upon Professor Bonfigli and beat him. They jeered a magistrate because he thought it his right to rise from his seat in a theatre when he saw fit. With the aid of police in uniform and in plain clothes, they lifted the critic of the *Avanti* bodily from his seat at the Scala and threw him out of the building because he refused to rise when the 'Royal March' was being played."

usual because a single cause and a single effect are involved, and because the change has taken place in such a short time. But they are in all respects similar to developments in criminal law where numbers of causes are mixed in together with many effects and which take place over longer periods of time. Criminal law reflects residues more directly than civil law. That is why civil law is oftentimes more logical than criminal law.

1303. Religions involving metempsychosis have souls reborn in human beings or animals for purposes of purification. Plato too speaks imaginatively of such a thing in the *Republic* and the *Timaeus,* books in which that illustrious dreamer, who still has his admirers among the people of our time, delivers himself of the grossest absurdities conceivable as to the manner in which this world of ours is made.[1] But even towards the person who is removed for good and all from this Earth, a sentiment of integrity endures that combines the many residues of Class II to determine the conduct of the living towards the dead.

1304. In the *Iliad,* XXIII, vv. 71-74, Patroclus asks Achilles to bury him promptly, that he may enter the abode of the dead.[1] So and for the same reason in the *Odyssey,* XI, vv. 51-56, the shade of Elpenor appeals to Ulysses. Virgil's Aeneas, *Aeneid,* VI, vv. 325-30,

1303 [1] *E.g., Timaeus,* 90-92: "Those among created men who were effeminate and led unholy lives were doubtless changed into women in their second existence." And the good soul goes on to impart "that then the gods set about creating a desire for copulation"—and explains at length how such union takes place. There are many other interesting things. He says for instance, 91E, that the simple and the naïve become birds, counting in that class anybody not altogether satisfied with his metaphysical poppycock. People ignorant of philosophy become four-legged animals and beasts of prey. The worst of them do not even get legs, but crawl on their bellies. Idiots and dullards (92B) generally become fish, because the gods did not deem them worthy of breathing a purer air.

1304 [1] "Bury me betimes that I may pass within the portals of Hades. The souls of the dead are keeping me off and allow me not to join their company beyond the river. So am I left wandering about Hades." On v. 73 the scholiast remarks (Dindorf, Vol. II, p. 250): "The [verse is marked with] a critical sign, because unburied souls remain without the river and mingle not with those who are in Erebus. The [same] critical sign also marks verses that are to be suppressed (*Odyssey,* XI, vv. 38-43)." The implication would be that the tradition was not Homeric. But that fact has no bearing on our study here. It is enough for our purposes to know that it was current in ancient Greece.

sees the souls of unburied bodies wandering about for a hundred years before they are allowed to enter Erebus.[2] Dante, *Purgatorio,* III, vv. 136-41, sees the souls of those who died in contumacy of Holy Church detained in the ante-Purgatory for thirty times as long a period as they spent in their presumption.[3] Residues remain the same, while derivations expand, diversify, change.

1305. This residue, again, underlies the Catholic derivation of Purgatory and the various liturgical devices for restoring the integrity of souls detained there. Jesting in the *Philopseudes,* 27 (Harmon, Vol. III, pp. 361-63), upon the superstitions of his time, Lucian has Eucrates describe the apparition of his wife, Demaenete, to him after her death: "On the seventh day after her death I was lying on this couch just as I am now. . . . And lo, Demaenete herself enters and sits down at my side. . . . At sight of her, I threw my arms about her and began to weep and moan. But she bade me dry my tears, and began upbraiding me because I had promised to offer her in sacrifice her whole trousseau, yet had I not burned one of her gold-embroidered sandals; and she told me that the sandal would be found under the chest, whither it had fallen—and for that reason

---

1304 [2] Lines 329-30 are an imitation of the passages in Homer:

> "*Centum errant annos volitantque haec litora circum,*
> *tum demum admissi stagna exoptata revisunt.*"

("A hundred years they wander flitting about the shores [of Acheron]. Then, admitted at last, they come to see the pools they so long to reach.") The line preceding, v. 325, reads:

> "*Haec omnis quam cernis inops inhumataque turba est.*"

("All these you see here are a throng of the poor and unburied.") Servius comments (Thilo-Hagen, Vol. II, p. 56): "People without legitimate, even symbolic, burial. Poor, without (*inopem*) [the rite of] throwing earth [upon the dead], *ops* meaning earth, in other words, without burial. He wants to show that symbolic burial [as in the cenotaph (*inanem*)] is as effective as plenary burial."

1304 [3]

> "'Tis true who in contumacy hath died
> Of Holy Church, though he repent at last
> Still needs must wait upon this shore outside
> Full thirty-fold the time that obdurate
> He hath been in presumption, if such ban
> Do not indeed deserving prayers abate."

(Fletcher translation.)

we had not found it and so had burned only one. We had still a great deal to say when a bark came from a wretched Maltese terrier that was under the bed, and at that sound she vanished. We found the sandal under the chest, and made haste to burn it." In the same work, 31 (Harmon, *loc. cit.,* pp. 367-69), Lucian has Arignotus tell a story of a ghost who had been haunting a house but disappeared when the body was found and buried.

1306. That story has numberless counterparts among pagans and Christians alike. The person who has died appears as a ghost and haunts people until provision has been made, among the pagans for his burial, among the Christians for his burial plus masses, prayers, and other rites in his behalf. The origin of the derivation is apparent enough. Pliny the Younger, *Epistulae,* VII, 27, tells a story of a house in Athens that was haunted by a ghost. The philosopher Athenodorus rents the house at a bargain. A ghost in chains appears. He follows it till the ghost vanishes at a certain spot. On digging into the ground there, bones are found in chains. They are given honourable burial, and the ghost gives no more trouble.[1]

1307. Among Christians the ghost asks for prayers. But the derivation lengthens and lengthens, since there may be doubt as to whether the request is not made by a devil rather than by the soul of the dead.[1] Says Tertullian: "We make yearly oblations for the dead, and on the birthdays of martyrs. . . . If you ask Scripture for light on these disciplines and others of the kind, you find nothing. But it will

1306 [1] Suetonius, *Gaius Caligula,* 59: "His [Caligula's] body was secretly conveyed to the gardens of the Lamian family, half burned on a hastily constructed pyre, and covered with a little earth. Later on it was disinterred, burned, and buried by his sisters on their return from exile. It is well attested that before that was done, the custodians of the gardens were pestered by ghosts."

1307 [1] Calmet, *Dissertations sur les apparitions,* XLIII (pp. 129-30): *"One should beware of ghosts that ask for prayers.* Ordinarily apparitions of the dead ask for prayers, masses, pilgrimages, restitutions or payments of debts that they had not met, which would go to show that they are in Purgatory and need the help of the living in their sufferings. . . . But one must be on one's attentive guard against such apparitions and solicitations. . . . In his *De la démonomanie* (Bk. 3, cap. 6, p. 157) Bodin mentions more than one example of demons that have appeared in that manner, asking for prayers and even assuming the guise of persons praying over the graves of the dead to give the impression that the soul in question needed prayers."

be shown you that their authority is tradition, their evidence custom, and their observance faith."[2] That, really, tallies exactly with the known facts. The residue of restoration of integrity gives rise to this or that derivation which appears in tradition, is confirmed and modified by custom, and ends by becoming a matter of faith.

1308. In its doctrine of Purgatory the Catholic Church merely gives definite form to derivations from a residue that is as ancient as the history of our Western races, and of many other races too, and which has come down to our time from a day when libations were being poured on the graves of the dead in many countries in Europe.[1] The doctrine may have profited by the existence of the residue, as it may have profited by other social forces; but it cannot have created it, since it had existed for centuries and centuries before the Church was born. Dom Calmet therefore is altogether in the right when he says, *Op. cit.,* LXXX, p. 239: "Those who contend that all the talk about ghosts and apparitions of souls is a mere invention of members of the clergy selfishly interested in holding people to such beliefs, overlook the fact that the ancient pagans, who derived no advantage from such apparitions, and the Barbarians, for instance those of the North, who never went into subtleties in such matters, speak of spirits, apparitions, hobgoblins, demons, and good genii in virtually the same terms as Christians and churchmen." But a

1307 [2] *De corona militis,* 3-4 (*Opera,* Vol. IV, pp. 293-94; English, Vol. I, pp. 336-37): *"Oblationes pro defunctis, pro nataliciis annua die facimus. . . . Harum et aliarum eiusmodi disciplinarum si legem expostules scripturarum nullam invenies. Traditio tibi praetendetur auctrix, consuetudo confirmatrix et fides observatrix."*

1308 [1] The Annamites of China have rites for delivering the souls of the dead from torment. Diguet, *Les Annamites,* pp. 192-93: *"Rite of the 'Lam Chay,' or solemn fast for the delivery of souls in torment.* These rites have the sole purpose of getting out of Hell certain souls that may be detained there on one account or another and may as a consequence of their unhappiness become harmful to their former families. When a person has died on an unlucky day or his grave is located in an ill-chosen spot, or even if some one of the countless rules for ritual that govern funerals has been omitted, Annamite families are convinced that all their misfortunes are ascribable to that untoward circumstance. . . . Among the reasons that may bring a soul to distress must be counted sins of all sorts that have to be purged by sufferings in the other world. . . . Rites during the fast are directed by the magician, or Thay-phu-thuy ('Master-Wood-Water'), who gets his name from his use of a wand and of holy water during services. . . . The delivery of the dead is sometimes made the occasion for a great memorial festival to which hundreds of guests are invited."

further error is common enough. That is to conclude that since such phenomena are not fraudulent they must necessarily be genuine. No such dilemma confronts us. There is a third hypothesis that oftentimes accords with the facts, namely, that the phenomena in question merely manifest the subjective existence of certain residues, which persist in time and assume numerous and ever changing forms.

1309. The Council of Trent declares it to be the teaching of the Catholic Church that "there is a Purgatory and that the souls therein detained profit by the prayers of the faithful and especially by the very acceptable sacrifice of the altar."[1] If one chose to epitomize in similar language the beliefs of our Graeco-Roman and, more generally still, of our Indo-European ancestors on this subject, one might say that "there is a place (the abode of ῞Αιδης, the abode of the *inferi*) where the souls are detained, and that such souls profit by the religious rites which the living perform in their honour and that each soul profits by the food which his descendants place on his grave." Ordinarily people who lay the prime stress on derivations feel that there is an abyss between the two beliefs. Those who regard the study of social phenomena as a mere pretext for preaching "virtue" or "progress" will be outraged that anyone should dare to compare a belief where the peace of the dead depends, in part at least, on their righteous behaviour on Earth with another belief in which it depends upon mechanical acts such as libations and offerings of food.

1310. Both are right if we look at things from the standpoint from which they are pleased to consider them. But there is another

1309 [1] *Canones et decreta Concilii Tridentini, sessio XXV (De Purgatorio)* (Richter, p. 391; Schaff, Vol. II, p. 198): "*Cum catholica ecclesia . . . docuerit purgatorium esse animasque ibi detentas fidelium suffragiis potissimum vero acceptabili altaris sacrificio iuvari.*" And *cf. Ibid., sessio* VI: *De iustificatione,* 30 (Richter, p. 33; Schaff, Vol. II, p. 117): "If anyone shall say that after the acceptance of the grace of justification the sin of any penitent sinner is so remitted, and the guilt of eternal damnation is so obliterated, that no guilt remains [requiring] temporal [temporary] punishment to be paid in this world, or in the world to come in Purgatory, before entrance to the Kingdom of Heaven can be granted (*patere*), let him be anathema."

standpoint, the strictly scientific standpoint, from which social phenomena are studied much as the naturalist studies plants and animals. From that standpoint the two beliefs are in every respect similar. They are derivations from residues of group-persistence and residues of restoration of altered integrity.

1311. The integrity of the corpse as well as the integrity of the soul may be altered. There are many stories of the dead bodies of excommunicates rising from their graves and leaving the churches where they were buried at the words, read by an acolyte, "Let non-communicants retire." [1] There is another pretty story about the incorruptibility of bodies of excommunicates. Says Dom Calmet, *Op. cit.,* pp. 344-45: "There is a very ancient belief that the bodies of excommunicates do not decay. That appears in the life of St. Libentius, Archbishop of Bremen, who died January 4, 1013. That

1311 [1] St. Gregory (the Great), *Dialogi,* II, 23 (missing in Migne; Gardner, pp. 84-85): Two nuns were great gossips, and their sins were reported to St. Benedict: "On hearing this of them, the man of God sent to them at once, saying: 'Chasten your tongues, for if you do not mend your ways, I shall excommunicate you.' This sentence of excommunication he uttered not as a pronouncement but as a threat. But they in no wise changed from their original habits, and within a few days died and were buried in the church. And it came to pass that whenever masses were being celebrated in the church, at the customary words called aloud by a deacon, 'Let non-communicants retire,' their nurse, who had all along been making offerings to the Lord for masses in their behalf, would see them rise from their graves and leave the church. After remarking several times that they left the church at the summons of the deacon and were unable to remain within, she recalled the words that the Saint had said to them in their lifetime, that he would bar them from communion unless they mended their ways and words. When this thing was reported to the Saint, he was filled with great sorrow and straightway made an oblation in his own behalf with the words, 'Go, and have a mass said for them, and they will no longer be excommunicate.' And when the oblation had been offered in a mass, at the customary summons of the deacon that non-communicants should retire from the church, they were no longer seen to depart." Their integrity, in other words, had been restored by the oblation and their bodies were no longer constrained to leave their graves. In the same dialogues, II, 24 (Gardner, p. 86), Gregory tells of a monk who died in a state of disobedience to his abbot. He was buried, but every time his body was put under ground, the earth vomited it forth. St. Benedict ordered that a consecrated host be placed on the breast of the body, and it was never again cast forth by the earth. Admirers of mediaeval "science" should not forget that in those times so dear to them little stories such as the above were accepted as true by everyone. The judgment passed upon them in our day is more in conformity with the facts.

holy prelate had excommunicated a number of pirates. One of them died and was buried in Norway. Seventy years later his body was found whole and without trace of decay, and it fell to dust only when it had received absolution from Bishop Alvaredo. To win prestige for their schism and show that the gift of miracles and the episcopal prerogative of binding and loosing subsists in their Church more visibly and certainly than in the Latin and Roman Church, the modern Greeks maintain that with them too the bodies of excommunicates are incorrupt." [2] It is a matter of common knowledge that the bodies of saints are also incorruptible. As usual the same derivation proves now heads, now tails.

1312. V-δ: *Restoration of integrity by acts pertaining to the offender.* There is a sentiment that impels animals and human beings to hurt those who have hurt them, to return evil for evil. Until that has been done a person experiences a sense of discomfort, as if something were wrong with him. His integrity has been altered, and it does not recover its original state until he has performed certain acts pertaining to his aggressor. Typical are the sentiments underlying vendettas or duels.[1]

1313. V-δ1: *Real offender.* This is by far the most important variety, in fact virtually the only one we need to consider. The offence

1311 [2] Dom Calmet further states, p. 346: "The modern Greeks tell the story that under Manuel (or Maximus), Patriarch of Constantinople in the fifteenth century, the Turkish Emperor of Constantinople determined to know the truth as to the claims the Greeks made about the incorruptibility of people who died in their excommunication. The Patriarch ordered the opening of the grave of a woman who had had criminal commerce with an Archbishop of Constantinople. Her body was found intact, blackened and greatly swollen. The Turks enclosed the body in a coffin under the Emperor's seal. The Patriarch offered prayer, giving absolution to the dead woman. Three days later the coffin was opened, and the body was found to have fallen to dust." On such beliefs, Huet, Bishop of Avranches, comments (Lenglet-Dufresnoy, *Traité . . . sur les apparitions,* Vol. II, p. 175): "I am not considering whether the facts as reported are true or whether it is just a question of a popular error. Certain it is that they are vouched for by so many skilled and trustworthy writers and by so many eyewitnesses that one must be very careful in reaching a decision."

1312 [1] Cunningham, *Two Years in New South Wales,* Vol. II, p. 34: "In common with almost all savages, revenge with them is never satiated till quenched in the blood of an adversary. Like the Chinese, they are not particular about the person, but if a *white* injures them, they generally satisfy their rage upon the first of that colour they can conveniently meet with."

frequently affects more or less extensive groups even if it is done to one individual member. Relatives of the victim, his dependants, companions, fellow citizens, and even animals—the dog defending its master, for example—may feel the offence as done to them, that their integrity has been altered; and so the need of a restoration of integrity may arise in them and prompt them to react against the offender. Whence, in their many varieties, the obligation of vengeance and the right to blood-money, which are observable among barbarous or semi-civilized peoples. Such residues often blend with the residues of the V-α variety (social equilibrium). Even among civilized peoples of our day, if a citizen of one country is harmed in a foreign country his government often takes the offence as a pretext for exacting indemnity. That is a mere logical act. But many people are led to approve of it by the identical sentiment that in olden times made vengeance a duty. A European is murdered in an uncivilized country. A village where none of the guilty parties are to be found is bombarded and numbers of innocent people are killed. The integrity of the citizens of the civilized country is restored at the expense of the inhabitants of the uncivilized country. The sum of sentiments designated by the term "hatred" may be at least partially classed with this variety. Fear very often lies at the bottom of hatred both in men and in animals. In many cases when the fear goes, hatred turns to contempt. In general terms, hatred arises from a desire to repel an attack on one's integrity. Vigorous conviction is an element in integrity, and that explains the violence of theological hatreds. Hatred wanes when faith wanes, or when the individual no longer considers the faith an essential part of his personality. The artist, the writer, the poet, are led not only by vanity, but also by a profound feeling for their arts, to see an offence to their individual integrity in any contrary expression of opinion, or even in mere silence. Oftentimes any change in the existing state of things is deemed an offence and is repelled by attachment to tradition—neophobia.

1314. Tatiana Leontiev was let off with a light penalty by a very enlightened jury at Interlaken. She had killed an unlucky individual by the name of Müller, mistaking him for the Russian minister Durnovo, upon whose person the heroine had intended, so she averred, to wreak vengeance for the mistreatment of Socialists in Russia. Asked by the Court whether she were not sorry for her mistake, she replied in the negative: "Anyhow, this Mr. Müller was a *burjui* too!" The harpy's reasoning—it was accepted, notice, by those kind-hearted jurymen—may be stated as follows: A *bourgeois,* Durnovo, had offended the Russian Socialists. It was therefore "just" to kill a Mr. Müller who had not the remotest share in the doings of Durnovo, but was, however, a *bourgeois.*

1315. From the logical standpoint the reasoning is idiotic. But it gets its force not from its logic but from the sentiments that it expresses—and they correspond to residues of restoration of integrity. To avenge one of its subjects the Russian Government kills people who have in no way offended the subject, but are of the same nation as the offender. To avenge certain of her friends (among whom some were shown to have been very friendly indeed) Tatiana Leontiev murders an unlucky Müller who has had no imaginable part in the offences complained of, but who did belong to the same class as the offender—the *bourgeoisie.* In both cases the integrity of certain *A*'s has been altered, and it is restored by altering the integrity of certain *B*'s. As for the jurymen, they thought that the integrity of certain humanitarian beliefs of theirs had been impaired by the Russian Government and therefore regarded as excusable any act that had as its cause or pretext a design to restore that integrity.

1316. Why Tatiana Leontiev should have fixed upon Mr. Müller as the scapegoat remains a mystery. She might have chosen her own father. He was not only a *bourgeois* but actually an employee of the Russian Government. She might have chosen one of those jurymen, for they, good souls, were also *bourgeois.* Why, furthermore, should she have thought it proper to lead a life of luxury on the money that she received from a *bourgeois* father and which came from the Russian Government? Why, finally, should humanitarians be so particular about killing a mad dog when they are quite willing to leave the world at the mercy of the worst criminals or half-wits? However, it is altogether idle to look for logical reasons for non-logical conduct.

1317. An individual who is barred from a group finds that his integrity has been altered in that simple fact, and the alteration may be felt so keenly as to serve as a very heavy penalty indeed. Even though there is no actual exclusion, the mere declaration that a person's integrity no longer subsists may be equivalent to a penalty inflicted by force.

1318. That explains why in a number of primitive legal systems sentences without sanctions of any kind, and for the execution of which no public authority is designated, are quite the rule. Jurists who are surprised at such things need only reflect that in our own day we still have decisions by "courts of honour" which are of the very same nature. There is no force of public authority to execute such decisions. The mere statement of one may be a penalty much more severe than the day or so in prison inflicted by formal sentence of an ordinary court. There may be indirect sanctions for a sentence that has no direct sanctions, for the integrity of the individual upon whom it bears is altered by it, and in consequence of it he no longer stands on a par with other individuals previously his equals. But such a consequence is in any event accessory. The prime fact is that integrity has been declared altered by certain authorized persons. Caesar, *De bello Gallico,* VI, 13, observed that in Gaul sentences passed by the Druids derived their force from just such indirect consequences.[1] He might have compared that with the *nota censoria* of the Romans or with the *sacer esto* declaration of ancient Roman

1318 [1] "They [the Druids] rule on almost all disputes public or private. If a crime has been committed, a murder for instance, if there is some dispute about an inheritance or over property-bounds, it is they who decide, making awards and fixing punishments. If any one, be he a private individual or an official of state, does not abide by their decree, they bar him from the sacrifices. [Likewise the only weapon available to the Christian priesthood when their faith was still persecuted and had not as yet won the support of the secular power.] That penalty is a very serious one with them. A person under such interdict is classed with the impious and criminal. [Alteration of integrity, the main effect of the declaration or sentence.] He is shunned by everyone. No one will talk to him or be seen in his company, lest some untoward consequence be incurred from the contact. He cannot sue

law.[2] In the concrete case a number of different residues are usually operative. But outstanding in the instances mentioned is a residue whereby the wrongdoer is declared stripped of his integrity. He loses status: he is expelled from the group. The ancient laws of Ireland yield similar cases, which Maine appositely compares with others arising under Hindu law to which we have already alluded (§ 551).[3]

1319. The state of mind in which one alteration of integrity is met with another alteration of the same sort gives rise to the exceedingly numerous rules that determine the nature and amount of the compensatory alteration. As for the quantum, we start with the very simple rules of the old-time "head-money" (*talio*) and come down

for justice, nor obtain any public office (*honos*)." [Indirect consequences of the alteration of integrity.]

1318 [2] Jhering, *Geist des römischen Rechts,* Vol. I, pp. 279-81 (Pt. I, § 18): "The *homo sacer* lived in a state of religious and temporal proscription. Handed over (*sacer*) to the vengeance of the divinity he had outraged by his crime, barred as a consequence from all human intercourse, his property confiscated and sold for the benefit of the treasury of the gods, he could be killed by anybody at will. Did status as *sacer* carry any penalty with it? I believe not. Of course, if by penalty one means the troubles ensuing on a crime, to be declared *sacer* was the heaviest penalty imaginable. There was no terror that it did not involve. It represented the extreme degree of persecution and humiliation. The [public] enemy had no rights, but what made the situation of the *homo sacer* worse was the psychological element, his consciousness of being an object of loathing, horror, execration, to men and gods, of being a source of mortal contagion [The most extreme form of alteration of integrity.], of being shunned by everyone. [Consequences of the alteration.] Once existing, the declaration *sacer esse* was a resource the law may have used, but it was not established by legislation, any more than the infamy that went with it. [Residues provoke legislation. They never derive from legislation save in some few exceptional cases.] The lawgiver never thinks up such institutions as the penalty of the *sacer* or infamy, or if he does, as when the privilege of wearing the national cockade is withdrawn, he altogether misses fire. Institutions of that sort emanate from the very heart of the people and from nowhere else. They are a spontaneous expression of the moral sense of the public at large. [Drop the "moral" and that may stand.] They are a sentence of condemnation pronounced and executed by the people as a whole." [No, they express majority sentiments and nothing more.]

1318 [3] *Early History of Institutions,* p. 43: ". . . in ancient Ireland it is at least doubtful whether there was ever, in our sense of the words, a central government; it is also doubtful whether the public force at the command of any ruler or rulers was ever systematically exerted through the mechanism of Courts of Justice; and it is at least a tenable view that the institutions which stood in the place of Courts of Justice only exercised jurisdiction through the voluntary submission of intending litigants." That is true, translating ancient psychology into modern juridical terms. Using the language of the time, we would say that the pronouncements of the

to the "dosimetric" system—as Enrico Ferri styled it—of the Zanardelli code in Italy, a system as ridiculous as it is "scientific." [1]

1320. **V-δ2:** *Imaginary or abstract offender.* This residue is clearly apparent in cases where people pick quarrels with their fetish, or with some saint, spiritual being, or god. The countless examples that might be cited may be epitomized as follows:

1. Men treat the imaginary being as a real being. They praise him, blame him, glorify him, revile him, bargain with him, vowing him gifts if he gets them what they want, threatening him with harm if he fails to stand by them; decking his image with garlands if he satisfies them, neglecting him, insulting him, even thrashing him, if he disappoints them.

2. These simple associations of ideas and the non-logical actions corresponding to them are subsequently explained and justified by derivations. The imaginary being may be regarded as uniformly good. The pact then takes the form of a simple promise to show gratitude with gifts—for instance, the contract which the Romans used to make with Jupiter that he might bring them victory, or the vows of gifts made by modern Catholics to St. Anthony of Padua if he enables them to recover articles they have lost. He may be considered sometimes good and sometimes evil, and the effort then is to treat him in such a way that he will be good. Or he may be considered chiefly or exclusively evil, and the effort then is to humour him by treating him well, or to punish him by abuse. Finally he may be considered as essentially evil—the case of the

Brehons (Irish jurists) had the prerogative of declaring what a man was, of judging the character of his conduct. It was that declaration, supported by public opinion, which dealt the more or less serious blow to the man whose integrity was altered by it. Of the Brehons Maine writes, p. 52: "No authority of our day is possibly comparable with that of the men who, in an utterly uncritical age, simply said of the legal rule, 'So it has been laid down by the learned,' or used the still more impressive formula, 'It is written.'" But "courts of honour" in our time function in exactly the same way, and the most that they can say of the laws they follow is, "Such is the custom!"—a procedure no whit less arbitrary than saying, "It is written."

1319 [1] This is not the place to go into such questions. The situation is complicated, showing a substratum of residues of one sort or another overspread with derivations of greater or lesser complexity.

Devil of the Christians. He then deserves nothing but abuse.[1] So we go step by step from the simple association of ideas to the ingenious and complicated theology; but residues remain under the varying derivations essentially the same.

1321. Well known the fact that peoples who have fetishes discard or abuse them on proper grounds of dissatisfaction, and without, apparently, any great amount of thinking.[1] So it is with Italian peasant women of our day when they abuse the image of a saint who has not done them the favour asked, and with people who curse and swear not out of bad manners, but in the deliberate intent of insulting God or the Virgin—and the trait is by no means confined to illiterates. Ancient Greece admired the poems of Homer, which represent mortals as quarrelling and battling with gods. In more ancient times that does not seem to have been in the least shocking. Later on, Plato waxes wroth at the adventures of Homer's deities, and still later, in annotating the Homeric poems the Alexandrines try to reduce them to less impious readings. In the *Iliad*, XXII, v. 20, Achilles addresses Apollo exactly as Letourneau's Negro did his fetish when he says: "Surely I would avenge myself on thee

1320 [1] In *L'évolution religieuse dans les diverses races humaines*, pp. 70-71, Letourneau notes that the Kaffir *morimo* "is a general term serving to designate spirits and ghosts. . . . All calamities are ascribable to the *morimos*, and they are ordinarily heaped with abuse. The missionaries found it impossible to convince the natives that God, the Christian God, could disapprove of their insulting the *morimos*. The Kaffirs think of the *morimos* as invisible human beings, and they would be glad enough to kill them if that were possible. 'If I could only get at him, and run him through with my spear!' said a Kaffir chief in speaking of a *morimo*." The Kaffirs, according to Letourneau, have another term, *thiko*, which Moffat defines as a "malignant, devil-like spirit—sometimes Death. The Hottentots are thinking of the *thiko* when they shoot poisoned arrows at the sky during a storm, evidently hoping to hit him and kill him." [Surprising that Pareto did not comment that the *thikos* and *morimos* are variables—derivations. The theme of "shooting God" or "killing God" is trite in European folk humor. In Jean Aicard's *Adventures de Gospard de Besse*, an episode is entitled: *L'homme qui a tué Dieu*. A marksman misses a partridge on a point blank shot, attributes the humiliation to the Eternal Father, and shoots his remaining cartridge at the sky.—A. L.]

1321 [1] Letourneau, *Ibid.*, p. 95: "For that matter, unless a fetish is particularly feared it is dropped as soon as it fails to give satisfaction. The Negro in Guinea treats his fetish exactly like a human being. Before changing one he will give it a thrashing to teach it to obey. If he wants to conceal his conduct from a fetish, he hides the fetish inside his belt."

had I power in me!" Diomed, *Iliad,* V, vv. 383-402, assaults Aphrodite and afterwards Ares too. There is a show of justification, since Athena stands as counsellor and protector of Diomed, who may so be regarded as a tool that Athena uses in striking at Ares. To console Aphrodite, her daughter Dione reminds her that many gods have had to endure terrible sufferings at the hands of mortal men. Again in the *Iliad,* III, vv. 390-417, Helen gives Aphrodite a piece of her mind.[2] At a much later period we find a similar incident in the *Dionysiaca* of Nonnus of Panopolis, XLVIII, vv. 689-98, where, furious at her violation by Dionysus, the nymph Aura runs to the temple of Aphrodite and flogs the statue of the goddess.[3] From the standpoint of historical reality the two stories are equally imaginary. As indices of sentiments, the values are not quite the same. The popularity of the *Iliad* in the early days proves that Helen's blasphemy did not shock the Greeks of those times; the story of Helen therefore registered very general sentiments. The story of Aura in the *Dionysiaca* merely registered the sentiments of a limited number of lettered people, and may be nothing more than a poetic device.

1322. Plato's indignation at the poets for the stories that they tell of the gods [1] is a reaction of logic against such associations of non-logical ideas. But the people who believed such tales by no means drew from them all the logical implications they might contain, and their reverence for the gods was not in the least diminished by them. So in our day a woman may berate a saint for not granting her favours and still not lose her reverence for him; just as the revivalists in Wales lose none of their esteem for leaders who show themselves skilled gamblers in the stock-market; nor our "proletarians" theirs for leaders who coin money with their Socialism, or rate as "prole-

1321 [2] Aphrodite is trying to induce Helen to make up to Paris. Helen is unwilling and loses her temper with the goddess: "Go and sit by his side yourself! Withdraw from the pathways of the gods and never again set foot on Olympus!" Aphrodite replies: "Provoke me not, wench that thou art!" The scholiast, v. 395 (Dindorf, Vol. I, p. 162), finds Helen's rebuke blasphemous and the goddess's rejoinder unseemly.

1321 [3] In *Ibid.,* XXX, vv. 192-208, comes the story of the death of Alcimacheia, who had gone so far as to flog the statue of Hera.

1322 [1] *Respublica,* II, 17, 377D-78; III, 3-5, 389-92.

tarians" by the labels they flaunt but as wealthy *"bourgeois"* by their bank-accounts.[2]

1323. Pausanias, *Periegesis,* III, *Laconia,* 15, 10-11, mentions a statue of Aphrodite that had shackled feet and explains that according to one legend it was an allegory devised by Tyndareus to show that women ought to be subject to their husbands. According to another it was his revenge on Aphrodite for her share in the crimes of his daughters, Helen and Clytemnestra. Pausanias thinks it ridiculous to imagine that one could get even with a deity by punishing a wooden image of her in that manner. Arrian, *De expeditione Alexandri,* VII, 14, repeats a story, though without any great faith in it himself, that in his great sorrow for the death of Hephestion Alexander the Great ordered the temple of Aesculapius destroyed to punish that god for not saving his friend. On the day when Germanicus died, according to Suetonius, *Gaius Caligula,* 5, "mobs stoned the temples of the gods and demolished their altars, some families casting their household gods into the street and exposing all infants born on that day."[1] Weird as such sentiments may seem, they have their counterparts even in our time, and not only in the ignorant crowds in Naples who hoot at San Gennaro if the blood is slow in coming to a boil, but among the educated as well.[2]

1322 [2] When Bebel died in 1913, he left a fortune of almost a million francs. Even granting the reductions his friends insisted should be made, it still amounted to several hundred thousand francs.

1323 [1] *"Qvo defunctus est die lapidata sunt templa, subversae Deum arae, Lares a quibusdam familiares in publicum abiecti, partus coniugum expositi."*

1323 [2] Consider, for example, the notion of some humanitarians that strict solidarity exists between man and God. But that is mild; one of them, a Protestant pastor, urges mankind to encourage God and bids Him have no fear: Monot, *Un athée,* pp. 36-37 (The preacher voices the opinion that if evil exists in the world, it is because God cannot prevent it): "Well, that vanquished God I hear speaking in my heart! . . . God strives to abolish evil and does not always succeed. . . . At such times, as we contemplate spectacles of iniquity or unexplainable unhappiness, we might use the following language for our faith, in a sublime talk with our heavenly Father: 'Fear not, I have no suspicion of Thee! I know that Thou hast not deceived us in these things. If I believed that, I should be in despair!' . . . All the same, to pray to the Father . . . is to ally our impotence with His impotence and say to Him: 'If we are defeated we shall fail together! Nothing is lost! I am still Thy child!' " A person who takes such gibberish seriously might just as well believe that Diomed struck Aphrodite with his sword.

1324. Class VI: *The sex residue.* Mere sexual appetite, though powerfully active in the human race, is no concern of ours here, for the reasons stated in § 852. We are interested in it only in so far as it influences theories, modes of thinking—as a residue. In general terms, the sex residue and the sentiments in which it originates figure in huge numbers of phenomena, but they are often dissembled, especially among modern peoples.

1325. Graeco-Roman antiquity thought of the sexual act as satisfying a bodily need, on a par with eating, drinking, adorning one's person, and the like; and all such things the ancients regarded with indifference, generally condemning abuses, and less frequently excessive refinements, in pleasures. A passage in an oration of Demosthenes against Neaera has remained famous: "We have," says he, "hetairae for our pleasures, concubines for the daily health of the body, wives to give us legitimate children and faithfully to attend to our households." [1] In Rome we get first a legal distinction between women who were obligated to chastity and women who were not. The law evidently had strictly civic objectives in view, enforcing certain duties that were considered beneficial to the state upon free-born women, but leaving men free in matters of sex so long as the exercise of freedom did not prejudice interests of the state. [2] For

1325 [1] *In Neaeram,* 1386 (Auger, Vol. X, pp. 448-49): Τὰς μὲν γὰρ ἑταίρας ἡδονῆς ἕνεκ' ἔχομεν, τὰς δὲ παλλακὰς τῆς καθ' ἡμέραν θεραπείας τοῦ σώματος, τὰς δὲ γυναῖκας τοῦ παιδοποιεῖσθαι γνησίως καὶ τῶν ἔνδον φύλακα πιστὴν ἔχειν.

1325 [2] Mommsen, *Römisches Strafrecht,* pp. 688-89: "The free-born woman in Rome was obligated by moral law to abstain from all carnal intercourse with men before marriage, and to keep to her husband after marriage. The man, on the other hand, was subject to the same moral code only to the extent of not impairing the chastity of a virgin or another man's wife in complicity with the woman." The Republic went to few pains in legislating on such matters, leaving crimes of that sort to domestic tribunals. Augustus and his successors instituted legal punishments under Imperial law, *Ibid.,* pp. 691-92: "The law took account of immorality only if it involved a free-born woman obligated to chastity (*matrona, materfamilias*); but in such cases the punishment always extended to the male accomplice. Female slaves were not subject to that law, nor were married or unmarried women who were not held to moral strictness by their manner of livelihood, namely: prostitutes, so long as they practised their profession; keepers of public resorts; actresses; keepers of places open to the public; women living in open concubinage. However, the mere fact of leading a dissolute life did not exempt the free-born woman in Rome from the legal consequence of her immorality. . . . [In a note:] Impunity could be

our Purity-campaigners today all love out of wedlock is illicit. For the Romans some forms were legitimate, some illegitimate.[8] They were not as tolerant of adultery in married women as sex-reformers of our day are, just as they did not have the sectarian rages of our moderns at amours with freed women or other women of the kind.

assured only by formal registration on the lists of prostitutes or by the fact of embracing a calling that implied the same looseness." The essentially civic character of the legislation comes out in that. Later on, towards the end of the Roman Empire, St. Augustine could write, *Sermones* (*Opera,* Vol. V), CLIII, 5, 6, that fornication and drunkenness were forbidden not by human but by divine laws: "You see the man enamoured of his carnal lusts . . . go seeking his pleasures on all hands in drunkenness and fornication, to mention no other things. And those things I mention because they may be committed under the law of man but not under the law of God. For what man is ever brought before a judge because he has entered the resort of the harlot, or who before a court because he has become (*defluxit*) licentious and unclean through his debaucheries (? *lyristrias*)? Who has ever been charged with crime (*crimen invenit*) because, though married, he has violated a slave? But so in the forum of man, not in the forum of Heaven, so in the law of the world, not in the law of the Creator of the world." In that the Saint draws a distinction, too soon to be forgotten, between law and morality. Custom came to establish a number of distinctions among public women. Nonius Marcellus, *De compendiosa doctrina,* 5 (Mercier, p. 423), mentions two such categories: "There is this difference between the *meretrix* and the common prostitute (*prostibulum*): the *meretrix* is of a more respectable place and occupation, being so called from the fact that she serves for pay, but only at night; the *prostibulum* is so called from her standing in front of her house by day and by night for purposes of gain." There were also categories corresponding to prices. Festus, *De verborum significatione,* IV, *s.v. Diobolares* (London, Vol. I, p. 224): "*Diobolares meretrices dicuntur quae duobus obolis ducuntur.*" Celius insulted Clodia with the epithet *quandrantaria*—"to be had for a fourpence."

1325 [8] Ovid is careful to state over and again that he sings only of legitimate passions. *Ars amatoria,* I, vv. 31-33:

> "*Este procul vittae tenues, insigne pudoris;*
> *quaeque tegis medios instita longa pedes!*
> *Nos Venerem tutam concessaque furta canemus!*"

("Hence, ye vapoury headbands, symbols of purity, and ye long skirts that half cover the feet! We are to sing to a harmless Venus, and of thefts within the law!") The *vittae* were worn by Vestals, matrons, and young girls: Servius, *In Vergilii Aeneidem,* VII, v. 403 (Thilo-Hagen, Vol. II, p. 156): "Fillets for the hair were worn only by matrons, never by prostitutes." Ovid repeats vv. 31-32 in *Tristia,* II, v. 247; then instead of v. 33 he writes, v. 249:

> "*Nil misi legitimum concessaque furta canemus.*"

("We sing of nothing but fair game and of thefts within the law.") And *cf.* his *Remedia amoris,* vv. 385-86, and *Ex Ponto,* III, 3, v. 51; Tibullus, *Delia,* 6, v. 67;

They were inspired not by sex residues, but by considerations of public utility. An inscription found at Isernia shows taverns posting in conspicuous places not only prices of victuals, but the tariffs for the women provided for public accommodation. A traveller spends one *as* for bread, two *asses* for the food served with the bread, eight *asses* for a girl and two *asses* for the hay for one mule.[4] Ulpian

Plautus, *Miles gloriosus*, ll. 789-93. In the *Ars amatoria*, III, vv. 57-58, 483-84, 613-16, Ovid repeats:

"*Dum facit ingenium petite hinc praecepta, puellae,*
    quae pudor et leges et sua iura sinunt. . . .
Sed . . . quamvis vittae careatis honore,
    est vobis vestros fallere cura viros. . . .
Nupta virum timeat, rata sit custodia nuptae:
    hoc decet, hoc leges iusque pudorque iubent.
Te quoque servari modo quam vindicta redemit
    quis ferat? Ut fallas ad mea sacra veni!"

("While still she [Cythera] inspires me, seek of me, O maidens, the precepts that modesty, the law, and your oaths, allow. . . . Even though you lack the honour of the headband, it must still concern you to know the arts of deceiving your men. . . . Let the bride respect her husband. Let every care be taken for the protection of the wife. That is all proper enough. That much the law, justice, decency, require. But who could tolerate that you, who have just been freed by touch of the praetorian rod, should continue a slave? Come to my oracles to learn the arts of deception!")

1325 [4] *Corpus inscriptionum Latinarum*, Vol. IX, no. 2689 (p. 251): "'*Copo* (*caupo*, innkeeper) *computemus.*' '*Habes vini* [*sextarium*] *unum: panem, assem unum; pulmentarium, asses duos.*' '*Convenit.*' '*Puellam, asses octo.*' '*Et hoc convenit.*' '*Faenum mulo, asses duos.*' '*Iste mulus me ad factum* (sic. ? that mule will be the ruin of me).'" The stone shows a carving of a traveller holding a mule by the halter and settling his accounts with a woman. Ulpian, in *Digesta*, XXIII, 2, 43 (*Corpus iuris civilis*, Vol. I, p. 370; Scott, Vol. V, pp. 251-52) (defining the word *palam*): "We regard as publicly prostituting not only a woman who has sold herself in a brothel but a woman who, as the custom is, has not spared her virtue in a public hostelry or some other such place. We also interpret the term 'publicly' quite generally in the sense of 'without love.' It applies not to the woman who has succumbed to an adulterer or ravisher but to the one who has played the rôle of prostitute [*i.e.*, for money]. . . . If a woman keeping a hostelry has mercenary women [in her employ], as the custom is with many women who keep prostitutes under guise of servants (*instrumenti cauponii*), it is to be ruled that such a woman comes under the term of procuress." *Codex Justiniani*, IV, 36, 3 (*Corpus iuris civilis*, Vol. II, p. 279; Scott, Vol. XIII, p. 117): "*Imperator Alexander.* . . . That said law be not evoked, such a woman [a slave sold for honourable purposes] must never have made money with her body nor practised prostitution in a public hostelry under guise of service." A law of Constantine distinguishes the proprietress of an inn from the women who serve the customers. The former may be accused of adultery; the

implies that many brothels were kept in places belonging to respectable people.[5] Later on, towards the end of the Roman Empire, and for causes that are still in part obscure, considerations of sex became a tyrannical obsession in the minds of men and assumed religious forms, often asserting themselves as a sort of religious horror. It is a curious fact that among the civilized peoples of our day the sex religion has survived as the last to which the support of the secular arm is still lent. One may blaspheme God and the saints with impunity, one may preach civil war, destruction, expropriation—but one cannot publish obscene books or licentious pictures. So the Wahabis (§ 1123) regard tobacco-smoking as the worst of crimes, something far more infamous than murder or theft. Such an inverting of the scale of seriousness in crimes—and an inversion it can only seem to a person not sharing certain religious sentiments—is an essential trait in the punishment of religious heresies and an index of the sway the persecuting instinct exerts over men who are playthings of their prejudices and feelings.

1326. In our Western races three abstinence taboos come down

latter not, because of their lowly estate. See *Codex Iustinianus*, IX, 9, 28 (*Corpus iuris civilis*, Vol. II, p. 588; Scott, Vol. XV, p. 15); Virgil, *Copa*; Philostratus, *Epistulae*, 32 (25), 33 (24), 60 (23). The distinction drawn in Justinian's law clashes with the Christian taboo, which is well formulated by St. John Chrysostom, *Homilia V, in I ad Thessalonicos*, I Thess. 1:1-4 (Gaume, Vol. XI, p. 533; Prevost, p. 344). That saint refuses to consider any distinction. According to St. Paul, he says, one must eschew commerce not only with the wife of a Christian brother "but with other women, both married and public. One must abstain from all fornication." In the *Digesta*, III, 2, 4, § 2 (*Corpus iuris civilis*, Vol. I, p. 98; Scott, Vol. III, p. 9) Ulpian writes: "Guilty of pandering is an individual who keeps female slaves for purposes of prostitution; but the person who makes a business of prostitution even with free-born women is in the same case. Whether that is done as the main business, or as an accessory to some other business (as the keeper of a tavern or lodging-house (*stabularius*) who has had such slaves as servants but practising prostitution on the pretext of such service; or again, the keeper of a bath-house, who keeps female slaves who ply that trade in said bath under pretext of taking care of the clothing of customers of said bath, as is commonly done in some of the country districts), said individual is to be held to the penalty for pandering." If prostitutes were available in all such places, there must have been a plenty of them.

1325 [5] In the *Digesta*, V, 3, 27, § 1 (*Corpus iuris civilis*, Vol. I, p. 149; Scott, Vol. III, p. 188): "Taxes that have been collected on rents of urban properties will be applied to that purpose, even if they have been collected from brothels, for brothels are kept on many properties belonging to reputable people."

across the ages, and in order of increasing virulence: abstinence from meat, abstinence from wine, abstinence from everything pertaining to sex. Abstinence from meat can be traced as far back as Pythagoras. Surviving from Plutarch are two tracts against the use of meat, *De esu animalium* (Goodwin, Vol. V, pp. 3-16), to say nothing of a whole treatise on the same subject by Porphyry. The Christians recommended abstinence from meat and enforced it in one form or another. Last in line come the vegetarians of our own day.[1] There was a great deal of talk in ancient times on moderation in the use of wine, but little or none on total abstinence. The early Christians advised a moderate use of wine, or indeed abstinence from it as well as from meat, first as a means of doing penance, but also and more especially as a means of attenuating impulses to carnal sin. There are plenty of prescriptions in such regards by the Church Fathers.[2] However, the Catholic Church has always aimed at a golden mean. Requiring abstinence from meat on certain days, it permitted the use of wine, so showing itself more liberal than many a modern pseudo-scientist. The prohibitionists of our time are re-enacting the feats of the religious fanatics of old. Abstinence from amorous indulgences and from everything even remotely calculated to suggest them is observable, in theory at least, among the early Christians,

1326 [1] Guérin, *Les conciles généraux et particuliers,* Vol. I, p. 55 (*Concile d'Ancyre en Galatie, l'an 314* [Labbe, Vol. I, p. 1503]): "Canon XIV orders priests and acolytes who were eschewing meat not to do so out of contempt for it as though meat were an unclean thing. It goes on to enjoin them to partake of meat and to eat it with vegetables that have been cooked with it, in order to show that their abstention from it was not due to any loathing for it or any idea that it was a wicked thing. . . . That ordinance by the council was a wise precaution against Ebionites, Manicheans, and some few other heretics, who were condemning the use of meat as wicked; for the faithful might have been led to imagine that the priests and acolytes in question in the canon were intending to favour the errors of such heretics. The use of meat is therefore not wrong in itself, though it may be meritorious to abstain from it in a spirit of penance, or as a matter of duty, at the times specified by the Church." Had the Church not safe-guarded personal freedom in the choice of foods in that manner, champions of purity might be going about in our time browbeating governments into putting people who eat meat into prison.

1326 [2] Fra Bartolommeo da San Concordio, *Ammaestramenti degli antichi,* 24, 3, 1: "The palate is a cause of sensuality. . . . (24, 4, 1) The use not only of food but also of wine must be temperate. . . . (24, 4, 5) Wine is beyond any doubt a breeder of sensuality."

and in our day, still in theory, it has again given rise to a patholog-ical fanaticism of purity.

1327. Residues in these phenomena are compounds. At least three elements are discernible in them.

1. Least important is a residue of combinations, in view of which members of a sect have some sign or other to distinguish them from the generality of men, from outsiders, from members of other sects. Prohibitions of certain foods are observable among many many peo-ples. The Bible prohibits the flesh of the hare. No consideration of asceticism or the like can be detected in the prohibition (§§ 1276 f.) —it is a plain residue of combinations. That residue is often com-bined with another relating to personal integrity—to pride. The compound serves not only to distinguish, but to glorify.[1] Residues of that sort may very probably have figured in the effort of the Christians to keep themselves distinct from the heathen.

2. The element most important for the first two taboos (meat and wine), and of considerable importance for the third as well (sex), is a residue of asceticism. It manifests its presence in the fact that such taboos are accompanied by abstentions and mortifications that certainly belong to asceticism. That is strikingly apparent in the case of the Christians, less apparent in other abstainers, barely if at all perceptible in still others. The prohibitionists of our day pretend to be interested strictly in public welfare. But it is by no mere chance that they are also as a rule humanitarians, religious zealots, moralists, and champions of sexual purity. Not a few of them, though they may not be aware of it, may not be altogether unaffected by the ascetic residue.

3. Sentiments incidental to asceticism, such as conceit, envy of others who are enjoying what one cannot afford, eagerness for the esteem and admiration of this or that group, and so on.[2]

1327 [1] Renan, *Marc-Aurèle*, p. 570: "It is pleasant to think of oneself as belonging to a little aristocracy of truth-holders, to imagine that one possesses the treasure of the good with a few other privileged souls. Pride has its share in that attitude. The Jew and the Syrian *metuali*, humiliated, despised by everybody, are at bottom scorn-ful, contemptuous creatures. No insult touches them. They are so proud to be of the chosen people!"

1327 [2] With those things we dealt in §§ 1169-71.

4. A need for expressing one's faith, in this case an ascetic faith, by external acts (Class III residues, § 888).

1328. Religious exaltation sometimes figures in the three taboos. The meat taboo assumes a religious form in India, not so in our Western countries. Scattered examples in connexion with the wine taboo are observable here and there among our contemporaries. With the sex taboo the fact is general all the way along from antiquity down to our own time.

1329. There are actually localities where the meat and wine taboos are more or less scrupulously observed, where, that is, groups of people actually abstain from meat and fermented drinks. For that matter, in such communities or countries the abstinence is at times merely apparent, as is the case in present-day Turkey. But as regards the sex taboo, differences in substance are negligible, there being notable differences only in forms. Prostitution is prohibited in Mohammedan countries, but it has substitutes in concubinage and in even worse practices. It was also prohibited in our parts of the world in days when morals were far from being better than they are at present. The sex taboo is one of the many cases in which sentiments are so powerful as to render substance virtually constant, admitting only of changes in forms. The contrast is so great that one is tempted to adopt the paradox that immorality is greatest there, precisely, where it is most severely condemned by morality and by law. Many indications lead to the belief that that is true of several states in the American Union—though one should not derive a general law from particular instances.[1]

1329 [1] It has been proved, of late, that there is much truth in Casanova's *Mémoires*. On the score of immorality, there were great differences as to forms, very slight differences as to substance, in the countries he visited. Salvatore di Giacomo, in *Giornale d'Italia*, Feb. 11, 1913: "Was Giacomo Casanova lying or telling the truth when, in his laborious solitude in the library which the good Count Waldstein had entrusted to his patient and learned reorganization, he told, among other things, the things that he had seen in Naples or which had happened to him during his sojourn there? Were the names of the people he knew in Naples really the names that he gives? And the Neapolitan society of those days—the people, the army, the clergy, our fatuous nobility, our attitude of frivolity, and that marvellous and almost inconceivable breath of noble ideas, of economic scholarship, of a new and inspiring philosophy in some few individuals, in whose austere ethical codes

1330. In the religion of sex, as in many other religions, inflexibility in forms gives rise to perversion and hypocrisy; the fable of the forbidden fruit is of all periods of history.[1] In the Middle Ages, and even somewhat later, when religious frenzies were rife, evocations

one already senses as it were a warning criticism of the times—were they as the observing adventurer describes them? We shall see. But meantime, if I may express in general terms an opinion that I have reached on the stories of Casanova which have to do with Naples, I can only say that he has surprised me not only for his having kept over so many years such a good memory of episodes and in their minute details, but for the literal accuracy of his account, which stimulated me to run down in our archives not the phantoms of an excited imagination, but persons and things that really existed, nay, that are almost alive today!"

1330 [1] Noting in his *Mœurs, institutions et cérémonies des peuples de l'Inde,* Vol. I, pp. 440-41, 437-38, how wide-spread and offensive he found incontinence to be among the Brahmans, Dubois adds: "And yet—who could imagine such a thing after what I have just been saying?—there is no country in the world where the outer semblances of decency, properly so called, are more generally observed. What we call *galanterie* is altogether unknown to them. That free, *risqué* chatter, those insipid allusions, that endless flattery, that boundless solicitude and attentiveness that is the stock in trade of our parlour 'dandy' would seem insulting to a Hindu lady, even to one not very strict in her morals, if she were offered them in public. If a husband ventured on any familiarities with his legitimate wife he would be set down as a ridiculous person of no very good taste." That may be repeated to the letter for many countries in Europe and America where words are hypocritically chaste and conduct unpleasantly indecent. So for another remark of Dubois: "Though adultery in a woman entails disgrace and is condemned by the rule of the Brahmans, it is nevertheless not punished in their caste as severely as in most others. If it is kept secret, little importance is attached to it. Publicity is the only thing that worries them, and in case of gossip, husbands are the first to contradict aspersions on the honour of their wives, in order to avoid the consequences of a public scandal." In one respect however, India is free of the hypocrisy observable in Western countries: "Relations with a prostitute or an unmarried person are not regarded as crimes by the Brahmans. Those men, who have associated notions of sin with violations of the most inconsequential rules, see no sin whatever in the extremest gratifications of sense. It was largely for their benefit originally that bayaderas and prostitutes were attached to service in the temples. They may often be heard reciting a scandalous line to the effect that 'commerce with a prostitute is a virtue that erases all sin.'"

Thinking of the pleasures of love Ovid observes, *Amores,* III, 4, v. 17:

> "*Nitimur in vetitum semper cupimusque negata.*"

(We strive for the forbidden and yearn for what is denied.) And he had said, *Ibid.,* III, 4, v. 9, that "she to whom erring is free, errs less": *Cui peccare licet peccat minus.* And, *cf. Ars Amatoria,* III, v. 603:

> "*Quae venit ex tuto minus est accepta voluptas.*"

(The pleasure that involves no danger is the least enjoyed.)

of the Devil and pacts with him were frequent. Who would dream of doing such things in our day, when the religious mania has, to a very large extent, abated? Many obscene expressions of lust may have, in part at least, very much the same origins as the old evocations of the Devil. Henry III of France was forever shuttling back and forth between rites of religious asceticism and offences against nature. He is just the type of a very large class of individuals. In our day, the very countries that lay greatest stress on purity reveal the worst cases of obscenities. Whenever the worship of Cythera is banned, the rites of Sodom and Lesbos come into vogue. The residue is constant. If its natural forms are interfered with, it assumes others.

When a person is under the sway of an all-absorbing idea, he is inspired to ridiculous conduct that provokes nothing but hilarity in those who are free of his impediment. That is why many rites of worship among savage and even civilized peoples seem fit subjects of mirth. Expressions of the sex residue are no exception to that rule. In England, Germany, and the United States in our day, instances of sex prudery, whether sincere or hypocritical, come to light every now and then that are as ridiculous as the most outlandish taboos.[2]

1330 [2] *Liberté*, Feb. 14, 1912: *Berlin*, Feb. 12: "Six years ago the widow of a captain in the Prussian army set up a little farm near her villa at Tetlow and living in peace there ever since have been two sheep, a pony, three ducks, a number of rabbits, and a flock of hens with a cock. For six continuous years quadrupeds and bipeds alike knew only the joys of a well-fed, happy existence. But the other day the thunderbolts of justice fell on their peaceful abode. It is quite a story. Across the way from the barnyard stands a primary school, and at recess-time the little Prussians had been in the habit of watching the antics of hens, ducks, and sheep. The schoolmaster chanced to follow his charges one day as far as the barn-yard fence and what he saw filled him with indignation. He took his most eloquent magisterial pen and addressed the burgomaster of Tetlow in part as follows: 'The daily spectacle of unaesthetic sexual inclinations on the part of the feathered tribe is exerting a most deleterious influence on the morality of the children in this school.' The conduct of the widow's enterprising rooster had shocked the good soul in his tenderest aesthetic sensibilities! Stranger still, the burgomaster, also best of souls, forthwith directed the lady *by police order* to shut up the cock behind closed doors. She, however, was deaf in that ear and sought an injunction of the courts. The Crown's attorney supported the mayor with a speech in which he roundly condemned the growing looseness of Prussian morals. The defence sought

1331. The sex residue is active not only in mental states looking to unions of the sexes or lingering on recollections of such things, but also in mental states that evince censure, repugnance, or hatred towards matters of sex. Strange as it may seem, there are data

to bring out the comic aspects of the case and made a motion that the 'Court proceed to an inspection of the farm and order the schoolmaster to present the rooster for a demonstration of immorality.' The court-room being in a tumult of laughter, the Court had the good sense to quash the police order issued by the mayor and to condemn the state to the costs." Another instance of soft-brained sex hypocrisy: *Gazette de Lausanne*, Jan. 1, 1913: "Is it lawful for a man to kiss his wife in a train in England? The Bavarian Government recently fined a man for just such an offence. Very properly stirred, a large English daily sent one of its best reporters to consult a high official of the British railways to determine whether travellers on trains in England were exposed to similar risks. The reassuring oracle emanating from that distinguished source was as follows: 'Patrons of the English railways have nothing to fear. A man may under most circumstances kiss his wife or any other duly authorized person on a station platform or in a train at a moment of arrival or departure or even during a journey. He may hold his companion's hand or even press it against his body. He may also allow his wife to rest her head on his shoulder whenever she feels fatigued.' These lucky Englishmen! At last they have their Charter of Necessary Liberties!" Stories of this kind are ordinarily taken as jests, but they are not jests; they are extreme manifestations of the sex residue, which assumes gigantic proportions in certain minds, fascinates and obsesses them, and deprives them of that sense of what is real and what is ridiculous which continues to function in minds not so seriously affected. Such things are observable in all times and places. They are the rule among the Christian ascetics and not rare among the Jews. Hosts of examples might be quoted from the Talmud. Suffice the following: Talmud of Jerusalem, Tract Taanith, I, 6 (Gemara) (Schwab, Vol. VI, pp. 149-50; Danby, p. 195): ". . . At the time of Noah's entry into the Ark, cohabitation was forbidden him, as it is written (Gen. 6:18) . . . but on coming out the privilege was restored to him in the words . . . (Gen. 8:16). . . . Rabbi Hiya b. Aba remarks: 'The expression "They left the Ark according to their families" means that it was for having preserved their lineage *sine coitu* that they were lucky enough to escape the Flood. The correctness of that interpretation is proved by the fact that the three who sinned against nature in the Ark, Cham, the dog, and the raven, were punished.'" Spicy details as to the misconduct of the raven in question are supplied by another Rabbi: *Commentarius Rasche* in *cap*. VIII, Genesis (8:7), (Scherzer-Abicht, *Selecta rabbinica-philologica*, p. 196): "*Exeundo et redeundo* ["And he sent forth a raven which went to and fro . . ."] He went to and fro about the Ark and did not fulfil his errand, because he had suspected Noah of designs on his wife *ne coiret cum illa in absentia*." That is pretty good, but there is better yet. Scherzer-Abicht translate (*Ibid.*, p. 18) a note by another Rabbi on Genesis. "Scripture teaches that Adam visited all animals and beasts and found his appetites unsatisfied by any of them"; and they add (pp. 66-67): "Reuchlin, *Cabbala*, I, f. 626 [Hagenau, f. VII, N] quotes Rasche as follows: 'Adam visited all animals and beasts of burden, but his senses were not inflamed till he came to his wife.' The last words are missing in my text. In this connexion Capnio, in person

a-plenty for showing that the very thought of chastity, when it assumes any prominent position in the mind, may have an underlying sex residue, and many individuals have been led over the road of purity to solitary vices.[1]

of Simeon the Jew . . . says that with those words, incarnate devils and fury-like spirits, rather than men, were preparing to raise the wrath of Christendom against us . . . for [the Christians] interpreted the line to mean that at that time Adam had foul commerce with all beasts and animals. But how could such a big man as Adam, and such a great one, have knowledge in a female way (*feminaliter*) of a flea, a fly, a cicada, a cimex?" It would seem impossible that the human being could sink to such depths of sottishness and that such a race of idiots could have survived to our day. Talmud of Babylon, Tract Berakoth, I, 5 (2) (Schwab, Vol. I, p. 260; Cohen, p. 59): "Suckling his mother's milk, he—David—perceives her breasts and breaks forth into song in these terms: 'Bless the Lord, O my soul, and forget not all His benefits' [Ps. 103:2]. 'What are those benefits?' 'His having,' answers Rabbi Abahou, 'placed the breasts of the mother in the seat of intelligence.' 'Why?' 'That the child,' answers Rabbi Juna, 'should not see nudity (as is the case with the females of animals),' or, according to Rabbi Matna, 'that the suckling of the child should not take place from an unclean part of the body.'" We are still

1331 [1] Renan, *Marc-Aurèle*, pp. 245-47: "One of the mysteries most deeply glimpsed by the founders of Christianity was the fact that chastity is a form of voluptuousness, and modesty one of the forms of sexual passion. Men who are afraid of women are, as a rule, the ones most attached to them. How often may we not say in all soundness to the ascetic: *Fallit te incautum pietas tua!*?" There is no mystery in the thing. It is nothing more than the "theory of veils," so called. Renan is well describing, but not so well interpreting, when he goes on to say: "That explains the strange mixture of timid modesty and sensuous languor that is characteristic of the moral sentiment in the primitive churches." A plain case of the sex residue. However, Renan feels in duty bound to append a bit of declamation: "Away with the base suspicion of the vulgar débauché who cannot comprehend such innocence! All was purity in those holy liberties! And furthermore, purity was essential to an enjoyment of them. [Renan of course was there in person and can testify that everything was purity itself.] Legend represents the pagans as jealous of the privilege of the [Christian] priest to see for a moment in her baptismal nudity the woman who was to become his spiritual sister as a result of that sacred immersion. What words to describe the 'holy kiss' which was the ambrosia of those chaste procreations?" All the same, those very Christians soon became aware that danger lurked in the "holy kiss" where men and women were involved. Athenagoras, *Legatio pro Christianis*, XXVIII: "If one kiss a second time for the pleasure of it [he sins] . . . so it is meet that we be cautious in the kiss, and more so in the salutation; for if our thought be defiled however so little or in any way, we are banished from eternal life." In the *Paedagogus*, III, 11 (*Opera*, Vol. I, p. 659; Wilson, Vol. I, p. 330), Clement of Alexandria would have the kiss not "immodest" but "mystical" and delivered "with chaste lips, closed" (διὰ στόματος σώφρονος καὶ μεμυκότος). With all due respect to Renan, this last prescription is not so terribly pure as purity goes. And *cf.* § 1394.

1332. The sex residue may figure in relations that are altogether innocent and chaste, and it is a manifest error to assume that wherever it is present relations of a physical character are necessarily envisaged. There are instances without end of women who have followed men at the bidding of a deep religious passion and treated them with great affection without hint of physical interest. That was apparent in the Welsh revival of 1904, where Evan Roberts was made the target of tenderest admiration on the part of women who seem really to have been pure of heart.[1] Such cases should put us on our guard against too ready acceptance of charges that adversaries hurl at one another on this score. It has been said that the Countess Matilda's feelings for Pope Gregory were those of a lover rather than a daughter. That seems not at all likely.

1333. On the other hand, the fact that the sex residue may be active in speech and writing that are altogether chaste, as well as in the frankly obscene, should serve to remind us that as regards stimulating physical passions the chaste may be as effective as the obscene and *vice versa*. It all depends on the individual. Some people

waiting for our respectable and brainy virtuists to pass a law ordering infants to close their eyes in drawing at their mothers' breasts. *Liberté,* Dec. 6, 1912: *"Purity in Australia.* At the instance of the Australian Government, the federal customs of Australia have just prohibited importation of indecently illustrated postcards, and so far, so good. But Australian customs agents have been instructed to interpret the term 'indecent' in the broadest sense to include anything of a blasphemous, indelicate, 'immodest,' or uncouth character. 'Immodest' is a very elastic term. Under it postcard prints of Rodin's 'Kiss,' of 'Alone at Last,' of 'Cupid and Psyche,' to keep to works of art, will be forbidden in Australia. One used to say 'Chaste Albion.' A prize for a word to give to Australia!" Gossip has it, meantime, that that well-chaperoned country knows all it might be expected to know of unnatural vices. *Journal de Genève,* Mar. 31, 1911: "A sentence just passed on Mr. X Y, editor-in-chief of a London weekly, is an indication of the vigour with which England is resolved to push her campaign against pornographic literature. Speaking for the Crown, Mr. Muskett declared to the Chief Justice, Mr. Marsham, that a number of the weekly edited by Mr. X Y contained an obscene paragraph. After a severe arraignment of Mr. X Y, the justice condemned him to a fine of ten pounds and costs." But absconders from the Continent find a safe refuge in England in view of the complications of extradition proceedings.

1332 [1] Bois, *Le réveil au pays de Galles,* pp. 437-38, 459. The story is told by Evan Roberts, the *dramatis personae* being as follows: "Mary, a Miss Mary Davies of Gorseinon, unrelated to the two better-known Davies girls, Annie and Maggie, who are sisters of Maestey; then Dan, Evan Roberts's brother. Says Evan Rob-are sensuously susceptible to talk and writing of the chaste variety, others rather to indecent literature. It has been said, and perhaps truly, that Guarini's *Pastor fido* has led more women astray than Boccaccio's *Decameron* ever did.[1]

1334. The sex residue figures actively in the vastly larger portion of literature. Tragedies, comedies, poems, novels, can hardly do without it. Moderns draw a distinction—along what lines is not quite clear—between a literature that is allegedly "moral" and a literature that is allegedly "immoral." The drawing of it oftentimes is a mere matter of hypocrisy, people shrinking at the word and not at the thing, and doing the thing but avoiding the word. At any rate, if it is not actually impossible to write an entertaining novel, comedy, or tragedy without the love-interest, successful ones in which love does not figure to some extent are as rare as white blackbirds—and that is enough to show the tremendous power of the sex residue. The public crowds in throngs to the criminal courts to listen to trials where passions are at issue and attention is the more greedy, the more obscene the matters discussed. Such audiences count no

erts: 'Just then a voice said to me: "You must observe silence for a whole week." The Davies sisters had just come in. When Mr. Mardy Davies had left the room, I asked them in writing to sing Newman's hymn "Lead, Kindly Light." . . . They did so. It was touching, solemn. When they came to the words "One step enough for me" there were tears in their eyes. Then they sang "I need thee every hour." Then one of them asked me, "What are we to do?" My answer was, "Wait until I get a definite message from Heaven." Heaven *suggests* [The word "suggests" was doubly underlined in the notebook in which Roberts wrote his responses.] that one of you go home and the other remain with me.' After a long time spent in prayer, my answer was ready: 'Annie is to stay here and take care of me. Mary will go home and rest or else go with Maggie and Dan.' " Annie Davies remains and Roberts hands her her instructions in writing: "No one but you is to see me during this coming week, not even my father and mother." And the girl nursed the prophet for a week without once hearing him utter a word. Bois comments: "One thing in all this might well surprise, not to say shock, a French reader—the assurance with which Roberts represents as a definite communication from Heaven an alleged command to keep a young girl all alone with him, while all others are sent away and he refuses to see anyone for a whole week. . . . The Holy Spirit had of course forbidden Roberts to speak, but he was still free to listen, write, and read. Many people besides Roberts might have seen in that suggestion rather a temptation than a divine command."

1333 [1] *Journal des Goncourt*, Vol. III, p. 6 (Jan. 1, 1866): "The French woman is more often led astray by the romantic in what she reads than by anything obscene."

end of men, and especially women, who in other places are energetic defenders of morality and wage frantic war on immorality.[1]

1335. We have had occasion time and again to note that the sex residues manifest themselves in phenomena quite similar to what is commonly called religion, and that they therefore as a whole may properly be classified with religious phenomena. The sex religion, like other religions, has its dogmas, its believers, its heretics, its atheists (a fact, also, to which we have made frequent allusion). But since that view is at variance with views more generally held, it will not come amiss if we add some further proof to those already given.

1336. Our single concern, remember, is to determine whether certain phenomena present, or do not present, certain specified traits—and not to evaluate their effects upon individuals or societies (§ 74). When we have recognized that the phenomena in question make up a group similar to the group known as religion, we still know nothing as to the good or the harm they may do. There are harmful religions, beneficial religions, religions that are neither the one nor the other; and nothing we have so far said will give any inkling as to the class in which the sex religion has to be located.

1337. In general religions do not admit their subjective character. They pretend to be objective, and hold that logico-experimental science confirms their dogmas throughout. In their primitive stages they are satisfied with their material elements. Becoming more advanced, they are inclined to take on intellectual, abstruse, and especially mysterious elements. Certain objects of worship are kept hidden from view, certain names are never pronounced, or if they are, only with holy reverence or holy horror. The Jews did not utter the name of their God. The Romans had a name for their city that was unknown to the public. The Athenians had severe punishments for anyone attempting to unveil the Eleusinian mysteries. Oftentimes in religions one gets a sentiment of mingled love and fear, even of terror, for the beings worshipped. Dogmas, like the prescriptions in taboos, are the premises, never the conclusions, of logical develop-

1334 [1] Carducci's poem, "*A proposito del processo Fadda*" (see §§ 1136 [1], 1297 [1]), is not a mere poem: it is a sound description of commonplace facts.

ments. The mere denial of them is a crime, or at least the index
of a perverse nature. The ardent believer is shocked at objections to
his faith, and often meets them not with arguments, facts, remarks,
in rebuttal, but with a resort to force, either direct or through some
public authority. As likely as not a prosecution for impiety will not
be held subject to the general rules of legal process. The mere charge
of a crime so serious is enough to deprive the accused of traditional
guarantees that are never denied in cases of other crimes. Defence
of a given religion becomes a defence of "morality," "justice," "decency," and must therefore be encouraged even by persons not holding that faith, so long as they are at least "moral" or "honest."
"Moral" or "honest" no one not a Christian could be in the Middle
Ages nor, in the view of many Mohammedans, can a non-Moham-
medan be today. Now all of those traits, in their varying degrees,
are recognizable in the mass of phenomena that go to make up the
present day Religion of Sex. Not only that. The sex religion also
adopts those time-honoured principles of conduct known as *raison
d'état,* whereby the end is held to justify the means, so that when
the end is of supreme importance, one need not scruple to smite the
innocent, provided in so doing no guilty person escape (§ 1012[1]).

1338. Among the peoples of antiquity and barbarous peoples of
modern times, the sex organs and sexual acts are just part of a general fetishism. We moderns, judging things according to our own
notions, distinguish the two types of fetishism, so that the sex fetishism endures, while other fetishisms have disappeared or lost most
of their force. It would be beside our point to cite cases and proofs
of sex fetishism among various races;[1] but since it is our duty to
become acquainted with all the residues that have a bearing on the
social equilibrium, we must mention a number of facts that go to
show the importance and the continuity of the sex residue in our
Western countries; and as usual let us devote our main attention to
the civilization that has come down to us from Greece and Rome.

1338 [1] On the one hand the facts are well known, and on the other hand, they
are a subject not for a general sociology, but for a special sociology dealing with
fetishisms.

1339. We have seen that among the ancient Romans almost all the non-logical actions of life gave rise, by virtue of the residues of group-persistence, to concepts that eventually appear as minor deities (§§ 176 f.). There were little gods for all the acts of life, from conception to death. If we arrange such concepts in order, category by category,[1] we observe that for us moderns a considerable hiatus develops between certain points, whereas for the ancients the series is continuous.

1. Gods for acts occurring before the consummation of matrimony: Juno Juga or Juno Pronuba, who joins in marriage; Deus Jugatinus, who presides at the marriage union; Afferenda for the delivery of the dowry; Domiducus, who leads the bride to the husband's house; Domitius, who keeps her there; Manturna, who makes her stay with her husband; Unxia, who presides over the anointing with oil which the bride performs on the threshold of her new home; Cinxia, who presides over the removing of the bride's girdle; Virginiensis Dea, who keeps watch over the bride's virginity.[2] On all such matters the moderns speak freely, and even

1339 [1] I follow Marquardt's enumeration, *Römische Staatsverwaltung: Sacralwesen*, pp. 10-17.

1339 [2] Martianus Capella, *De nuptiis inter Mercurium et Philologiam*, II, 149 (Berne, p. 61. For the beginning of the quotation see our note next following, § 1339 [3]): "Thee [Juno] mortal brides should summon to their nuptials as Interduca [variant, *Interdua*] and Domiduca, Unxia and Cinxia, that thou mayest protect them on their way and take them to their longed-for homes and destroy evil omens [Marquardt suggesting *funestum* for *faustum*.] as they anoint the doorposts, and not desert them as they lay aside their girdles in their nuptial beds." Romans and Greeks alike attached a religious significance to the removal of the virgin's girdle. Festus, *De verborum significatione, s.v. Cinxiae* (Amsterdam, 1699, p. 150): "The name of Juno Cinxia was regarded as sacred in marriage rites, the girdle with which the new bride was girt being removed at the beginning of marriage." Suidas, *Lexicon, s.v.* Λυσίζωνος γυνή ["a girdle-loosing woman"]: "A woman having intercourse with a man, for on the point of consummation virgins dedicated their virginal girdles to Artemis." "Whence," as the scholiast on Apollonius, *Argonautica*, I, 288, remarks, "the temple in Athens to 'the girdle-loosing Artemis.'" And *cf. Orphica, Hymnus* 35 (36), 5 (Leipzig, pp. 299, 576-77; Taylor, pp. 85-86); Callimachus, *Hymnus in Jovem*, v. 21 (". . . *temporis quo Rhea zonam solvit"*); Homer, *Odyssey*, XI, v. 245 (though Zenodotus omits the verse and Aristarchus rejects it). Hence also the expressions *zonam solvere*, ξώνην λῦσαι "to loose the girdle," used of a woman having commerce with the opposite sex. A woman who had married but once could say that she "had loosed the girdle

with satisfaction. No fetishism has survived for any of the acts mentioned. The hiatus develops with the group next following.

2. Gods presiding over consummation. They are as numerous as the gods in the other groups. For the Romans this type of fetishism was in no sense different from any other fetishism; but it is the only one the moderns have kept—they have dropped the others. Bridging the hiatus, we get the following categories, of which, again, the moderns speak freely, the gods and goddesses of parturition forming a transition between the two groups.

3. Gods of birth: Juno Lucina, invoked by women in childbirth; Diespiter, who presided over birth itself; Candilifera, so called because a candle was lighted at birth; the two Carmentes, Prorsa and Postverta (relating to the manner of the child's presentment); then Egeria and Numeria.

4. Gods invoked just after birth: an Intercidona (who protected the house against Silvanus); a Deus Vagitanus, who opened the child's mouth that it might utter its first cry; a Cunina, who attended to the cradle, and so on—ten in all.

5. Gods of infancy. Potina and Educa taught the child how to eat and drink—thirteen in all (§ 176 [2]).

6. Gods of adolescence—twenty-six in all. Then come numberless gods and goddesses, dealing with all the occupations of life until with death Libitina and Nenia come on the scene.[8]

for only one man: *Greek Anthology*, VII, 324 (Paton, Vol. II, pp. 174-75): μούνῳ ἐνὶ ζώναν ἀνέρι λυσαμένα." Theocritus, *Idyllia*, XVII, v. 60 (Edmonds, p. 215), uses the locution of a woman in childbirth.

1339 [8] The chief gods in the hiatus were: Mutinus, Subigus, Prema, Pertunda, Perfica, Janus Consivus, Liber and Libera, Fluonia, Nona, Decima, Partula Vitumnus, Sentinus. Ample information about them survives in the Church Fathers. To the passage quoted from St. Augustine in § 177 [8], the following may be added from the *De civitate Dei*, VII, 2-4, 11—the Saint is saying that the "chosen" gods of Varro are one and the same with others that were assigned to humbler offices [He is not, however, ridiculing the pagan gods altogether, but sustaining an argument for monotheism by analogy: since all the pagan gods come down in the end to one god, Jupiter, the pagans might just as well accept the one God of the Christians.— A. L.]—"In the first place Janus himself *aperit aditum recipiendo semini* at the time the infant is being conceived, all the business taking its beginning from that, each little thing being assigned to its respective little god. Saturn is there *propter ipsum semen,* and Liber *qui marem effuso semine liberat;* and there too Libera, who

1340. The hiatus appears in a distinctly religious guise in the writings of the Church Fathers; and as long as it remains of that character no judgment can be passed upon it by anyone who is concerned to keep to the experimental field and must therefore con-

is said to be Venus, and performs the same service for the woman *ut etiam ipsa emisso semine liberetur*. These are the only ones in the lot who are called 'chosen' gods. But the goddess Mena is also there to preside over the female period. A daughter of Zeus, she is none the less a menial (*ignobilis*) on that account! This province of the female period the same writer [Varro] assigns to Juno, no less, in his list of select gods, and she is even queen among them! And there also Juno Lucina presides over the same mess (*cruori*) with the same Mena, her stepdaughter. Two other gods are there, very vague individuals, Vitumnus and Sentinus, the one to bestow life, the other sense (*sensus*) on the child." And the Saint's argument is sound; it would have been very stupid of the Romans to assign such menial functions to the greater gods already existing. However, the Romans did not go from the gods to the acts: they went from the acts to the gods. The Saint is led astray by the preconception that essentially non-logical actions have to be logical: "Vitumnus, the life-giver, and Sentinus, the sense-giver, ought rather to be ranked among the chosen gods than Janus the introducer of the seed, Saturn its giver or sower, and Liber and Libera *seminum commotores vel emissores*, for [surely] it is a degrading thing to be concerned with such seed (*quae semina . . . cogitare*) before it has attained life and sense." The Saint goes on to say, IV, 11, that Jupiter may be everything that is claimed for him, but that all the same "he is the lowest in all that herd of menial gods. Under the name of Liber, *praesit . . . virorum seminibus* and under the name of Libera [*praesit seminibus*] *feminarum*. He is the Diespiter who leads the child to light of day, and the goddess Mena who has been put in charge of the female period. He is the Lucina on whom mothers in travail call. No other than he lends succour to the infant at birth in rescuing it from the bosom of the Earth, and so is called Opis (*opem ferat: Opis*). . . . He is called Paventia from the terror (*pavore*) of the child, Venilia from the hope of its coming (*de spe quae venit*), Volupia from the lust of procreation, Agenoria *de actu*, Stimula *de stimulis quibus ad nimium actum homo impellitur*, Strenia *strenuum faciendo*, Numeria *quae numerare doceat*. He it is in person of the god Jugatinus who unites bride and groom, and he it is in person of the *Dea Virginiensis* whose name is called when the girdle of the virgin bride is loosed. He is that Mutunus or Tutunus who is known as Priapus among the Greeks. All these things which I have mentioned, with due apology to chaste ears (*si non pudet*), and all the many things that I have not mentioned, for I think that some of them should not be— all these gods and goddesses in short come down to one god, Jupiter, or else they are, as some claim, parts of him, his powers." That treats on a par gods which later Christians were to sever with a hiatus. Tertullian, *Ad nationes*, II, 11 (*Opera*, Vol. V, p. 148; English, Vol. I, pp. 488-89): "They divide the whole life (*statum*) of man from his very conception in the womb into separate domains. A certain god Consevius presides over the amorous combat, and a certain Fluviona prevents miscarriage (*infantem in utero retineat*). Then Vitumnus and Sentinus, through whom the child first acquires life and sense, and then a Diespiter, who brings on birth. At the moment of birth there was a [goddess] Candilifera, for a candle was lighted

sider religious phenomena from the strictly extrinsic standpoint as social facts.

1341. Interesting from that standpoint is the fact that when the war on paganism was over, the religious character of the hiatus

at that time, along with other goddesses who derive their names from services connected with parturition. . . . They say it is the province of a Postverta to help a child if it is in wrong position, of a Prosa Carmentis if it is in normal position. . . . Speaking of the wedding itself, an Afferenda is placed in charge of providing the dowry [Never any trace of hiatus in that connexion!]; but, oh, for shame! there is a Mutunus and a Tutunus, a Pertunda, a Subigus, a Prema, a Perfica. [Now plenty of hiatus in Tertullian.] Mercy, ye gods of indecency: *Luctantibus sponsis nemo intervenit!*" Tertullian again in *De anima*, 37 (*Opera*, Vol. IV, p. 253; English, Vol. II, p. 498): "Roman superstition invented a goddess Alemona for nourishing the unborn child, a Nona and a Decima, so called from the critical months, a Partula to attend to parturition, and a Lucina to bring the child forth. We believe that those are divine functions belonging to angels (*Nos officia divina angelos credimus*)." Interesting this last remark. It is, after all, a mere question of competing theologies. Arnobius, *Disputationes adversus gentes*, IV, 7, and III, 30 (Bryce-Campbell, pp. 189, 171, 193-94) (proving that such gods do not exist): "Are we to count as one of the gods that Perfica who causes (*perficit*) those obscene and filthy enjoyments to proceed to the end with uninterrupted pleasure? Or that Pertunda who presides in the bedchambers over *virginalem scrobem effodientibus maritis?* Or that Tutunus, the wearing [*cuius . . . inequitare:* "whose riding of your matrons by"] of whose monstrous emblems and disgusting amulets (*fascino*) by your wives and matrons you regard as a favourable omen and insist on having (*optatis*)? . . . And does not an identical reasoning eliminate Juno from the list of the gods? For if Juno is the air (*aer*), as you commonly say in jest, transposing the letters of her Greek name [ʽΗρα], no wife and sister of Jupiter the Omnipotent is any longer left [and with her go her special manifestations as] Fluonia, Pomona, Ossipagina [§ 176 [2]], Februtis [purification], Popolonia [fertility], Cinxia [§ 1339 [2]], or Caprotina [she who gave warning of the approach of the Gauls from a wild fig-tree]; and so it develops that there is nothing whatever behind that vacuous semblance of a name (*inanissima nominis fictio*) which has been made so famous by the fatuous beliefs of men." (The usual error of regarding non-logical conduct as logical.) Festus, *De verborum significatione*, VI, *s.v. Fluonia* (London, Vol. I, p. 270): "Women worshipped Juno Fluonia in the belief that she prevented hemorrhages in childbirth." Martianus Capella, *De nuptiis inter Mercurium et Philologiam*, II, 149 (Berne, p. 61) (invocation by Philology personified): "Beautiful Juno—though the heavenly fellowship would supply thee with another name, we call thee Juno because of the help thou dost give us (*a juvando*). . . . Or shall we call thee Lucina (or even Lucetia), from the light thou bringest to new-born babes? Do not expect me to call upon thee as Fluonia or Februalis or Februa, since I am undefiled of sex and have suffered no bodily pollution." The quotation is continued just above, § 1339 [2]. Lactantius Firmianus, *Divinae institutiones*, I, *De falsa religione*, 20, 36 (*Opera*, Vol. I, p. 77; Fletcher, Vol. I, p. 57): "A Cunina, too, is worshipped, as standing guard over infants in the cradle and keeping off the evil eye; and a Sterculus, who first established the custom of manuring the

seemed to be something quite incidental to the Christian faith; but while the conflict was acute the sex religion was called in to re-enforce Christianity and testify to its truth. Manifestly the idea of St. Augustine and others is that the pagan religion was false because it was obscene. The fact that sex sentiments could be appealed to as arbiters is evidence of their great strength. It is also manifest that the claim so often advanced down to our own time that the world owes its cult of purity to Christianity is untenable. Quite to the contrary, the cult of purity, sincere or hypocritical as it may have been, was a powerful factor in the triumph of Christianity. One need only read the Church Fathers to see at once and unmistakably that in defending their derivations they relied upon sentiments favouring chastity and hostile to sex indulgences, which were quite as current among the pagans as in their own circles. They used those sentiments, indeed, to reach minds which were closed to their theological dogmas, and persuade them that they ought to accept a religion that so well expressed sentiments of which they already approved. Such a thing will not strike the reader as surprising after the many proofs we have given that derivations follow, and do not precede, sentiments, though, of course, they may then serve to re-enforce them. Nor is it new for us to see sentiments of sex called in to judge competitions between religions and religious sects. This case is just one of a long long series of similar cases. Religions and sects are for ever accusing one another of obscenity and immorality. The pagans dubbed the agapes of the early Christians "obscene promiscuities of men and women," and at a later day orthodox Christians were to heap the same charges on the "meetings" of heretics. Protestants made effective use of the hackneyed charges of indecency and immorality against the Catholic clergy, and all Christians have with

fields; and a Mutinus, in whose naked (*pudendo*) lap brides seat themselves on the eve of their weddings [And see St. Augustine, *De civitate Dei,* VI, 9, who, etymologizing for Priapus, writes *prius sedent* for *praesident*], that he 'may be the first' to have impaired their purity." *Cf.* Arnobius, *Disputationes adversus gentes,* IV, 11, and Tertullian, *Apologeticus,* XXV, 3, 10-11 (Glover, pp. 137-39). Festus, *Ibid.,* XI, *s.v. Mutinus* (London, Vol. I, p. 445): "There was a shrine to Mutinus Titinus in Rome whither women went in broad-bordered togas to sacrifice to him."

one accord pressed it against atheists—time was when "liberal" and "libertine" were synonymous terms.[1] The philosophers of the eighteenth century used the sex weapon relentlessly against the Church, and the same blade, which has never yet grown rusty, is continually being brandished in France and Italy, where if not the only, it is at least the chief, argument put forward by many newspapers against the Church.

1342. How true or how false such charges may be or have been

1341 [1] Perrens, *Les libertins en France au XVIIᵉ siècle*, pp. 5-10: "The sixteenth century applied the term 'libertinage' to the spirit of unbelief, which had been a very ancient thing in France. . . . The great heresiarch, Calvin, fought bold thinking, licentious habits, and the conservative party at large in his 'young ones of Geneva.' . . . Unluckily the opposition interpreted the word 'liberty' not only in a political sense but in the voluptuous sense so popular among young men. . . . Was there so much licence? Probably not, for fires were lighted about the stakes on the basis of doctrines. [So today our Inquisitors on Purity use imprisonment and fines in lieu of arguments they are unable to find in their wretched brains.] . . . Calvin now began to add moral accusations to charges of false doctrine. . . . His appointed victims became 'licentious Christians fallen from grace and given over to the demon of the flesh, Anabaptists, the abomination of despair.' [That could very well come from Senator Bérenger or some other idiot of the same breed.] . . . In his copious vocabulary of invective one finds the term 'libertine,' which he seems to have been the first to introduce into French. The word as an epithet for an adversary does not appear in any manuscript of the sixteenth century. *Libertin* and *libertinage* are words not to be found in the oldest French lexicons. The Jesuit Philibert Monet was the first to make up his mind to naturalize the two new-comers in ordinary French parlance (*anno* 1635). . . . Independence in religious thinking was the main thing that Calvin branded as 'libertinage.' To use it as he used it would have been an abuse. He had burned the bridges behind him. . . . But in the long run the bridges were rebuilt. Those who insist on crossing them in the seventeenth century are forcing the hand of their time. . . . As regards individual conduct, the honourable denotation is new, but there are cases of it. Mme. de Sévigné writes: 'I am such a libertine when I sit down to write that the first turn I take controls all the rest of my letter.' Whereas Furetière, who harks back to the regular usage, declares a 'libertine' the schoolboy who plays hookey from his classes or disobeys his teacher, the disobedient wife or daughter, the man who is restive under constraints and follows his own inclinations *without however departing from the rules of virtue or good manners*. He is as particular as Richelet is in stressing that significant qualification, for he adds that a woman may say of herself *in a good sense and with altogether proper connotations* that she was a born *libertine*. Voltaire too thinks of a libertine as a man who wants his independence [*Dictionnaire philosophique, s.v. Liberté*]. But it was inevitable that in an age of believers the independent spirit should be regarded as a scandalous thing if it was extended to matters of faith. Whence a derived meaning, which readily became the main one."

is not the question at issue here. We can stop at the fact that their regular recurrence in such great abundance in the whole course of so many centuries down to our own times bears incontestable witness to the great influence that sentiments of sex have upon human societies, a truth that is further corroborated by other facts in large numbers.

1343. Worship of the organs of sex has had its day in many lands. The fact should not seem surprising once we reflect that such cults were just a part of the general fetishism everywhere where the hiatus described above (§ 1339) had not developed. In Graeco-Roman antiquity phallic worship is observable not only among peoples of exuberant imagination, the Greeks, for instance, but even in earnest, unimaginative Rome. In Rome it appears as in no sense a product of decadence, but as a fetishism surviving others that had gradually died out. Triumphant Christianity found phallic rites still in full vigour; nor did it succeed in extirpating them altogether. They hung on throughout the Middle Ages. In the very times when Christian faith was most ardent obscene figures continued to be carved on sacred edifices and painted in miniature in sacred books, while certain Christian saints inherited the functions of the gods of generation and the Church had no little trouble in putting an end to these various kinds of obscenity.[1][2]

1343 [1] An epigram of Antiphilus of Byzantium in the *Greek Anthology*, IX, 263 (Paton, Vol. III, pp. 138-41), shows a case of fetishism identical with the cults observable today among African Negroes: "When the old woman Eubule had something in mind, she was wont to regard the first stone that she found in her path as an oracle of Phoebus, and she would pick it up and weigh it in her hand. If she chanced to want nothing, she would find it heavy; if she had some wish, it would be lighter than a leaf. So she did whatever she pleased. But if things turned out badly she ever blamed Phoebus for the work of her own hands." Ancient

1343 [2] Cabanès, *Mœurs intimes du passé*, 3d ser., pp. 20-23, 110-11: "*The grotesque faun of the cathedrals:* So-called indecent figures come down very late even on religious monuments, and they have been noted in many places more or less mutilated but still so readily visible as to leave no doubt of their former existence. That they are still to be seen in fairly large numbers is indicated by the fact that in 1901 the Pope instructed the clergy to make a very careful examination of church buildings for the special purpose 'of destroying or rectifying all paintings either in the nude or insufficiently clothed.' The Sovereign Pontiff might have mentioned

1344. As usual, residues abide while derivations change. Nowadays it is the fashion to justify the hiatus that has developed in the series which was unbroken under the Romans with the pseudo-scientific arguments our times insist on having, so transmuting non-

heroes swore by their spears: Justinus, *Historiae Philippicae*, XLIII, 3 (Clarke, p. 302): ". . . In the beginning, our forefathers worshipped their spears as immortal gods, and we have a survival (*memoriam*) of that worship in our day, when spears are offered to the statues of gods." Aeschylus, *Septem adversus Thebas*, vv. 514-15 (529-30), says of a warrior: "He grasps a spear which in his assurance he holds in higher honour than a god and more precious than his eyes, and by it he swears an oath." [Smyth translation.] And *cf.* Virgil, *Aeneid*, XII, vv. 95-96; Valerius Flaccus, *Argonauticon*, III, vv. 707-11; Homer, *Iliad*, I, v. 234. The fetishisms in which Priapus figures were of the very same kind. Literature and inscriptions abound in allusions to him and there is nothing obscene about them: *Corpus inscriptionum Latinarum*, Vol. XIV, no. 3565 (p. 379): [On the top of a block of stone:] "To the genius of the god Priapus, powerful, mighty, invincible, Julius Agathemerus, freedman of Augustus [dedicates this stone in gratitude for] being warned in his sleep by the kindness of friends." (On the bottom:) "Hail, Holy Priapus, father of all things, hail. Grant me an untiring youth. . . . Grant me the power to charm fair maidens with the spell of wanton eye. Grant me to dispel soul-destroying cares in constant gaming and good times. Let me not fear old age too much nor be tortured by the fear of wretched death that is to bear me to the unwelcome mansions of Avernus where the King [Pluto] enchains (*coercet, sc. vinculis*) the vapoury (*fabulosos*) souls of the dead (*mortis quae ad domus trahet invidas Averni Fabulas manes ubi rex coercet*) and whence Fate allows no one to return. Hail, Holy Father Priapus, hail." (On one side:) "Come, all of you together, all you maidens [the Dryads and Naiads] who attend the sacred grove, all you maidens who worship the sacred waters." (On the other side:) "O Priapus, mighty, beloved, hail! Thy name chaste virgins invoke in prayer that thou shouldst loosen a girdle too long tied. Thee the bride invokes." (Here we follow the notes of De Ruggiero (*Syll. epig.* [?], Vol. II, pp. 23-24), who amends "*fabulas*" to "*fabulosas*," modifying "*manes*," and renders as "*inanes.*") Dessau, *Inscriptiones Latinae selectae*, no. 3581: "*Faustus Versenni P. ser. Priapum et templum d.s. peculio f.c.*" (Faustus, slave to Publius Versennus, had ["*f.c.: faciendum curavit*] this Priapus [*i.e.*, the statue] and temple reared at his own expense.") *Ibid.*, no. 3582:

sculpture as well as paintings; though it is only fair to state . . . that church buildings are not the only ones which reflect the manners and morals prevailing at one time or another in their ornaments. To say nothing of the winged Priapi on the Arena at Nîmes, or the sandstone monoliths in phallic form in the square at Préciamont (Oise), naturalia of a doubly inferior art have been observed more or less everywhere. The brush of the illuminator was neither more chaste nor more reticent than the chisel of the sculptor. There is a Bible with fairly skillful illustrations that were long attributed to John of Bruges. It portrays as naturally as can be the biblical episode of Lot and his daughters [Gen. 14:31-38]." *Cf.* § 1380. Such cases are not the few and the exceptional; they are the many and the commonplace. To describe them Witkowski needed three very fat volumes.

logical conduct into logical. Prosecutions of individuals who fail to respect a hiatus non-existent for the Romans are represented as necessary if we would have the younger generation strong and vigorous. But the younger generations in the Rome that conquered the whole

"Priepo Pantheo P.P. Aelii Ursio et Antonianus aediles col. Apul. dicaverunt Servero et Quintiano cos." ("Ursio and Antonianus, aediles of the colony of Apulia, dedicated this statue [*Pantheo for Pantheon*] to Priepus in behalf of [*P.P.*] Aelius during the consulship of Serverus and Quintianus.") St. Augustine, *De civitate Dei*, VII, 24: "In the rites of Liber a reputable matron placed a crown on the phallus in the presence of a throng of onlookers, among whom, blushing and sweating [we may imagine], if there be any shame (*frons*) in men, stood mayhap her husband. In the celebration of a wedding the new bride was bidden to sit down on a pyle of Priapus." But that is nothing compared to the indecencies in the mysteries of Cybele, the "Great Mother." In *Ibid.*, VII, 21, the Saint states that altogether respectable married women publicly crowned the phallus to obtain good harvests: "In the hamlets (*compitis*) of Italy certain rites of Liber are celebrated with such disgusting licence that male organs are worshipped in his honour and not [*nam* misprint for *non*] in a somewhat modest secret at least, but with a brazenness that shouts aloud in the public squares (*in propatulo exsultante*). On the holidays of Liber the obscene member was set up over every door in great honour and then carried about in parade, at first in the streets of small country towns, but eventually in Rome itself. In the town of Lavinium a whole month was dedicated to Liber, and on all those days everybody used obscene language until finally the image was paraded through the forum and restored to its accustomed place. It was necessary for a married woman of unimpeachable reputation to place a crown on the obscene object. For the god Liber apparently required so much placating for the sprouting of the seed, so much was needed to keep the evil eye (*fascinatio*) from the fields, that a respectable woman was forced to do in public a thing that a prostitute would not be allowed to do on the stage if married women were in the audience." All the same, in the more ancient times when those rites were customary "the altars on the Capitol glistened with trophies of Gallic and German kings"; while it was mystics of the Augustinian brand who "beckoned to barbarian swords to batter down the noble walls of Rome." [First allusion to Carducci, *"Agli amici della valle tiberina,"* *Poesie*, p. 393. The second, ?—A. L.] Lactantius Firmianus, *Divinae institutiones*, I, *De falsa religione*, 21-25 (*Opera*, Vol. I, p. 83; Fletcher, Vol. I, p. 61): "At Lampsacus [on the Hellespont] the ass was the prescribed victim for Priapus," and Lactantius gives an obscene reason for the custom that very probably was invented to explain it. Arnobius cries, *Disputationes adversus gentes*, IV, 11 (Bryce-Campbell, p. 193): "If we did not bend the knee as suppliants to Mutunus and Tutunus, would that be the end of the world, would everything go topsyturvy?" And he is right; for if one thing is certain it is that worshipping or not worshipping one god or another was a matter of utter irrelevance to the welfare of Rome. And *cf.* Pausanias, *Periegesis*, VI, *Elis* II, 26, 2; and IX, *Boeotia*, 31, 1-2. Diodorus Siculus, *Bibliotheca historica*, IV, 6, 1-4 (Booth, Vol. I, pp. 222-23), states that Priapus was worshipped not only in temples but also in the open fields, as their guardian, and that he was thought to be effective against spells. The cult of the phallus had a long life. There are traces of it as late as the

Mediterranean basin—were they a race of weaklings?[1] The soldiers of Caesar conquered the Gauls and other peoples, to say nothing of the legions of Pompey—were they weaklings? Can it be that Senator Bérenger is more of a fire-eater than Julius Caesar?[2] Such perse-

sixth century. Evagrius, *Ecclesiastica historia*, I, 11 (Migne, p. 2451; English, p. 23): "A person might very properly laugh at the phalli of the heathen, their Ithiphalli, their Phallagogy, their grotesque Priapus and that Pan of theirs who is worshipped in the obscene member." Nicephorus Callistus also mentions the thing in his day, *Ecclesiastica historia*, XIV, 48; and *cf.* Suidas, *Lexicon*, *s.vv.* Ἰθύφαλλοι, Φαλλοφόροι, Φαλλοί; Hesychius, *Lexicon*, *s.vv.* Ἰθύφαλλοι, Εἰθύφαλλον, Φαλλός; Harpocratio, *Lexicon in decem oratores Atticos*, *s.v.* Ἰθύφαλλοι; Demosthenes, *In Cononem*, 1263 (Auger, Vol. VI, pp. 348-49); Athenaeus, *Deipnosophistae*, IV, 3; XIV, 16; Eustathius, *Commentarii ad Homeri Odysseam*, I, v. 226 (Vol. I, pp. 52-53). If we are to believe the author of the *Philosophumena*, V, 4 (Cruice ed., p. 237), Priapus figured largely in the Justine heresy, and got his name from the fact that he was "created before" (*priapus* from *prius*) anything else: "That is why he has a place in every temple, is honoured by all Creation, and has the fruits of the created world draped about him when he is carried about the streets, since he is the cause of creation." Well known the rôle of Priapus as the guardian of gardens: Virgil, *Georgics*, IV, vv. 110-11:

> "*Et custos furum atque avium cum falce saligna*
> *Hellespontiaci servet tutela Priapi.*"

("Let the guardianship of the Hellespontian Priapus with his willow sickle serve as protection against thieves and birds.") *Eclogues*, VII, vv. 33-36:

> "*Sinum lactis et haec te liba, Priape, quot annis*
> *exspectare sat est: custos es pauperis horti.*
> *Nunc te marmoreum pro tempore fecimus, at tu*
> *si foetura gregem suppleverit aureus esto.*"

("This cup of milk and these cakes are all you can expect, O Priapus, year after year. You are the guardian of a poor man's garden. For the present we have

---

1344 [1] As a measure for restoring discipline in his camp in Spain, Scipio expelled a large number of sutlers from it and prostitutes to the number of two thousand. Valerius Maximus, *De dictis factisque memorabilibus*, II, 7, 1: "... *nam constat tum maximum inde institorum* [pedlars] *et lixarum* [camp-followers] *numerum cum duobus millibus scortorum* [prostitutes] *abisse.*" Xenophon did much the same for the Ten Thousand (*Anabasis*, IV, 1, 14), but as a measure for conserving food-supplies.

1344 [2] Suetonius, *Divus Julius*, 65: "He [Caesar] judged his men not by their good morals nor by their families, but by their prowess as soldiers, treating them all with the same strictness and the same indulgence." *Ibid.*, 67: "A merciless disciplinarian when it came to desertion and mutiny, he winked at other things. Sometimes after winning a great battle he would relax routine duties and give the men free rein in satisfying their lusts. It was a saying of his that 'his soldiers were fighters even when smelling from women.'" And *cf.* Dio Cassius, *Historia Romana*, XLII, 55.

cutions are held to be necessary to protect family virtues, as if those virtues were few or weak among the ancient Romans in the days when the image of the phallus was protecting children, men, and even victorious generals from the evil eye. And they are said to safe-

made you of marble, but you shall be of gold if the coming lambs fill out the flock.") And Ovid, *Fasti*, I, v. 415: *"At ruber hortorum decus et tutela Priapus . . ."* ("And ruddy-thighed Priapus, the ornament and guarantor of the gardens.") And *cf.* Tibullus, *Delia*, I, vv. 17-18; Columella, *De re rustica*, X, vv. 29-34 (Vol. I, p. 399); Horace, *Saturae*, I, 8 [Fairclough: "How Priapus put the witches to rout."]; *Greek Anthology*, XVI (The Planudean Appendix), 236-43 (Paton, Vol. V, pp. 300-05). The cult of Priapus appears in places where it cannot possibly have implied any obscene allusion. He was the guardian of tombs, for instance. Dessau, *Inscriptiones Latinae selectae*, no. 3585 (Now in Paris, found in Rome among the ruins of tombs along the Via Appia): *"Custos sepulcri pene destricto deus Priapus ego sum. Mortis et vitai locus."* ("I the god Priapus of the *penis destrictus* am the guardian of this tomb. This is a place of death and life.") *Ibid.,* no. 3586 (Verona inscription): *"dis manibus . . . Locus adsignatus monimento in quo est aedicla Priapi."* ("Sacred to the gods of the dead . . . A place devoted to burial which is the home of Priapus.") In the *Greek Anthology*, VI, 33 (Paton, Vol. I, pp. 314-15), Priapus is designated by the poet Maecius as protector of the sea-shore. And *cf. Ibid.,* VI, 89 (Paton, pp. 346-47); VI, 193 (Paton, pp. 398-99—the poet Flaccus); and X, 1 (Leonidas) and 2 (Antipater) (Paton, Vol. IV, pp. 2-5). This latter contains an exhortation to sailors to put to sea, and ends with the words: "This I say to you, I, the Priapus that stands in the harbour, son of Bromius." An image of Priapus is stamped on coins from Lampsacus. Strabo, *Geografica*, VIII, 6, 24 (Jones, Vol. IV, p. 205), speaks of a town that was called Priapus because that god was worshipped there. [This is a misapprehension on Pareto's part. Strabo says (Jones translation): "Orneae is named after the river that flows past it. . . . It was from Orneae that the Euphronius who composed the *Priapeia* calls the god 'Priapus the Orneatan.' "—A. L.] Lajard, *Recherches sur le culte de Vénus . . . en Orient*, pp. 51-54: "Significant the presence of the very organ of female generative capacity among the emblems that are grouped around the androgynous figure which I take to be the Assyrian Venus, or Mylitta. . . . Another cone even shows a priest dressed in an Asiatic costume and performing an act of worship before an altar visible on which are a κτείς and the star of Venus, or else the Sun. There the κτείς seems to be the emblem of the goddess herself. The presence of such an attribute on all these different monuments seems to me to characterize the cult of the oriental Venus with that same forcefulness, that ingenuous crudeness, which was doubtless stamped in the beginning on the religious doctrines current among the Assyrians and Phoenicians. Reaching over the centuries and over a long series of religious or political revolutions, those doctrines have left such deep imprints on the soil of Western Asia that on examining the manners and morals of the peoples living there today one gets the gloomy impression that despite the successive efforts of Christianity and Islam, worship of the κτείς has not disappeared in certain religious sects of the Near East and notably in a locality that was famous in a day gone by for the worship of Venus that was practised there. In our day, in fact, the Druses of the Lebanon district pay a real

guard the chastity of women, as though Roman matrons in the heyday of the Republic were any less moral than the emancipated women of the United States, which of all countries is the paradise of sex hypocrisy.[8]

worship to the female organ of sex in their secret vespers, and so worship every Friday evening, the day, that is, that was consecrated to Venus of yore, and also the day on which the Mussulmans are required by Mohammed's code to perform the double duty of going to mosque and attending their wives. . . . As regards these vespers . . . we are told that each initiate . . . is obliged to make a general confession and that the greatest of all sins is fornication with 'sisters' or female initiates. But the Nozaïrians, who have also kept the ceremonies of κτείς worship, regard carnal commerce as the only means by which perfect spiritual union is attainable." Athenaeus, *Deipnosophistae*, XIV, 56: "Μυλλοί: Heraclides of Syracuse says in his *De ritibus* that at Syracuse on the day of the Thesmophoria [festival in honour of Ceres] [cakes in the form of] female *pudenda* were made of sesame and honey and passed around in honour of the goddess. They [the cakes] were known throughout all Sicily as *mylli*." Cf. Martial, *Epigrammata*, XIV, 69 [This epigram refers to a sweetmeat shaped like a Priapus. Pareto gives another reference to Martial, IX, 3, v. 3. This is mistaken. If he was thinking again of a Priapine pastry the reference might be to VI, 73, v. 2.—A. L.] And see further: D'Ansse de Villoison, *De triplici theologia mysteriisque veterum commentatio*, quoted by Sainte-Croix, *Mémoirs pour servir à l'histoire de la religion secrète des anciens peuples*, pp. 246 f.

1344 [8] On a line in Horace that deals with the symptoms of advancing age, *Epoda*, VIII, v. 18, *"Minusve languet fascinum?"* ("Is your spell any the weaker?") Porphyrio comments: "An allusion to the male organ, for it was customary to place that ugly object in front of things that were likely to be cast under a spell." Pliny, *Historia naturalis*, XXVIII, 7 (4) (Bostock-Riley, Vol. V, p. 290): "If a stranger enters the room, or if someone looks at a sleeping child, the nurse spits three times, though they (*illos*, the children) are already protected by the god Fascinus, who is the guardian not only of children but also of generals. He is worshipped by the Vestals as a god among other Roman gods and an image of him is hung from the floors of the chariots of generals as they ride in triumphal processions and protects them like a physician ever at hand against the evil eye of envy." Varro, *De lingua Latina*, VII, 97 (Goetz-Scholl, p. 119): "Obscene things are so called, perhaps, because of the indecent images (*obscaena*, i.e., *virilia*) that are hung about the necks of children to protect them from the evil eye." Daremberg-Saglio, *Dictionnaire*, s.v. Fascinum, Fascinus: "The phallus was carved in bas-relief on the walls of cities and all sorts of buildings public or private. An example unearthed at Pompeii also has an inscription, *Hic habitat Felicitas*, an assertion of good omen designed to bar the door to bad luck. The phallus was one of the commonest constituents in amulets worn on the person. Countless objects have been found ornamented with that design. Hardly a collection of antiquities is without one. Sometimes, to increase the effectiveness of a charm, several phallic designs would be grouped together to make up a sort of monstrosity. Then again the phallus would be given wings and legs. The licentious fancy of the ancients gave itself free rein in such grotesque compositions. . . . In cases of any immediate danger

1345. The United States mails refuse to carry an English novel because it is deemed too "sensuous"; but they carry without the slightest scruple publications that preach slaughtering the moneyed classes and robbing them of their property. But, really, can anyone keeping strictly to logic and experience consider such activities less harmful to individual and society than a little "sensuality" in print? [1]

from the evil eye, one could extricate oneself quite readily by making a gesture that is still familiar in Italy and other countries as 'the fig' (*far la fica*). . . . Inserting the thumb between the fore and middle fingers, one got a suggestion of the two sexes in union. To represent the two organs one by one was a very effective prophylactic." Of such things Pliny says, *Op. cit.*, XI, 109 (49) (Bostock-Riley, Vol. III, p. 92): "There is no difference between peoples in this respect, and universal also are such rites." After his allusion to the crowning of the phallus by respectable matrons (§ 1343 [1]), St. Augustine exclaims of Varro (*De civitate Dei*, VII, 21): "And he would call such acts of sacrilege sacred rites (*sacra*)!" Theodoret, *Graecarum affectionum curatio, Sermo* III, *De Angelis* (*Opera*, Vol. IV, p. 890): "At the festival of the Phallagogia, those who are celebrating the orgy pay honour to the little creature Priapus, with his *ingenti et exporrecto membro,* and so to the phallus of Liber, his father. In the same way the female *pecten* (*cf.* κτείς, § 1343 [1])—so the female organ is called—is worshipped with divine honours by female initiates to the Thesmophoria [of Ceres]."

1345 [1] *Liberté,* Jan. 9, 1913: "From the summer months of 1905 down to February 1912, when arrests took place on a large scale, unionist dynamiters had been trying by a 'nitro-campaign' to intimidate employers of non-union labour. Their activities spread terror in every shop and factory from New York to California. The Los Angeles *Times* building was blown up on Oct. 1, 1910, the deaths of twenty-two non-union type-setters resulting. That outrage required energetic action. It was then discovered that the International Association of Bridge and Structural Iron Workers was ordering the systematic destruction of shops, mills, and factories that disregarded the mandates of organized labour. The forty thousand exhibits that appear in the case, to say nothing of the oral testimony of witnesses, show that the Bridge and Iron Workers' Association had organized that agency of 'agitation' and that it was functioning with some efficiency. A secret budget of a thousand dollars a month was being devoted to purchases of dynamite. All the great industrial centres had information bureaus that kept the central committee supplied with the data required for prompt and direct action. When a company refused an increase in wages or took on 'yellow' help, when an employer undertook to guarantee the independence of non-union labour, when a non-unionized enterprise was competing with a unionized business in such a way as to lower wages and therefore had to be ruined, the dynamiters came on the scene; one of their delegates was sent to the place and a bomb exploded. One of these audacious terrorists, Ortie MacManigal, has told the story of his expeditions to the court in abundant detail. He has participated in fifty 'jobs,' most of them successful, in the five years since he began his propaganda by action. Let us give him the floor. 'In 1907,' says he, 'Herbert S. Hockin, secretary-treasurer of the Bridge Workers, came to see me in Detroit. "You are used to working in the quarries," he said, "so you know how to handle explosives. From now

Senator Bérenger goes around scrutinizing the costumes of chorus-girls with a view to safe-guarding morality. But he is also the author of a probation law that turns hosts of criminals loose upon the public to resume their former feats of prowess. Yet are crimes of violence really less reprehensible than a glimpse at a pair of legs, or even at a pair of thighs, on a stage? In some cities in the United States the authorities send policewomen about the streets to provoke "mashers" and arrest them, but they never hire detectives to provoke Anarchists to crimes of violence and then arrest them. Can logic and experience ever have shown them that a lewd remark to a woman on the street does greater harm to individual and society than a crime of arson, a murder, or a theft (§ 1325)? On March 28, 1913, the French Chamber debated an amnesty bill. It was proposed to vote pardons for all persons convicted of anti-militaristic agitation. The propa-

on you are in the pay of the union. It needs you." I tried to object, but he gave me to understand that if I refused the Executive Committee would black-list me and that I would be out of a job. In the end I gave in.' From that time MacManigal had a busy life. He started 'work' in Ohio, Illinois, Massachusetts, New York. He had a liberal expense allowance from the union heads. On occasions when his bombs failed to go off or were discovered in time to prevent explosion, he got only travelling-expenses. He communicated with headquarters only by telegrams of apparently insignificant content. When things went well he would simply send the newspaper item. . . . Ortie MacManigal tells his story in a matter-of-fact way. His confession, which is a real novel, is not less than seven hundred pages long. Here is a specimen from it. 'In June, 1908, I was on a job at Evanston, Illinois. Hockin paid me a visit. He had come to tell me that he had got hold of a new invention that would do wonders. It was a sort of clock device with a charge of nitroglycerin, which went off one hour, five hours, even ten hours after setting, according to the way you regulated it. It was very easy to work, and it gave you time to get far enough away to establish an alibi. He wanted me to start using it at once. I refused. "But we have tried it," he said, "at Steubenville, Cincinnati, Indianapolis. It works fine." ' " As regards police corruption in the United States, to say nothing of corruption in other public departments, there are documents without end. Here is one: *Journal de Genève*, Mar. 1, 1913: "Mayor Gaynor of New York, testifying before the commission investigating corruption in the police department, declared: 'At the time I came into office police inspectors were retiring millionaires. Some of them had town and country homes, yachts, automobiles. The police were collecting three millions annually in graft from disorderly houses alone. That situation no longer prevails today. There may be one or two exceptional cases of graft. But don't imagine the newspapers are altogether clean of graft. For twenty-five years they have been in it up to their necks.' "

ganda in question had urged citizens not to answer the call to arms, or if forced to do so, to fire on their officers rather than on the enemy. It had also given instructions for damaging a cannon so that it could not be used. The bill was defeated, after impassioned debate, by a vote of 380 to 171. At the same session a bill was introduced to grant amnesty to persons convicted of agitation for birth-control. That bill was defeated by a vote of 471 to 16. What are we to conclude? That betraying one's country, murdering army officers, destroying war materials, and handing the country over to an enemy are less important crimes than expressing one's opinion freely as to whether one should or should not take economic circumstances into account in bringing children into the world? Such a reasoning does not hold, and the non-logical, religious character of the whole procedure is evident enough.[2]

1346. Much less pretentious but no whit better is the argument which would justify the hiatus by the claim that it is designed to prevent minds from dwelling on loathsome things. But what more loathsome than a corpse in a state of decomposition, swarming with maggots, let us say? Yet one can speak of such a thing freely, and feel no compulsion to use Latin words or Greek letters for either the corpse, the decomposition, or the maggots. Obviously, therefore, the hiatus must have developed in response to some other sentiment than a feeling of revulsion for unclean things.

1345 [2] Frequent is a derivation that is designed to give a semblance of practical utility to prescriptions of a religious character. So the prohibition of pork among the Jews has been represented as a measure of hygiene. In the same way birth-control propaganda is said to be condemned only on patriotic grounds as tending to decrease the number of men available for a country's defence. If that argument were sound, the 471 French Deputies who condemned birth-control agitation ought *a fortiori* to have condemned an agitation designed to deprive the army of the weapons required for fighting an enemy. It is also somewhat ludicrous to be so fussy about increasing the number of men available for an army, just to have them killed by their comrades later on if they have brains enough to become officers. Much more consistent were those German women who, copying Lysistrata, preached a "mother's strike" to stop supplying the *"bourgeoisie"* with slaves and the Empire with soldiers. It is true that the considerations underlying a vote taken in a legislative body are very complex, and that logic is the last thing one should ask of them. In view of that, if the vote in France stood alone it would prove nothing. It acquires significance, however, from the fact that it is typical of an exceedingly large number of cases.

1347. The sentiment in fact is of a class with the sentiments that prompt people to have an element of mystery in their religions. The hiatus as it exists today is a reticence of form rather than of substance. It appears very much as an oscillation in the degree to which mystery is carried. Mystery was not unknown among the ancient Romans, but in our time it shrouds many things that were formerly left in the light of day.

1348. If we would keep to the logico-experimental field in dealing with such facts, we must not in any way share in the religious sentiments in which they originate, or at least must put our sentiments aside so long as we are dealing with them.

1349. These sentiments may be of great practical utility in the conduct of social life. They are certainly fatal to theoretical investigations conducted in the logico-experimental field. Anyone not feeling his mind altogether at ease would therefore do better to read no farther in this chapter, just as people who believe in the divine inspiration of the Koran do well in not reading historical criticisms of that book or of the life of Mohammed.

1350. A man may be a scientific sceptic in one field and a man of faith in another field; but he cannot, "because a contradiction there consents not," be a sceptic and a believer in the same field. The believer, precisely because he is one, can only regard his own religion as true and other religions as false. He therefore judges, as he has to judge, the facts by that standard. From the experimental point of view two actions may be in all respects similar, but he will judge them now good, now bad, according as they belong to his own religion or to some other. He readily sees the mote in his neighbour's eye. He cannot see the beam in his own.

1351. Like the believer in any other religion, the believer in the Religion of Sex rejects *a priori* every argument that runs counter to his faith; and he feels in duty bound to constrain others to assent to his faith, though he would complain bitterly enough if anyone tried to force some other faith upon him. Wherever he has the support of the secular arm he achieves by force what he cannot achieve by persuasion. In many Christian countries it is possible to blaspheme Christ as much as one pleases and no court of law will effectively intervene. But the same courts will condemn an obscene postcard with swift despatch.

1352. The Romans read without trace of indignation the verses (*Epoda,* VIII, XII) in which Horace alludes to organs of the female body under their exact Latin names; but the Romans would never have tolerated either anti-patriotic or anti-militarist utterances. Many moderns will tolerate these latter but cry aloud for dire punishment on anyone who writes as Horace wrote. When the high-priest, Caiaphas, heard words of Jesus offensive to his religious sentiments, he "rent his garments"—*scidit vestimenta sua,* wailing, "He hath uttered blasphemy." So Senator Bérenger, high-priest among our pedlars of purity, waxes wroth at the mere thought that Mme. Regina Badet should appear on the stage in skirts a little short. The Moslems hold the hog in horror and would not taste its flesh at any price; but they speak freely of sexual intimacies. Our sex-reformers feel, or pretend to feel, horror at such discourse, but eat pork with the best of appetites. Dubois relates:[1] "A European of my acquaintance had written a letter to one of his friends in favour of a Brahman whom I had recommended to him. On finishing the letter he sealed it with a sealing stamp, which he moistened with the tip of his tongue. The Brahman noticed it, refused to receive the letter, left in a bad temper as though he had been grievously insulted, and preferred losing the advantages he might have gained from the recommendation to being the bearer of a missive polluted in such a fashion." Our sex-reformers of the prolific breed that is so deft at finding the mote in a neighbour's eye would ridicule the stupidity of that Brahman, without remembering that their behaviour would be precisely the same if the stamp on the letter was engraved with an image of the phallus, which the ancient Romans used without trace of scruple in warding off the evil eye.[2]

1352 [1] *Mœurs, institutions et cérémonies des peuples de l'Inde,* Vol. I, p. 252.

1352 [2] The Catharists exchanged a kiss of peace; but their Perfects were not allowed to touch a woman, so they imparted the kiss by way of a copy of the Gospel: Guiraud, *Cartulaire de Notre-Dâme de Prouille,* Vol. I, Preface, pp. cxcix: "The Perfects kissed each of the faithful on both cheeks . . . and there was no difficulty about that so long as the ceremony was between men. It grew complicated when there were women in the congregation. A Perfect could in no case touch a woman

1353. The sex residue appears in combination with other residues in many social phenomena, and here therefore we have to repeat in part what we said of asceticism.

1354. Let us as usual ignore the case of plain hypocrisy, which is much rarer, after all, than is ordinarily supposed. Hypocrisy is often-times a device for executing certain logical purposes and therefore has no place among the residues.

1355. The sex residue figures in many religious effusions. At times it is recognizable out of hand, then again it is almost impossible to identify it as something apart from the strictly religious sentiment.[1] Enemies of the Roman Church have pretended to find it where it certainly was not. Friends of the Church have tried to deny its presence even where it was in striking evidence. Many of the priests who leave the Church are moved to do so, now consciously, now unwittingly, by interests of sex. The same urge is not without its influence on much of the criticism of the Modernists, just as in their disposition to play up to democracy lurks a hope of securing advantages thereby.[2]

even with the tip of a finger. With all the more reason was it forbidden him to kiss one. The rule was so strict that in the rite of the blessing, which involved the Perfect's resting his palms on the head of the convert [or invalid], he was directed, if the recipient was a woman, to hold his hands above her head without touching her—*tenendo manum super caput infirmi, non tamen tangendo si sit mulier.* The same difficulty had to be evaded in the rite of the kiss, and what the Catholic liturgy calls an 'instrument of peace' was used for the purpose. The kiss is deposited on some object of particular veneration, and then the individual who for one reason or another cannot be kissed goes and gets it there. . . . The Perfect in charge of a Catharist ceremony kissed a copy of the Gospels and handed it to the women to kiss. . . . They did so and then kissed one another." The sex-reformers of our day, who are the most perfect idiots of whom human history makes mention, differ from the Catharists in dogmas but not in the sex residue.

1355 [1] *Cf.* I Cor. 5. If all sex-reformers were Christians, one might have no certain means of distinguishing the sex residue from the purely religious residue; but free-thinkers sometimes go in for purity and the religious residue does not figure in that case. Says the good St. Ambrose in *De virginibus,* I, 8, 52 (*Opera,* Vol. II, p. 159): "*Castitas enim angelos fecit. Qui eam servavit angelus est, qui perdidit diabolus.*" ("Chastity hath made angels; for he who hath preserved his chastity is an angel, he who hath lost it, a devil.") Free-thinkers have—or pretend to have—neither angels nor devils. They cannot take advantage of such a language.

1355 [2] Traditional pleasantries often state facts in vivid form. Take a story in Sorbière, *Sorberiana, s.v. Moine* (pp. 145-46): "A certain monk having put off

1356. The cult of woman figures explicitly or implicitly, openly or thinly veiled, in many religions—a thick book might be written on the subject. One should not forget the many genealogies of divine beings that all show a sex residue, nor allegories and personifications, male or female, of abstractions or other fantastic aggregates. All such things go to show how at all times thoughts of sex crowd into the human mind. Certain it is that forced chastity, especially when it is scrupulously observed, tends to introduce amorous sentiments into situations where there is, and can be, no question of erotic relations. That is already apparent, in germ, in the extreme fondness of a little girl for her doll, an animal, her friends, and sometimes, though she may be unaware of it, for her parents. The fact can be proved, for when the girl marries or comes into contact with a man in some way or other, such forms of affection either disappear or diminish in intensity. Cut off from men, a woman oftentimes entertains for a pet sentiments that have—though she may not be aware of it—an erotic element. Other women, in the same cir-

the frock applied for assistance to the late Prince Maurice of Orange. [The same story is often told with other names and so, probably, is fictional in character.]: "*Cuius causa huc venisti?*" asked the Prince. "*Religionis,*" answered the friar. "*Religio cuius generis?*" "*Foemininil*" "*Ergo,*" the Prince concluded, "*tu huc venisti propter genere foemininum.*" [The phrase "*religio cuius generis*"—in case the jest is not apparent to anyone—has a double meaning: "What sort of religion?" "Of what gender is the word religion?" The friar, thinking his Latin is being tested, answers: "Feminine gender." "I see!" concludes the Prince, "You came here looking for a woman."—A. L.] In the *Journal de Genève,* Sept. 17, 1913, a friend of Father Loyson (Father Hyacinthe) reports a conversation that took place in Rome between the ex-priest and Prince Baldassare Odescalchi: "Said the Prince (the details of the conversation I got both from M. Loyson himself and the Prince): 'But, Father, since you continue to call yourself a Catholic priest, why should you not return to the Roman fold?' 'Why, Prince Odescalchi . . . you forget that there are difficulties!' 'What difficulties?' 'Well, first of all, there is the question of infallibility!' 'Oh, infallibility!' said Prince Odescalchi. 'There are ways of coming to an understanding—there are interpretations! That could not be an insuperable obstacle.' 'But then there's the matter of my marriage.' 'Yes, your marriage, of course. There's some difficulty there, but not insuperable either. You are as well aware as I that Catholic priests of the oriental rites marry. You might be transferred to some oriental rite.' [The Pope, Leo XIII, appointed Father Vives, a Capuchin friar, to handle negotiations. Nothing came of them.] . . . M. Loyson has repeatedly asserted that the conferences failed primarily because of his inability to accept the dogma of papal infallibility. But the question of his marriage was a much more serious difficulty than Prince Odescalchi ever imagined."

cumstances, devote themselves to charities, social agitation, or religious activities. The so-called feminist is often just a hysterical woman in want of a mate.[1]

1357. Veneration and hatred for a given thing may likewise be forms of a religion which has that thing for its object of worship. The religious trait is eliminated only by indifference (§ 911). That is why the hiatus in the sex series is more of form than of substance. The Negro in maltreating his fetish, the Catholic in reviling his saint, are both manifesting a religious mood not shared by the man who is indifferent to fetish and saint alike. That is a matter of common knowledge as regards love. It was observed of old that love and hatred are kindred things, the opposite of both being indifference. It is also a trite remark that the men who most malign women are the ones who can least do without them.[1]

1358. We need therefore not be surprised that strong sex impulses often lead to loathing for the sexual act and, in the Christian saints, to misogyny. Often enough in their invectives one detects a combination of a sentiment of pure asceticism with a sentiment of unsatisfied sexual interest. The sex-urge may become so violent as to provoke hallucinations, and the Christian becomes convinced that the Devil is tempting him to sins of impurity. And the Devil in question was not altogether without his reality. He is actually present in the mind of the human being, though he is more effectively banished by a sexual act than by any rite of exorcism.

1356 [1] Bayle, *Dictionnaire historique, s.v. Junon:* "I would go so far as to say that the extremes to which the Christian went in regard to the Virgin Mary and which surpass anything the pagans ever invented in the worship of Juno [Because to a greater degree than the Christian their religion offered other channels for the expression of the sex residue.] came of the same source, from the habit, I mean, of honouring and courting women with more devotion and more respect than is paid to the other sex. [From the sex residue, in other words.] It is impossible to dispense with women either in civil or in religious life. Strip the Roman communion of its worship of female saints, and especially of the woman who is called Queen of Heaven or Queen of the Angels, and terrible gaps would be opened in it. What would be left would fall to pieces like *arena sine calce, scopae dissolutae.*"

1357 [1] Athenaeus, *Deipnosophistae,* XIII, 5: "Someone remarked to Sophocles that Euripides was a misogynist. 'In his plays, yes,' said Sophocles. 'But in his bed he is a philogynist.'"

1359. One needs to read only a portion of what the worthy Friar Bartolommeo da San Concordio has to say in disparagement of women, and the remarks the Church Fathers devoted to the subject would fill a fair-sized library.[1]

1360. Persons who feast on such exhortations may likely enough be brought to such a pass by the sheer ardour of unsatisfied senses as to have the female of the species constantly on their minds, to shun women in fear of the danger they represent, to hate them out

1359 [1] Says Fra Bartolommeo, *Ammaestramenti degli antichi*, 25, 10, 1-10: "To have converse with women is to expose oneself to the perils of sensuality. *Ecclesiasticus*, 42:12-13. 'Sit not in the midst of women, for from garments cometh a moth, and from women wickedness.' Jerome to Oceanus [Frankfurt, 1684, Vol. IV, p. 213: *Ad Oceanum, De vita clericorum*]: 'Especially do I warn thee to be watchful; for it is the clerk's temptation to go oft unto women. . . .' 'Converse with women is the door to the Devil, the road to iniquity, the sting of the scorpion. . . .' 'With a flaming fire doth woman singe the spirit of him who abideth with her.' 'Verily he cannot of his whole heart walk in the path of the godly who hath converse with women. . . . Art thou chaste? Lo, thou dost tell a great lie; for if thou seekest chastity, why goest thou with women? The woman of pleasing converse love thou of the mind and not of the body.' Gregory, in the third of the *Dialogues* [III, 7 (*Opera*, Vol. III, p. 229; Gardner, p. 113)]: 'Those who order the body to continence presume not to abide with women.' *Idem, In registro* [*i.e., Epistolae*, IX, 2, 60 (Migne, Vol. III, p. 997; Barmby, Vol. II, p. 85)]: 'It is written of the blessed Augustine that he refused to live with his sister, and he said, "The women who are with my sister are not my sisters." ' The caution of a man so great may well be a firm lesson unto us. Isidore, in *Synonima*, II [17 (4) (Migne, p. 849)]: 'If thou wouldst be secure against fornications, keep in body and in gaze aloof from woman; for dwelling near the serpent not long wilt thou hold off from him; abiding near the fire but in danger, not long shalt thou be safe; for thou shouldst be of iron, yet shouldst thou sweat of some heat.' Jean Plantavit, in his *Florilegium rabbinicum*, p. 458, relates that 'a certain wise man looking upon a small but pretty woman said: "Small is the beauty, but the evil is great." ' And he comments: '*The evil is great:* the wicked woman is worse than evil, as Chrysostom well said in words which Antonius Melissa quotes [in his *Sententiae*], II, 34 [Migne, p. 1090], and as we have elsewhere cautioned. For he says: "O Evil! A wicked woman is worse than any evil! Deadly are dragons and poisonous snakes, but the deadliness of a woman is deadlier than the poison of serpents. The wicked woman is never chastened: treat her sternly and she rageth, mildly and she runneth wild. Easier is it to melt iron than to tame a woman. He who hath a bad wife may know that he hath received the reward of his sins. There is on earth no wild beast to be compared to a bad wife. What quadruped is fiercer than the lion? None, save a bad wife! What serpent is deadlier than the dragon? None, save a bad wife!" ' " And *cf.* Athenaeus, *Deipnosophistae*, XIII, 6-10 [This, however, is a light-hearted treatment of the theme.—A. L.] Such the usual attitude of men who malign women out of morbid attachment to them.

of attachment to them, and to envy those who they see are enjoying them; and just such envy creeps into their glorifications of virginity, the praises they shower upon married couples who live in continence and their horror for fornication. They, meantime, seem to be in the utmost good faith—that, indeed, is the thing which sharpens and intensifies their sentiments.

1361. Others, too, may be in good faith. The zeal evinced by priests and moralists in safe-guarding women from "temptations" may express an unmixed religious or moral enthusiasm. But not seldom sex jealousies enter in. Such sentiments can function quite apart from any actual sex relation. Eunuchs, as is well known, are often susceptible to jealousy—they are usually jealous, in fact, and in our parts of the world the violence that jealousy may assume in the sexually impotent is a matter of common observation. Then there are the professional prudes of the humanitarian cult, and women who are aged or ugly and have no hope of romance in their lives. Such women are prone to jealousy and quite lose their heads if they see a young man looking at a young or pretty girl or going so far as to speak to one. All this may happen quite apart from any perception on the individual's part that the sex residue is influencing his conduct. So envy may be so intimately blended with the sex residue as to be indistinguishable from it even by the person who is experiencing the complex sentiment.

1362. Towards the end of the eighteenth century and the beginning of the nineteenth the view generally prevailed that Christian theologians were alone responsible for the efforts to deprive mankind of the pleasures of the senses and therefore of those sexual pleasures which "Nature" had vouchsafed to men. But developments after that time, and especially since 1900, show that the theologians of free-thought are no less valiant in repressive zeal than the theologians of Christianity, and that modern inquisitors of "heretical depravity" in the Religion of Sex are a good match for the old-time inquisitors of "heretical depravity" in the Catholic Church.[1]

1362 [1] The old misapprehensions arose from the fact that the free-thinkers of the time were trying to take advantage of the ever present and ever vigorous residues

1363. It is a curious fact that while the Christian, and especially the Catholic, Church denounces amorous pleasures, it is from them in the main that it derives the metaphors through which it expresses manifestations of faith. The Church is the Bride of Christ, to say nothing of the interpretations of erotic elements in the Song of Songs, which turn a love-song not a little coarse and not a little absurd, to tell the truth, into an epithalamium of the Church as the Bride of Christ. Christian nuns are "brides of Christ." To Him they

of sex in their battle with Christianity. Once they had won that fight, they did more and worse than their sometime adversaries. Not even as able a thinker as Buckle avoids the misapprehension alluded to. In his *History of Civilization in England,* Vol. III, pp. 270-72, he begins very judiciously: "The happiness derived from gratifying the senses, being thus diffused over a wider area, and satisfying, at any given moment, a greater number of persons than the other form of happiness is capable of, does, on that account, possess an importance which many who call themselves philosophers are unwilling to recognize. Too often have philosophic and speculative thinkers, by a foolish denunciation of such pleasures, done all in their power to curtail the quantity of happiness of which humanity is susceptible." But then he goes on to say: "If, then, we review the history of opinion in connexion with the history of action, we may probably say, that the ascetic notions of philosophers, such, for instance, as the doctrines of the Stoics, and similar theories of mortification, have not worked the harm which might have been expected, and have not succeeded in abridging, to any perceptible extent, the substantial happiness of mankind. . . . But, though philosophers have failed in their effort to lessen the pleasures of mankind, there is another body of men who, in making the same attempt, have met with far greater success. I mean, of course, the theologians, who, considered as a class, have in every country and in every age, deliberately opposed themselves to gratifications which are essential to the happiness of an overwhelming majority of the human race. Raising up a God of their own creation [That overlooks free-thinkers.], whom they hold out as a lover of penance [That overlooks at least some of the pagans.], of sacrifice, and of mortification, they, under this pretence, forbid enjoyments which are not only innocent but praiseworthy. For, every enjoyment by which no one is injured, is innocent. . . . The theologians, however, for reasons which I have already stated, cultivate an opposite spirit, and, whenever they have possessed power, they have always prohibited a large number of pleasurable actions, on the ground that such actions are offensive to the Deity." That [logic], however, is not the cause of their conduct—their conduct is non-logical: it is the derivation with which they justify their conduct; and that that is the case is apparent from the fact that free-thinkers who have no Deity to consider offended deport themselves in exactly the same manner, but using different derivations denouncing "offences" against "modesty" or "morality" or some other fetish of theirs. Buckle's remarks are therefore not in strict accord with the facts, if by "theologians" we understand the theologians of Christianity or any other religion. They come into exact line with the facts if by "theologians" we mean fanatics of every breed who take pleasure in annoying their neighbour.

consecrate their virginity, and for Him they nourish a passion in which the sacred blends with the profane. Nor is that the whole story. The Church Fathers are unable to speak for any great length of time without alluding, if only by metaphor, to sex. The vision of woman hovers before their eyes. Banished in one direction, back she comes from some other.

1364. Even in the Gospels there are passages in which the sex residue comes into view, in a very incidental way, to be sure. There is no apparent reason why in place of the parable of the ten virgins something else could not have been found less likely to fix attention on virginities and consummations. But woman dominates the later stages of Christianity more especially, till she is finally exalted to the splendours of a heavenly throne in the person of the Virgin Mary.

1365. Compare such things with Xenophon's *Memorable Sayings of Socrates*. For Xenophon sex is a physical need like any other, the satisfaction of it being condemned only in the excess. Xenophon is not greatly concerned with it, any more than he is with other physical needs—eating, for instance. It is not on his mind. His main concern very evidently is with something else. But it weighs like an incubus on the mind of the Church Fathers, provoking in them something like the hankering of the thirsty soul in Dante's *Inferno* for the water he longs for.[1]

1366. In a well-known passage St. Paul accepts matrimony as the lesser evil: it would be better for a person not to have commerce with the opposite sex, but if one is not of that fibre, marriage may be allowed. St. Paul was undeniably a misogynist. But we know too little about him to say whether that attitude sprang from some physical deformity, as in the case of Leopardi, from lack of success

1365 [1] *Inferno,* XXX, vv. 64-69:

> "The little brooks that down each verdant hill
>   Flow into Arno from the Casentine
>   Making their beds so fresh and cool, are still
> Ever before me, and not all in vain;
>   For more their image parches than this plague,
>   Howe'er the flesh from off my face it drain."
>   (Fletcher translation.)

with women or some other such cause, or from pure mysticism.[1]

1367. Of truly celibate nuns St. Cyprian declaims: "Now we come to those who are virgins of body and in them our interest must be the greater in proportion as their glory is the more sublime. They are the flower of the ecclesiastical vine, the honour and ornament of spiritual grace. They are the character beautiful, the perfect and undefiled achievement of glory and of honour. They are the image of God that corresponds to the sanctity of Our Lord, that part of Christ's flock which is most glorified. Through them the glorious

1366 [1] I Cor. 7:1-2: "Now concerning the things whereof ye wrote unto me: It is good for a man not to touch a woman. Nevertheless, to avoid fornication, let every man have his own wife, and let every woman have her own husband." The passage was a hard nut for the Christians to crack. Some took it in an obviously false sense as addressed only to priests. Some toned it down, explaining that if virginity held first place, the married state came second. Others still observed that the old Law bade mankind to increase and multiply at a time when the Earth had not been populated. Now that it was covered with people, the injunction no longer held. But after all the passage could hardly be clearer: it is the dictum of a virtuist who abhors the carnal act and yields to marriage only as the lesser of two evils. St. Jerome notes on the passage, *Commentarius in epistolam I ad Corinthios* [Pareto quotes *Opera*, Paris, 1623-24, Vol. VIII, p. 199; missing in Migne]: "What I preached at the outset was the sound doctrine (*bonum*), to wit, that one should not touch a woman according to the habit of marriage. But since you tell me that many incontinents are violating that teaching, let a remedy be granted them that they die not in fornication. Virginity and continence are therefore preached as most desirable (*in primis*) following this example of the Apostle; but if anyone is not too ashamed to confess himself incontinent and demands the relaxation of incontinence, let the remedy of marriage not be denied to him, just as when the patient is restless and avers he cannot abstain from all fruit, the shrewd physician will allow him somewhat of it lest he take such as will do him harm. . . . But the lust-lovers commonly answer: 'Why then did God in his first blessing bid men to be fruitful and multiply?' That, of course, the Earth might be filled with people. But now that it has been so filled we must restrain ourselves from incontinence." St. Anselme of Laon [see § 1803 [5]], in his commentary, *In epistolam I ad Corinthios* (7:1-2), likens woman to a fire that burns at the touch: "Note the wisdom of the Apostle: he does not say that it is good not to have a wife, but that it is good not to touch a woman, as though the danger lay in the contact, as though he who touches a woman is lost. Just as one is burned on touching fire, so at the touch of man or woman one senses one's nature and becomes aware of the difference of sex. It is good not to touch! *But to avoid fornication* let each man have his *legitimate wife*, not a concubine, and each woman her husband. Nothing but the fear of fornication explains such a concession." *Canones et decreta Concilii Tridentini, sessio* XXIV, 10 (Richter, p. 216; Schaff, Vol. II, p. 197): "If anyone shall say that the conjugal state is to be preferred to virginity or celibacy and that it is not better and more holy to remain virgin and celibate than to marry, let him be anathema."

fecundity of our Mother Church rejoices. In them she flourishes the more bounteously, and the more virginity adds to its numbers, the greater is the Mother's joy." In penning those torrid lines the Saint probably imagined that he was responding to a purely religious sentiment; but it is more than probable that without his knowledge a sex residue was at work in him.[1]

1368. St. Augustine relates that he frequented women in his youth, but that after his conversion he became averse to all such contacts, even legitimate.[1]

1367 [1] *De disciplina et habitu virginum*, III (*Opera*, p. 443; Wallis, Vol. I, p. 336): "*Nunc nobis ad virgines sermo est, quarum quo sublimior gloria est maior et cura est. Flos est ille ecclesiastici germinis, decus atque ornamentum gratiae spiritalis, laeta indoles, laudis et honoris opus integrum atque incorruptum, Dei imago respondens ad sanctimoniam Domini, illustrior portio gregis Christi. Gaudet per illas atque in illis largiter floret Ecclesiae matris gloriosa fecunditas, quantoque plus copiosa virginitas numero suo addit tanto plus gaudium matris augescit.*" St. Augustine, *De doctrina christiana*, IV, 21, 47 (*Opera*, Vol. III, p. 112; *Works*, Vol. IX, pp. 157-58), quotes the lines as an example of style. Many other equally vivid expressions of the kind are to be found in the Church Fathers. Coming upon them one thinks of an epigram of Rufinus in the *Greek Anthology*, V, 77 (Paton, Vol. I, pp. 166-67), and is tempted to suspect that the sentiment would be less colourful had the Fathers been better acquainted with the things they were raving about: "If women had such charm after the bed of Cypris, no man surely would ever be sated after love of his wife. For after Cypris all women are a bore." And *cf*. Tatius Achilles, *Leucippe et Clitophon*, IV, 8.

1368 [1] *Soliloquia*, I, 17 (*Opera*, Vol. I, p. 878; Starbuck, p. 543) (a dialogue between Reason and the Saint): "*Reason*. What about a wife? Are there not consolations in one that is beautiful, chaste, well mannered, well educated? *Augustine*. However attractive the colours in which you paint her, with whatever virtues you endow her, I have decided that there is nothing that I must more studiously shun than such intercourse. In my judgment nothing lowers a man's spirit farther from Heaven (*ex arce*) than the caresses and physical contact of a woman—and if one has a wife such things cannot be avoided." *Idem, Contra Julianum, haeresis Pelagianae defensorem* (*Opera*, Vol. X, pp. 641 f.), III, 24, 42: "*Concupiscentiae carnalis qui modum tenet malo bene utitur; qui modum non tenet malo male utitur; qui autem etiam ipsum modum sanctae virginitatis amore contempserit malo melius non utitur.*" [This pious gibberish is unintelligible apart from its context. It is the mechanically constructed counter-thesis to a declaration of Julianus, who held that the sex instinct (*naturalis concupiscentia*) having been placed in man by the Creator must be a good thing, though conceding that the practitioners of ascetic chastity were essaying a "glorious emprise." Said he: *Concupiscentiae naturalis qui modum tenet bono bene utitur, qui modum non tenet bono male utitur, qui autem etiam ipsum modum sanctae virginitatis amore contempserit bono melius non utitur, confidentia quippe suae salutis et roboris contempsit remedia ut gloriosa possit exercere certamina.* This, with some goodwill, is intelligible: "He who (follows the way

1369. In St. Jerome the strength of sentiment in respect of everything pertaining to women and sensuous pleasures is something quite exceptional. The Saint is for ever counselling virgins and widows, comforting, advising, rebuking them. He is much less interested in married women and actually gives the impression of regarding husbands unconsciously as his rivals. He feels hurt that certain heretics were mean enough to accuse him of condemning matrimony; but one must say that he gave quite a few grounds for such charges.[1]

1370. In an epistle to the Virgin Eustochia he stresses the evils of matrimony from a worldly standpoint: the annoyance of pregnancy, the crying of children, the jealousy of a husband's mistresses, household worries; and he has his virgin express her unwillingness to fall under the sentence pronounced in Genesis: "In sorrow thou shalt bring forth children."[1] "That is a law for women, not for

of ?) natural concupiscence makes a good use of a good thing; he who eschews that path makes a bad use of a good thing; but he who spurns it altogether through love of holy chastity eschews the use of a good thing to better advantage inasmuch as in confidence as to his strength and security he has spurned legitimate remedies in order to essay a glorious emprise." Augustine states that his one difference with Julianus here is as to whether the sex instinct is a good or an evil, it being for him an evil. He accordingly adopts the form of statement of Julianus, but replaces the word *bonum* with the word *malum*.—A. L.]

1369 [1] *Epistolae*, 48, 10-12 (*Ad Pammachium pro libris contra Jovinianum*) (*Opera*, Vol. I, p. 499; Schaff-Wace, p. 40): "My opinions on the subject of those who are pure, on widows and married people, must be sufficiently clear from the passage in my Commentary on the Apocalypse [where I wrote] (*Adversus Jovinianum*, I, 40; *Opera*, Vol. II, p. 269; Schaff-Wace, p. 378): 'The pure are they who sing the new song which no one can sing save he be pure. . . . They are the first-fruits of the Lord, Lambs of God, without blemish.' And if virgins are the first fruits of the Lord, it follows that the widowed and those who are continent in marriage come after the first fruits in a second and third degree. I give second and third place to widows and married women, yet I am charged (*dicimus* misprint for *dicimur*) by heretical madness with condemning marriage!" And he goes on, *loc. cit.*, 12, to beg his reader's indulgence and claim extenuating circumstances: "A thoughtful and kindly reader should judge things apparently harsh from all that I say (*de caeteris*) and not accuse me of expressing different sentiments in one and the same book. For who could be so stupid, so unskilful in writing, as to praise and condemn the same thing?" [So failing to take due account of the predicament of the man who has a thought but cannot in view of this or that consideration express it in full.]

1370 [1] *Ad Eustochium de custodia virginitatis*, Epistola, XXII, 2 (Wright, p. 57): "*Nec enumeraturum molestias nuptiarum, quomodo uterus intumescat, infans vagiat,*

me!" she cries. In his qualms about pregnancy the Saint must be reckoned a predecessor of the birth-control advocates of our day, and Senator Bérenger, who has a mania for indictments, ought to have the French Attorney-General hale him into court. That being impracticable in view of the Saint's having been dead for so many centuries, his books at least might be expurgated. The Saint, however, might get some consideration from the fact that, though plain-clothes men were unknown in those days, he had other ways of dealing with people who tampered with the morals of virgins.[2]

1371. The thought of woman exacerbated by unsatisfied hankerings tormented the poor Saint and survived his practices of morti-

cruciet pellex [concubine], *domus cura solicitet, et omnia quae putantur bona mors extrema praecidat* [and in the end death cuts off everything that is called a blessing]." *Adversus Helvidium de perpetua virginitate Beatae Mariae*, XX (*Opera*, Vol. II, p. 204; Schaff-Wace, p. 344) (Married women are distracted from their religious duties by family worries): "Do you think it is the same thing to attend to your prayers and fasts by day and by night, and to stop what you are doing at the coming of your husband (*gressum frangere*) and brighten your face and simulate affection? Here the children are crying and the family is in an uproar. The children are calling for your kisses and for a word. The bills have to be figured up, the accounts settled. There are the army of cooks with their sleeves rolled up (*accincta*) grinding the meats. In the other room a group of seamstresses are making a noise. And there is your husband with his friends! The wife darts hither and thither like a swallow about the whole house, to see if the dining-couch has been set up, if the floors have been swept, if the wine-cups have been crowned, if the dinner is ready. Tell me, I pray you: Where in all that is there time to think of God? And I have described a happy home!" Striking the contrast between that civilization and the ancient Roman. The things the Saint disparages here were the pride and glory of the matron in the heyday of Rome.

1370 [2] *Epistolae*, V, *Ad Laetam de institutione filiae* (*Opera*, Vol. I, pp. 872-73; Schaff-Wace, p. 191): "At the command of her husband, Hymettius, who was grandfather to the virgin Eustochia, Praetextata, a very noble woman, changed the styles and ornaments of the virgin and redressed her unkempt hair in the worldly fashion, thinking so to thwart her designs and her mother's expressed wishes. And lo, on that same night an angel appeared before her, threatening woe unto her in dread voice, and crushing her to earth with these words: 'Hast thou the boldness to prefer a command of thine husband to the will of Christ? Presumest thou to lay impious hands on the head of God's virgin? Verily those hands shall soon wither, in punishment for what they have done, and finished this fifth month thou shalt be carried away to Hell; and if thou dost persist in this sin, thou shalt lose husband and children all.' And so it came to pass in due course, and the death of the unlucky woman bore witness to the too great delay in her repentance."

fication. Retiring to the desert, he relates, "to the society of scorpions and wild beasts," he "was frequently molested by troops of dancing girls. My face paled from fasts, but my mind flared hot in a cold body. In the dead flesh of a man there burned naught but the fires of lust." [1] Such hallucinations are familiar things in the writings of the Fathers. Demons were forever besetting the saints of asceticism and tempting them under female forms. St. Jerome mentions other instances in addition to his own, and in general the lives of the saints are replete with them. [2] It is readily comprehensible that harbouring a sex residue of such power, St. Jerome should have been accused of taking too much pleasure in the society of women—a charge that he, of course, indignantly and probably in all honesty denies. "Many virgins," he explains, [3] "oftentimes gathered about me, and to not a few of them I expounded divine Scripture to the best of my ability; and our readings inspired assiduity, assiduity familiarity, and familiarity confidence. Let them bear witness whether they ever found aught in me unbecoming to a Christian. Have I ever accepted money? Have I not spurned gifts, whether great or small? Has the coin of others ever clinked in my hand? Have I been immodest

1371 [1] *Ad Eustochium de custodia virginitatis, Epistola* XXII, 6 (Wright, pp. 67-69).

1371 [2] The case of St. Hilarion, which I choose at random: St. Jerome, *Vita sancti Hilarionis*, VII (*Opera*, Vol. II, p. 36; Schaff-Wace, p. 304): "Many his temptations, and ingenious the traps laid by the devils by day and by night. . . . How many times did naked women appear before him as he lay on his cot? How many times were luscious banquets spread before his famished eyes?" A young woman and a square meal would have done for all those demons. A great many saints were tempted in just such ways. The story of St. Anthony is even too well known. St. Francis also had his troubles (§ 1184 [2]) and his disciples as well as he. The Protestants were enemies of the Franciscans, of course; but they make a sensible remark anent a temptation of Brother Aegidius, though it is garbed in one of the inevitable derivations: *L'Alcoran des cordeliers*, II, 186: "While Brother Aegidius was at Spoleto he had a greater temptation than he had ever experienced before through hearing the voice of a woman. However, by prayers, flagellations, and divine rites he cast her forth from him and so was completely freed." The editor of the *Koran* comments on the vision itself: "Is it any wonder these presumptuous charlatans (*caphars*) are always stewing day and night in the secret fires of roistery, since they have rejected holy matrimony, which is the God-given cure for such temptations?" And on the flagellation: "Such thrashings are inventions of Satan and are nowhere approved by God."

1371 [3] *Epistolae*, 45, 2 (*Ad Asellam*) (*Opera*, Vol. I, p. 481; Schaff-Wace, p. 59).

either of speech or eye? I am reproached of nothing save my sex; and of that I am reproached only because of the journey of Paula and Melania to Jerusalem."

1372. All the same his conversation was inclined to tread dangerous ground, and his continuous harping on erotic pleasures was of a sort calculated to put chastity in peril. To the virgin Eustochia he writes:[1] "It is difficult for the human soul not to love something: to something our spirits must needs turn in affection. But carnal love is vanquished by spiritual love, desire is quenched in desire [Most suggestive language.]; and carnal love is certain to diminish as spiritual love increases. Repeat often as you lie on your pillows: *By night on my bed I sought him whom my soul loveth.*" The quotation is from the Song of Songs, 3: 1. It refers—or rather, the Saint thought it referred—to a spiritual bridegroom. But, alas, it suggests, especially when a girl utters it on her pillows, the image of a physically real bridegroom. In all such utterances, even if they are uttered in all innocence, the sex residue figures, just as it figures in the piety of a certain French pastor who, out of loathing for pornography, goes to a show to measure the length of the ballet's skirts and the precise amount of ankle and thigh they leave exposed.[2]

1373. Heretics went as far as the orthodox in their worries over sex. As already suggested (§§ 1341 f.), the charges of indecency that are hurled back and forth by various religious sects are not to be taken too seriously; but they suffice to show the force of the sex

---

1372 [1] *Ad Eustochium de custodia virginitatis, Epistola XXII,* 17 (Wright, p. 89).

1372 [2] In the same letter to Eustochia, 25 (Wright, p. 109), the Saint makes a long comparison between the heavenly and the earthly bridegroom, with quotations from the Song of Songs: "Always let the secret of your chamber be your shelter and protection. Always may the Bridegroom sport with you within (*laudat* misprint for *ludat*). Are you in prayer? You are conversing with your husband. Are you reading? He is talking to you. And when you fall asleep, He will come to the door and put His hand through the hole in the door [Song of Songs, 5:3] and touch your breast [Exquisitely physical imagery for spiritual acts.]; and awakening you will arise and say: 'Thou hast ravished my heart' [*Ibid.,* 4:9 (?): Vulgate, *Vulnerata caritate ego sum*—"I am sick with love"]; and from Him you will hear: 'A garden enclosed is my sister, my spouse, a spring shut up, a fountain sealed' [*Ibid.,* 4:12]. . . . Jesus is a jealous husband (Wright, p. 111); He does not wish your face to be seen of other men" (*Zelotypus est Iesus: non vult ab aliis videri faciem tuam*).

religion, which is great enough to provide the weapons men need for their battles and to enable it to serve so many religions in all periods of history as the pretext for persecutions great and small.

1374. Not a few accusations of immorality are brought rightly or wrongly against heretics in St. Augustine's treatise on heresies, *De haeresibus ad Quodvultdeum* (*Opera,* Vol. VIII, p. 21). The Saint deals at length with the Manicheans or Catharists (Perfects), on the one hand describing them as finding evil present in all matter and therefore as very strict in rejecting everything carnal, and on the other hand accusing them of licentious depravities.[1] To judge them

1374 [1] To summarize the Saint's accusations at large: The *Simonians* taught the detestable depravity that commerce with women was a matter of scant importance. The *Saturnians* imitated the depravities of the Simonians. On being rebuked for too great love for his wife, a most beautiful woman, and desiring to purge himself of the charge, Nicolas, leader of the *Nicolaitans,* gave notice that anyone who chose might have her. The *Gnostics* were called *Borborites* (Greek, mud-lovers) because of their gross immoralities. The *Carpocratians* taught all sorts of depraved practices. The *Cerinthians* believed that after the Resurrection mankind would live a thousand years in Christ's earthly kingdom, spending the time in gluttony and all sorts of lusts. The *Secundians* differed from the *Valentinians* only in degree of depravity. The *Cainites* honoured Cain and the inhabitants of Sodom. The *Tatians* condemned marriage and held it to be on a par with fornication and other vices, nor would they admit married people to their sect, whether men or women. The *Kataphrygians* held a second marriage equivalent to fornication and were said to have celebrated licentious mysteries. The *Peputians* or *Quintillians* gave great authority to women. The *Adamites* imitated the nakedness of Adam in Paradise before the Fall. They condemned marriage on the ground that Adam had no commerce with his wife either before the Fall or before he had been driven from Paradise, and that therefore had no one ever sinned there would have been no marriage. They went naked to their meetings and listened to their sermons and took their sacraments naked, thinking of their church, in fact, as Paradise itself. The *Elcesaites* or *Sampsaeans* worshipped two women. The *Valesians* practised castration. The *Catharists* condemned second marriages. The *Apostolics* rejected married people. The *Origenists* practised unmentionable depravities. For the *Manicheans* or Catharists, see below, § 1374 [2]. The *Hieracites* admitted only celibates as members. The *Antidicomarians* denied the virginity of Mary, on the ground that after the birth of Jesus she had relations with her husband. The *Priscillianists* forbade the use of meat, and separated husband and wife on the ground that flesh was created by the Devil and not by God. The *Paternians* "think that the human body below the waist was created not by God, but by the Devil. They therefore allow all sorts of licence to the nether parts of the body and lead most impure lives." St. Augustine claims to have had personal knowledge of the *Abeloites:* "They had no commerce with their wives, yet the dogmas of their sect did not permit them to live unmarried. Man and woman, they lived together in continence, and adopted a boy and a girl who were to succeed them in their pact of comradeship."

by what we know of their successors in the Middle Ages, the Albigenses, it would seem probable that they practised an exceedingly
rigorous asceticism entirely free of depravities. We can of course not
be altogether sure. St. Augustine taxes them with believing that the
holy virtues turned into males in order to attract the women of
hostile sects and into women in order to appeal to males. True or
fanciful as this picture of Manichean doctrine may be, the fact remains that the sex residue played an important part either in their
thinking or in the arguments of their adversaries.[2]

1374 [2] Guiraud, *Cartulaire de Notre-Dâme de Prouille*, Vol. I, Preface, pp. cii-iii:
"The norms of the Manichean ethics were very austere. In its absolute rule of celibacy and in the strictness of its abstinences, it went far beyond the severest monastic
disciplines. It is easy to see why those who observed them readily gained reputations
for sanctity in the easy-going moral atmosphere that prevailed in the South of
France. . . . Not being able to deny the astonishing results, the Catholic preachers
were reduced to declaring that such Puritanism was mere hypocrisy and that its
grim outward semblances concealed only a more shameful viciousness. Catholic
writers of our own day have adopted that thesis and also declared, without shred
of proof, that Catharist virtue was an artificial pose designed to deceive the simple-
minded. . . . There is no occasion for resorting to such gratuitous and facile speculations to explain the rigour of Catharist morals. It is sufficient to note that far from
appealing to the crowd at large regardless of persons and conditions, the Manichean
rule was practised only by a small *élite* that was carefully prepared to accept it and
live up to it." Guiraud is a Catholic historian, hostile to the "Perfects."

See St. Augustine, *Ibid.*, I. As regards the asceticism of the Manicheans (Catharists): "They have divided their Church into those two professions, the Elect, that
is, and the Auditors. In other people, and even in their own Auditors and especially
in those who have children, they think that that element of good and divine substance which is mixed and combined into foods and drinks is present in a scantier
(*artius* for *arctius*) and less pure mixture. . . . They do not eat meats . . . nor
even eggs . . . nor do they partake of foods containing milk. . . . They do not
drink wine . . . saying that it is the gall of the princes of darkness. Though they
do eat grapes, they will not drink the fermented juice (*musti*) nor the fresh. . . .
They regard trees and plants as so much alive that they feel the life that is in them
and experience pain when they are hurt. . . . For that reason they consider it
wicked to clear a field of brush. . . . They condemn marriage out of hand and
prohibit it so far as they can, since they forbid the generation of children, which is
the reason for marriage unions." And as regards Manichean (Catharist) abomina-
tions, the Saint says: "On that pretext, or rather under the constraint of an execrable
superstition, their Elects are obliged to take as it were their Eucharist *conspersam
cum semine humano*, that in that way, as is the case with the other food they take,
it may be cleansed by a divine substance. But they deny that they do any such
thing, asserting that other persons unnamed do it under pretence of being Manicheans." But the Saint points, in rebuttal, to the testimony of two girls who had confessed to participating in the obscene rite, and adds: "Not so very long ago, a num-

1375. St. Augustine derives some of his information from St. Epiphanius, who adds further indecent details, in the case of the Gnostics especially, quoting, in his turn, St. Irenaeus. It seems hardly possible that such particulars could be altogether true. Some of them at least must have been imagined by a brain fermenting with prurience.[1]

1376. A community in which sexual unions were altogether prohibited would soon disappear unless, as was the case with the Essenes, it were replenished by recruits from other communities. A religion that aspires to become universal or at all wide-spread, unless it preaches the extinction of its disciples or the human race must necessarily permit marriage and rest content with regulating it. St. Paul seems not to have thought of that. His idea in allowing marriage was merely to avoid the very serious sin of fornication. But such considerations figured to some extent in the policy of the Catholic Church towards marriage, the moment the Church became a force of importance in society and began aspiring to supreme leadership over the destinies of men. Small heretical sects might here and there rescind the concession made by the Apostle and condemn sexual commerce absolutely and for all; and here and there one of them might even go so far as to recommend or require castration as a surer guarantee that the abhorred union would be eschewed. The Church, however, managed to hit on the golden mean, taking the position that matrimony was a praiseworthy state though less

ber of them were discovered and taken to Church, according to the Bishop's report that you have sent to me. Under severe examination they confessed that [the rite in question] was not a sacrament but an incantation in witchcraft (*non sacramentum sed execramentum*)."

1375 [1] St. Epiphanius, *Panarium adversus haereses, Lib.* I, *Tomus* II, *Haeresis* 31, 3 (*Opera*, Vol. I, pp. 474-543). St. Irenaeus, *Contra haereses*, I, 6, 3 (Migne, p. 507; Keble, p. 20): "Some of them, insatiable devotees of their carnal pleasures, say that things of the flesh should be matched with things of the flesh, things of the spirit with things of the spirit. And some of them secretly corrupt the women whom they instruct in their doctrine, as many of their victims, on reconversion to the Church of God, have confessed, with all the rest of their error. Some indeed quite openly and without trace of shame make such women as happen to strike their fancy their brides, taking them away from their husbands. Others begin more modestly, pretending to be living with their sisters, till in course of time it all comes out, the sister being found with child of the brother."

saintly than virginity. Rulings on successive marriages were to vary: now they were permitted but not recommended; now they were permitted but under censure; then again they were flatly prohibited. That is the case with divorce, and many other subjects that we need not here go into.

1377. But all Christians—except for some few heresies, which are for that matter not very well authenticated—agree with St. Paul that unchasteness is among the gravest sins; and in that notion, which is shared also by many unbelievers and atheists of modern times, the sex residue is clearly manifest, the residue enduring, the religious derivations that cloak it changing.

1378. Has this reprobation of carnal sin proved very effective in suppressing it in the concrete? If one reads history with unprejudiced eyes, looking for the actual facts rather than for what one might wish the facts to be, one can only doubt that it has. In the first place, and in general, if we were to find that with the growth of faith in a given religion that disapproved of carnal sin there were a diminution in immorality, or *vice versa,* one might take the coincidence as a certain indication of the probable effects of moral theory upon conduct. But if we find that periods of eager faith are also ages of great immorality, we are obliged to conclude, not that faith fosters immorality, since it is evident enough that other causes have been functioning, nor that faith has done nothing to promote morality, since after all we cannot be sure that the immorality would not have been worse had there been no faith; but that the sex residues are so powerful that in many cases they are able to override the prescriptions of faith. In so concluding we should be doing nothing more than epitomizing a multiplicity of facts in a general statement, and the conclusion may also be accepted by ardent believers, by ardent Catholics, for example—only they would express it in different language: where we speak of the power of the sex residue, or, better, of the sentiments registered by the sex residue, they would speak of the power of a Devil who is going about *quaerens quem devoret.* Nor could they, if they were at all inclined to be logical, deny that the facts seem to show the scant effects of moral theories on conduct; for they assert that very thing in different words when they say that to escape the traps of the Devil the human soul needs the support of divine grace.

1379. There are facts without end to show that among certain peoples and in certain periods of history enthusiastic faith may go hand in hand with immorality. Have we, from the earliest centuries of Christianity down to times very near our own, heard aught else than complaints as to the moral laxity of Christians? Even making liberal allowance for exaggerations by our censors, and granting that the evil has loomed larger in their eyes than it has been in reality, we can hardly imagine that none of the complaints had any foundation in concrete fact. And then, leaving talk aside, there are the facts themselves. Granted that some of them have been fabrications, can they all have been? To assume such a thing would be to cast doubt upon every historical certainty. At no time has there been any lack of sophistries to disprove the truth. Some have contrasted the vices of the present with the virtues of a past that was never a present for any living soul and which has existed only in their imaginations. Some have contrasted the vices of their own countries with the supposed virtues of other countries. That was one of the motives of Tacitus in writing his *Germania,* and the same prejudice inspired the declamations of Saint Salvian of Marseilles. Salvian goes to many words in contrasting the vices of the Romans with the virtues of the Barbarians. But if he spoke truth, we can only conclude that the Barbarian virtues must have lasted for a very short season; for hardly a century after Salvian's time the *History* by St. Gregory of Tours is portraying those same Barbarians as a blood-thirsty, avaricious, lustful crew.[1][2] (For footnote 3 see page 858.)

1379 [1] For that matter, Tacitus himself says, *Germania,* 15, that when the Germans were not engaged in warfare, they spent much time in hunting "but even more in idling, sleeping, and guzzling (*dediti somno ciboque*)." In *Annales,* XII, 27, 3-4, he tells how the Romans managed to surprise the Gauls because the latter were half-asleep after spending their booty in one round of carousals.

1379 [2] Says Salvian, *De gubernatione Dei,* III, 9 (Sanford, p. 92): "It is God's command that every Christian should keep even his eyes chaste. Yet how many are they who are not sunk in the mire of fornication? And what else? Grievous and painful is what I am about to say! The Church herself who should be the consoler

1380. Admirers of the Middle Ages in our day refuse in any way to grant that those were times of brutish immorality, and they will accept any sort of sophistry so only to escape the plain evidence of the facts. There is the argument, for instance, that the obscene paint-

of God in all things—what is she but an irritation to Him? With the exception of some few who shun evil things, what else is almost any forgathering of Christians than a cesspool of vice? How many men can one find in the Church who are not either drunkards or gluttons, either adulterers or fornicators, either seducers of maids or pursuers of women, either thieves or murderers? [Such things are not confined to the slave, the low-born, the soldier: they are sins of the well-born (III, 10; Sanford, p. 96):] Tell me whether any one of them is innocent of the two crimes that may be considered capital—murder and rape? Is there one of them that is not either dripping with blood or reeking with slimy impurity? . . . [IV, 5; Sanford, p. 107:] How many are there among the rich who keep their marriage sacraments, who are not swept headlong by lustful furies, who do not use their own homes and families as brothels, and who do not follow their mad impulses against whatever persons the flame of wicked lust has drawn them? Exactly as is written in the Scripture of such things: 'They are as fed horses in the morning, each one neighing after his neighbour's wife' (Jer. 5:8). What else does a man prove of all this except that it is true of him, when he tries to possess in intercourse whatsoever woman has caught his eye? It may seem unfair that anything should be said of concubines, for in comparison with the crimes I have mentioned concubinage is a sort of chastity—it is confined to a relatively few married men and serves to bridle lust among a certain number of husbands and wives. I say husbands and wives, because things have come to such a pass of thoughtlessness that many men think their housemaids are their wives. And if only they would stop at that! [Literally: would that just as they are thought of as almost wives, so they might be considered as the only wives.] [On the lookout, as usual, for antitheses, Salvian finds one in a contrast between the morals of masters and slaves (IV, 6; Sanford, p. 108):] The slaves taken on the whole are immune to such crimes or greater ones. Is there any slave that has a flock of concubines? Is any one of them disgraced with the evil of having many wives? Does any one of them—after the manner of dogs and swine—think he has a right to any woman whom he can induce to submit to his lust? [Salvian compares Romans and Barbarians (IV, 13; Sanford, p. 121):] There are two kinds of people among the Barbarians as a whole—either heretics or heathen. As regards the divine law we are incomparably their superiors, but as regards living and the conduct of life I am exceedingly sorry to say that we are worse. To be sure, as I have cautioned above, I do not say this of absolutely the whole Roman people. I except first of all the churchmen, and then not a few laymen who are the equals of the church-men. But all or almost all the rest have far worse morals than the Barbarians. [However, Salvian concedes that the Barbarians are of no great account either (IV, 14; Sanford, p. 122):] The Barbarians are cheats, and so are we. The Barbarians are grasping, and so are we. The Barbarians are lecherous, and so are we. The Barbarians are full of all sorts of wickedness and impurity, and so are we. [Not worrying over his inconsistency, he returns to the charge: the Romans are worse than the Barbarians. He begins with a bitter thrust at the Aquitanians (VII, 3; Sanford, p. 193):] I am sure there is less wickedness in a brothel. The whores that

ings and sculptures that have come down from the Middle Ages
(§ 1343 [2]) and the scurrilous language used in the romances and
fabliaux and other mediaeval writings, far from revealing corrupt
morals, show the healthy moral poise of people who can in all safety

are to be found in a brothel have never taken a marriage vow, and they therefore
cannot be said to violate a sacrament they know not of. They are amenable to punishment for inchastity, but not for the crime of adultery. Furthermore, not many
brothels are permanent things, and few the prostitutes who damn their unhappy
lives in them. But among the Aquitanians, what city as regards its wealthier and
nobler sections but has been virtually a brothel? Who of its rich and leading men
but has lived in the mire of debauchery? Who has not taken his plunge into an
abyss of filthiest sewage? Who has ever kept faith with his wife? [He accuses owners of ruining their female slaves (VII, 4; Sanford, p. 195):] One can gather from
that what a filth of loathsome strumpets there must have been when a woman
under a lecherous master was not allowed to be chaste even if she wanted to be.
[It seems that in view of all these offences against chastity the Lord brought
the Romans under Barbarian dominion (VII, 6; Sanford, p. 196):] Though God
has handed them over to the Barbarians because of their corrupt lives, even under
the Barbarians they have not abandoned their lecheries. [Again borne aloft on
the wings of his mania for declamation, Salvian credits the Barbarians with all
the virtues (VII, 7; Sanford, p. 196):] Among the chaste Barbarians we are the
unchaste. I will go farther still: the Barbarians are disgusted at our lewdness! [He
sounds something like Senator Bérenger—or some other person who has lost his
mind—when he prattles on, in conclusion (*loc. cit.*):] It is not lawful among the
Goths for a Goth to be a whore-monger. Among them lewdness is permitted only
to the Romans, to the prejudice of their race and name. And what hope have we,
I ask, before God? We love lechery, the Goths hate it. We abhor purity, they worship it. Fornication with them is a crime and a disgrace, with us it is a distinction." To make a long story short, Salvian lived at a time when morals were no
worse than they had been in the past, when Rome was conquering the Barbarians.
He disregards that fact, and imagines that the Romans had been conquered because
of their immoralities.

1379 [8] The dissoluteness of the Frankish kings as recounted by Gregory of Tours
is too well known to require detailed mention. Here are a few facts gleaned from
the *Historia ecclesiastica Francorum* and from its sequel, known as the *Chronicles
of Fredegarius*, II, 12 (*Opera,* p. 209C; Dalton, Vol. II, p. 56): "When Childeric,
who was a dissolute man of excessive licence, became king over the Franks, he
began lecherously to rape and mislead their daughters." Of Duke Victor Gregory
writes, II, 20 (*Opera,* p. 216B; Dalton, Vol. II, p. 60): "He fled to Rome and trying
to carry on a similar licence there, he was stoned to death." II, 42 (*Opera,* p. 238C;
Dalton, Vol. II, p. 80): "At that time Ragnacharius was king at Camaracum. He
was so bent on licence that he could hardly be brought to spare his close relatives.
He had Farro for his counsellor, a man smirched with the same vices." Theodobert
(III, 21-26; *Opera,* pp. 260-62; Dalton, Vol. II, pp. 103-05) takes up with a certain
Deuteria who was occupying the Castle at Capraria: "Deuteria came forth to meet
him, and he, seeing that she was a handsome woman, fell enamoured of her and
joined her to his bed." After a time he marries her: then, "seeing that her daugh-

call a spade a spade. To believe some writers, one would imagine that men and women of the Middle Ages were so many Daphnises and Chloes. Arguments of that kind might be passed if the mere existence of obscene statues and pictures and the mere use of in-

ter was full grown, and in fear that her husband might lust after her and take her as a mistress, she had her placed in a litter to which two unbroken bulls had been hitched and pulled off a bridge." IV, 13 (*Opera,* p. 278C; Dalton, Vol. II, p. 125): "In those days Chramnus was in residence at Arvernum, and he did many irrational things. . . . He had no affection for any man of whom he might have had good or useful counsel, but gathered about him persons of low birth and still in the unstable years of youth, and gave all his favour to them, listening to their counsel, so that he ordered by royal decree that the daughters of Senators should be taken away from them by force." V, 21 (*Opera,* p. 340C and see p. 342C; Dalton, Vol. II, pp. 195, 197): Of two bishops he says that on attaining their posts they began to run riot "in invasions of property, massacres, murders, and adulteries." And he adds: "Nor was there any lack of women to connive with them in such corruption." VI, 36 (*Opera,* p. 403A; Dalton, Vol. II, p. 267): "There was a priest hailing from a city of the Cenomanni [Northern Italy] who was an exceedingly licentious man and a great lover of women, of the table, and other sensuality, and was addicted to every kind of vice. Having often frequented the wife of a certain individual who was a harlot . . ." VI, 46 (*Opera,* p. 414A; Dalton, Vol. II, p. 279): Of Chilperic Gregory says that "No lust or license could be imagined in thought which he had not perpetrated in deed." VIII, 19 (*Opera,* p. 461C; Dalton, Vol. II, p. 344): "Though Dagulfus, an abbot, was often censured for his extravagances, since he had committed several thefts and murders, he was none the less dissolute in his adulteries. At one time when the wife of a neighbour had caught his fancy and he was intriguing with her, he sought various pretexts whereby he might entice the woman's husband inside the precincts of the abbey and do away with him. Finally the man replied to him that if he came near his wife again, he would be punished." IX, 13 (*Opera,* p. 492B; Dalton, Vol. II, p. 383): "The wife of Wiliulf himself was living with a third man, the son of Duke Beppolenus, and he himself, by common knowledge, had left two wives living. For he was a frivolous, sensuous man. In his inordinate fondness for women, he would leave his own wife and take up with her maids. Despising legitimate marriage, he was always on the look-out for something else." IX, 20 (*Opera,* p. 502A; Dalton, Vol. II, p. 394): The King had summoned a synod of bishops. Questioned as to his reasons for doing so, he answered: "Many improper things have been going on and have to be attended to—immoralities, for one thing." IX, 27 (*Opera,* p. 506A; Dalton, Vol. II, p. 398): "Duke Amalo sent his wife to another of his properties to look after matters there. While she was away, he fell enamoured of a certain girl, free-born; and one night, after an orgy of wine at table, he sent his sons to get possession of the girl and bring her to his bed." IX, 33 (*Opera,* p. 511A; Dalton, Vol. II, p. 404): A man complains to a bishop: "You carried off my wife with her maids. Now see, that is not becoming in a priest, for you have committed adultery—you with my maids and she with your men." Now from Fredegarius, *Chronicum,* 36 (p. 624B): King Theodoric pays frequent calls on Saint Columban: "And since he came very often, the man of God began to rebuke him for living in adultery with concubines and

decent language were to be taken as proving sexual immorality. It is true enough that severely impeccable modes of speech may go hand in hand with morals far more corrupt than anything connected with indecencies in speech. However, the argument is false. In the writings in question, not forms only are obscene; the substance is obscene. Translate the romances and the *fabliaux* into words as chaste as one may wish, couch in elegant periphrase the things they say with brutal frankness, and the substance is still there —and it is obscene in the highest degree.[1]

1381. In addition to literature, there are the facts, as reported in chronicles and other documents; and in truth nothing more is needed to assert in all assurance that the period of the Middle Ages was not more chaste than ours, and seems, indeed, to have been more corrupt. There are those who reject immorality in the clergy as proof of the general immorality of the times, and they lay it to the account of religion, "Catholic idolatry," or "Papism," to use terms of the Protestant reformers. But that is another fallacy which is at war with the facts. Immorality was not worse in the clergy than in the public at large—in fact it was not so bad. If there were the many bishops to match the many corrupt barons, there were clerics who set examples of virtue hardly to be matched in the laity. It is often apparent that when certain mediaeval chronicles speak of im-

not preferring the legitimate affections of his wife." *Ibid.*, 42 (p. 653C): King Clothaire is criticized "for betaking himself too assiduously to hunting and for too ready response to the advances of women and girls." *Ibid.*, 48 (p. 637A): "The Chuni went every year to pass the winter season among the Slavs, and made paramours of their wives and daughters." [Such the morals of the good Salvian's Barbarians in the mass!] *Ibid.*, 60 (p. 644B): King Dagobert "was exceedingly addicted to pleasure. He had three queens, in imitation of King Solomon, and no end of concubines. The names of the queens were [He gives them.] . . . but the names of the concubines would be far too many to include in this *Chronicle.*" *Ibid.*, 70 (p. 650C): King Clothaire "was at all times roistering with concubines." Such the morals of the kings! One may imagine that the morals of their subjects could not have been much better!

1380 [1] To point the contrast—the *Malleus maleficarum* of Sprenger and Krämer contains obscene descriptions; but they are not essentially obscene in the intent of the authors. The *Roman de Renart* contains obscene terms (*e.g.*, vv. 12386-486). With some goodwill one may again grant that the indecency is primarily in the expression. No such excuse is possible with many *fabliaux*.

morality in the clergy, they take immorality in the laity for granted, and that the special wrath is due to the mere fact that the clergy is at fault.[1] The measures taken against immoralities by Church councils, lay rulers, and other authorities of every sort and description prove the prevalence of immoralities. A thing that does not exist is not for ever being prohibited. The taxes imposed on prostitutes in many places show that their numbers could not have been small, for in that case the tax would not have been worth the bother. We have records of many trials for "bestiality," and many animals so misused were publicly burned. On the immorality of the Crusaders a library of books might be compiled. It may well be that some of their doings have been represented as worse than they actually were; but they cannot all have been invented out of whole cloth.[2][3][4] (For footnotes 3 and 4 see page 862.)

1381 [1] This chapter would become far too long were we to document even in very small part the huge number of facts available to show the immorality in deed, as well as in word, that prevailed in the Middle Ages, to say nothing of times earlier and later. And it would be of little use to expatiate on things known to everybody and which only partisan passions can overlook.

1381 [2] As for decrees on immoralities, cf. Council of Auch (Eliberritanum), anno 309, 12 (Labbe, Vol. I, p. 994; and see addendum of Mansi, Vol. I, p. 128): "If a mother or any relative or any Christian shall have procured [for a female child], communion shall be withheld even in extremis." 71 (Labbe, Vol. I, p. 999): "Communion shall be withheld to violators of boys even in extremis." Council of Ancyra, anno 314, 15-16 (Labbe, Vol. I, pp. 1495, 1498): "Cohabitors with males, or cattle . . . : "Cohabitors with males or cattle are ordered by the Sacred Synod to do penance (orent) on a footing with persons bewitched (? hiemantes) or possessed by devils . . ." 20 (Labbe, Vol. I, pp. 1499, 1505): "Women who kill children born of fornication shall do penance for ten years." Council of Toledo, anno 693, 17 (3) (Labbe, Vol. VIII, p. 60): "Such as may be found guilty of acts of sodomy and have frequently permitted themselves such wickedness, in case they shall be bishops, priests, or deacons . . ." Council of Ratisbon, anno 742, VI (Labbe, Vol. VIII, p. 271): "Any servant of God or handmaid of Christ who shall fall into sin of fornication . . ." Council of Tours, anno 813, 41 (Labbe, Vol. IX, p. 355): "Many individuals have been found here who are guilty of incests, parricides, and murders, and some we have already excommunicated; but they take that very lightly and persist in the same crimes, wherefore may your mercy decide what henceforward is to be done with them." Council of Treves, anno 895, 43 (Labbe, Vol. XI, p. 650): "If anyone shall be guilty of fornication with a woman and without his knowledge his son or brother likewise unknowingly shall have fornicated with the same woman . . ." Council of Milan, anno 1565, Decretum 65 (Labbe, Vol. XXI, p. 73): "That harlots may be clearly distinguishable from

1382. It is one of the dogmas of the present-day religion of sex that prostitution is an absolute "evil," and like every other religious dogma, it is not debatable. But from the experimental standpoint it is still a question whether prostitution may, or may not, be the occu-

respectable women, let the bishops make provision that they wear some sort of conspicuous veil."

1381 ⁸ As for taxes on vices, *cf.* Pertile, *Storia del diritto italiano,* Vol. II, Pt. I, p. 435, note 51: "The public decrees of Lucca for the year 1351 (*Bandi Lucchesi,* no. 313) publish a rental contract for a brothel at 120 gold florins a year for that year. Sometimes there was a show of palliating the taint of such revenues by applying them to some purpose of public welfare. *Anno 1404,* Catherine, duchess of Milan, regent for her son Giammaria: "We hear that the money deriving from taxes on resorts and harlotries in the commune of Milan and which have been paid have been specially appointed to the payment of expenses incurred in repairing the fortresses of that city and in payment of assignments for wolves and foxes [*i.e.,* "bounties" for people killing such animals] and for other such purposes'—and she orders that that arrangement be continued. . . . *Cf.* Osio, [*Documenti diplomatici,* Vol. I, p. 257]. In order to increase revenues from brothels it was ordered in Mantua (*Stat. iud. dac. Com. Man.,* f. 143) that [legal tariff restrictions on prices be abolished] and 'that the buyers of such taxes [*i.e.,* licences] should not have a price fixed by the commune which they may ask for their wares, but that it is allowed them by the commune to sell their wares for the best prices they can get and according as trade and customers shall be found.' "

1381 ⁴ As regards the morals of the Crusaders, there is the Mussulman testimony, which we may disregard as suspect of bias, *e.g.,* the *Book of the Two Gardens,* Vol. IV, p. 433. (While the Franks were besieging St. John of Acre, A.D. 1189-90, *anno* 585 of the Hegira): "a vessel brought them three hundred women of very unusual beauty. They had been recruited here and there among the islands [of the Mediterranean], having enlisted for that shameful service. Voluntary exiles for the consolation of those abroad, they had left their homes to become the mistresses of those wretches. Far from withholding their favours from monks and priests (*célibataires*), they offered themselves to them of their own accord, regarding the offering as the more meritorious and deeming that no sacrifice could be greater than theirs if the man to whom they gave themselves had the double status of foreigner and celibate. [A transparent invention.] Some of our Mamelukes deserted our camp [Something much more probable.] under the lash of carnal desire to follow that path of damnation, like the ignorant wretches they were." But the testimony of Christian writers is not to be tossed aside on the same grounds: *e.g.,* Gauthier le Chancelier, *Histoire des guerres d'Antioche,* pp. 104-05 (*anno* 1115-19). "Some, sworn enemies of fasting and followers of the pleasures of the table, did their utmost to imitate the rule of life not of those who live well but of those who feed well. Others, in addiction to lechery, frequented the resorts of harlots and overstepped the bounds of all decency. . . . They used the gold and precious stones of Arabie to make ornaments and coverings for *les parties sexuelles de leurs épouses,* and they so did, not to hide such parts from view nor to quench the flames of lust, but to the end that 'those who had lost their taste for lawful pleasures might be stimulated the more keenly by the unlawful, so intensifying crime with crime,

pation best suited to the temperaments of certain women, as being more congenial to them than any other that they might follow; and whether prostitution is, or is not, within certain limits beneficial to society as a whole (§ 1382⁴). Followers of the modern religion of

thinking, as we may suspect (*? ut praelibaremus*), that they were adorning (*? dealbare*) their women and satisfying them, since they were trying in that way to imitate their lusts.' The women had nothing saintly, nothing well-bred, in their manner of enjoying the pleasures of the senses. Scornful of their husbands' beds, they resorted to places of assignation to practice impurities there. They spent night and day in one round of pleasures, amusements, feastings." An age in which such a passage could be written could not, making all due allowance for fabrication, have been an age of such innocence as not to relish the flavour of obscene stories and pictures. Robert le Moine, *Histoire de la première croisade*, p. 407 (Jesus is speaking, having appeared in a dream to a priest to complain of the doings of the Christians): " 'I have permitted all these tribulations and hardships which they are facing because many things have gone on with women, Christian and heathen, that are grievously painful to my eyes.' " Foulcher de Chartres, *Histoire des croisades*, p. 40, also regards the sufferings of the Crusaders at Antioch as a punishment for their immoralities: "Numbers of them weakly and shamelessly gave themselves over to pride, licentiousness, and brigandage. A council was therefore called and all women, whether legitimate wives or concubines, were banished from the army, lest our men should bring the wrath of the Lord down upon themselves by their crimes of debauchery." The same detail is given by Guibert de Nogent, *Gesta Dei per Francos*, V, 17 (*Recueil*, p. 195; Migne, pp. 760-61). And *cf.* Jacques de Vitry, *Histoire des croisades*, pp. 271-72. Book II is entitled: *De la corruption des contrées de l'occident et des péchés des occidentaux*. ". . . Continence," says the author, "so beloved in the heavenly mansions and so pleasing to God, was despised as a worthless thing. The men turned indiscriminately and shamelessly to lustful pleasures, and like hogs wallowing in the mire took delight in such filth. . . . Marriage bonds became very flimsy between relatives and allies, and unbridled licence was not halted even by differences in sex." Ernoul, *Chronique* (Mas Latrie ed.), pp. 86, 91, 216-17, *anno* 1180-84): "Now I must tell you of his manner of life [of the Patriarch of Jerusalem]. When he returned from Rome he became infatuated with the wife of a merchant who lived at Neapolis, some twelve leagues from Jerusalem. And he often sent for her and she went. He gave her much property in order to stand well with her husband. It was not long before her husband died. Then the Patriarch came and took her to live with him in Jerusalem, and he bought her a fine stone house. [The morals of the Greeks were no better:] Now we shall tell you of Andronicus, who was emperor of Constantinople. There was not a pretty nun in the whole land, nor daughter or wife of gentleman or burgher so only she were pretty, that he did not take her and force her to be with him." Jerusalem is besieged by Saladin. The inhabitants pray for rescue, but "Our Lord, my Lord God, could not hear any plaint or prayer that was made in the city because the stench of lust and adultery and sins against nature which was in the city did not allow any prayer that was made before God to rise to Heaven." Evidently such things explain the general opinion prevalent at the time that a man came home from the Crusades worse than he went. In the days of St. Louis, Rutebeuf

sex offer no proof whatever in support of their answers to those questions. Their assertions have to be believed in just as one believed in Zeus in a day gone by and just as now the Mussulman believes that contact with a pig is a source of very serious blemish.

wrote a dialogue (*Œuvres*, Vol. I, p. 156) between a man who wanted to go on the Crusades and one who did not, and the Crusaders come in for some sharp criticism: *La desputizons dou Croisié e dou Descroisié:*

> *"Mult vont outre meir gent menue,*
> *sage, large, de grant aroi. . . .*
> *Si ne valent ne ce ne quoi*
> *quant ce vient à la revenue."*

("All sorts of people go overseas, the poor, the rich, the strict, the easy—but they are not worth *that* when they return.") Guillaume de Nangis, *Chronique* 7, *anno* 1120: "William and Richard, sons of Henry, King of England, the daughter and the niece of that king with a large company of lords and gentlemen of England, were lost at sea in trying to cross from Normandy to England, though the sea was calm and there was no wind. It was said, and in all truth, that they were almost all tainted with the crime of sodomy." Guibert de Nogent, *Vie . . . par lui-même*, III, 3 (pp. 5-7): "There was, in fact, a certain . . . Enguerrand de Boves, who was a generous, prodigal, exceedingly wasteful person. He affected limitless respect and munificence toward the Church, having learned to think that religion was a matter of such things and nothing else. But in another direction he was so fond of women that he always had about him a number of them, bought or borrowed, and in general did nothing except what their effrontery encouraged him to do. Having always failed in his efforts to get a wife, he began to chase the wives of others, managed furtively to seduce the wife of the Count de Namur, a relative of his, and after urging her secretly to crime, finished by living publicly with her as his legitimate wife. . . . The woman was a daughter of Roger, Count of Portian. . . . All those . . . who have known him agree that we should have too great cause for blushing not only in detailing the course of his escapades but even in adverting to them in this history." Regord (Rigot), *Vie de Philippe-Auguste*, p. 139: "In the year of Our Lord 1198, the Foulques here in question took a priest as his assistant to help him in his preaching. . . . Every day, in accompanying the various sermons, he saved some soul from the sin of usury and what is even more from the sin of lust. He even managed to bring back to conjugal continence women who had been living in places of prostitution, there giving themselves to all comers at negligible prices, not even choosing their accomplices." Mathieu Paris, *Grande chronique*, Vol. III, pp. 400-02 (*anno* 1229), gives an account of riots among the students in Paris. They were accusing Queen Blanche of an affair with the Papal Legate and an obscene song was going the rounds:

> *"Heu, morimur strati, vincti, mersi, spoliati:*
> *mentula legati nos facit ista pati."*

Muratori, *Antiquitates Italicae, Dissertatio* 20 (Vol. IV, pp. 251-53; missing in *Dissertazioni*): "During the tenth century of our era, which was the most corrupt that Christian Italy ever saw, licence was given such an inordinately free rein that

Such dogmas may, or may not, be useful to society under certain circumstances. Sacred prostitution has prevailed among many peoples. The fact may seem surprising to anyone labouring under the influence of the hiatus mentioned in § 1339; but not to one who is free of that influence and realizes that such a rite in no sense differs in character from the sacrifices of one kind or another—human sacrifice included—that were offered to the gods, nor from such consecrations as the *ver sacrum* of the Romans (§ 930).[1] Common prostitution is observable among all civilized peoples and in all periods of history. It prevailed among the Hebrews, a people chosen of God, and among the pagans. The Greeks and Romans regarded the harlot's profession as of a lower order than others, but no less necessary. The institution survived the Greeks and Romans. Christianity failed to suppress it. It has held its own down to our own day, and one may reasonably guess that it will live on in future ages despite the wrath

even the leading princesses openly treated themselves to every form of loose morals. Special notoriety for that sort of thing was acquired, around the year 925, among the Lombards by Hermengarde, wife of Adelbert, Marquis of Ivry (*Eporedia*) and among the Romans by Marogia, mother of Pope John XI and wife of the Marquis Alberico the Elder, her mother, Theodora, and another Theodora, her sister. The record of their vices has been transmitted to posterity in a rather free style by Liutprand, the historian of those days. In that same century the clergy likewise began to despise the continence that had been observed in the West from the foundation of the Church, and the unhealthy spirit went so far that priests, deacons, and subdeacons kept women as their wives under the public eye on the plea that what was in no sense unlawful among the Greeks should not be unlawful for them. Verily do the vices thrive more easily by far than the virtues. The pestilence in question gradually pervaded almost all the cities of Italy and the *Urbs* itself. The wicked leaders connived at the thing, the good ones resisted. . . . On the margins of a very ancient manuscript of sacraments owned by the Canonicate at Modena I note the following: 'I, Andrea, a priest, promise before God and all the saints, and before you, Bishop Guarino, that I shall not practise carnal intercourse, and if I should do so, may I lose my post and benefice in the Church.' And another similar oath follows: 'From this time on, I, Giovanni, archpriest, promise you, Guarino, my bishop, that in all the days of my life I shall not commit adultery with the wife of another man, nor fornication with an unlawful harlot, and if I should do so, I hereby declare myself in [mortal] danger.' "

1382 [1] The subject in itself does not properly concern us here. It is a matter for a special sociology. Nor are we interested in the question of the utility of prostitution. In these chapters we are concerned strictly with determining the character of the various residues and the intensities with which they function.

of some of our contemporaries who are often more chaste in theory than in practice. In view of the hypocrisy of ideas about sex, first in mediaeval and then in modern times, governments have now and again been induced to fight prostitution by law. Such efforts have had little or no success, and that is another indication of the power of the sex residues. Prostitution was rife among the devoutly Catholic peoples of the Middle Ages, as witness the many regulations that were made with regard to it and the threats of punishment that were incessantly addressed to prostitutes, the very fact of the constant reiteration proving their inefficacy. Prostitutes are already mentioned in the laws of the Barbarians. The *Capitularies* of the pious Charlemagne represent prostitutes as plying their trade in the very palace. They further allude to grave depravities that were threatening the welfare of the realm, and fix penalties for unnamable vices. The constitutions of the Kingdom of Sicily prohibit the forcing of harlots by violence.[3][4][5][6][7] (For footnotes 3-7 see pages 867-871.)

1382 [2] As regards sacred prostitution, it is noteworthy that courtesans played a part even in Roman worship, which was very austere on the whole. In the *Fasti Praenestini* one reads (*Corpus inscriptionum Latinarum*, Vol. I, Pt. I, p. 236): "*Robigalia: Feriae Robigo via Claudia ad miliarum [quintum], ne robigo frumentis noceat. Sacrificium et ludi cursoribus maioribus minoribusq(ue) fiunt. Festus et puerorum lenoniorum, quia proximus superior meretricum est.*" (*Robigalia*: Holidays, Robigo, on the Via Claudia at the fifth milestone. A sacrifice to keep the rust from harming the crops, and games with major and minor races are held. Also the feast of panderers, because the feast next preceding [The Vinalia, coming on April 22, the Robigalia on April 25.—A. L.] is for prostitutes.") The feast of the Vinalia was celebrated by prostitutes: Ovid, *Fasti*, IV, vv. 865-68:

> "*Numina vulgares Veneris celebrate puellae:*
>   *multa professarum quaestibus apta Venus.*
> *Poscite ture dato formam populique favorem;*
>   *poscite blanditias dignaque verba ioco.*"

("Pay honour, ye girls of the public, to the divinity of Venus, the Venus who grants great profits to the business of her devotees. Make your offering of incense and then ask for beauty, and popularity, and the arts of love, and the gay words that go with your play.")
For the festival of Flora, see *Ibid.*, V, vv. 331-34, 349-50:

> "*Quaerere conabar quare lascivia maior*
>   *his foret in ludis liberiorque iocus:*
> *sed mihi succurrit numen non esse severum*

1383. The good king St. Louis discovered that brothels had been established in his camp at Damietta near the royal pavilion. The many allusions to the "King of Harlots" mention the prostitutes who followed the French Court and others who were under

> *aptaque deliciis munera ferre Deam. . . .*
> *Turba quidem cur hos celebret meretricia ludos*
> *non ex difficili causa petenda subest.*"

("I was about to ask why there should be greater licence in these games and a freer speech; but it occurs to me that the divinity they celebrate wears no long face, that she has functions conducive to pleasures. . . . As to why these games should be celebrated by a throng of harlots, the cause is not hard to imagine.") Well known the fact that at Corinth the city's prayers to Aphrodite were offered by prostitutes, and supplications were addressed to that goddess at the time of the Persian invasion. A scholium on Pindar tells of a man who brought a hundred young courtesans to the sacred forest of the goddess to show his gratitude for a favourable answer to his prayers. And *cf.* Athenaeus, *Deipnosophistae*, XIII, 33. Athenaeus also gives, XIII, 31, a list of temples and festivals that were named after hetairae.

1382 [8] Prostitution among the Hebrews: For one thing, prostitution is explicitly prohibited in Deut. 23:17 ("There shall be no whore of the daughters of Israel"); and there are plenty of other allusions in the Bible to show that such a thing was not unknown among the Jews. To reconcile the law with the fact it has been claimed that the law in Deuteronomy referred to sacred prostitution only and the fact to common prostitution. John Spencer vigorously defends that view, *De legibus Hebraeorum ritualibus*, Vol. I, Bk. II, § 35 (p. 561). Quoting the passage in Deuteronomy, he observes: "What is prohibited in those words is not the common prostitute who gives her body for money or in mere quest of pleasure, but the so-called sacred harlot who is consecrated to some foul god of the heathen and practises all sorts of abomination in his honour." That may well be, but it may just as well be that, as is the case among all peoples in such matters, there was some divergence between a theoretical prohibition in the law and a practical toleration in the fact. In any event, prostitutes there were among the Jews, otherwise there would have been no sense in forbidding a priest to marry one (Lev. 21:7). In Judg. 11:1, there is mention of a Jew (Jepthah) who was the son of a harlot. The famous judgment of Solomon (I Kings, 3:16) was rendered in a dispute between two harlots (". . . There came two harlots unto the king"). The story of Tamar (Gen. 38), who traps Judah as a harlot after he had refused her as a wife, could not have been written in a society where prostitution was unknown. And it is told without trace of censure: "When Judah saw her, he thought her to be an harlot because she had covered her face," and he proceeded to cohabit with her. [Judah does say, "She hath been more righteous than I."—A. L.] One of the Proverbs (VI, 26) declares that "by means of a whorish woman a man is brought to a piece of bread." Samson went to Gaza (Judg. 16:1) and "saw there a harlot and went in unto her"; and there is no word of censure in Holy Writ. Many passages in the Talmud show the common divergence between theory and practice in the matter of chastity: Talmud of Jerusalem, Tract Berakoth,

the jurisdiction of that same official. When we come at a later date, the sixteenth century, upon a veritable outburst of corruption we must remember that it is not a thing appearing *ex novo,* but just one of many oscillations over a continuous curve. In a word, prostitution

III, 4 (Gemara) (Schwab, Vol. I, p. 65; Schwab, *Berakoth,* Vol. I, p. 67) (in question the *thebila* (*tefillah*)—a bath of purification taken after carnal pollution): "*Comment la thébila nous empêche-t-elle de pécher? En voici un exemple: Il est arrivé qu'un surveillant de jardins était prêt à commettre un péché avec une femme mariée; mais ils voulaient d'abord s'assurer de pouvoir se purifier immédiatement après* [Striking here the mechanical character of the purification. *Cf.* § 1257]; *pendant ce temps des étrangers arrivèrent et ils furent empêchés de commettre le péché. Un autre, ayant voulu séduire une esclave du Rabba, reçut d'elle cette réponse et ce refus: 'Je ne puis prendre la thébila que quand ma maîtresse en prend.' 'Toi, [esclave], tu n'es considérée que comme une bête,' lui dit le séducteur, 'donc tu n'as pas besoin de thébila.' 'As-tu oublié,' répondit celle-ci, 'qu'il est écrit: Celui qui pèche avec une bête doit être mis à mort (lapidé)?' Et ils ne péchèrent point.*" Talmud of Babylon, Tract Berakoth, III, 5 (Gemara) (Schwab, Vol. I, p. 313; Schwab, *Berakoth,* p. 67; Cohen, pp. 150-51), tells a similar story of the phylacteries worn by Jews: "*Les rabbins ont enseigné qu'avant d'entrer aux cabinets on retire ses phylactères à la distance de quatre coudées . . . il faut les tenir à la main ainsi enveloppés, puis les placer dans des trous à proximité des cabinets, mais ne donnant pas sur la rue, de crainte que les passants ne les prennent et ne donnent lieu à de faux soupçons; car il arriva ceci à un étudiant: ayant laissé ses phylactères dans des trous situés sur la rue, une femme de mauvaise vie vint les prendre et les apporter à la salle d'étude, en disant que cet étudiant les lui avait donnés pour récompense (de son libertinage). Le jeune homme en entendant ces mots monta sur le toit et se jeta en bas par désespoir.*"

1382 [4] According to tradition (Athenaeus, *Deipnosophistae,* XIII, 26) Solon was the first to establish brothels in Athens, διὰ τὴν τῶν νέων ἀκμήν: "because of the exuberance of the young men in the city." Horace, *Saturae,* I, 2, vv. 31-35:

> "*Quidam notus homo cum exiret fornice, 'Macte*
> *virtute esto,' inquit, sententia dia Catonis.*
> *Nam simul ac venas inflavit tetra libido,*
> *huc iuvenes aequum est descendere, non alienas*
> *permolere uxores.*"

("On seeing a man he knew issuing from a brothel he said: 'Congratulations!'—an opinion of divine wisdom by Cato. 'For as soon as a noisome lust begins to swell the veins, it is a good idea for young men to come here and not go pestering other men's wives.'") Pseudo-Acron, *Scholia in Horatium* (Paris, 1519, f. 175): "A certain individual came out of a brothel just as Cato was going by. The man took to his heels, but Cato called him back and commended him. But on seeing the man issuing again from that same brothel, he is reported to have said, 'Young man, I commended you for coming here, not for living here.'" The anecdote reflects the Roman's tolerance of the use, and reprobation for the abuse, of sex. Porphyrio, *Commentum in Horatium* (Paris, 1519, f. 175): "On seeing a respectable man issuing from a brothel, Marcus Cato, the Censor, commended him, deeming that there was nothing wrong in a man's satisfying his natural desires." In Athenaeus, *Op. cit.*, XIII, 26, the poet Zenarchus is made to rebuke young men for pursuing married women instead of contenting themselves with prostitutes: "Dreadful [dreadful and intolerable] things are the young men of this city doing. The brothels are full of most beautiful girls. There they stand in proper line, warming themselves in the sun, their breasts bare, their bodies naked." And he wonders that the young men can so soon be so forgetful of Draco's laws against adultery. In his oration *Pro Marco Coelio*, 20, 48, Cicero defends his client for frequenting prostitutes: "But anyone contending that a young man is forbidden commerce with mercenaries is altogether too strict. I cannot deny the fact [of the interdiction], but it is at variance not only with the licence of our times, but with the custom of our forefathers [A most interesting statement.] and the things they deemed allowable. When have such things not been done? When have they been rebuked, when not permitted? When, finally, has it ever been that a lawful thing was not allowable?" And *cf.* Marcus Seneca, *Controversiae*, II, 12, 10 (*Nepos ex meretrice susceptus*, Bouillet, p. 211): "He has done no wrong, he says. He is enamoured of a harlot—a quite usual thing. He is a mere boy! Wait a while! He will mend his ways, and take a wife." Terence, *Adelphoe, ll.* 102-03, and Prudentius, *Contra Symmachi orationem, Hymni*, I, vv. 134-38 (*Opera*, Vol. II, p. 138) [However the lines of Prudentius are not just to this point.—A. L.]. Roman law upheld the dignity of matrons but left broad liberties to courtesans and their patrons: Suetonius, *Tiberius*, 35: "To be free of the rights and obligations (*dignitate*) of matrons and evade the penalties imposed by the laws, women of compromised reputations began to enroll as prostitutes." Tacitus, *Annales*, II, 85: "In that year [A.D. 19] the Senate passed severe laws against profligacy among women and decreed that no woman whose father, grandfather, or husband had been a Roman knight could register as a prostitute. That was because a woman of praetorian rank named Vestilia had so registered with the aediles, as was permitted by the ancients, who deemed it a sufficient deterrent for a woman well born that she should make public declaration of her infamy." Papinian, in *Digesta*, XLVIII, 5, 10, § 2 (*Corpus iuris civilis*, Vol. I, p. 896; Scott, Vol. XI, p. 35): "A woman who has registered as keeper of a house of prostitution or hired out her services [as an actress] on a public stage for the purpose of evading the penalties of adultery can be indicted for adultery and condemned by decree of the Senate." Livy explains, *Ab urbe condita*, XXXIX, 9, how the Bacchanalian orgies came to be discovered: "A famous courtesan, the freedwoman, Hispala Fecenia, a person worthy of a better lot, continued practising the profession that she had practised as a girl slave even after she had won her freedom. She had established relations with one Aebutius because they were near neighbours, and doing no harm to him either in his property or reputation. She had loved him and sought him of her own accord, and since he was ever in need because of the niggardliness of his family, the courtesan had helped him, out of the kindness of her heart." Even Fathers of the Church recognized prostitution as a necessary evil. St. Augustine, *De ordine*, II, 4, 12 (*Opera*, Vol. I, p. 977), observes that there are necessary evils, such as executioners, prostitutes, panderers: "Can anything be called more loathsome, farther removed from decorum and more fraught with wickedness, than prostitutes, panderers, and other pests of that kind? Yet remove the prostitute from society and everything would be corrupted by lust. Give the harlot the ranking of the matron and you bring the matron into disrepute and defilement. That is why that class of women who are so exceedingly corrupt in their manner of living as regards their morals are assigned to the lowest station by the laws of social ranking." St. Thomas, *Summa theologiae*, II*ᵃ* II*ᵃᵉ*, qu. 10, art. 11 (*Opera*, Vol. VIII, p. 93: *Utrum infidelium ritus sint tolerandi*): [Just as God suffers certain evils to avoid greater ones] "so those who preside over human governments properly tolerate certain wrongs lest certain good things have hurt or even worse evils be incurred, as Augustine says." And he quotes the lines just mentioned. The pagan Emperors taxed prostitutes in Rome and Christian Emperors did the same at Constantinople: Suetonius, *Caligula*, 40: "This strange and unheard-of tax Caligula first collected through the civil tax-collectors [publicans] and then through the centurions and the praetorian tribunes." He taxed the earnings of prostitutes to the amount of the proceeds from one venture, the law furthermore requiring registry of prostitutes and keepers of disorderly houses. Aelius Lampridius, *Alexander Severus*, 24, 3 (Magie, Vol. II, p. 223): "He would not allow the proceeds of the tax on disorderly houses, prostitutes, and mendicants [? *exoletorum;* Magie: "catamites"] to be paid into the sacred treasury, but assigned them to the public budget for the upkeep of the Theatre, the Circus, the Amphitheatre and the Stadium (*aerarii*, read *stadii*)." Zonaras, *Epitome historiarum*, XIV, 3 (Migne, Vol. 135, p. 54), states that the Emperor Anastasius laid a tax called the *crisagyrium* (gold and silver tax, Latin, *aurargenteum*) on "all paupers, mendicants, and courtesans." In his fourteenth *Novella* (III, 1) *De Lenonibus* (*Corpus iuris civilis*, Vol. III, pp. 94-98; Scott, Vol. XVI, pp. 78-80), Justinian complains that prostitutes were flocking to Constantinople from all parts of the Empire and "the place and its environs were full of brothels." He therefore enjoins on all his subjects to help remedy the situation by "conducting themselves chastely to the best of their ability." What a pulpit for that sort of sermon!

1382 ⁵ As for Barbarian legislation, *cf.* the *Codex legis Wisigothorum*, III, 4, 17 (Canciani, Vol. IV, pp. 97-98): "Matter of prostitutes whether free-born or slaves, or in case judicial authorities have been lax in prosecuting and punishing their crime. If a girl or woman free-born shall be shown to be a prostitute publicly practising her profession in a city and though frequently taken in adultery evinces no shame but is shown to have gone on soliciting many men through her evil habit, she shall be arrested by the Count (*Comes*) of such city."

1382 ⁶ As for the court of Charlemagne, *cf. Capitularium de minesterialibus palatinis*, 1: "Each attendant at court shall by a diligent taking of the roll (*discutiat*) first among his men and then among his peers see whether he can find hiding among them or at our court any unknown person or prostitute." *Capitularium regum Francorum*, VII, 143 (Canciani, Vol. III, p. 320): "But since with the help of God and through the merits and intercession of the Saints and servants of God whom we have at all times tried, as we still are trying, to honour and glorify, we and our successors have so far acquired realms and territories and won many victories, so it must henceforward be the concern of all of us that we should not be deprived of such things—which God forbid—because of the foul and unlawful vices that we have mentioned. For many lands which have practised encroachments, robberies, confiscations, invasions and abuses of church properties and oppressions of priests and other servants of God and other sorts of wrongs, or unlawful things such as adulteries, sodomies, or frequentings of prostitutes, have never long endured strong in secular war or abiding in faith. And in what measure the Lord has permitted avenging punishments to come upon and serve those who

prevails among almost all civilized peoples and in all periods of history. There are very considerable variations in forms, very few in substance.[1][2][3] (For footnote 3 see page 873.)

1384. So far we have been speaking of people in general. Let us

are guilty of such crimes now through the Saracens, now through other peoples, is apparent (*liquet*) to anyone reading their histories. And unless we beware of such things, we have no doubt that similar punishments will overtake us also, for God takes His vengeance for all such things." Virtually the same words are repeated in the Fourth Appendix (*Additio quarta*) to the *Capitularium*, sec. 160 (Canciani, Vol. III, p. 408), but with this adjunct: "Such immoral women, whether of the monasteries or of the laity, oftentimes and in large part kill the offspring they have conceived in sin, so sating the other world with unhappy souls and filling not the churches with adoptive children but the graveyards with dead. God grant that (reading *pereatis*) ye perish not from such things and that we fall not with our realm (reading *peccatis*: "that we fall not with our realm because of such sins")." As we shall see further along (§ 1391 [3]), Charlemagne notes that priests and clerics were frequent sinners with the women with whom canon law, assuming such contacts to be innocuous, permitted them to live. Morals in the people generally were no better. *Capitularium cit.*, VII, 336-56 (Canciani, Vol. III, 340-41): "*That concubines are unlawful:* A man who has a wife cannot at the same time have a concubine nor shall love of a concubine keep him apart from his wife. . . . On men who have had intercourse with animals (*pecorum*) or who after the manner of animals have committed incest with relatives within the limits of blood-relationship or have had commerce with males." And *cf. Ibid.*, Bk. VI, 27 (Canciani, Vol. III, p. 264).

1382 [7] As for the laws of Sicily, see *Constitutiones regni Siculi*, Bk. I, 20 (Canciani, Vol. I, p. 311): "*On forcing prostitutes* [*against their will*]: Laws of King William: Those unfortunate women who are distinguished by the nefarious trade of the prostitute shall have our favour, in response to their petition (*gratulantes*), to the extent that no man shall force them to do his pleasure against their will." *Ibid.*, Bk. III, 53 (Canciani, Vol. I, p. 372): "*On penalties for a mother who makes her daughter a public prostitute:* Laws of the Emperor Frederick: We ordain that mothers who publicly prostitute their daughters shall be subject to the penalty fixed by the late (*divus*) King Roger of having the nose cut off. We think it not so much unjust as severe that there should be penalties for other women who merely abet (*consentientes*) and offer to the pleasures of men daughters whom poverty prevents them from marrying off or supporting and who thereby earn livelihood or favours."

1383 [1] For conditions in the French camp at Damietta, read Joinville, *Histoire de Saint Louis*, XXXVI, 171: "The rank and file took to light women, so that the King banished all such individuals from the army in one sweep when we came back from taking the town [*prison*]. I asked him why he had done that, and he told me that he had discovered that the people whom he had sent away had set up their brothels within a stone's throw of his tent and that too at a time when the army was in the direst straits it had ever been in."

1383 [2] On the "King of Harlots" see Pichon, *Le roy des ribauds*: C. Fanchet, p. 25: "It is said that the light women who followed the court were obligated

now look at various classes of people in particular. If in so doing we were to find that immorality is not observable among individuals highly placed in religious orders that condemn carnal indulgence, an influence of doctrines upon conduct would be plausibly indicated. But if that is not the case, if morality is none the greater where faith seems greatest, we shall again conclude, as we have previously concluded, not that faith is a bad thing, nor even altogether without influence, but that in many cases it is not powerful enough to subdue the sex residues.

1385. Beginning with the reproaches addressed of old to the philosophers of Greece and Rome, coming on through the accusations brought against the Catholic clergy, or the Christian clergy in general, we finally reach our own time, when similar charges can be lodged against our virtuists.

during the month of May to make the bed of the Provost of the Mansion. They had come to be called *ribaudes* because of their bold impudence and immodesty." According to Bouteillier, an author writing about 1459, and who is also quoted by Miraumont (p. 37), the King of Harlots "collected a tax of two sous a week from all brothels and from the women in them." Du Tillet, quoted by Estienne Pasquier, *Recherches de la France*, VIII, 44 (p. 750), quoted by Pichon, *Op. cit.*, p. 78, repeats the detail of the bed-making: "The harlots who follow the Court are under the charge [of the King of Harlots] and are obliged to go and keep his room in order all through this month of May." Du Cange, *Glossarium . . . mediae et infimae Latinitatis, s.v. Ribaldi*, quotes the privileges of the King of Rogues at Cambray: "Said King may have, take, collect, receive from each woman who goes with a man, when she has earned her money and provided she has rented or is renting a house in the city, five sous of the Paris mintage for each time. 2. From all women coming under the law who enter the city for the first time, two sous of the mintage of Tours. 3. From each woman coming under the law who moves from one house or resort (*estuve*) to another to live, or who goes out of the city and stays one night, twelve pence." Criticizing the remark of Bouteillier, above, Gouye de Longuemare (pp. 96-97) [*i.e., Eclaircissemens, etc.*, pp. 223-24] none the less substantiates the prevalence of [Court] prostitutes: "As for what Bouteillier says of his [the "king's"] jurisdiction over 'brothels and the women in them,' one must understand that his function was to visit such places and enforce the observance of a certain orderliness. . . . The houses and the women who lived in them had to pay a tax of two sous a week. . . . Immorality would seem to have been permitted at the time in the retinue of our Kings. All the same it should be noted that it was only tolerated there, just as disorderly houses were tolerated in Paris. . . . It seems indeed that the purpose of the tolerance was merely to avoid still greater irregularities." [Whatever the motives underlying the fact, the fact remains a fact.] Le Bibliophile Jacob, *Curiosités de l'histoire de France*, pp. 163-64: "Rogues' Royalty went to the distaff on the passing of the good Lord of Gri-

1386. People who are inclined to attach great or exclusive importance to logical conduct are tempted to infer from the fact that a few or many believers in a given religion are dishonest that that religion is "false," useless, harmful. But those who understand the important rôle non-logical conduct plays in human life also understand that such a conclusion is not warranted. Philosophy is not to be condemned because there have been dishonest philosophers, nor the Catholic religion because there have been criminal priests, nor the religion of our Inquisitors on Purity because dissolute individuals are to be counted among them. Such religions, all religions, are to be judged by different standards. Even disregarding non-logical conduct and keeping strictly to the logical, the accusations in question are in many cases unjustified.

1387. The bitter censure that has been heaped upon the Jesuits

gneaux. 'A lady, and sometimes a great lady,' says Rabutaux in his interesting *Mémoire sur la prostitution en Europe,* 'had charge of policing the women at court. In 1535 her name was Olive Sainte, and she received an allowance of ninety pounds from Francis I 'to help her and said girls to live and meet such expenses as they should properly make in ordinarily following the court. . . .' Several ordinances of the same sort, issued between the years 1539 and 1546, have been preserved, and they show that every year during the month of May all the girls about the court were allowed the honour of offering the King the 'Spring bouquet' (*bouquet du renouveau*) or 'valentine,' which welcomed the return of spring and amorous pleasures." P. de Miraumont quotes (p. 41) an order of July 13, 1458, also referring to the superintendence by a woman. It "expressly enjoined and ordered upon all prostitutes and others not on the registers of the mistress in charge of said girls, to vacate the court forthwith on publication of said order, girls on the registers meantime being forbidden to go about in the villages, and carters, muleteers, and others to transport them out or back or give them lodging, and further to swear and blaspheme the name of God."

1383 [8] As for the success of repressive measures see Lamare, *Traité de police,* I, *Lib.* III, *tit.* V, ch. 6, pp. 521-22: "St. Louis set out to abolish prostitution: his Ordinance of 1254 begins with just that reform. It states that all prostitutes, girls or women, shall be driven from towns and villages alike. . . . But long and sad experience showed at last that prostitution could not be totally abolished without occasioning other irregularities incomparably more dangerous to religion, to morals and the state. . . . It then became the policy to tolerate those unhappy victims of impurity . . . An Ordinance of the Prefect of Paris, September 18, 1367, orders all women of dissolute life to go and live in the brothels and public places assigned to them . . . and other persons are forbidden to rent them houses in any other places on pain of confiscation of the rents; and the women themselves are forbidden to buy houses elsewhere on pain of losing them."

for discussing cases of conscience relative to sex in their treatises might be logically justified if it came of the conviction that neither morality nor law should interfere in matters of sex. It is not justified if it comes, as it usually does, from people who believe that morality and law ought to interfere in sex. Obviously it is impossible to regulate a thing without discussing it. The Jesuits, moreover, were far from being the only ones to harp on sex. They had predecessors in the Church Fathers and successors in all those who, believers and infidels alike, have since set out to regulate sex relations.[1]

1388. The "abolitionists" of our day who would abolish prostitution root and branch use language more indecent than the Jesuits ever did; and a language furthermore that is common to everybody, whereas the Jesuits used Latin. Our puritans also fight immorality, at times in such ways as to make one's mouth water for sin. I say nothing of those who under pretext of educating the young to chastity write books to impart all the details of the sexual act.

1389. The evidence that, as regards morality in individuals, theories and facts are far from always corresponding is exceedingly abundant, too abundant indeed. We must be on our guard against it and reject not a little of it. But meantime the evidence on the other side is also suspect, because it may, even when produced in good faith, express a mere ill will that takes advantage of the powerful weapon provided by the sex residue to vent its spleen. The evidence furnished by neutrals is also not always above suspicion, for the impression left upon our minds by the contrast between fine

1387 [1] There is no good reason for doubting the utter good faith of St. Alfonsus Liguori when, *Theologia moralis*, Vol. I, p. 228, he confesses his repugnance to dealing with violations of the Sixth and Ninth Commandments: *"Treatise on the Sixth [i.e., Seventh] and Ninth Precepts of the Decalogue:* Reluctantly now we approach the consideration of a subject the very name of which corrupts the minds of men. Would that I could express myself more briefly and in a language more veiled. But since it is the more frequent and abundant topic in confessions and the thing that drags the greater number of souls to hell—indeed I do not hesitate to say that all who are damned are damned because of this one vice of impurity or at all events not apart from it—I have been obliged to express myself clearly (though as chastely as possible) and to discuss many many things in detail for the instruction of those interested in mastering moral science."

preaching and bad practice tends to magnify shortcomings in preachers of virtue. Not even the testimony of loyal believers in a religion against its priesthood is always to be accepted at face value. There is a natural inclination in the human being to exaggerate an evil the better to correct it, and to substitute preaching for impartial observation. As regards the neutral and the believer, such reservations apply more especially to comments upon the facts, little if at all to the bare facts themselves. Everything is possible, but it is not very probable that a believer will invent a fact outright for the mere pleasure of slandering people who hold the same faith as he. Nor is it very likely that an unbiased person interested in having an accurate record of facts would invent the things that he records. In a word, the causes of error that we have indicated have their influence on all historical documents. If we would reject absolutely everything in which they figure, we should have to give up all history of whatever kind as a hopeless business.

1390. St. Jerome betrays the fact that in his early day there were priests who for all the world resembled the cassocked "dandies" of the eighteenth century, as well as women very very like the petti-coated sex-reformers of our day who for sheer love of purity cannot get their minds off prostitution. The allusions of the Saint, along with the laws that the Emperors had to proclaim against too close intimacies between women and clergy, remove any doubt we may have held that the remarks of Ammianus Marcellinus on the Roman pontiffs of his time may have been slanders. "Considering," he writes, *Res gestae*, XXVII, 3, 14, "the magnificence of that office in the city of Rome, I can understand the excessive eagerness some people manifest for obtaining it and why it is fought for with such bitterness. The person who secures it is sure of growing rich through the gifts of Roman matrons, of having a carriage to ride in in robes of the most elegant fashion, and of enjoying banquets that surpass the feasts of kings in splendour."[1]

1390 [1] St. Jerome, *Ad Pammachium adversus errores Ioannis Hierosalemitani* (*Opera*, Vol. II, p. 561; Schaff-Wace, p. 428): "Poor Praetextatus! He died just as he had been named consul! A sacrilegious soul and a worshipper of idols, he used to say playfully to the blessed Pope Damasus: 'Make me bishop of the city of Rome, and I'll turn Christian at once!' "

1391. The Theodosian Code had a law that forbade ecclesiastics and self-styled "continents" to frequent the homes of widows and female orphans, and to accept gifts from such women under pretext of piety. Another law forbade them to keep women in their houses when a scandal was likely to result. Laws of that kind are to be found in other codes, notably in Charlemagne's Capitularies. The battle the Popes waged all through the Middle Ages against a concubinary clergy is too well known to require documentation.[128]

1391 [1] As for the protection of widows and orphans, *cf. Codex Theodosianus,* XVI, 2, 20 (Haenel, pp. 1492-93): *Imperatores Valentinianus, Valens et Gratianus Augusti (AAA) ad Damasum Episcopum urbis Romae.* "Priests or ex-priests or those who choose to call themselves 'continents' shall not enter homes of widows and female wards, but they shall be banished by public sentence if hereafter relatives of such women or members of their families shall see fit to have them brought to .trial. And we likewise ordain that such individuals shall not be allowed possession of anything from the liberality or last wills of any woman to whom they may have secretly attached themselves under pretext of piety, and any legacy made by any such woman to any such person shall in all respects be null and void so that they shall receive nothing even through a third (*subjectam*) person from any gift or testament." Godefroi annotates (Vol. VI, p. 48): " 'Continents' were individuals inspired by personal zeal for a better life, following a vow to live more austerely apart from the consolations of legitimate matrimony. The ἀποταττόμενοι practiced celibacy. The word ἐγκρατευόμενοι means 'the temperate.' "

1391 [2] As for priests keeping women in their homes, *Ibid.,* XVI, 2, 44 (Haenel, p. 1514), *anno* 420: "It is not becoming that a man who is ostensibly practising a rule of life before the laity should be compromised (*decolorari*) by any so-called sororial association. All persons whatsoever therefore who are supported by the priesthood of whatever grade or who are distinguished with the honour of the priesthood, should know that association with women not their kin (*extranearum*) is forbidden them. . . . *Interpretation:* All persons practising the profession of priest are forbidden to associate on terms of intimacy with women not their kin. Notice is served (*noverint*) that the attendance (*solatia*) of mothers, sisters, or daughters is all that is permitted them in their homes, for the law of nature does not allow that any wicked deed or thought should arise in connexion with such persons. Even of such women, however, they are to be chosen as attendants who have been married before service with a priest." And see the long note by Godefroi, Vol. VI, p. 86.

1391 [3] For the allusion to Charlemagne, *cf. Capitularium regum Francorum,* VII, 376 (Canciani, Vol. III, p. 343): "*That females shall not live with priests or other clerics nor act as their servants nor stay in their houses nor approach the altar.*" Charlemagne bars women who were passed by the old canons, "because it is our experience that at the instigation of the Devil crime has frequently been committed with even those women." And *cf. Ibid.,* VII, 452 (Canciani, Vol. III, pp. 353-54). The Third Appendix (*Additio tertia*), 117, reads (Canciani, Vol. III, p. 386): "*On the introduction of women* [into homes of priests]: It shall be strictly for-

1392. It had been a long-standing evil, and one must say that if it is to be counted a degeneration of Christianity, the corruption set in at a very very early stage. St. Cyprian expatiated at length on the subject and he was a man of the third century. In a letter he writes to one Pomponius, *Ad Pomponium de virginibus,* conjointly with other priests, he expresses himself as follows: "Very dear Brother: We have read the letter that you sent us by our brother Pacomius, urgently requesting in answer our opinion as to those virgins who, despite their vows to remain in their state and observe continence, are found to have slept in the same beds with males, among whom, you state, a deacon, and who, though openly confessing to so sleeping with men none the less aver that they are still virgins." The Saint condemns that sort of household on the strength of biblical quotations: ". . . Virgins cannot be allowed to live with men—I do not say to sleep with men, but even to live in their houses. . . . How many the men who are ruined in that way, and how many the virgins who are corrupted by that illicit and dangerous contiguity to the supreme sorrow of our soul! . . . If they really will not, or cannot, persevere [in their state], it is better for them to marry than to fall into hell-fire by sinning." According to St. Jerome married women and widows who hobnobbed too intimately with priests behaved no better.[1]

bidden for any priest to have a woman with him in his house save as permitted by the canons."

1392 [1] St. Cyprian, *Epistolae,* 62, 1-2 (*Opera,* pp. 364-65; Wallis, Vol. I, p. 204). And *cf. Ibid.,* 62, 3 (*Opera,* pp. 367-69; Wallis, Vol. I, p. 206): "*Nec aliqua putet se hac excusatione defendi, quod inspici et probari possit an virgo sit cum et manus obstetricum et oculus saepe fallatur. Et si incorrupta inventa fuerit virgo ea parte sui qua mulier potest esse potuerit tamen ex alia corporis parte peccasse quae violari potest et tamen inspici non potest. Certe ipse concubitus ipse complexus ipsa confabulatio et osculatio et coniacentium duorum turpis et foeda dormitio quantum dedecoris et criminis confitetur!*" (See below, § 1394 [6]). More chaste and by far than such women was the Roman matron who used an image of the phallus to protect her children from the evil eye; nor would a paterfamilias of the better Roman days have allowed daughters of his to submit to such indecent inspections. To cap the climax Saint Cyprian adds a touch about divine jealousy which had better stay in Latin (*loc. cit.*): "*Si superveniens maritus sponsam suam iacentem cum altero videat nonne indignatur et fremit? Et per zeli livorem fortassis et gladium in manum sumit? Quid? Christus Dominus et iudex noster, cum virginem suam sibi dicatam et sanctitati suae destinatam facere cum altero cernit,*"

1393. The censures heaped by the Fathers and dignitaries of the Church on immoralities in the clergy are usually met with the defence that they were not descriptions of literal fact, but assumed the existence of evils in order to point a lesson. That objection was raised against Cardinal Peter Damian for one among many others. But can we possibly imagine that St. Cyprian invented the letter of Pomponius, which he answers, out of whole cloth? Can everything he says be fiction? Even granting all that, it would still not be enough. The acts of the Councils and no end of other documents are there to vouch for the fact that women commonly lived with priests. But to defend the clergy it is unnecessary to brand all such evidence as false. It is sufficient to observe that, after all, the morals of the clergy were no worse, indeed they seem to have been on the whole better, than the morality generally prevailing at the time.[1]

quam indignatur et irascitur! Et quas poenas incestis eiusmodi coniunctionibus *comminatur!*" For Jerome's picture of the merry widows of those days see his letter *Ad Eustochium, Epistolae,* XXII, 6 (Wright, p. 85) (Widows affecting chastity in question): "Their houses are full of flatterers, full of guests. The very priests whose rôle would better seem to be that of the teacher who is feared kiss them on the foreheads, or hold out their hands—to bless them you might think if you did not know—to receive the rewards of the greeting. The widows, meantime, seeing that the priests need their help, become conceited and proud and to the rule of a husband that they have experienced they much prefer the freedom of widowhood, call themselves 'continents' and nuns and after equivocal suppers (*post cenam dubiam*) see Apostles in their dreams!"

1393 [1] As for the Damian incident: That saint had brought the immorality and vices of a number of ecclesiasts to the attention of the Pope: St. Peter Damian, *Liber Gomorrhianus ad Leonem IX, Romanum Pontificem (Opera,* Vol. III, p. 73): "Argument: [St. Peter Damian] deplores the detestable, nay, unspeakable criminality into which men of his time who were consecrated to God were falling. He argues that they should be removed from the sacred orders as unworthy and begs the Roman pontiff Leo to restrain such foul sinners with all his authority." And *cf.* Burchard, *Diarium,* May, *anno* 1493 (Vol. II, p. 79): "[Pope] Alexander [VI] has carried on the policy of marrying his female progeny that Innocent began and has improved upon it. The whole clergy therefore is falling to with a will to the business of raising families. From highest to lowest they are living with concubines very much as wives and indeed publicly. Unless God forfend, this corruption will extend to the monks and friars, though virtually every monastery in the *Urbs* is already a brothel, with nobody objecting." Thuasne, Burchard's editor, comments (*loc. cit.*): "This comparison of brothels and convents is a common theme with writers of the fifteenth century"—and he mentions examples. Infessura, *Diario,* pp. 259-60: "Among other things also that may be ascribed to those times [*anno* 1490] is the fact that the Reverend Father, the Vicar of the Pope in the City and District, think-

1394. The women who live with the clergy were variously designated: *subintroductae* (*i.e.*, secretly), "strangers" (*i.e.*, not of one's kin), "sisters," "agapetes" (lovers in Christ), and there is frequent allusion to them in the acts of the Councils.[1] St. John Chrysostom has

ing as befitted a kind soul to shelter the lambs of the flock entrusted to his care, issued an edict prohibiting laymen and clergy of whatever rank or condition, and among other things, on pain of excommunication, suspension, and loss of benefices, from keeping concubines either privately or in public, since he had learned that that was being turned to the discredit of divine law and against the reputability of the clergy, there being many, in fact countless numbers of priests, both high prelates and ordinary clerics, who were keeping concubines, so that that was not judged a proper manner of living in them and they were diminishing the devotion and faith of the laity. When the Holy Father heard of that, he hastily summoned said Bishop and Vicar to him and sharply reprimanded him for issuing the interdict and bade him rescind it at once since, he said, the thing was not prohibited, because the manner of living of priests and attendants at the Curia had come to such a pass that hardly one could be found who was not keeping a concubine or at the very least a prostitute to the glory of God and the Christian faith. That may be the reason why, as competent authority avers, the number of prostitutes practising publicly in Rome at that time has been estimated at 6,800, not counting those who were living as concubines and those who were plying their trade not publicly but in secret with five or six others, each one of them having one or more procurers." In his *Diarium*, Vol. II, p. 400, Burchard mentions a service that took place in August, 1497: "Harlots and other disreputable persons were present everywhere between the altar and the Cardinals." And, *Ibid., anno* 1501 (Vol. III, p. 167), he describes the famous banquet with the fifty courtesans offered by Pope Borgia: "That evening fifty prostitutes, more chastely known as courtesans, had supper with Duke Valentine in his apartment in the Apostolic Palace, and after the meal they danced with the servants and the others there present, first in their costumes and

---

1394 [1] Speaking against Paul of Samosata in his *Historia ecclesiastica*, VII, 30, 12, Eusebius uses the term συνεισάκτους, " 'taken in with,' as the people of Antioch call them, and those of the priests and of the deacons who live about him . . . and we know how many [priests] have fallen as a result of allowing women near them." And *cf.* Nicephorus Callistus, *Ecclesiastica historia*, VI, 30. In his letter to Eustochia, *De custodia virginitatis*, Epistola XXII, 14 (Wright, pp. 81-83), St. Jerome cries: "I shrink from mentioning such profanity. Sad is it yet true! How did this pest of the 'agapetes' ["sisters in Christ"; Wright: "dearly beloved sisters"] get into the Church? How is it we have come to have another name for unmarried wives? Whence this new sort of concubine? I will speak more plainly: Whence this whore who keeps to one man, one house, one chamber, often indeed one bed! And they call us evil-minded if we suspect something (*suspiciosos nos vocant, si aliquid extimemus*)! Here a brother leaves an unmarried sister to her own devices. There a maid will have none of her unmarried brother. No indeed! She must have a 'brother' not her kin! And since they both pretend to be of one mind on that point, they seek the spiritual solace of 'strangers,' but for the purpose of carnal pleasure amid all the comforts of home (*ut domi habeant carnale commercium*)!"

two whole sermons against them. In the first [2] he says that the fore-fathers knew two reasons for a woman's living with a man: one of them was righteous and rational—matrimony; the other, more modern, was unrighteous and illegal—fornication, which was the

then naked. After dinner also the common candlesticks were taken from the table with candles lighted and set on the floor and chestnuts were strewn over the floor among the candlesticks set in line (*projecta*) and the harlots gathered them up scrambling on all fours among the candles, the Pope, the Duke, Milady Lucretia, the Duke's sister, being present and looking on. At length the last gifts were brought out, silk dresses, boots in pairs, caps, and other things for those *qui pluries dictas meretrices carnaliter agnoscerent quae fuerunt ibidem in aula publice carnaliter tractate arbitrio presentium,* the gifts being distributed to the winners." Thuasne notes: "The [story of the] banquet of the fifty courtesans is corroborated by Materazzo who, however, speaks of lords and ladies of the court instead of the servants and courtesans in Burchard's story [See *Archivio storico italiano,* Vol. XVI-2, p. 189]; by a letter of Silio Savelli . . . which Sanudo inserts in his diary, and finally by the Florentine orator, Francesco Pepi. . . . Early in the eighteenth century the French regent gave a series of twelve balls at the Little Luxembourg, where dancers male and female and entirely nude revived the gay festivities of the Vatican." Machiavelli, *Vita di Castruccio Castracani* (*Opere,* Milan, 1804-05, p. 153): (After the defeat which Castruccio inflicted upon the Florentines) "he halted with his people on the plain of Peretola . . . where he lingered for many days dividing the booty, celebrating the victory, and having medals struck in contempt of the Florentines and racing horses, men, and courtesans." Burchard, *Diarium,* Vol. III, p. 146 (June 19, 1501): "A place near the Acqua Traversa was appointed . . . for the lodging of attendants of the King of France on their way to Naples. . . . Fences were built about the place, and supplies of bread, meats, eggs, cheese, fruit, and all other necessaries laid in, and by special order sixteen harlots to provide for the needs of those people." Familiar the fact that concubinage was wide-spread among priests in the Middle Ages and that in many instances lay and religious authorities sold the privilege of keeping concubines at certain rates. It was an evil of long standing, and many chroniclers allude to it, *e.g.,* Mathieu Paris, *Grande chronique,* Vol. I, p. 293 (*anno* 1129): "That same year, on August 1, King Henry held a great Council in London to prohibit concubinage in the clergy. William, Archbishop of Canterbury, Thurston, Archbishop of York, and their followers attended. Thanks to an awkward blunder of the Archbishop of Canterbury, Henry fooled all the prelates roundly. He indeed got high justice on clerical concubinage, but the business was to end in a great scandal, for the King made a fortune by selling back to the priests the right to keep their concubines." Things are much the same in our day in places where sex-reformers have got purity into the law, the profits going to the police, who know how to tolerate immorality in practice. *Ibid.,* 286-87: "In the year of Our Lord 1125, Jean de Crème, Cardinal of the Holy Apostolic See, visited England with the King's permission and went from diocese to

<hr>

1394 [2] Gaume, Vol. I, pp. 279-326: Πρὸς τοὺς ἔχοντας παρθένους συνεισάκτους. Gaume's editor, Savil, paraphrases: "*Adversus eos qui apud se fovent sorores adoptivas quas subintroductas vocant.*"

work of the Devil. In his own day another reason strange and para-
doxical had come into vogue; for there actually were men who took
girls into their houses without marrying them and apart from considerations of sex and lived with them to old age. The reasons alleged

diocese, from abbey to abbey, not without everywhere collecting bounteous presents.
On the day of the Nativity of the Blessed Mary he held a solemn council in London, where he preached forcefully against concubinage among priests, declaring it
an abominable crime to go from the arms of a courtesan to partake of the body of
Christ. But after communing that day, he was found spending the evening with a
courtesan." Similar mishaps have befallen sex-reformers in our day. The centuries
roll by, human nature remains the same! There is a passage in Cornelius Agrippa
that certainly oversteps the truth, but which no less certainly is in partial accord
with the facts. Appearing in the Antwerp edition of 1530, the passage was deleted
in the Lyons edition of the *Opera omnia*. On the point see Bayle, *Dictionnaire historique, s.v. Agrippa*. The copy at my disposal begins: "*Splendidae nobilitatis viri et
armatae militiae Equitis aurati . . . Henrici Corneilii Agrippae ab Nettesheym De
Incertitudine et Vanitate Scientiarum et Artium atque excellentia Verbi Dei Decla-
matio*"; for a colophon: "*Iona. Grapheus excudebat anno a Christo nato MDXXX,
mense Septemb. Antuerpiae*." The pages are not numbered; but there is a register
of the sheets. In the chapter *De arte lenonia* (sheet *z*, recto, last page) Agrippa
fiercely declaims against the immorality of his age: "The jealous husband is pacified
by gold, by gold is the heart of the relentless rival softened. Guards most scrupulous
are vanquished by gold, for gold doth every door swing open. Every marriage-bed
has its price in gold. The stoutest door-bar, the hardest rock, the unsunderable bonds
of matrimony, are broken in twain by gold. What wonder that virgins, maids,
matrons, widows, nuns (*vestales*), are venial, if Christ Himself is sold for gold?
With gold the panderer as leader, countless are they who have risen from lowliest
station almost to the supreme heights of nobility. This man prostitutes his wife and
he is made a Senator, that one prostitutes his daughter, and lo, he is a Count. A
third solicits the embrace of a married woman for his prince, and straightway he is
a royal chamberlain deemed worthy of an ample salary. There are those who have
become important men and been placed in charge of public bureaus by marrying
royal mistresses. Many cardinals and Popes have won many rich benefices by those
same arts nor is any road in the Church more expeditious. . . . [Agrippa turns to
ancient examples of the use of religion for purposes of pandering, and then goes
on:] Nor if I chose to mention them would I find any lack of modern examples.
For priests, monks, friars, lay brothers, and the women they call 'sisters,' have the
special prerogative of pandering, since under guise of religion they are free to go
anywhere and to talk without witnesses to anybody as long, and as often, as they
wish under pretext of visitation, consolation, and secret confession, so piously are
their panderings accoutred; and there are those among them who call it a pain and
a punishment to touch hand to money, but who are not at all stirred by the words
of St. Paul: 'It is good for a man not to touch a woman' [I Cor. 7:1], and who
time and again touch them and with unchaste hands, who stealthily slink to the
brothels, corrupt consecrated nuns, seduce widows and the adulterous wives of those
who offer them hospitality." Then (sheet *a*, p. 1, recto) comes the passage discussed
by Bayle and which appears in a very free French translation in the 1603 ed., n.p.,

for such a practice the Saint deems ill-founded. He thinks the main consideration was that "a certain sensuous pleasure comes from living with a woman, not only in a conjugal relationship, but also quite apart from marriage or physical relations." [8] And that pleasure indeed he finds greater than the joys of marriage, since in marriage a man tires of his wife through frequent contact, and a wife ages sooner than a spinster. It would seem that those spiritual intimacies were carried a bit far; for, after quoting an apothegm stressing the danger of the kiss, the Saint adds: "I need hardly say as much to those who kiss and caress the women who live in their homes." [4] And he runs on at length to confute the various pretexts advanced in justification of such practices. In his second sermon [5] the Saint deals with the women involved. In general he thinks it wrongful for consecrated virgins to dress fastidiously. As for those who live with men, the Saint would have them buried alive. He flouts the shameless proofs they give of their virginity. [6] He confutes, preaches, groans, exhorts. Strange indeed if for so much smoke there were no fire whatever in actual life. As a matter of fact it is transparent proof that the scandal existed and was no small scandal at that; and there is plenty of other evidence to the same purport.

p. 394: "The laws and the canons are also enlisted in that army [of vice], and serve to foment immorality by working in favour of the powerful for the validation and legitimizing of wrongful marriage and in breaking up marriages that are legitimate and holy, and by forcing priests to cowardly secret lusts by forbidding them honourable marriage. The law-breakers have found it better that men of the Church should lead disgusting lives with concubines than respectable orderly lives with married wives, perhaps because the profits and conveniences that they derive from the concubines are the greater. For we read that a certain bishop made boast at a banquet that he had eleven thousand priests in his diocese who kept concubines and that they paid him every mother's son at the rate of a pound apiece a year."

1394 [8] Δοκεῖ μοί τινα ἡδονὴν ἔχειν τὸ συνοικεῖν γυναιξὶν, οὐ νόμῳ γάμου μόνον, ἀλλὰ καὶ γάμου καὶ συνουσίας χωρίς.

1394 [4] Ἐγὼ δὲ τοῦτο μὲν οὐκ ἂν εἴποιμι ὅτι τὰς συνοικούσας φιλοῦσιν ἢ ἐπαφῶνται.

1394 [5] Gaume, loc. cit.: Πρὸς τὰς ἐχούσας ἄνδρας συνεισάκτους: [Savil] "Adversus eas qui viros introductorios habent."

1394 [6] The passage reads in Latin translation: "Obstetricis enim ars et sapientia hoc solum potest videre: an congressum viri corpus tulerit. An liberum [sit] et adulterium ex osculis et corruptionum amplexibus effugerit, dies illa tunc declarabit quando verus Dei sermo qui occulta hominis in medium adducit et praesens nunc his quae clam fiunt omnia et exuta ante omnium oculos ponet: tunc sciemus bene an ab his sit purum et undequaque incorruptum corpus." (§ 1392 [2].)

1395. The nineteenth canon of the Council held at Ancyra in Galatia, in the year 314 (canon XX, Labbe, Vol. I, p. 1494), forbids virgins to live with men as "sisters." The Council of Nicaea eleven years later (*anno* 325, canon III, Labbe, Vol. II, p. 34) forbids the clergy to keep in their houses *subintroductae* other than mothers, sisters, aunts, or other women above suspicion.[1] Nor did the Church relax its battling in later times to prevent its priests from keeping paramours or concubines. But results were negligible. What serious proportions the task of suppressing a concubinary clergy in the Middle Ages assumed is a matter of common knowledge. There were, to be sure, Popes who attached little importance to sexual morality, but there were others who, no less certainly, did their utmost to enforce it. In the end, after great efforts public concubinage was abolished, but not much was accomplished as regards substance.[2]

1396. If one consider on the one hand the immense power that the Church held through the spiritual, moral, and material weapons it had at its disposal, and on the other the insignificance of the results achieved, one gets some conception of the tremendous power of the sex residue, and comes to realize how ridiculous certain fatuous pygmies of our day are in even dreaming that they can repress it.[1]

1395 [1] See Du Cange, *Glossarium . . . mediae et infimae Latinitatis, s.v. Subintroductae;* and *Idem, Glossarium . . . mediae et infimae Graecitatis, s.v.* Συνείσακτοι.

1395 [2] In a number of countries the clergy are more moral today than they ever were in times past; but that fact is due rather to the selection that is now exercised, all candidates who fail to give certain promise of genuine vocation being rejected.

1396 [1] [In his treatment of the sex residue Pareto is less objective than is his wont, and his exposition may be perfected in some important respects. For instance when he comes to the matter of the combination of the sex residue with other residues, one would have thought that he would follow his classification and show how the combination is effected with each class of residues in turn and the consequences of the combination. Some interesting analyses would have resulted. General: The general effect of the sex residue in combination with others is to intensify those others, so that if a sex slant can be introduced into a non-logical impulse, the latter flares on high. This is so true that one of the ways to gauge fluctuations of intensities of sentiments in history is to watch the effects that various transformations have on the status of women. Historians have commonly noted that one of the most striking results of the so-called Christian revolution was the abolition of the Graeco-Roman harem and a step toward the equalization of women with men. This can be stated in Paretan language in terms of a sudden intensification of Class V residues in the ruling classes. So a contrast between the treatment of women by the law before the eighteenth century and their modern status brings out the rapid development of humanitarian sentiments (Class IV and Class II residues). Particular: 1. Pure and generic manifestations of sex, so frequent in ancient and medieval times, nay, so unconscious, have been reduced to a sub-social level and are punished by law in all Western countries. Examples, the obscenities that are drawn or written on walls and bill-boards in public places. 2. Combinations with Class I residues. The chief manifestation here is in wit: the risqué story, sub-rosa and in art. The phenomenon presents wide variations in time and in space, and accounts for certain aspects of our Western national literatures. 3. Combinations with Class II residues. Important is the phenomenon of Platonic love. Not less than a dozen professorial chairs have been created to produce literary drool on this subject, and all to no scientific purpose, the Platonism, so-called, being nothing but a combination of the sex residue with certain persisting abstractions, God, Eternity, Virtue, and the like. 4. Combinations with activity residues. Example: obscene oaths, past and present. A subject to which not less than fifty doctoral dissertations in Germany have been devoted, to the great distress of bibliographers and librarians and to no corresponding scientific advantage.

One may wonder, further, whether, in a strictly sound Paretan classification, the sex residue would be a class by itself, or a genus of a much larger class, which I would define as residues connected with parts of the body and their functions. I will not go into this matter save to point out that apart from what I will call a "stercorary residue" German humor and French humor simply would not exist; that the juvenile literature of many continental countries would take far different forms, and that an American writer named Chick Sales would have had to find a different route to immortality. I am not sure that musical criticism would not be able to issue from its present theological stage (to use language of Comte) if it could be brought to consider certain "auditory residues." Oriental literatures have a veritable cult for the navel, Western literatures for visual residues, Papal encyclicals for the "olfactory." It is a gross mistake to reduce all these attitudes to sex, in the bad sense under the term "obscenity," and in the good sense under the term "beauty."—A. L.]

Printed in the United States
1504100001B/132